Against the Hounds of Hell

THE AMERICAN SOUTH SERIES

Elizabeth R. Varon and Orville Vernon Burton, Editors

AGAINST THE HOUNDS OF HELL

A LIFE OF HOWARD THURMAN

PETER EISENSTADT

UNIVERSITY OF VIRGINIA PRESS
Charlottesville and London

University of Virginia Press
© 2021 by the Rector and Visitors of the University of Virginia
All rights reserved
Printed in the United States of America on acid-free paper

First published 2021

1 3 5 7 9 8 6 4 2

Library of Congress Cataloging-in-Publication Data

Names: Eisenstadt, Peter R., author.
Title: Against the hounds of hell : a life of Howard Thurman / Peter Eisenstadt.
Description: Charlottesville : University of Virginia Press, 2021. | Series:
The American South series | Includes bibliographical references and index.
Identifiers: LCCN 2020037902 (print) | LCCN 2020037903 (ebook) |
ISBN 9780813944524 (hardcover) | ISBN 9780813944531 (ebook)
Subjects: LCSH: Thurman, Howard, 1899–1981. | Baptists—United States—
Biography. | African American Baptists—Biography. | Theologians—United States—
Biography. | African American theologians—Biography. | Educators—
United States—Biography. | African American educators—Biography.
Classification: LCC BX6495.T53 E39 2021 (print) | LCC BX6495.T53 (ebook) |
DDC 280/.4092 [B]—dc23
LC record available at https://lccn.loc.gov/2020037902
LC ebook record available at https://lccn.loc.gov/2020037903

Cover photo: Rev. Dr. Howard Thurman. (Stuart A. Rose Manuscript,
Archives & Rare Book Library, Emory University)

To Jane, always,
and Harold Weschler, of blessed memory

Whenever [Jesus'] spirit appears, the oppressed gather fresh courage; for he announced the good news that fear, hypocrisy, and hatred, the three hounds of hell that track the trail of the disinherited, need have no dominion over them.

—Howard Thurman, *Jesus and the Disinherited*

Contents

Illustrations

Acknowledgments

The beginning of my personal and professional odyssey with Howard Thurman began on Thanksgiving Day 1995, with a drive from Brooklyn to Rochester with my wife, Jane, and my late brother, Freddy. For the past quarter century, with a few extended breaks, I have been trying to take the measure of this extraordinary man. What began as a job has become a calling and a mission, my track to the water's edge.

This book reflects many years of work with the Howard Thurman Papers Project and its documentary edition, *The Papers of Howard Washington Thurman*. I have followed its wanderings from Colgate Rochester Crozer Divinity School, to Morehouse College, to Boston University. To say that this book would not have been possible without the opportunity the Thurman Papers Project gave me to immerse myself in his life and works barely requires stating. However, this book is not an official product or publication of the Thurman Papers Project, and let me emphasize and underline the standard disclaimer: all opinions, mistakes, misjudgments, and errors of commission or omission are entirely my own. From the beginning of my work with Howard Thurman, my friend on this journey has been the Rev. Dr. Walter E. Fluker, the project's only begetter, director, and muse. This book would have been impossible without his unstinting support. Walter knew Thurman well, and his affection, passion, and deep intellectual seriousness about Thurman has always been my inspiration. Above all, I have tried to stay in the light.

I have worked with many people on the Thurman Papers Project over the decades, unfortunately, far too many to call them all out individually. A few deserve special mention as friends and colleagues: Quinton Dixie, my *Visions of a Better World* coauthor; Kai Jackson Issa; Silvia P. Glick; and Jamison Collier. This book is built on our many years of fruitful work together. In the years I have been working on Howard Thurman I have made the transition, much to my surprise, from Brooklynite to upstate New Yorker to Carolinian. The first sweltering summer day I ever stepped onto the campus of Clemson University, wondering what it would be like to live in a place as exotic to me as South Carolina, Vernon Burton was there to greet me. Vernon, a peerless and courageous historian of the South, has provided boundless encouragement, intellectual stimulation, close readings, and practical assistance in the birthing of this book. He and his wife, Georganne, have become two of our closest friends. Vernon is one of our greatest Lincoln scholars, and he has engaged me in his life quest to fulfill Lincoln's unfinished work. I see this book as part of our shared journey.

Thurman wrote of the need of an "intimate circle of a close fellowship" to provide the "other-than-self reference" needed to sustain oneself. Rob Snyder, Daniel Soyer, Marc Korpus (who also is the book's superb cartographer), Julie Miller, Cathy Harris, Ayala Emmett, Maggie Kearney, and Alison Parker are all members of my fellowship. I have also learned much from other Thurmanites on this sojourn, among them Rev. Luther Smith, the dean of Thurman scholars, the Rev. Paul Smith, Kipton Jensen, and Rabbi Or N. Rose. Ryan Hendrickson and Sean Noel of the Howard Gotlieb Archival Research Center of Boston University have been unstintingly helpful. I would like to extend my thanks to Thurman's grandchildren, Anton Wong and Suzanne Chiarenza, for their support. I remember with great fondness the illuminating conversations I was privileged to have with Thurman's daughter, Olive Thurman Wong, and with Thurman's student Reb Zalman Schachter-Shalomi, both of blessed memory.

Let me thank Martin Doblmeier of Journey Films for his support and Clemson University provost Bob Jones for financial assistance in completing this work. Dick Holway, Helen Chandler, and the staff of the University of Virginia Press worked heroically during the pandemic to produce this book. Bea Burton was an indexer nonpareil. Susan Murray's Argus-eyed copyediting greatly improved the book, and let me give a special shout-out to Nadine Zimmerli for her superb editorial skills, and the exacting though nurturing ministrations she delivered to my slack and meandering prose. I would also like to thank Paul Harvey for his response to an earlier draft of this manuscript. A special thanks to the eminent scholars who consented to review the manuscript that became this book: Walter Fluker, Luther E. Smith, Edward Kaplan, and Vernon Burton.

Three dedicatees. Aaron Braveman, a dear friend and a pillar of Rochester's Jewish community, accomplished much in his long and useful life. For me, his outspoken quest for a true peace between Israel and Palestine was an enduring inspiration. Another Rochesterian, Harold Weschler, was a rare gentleman, a singular scholar, a mensch among mensches, a baseball fanatic extraordinaire, a boy of summer, and a great source of intellectual and moral support. The foul ball I caught sitting next to him is always on my desk. As Harold liked to say, the world is reborn every year when pitchers and catchers report. Without Harold, and after a strange spring without baseball, the world has a heavier heart. I always root for my home team. In every inning, Jane DeLuca, bella figlia dell'amore, has been batting for me. This book, like my life, is hers. And, as Jane would insist, don't forget to mention the cats.

A few words on the text. This is the book of a historian, not a theologian, though of course you cannot write a life of Howard Thurman without writing a lot about his religion. I see this book as a supplement to the abundant and rich theological literature on Thurman, not in any way its substitute or replacement. When he was writing his own life's story, Thurman wrote that he would try to write "the inner story of the unfolding of my own spirit as it grappled with the realities of my life as a black man growing up in American society. It is rather interesting that the span of my life covers precisely the first three quarters of this century." An autobiographer and a biographer have somewhat different tasks, but this is the story I have tried to tell as well. I wish I could have documented the remarkable marriage between Howard and Sue Bailey Thurman in greater detail. If I sometimes call her Sue in this book, it is not because of an unearned informality on my part but because constantly using Sue Bailey Thurman sounds too fussy. When they are mentioned together in the book, they are always Howard and Sue. Throughout his life, Thurman used masculine language to refer to people collectively, and his word choices have not been altered.

"There is," Thurman wrote, "something incomplete about coming to the end of anything." Howard Thurman is an elusive subject for a biographer. Whenever I thought I was getting close to fully understanding him, I heard his hearty laughter ringing in my ears, encouraging me to keep on searching. I still hear his laughter. During my work on this book I have kept in mind the closing words of *With Head and Heart*: "And this is the strangest of all the paradoxes of the human adventure: we live *inside* all experience, but we are permitted to bear witness only to the *outside*." This is true for all of us, and all the more so for a person who was as complex, and as private, as Howard Thurman. Whatever part of Howard Thurman I have managed to capture in this book, I hope it is a fair representation of the larger, deeper, whole.

If Thurman had a favorite quotation, it was surely the words of Eugene V. Debs on being sentenced in 1918 for sedition for his opposition to World War I: "While there is a lower class, I am in it; while there is a criminal element, I am of it; while there is a man in jail, I am not free." A century on, Debs's words have lost none of their salience. As long as any of us have to "stand with our backs against the wall," we are all still standing there. I also dedicate this book to all of those who are working to create a world without walls, where we can all live together, warmed by a friendly sun, beneath a friendly sky.

Against the Hounds of Hell

Introduction
"With Our Negro Guests"

On 21 February 1936, Howard Thurman, his wife, Sue Bailey Thurman, and Edward Carroll arose around midnight from their hostel in Bombay. They comprised three-fourths of the Negro Delegation sent by the American Student Christian Federation on a "Pilgrimage of Friendship" to their Indian counterparts. (The fourth member of the delegation, Edward Carroll's wife, Phenola Carroll, was indisposed.)[1] By 21 February the delegation had been on an extended speaking tour of British colonies in South Asia for four months.[2] This night was special. After getting ready, Howard, Sue, and Edward Carroll boarded a train. About four hours later, they arrived at Navsari Station, about two hundred miles north of the city. They were met by Mahadev Desai, Mahatma (Mohandas) Gandhi's longtime personal secretary. While Sue and Edward Carroll rested in a bungalow, Howard chatted with Desai. At dawn they all got into Desai's battered Model T Ford for the twenty-mile drive over a badly rutted dusty road to Dharampur in the native state of Bardoli, where the Indian Congress Party had a compound. (In the political patchwork that was British India, Bardoli was one of the more than 550 princely or native states, areas that enjoyed a slightly greater measure of self-governance than areas directly under British control.) The three would shortly become the first African Americans to formally meet with Gandhi, the world-famous leader of the Indian independence movement.

Gandhi bounded out of his tent bungalow to meet the visitors. Desai told Thurman he had never seen Gandhi greet visitors so effusively or enthusiastically. The first thing Gandhi did was to pull out a pocket watch from under his dhoti and say, "I apologize, but we must talk by the watch, because we have so much to talk about and you have only three hours before you have to leave to catch your train back to Bombay." Mahadev Desai kept notes from the meeting with Gandhi and the Negro Delegation and would publish an account of the meeting the following month in Gandhi's magazine *Harijan,* under the title "With Our Negro Guests."[3]

Gandhi started to pepper the delegates with questions. "Never in my life," Thurman would later write, "have I been a part of that kind of examination: persistent, pragmatic questions about American Negroes, about the course of slavery, and how we survived it." Gandhi asked questions about voting rights, lynching, discrimination, public school education, and Black churches. Thurman provided a short history of African Americans since Emancipation, explaining to Gandhi "the various schools of Negro thought," in Desai's words, "with the cautious and dispassionate detachment characteristic of a professor of philosophy."[4]

Thurman began with Booker T. Washington. Throughout his time in India, Thurman emphasized Black accomplishment and what had been achieved in the seventy years since Emancipation, an anniversary he often mentioned in his talks. He was always complimentary to Washington, emphasizing less his racial compromises than what he had achieved and built despite the formidable barriers he faced. The previous November, in Palamcottah, a newspaper account of Thurman's talk, "The Faith of the American Negro," reported that Thurman spoke of how Washington and his peers tried to uproot "the slave mentality of the race. They soon brought into existence a new way of knowledge and thinking and understanding. They developed in the minds of the Negroes a deep faith in their own strength and abilities."[5]

If Thurman admired Washington, he also thought that his era had passed. He told Gandhi that Washington's ideas no longer made sense in an era of urbanization, mass production, and industrial unionism. Citing W. E. B. Du Bois's recently published *Black Reconstruction,* Thurman provided a history of the South that emphasized the role of white working-class resentment in shaping racial attitudes. At the end of the Civil War, as Desai summarized Thurman's words, "the economic situation was paralyzed, leaving the whole structure in the hands of the poor Whites who smarted under the economic competition of the Negro." As he told the audience in Palamcottah, rather than Blacks competing directly with whites, Washington's theory was "that in order that the American Negro should survive in American society, he must be taught to produce goods which could be exchanged in the market, as a result of which he could have economic security" and "free [himself] from the great burden of hunger."[6] But the point of Thurman's quasi-Marxist history of the South was that Washingtonianism, with its presupposition of Blacks remaining largely rural, agricultural, southern, and mostly apart from white workers, was no longer a viable strategy. In the 1930s, along with many like-minded colleagues at Howard University—notably his close colleague, the political scientist Ralph Bunche—Thurman felt that America's racial problems could only be seriously addressed if white and Black workers formed industrial unions and fought against both the excesses of capitalism and the realities of racism.[7]

Thurman told Gandhi of the "theory of the separate but so-called 'equal' education of the Negro." He had told an audience some two months earlier that the goal of Black education since Emancipation was not to build Black institutions for their own sake but to give Blacks "a certain social attitude that can be injected into American society, so that it will become increasingly impossible to have separate schools for whites. The Negro attack is directed against segregated institutions of the present day."[8] In other words, the justification for segregated educational institutions was educating their students to question the existence of segregated institutions.

When Gandhi asked, "Is the prejudice against color growing or dying out?," Thurman's answer was ambivalent: "It is difficult to say." He seemed most optimistic, somewhat surprisingly, about the situation in the South, where, probably reflecting his interaction with southern white students, Thurman found a "disposition to improve upon the attitude of their forebears." However, he added that the "economic question is acute everywhere," and that "in many of the industrial centers in [the] Middle West the prejudice against Negroes shows itself in its ugliest form," and he worried about clashes between white and Black workers. When Gandhi asked, "Is the union between Negroes and the Whites recognized by law?," Edward Carroll told him that such marriages were illegal in a majority of the states and that as a Black minister in Virginia he had to post a five-hundred-dollar bond and forfeit it if he ever solemnized an interracial marriage. Thurman, a strong feminist, added that these laws especially hurt Black women: "But there has been a lot of intermixture of races as for 300 years or more, the Negro woman had no control over her own body." A possible subtext to this part of the conversation was Gandhi trying to make amends for a controversial 1930 book in which he seemed to oppose interracial marriage. This provoked outrage among some of Gandhi's African American supporters, leading to his statement in the *Baltimore Afro-American* in 1934 that "prohibition of marriage between colored people and white people I hold to be a negation of civilization."[9]

The discussion then turned to the appeal of Islam. Gandhi stated that it "is the only religion in the world in which no lines are drawn from within the religious fellowship." Thurman agreed. No doubt thinking of a recent disagreement he had with an American missionary in Lahore, he told Gandhi: "We are often told that but for the Arabs there would have been no slavery. I do not believe it."[10] The previous month, while in Calcutta, Thurman attended a service in a huge public park for Eid al-Fitr, celebrating the end of Ramadan: "There were the rich and the poor, the educated and the uneducated, those who stood high and those who stood low in the community—they were all there, side by side, without distinction. Only one who has lived my life can know the thrill that a spectacle of that sort gives."[11] Thurman was one of a long line of African American observers who were impressed by what they saw as the universal, racially inclusive scope of Islam.[12] Thurman often told the story of a Nigerian Muslim who had once told him that Allah laughs at the stupidity of First Baptist Church, colored, and First Baptist Church, white.[13] As the conversation with Gandhi continued, in the words of Mahadev Desai, "the whole discussion led to many a question and cross-question during which the guests had an occasion to see that Gandhiji's principle of equal respect for all religions was no theoretical formula but a practical creed."[14] This was Thurman's creed as well, confirmed during his time in Asia, when he was exposed to Hinduism, Islam, Zoroastrianism, and Buddhism (the latter primarily in Ceylon and Burma), as well receiving many lessons on the inadequacies and Western biases of Indian Christianity. Writing in 1938, he said of India that "in some ways it seemed to be God-intoxicated. Despite all of the superficialities and leaches that are present in all developed religions, more than any place I have ever known India seems capable of grasping a religion that inspires overwhelming personal sacrifices and complete moral and ethical devotion."[15] As God-intoxicated as he was, Thurman was never quite satisfied with just one religion, and certainly not with any version of his own religion, Christianity, that did not place passionate "ethical and moral devotion" at its core.

At this point, it was the visitors' turn to ask Gandhi questions. Sue, whom Desai credited as being "nobly sensitive to the deeper things of the spirit," posed some of the knottier ones: "Did the South African Negro take any part in your movement? [during the two decades, from 1893 to 1914, that Gandhi lived in South Africa]." "No," answered Gandhi, "I purposely did not invite them. It would have endangered their cause. They would not have understood the technique of our struggle nor could they have seen the purpose or utility of non-violence." This was a questionable defense of a dubious strategy. Gandhi's comments to the Negro Delegation indicate that he was still not free of stereotypes of Africans as unusually violence-prone. As for practical results, the policy of excluding Africans from Gandhi's campaigns might have resulted in some short-term term tactical victories, but it is difficult not to conclude that this decision significantly contributed to the ultimate failure of his South African satyagraha campaign.[16]

The conversation then turned to, in Desai's words, "a discussion which was the main thing that had drawn the distinguished members to Gandhiji," the philosophy of nonviolence. Although "nonviolence" is a term that Gandhi coined—his is the earliest citation in the *Oxford English Dictionary*, from 1920—he never liked the term, as he told the delegation, because, of "the negative particle 'non.'" "It is no negative force," he said, but is rather "the greatest and the activest force in nature," a translation of the Jainist concept of ahimsa, respect for all living things, Gandhi's Sanskrit term for the concept. ("Satyagraha" is giving ahimsa a concrete political task to accomplish.)[17] "Superficially," he told Thurman and the others, we are "surrounded by life and bloodshed, life living upon life," but ahimsa is the deeper and truer reality, "a force which is more positive than electricity and more powerful than [the] ether." When Thurman asked if nonviolence "overrides all other forces," Gandhi replied, "Yes, it is the only true force in life."[18] Nonviolence, or ahimsa, for Gandhi was less an idea than a physical and moral reality. It was the Force.

This force could be channeled by its masters. Worldly goods and material possessions limit its effectiveness. "It possesses nothing, therefore it possesses everything." And though it was open to everyone and anyone—"if there was any exclusiveness about it, I should reject it at once"—very few had mastered it. Gandhi, who could toggle easily between abject humility and extraordinary hubris, suggested to Thurman that if just one person had grasped and learned the meaning of ahimsa, it might be possible for just "one single Indian to resist the exploitation of 300 million Indians." He hoped to accumulate sufficient "soul-force" to do this, but he acknowledged to Thurman that he was still far, very far, from this goal.

The British still controlled India, Gandhi continued, because ahimsa had yet to be adopted by the Indian masses. And this was because the Indian masses lacked "vitality," a vitality to be drawn from the force of ahimsa. For both Gandhi and Thurman, vitality meant something akin to drawing on the life force. The masses were too hungry and too focused on their immediate physical needs to easily do so. (It's hard to convince a starving person of the spiritual importance of fasting.) British imperialism had robbed them of their self-reliance and ability to take care of themselves. And to some extent, Indians had brought it on themselves, because of the persistence of untouchability. (However, while Gandhi anathemized untouchability, he did not oppose the caste system as such. Thurman was, oddly, sympathetic to Gandhi's distinction, writing in 1938 that he did not "know enough" to say whether the caste system was "good or bad" for India but that untouchability is a "very, very terrible thing.")[19]

Gandhi told the delegation that the ultimate test of one's mastery of ahimsa was the ability to convince others, current foes and potential allies alike, of the rightness of one's cause, and in this Gandhi felt he had failed. Successful non-violent protests for Gandhi were ultimately exercises in persuasion, an effort to strip away from the target of the protest their self-confidence and their belief in the morality, necessity, or sustainability of their actions. When Thurman asked whether one could fully realize the possibility of ahimsa, Gandhi told him that "no one had yet been found to express ahimsa in its fullness" and that "there is no royal road, except through living the creed in your life which must be a living sermon," adding, with a karmic twist, that this would probably require several lifetimes to accomplish. "Seek ye first the kingdom of Heaven and everything else shall be added unto you," Gandhi told the delegation, quoting Matthew. However, he added, "the Kingdom of Heaven is Ahimsa."

Sue, no doubt slightly wearying of this airy metaphysical discussion, tried to bring the conversation around to some of the practical consequences of ahimsa and satyagraha: "How am I to act, supposing my own brother was lynched before my eyes?" There is, Gandhi replied, "such a thing as self-immolation." Self-immolation was a difficult doctrine indeed, as difficult as it sounded. It was a recognition that nonviolence rested on personal suffering and absorbing sufficient suffering to change the behavior of others: "I must not wish ill to these, but neither must I co-operate with them." If your liveli-hood is in any way dependent on the community of lynchers, one must find alternative means of support, refusing "even to touch food that comes from them, and I refuse to co-operate with even my brother Negroes who tolerate the wrong." The only life you can take to address evil and injustice is your own: "One's faith must remain undimmed whilst life ebbs out minute by minute." Perhaps sensing that the delegates were not entirely persuaded, Gandhi added that he was "a very poor specimen of the practice of non-violence, and my answer may not convince you." But this was his faith. He had given the dele-gates much to consider.

The conversation began to draw to a close. The delegates begged Gandhi to come to America. Sue was even more specific: "We want you not for White America, but for the Negroes, we have many a problem that cries out for solution, and we need you badly." Gandhi said it was impossible. "How I wish I could," but he had to "make good the message here before I bring it to you." In any event, he implied, what Black Americans needed wasn't Gandhi in the flesh but their own Gandhian movement, authentic to their own needs and ideals.

Gandhi asked the delegation to sing a few spirituals before they left. This was a sensitive issue. Before the delegation left, the request had come from the Indian sponsors that they wanted its members to be "expert singers." This worried the American organizers of the tour, writing their Indian counterparts that the delegation would not be put "on exhibition either as singers or anthropological specimens" and that "sending a good tenor or bass to India was no concern of ours."[20] The Indian sponsors endeavored to clear up the confusion. They did not want a minstrel show. However, if the delegation could talk about Negro spirituals and, perchance, sing a few as well, that would be most welcome. Indians were mad about spirituals, the first of many genres of distinctively African American music to attain worldwide fame, and to hear them sung by African Americans would be thrilling.[21] Howard had written about the spirituals, and Sue, a trained musician with a degree in musical performance from Oberlin College, had often sung them, so they agreed to make it part of their lectures in Asia.[22]

In any event, whatever their reservations, and even if the delegation had voices that sounded like a trio of croaking frogs on a log, they were unlikely to have wanted to disappoint Gandhi. With Sue in lead, they sang "We are Climbing Jacob's Ladder," which in Desai's words "gave expression to the deep-seated hope and aspiration in the breast of every oppressed community to climb higher and higher until the goal was won." And they sang, at Gandhi's request, "Were You There When They Crucified My Lord?" Gandhi told Thurman that this spiritual expressed "the root experience of the entire human race under the spread of the healing wings of suffering," the message that all of us, not only Jesus, must be prepared to die for the sins of others.[23]

There are two different accounts of the end of the meeting. In his autobiography, Thurman writes that at parting, he asked, "what is the greatest handicap to Jesus Christ in India?" Gandhi told him that it was "Christianity as it as practiced, as it has been identified with Western civilization and colonialism." The greatest enemy of the message of Jesus in India is "Christianity itself." This was a sentiment Thurman had heard many times while in India, and it was one with which he heartily agreed.[24]

But the Desai account, "With Our Negro Guests," published in 1936, became the main reference for the interview. In Desai's retelling, Thurman told Gandhi that "the Negroes were ready to accept the message" of nonviolence, and Gandhi replied, in his closing comment as he said good-bye, "Well, . . . if it comes true it may be through the Negroes that the unadulterated message of non-violence will be delivered to the world." The civil rights movement, of course, has no single starting date, and the question of when it began has been vigorously if inconclusively debated. But if one had to pick a day, 21 February 1936, the date of Gandhi's benediction to the budding Negro revolution, is as good as any. Some two decades later, in early 1957, at the end of the founding meeting of what would become the Southern Christian Leadership Conference, Bayard Rustin was talking to Martin Luther King, Jr. Rustin quoted the "prophetic statement" made by Gandhi to Thurman. Perhaps, Rustin suggested, Gandhi's torch had been passed to a new people and a new continent.[25]

On 21 September 1935, Thurman embarked on the *Ile de France* from New York harbor for the first leg of the journey that would take the Negro Delegation to Asia. He was thirty-five years old. In those days before the advent of widespread commercial air travel, it would take a month, with two intervening continents and two long ocean voyages, to arrive at their destination, on 21 October, in Colombo, Ceylon. He was chair of the four-person delegation, sent by the American Student Christian Movement—basically an amalgam of the YMCA, the YWCA, and the Student Volunteer Movement—to its counterpart, the Student Christian Movement of India, Ceylon, and Burma. At the time of his departure for India, Thurman was a professor of religion and the campus minister at Howard University. (Shortly after his return to the United States, in April 1936, he would be named dean of chapel at Howard, the first African American minister to be given that title.) He was widely hailed, by Blacks and whites alike, as one of the leading ministers and preachers of his generation.

Howard Thurman was born in Florida as the nineteenth century was expiring, in November 1899. He was raised in the growing resort town of Daytona. The area's salubrious climes were attracting some of the wealthiest people in the United States to the area. Thurman knew a different Daytona. He was born poor and Black and, from an early age, was fatherless. He came to manhood as the vise of Jim Crow was tightening throughout the South. He demonstrated extraordinary intellectual capacities, and by dint of hard work and a little luck was able to attend and graduate from high school at the Florida Baptist Academy in Jacksonville. (There was no public education for Blacks in Daytona beyond the seventh grade.) As valedictorian, he was awarded a scholarship to Morehouse College in Atlanta, where, after once again graduating as valedictorian, he continued his education at Rochester Theological Seminary (RTS), a prominent liberal Protestant seminary in upstate New York, completing his formal education, once again graduating at the head of his class, with a B.D. degree in 1926. After two years ministering to a Black Baptist congregation in Oberlin, Ohio, and arranging to take some time off for a semester of postgraduate study, he returned to Atlanta to teach religion at his alma mater, Morehouse, and its sister institution, Spelman College. In 1932 he moved from Atlanta to Washington to take a position at Howard University.

Accompanying Thurman to India was his wife, Sue Bailey Thurman, born in Pine Bluff, Arkansas, in 1903. She was a graduate of Spelman and Oberlin Colleges, and a former national secretary of the YWCA. They had been married in the summer of 1932, just before their move to Washington. She was an effective administrator, an elegant, forceful, and accomplished public speaker and educator, and an excellent musician, well known and admired in progressive Christian circles. It was her first marriage, his second. Thurman's first wife, Katie Kelley, whom he married on graduation from RTS, had died of tuberculosis in December 1930. Thurman had two daughters, one from each marriage: Olive, born in 1927, and Anne Spencer, born in 1933.

By September 1935, Thurman had been waiting and planning for the trip to India for a year and a half. The original inspiration for the Negro Delegation's trip to India came from the Rev. Augustine Ralla Ram, in his capacity as the executive secretary of the Student Christian Federation of India, Ceylon, and Burma. Augustine Ralla Ram was born in 1888, the son of Indian converts, and like his fifth-century CE namesake, he was very worried about whether Christianity in his country could survive the crumbling of the structures and specific cultural forms imparted to it by a fading empire.[26] In the fall of 1931 Ralla Ram had traveled to the United States and had toured American colleges speaking about India and Indian Christianity. One of his stops was at Spelman College, where he had spoken of Gandhi, a friend, as "a second corporate Christ, the living spirit of Christianity." The Spelman College newspaper reported that Ralla Ram took a special interest in "the social and class distinctions to which Negroes are subjected" because they so closely paralleled caste divisions in India.[27] The World Student Christian Federation often sent "Pilgrimages of Friendship" from one country to another, in order to familiarize both the giving and receiving countries with the realities faced by Christians elsewhere.[28] On return to India, in 1933, he contacted his counterparts in the American Student Christian Movement, requesting a Negro delegation to tour his country because Christianity in India is seen as "the 'oppressor's' religion, [and] there would be a unique value in having representatives of another oppressed group speak on the validity and contribution of Christianity."[29]

The American Student Christian Movement liked the suggestion. A committee of six people, the Committee on the Negro Delegation to India (hereafter the India Committee) was set up to plan and raise money for the tour. There were six members of the committee; three men, three women, four whites, and two Blacks. The two African Americans, both good friends of the Thurmans, Frank T. Wilson and Marion Cuthbert, were YMCA and YWCA secretaries, respectively. However, the real leadership of the India Committee was in the hands of its cochairs, Betty Harrington, and A. R. "Roland" Elliot, who made most of its decisions. The India Committee drew up a list of objectives for the tour and criteria for selecting its members. The delegation would have four persons, a team with complementary talents, an equal number of men and women, all under the age of forty, and one person under the age of twenty-six.[30] There was some discussion of including one or two whites in the delegation, but the committee, wisely, decided to adhere to Ralla Ram's original request.[31]

The next task of the India Committee was to select the four delegates. They wanted their choices to be able to combine the "philosophical, mystical approach of personal religion" with a "practical and ethically compelling demand for social justice." The committee also sought persons who were articulate public speakers, thoughtful leaders of discussions with small groups of persons, flexible and adaptable, sturdy enough to withstand the rigors of extensive touring, and able to put their lives on hold for the better part of a year to participate in the delegation. By March 1934 the India Committee had assembled a list of fifteen potential candidates, most of whom had long histories in the YMCA-YWCA speaking circuit. After further discussion they were able to whittle down to six names, including Thurman, Benjamin Mays, and one member of the India Committee, Frank Wilson.[32] Howard Thurman headed the list.[33]

On 3 April 1934, in a joint meeting of the YMCA and YWCA, Thurman was the first selection of the committee, with the only objection being that at thirty-five, he was a bit long in the tooth to be described as a "student."[34] The cochair of the committee, Elizabeth Harrington, was authorized to negotiate with Thurman over his participation in the delegation. Thurman said no. "Under no circumstances would it be possible for me to accept," he later wrote. His reasons were ideological, not personal. "How could I, a member of an exploited race in America," Thurman asked, defend American Christianity, "which make[s] its peace with the powerful of the earth . . . against the weak and with the strong." He had "certain misgivings that led me to believe that we would be considered as the spearhead of some kind of evangelistic movement from the West."[35] Thurman was adamant that he would not be an evangelist, either for America or for American Christianity. Part of this reflected Thurman's suspicions about the Student Christian Movement. He had written a month before that the movement was too stuffy and hidebound, too conventional in its politics and its Christianity, in all, containing "a lot of deadness."

Combining the YMCA and YWCA to form the Student Christian Movement accomplished nothing: "Zero multiplied by infinity is still zero."[36]

After Thurman had initially turned down the invitation, the India Committee wisely sent Winnifred Wygal, a national secretary of the YWCA and an old associate of both the Thurmans who had a speaking engagement at Howard University, to see if she could persuade him. Howard writes in his autobiography that he and Sue and Wygal "talked far into the night" and with the "sort of communication that is possible only in a climate of honesty and trust," and Wygal convinced Thurman that he should go to India because of and not despite his objections. It was precisely because he would not apologize about America or American Christianity that he needed to go to India. It seems likely as well that to make the trip more attractive, Wygal presented the Thurmans with a sweetener: Sue Bailey Thurman could accompany her husband as a member of the delegation. Certainly the possibility of a half year traveling together was more attractive than a half year of separation.[37]

By May, the Thurmans were committed to the trip.[38] There were skeptics who doubted that they would be able to accomplish much. Howard's closest friend, Herbert King, thought that the trip would be worthwhile "despite the *auspices* of the thing," and others wondered whether Thurman would or could be honest in what he said about America or American Christianity. One correspondent commiserated with Thurman that he would be "suppressed . . . by the conservative YW" during his time in India. Others thought that Thurman would sentimentalize American race relations and avoid unpleasant topics, or even that the delegates, all with southern backgrounds, had been chosen because "southern Negroes [unlike those from the North] are noted for their tolerant, kindly, more or less weak, stand with reference to the American white man."[39]

The Thurmans were determined to prove the doubters wrong. He wrote the India Committee that he wanted Blacks to support the endeavor because he would testify to "the limitations of American life" faced by the "masses of Negroes" with no attempt to make apologies. He would not testify what "the grace of God" had "done for us people in American society."[40] He could not represent American Christianity because "I did not have any confidence in the aspect of American Christianity with which I was familiar."[41] He went to India to explain his version of Christianity to non-Christians and not to troll for converts.[42] (Thurman was mightily annoyed when a prominent American Methodist missionary in India announced that the delegation was coming to Asia as "singing, soul saving evangelists.")[43] The Thurmans would represent only themselves. After being named to the delegation in May 1935, they spent much of the next year preparing for their time in Asia. Sue, with her deep interest in artistic production of all kinds, took an extended trip to Mexico over the winter of 1934–35 to study "the whole of American Culture in preparation for the contacts we would make with a significant culture of the East," as Thurman later wrote.[44] (The only problem, as the Thurmans discovered, was that Mexican immigration policies made it difficult for African American tourists to enter the country.)[45]

Howard did not accompany Sue to Mexico, but he was doing plenty of preparation of his own. He gathered differing opinions on the state of Black America, from racial moderates such as Robert Russa Moton, the former president of Tuskegee Institute, to the socialist labor leader A. Philip Randolph.[46] He spoke to Indian academics and students studying in the United States and persuaded Madeleine Slade, known as Mirabehn, daughter of a British admiral who was a member of Gandhi's ashram, to speak at Howard University.[47] He also undertook a rigorous reading regimen covering many subjects including books on Indian, American, African American, and American Indian history, texts on comparative religion, and "a study of imperialism, both from the orthodox and Marxian point of view."[48] The delegation found Asian audiences to be very interested and knowledgeable about American politics and history, and they were quizzed on domestic American matters such as the current state of Fourteenth Amendment jurisprudence and the status of the Scottsboro case.[49] In India, Thurman gave a number of talks on American politics. (This was in contrast to his practice in the United States, where he rarely spoke about the politics of race before white audiences, in large part because he felt that this was the only topic many white audiences felt Blacks were capable of discussing.) Indian politics was another matter. The delegation took Ralla Ram's advice and avoided direct mention of the question of Indian independence.[50] Despite this, the delegation was shadowed by British intelligence officers throughout their stay.[51] Indeed, had it not been that 1935 marked a relative lull in the usually explosive politics of British India—for one thing, Gandhi was not in prison—it seems unlikely the British authorities would have granted permission to the Negro Delegation to enter the colony.

The finances of the tour were complex as well. At the request of the India Committee, Thurman doubled his usual number of summer lecture appearances in 1935 to raise money. The funding proved inadequate. He complained during his time in India that "in practically every place it becomes necessary to resort to taking public collections to help with the expenses."[52] Thurman took an unpaid sabbatical from Howard to participate in the delegation, resulting in what he later called an "overwhelming hardship." When he returned to the United States, he tried to replenish his coffers with punishing speaking tours, with deleterious physical and psychic effect.[53]

The biggest problem facing Thurman and the India Delegation in the spring of 1935 was the selection of the delegation's personnel. Edward Carroll, a twenty-five-year-old Methodist minister in Virginia and graduate of Yale Divinity School, was chosen shortly after the selection of the Thurmans was announced, as was Grace Towns Hamilton, a twenty-eight-year-old professor of psychology at Le Moyne College in Memphis. But Hamilton decided early in 1935 that she couldn't leave her young child alone for the extended period the trip would have required. The India Committee dithered on choosing her replacement, and, after rejecting Thurman's suggestions, the committee in July finally chose Phenola Carroll, the wife of Edward Carroll. Thurman was furious. He felt Phenola was unqualified—he also had doubts about her husband—and the late date of her selection would not give her adequate time to prepare for her responsibilities. And he felt that her selection made it appear that the wives were chosen to accompany their husbands rather than, as surely was the case for Sue Bailey Thurman, being worthy of selection in their own right. The Thurmans threatened to resign, and Howard wrote some of the darkest, angriest letters of his life.[54]

The Thurmans decided that they had invested too much time and effort into preparation for the trip to walk away, but hard feelings remained, and they remained convinced that Phenola was not up to the responsibilities assigned to her. Thurman wrote a blistering letter to that effect to the India Committee, three months into the tour.[55] It was so negative in tone that the committee became convinced, without evidence, that Thurman was trying to undermine their work.[56] It left Thurman permanently estranged from some of the members of the India Committee, but the Thurmans did not take out their anger on the Carrolls. It was not Edward Carroll's fault that, like Thurman, he wanted his wife to accompany him to India, nor was it Phenola's responsibility that she had been selected for the delegation only two months before they sailed, without adequate time to prepare. As far as one can tell, during the six months the Thurmans and the Carrolls were daily in each other's almost uninterrupted company from rising to retiring, they seem to have gotten along reasonably well, and they remained close, if not intimate, friends for the remainder of their lives.[57]

After all the preparations were complete, the Thurmans and the Carrolls left for South Asia in late September 1935. Thurman had wanted second- and not third-class passage for the crossing, as he wrote the chair of the India Committee, not out of a desire for "deluxe travel" but because "the tendency to discriminate against Negroes in third class is much more marked than in second class." (His wishes were not honored.)[58] But the biggest problem on the crossing wasn't racism but rough seas. Thurman, a connoisseur of stormy weather from his boyhood on Florida's hurricane-prone east coast, was enthralled by the gales and experienced a storm during which "the very roots of my being were exposed by the raw energy of the sea." Thurman seems to have been the only member of his party who felt this way, as the others were confined to their cabins. Thurman mentions in his autobiography, with some pride, that he was one of the few passengers never to miss a meal.[59]

Two passengers who definitely did not appreciate the blustery weather were the Thurmans' two young daughters, Olive and Anne. Thurman remembered the "quivering muted whimper of terror that came from the children's lips" when the ship shuddered and rocked.[60] They were traveling with their parents, as was the girls' aunt, Thurman's sister Madaline, on the first leg of the journey. Their destination was Geneva, where Madaline would serve as their surrogate parent while Howard and Sue toured India. Madaline was a last-minute addition to the traveling party after Howard and Sue agreed with Frank Wilson that there might be a "possible moral embarrassment" if their daughters were cared for exclusively by whites during their stay.[61] (Olive, then aged eight, later remembered that the exotic skin color of her and her sister and aunt was the subject of considerable gawking by Genevans.)[62]

After Geneva, the Thurmans rejoined the Carrolls in Marseilles. The sultry weather on the passage through the Mediterranean and Suez Canal sharply contrasted with that of the North Atlantic—"at night always music, the moon, and passing ships"—but the region's politics were anything but calm.[63] The possibility of war between Ethiopia and Italy was much in the air. The delegation would get close to the impending conflict, stopping for a port of call in Djibouti, in French Somaliland, days before the invasion commenced from neighboring Italian Somaliland in early October 1935.

This was Thurman's first time in sub-Saharan Africa (and the last time until 1963), and he experienced, almost immediately, a direct taste of how imperialism can divide. He had, with the other passengers on his ship, intended to pass a few hours in Djibouti. All of the other twenty or so passengers on the launch, all but him white, passed through a gate without problems and without being asked questions. Thurman was stopped and searched thoroughly by a "tall, fine looking African." While he was being searched he told the guard: "I do not know whether you speak my language but I think your eyes speak my language. Let us not make the man who is making you do this make me your enemy and you my enemy. For, if we do, then this enmity between us will erect a wall. And when it is high enough, he will sit on that wall with one foot on your head and another foot on mine."[64] After this delay, Thurman was allowed to enter the city.

After Djibouti, the Negro Delegation continued, east of Suez, across the Indian Ocean, and on 21 October they finally disembarked at the old Dutch port of Colombo, their arrival in Asia timed for the end of the monsoon season.[65] Thurman's first encounter in Asia was with officious British bureaucrats, who delayed the exit of the delegation for several hours until they were convinced the delegation's papers were in order. The delegation emerged from customs to enter a country that was overwhelmingly nonwhite: "The dominant complexions all around were shades of brown, from light to very dark."[66] It was a country where whites, however powerful, were the outsiders and a tiny minority, while the majority, even if they didn't control their government, knew the country belonged to them. Thurman soon discovered a color line in Ceylon and India that was, if anything, more vertiginous than its American cousin, with the difference being that as Westerners the delegation's members were treated as honorary whites.[67] As he noted: "Servants were everywhere. Rickshaws pulled by men were everywhere. Servants were called 'Boys.' Shades of Southern United States."[68]

Thurman and the other members of the delegation faced numerous questions about their intentions: "Everywhere we went in the colleges, why are you here if you are not the tools of the European white people?" With "very few exceptions," whether in "private conversations, group meetings, or discussions," the same question and dilemma was raised: "If Christianity is not powerless, why is it not changing life in your country?" And if Christianity is powerless to change the condition of American Blacks, "why are you here representing it?" Out of the "churning" this line of questioning raised, a "fresh sense of authority began to emerge," and it "became the contagion that swept us along from town to town, campus to campus, church to church."[69]

Thurman's most memorable encounter on these matters occurred at the very beginning of the tour, probably on his very first evening in Colombo. He described the meeting many times, most memorably in the opening pages of his most influential book, *Jesus and the Disinherited*. Thurman had just given a lecture at the Law Club of Ceylon on "American Negro Political Questions" when he was stopped by a man, whose name Thurman never provides, variously described by him as a law student, a lawyer, or a law professor. Whatever his legal training, he knew how to prepare an indictment. He told Thurman he hadn't been going to bother speaking to him, thinking him just a lackey, but to his surprise he seemed intelligent and honest about the condition of Negroes in America. That only made it worse. Didn't he realize that a person like himself "in our country on a Christian enterprise" was a "a traitor to all of the darker people of the earth?" and that "any black Christian is either a fool or a dupe." He proceeded to provide Thurman with a well-informed history of the complicity of Christianity in African slavery and the subsequent oppression of American Blacks, dating back to the origins of the Atlantic slave trade up to the present, when he claimed Thurman lived in "a Christian nation in which you are segregated, lynched, and burned." Thurman told him he hadn't come to Asia to defend Christianity or to be "exhibit A as to what Christianity has done for me and my people." As for the racism tolerated by American Christianity, as a Ceylonese, he didn't know the half of it. Having lived within it his entire life, "my judgment about slavery and racial prejudice is far more devastating than yours could ever be." He believed, he said, not in Christianity, but the "religion of Jesus." As for the former, Christian churches and Christian institutions "are built and prevail upon the assumption that the Strong man is superior to the weak man" but that he was part of a "small minority of Christians who believe that society has to be completely reorganized in a very definite egalitarian sense if life is to be made livable for most of mankind."[70] In various forms, this was the message that Thurman and the other members of the Negro Delegation had brought to Asia. Over the next four months they would travel to fifty cities, traversing the breadth and width of South Asia, from subtropical Ceylon to the foothills of the Himalayas, from the Irrawaddy River in Burma to the mountain passes of the Indian border with Afghanistan. Their visits were anchored by the large network of Christian colleges and schools throughout South Asia.[71] After traveling through Ceylon, they spent over a month touring southern India, stopping in cities such as Madras and Bangalore. (At a break at Christmastime the Thurmans traveled to Darjeeling, where Thurman, after the clouds parted, just for a minute caught a glimpse of the peak of Mt. Everest, which became a "transcendent moment of sheer glory and beatitude, when time, space, and circumstance evaporated." He would "never, never be the same again.")[72] On New Year's Eve the delegates were in Rangoon, Burma, and serenaded at midnight by members of the local YMCA and YWCA singing "Auld Land Syne." After Burma they toured Bengal, spending several days in Calcutta, and then on to the major cities in the north, the spine of Mughal India—Delhi, Agra, and Lucknow. The delegates then traveled into what is now Pakistan, stopping in Lahore, Rawalpindi, and Peshawar. In mid-February they were in Bombay and finished the work of the Negro Delegation in early March 1936.[73] Then after another month on the return voyage, the Thurmans, reunited with their daughters, arrived back in the United States.

By the time the Pilgrimage of Friendship was complete, in early March 1936, the delegation had logged tens of thousands of miles, offered at least 264 formal lectures or sermons, and conducted many more informal gatherings

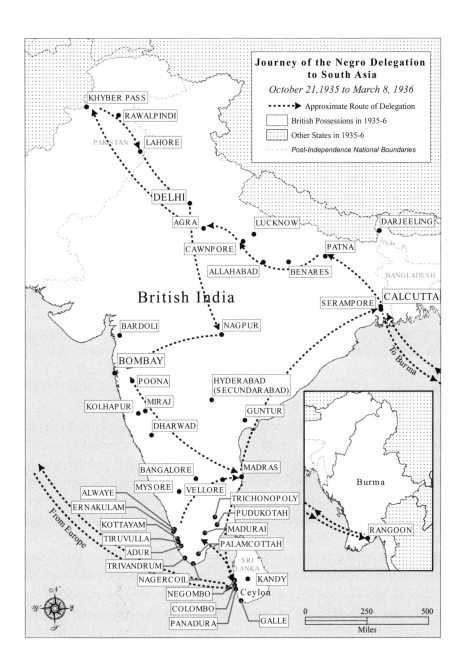

Journey of the Negro Delegation to South Asia
October 21, 1935 to March 8, 1936

- - - - ▶ Approximate Route of Delegation
☐ British Possessions in 1935-6
⫶ Other States in 1935-6
- - - Post-Independence National Boundaries

KHYBER PASS
RAWALPINDI
PAKISTAN
LAHORE
DELHI
AGRA
LUCKNOW
DARJEELING
CAWNPORE
PATNA
ALLAHABAD
BENARES
BANGLADESH
British India
SERAMPORE
CALCUTTA
NAGPUR
To Burma
BARDOLI
BOMBAY
POONA
HYDERABAD
(SECUNDARABAD)
KOLHAPUR
MIRAJ
GUNTUR
DHARWAD
Burma
BANGALORE
MADRAS
MYSORE
VELLORE
ALWAYE
TRICHONOPOLY
ERNAKULAM
PUDUKOTAH
KOTTAYAM
MADURAI
RANGOON
TIRUVULLA
PALAMCOTTAH
ADUR
From Europe
TRIVANDRUM
SRI LANKA
NAGERCOIL
KANDY
NEGOMBO
Ceylon
COLOMBO
PANADURA
GALLE
0   250   500
Miles

and meetings. Thurman was the most prolific speaker, with at least 135 speaking engagements, on a grueling schedule.[74] A typical day for the delegation, in Madura on 11 November 1935, had them up early for their first of the ten events scheduled, a meeting with students at 8:00 a.m., followed by lectures in three different colleges (divided among the delegates) by noon, lunch with another student group, an afternoon rest followed by visits to Hindu temples and dignitaries, a meeting with college faculty, and three addresses in the evening, all topped off with dinner at 8:00 p.m.[75] (These were often multicourse Indian banquets.) In addition to the pace, the delegates, despite all being sons and daughters of the South before the advent of air-conditioning, found the heat enervating. It is not surprising that all the delegation's members, at one time or another, had to take time off from the tour to tend to aliments, and the group as a whole decided to drop their schedule in Delhi for a few days, all of them suffering from nervous exhaustion.[76]

But there were many compensations. Throughout the trip they met local dignitaries and many persons with national and international renown, including Madame Vijaya Lakshimi Pandit, the sister of Jawaharlal Nehru (and subsequently the first female president of the United Nations General Assembly).[77] Near Calcutta they spent several days with Rabindranath Tagore, the first non-Western winner of the Nobel Prize in Literature, at his school, Santineketan. Thurman was a little disappointed with Tagore, whom he found distant and oracular, but he had a different experience with Tagore's associate, Kshitimohan Sen, a leading scholar of Hindu mysticism. Their intense conversation on the nature of religion he would later describe as "the most primary, naked fusing of total religious experience with another human being of which I have ever been capable."[78]

The delegation met with Asians from all walks of life, getting to experience other religions on a firsthand basis and regularly drawing large and enthusiastic crowds. They spoke about life in America, and what Black Americans had accomplished since Emancipation despite the combined efforts of church and state to hold them back. Thurman soon discovered that there was no need to speak about Indian politics directly. Talking about the situation in the United States was sufficient. Indians were more than capable of drawing the appropriate comparisons, from one dark-skinned people smarting under the Anglo-Saxon thumb to another. One correspondent wrote Thurman thanking him for providing ammunition for "the great conflict in [the] future," which will be "a question of white races against brown and black."[79] Another correspondent, an Indian Christian, thanked Thurman for his insight into the "economic exploitation, political disenfranchisement, Educational inequalities, lynching" perpetrated against Blacks in the South, offering him "great heart and head sympathy," convinced that "like the Indians you are concerned with the liberation of your people" and that his religion was sincere, reflecting the true meaning of the "crucified and risen Christ of Nazareth" rather than the Christianity of the "imperialistic animals of the white Americans," whose missionaries are but "one more example of patronizing oppressors preaching love."[80]

A reporter for a Madras newspaper, after hearing Thurman speak about the history of Black advancement since Emancipation, offered unstinting praise: "The like of it has not been heard before" and was comparable only to when "Mahatma Gandhi, in his pre-Indian career came as the messenger of suffering Indians in South Africa." What made Thurman's talk special was "the response of hearts that felt their linking up with another race as the lecturer proceeded with the interpretation of his people, defending them against false judgment, proclaiming the grit and character that was evolved under great stress, tracing the moods through which they have passed and expressing the bases of their confidence, while betraying no bitterness against their environment." Thurman's talk was no "cold intellectual presentation" but rather "the soulful expression of the faith of the meek that rose conqueror over trials and suffering."[81]

Not all Madrasis were equally complimentary. T. K. Jagannanthacharya, who saw Thurman lecture in the city, lambasted Thurman, starting with his choice of marriage partner: "By marrying a lady, who, I guess, is not a Negro, certainly has led you away from your duty towards the preservation of your Negro Race." (Sue Bailey Thurman, whose maternal grandfather had been the owner of her maternal grandmother, really wasn't all that light-skinned, but perhaps was light enough to confuse Indian observers concerned to uphold a high standard of racial purity and unused to the practical implications of America's one-drop rule.) Even Thurman's deep ebony skin color wasn't black enough. Mr. Jagannanthacharya asked to be put into contact with "a pure Negro—an English-educated [Negro] who is born of Negro father and Negro mother who is not a Christian," from whom he could "learn more of pure Negro customs, culture, etc. and of life."[82] No response by Thurman is extant, but letters and comments of this sort certainly contributed to his feeling that in Asia he had been "challenged as I was in the vastness of Indian life, all the thinking and the working out of this problem that I had done over the years on the word of Jesus to the disinherited now came to the fore."[83]

One of Thurman's hopes from the time the tour was announced in March 1934 was the possibility that he might be able to meet with Gandhi. Thurman had been an admirer of Gandhi for many years. He had been a pacifist, active in the prominent pacifist organization the Fellowship of Reconciliation since his sophomore year at Morehouse College. As of yet, no African Americans had been able to arrange a visit with Gandhi, primarily because of logistical complications.[84] But the lack of physical contact didn't prevent a steady stream of mutual admiration between Gandhi and African Americans. In 1921 the *Chicago Defender* called Gandhi "the greatest man in the world today," and W. E. B. Du Bois, writing in the pages of *The Crisis,* only slightly

Sue Bailey Thurman with Mahatma Gandhi in Bardoli, India, 21 February 1936

qualified this, calling him the "most famous colored person in the world." Gandhi returned the compliment, writing a special message "To the American Negro" in *The Crisis* in 1929.[85] Muriel Lester, a prominent English pacifist and social reformer, was a close associate of Gandhi, and he had stayed during his 1931 visit to Britain at her London settlement house, Kingsley Hall. When she heard about the forthcoming trip of the Negro Delegation, she was so excited that she insisted that Thurman, at her expense, travel from Washington, D.C., to Berkeley, California, where she was staying, to talk with her for a few hours.[86] After the meeting, she contacted Gandhi about the delegation's plans, and Thurman wrote to Gandhi on his own as well. When the delegation arrived in Ceylon, a postcard from Gandhi was awaiting the Negro Delegation, inviting them to visit him.[87]

The delegation tried to arrange their meeting with Gandhi from the time of the arrival, October 1935, but the complexities of their schedules, Gandhi's bad health, and the weariness and illnesses of the delegation caused several opportunities to be missed. And when, around 19 February 1936, the delegation arrived in Bombay, they knew that if there was to be a meeting with Gandhi, it was now or never. Gandhi felt the same way. When he learned that they had arrived in Bombay, he sent an emissary to contact them, with a letter that expressed his willingness, despite his ill health, to come to Bombay to meet them.[88] When Thurman was going to the nearest telegraph station to contact Gandhi, he passed a man wearing a Gandhi cap. They walked past each other, then turned around, and each knew, without asking, each other's errand. Thurman, both a skeptical rationalist and a mystic, looked upon such events as examples of portals to a hidden level of reality.[89]

When Thurman met Gandhi he was likely still thinking of another event that had occurred two weeks before. During a visit to Peshawar (now in Pakistan), on the border with Afghanistan, the Negro Delegation spent a morning doing some sightseeing, visiting the famous Khyber Pass, the passage through the towering Hindu Kush mountains that had for millennia provided an entrance into South Asia for conquest and commerce, the path of a human river that had helped create its vast civilizational stew of peoples, ethnicities, and religions. He had an epiphany in the Khyber Pass. When he returned home, he would try to create "a religious fellowship developed in America that was capable of cutting across all racial barriers, with a carry-over into the common life."[90] It would be a community committed to racial equality and religious openness. Thurman would spend the rest of his life trying to fulfill this vision. "The genius of Christianity," he would write in 1938, contrasting it to religions in Asia, "tends to be exclusive. It is an either-or genius."[91] Thurman was not blind to the challenges and tensions within and between the religions in India, but he was fascinated by their complex entwining. He would try to develop a version of Christianity that wouldn't define itself by its dichotomies, exclusions, and prohibitions.

The time Thurman spent in India was less transformational than conformational. None of his basic beliefs changed; all of his beliefs were challenged and intensified, provided with a new impetus, immediacy, and urgency. He experienced race and the clash of white and nonwhite as he never had before and never would again, and he returned to the United States with an incandescent hatred of imperialism. Thurman's time in India remains, properly, the best-known episode in Thurman's life, six months of a life of eighty years. It is at its center, midway through his life's journey, rippling in all directions like a stone thrown in a pond, back to his earliest days, and forward to the challenges ahead.

1

Deep River

A Daytona Boyhood

The census enumerator came on a June day in 1900. Little Howard Thurman was about seven months old. Living in the same West Palm Beach, Florida, household were his sister, Henrietta (aged three); his mother, Alice Ambrose Thurman (aged twenty-eight), and her husband, Saul Solomon Thurman (aged fifty.)[1] West Palm Beach was just a speck, with a total population in 1900 of only 564 and, like young Howard, newly fledged, incorporated only in 1894. The Thurmans were living in this still quite out-of-the-way south Florida community because Saul Solomon Thurman was a laborer on the Florida East Coast Railway. Developing the nether regions of south Florida was the extravagant dream of Henry M. Flagler, a former Standard Oil executive. The new railroad was a key element in his plans. West Palm Beach was originally platted as a residence for servants in the two new hotels Flagler built in adjacent Palm Beach.[2] Alice Thurman had likely also been in West Palm Beach the previous 19 November, when Howard Thurman was born.

We aren't sure. Thurman rarely discussed his place of birth.[3] But we do know that the location of his nativity meant little to Thurman, since if he was born in West Palm Beach, he and his family moved, probably when he was still an infant, some two hundred miles to the north, to Daytona, the city he always thought of as his hometown. For most of his life he recorded his birth date as 19 November 1900, rather than 1899. Thurman, for various reasons, as we shall see, did not like to discuss the actual circumstances of his birth.

Daytona, like many central and south Florida cities, had no antebellum existence. The site of a failed attempt by white abolitionists to create a post-Emancipation settlement for Blacks, it received its name, in 1876, from one

Matthias Day, an Ohio businessman, one of the many northern whites who played important roles in the early history of Daytona. The red-letter year for the history of Daytona was 1888, when the Florida East Coast Railway was extended to the area. From a population of 300 in 1880, Daytona grew to 3,572 by 1910.[4]

Unlike nearby Daytona Beach and Seabreeze, all three to be eventually joined to form the City of Daytona Beach, Daytona was not on the famous beach. It was separated from the Atlantic Ocean and the main tourist trade by the Halifax River, a misnamed tidal estuary. Daytona, humbler than its all-white beachfront neighbors, always had a substantial Black population. Within Daytona there were three African American neighborhoods, Waycross, Newton, and Midway. Thurman grew up in Waycross, at 516 Whitehall Street, in a three-room clapboard house that still stands. Waycross was primarily a neighborhood of private homes, with one restaurant, one rooming house, several fraternal lodges, and two churches, Baptist and AME, which were the subject of a local rivalry. (Thurman was a Baptist, and his schoolyard banter included many heated conversations and the occasional fistfight with AME counterparts on the efficacy and scriptural warrants for pedobaptism.)[5]

Waycross was separated from Midway, the business center of Black Daytona, by the main line of the Florida East Coast Railway, which ran down the middle of Waycross. (With numerous unprotected grade crossings, an all-too-common occurrence in Black neighborhoods, both Waycross and Midway were on the wrong side of the tracks.)[6] Some sense of what Black Daytona looked like in Thurman's day can be garnered from a series of photographs of Midway taken by the famed photographer Gordon Parks for the Office of War Information in 1943. Midway comes across as a tidy town, where proud people lived in modest homes, worked hard in small businesses, and attended well-maintained churches.[7] For Thurman a visit to Midway, with its pool halls, movie theater, professional offices, and eateries, was always "like a country boy going to the city."[8]

That said, there was little that was countrified about the young Thurman. He sometimes categorized people as either rural or urban. (Jesus was rural; Paul was urban.) Rural people were more straightforward, and the "distance from the center" of their being "to the circumference was very short," whereas for city people "distance from the center to the circumference was very involved." If Thurman sometimes fancied himself as having a rural sensibility, he was urban to his core. (Even his abiding and abounding immersion in the world of nature was from the vantage of an observer rather than a tiller of the soil.) Thurman's Daytona childhood, with its many opportunities and stimulations, is a key to understanding the person he became. If Daytona during

Thurman's childhood was perhaps more of a town than a city, it was sophisticated in ways beyond the size of its population, and it was only the first of several urban areas and cities that shaped the complicated "city man" that he would always be.[9]

White Daytona, in its paternalistic fashion, was impressed by the civic energy of Daytona's Black residents. This from a 1900 city directory: "Here we see colored men and women at every step decently clad, healthy in look and well behaved. . . . Waycross has a population of 300, two good, large well-built nurseries, a public school and a kindergarten, drug store, grocery store, Masonic and Odd Fellows lodge. . . . There is abundant proof that here is a fairly industrious population, self-supporting."[10]

Black Daytonans felt the same way about themselves, without the condescension. A 1915 article in the *Chicago Defender,* "Southern City Making Wonderful Progress," asserted that "there are but few towns in the United States that offer men and women of the race better business and educational opportunities than this place. . . . It already has to its credit quite a number of the most successful business men and women of the race in this section of the country."[11] Daytona was the sort of town Booker T. Washington could, and did, love.[12] Black Daytona celebrated New Year's Day, doubling as Emancipation Day, the anniversary of the Emancipation Proclamation, with pomp and reverence. In 1913 the highlight was, as described in a local newspaper, a float with "four old mothers who were eyewitnesses to the liberating of the race." Two years later the event was celebrated "in a grand style . . . with a grand parade, consisting of floats, music, etc.," capped off with appropriate Emancipation Day oratory.[13] Thurman no doubt watched the parades from the sidelines.

Daytona had what passed for relatively moderate race relations in the Deep South, circa 1900–1910, at the perigee of the Jim Crow era. This was connected to the prominence of northern whites in its early history. A white former abolitionist in Daytona in 1887 praised "the spirit of the white citizens of East Florida toward the colored people," so much so that Blacks from South Carolina felt it was "like escaping from slavery to a land of freedom."[14] If this was laying it on a bit thick, it was not entirely untrue, either. By the time of Thurman's childhood, Daytona was a winter resort for some of America's wealthiest individuals (including, in nearby Ormond Beach, the wealthiest of them all, John D. Rockefeller Sr.). The presence of northern whites—the so-called "snowbirds"—in the town, Thurman writes, was a "tempering influence," making "contact between the races less abrasive than it might have been otherwise."[15] (One example of their charity was a private kindergarten in Waycross that Thurman attended, paid for by snowbirds.)[16]

A source of the civic pride of Black Daytonans was that theirs was the largest city in Florida in which Blacks continued to vote in large numbers throughout the Jim Crow era.[17] In 1898 Joseph Brook Hankerson, a Black barber and Baptist minister, was elected to the Daytona City Commission, and hopeful voices in the Black press hailed this as "the sign of the dawning of a new day in the South for capable and worthy Negroes."[18] This proved to be a false dawn, and there would not be another Black candidate for office in Daytona until after World War II. However, this did not mark the end of Black political influence in Daytona. In exchange for Black votes, Black neighborhoods were granted municipal favors such as new storm sewers, new schools, paved sidewalks, electric street lights, and even Black policemen.[19] (A Black reporter, driving through Daytona in 1912, was almost giddy after being stopped for speeding and admonished by a Black officer.)[20] In 1916 some of the white candidates for office went to a forum for Black voters promising to protect Black prisoners against lynch mobs.[21] The incorporation of the City of Daytona Beach in 1926, merging Daytona with its all-white neighbors, Daytona Beach and Seabreeze, was something of a municipal gerrymander, done in part to dilute Black voting strength. Still, Black involvement in the political process continued, and in Daytona Beach in the 1920s and 1930s there was a dominant political machine that relied on Black votes to foil an attempt of the Ku Klux Klan to take over local politics. In 1929, 30 percent of Daytona Beach's registered voters were African American.[22]

At the same time, Daytona was also a typical southern town, and one that became more so during the years Thurman grew up there, as more white southerners moved to the area. Black and white worlds, Thurman wrote, were "separated by a wall of quiet hostility and overt suspicion."[23] If the beachfront houses and resorts created numerous employment opportunities for Blacks, the beachfront communities were "sundown towns" where Blacks were not permitted at night.[24] Thurman wrote that he "could work in Sea Breeze and Daytona Beach, but I was not allowed to spend the night there, nor could I be seen after dark without being threatened." White Daytona was no better. It was "no place for loitering. Our freedom of movement was carefully circumscribed, a fact so accepted that it was taken for granted."[25] Sometime after 1900 Black store owners who catered to whites were forced from their downtown locations and moved their businesses to the African American neighborhoods, losing much of their customer base.

It was in the early years of the twentieth century that the full minatory apparatus of Jim Crow came to Daytona.[26] One account placed the arrival of complete racial separation in public places in the years 1902 to 1906, though Thurman remembered that in 1910, when famed auto racer Barney Oldfield set a new world speed record (131.72 mph) on the hard, flat sand of Daytona Beach, Black and white spectators were not separated, and the beach was "not segregated as it was later to become."[27] Daytona was not free of the most heinous aspects of the South's racial regime. In 1907 there was a lynching, and the dead man was carried through the Black neighborhoods as a reminder for Blacks "not to get out of their place."[28]

Thurman often told the story that when he was a young boy, while engaged in one of his first jobs, raking leaves for a white family, a young girl came up to him with a straight pin and stuck him. When Thurman yelped, the girl was confused, telling him she thought Black people couldn't feel pain.[29] For Thurman, this was a metaphor for the way Blacks and whites did their best to pass by each other with the least amount of contact, understanding, or empathy. Thurman's Black world was emotionally "sealed off from the white world" in which greater dangers lurked than oblivious little girls with straight pins.[30] For Thurman, as a young boy, on his side of the Halifax River, there was "serenity, honor, and peace in the Black community." On the other shore "was chaos, cruelty, and indecency."[31] Christianity, the religion that whites and Blacks shared, only exacerbated the tension. Not only was there "no communication between the white church . . . and the Negro church," but in Thurman's opinion "the white people in our town who were the most friendly and less antagonistic were numbered principally among those who were not members of any church."[32] Waycross was Thurman's world, a tight one in which "any child belonged to the whole immediate community, so that if an adult saw me and wanted me to do an errand I did not have to go home to ask my mother's permission. I would simply do it, because if I said Mrs. Thomas told me that was all that was necessary."[33] One of the female guardians of Waycross was Thurman's grandmother, Nancy Ambrose. With his mother often in service as a cook, his grandmother was the dominant figure in his household.[34] As he told an interviewer: "She was really a positive, strong, tender human being. Tender as over against soft, you see? And she was kind without being sentimental. She could sit on the front porch and control all the children in three blocks, just without ever moving from her chair." When the interviewer asked if he was included in her scope of supervision, he was surprised at the question: "Oh, my . . . that was automatic."[35]

Nancy Ambrose had been born into slavery, around 1844, in Madison County, Florida, in the northern Florida area then known as Middle Florida, on the Georgia-Florida border, in the only region of the state that was extensively developed in the antebellum era. After its acquisition by the United States in 1821 from Spain, Middle Florida rapidly became a part of the South's burgeoning cotton economy. Madison County was an area characterized by

Nancy Ambrose, Thurman's grandmother

large plantations, with the Suwannee River running through it. In 1860, of the 7,779 people living in Madison County, 55 percent were enslaved.[36] Nancy Ambrose had roots in South Carolina, where both of her parents and her husband were born.[37]

Before Emancipation, Nancy had been the property of a man she disparaged as "old man McGhee," or John C. McGehee (1802–1882), the second-largest slaveowner in Madison County, with more than one hundred enslaved persons in his possession in 1860. Nancy (and probably her husband, Howard Ambrose, Thurman's namesake) lived at a 2,400-acre plantation in the town of Moseley Hall.[38] John C. McGehee was a native of upcountry South Carolina, as were many of his fellow Madison County planters.[39] A man of parts, McGehee was described by one historian as a "lawyer, circuit court judge, planter, scientific farmer, industrialist, buyer and seller of land [and one might add, of persons], and Presbyterian elder."[40] He took his Christian responsibilities seriously. His niece wrote that "he was the spiritual advisor of his slaves, visiting them in their cabins and reading to them from the Bible," though Nancy Ambrose complained to her grandson that McGehee's biblical selections seemed limited to those passages enjoining slaves to be obedient.[41] In 1860, after an escape attempt, several enslaved persons were shot by McGehee's plantation manager. The following year saw McGehee's most notable stint of public service as president of the secession convention in Tallahassee in January 1861, telling the convention that President-elect Lincoln was controlled by "an infuriated fanatical madness" that will "inevitably destroy every vestige or right growing out of property in slaves."[42]

Of Nancy Ambrose's life before Emancipation, her grandson knew relatively little. In Waycross during Thurman's childhood, the adults were the formerly enslaved and their children. He had been "conditioned so early" from hearing "terrifying stories about what slavery was like" from "the lips of people who had come through the experience."[43] Some who grew up in bondage told stories; others chose silence. Nancy Ambrose was one of the latter. This was not a matter of indifference; except for a few anecdotes, she found it too difficult to discuss her early life. Yet every summer she returned to the place of her birth, visiting her daughter and other relatives in the area, sometimes taking her grandson with her. As Thurman wrote in his autobiography: "It was Grandma's pilgrimage. The slave plantation where she grew up was in this area. She never spoke of it; she did not point out landmarks. Her thoughts were locked behind a fierce wall of privacy and she granted to no one the rights of passage across her own remembered footsteps."[44]

Nancy's husband, Howard Ambrose, was born about 1826 and was about two decades older than his wife. He was born in South Carolina and presumably came with the McGehees to their new home in Florida.[45] There is but a single reference by Thurman to Howard Ambrose: to his talents as a "calculator." Perhaps he kept accounts for McGehee. Perhaps he was one of those enslaved prodigies who amazed audiences with their arithmetical abilities, performing feats such as quickly multiplying together nine-digit numbers in their heads. Thurman mentioned his grandfather as one of those persons who though "bound by shackles and deprived of education" nonetheless became expert "thinkers and designers."[46] Howard Ambrose died in the 1880s.[47] Nancy and Howard's oldest child, of eight, Sarah, was born before Emancipation. Her youngest, Emily, with whom Thurman would be close and remain in contact, was born in 1880. Alice was born in 1878. Nancy outlived her husband by a half century, living into the 1930s.

How the Ambroses fared during Reconstruction is unclear. They stayed in Moseley Hall and probably supported themselves as farmers. Madison County, like all of the heavily African American counties, experienced the violence typical of the Reconstruction and post–Reconstruction-era South. Whites met Blacks' attempts to organize politically and economically with violence, beatings, lynchings, and night riding by the Ku Klux Klan.[48] The father of the minister of his Daytona church when Thurman was a young man, Arthur L. James, a Madison County native, was murdered by a white

Alice Thurman Sams, Thurman's mother

mob when young Arthur was five.[49] Thurman probably heard many similar stories of white violence growing up. At some point, Nancy and Alice moved, along with several other of Alice's siblings, out of Madison County downstate to Daytona and other locations nearby in Volusia County, either because of its slightly better racial climate or the availability of work. For the remainder of her life, Nancy Ambrose usually lived with her daughter, Alice. Alice generally worked as a cook and maid; Nancy was a midwife.

We know almost nothing about Saul Solomon Thurman and the other side of Thurman's family. Howard Thurman, no doubt deliberately, tells very little about him. At some point in the 1890s, probably in Daytona, Alice Ambrose met and married Saul Solomon Thurman. We know from census records that he was born in Florida around 1850. He was more than twenty years older than his wife, and he almost certainly spent his early years in bondage.[50] In the early years of the twentieth century, as noted above, he was working for the Florida East Coast Railway. He was likely employed on its so-called

"Overseas Extension." After putting the towns of the east coast of Florida on the map, Henry Flagler was determined to extend the line to Key West. This island-hopping extension of the line, through malarial wetland and over the ocean through the Keys, was a remarkable engineering feat, but it was also something of a folly, with its financial and human toll far outweighing its economic benefits. It opened in 1912 and lasted only until 1935, when it was destroyed in a hurricane. The line was never rebuilt.[51]

Building the Overseas Extension came at a high cost of human lives. A hurricane in 1906 killed more than 125 railroad workers. In the best of times, Flagler and other railway officials treated the workers with a tight-fisted indifference. The men endured terrible conditions in the camps where they lived, and the railway's treatment of contract laborers became a national scandal, with congressional hearings and a resultant outcry, though most of the attention was focused on the ignominy of white workers toiling in the conditions of unfreedom usually reserved for Blacks. On the other hand, for Black workers, building the railroad was a good, steady job, with some prestige, that paid better and more regularly than most alternatives. For Saul Solomon Thurman, whatever the compensation, working on the railroad destroyed his health.[52]

Saul Solomon Thurman would come home to his family in Daytona every other week. He was, Thurman tells us, quiet, fastidious, and soft-spoken.[53] Young Howard would wait for him at the barber shop when he tidied himself up before going home. One day in 1907 or 1908, Saul Solomon Thurman returned home midweek, desperately ill from a respiratory infection. Five days later he was dead of pneumonia. In those pre-penicillin days, there was no adequate treatment for serious respiratory infection, and whatever little was available to whites, there was less for African Americans. One prayed, tried some folk remedies—Thurman mentions several—and hoped for the best. For Saul Solomon all efforts were unavailing. In his last moments, being held down by his son and wife and Nancy, Alice asked him if he was ready to die. Gasping for air, he replied: "Yes, Alice, all my life, I have been a man. I am not afraid of death. I can meet it." He died shortly thereafter, and the long silence of mother-in-law, wife, and son "was broken only by the sound of our anguished weeping."[54]

Saul Solomon Thurman, Howard tells us, had an "original mind" about religion.[55] His last words, "all my life, I have been a man. I am not afraid of death," are almost the only words of his that Thurman preserved.[56] If it was his creed, it was a common one among Black men at the time, who thought that their only protection was their toughness and that complaining about things would not make them any easier or more palatable. It was a creed, often, for men who thought that religion was for womenfolk and that life was hard enough without being teased by religion's false hopes. Saul Solomon Thurman was not a Christian. On Sunday mornings he would sit on the porch and watch his family go to church. Thurman's mother, Alice, once said that Saul was afraid that "if he joins the church he will lose his soul because he felt that there was more religion, more honesty, and more virtue and all that sort of thing in people who did not join the church [and] did not have the pretension of the church."[57]

As Thurman tells us in his autobiography, there were other unbelievers in Daytona, such as his lifelong friend Dr. John Stocking, but in Black Daytona as almost everywhere else, belief was much better organized than unbelief. In his church, Thurman writes, "the 'sinner' was a unique isolate within the generally binding character of community. It was this ultimate isolation that made the sinner the object of such radical concern in the church of my childhood."[58] Death released Saul Solomon Thurman from the control and strictures of the believers. It did not release his family. Because Saul Solomon Thurman died "out of Christ," the minister of the Thurman's church refused to let the sanctuary be used for his funeral service. Nancy Ambrose, being her usual formidable self, marched down to the chairman of the board of deacons and told him that while ministers come and go, deacons do not, and deacons have the final authority to decide what does or does not happen in the church. The deacons relented, but Saul's family now had a place for the service without a minister to conduct it. Finally, a jackleg minister, an itinerant evangelist without a regular congregation, agreed to conduct the service. But he took the occasion to sermonize on the wages of sinfulness and preached the unbelieving Saul Solomon Thurman into hell. Thurman, sitting in the front pew, the "mourner's bench," listened to the eulogy with "wonderment, then anger, and finally mounting rage." Under his breath, he spoke to his mother, "He didn't know Papa, did he? Did he?"[59]

Later, coming home from the cemetery in a buggy, Thurman peppered his mother and grandmother with questions. Why did the reverend do that? Why would he say such mean things? Finally he announced, no doubt echoing what he had heard from Saul Solomon Thurman: "One thing is sure. When I grow up and become a man, I will never have anything to do with the church."[60] This was, for Thurman, a key event in his early life, a shattering transition from childhood innocence to the beginning of adult awareness that all was not right with the world. He opens his two extended autobiographical accounts with this episode and told the story many times.[61] Almost all African American autobiographies of that time and place have a primal scene, a blunt-force introduction to harsh realities, and they often relate stories that involve the humiliation of fathers and the discovery that when their fathers were confronted by whites, their powerful fathers became powerless.[62] But unlike most of these accounts, Thurman's story is one not of white racism but of Black callousness. For Thurman white supremacy was not only brutal, it was utterly insidious, an acid with the potential to leach into Black psyches and their institutions. Evangelical Christianity and Jim Crow, for Thurman, both operated on the principle of exclusion, dividing the world into the saved and the damned.[63] For Howard, Saul Solomon Thurman, in death as in life, was a victim of Jim Crow. His lifelong fight against all that was narrow and unfeeling done in the name of Christianity began in the buggy ride home.

The death and burial of Saul Solomon Thurman was one of the great traumas of young Howard's childhood, one that he spoke of and wrote of often, There was another hurt connected to Saul Solomon Thurman, one that Howard always kept a closely guarded secret. Saul Solomon Thurman was not his biological father. This was not a secret in Waycross. He was teased about it in mean-spirited tittle-tattle from his playmates. The identity of his biological father was also not a secret. Thurman did not discuss this in his autobiography or in his available papers, but he did write about it in a letter to his daughter Anne sometime in the 1970s.[64]

In a 1949 sermon, discussing a character in a novel, he was likely being covertly autobiographical when he stated: "Little by little the word began to get around that he was illegitimate, and it did something to him. It would be a very interesting thing for somebody who had the time and the incentive and the emotional and the intellectual resources, to make a study of the thing that has happened in terms of the projecting of the will of the individual upon the unresolved aspects of his world, growing out of the deeply lying consciousness that he is not within the folds of legitimacy." Those "born out of season," he continues, can either allow themselves to be crushed by the world's unfairness, or vow to prove the world's judgment wrong.[65] This is perhaps Thurman's only extant reference to illegitimacy. We can only surmise how much this condition contributed to what he often describes as his childhood alienation from other people, and his sense of being, in multiple ways, disinherited. And perhaps Thurman's choice of that word, "disinherited," as his favorite term to describe society's outsiders and outcasts, with its connotations of being cut off from a birthright, had a deeper resonance to him than he ever allowed.

We know few details of Thurman's family life after Saul Solomon Thurman's death. In 1907 his younger sister, Madaline, was born. Thurman writes in his autobiography that he was her babysitter and nursemaid, placing her within the handlebars of his bicycle, combing and braiding her hair. She and her brother would remain close throughout their lives.[66] Around 1909, when

Thurman's childhood home in Daytona Beach, with
live oak in backyard and unidentified girl

Thurman would have been in the third or fourth grade, his mother married a
"Mr. Evans" who lived in Lake Helen (about twenty-two miles from Daytona,
inland from the Atlantic). Thurman liked his stepfather, who was a skilled
operator at a sawmill and was respected by his employer. Thurman's family
lived in company housing, and Alice was able, perhaps for the only time in
her life, to stay at home with her children. (Presumably at this time Nancy
Ambrose remained in Daytona Beach, in the family house to which Thurman
would return.) Unfortunately, Mr. Evans died shortly thereafter, and Alice
and family moved back to Daytona, where Alice had to support herself again
as a maid and cook.[67] This was no later than the fall of 1913, when Thurman
was in seventh grade in Daytona. Alice remarried again, to James Sams, of
whom Thurman writes in his autobiography, with considerable understate-
ment, that he "did not feel as close to him as to Mr. Evans." (Their animus
persisted until after World War II.)[68]

Back in Daytona, as Thurman entered adolescence, he could be gregarious or solitary, depending on his mood, though by his account, he was more of a brooder than a joiner. He was a frequent subject of taunting and bullying. "In my early life I was ever haunted by a feeling of awkwardness in all of my relationships." He was pigeon-toed, not conventionally handsome, and, he writes, "fat," picked on by other boys. He had no "masculine back-up," no father, no big brother. He was not athletic.[69] "In my everyday experiences, I seemed to be passed over unnoticed, my company not welcomed by the girls, nor by boys in choosing sides for games. Among my peers I always seemed to be an 'extra.'"[70] (This did not prevent Thurman, who like many nonathletes dreamt of hitting home runs, from being a rather avid sports fan.) "Again and again," as "a boy, by the standards of my fellows, I was inadequate, a failure," writing toward the end of his life that "little failures, middle sized failures, big failures, have never deserted me."[71]

Thurman dealt with this punishing sense of inadequacy in various ways. Eventually, he came to place the bullying by his social circle "in the same category as the treatment by white men of my world," a radical unfairness that he had done nothing to trigger, did not deserve, and would not give in to, another example of how the pervasive meanness of Jim Crow could infect internal African American life.[72] Thurman found other ways to assert his sense of self-worth. He retreated into himself; he grew close to nature: "My world was surrounded by the Atlantic Ocean and the Halifax River . . . and a large wooded area in which there were huckleberries, wild grapes, and rattlesnakes, a very happy combination."[73] He "found more companionship in nature than I did among people. The woods befriended me." For a self-conscious young boy, often uncomfortable in social situations, "the quiet, even the danger of the woods provided my rather lonely spirit with a sense of belonging that did not depend on human relationships."[74]

Thurman loved the night sky. The night was "a presence, an articulate climate" covering "his spirit like a gentle blanket." In those far away pre-neon days, the nights on the Florida coast "were not dark, they were black." He spent "many nights alone along the seashore, the dark Florida night; the many, many bright stars, the vast ocean, the little boy." He "could hear the night think, and feel the night feel."[75] An early poem, from 1920, simply entitled "Night," concludes with this heartfelt if awkward quatrain:

A spell is thrown o'er land and sea
From all mankind there comes a fee
She reigns upon a throne of might
Her king is God, her name is Night.[76]

On the magnificent beach, which at low tide was over a mile wide, Thurman could be alone with the sand, the sea, and the sky, and "had the sense that all things" and "I were *one* lung through which all of life breathed."[77] He particularly cherished those moments, at daybreak and sunset, when these immensities appeared to merge into or come out of their primordial unity, as he described in one of his first published writings.[78]

Above all, Thurman loved the sublimity and power of Florida's many great storms, roaring up the coast, demanding that everyone give them their undivided attention, treating Black and white alike with an impartial and imperious disregard. At the height of a storm, he would run into his backyard and watch its giant live oak tree (which still stands, as of this writing), its branches swaying wildly but remaining secure and rooted. In storms, "the boundaries of self did not hold me. Unafraid, I was held by the storm's embrace. The experience of these storms gave me a certain overriding immunity against much of the pain I would have to deal with in the years ahead." The oak tree, "like the woods, the night, and the pounding surf," were his "earliest companions, giving me space."[79]

Thurman not only found his refuge in nature. He also found his God. (He would later compare the great storms of his childhood to "the numinous silence of sacrament." First the "stillness that pervaded everything" as the barometric pressure dropped, followed by the "maddening fury" of the hurricane, a "noisy silence" that proclaimed the "solidarity and the unity of life," an "act of consummation" before which all human stupidities seemed insignificant and puny.)[80] His sense of finding God in nature was likely at its most intense in childhood, when it was at its least mediated or intellectualized. When alone in nature, he found none of the artificial barriers imposed by human society enclosing his spirit. This was the response of a mystic. (I discuss Thurman's mysticism in detail in subsequent chapters.) Like most mystics, what he sought was a state of higher, exalted consciousness, an awareness of hidden connections. After telling an interviewer in 1976 that he would "go and sit with my back against the oak tree to talk to it about my problems," he explained: "I had a sense from my earliest memory of being a part of this whole rhythmic flow of life and my earliest religious experience. I would talk aloud to God in that setting. And if someone came along they'd wonder what on earth was going on, but this had more religious meaning for me than the things that happened in church."[81] In 1978 he told the journalist and historian Lerone Bennett Jr. that "ever since I can remember I have felt that there is no binding or absolute separation between the segment of life that is Howard Thurman and life."[82]

Thurman's nature mysticism likely had many sources. He was, certainly by his teenage years, an avid reader and enthusiastic writer of nature poetry, the sort of warmed-over Wordsworth that crowded the poetry columns in the popular press in the early twentieth century. At the same time, though Thurman never wrote about this, there were likely influences from African American religion and folklore, such as the practice of adolescents trying to find divine inspiration from solitude in nature, a practice sometimes called "seekin."[83]

He grew up in a household that believed in spirits. He entered the world with a caul, with the amniotic sac covering his face, a real instance of W. E. B. Du Bois's famous metaphor "born with a veil, and gifted with second-sight in this American world."[84] If Du Bois, in *The Souls of Black Folk,* was writing of the painful knowledge one learns being Black in America, Thurman grew up in a household that believed that those born with a caul would indeed develop second sight, the power of clairvoyance. His mother and grandmother also believed that this was a profoundly unlucky gift, as if young Howard would face enough challenges without being burdened with the dubious gift of prematurely knowing his fate. To counteract this, his mother and grandmother pierced his ears, to dissipate its power. But it didn't entirely work. "How deeply I was influenced by this 'superstition' I do not know," he wrote in his autobiography, adding that he had always believed that he had, in some measure, retained the ability of "second sight."[85] His grandmother warned him that nature was somehow uncanny and haunted, filled with specific dangers.[86] He believed in angels. As a child he believed in ghosts, though they seem to have been of the benign variety. Sometimes "they appeared in human form," but on dark nights ghosts "manifested themselves as currents of hot air that surrounded my face." For Thurman, this was the same as the "presence of God," something "real but invisible." As Thurman said in 1978, reflecting on his early years, that "when I refer to God—I am not talking about a thing, I am not talking about an object: I am talking about a Presence."[87] He did "not identify this sense of presence with Jesus." But his was a world, from his childhood to his final days, pervaded by manifestations of the divine.[88]

Alice taught Howard not to be afraid of God or God's creation. In a story he often told, in 1910, Halley's Comet returned, and many adults around him had acquired "comet pills" to be used as protection if the comet fell to earth. One night his mother woke him to view the comet at its most dazzling, its tail dominating the sky. He was afraid. Alice told him: "Nothing will happen to us, Howard. God will take care of us."[89] If there were numerous sources for his mysticism, in the end, it was less the product of his influences than his own spiritual creativity, a determination to find his own path, and his exceptional sensitivity to things usually hidden. From his earliest days, he felt that "when I was born God must have put a live coal in my heart, for I was his man and there was no escape."[90]

But if Thurman found his God in nature, he found something just as important in church, a community. Participation in the life of the Mount Bethel Baptist Church in Daytona was, of course, originally involuntary. From his earliest days, Thurman's Sundays were given over to the church, with Sunday school, twice-a-day services, in addition to Wednesday prayer meetings, fifth Sunday evenings, and so on. (One of his earliest memories was burying his head in the lap of his grandmother's taffeta dress to take a brief respite "during the endless hours of the worship service.")[91] But soon he discovered his own reasons to attend church. Like many lonely adolescents, Thurman found an acceptance in church he could not gain elsewhere. Everything in the Mount Bethel Baptist Church, a wooden structure with a single large room, emphasized a group sense of shared purpose.

Thurman's mother, Alice, "was very devout, a very conscientious worker in the church." How devout he would not realize until the 1940s, when he discovered, inadvertently (she had never told him) that she had a complete fast every Friday, devoting as many hours during the day as possible to prayer.[92] Thurman tells less about the specifics of the faith of his grandmother, except that she was "not quite as emotionally tied up in the church as my mother," but Nancy, with a more forceful personality than her daughter, became a not-to-be-trifled-with pillar of Mount Bethel Baptist.[93] When he was twelve, he was "converted" (with Thurman's scare quotes in the original) during a children's revival. He was excited by the prospect of being baptized. But when asked why he wanted to be baptized, he answered, because "I want to be a Christian." This was the wrong answer. Crestfallen, he went home to tell his grandmother, who "took me by the hand and carried me back to meet these same deacons and to say how dare you stand between this boy and the church. Who made you the judge?" The deacons did as they were told. Thurman's answer was no doubt innocent, but it revealed more than he knew. From his earliest days, he writes, Jesus was a companion, a friend to a lonely boy, rather than a God.[94] On some level, Thurman, assured as he was of the inner presence of the divine, probably found the evangelical emphasis on the externals of the conversion experience to be superfluous. He was less interested in accepting Christ and more interested in being accepted as a member of the church (though without ever quite forgetting that this was the same church that had ostracized Saul Solomon Thurman).[95]

And so he was baptized. On Baptism Sunday, in a candidate's white robes, he marched with the church members to the Halifax River, led by "old lady Wright," who would sing "in full and glorious voice" verse after verse, "Oh, mourner, don't you want to go / Let's go down to Jordan, Hallelujah." The minister dipped him in the river, baptizing him "in the name of the Father,

Son, and Holy Ghost," and he was helped to his feet by the deacons, accompanied by a loud chorus of "Amens" from the shore.[96] Thurman would later in life find that whatever doubts he had about the purpose or efficacy of a religious ceremony were often overcome by his appreciation of its majesty. Belonging to the church, he would write, gave him "a fontal sense of worth that could not be destroyed by any of life's outrages."[97] After his baptism, membership in the church opened doors and became a source of strength. His spiritual progress was closely monitored by two older sponsors, and soon he was conducting adult prayer meetings. Thurman thrived on the dense network of conferences and other special occasions within the Baptist and Christian world, going to interesting places and meeting interesting people. In August 1915, the *Chicago Defender* reported that one "Howard W. Thormon" had attended the Baptist Young People's Union and Sunday School convention in Melbourne, Florida.[98] For the next quarter century, the Christian circuit, especially the YMCA, the YWCA, and the Christian Student Movement, would be his second home.

Mount Bethel's Christianity was intensely evangelical, and its ministers were in the business of saving souls. The church held revivals, such as the campaign of September 1915, just as Thurman was preparing to leave for high school in Jacksonville. As described in the *Chicago Defender*, "Rev. Nay [a visiting minister] preached a red-hot gospel for eleven days and when the smoke of battle cleared away twenty-nine souls were converted and thirteen reclaimed otherwise."[99] Thurman almost certainly went through an evangelical phase as he understood it, and there are traces of evangelical language in his earliest letters and some other evidence of a conventional Christianity that he soon abandoned.

That said, the regular ministers at Mount Bethel were, Thurman tells us, "not 'whoopers.'" They preached from written texts, they emphasized moral responsibility, and they were "more thoughtful than emotional."[100] Most were college-educated, like Samuel A. Owen, minister during Thurman's teenage years, who was a graduate of Atlanta Baptist College (now Morehouse College) and later in life would be the president of one college and have another named after him.[101] Thurman was annoyed when the president of Rochester Theological Seminary, when Thurman was a student there in the mid-1920s, asked him to speak about attending camp meetings, as if all Black Christians spent their Sundays perseverating in the canebrake.[102] Mount Bethel emphasized education, and church members tried to help Thurman and others gain access to high school, not an easy feat in a city without a school for Blacks beyond the seventh grade.[103] The focus of the church and its ministers was how religion can provide the wherewithal for personal stability and success, and how this was necessarily a community-wide endeavor. W. J. Jackson, the pastor of Mount Bethel Baptist Church during Thurman's early years, had a "famous" oft-delivered sermon on the topic of "From Slavery to Honorable Citizenship."[104] For Thurman the importance of Mount Bethel was that it gave its members the spiritual courage to live their lives as free men and women in the turn-of-the-twentieth-century South. "There was a feeling of sharing primarily in community," he writes in his autobiography, "more than all the other communal ties, it also undergirded one's sense of personal identity," providing a sense "that whatever I did with my life mattered."[105]

Another task of "personal identity" in adolescence is growing into an adult body and its attendant challenges and responsibilities. Thurman, living in a household with four women, needed what he called "masculine idols," men who could bolster the shy, awkward young man's confidence and sometimes shaky sense of his masculinity.[106] He found dynamic, successful men who saw something special in the young Thurman. There was Dr. John T. Stocking, just beginning his practice during Thurman's adolescence. Like Saul Solomon Thurman, Stocking was a nonbeliever. And this, Thurman writes, "cost him: There was a feeling that in our community that if a doctor did not belong to the church as a devout Christian, he was out of touch with the spirit of God," and no one wanted to trust their health to someone so spiritually challenged. This changed when, one night, at a church food sale, Stocking, from across the street, saw Waycross's town bully and drunk charge into the social hall with a drawn pistol, and Stocking walked into the hall and coldcocked him. He got God-fearing patients thereafter but still had nothing to do with religion. He offered to pay Thurman's tuition at medical school and could not understand why such a bright young man would want to devote himself to something as useless as religion.[107]

The other masculine idol Thurman singled out was his cousin Thornton L. Smith, a one-time semi-pro baseball player and owner of a restaurant in Midway, which became "the largest soda fountain and wholesale and retail ice cream business in town."[108] Thurman, who churned ice cream in Smith's store as one of his first jobs, deserves a small sliver of the credit for the store's success. (Making his own ice cream for parties would long be a Thurman specialty.) Thornton was a civic leader and, in Thurman's words, "a wise man, unacquainted with fear," who worked to defeat the Klan in Daytona in the 1920s.[109]

Thurman's forays into adolescent self-discovery sometimes took him down some unexpected paths, such as entering the boozy, hypermasculine world of high-stakes card games. Another cousin, James Murray, encouraged Thurman's evident talent at card playing and convinced him to play with professional gamblers. Thurman was proud of his ability at "outwitting or outguessing" his opponents. He was developing a mystic's talent to peer beneath surfaces and intuitively reach the inner life of others, and if this gift was perhaps better devoted to more spiritual pursuits, it no doubt aided him in penetrating the poker faces of his playing companions. This included victories at the card table over one Adolphus Berry, a professional gambler with the reputation of murdering people who made him angry, but Thurman was apparently unfazed. His brief career as a card shark ended when he realized his cousin was betting on him without telling him, and making a fair amount of money doing so. This led him to briefly consider becoming a professional card player himself, but the thought so frightened him that he decided to foreswear card playing forever. For the rest of his life he had a "mental block" about card games of any sort, even when his daughters wanted to play friendly card games such as "Go Fish" with him."[110]

Whatever the meaning of this strange episode for Thurman, becoming a man primarily meant for him accepting the responsibilities of adulthood, and one lesson Thurman learned from John Thornton, from his grandmother, mother, and from almost everyone he met was the importance of hard work, of doing a task willingly and doing it well. For Nancy Ambrose, and for all Black Daytona—save perhaps its professional gamblers—industriousness was both an ideology and a practical necessity. Thurman was early on schooled in both. He worked all through his primary and secondary school years, long hours of toil in addition to long hours of study, doing both without complaint, often to the point of exhaustion. His varied work experience included the full range of vocational opportunities open to Blacks in urban areas. When his mother and grandmother took in laundry from white families in Daytona, he picked up and delivered the bundles. He raked leaves. He worked at a shoeshine stand but had neither "the skill nor the manner to be a successful bootblack."[111] He was the caretaker of the winter home of a wealthy snowbird during the summer, where his responsibilities included cooking meals for the owner's two bird dogs. He worked one summer as a baker (a notoriously hot and uncomfortable working environment) for six days a week, ten hours a day.[112] He also became a commercial fisherman, and by the time he was studying for his eighth-grade exams, he started the day at sea, took his catch to a stall, and "ran a fish market, studied my lessons at the market [illegible], went to school to recite them, immediately after reporting for my job."[113] Thurman's combination of precocious academic and entrepreneurial skills led to, in June 1915, what was likely the first mention of Thurman in print: "We are glad to note that Mr. Howard Thurman, a recent graduate of Daytona grammar school, is doing a fine business in his fish market."[114]

Thurman's lifelong friend, Daytona Beach
educator Mary McLeod Bethune, ca. 1916

In addition to Stocking and Thornton, there was one more crucial "idol"
in his early years. But not a masculine one. As Thurman remembered, he first
heard Mary McLeod Bethune speak at Mount Bethel Baptist Church before
he was wearing long pants. Their friendship ended only with her death in
1955, when Thurman delivered the main eulogy at her Daytona Beach funeral,
saying that "her life has been involved with my own life almost since I remember my own life," like a second mother, or second grandmother.[115] For many
years Bethune had been perhaps the most famous and honored Black person
in America (and certainly the most famous and honored Black woman). As
a young boy he regularly attended events at the Bethune Institute, the girl's
school she founded in Daytona in 1904, which, as the Bethune-Cookman
Institute, evolved into a four-year coeducational college. Like John Stocking and Thornton Smith, Bethune was deeply involved in local politics, but

unlike them, she expanded her ambit to a national stage, as the founder of the National Council of Negro Women, and later as one of the most prominent and influential members of Franklin Roosevelt's so-called "Black Cabinet." She was the model of the educated, spiritually aware, politically acute Black person, equally comfortable with Black and white audiences, a model that Thurman would spend a lifetime emulating, and she was no doubt a model for his burgeoning feminism as well.[116] From all of his Daytona idols he found examples of Black success, from persons who had gained the respect of whites while retaining the confidence of Blacks.

If there was one value that all of Thurman's idols placed above all others, it was education. He would pursue his education with a passionate intensity and an unsated omnivorousness. Education for African Americans raised in Thurman's time and place was always a collective enterprise. People worked together to realize the dreams of a select few, who were never allowed to forget just how fortunate they were and the responsibilities this entailed. The emphasis on education, respectability, propriety, and racial self-advancement known as "uplift" was a pervasive though somewhat amorphous ideology in the early twentieth-century South. It was not limited to the Black middle class and had passionate believers among the Black poor, such as Thurman's illiterate grandmother and grade-school-educated mother. Thurman remembered the separation tantrum he went through on his first day of kindergarten, but his mother left him at the school, telling the teacher, "I want my boy to learn." His kindergarten teacher, Miss Julia Green, whom Thurman remembered as "tall, very dignified, with large eyes," engaged the reluctant student in class activities. A half century later, in 1963, when a still far from completely desegregated Daytona Beach celebrated "Howard Thurman Day" with the mayor and other civic leaders in attendance, Thurman's highlight was being reunited with Julia Green.[117] School soon became a second home. And Thurman knew that he was going to school for his mother, his grandmother, and the generations of African Americans who never made it inside the schoolhouse door.

Thurman liked to relate the story his grandmother told, that when she was a little girl, she was the personal attendant of the young daughter of her master. The young girl, excited by her lessons, started to teach young Nancy the alphabet. When these surreptitious educational trysts were discovered, it led to a whipping all around and an end to instruction. "My grandmother felt that there must be some magic in writing and reading," Thurman said. Since whites would go to such lengths to prevent little Black girls from learning its secret, she told told herself that "if ever freedom came," she would unlock its mysteries.[118] Nancy Ambrose, unfortunately, never acquired the tools of literacy, but her grandson said she "insisted that we would learn or die. There was nothing in between."[119] Anything lackadaisical in his behavior or attention to his studies would lead to a hiding. (Howard first had to go outside and fashion the instrument of his punishment. He started by cutting relatively brittle switches from a peach tree, but Nancy got wise to that and insisted on oak.)[120]

In Daytona, as throughout the Black South, there was a ruthless winnowing of young Black bodies and minds from the classroom, as inadequate provisions and funding made regular school attendance a goal obtained only by the most determined. In 1915 in Volusia County, in which Daytona is located, the elementary school term for whites was 6 months, for Blacks, 4.9 months. Regular attendance rates were 98 percent for whites, 72 percent for Blacks; illiteracy rates, 2.0 percent for whites, 22.9 percent for Blacks; weekly teachers' salaries, $24.01 for whites, $4.94 for Blacks.[121] (And this compares favorably to the statistics for Florida as a whole, with only 58 percent of Black students aged six to fourteen attending school.)[122] Thurman's seventh-grade report card survives. He received a grade of 100 in deportment, reading, arithmetic, geography, grammar and language, U.S. history, physiology, and agriculture, with a 90 in spelling (never one of Thurman's strong suits) and a 91 in writing (if Thurman's execrable penmanship was part of the grade, that was generous).[123]

In Daytona, funds for educating Black students extended only to the seventh grade. In one of the innumerable catch-22s of Jim Crow, the argument against a public high school for African Americans was of course the fact that there was no eighth grade. Thurman was undaunted. His evident promise led the principal of his school, R. H. Howard, to offer to tutor Thurman on the eighth-grade curriculum on his own time. Thurman, fourteen years old, was working full-time, but teacher and pupil managed to get together for study during their respective lunch hours. The white school superintendent insisted on testing Thurman himself. He passed. The next problem was finding a high school. In all of Florida, there were, in 1910, only 492 Black secondary school students (about 3 percent of those age-eligible) attending two public schools and six private schools, all of the latter connected to religious denominations.[124] Thurman, probably helped by connections at his local church, was admitted to Florida Baptist Academy in Jacksonville.[125] But to go to a private school in Jacksonville was an obvious financial burden on Thurman's mother and grandmother. There simply was no money for tuition or room and board. As he wrote in June 1918, his mother, "God bless her holy name . . . toiled morning noon and night that we [Thurman and his two sisters] may be permitted to attend public schools," but when it came to high school, she said, "Son you go but I cannot do anything for you financially."[126] Thurman told his mother he wanted only her prayers. His mother evidently did provide some additional financial assistance, taking some sort of advance payout on an insurance policy to give him enough money to pay for his train fare to Jacksonville. He made arrangements to stay with a relative, doing chores to earn his keep.[127]

And this takes us to a story that had extraordinary power for Thurman, a chance meeting so significant that in 1979 he dedicated his autobiography "to the stranger in the railroad station who restored my broken dream sixty-five years ago." Thurman was beginning his journey with an old borrowed trunk, without handles, tied together with rope, a dollar and change in his pocket, and absolutely no margin for errors or additional expenses. As he was leaving, his grandmother told him that "there is one thing I want you to remember. Look up always, not down. Look forward always, not back. And remember, everything you get you've got to work for."[128] With this benediction and pithy condensation of the philosophy of uplift, Thurman left for the station. But sometimes hard work needs to be supplemented by good fortune. When he came to the station, the station master told him that regulations stipulated that the ticket must be attached to the handle, and since his trunk had no handles, it would have to be shipped express, for which Thurman did not have the money. So Thurman, so close to his dream of high school yet so far, sat down on the station steps and "cried my heart out." And then, in his own words:

> Presently I opened my eyes and saw before me a large pair of work shoes. My eyes crawled upwards until I saw before me the man's face. He was a black man, dressed in overalls and a denim cap. As he looked down, he rolled a cigarette and lit it. Then he said, "Boy, what in the hell are you crying about?"
>
> And I told him.
>
> "If you're trying to get out of this damn town to get an education, the least I can do is to help you. Come with me," he said.
>
> He took me around to the agent and asked, "How much does it cost to send this boy's trunk to Jacksonville?"
>
> Then he took out his rawhide money bag and counted the money out. When the agent handed him the receipt, he handed it to me. Then, without a word, he turned and disappeared down the railroad track. I never saw him again.[129]

The story had many levels of significance for Thurman. It was about leaving home for the first time, becoming a man, and then being reduced to crying like a child. What could Thurman do? He couldn't go to Jacksonville; he didn't have the money. And he couldn't go home, for the embarrassment, and because it would only put his mother and grandmother in the position of having somehow to raise more money for him, when it was clear that they had gone beyond their meager budget to equip him for high school in the first place. So he was stuck in the station, with no way to avoid deeper humiliation. And then comes his rescue. It was a tale of racism and Black solidarity, about finding oneself alone, isolated, and scared, and finding, when most needed, one's community, in the person of an anonymous stranger. (If the clerk's decision to charge more for the trunk was not result of racism, you never would have been able to convince Thurman.) It was about his family, with his rescuer, dressed like a railroad worker, who might have been the ghost of Saul Solomon Thurman, gruffly helping young Howard over the bumps of this crucial rite of passage. It was about the importance of education as a subversive act, honored by his mother and grandmother and the man at the station, none of them from the "respectable class" of Blacks, trying to grasp something precious that whites were trying so hard to keep out of their reach. Nancy Ambrose had often told her grandson that "your only chance is to get an education. The white man will destroy you if you don't."[130]

On some level it was also about religion, and the conviction that the seemingly random events that make up a life are never quite the result of happenstance. Providence would be perhaps too strong a term for Thurman's belief; luck is too weak. It was one of those uncanny linkages between two events, a brief moment when a hidden, benign undergirding and connectedness of the universe is glimpsed. If Thurman's God was in a live oak tree, God could also be found in a railway station. The episode marked the end of his childhood. He had to leave the tight-knit community of Waycross behind to obtain what he wanted. He left for Jacksonville. Never again would he make Daytona his permanent home.

2

"My People Need Me"

High School Years

The trunk with no handles was safely on the train. Thurman traveled the ninety miles from Daytona to Jacksonville. While on the train he promised God that if he ever obtained his education and earned a living, he would be able to tell his mother, "Now you can go home and not work anymore for anybody." She could tend her garden and "live [her] life without worry." He also vowed that "as long as I earned any money, a part of that money every year of my life would help some kid in school." He was able to keep both promises, the latter for more than sixty years.[1] Florida Baptist Academy awaited. Perhaps the episode at the train station was a sign that nothing during his high school years—except perhaps the academic work itself—would come easily. He needed tuition, he needed money for room and board, he needed part-time jobs to supplement his slender resources, and he needed time for his studies. Everything else was a luxury, including eating and sleeping. "The four years in high school were not easy years," he would write in his autobiography. "There was never enough food and my health began to suffer."[2] In his first year he lived with a relation of his uncle Gilbert Ambrose (his mother's brother), doing chores in lieu of rent, with a twice-a-day four-and-a-half mile walk to and from school. He ate one meal a day to cut down on expenses. When he returned to Daytona at the end of the school year his haggard look frightened his mother. Although always inclined to stoutness, he had lost fifteen to twenty pounds. On seeing him, his mother burst into tears: "I'd rather see you alive and ignorant than educated and dead."[3]

His mother refused to let him live off campus again, but boarding on campus required a lot more money (nine dollars per month), more than Thurman

Florida East Coast Railway station in Daytona Beach, ca. 1920, where
Thurman met "the stranger" who "restored my broken dream"

could possibly earn by working odd jobs. He decided that he would contact
a wealthy snowbird, James Gamble, of Proctor and Gamble, who had given
money to Mary McLeod Bethune's school. He did not know Gamble's Cincinnati address or have a way of finding it, but through one of those coinci-
dences that Thurman did not think were quite random—a "very ill-tempered
woman" yelled at him, "Boy . . . mail these letters," and one of those letters was
addressed to Gamble—he discovered it and wrote to him. Gamble agreed
to give Thurman five dollars per month, an arrangement that continued
throughout his schooling. They would eventually meet, and Gamble became
Thurman's "good and faithful friend."[4]

   If boarding at school led to some improvement in his physical and mental
condition, his deterioration at the end of his first year of high school is a
glimpse into the tightly wound, goal-oriented young man he was, relentlessly
pushing himself to and beyond the point of exhaustion. A feeling of unworthiness haunted Thurman, along with the need to prove himself, again and
again, despite the overabundant confirmation of his worth. In high school
the added obligation he felt to carry the entire Negro race on his shoulders
led to his adopting a Black Protestant ethic that combined a punishingly hard

devotion to duty and a sense of self-abnegation so intense that it could put Max Weber's Calvinists to shame.

This was a recurring pattern. At the end of his senior year he had something akin to a nervous breakdown, collapsing during a graduation reception, though he insisted on remaining on campus to deliver an address. But when he returned to Daytona he was confined to indefinite bedrest, writing one of his favorite teachers that he had been diagnosed with high blood pressure and was paying off his "big bill to Dr. Sleep."[5] It would be one lesson that would go unlearned. A few months later, as a college freshman, he wrote to the same teacher: "I am working, working, working. I preach real hard too. I must do my best even tho it is against my health."[6] Throughout his life he was prey to sudden falls from periods of hyperactivity into deep sloughs, balancing his need for social contact with the necessity of silence, solitude, and inaction.[7] Whatever the physical and psychic toll of these ups and downs, they proved effective. He graduated from Florida Baptist Academy as valedictorian, thereby winning a scholarship to Morehouse College, where, once more pushing himself to the point of exhaustion, he again graduated as valedictorian.

The seven years Thurman attended Florida Baptist Academy and Morehouse College, from 1915 to 1923, were at the core of his formal education, forever imprinting him in numerous ways. Thurman, whose ashes are interred in a monument on the Morehouse College campus, had a deep and abiding love for his educators and for Black educational institutions. He knew how fortunate he was, and how few of his peers from Daytona or elsewhere in the South were able to attend and graduate from high school, much less a four-year college. He learned of the daunting, almost insuperable challenges that Black educators faced in finding funding and political support for their work. But at the same time, he came to be dissatisfied with the sort of education and training he received at Florida Baptist and Morehouse, for reasons that were largely outside of the control of those in positions of authority at those institutions. They could transform students like Thurman, uplift them from poverty and obscurity, and instill in them the values, knowledge, and self-confidence that would last a lifetime. But Black educational institutions couldn't uplift their students from the crushing realities of Jim Crow and white supremacy. What to do about this was a lesson that could only partially be learned in a classroom.

Florida Baptist Academy—like so many other Black schools in the South founded in the years after the Civil War—had been originally indebted to the principles and pedagogical imperatives that had been established by Booker T. Washington: practical education; preparing students for a vocation;

impressing upon them their personal and collective responsibilities; and, underlying all else, avoiding needless political confrontations. Also, like many schools founded in the Washingtonian mode, by the second decade of the twentieth century, without rejecting its roots, it was moving toward a more academic orientation. During Thurman's four years in attendance, the school would change its name, its mission, and even the city in which it was located. It had been founded as Florida Baptist Institute in Live Oak in 1879, moving to Jacksonville in 1882 and becoming the Florida Baptist Academy. (Its campus was built on a former plantation.) In 1918, before Thurman's senior year, the school would move forty miles south, to St. Augustine, becoming the Florida Normal and Industrial Institute, its new name exhibiting its postsecondary aspirations.[8]

In 1914, a year before Thurman enrolled, the school was described as "a secondary school with a large elementary enrollment." In that year there were 404 students, of whom only 86 were in the secondary school.[9] This was not a school for loafers. It practiced an exacting Christianity, with daily chapel services and twice-weekly prayer meetings. The academy set itself a very ambitious goal: "Our aim is to perfect human character. Our method is a sound Christian education, putting every faculty and organ under complete control of Him who came to restore us to our original glory. Knowledge in the mind, divine love in the heart, and skill in the hands is our idea of a perfect education."[10] There still was a healthy dose of industrial education in the curriculum at Florida Baptist Academy. One of the school requirements in 1916 was that "all students must work at least one hour a day without pay." Presumably Thurman was not exempt and put in his time in agriculture, blacksmithing, or carpentry, along with all the other male students, adding to what was already an arduous day of work and study.[11]

But at the same time Florida Baptist Academy took academic education very seriously as well. (It took everything seriously.) The main task of the secondary school was producing teachers, not carpenters. At Florida Baptist, the secondary school was divided into two overlapping tracks for "normal" education (that is, teacher training courses) and a college preparatory track.[12] The college preparatory track was rigorous, and it is clear that when he finished hammering at the anvil or other industrial work, Florida Baptist was perhaps the most formative educational experience of Thurman's life, the place where his intellectual stirrings and strivings were encouraged and nurtured and where his understanding of himself and the world began to take on its mature contours.

By any standard, Thurman had a thorough high school education, very much preparing him for college. Thurman took four years of math, three years of Bible, and a year apiece for the traditional triad of biology, chemistry, and physics, and a year of psychology (which probably was largely a course in pedagogy), four years of Latin, and one year of Greek.[13] He would round off his foreign language training with two years of German and one year of Greek and French at Morehouse, and an additional year of New Testament Greek at Rochester Theological Seminary.[14] None of this took too deeply, however, and he would always regret the linguistic and intellectual limitations of being limited to English.[15] Thurman's favorite subject was English. During his time at Florida Baptist his required reading included orations from Edmund Burke to Frederick Douglass; a good deal of Shakespeare; and a steady diet of poetry from the nineteenth-century canon, much of which would stay with him for his entire life.

Florida Baptist taught its students both race pride and race prudence. The 1916 catalogue stated, with a perhaps understandable reluctance to make waves, that "the white and colored people in Jacksonville live together in the most perfect harmony, with no opposition to the education of the Negro."[16] The American Baptist Home Mission Society, the northern white Baptists, gave the school considerable support, and four of the Academy's nine trustees were white.[17] Yet African American topics were emphasized in history and English classes. One history course promised "especial study will be made of the rise and fall of American slavery." In addition to biographies of George Washington and Alexander Hamilton, the class read *Uncle Tom's Cabin,* and Benjamin Brawley's *Short History of the American Negro.* Students at Florida Baptist came away with a decent appreciation of the complexities and tragedies of African American history.[18] Intellectual stimulation was not limited to the classroom. Thurman was active in the school's YMCA chapter, which had a record player, a current events discussion group, and subscriptions to *The Crisis,* several Black newspapers, *Scientific American,* the *Saturday Evening Post,* and several YMCA periodicals.[19]

Of course, it is the teachers and not the curriculum that make any school. Three teachers stood out in Thurman's memory. Josephine Junius was a teacher of Latin. But in her Latin class, it was his English grammar that was suspect. One day, at the blackboard, he translated "veni" as "I have came" to class titters. Deeply embarrassed, he erased his work. Junius told the class to stop laughing and told Thurman to write the conjugation on the board again. She saw something special in him, and soon he was visiting her quarters after school, and they would read from a number of works, ranging from classic literature to opera librettos. He later wrote of her that "it was she who first exposed my mind to the beauty and purity of the English language. When I entered her class I had very little knowledge of correct speech. With infinite patience and great sensitivity, she opened up the whole magical world of poetry and creative prose."[20]

When Josephine Junius left the staff of Florida Baptist Academy in the fall of 1917, it prompted the writing of what are Thurman's earliest extant letters: "So often I find myself expecting to hear your voice, but alas, I find that it is only a condition of the mind and not reality" and that "my school year will not be the same because of *you* not being here." If this might sound to the letter's recipient like a schoolboy crush, Thurman endeavored to make clear "that I am understood," that his affection for his teacher, who likely was only a few years older, was only because "I have found none other of your sex who had a more genuine interest in my literary development than you. I may not come up to your expectations, but with the help of my God, I shall be worthy of . . ."[21] There the fragment of the letter cuts off. The strongest impression left by Thurman's early correspondence is of a young man desperate to be appreciated, to impress, to be mentored and acknowledged. In another letter to her, written a month later, he detailed his grades in six classes, apologizing for his low marks, which ranged from a 90 in geometry and astronomy, to a 94 in Cicero, to a 98 in history.[22] Since irony seems to have been beyond Thurman as a teenager, it seems more likely that he was devastated by his two marks of 90, a single integer away from descent in the mediocrity of the 80s. (Thurman knew he would need scholarships to attend college.) He would write in an unpublished draft of his autobiography that for the sake of his mother and grandmother, "I could not throw myself away, I had to become educated. At first it was for their sake, then for God's sake, and finally, for my sake."[23] For whatever complex of reasons this extraordinarily driven young man was pursuing his education, fear of failure and fear of disapproval from respected figures in authority was high among them.

Ethel Simons was another teacher who took an interest in Thurman, who demanded of him "perfect spelling and correct syntax and construction. If a student could not write clearly, it meant that he was either sloven, careless, or irresponsible."[24] But if Ethel Simons was exacting, she opened doors to the enchantments of poetry. Together they read the *Oxford Book of English Verse*, Edward Fitzgerald's translation of the *Rubaiyat of Omar Khayyam,* and some of the many anthologies the African American poetry editor William Stanley Braithwaite compiled.[25] Poetry was a key to Thurman's intellectual sensibility, and if he had some interest in the modern poets of the twentieth century, such as T. S. Eliot and Langston Hughes, his basic poetic tastes were rooted in Victorian and Edwardian poets and versifiers and their American counterparts, the sort of poetry that lent itself to recitation. Poetry, especially memorizing poetry, Elizabeth Yates suggested, gave Thurman, "a sense of power within himself, a transcendence over his immediate environment."[26] Thurman's affection for Ethel Simons, who was in her mid- to late twenties, was another schoolboy crush, one that continued after he graduated.[27] In June 1919, just after his graduation, he wrote her that "I miss you and I find myself actually wanting to be in your company."[28] When he arrived at Morehouse, he found his English courses vastly inferior to his high school instruction.[29]

A third high school teacher who left a lasting impression was the man who gave him his meager 90 in geometry, and the supervisor of the male dormitory, math teacher J. A. "Pick" Grimes. He was, Thurman told an interviewer in 1976, "the first strong distinct sustained masculine influence on my life."[30] (Although, as we have seen, he elsewhere suggested other, perhaps earlier candidates.) As dormitory supervisor, Grimes helped Thurman get through a personal problem of otherwise unspecified causes or dimensions, a "crisis, [an] internal crisis, about the meaning of life and the meaning of my own life," so painful that it felt as if "something in me was going to burst."[31] As math teacher, Grimes appealed to Thurman's need for rigor and precision, even though he was not much of a mathematician. Thurman often cited a stinging rebuke from Grimes, delivered after Thurman thought he had solved a difficult problem ahead of his classmates: "Howard, I want you always to do your own thinking, but remember, wisdom was not born with you."[32] In any event, if he wasn't Grimes's best student, he learned enough to deliver a mathematical proof of Black intellectual capacity to doubting whites. Thurman told with relish the story when he worked as an in-house dog sitter for a wealthy Daytona Beach family and talk came around to his high school studies. He was asked to provide the answer to the question what is $(a + b)^2$. When Thurman promptly answered $a^2 + 2ab + b^2$, all the startled questioner could say was, "I'll be goddamned," confronting for the first time in his life the fact that an African American could learn algebra.[33]

Thurman stayed in touch with all of his favorite teachers. Grimes lived to the mid-1970s. He remained in correspondence with Josephine Junius Harris and Ethel Simons Meeds, who lived to the age of 103, for the rest of his life.[34] What Thurman said of Grimes could be applied to all three. They had been "influential in helping me bring into focus the meaning of life, the values, a sense of the persona, that my grandmother and mother saw and chiseled" but had not made "articulate, because they did not have the tools, the skills" to shape Thurman's maturing academic personality.[35] Thurman also greatly admired and stayed in touch with Nathan W. Collier, Florida Baptist Academy's president from 1904 until his death in 1941. He wrote Collier in 1935 that he counted "my four years at the Academy as the four most significant years of my academic career. My high school education was much more cultural and much more thorough than my college education."[36] If Thurman outgrew his early immersion in the culture of Washingtonian uplift, he never quite left it behind. It was one of the great dilemmas of his later life that in his pursuit of interracialism and integration, he had somewhat neglected his first great pedagogical passion; bringing education and racial pride to the poor Black youth of the South.[37]

One family tragedy happened during Thurman's high school years. In June 1918 Thurman's older sister Henrietta died of typhoid. The disease was endemic in Thurman's Daytona: "We did not know the cause or cure of typhoid fever. All we knew was that every summer there would be a regular death toll of typhoid victims."[38] Thurman had been closer to his considerably younger sister, Madaline, six years his junior. As Thurman indicated later, at a difference of two years, the problem was the age-old tale of sibling rivalry, an older sister who would prefer to hang out with her cooler friends than with a pesky, importuning younger brother.[39] However, Thurman told of various adventures with Henrietta, such as when they heard the news about a nearby body, rushing to see their "first murder victim," a woman, bloodied, lying in the street, killed by her boyfriend, and then being embarrassed by their prurience. Or the time when, as a very young boy, he took his first train trip, with his grandmother to Jacksonville, and was so excited by his first ice cream cone that he packed several in his suitcase for Henrietta back in Daytona, with the inevitable soggy result upon his return.[40] Henrietta was an accomplished pianist and, like her brother, went away for school, first to Fessenden Academy in Martin, Florida—eighty miles to the west of Daytona—and then Edmund Waters College in Jacksonville.[41] In the last year of her life, she married a Mr. Register. Thurman had been unable to return to Daytona for the wedding. He was in Jacksonville in June 1918 when he had a sudden urge to pray and an image of Henrietta came to mind. He started to weep and then received a telegram telling him to come home at once. By the time he arrived, Henrietta, twenty-one years old, was dead.[42]

Thurman's high school years coincided with the worldwide vortex known as the Great War. For Thurman, as for other members of his generation, it was all-encompassing and life-changing. Within a few years of the armistice he would become a pacifist and with rueful disdain review the world's antebellum complacency, writing in 1924 that a decade earlier "the world was fast asleep having for its cozy bed the cradle of a crusted, but internally seething volcano." People believed "God's in Heaven, all's right with the world," while "in the hearts of men forces were at work which were soon to break loose into the most terrific and bloody carnage the world has ever seen." (Thurman presciently worried that the Great War might soon be in danger of losing the title of the most terrific carnage in human history to a younger rival.) The war had exposed the emptiness of conventional religion and conventional political thinking in dealing with the reality that "our social order is shot through with many inherently vicious principles working themselves out in a thousand human ills."[43]

Thurman had clear memories of both wartime excitement and the postwar sense of loss and abandonment. He wrote in 1940 that "it was not until the last war that the Negro became aware to some degree of his citizenship. Persona was conferred upon him by the dominant social group—he was made to feel that he counted—that the future of democracy was dependent upon him. For one breathless, swirling moment he became conscious of being a part and parcel of the very core of the nation." But the moment was short-lived. He reminded his audience of the events of the Red Summer of 1919, when, "like a tremendous octopus, American society sought to place the Negro back into his position of anonymity," which it accomplished, though not without "wild resentment" on the part of Black Americans, this little history lesson no doubt reflecting his own memory of anger and betrayal.[44]

In June 1918, the commencement address at Florida Baptist Academy was delivered by Emmett J. Scott, former private secretary to Booker T. Washington and currently special advisor to the secretary of war for the Negro soldier.[45] And on 5 June that year, Thurman was presumably one of the seven thousand persons who attended a mixed-race rally for the Third Liberty Loan in Jacksonville, sponsored by the city's Black residents. President Collier, in the words of the *Chicago Defender,* addressed the gathering "on loyalty and its significance." In the words of the reporter: "Professor Collier reviewed the matchless history of our people through all the struggling days of our country, when strong men were needed for the preservation of liberty" and envisioned the day when Black troops would reach Berlin, demanding the "surrender of the head of the Kaiser," singing "There Will be a Hot Time in the Old Town Tonight."[46]

The featured speaker was the African American author, civic leader, and Jacksonville native James Weldon Johnson (who would subsequently become Thurman's friend). He read his poem "The Young Warrior," with the following opening stanza:

Mother, Shed no mournful tears,
But gird me on my sword,
And give no utterance to thy fears,
But bless me with your word.[47]

Johnson was a strong, though hardly uncritical, supporter of the war effort. He knew the conditions under which Black soldiers had to fight. After the horrible miscarriage of justice in the Houston riot of August 1917, which resulted in the hanging of nineteen enlisted Negro soldiers, Johnson had led an NAACP delegation to the White House protesting the outrage and had a largely unsatisfying meeting with President Wilson.[48] He wrote of a recruiting poster circulated in Florida that wanted white men "experienced in the handling of the colored man" as "about the most conspicuous grouping of the Negro with the mule that has ever been brought to my attention." In an editorial that appeared in the *New York Age* the same month as his Jacksonville address, "Why Should a Negro Fight?," he argued that despite the many good reasons why a Negro might not want to fight, "America is the American Negro's country. He has been here three hundred years, that is, about two hundred years longer than most of the white people. He is a citizen of this country, declared so by the Constitution. Many of the rights and privileges of citizenship are still denied him, but the plain course before him is to continue to perform all of the duties of citizenship while he continually presses his demands for all of the rights and privileges."[49]

This ambivalent support of the war effort was probably Thurman's view as well. In any event he was no mere armchair patriot. From the beginning of August 1918 to mid-September, Thurman was one of seven hundred young Black men who tramped the fields and marched in the open spaces of Howard University in Washington, D.C., as a member of the Student Army Training Corps (SATC), learning the rudiments of "military science and training."[50] During their time in the SATC, the men were temporarily enlisted in the army as privates, receiving a private's pay (thirty dollars per month), as they learned to drill, use weapons, and experience the rigors of military discipline. The establishment of the SATC was demanded by Black leaders who wanted Black soldiers to be led by Black officers, and its goal was to develop a corps of young Black officers who would serve in the field. When the corps finished their training, before their return to civilian life, they crowded into Rankin Chapel on the Howard University campus (where Thurman would spend a decade as dean of chapel) to hear their efforts praised by Emmett J. Scott and Robert Russa Moton, Washington's successor as president of Tuskegee Institute.[51] One suspects their speeches were similar to what the influential Howard University dean Kelly Miller expressed at the time: "The chief beneficiary of the war is the Negro, and that the outlook for becoming a real American is more hopeful than ever before."[52]

In one of Thurman's earliest surviving letters, from June 1918, to his soon-to-be mentor Mordecai Wyatt Johnson, just before he entered the program,

Thurman sounded, if not excited, then at least resolved about military service. He and his fellow SATC members surely would have entered the army in 1919 had the war continued, and he worried that time in the army would seriously delay his plans to become, as quickly as possible, a minister of the Gospel.[53] If the question of his priorities were resolved by the Armistice, Florida Baptist, now renamed Florida Normal and Industrial Institute and relocated to St. Augustine, remained on a war footing. As Thurman explained in his autobiography: "It became my responsibility to teach the men drill regulation I learned at Howard. My duties were equivalent to those of a dean of men. I had to see that lights were out in the dormitory at ten o'clock."[54] (It is not easy to imagine Thurman, with his slow, contemplative voice, barking out orders like a drill sergeant.)

Thurman had learned many lessons from his brush with the war. He remained, at least at first, a fervid patriot. In what was probably the worst poem he ever wrote, "The Flag," appearing in the *Athenaeum* (the Morehouse-Spelman literary magazine) in January 1920, he pledged his "soul's enthralled" allegiance to the flag and, without a hint of ambivalence, to die for it, to pay any price to defend it, and to fall on the field thinking of "thy stars upon a field of blue / thy stripes of red and white."[55] A somewhat more sophisticated patriotism shaped "Our Challenge," an Emancipation Day oration he delivered at Morehouse on 1 January 1922.[56] He lauded Black military service, stating "our loyalty is unsurpassed from Bunker Hill to Carazel" (the latter referring to the Battle of Carrizal, during the anti–Pancho Villa invasion of Mexico in 1916, when the Tenth Calvary, a Black regiment, took heavy casualties, an episode celebrated in both the white and Black press).[57] But he balanced Black patriotism against the hostility of the white world, and the inadequate Black response to it. This tension, for Thurman, and for his generation of African American intellectuals, eager to participate fully in American life, uncertain of their welcome, would never be entirely resolved.

Thurman was never ambivalent about wanting to pursue a religious vocation. Knowing the trajectory of the rest of his life, this seems like a career path foreordained, but Thurman had many other options, and many who urged him to consider other options. At Morehouse his classmates were primarily future lawyers, entrepreneurs, and educators, not ministers. His Daytona mentor Dr. John T. Stocking had wanted Thurman to become a physician.[58] At Morehouse his main field of study was business and economics, and, Lorimer Milton, a business instructor and later very successful Atlanta banker, who would be Thurman's lifelong friend, saw Thurman as a protégé. When Thurman graduated from Morehouse in 1923, he was offered an instructorship in economics and a chance to "validate" his degree at the

University of Chicago. (Validation was a fifth year of undergraduate study at a predominantly white university for graduates of historically Black colleges, which typically lacked formal academic accreditation.)[59] Thurman turned it down in favor of studying at seminary.

Thurman writes about his aspirations in his earliest letter to Mordecai Wyatt Johnson. It is a long and ardent letter, filled with heart-on-sleeve teenage passion, anxious and beseeching, an intellectual love letter sent with the hope that its recipient would acknowledge and take note of the letter writer's existence. Written in June 1918, it began a lifelong friendship that would last until Thurman delivered a eulogy for Johnson at his funeral in 1976. Johnson was a decade older than Thurman, a Tennessee native, and he pioneered a career path Thurman would follow and emulate. He graduated from Atlanta Baptist College in 1911 (two years before it changed its name to Morehouse College) and then became deeply involved in work for the YMCA and the Student Christian Movement. (Johnson resigned his position as the YMCA secretary after the organization held a conference at a segregated hotel.) He received his ministerial training at Rochester Theological Seminary. When he received Thurman's letter, he was a parish minister in Charleston, West Virginia, and one of the most noted Black preachers and orators of his generation. For all they shared, there were differences between the two men, starting with what was most immediately obvious; although Johnson's parents had both been enslaved, he was light-complexioned enough to easily pass as white. (Thurman, though he rarely wrote about it, was well aware of color bias against very dark-skinned persons such as himself in the upper echelons of Black society, including higher education.)[60] Johnson was one of the titans of African American education in the first half of the twentieth century, best remembered for his three-plus decades at the helm of Howard University at a time when it was unquestionably the "capstone of Negro education," and he was the impresario of its "golden age" during the 1930s. And yet one senses that he has become something of a forgotten figure, an afterthought in African American history, his accomplishments as an institution builder and intellectual leader taken for granted. But, as an advocate for a theologically sophisticated, socially active African American Christianity with a mission to transform American society, Johnson blazed the path Thurman would follow.[61]

Thurman first heard Johnson speak at the annual YMCA summer conference for African Americans at Kings Mountain, North Carolina, in 1917.[62] Kings Mountain for Thurman was an introduction to another, wider world of Black possibility. "It was a place," he told an interviewer, "where you met everybody . . . all of the men who were shapers of thought and influence in the whole sweep of Negro life . . . these men came and you met them."[63] On one such occasion, at a vesper service in the early evening, sitting on a hillside, listening with rapt attention, he first heard Johnson speak.

Thurman tried to write his first letter to Johnson many times before sending it, and it would take a year, and another Kings Mountain conference, for him to summon his nerve: "I wanted to know you and wanted you to know me; I longed for a cheering word from a man like you; I yearned to tell you [of] my hopes, ambitions, and discouragements, but each time something hindered, something caused me to be denied that coveted privilege."[64] Writing in his still somewhat stilted prose, he promised that "as long as memory reproduces pictures, to me, you shall be a living inspiration. I admired your eloquence, bowed humbly before your sympathy, and rejoiced to know that you *cared*." He wanted Johnson to "listen while I tell to you my soul." Thurman went on: "I want to be a minister of the Gospel. I feel the needs of my people, I see their distressing condition" and want to help the "skinned and flung down" (a phrase evidently borrowed from Johnson's sermon, and Thurman's first term for what he would later call the disinherited). He indulged in a bit of teenage melodrama—"[I] have offered myself upon the altar as a living sacrifice"—and in a bit of teenage impatience, he worried that though he wanted a college education, if drafted, this would considerably slow his path to the ministry, and he wanted to become one right away, military service or not, college or not: "As you know, the war is on and young men are being snatched daily. I am patriotic; I am willing to fight for democracy but my friend Rev. Johnson, my people need me."[65] It is the letter of an eighteen-year-old in no doubt as to his racial priorities.

Above all, what Thurman wanted from Johnson was help ("please take a personal interest in me and guide me and God will reward you, for you are God's trustee") and support ("on every hand I am discouraged in my choice of the ministry"). Johnson wrote a kindly reply and gave Thurman good advice. He told him not to let the war dictate his future because it might soon be over, as indeed it was. He told him to stay in school, go to a good college, and not to take too many courses in religion in college because that was what seminary was for. Then attend a good seminary and be out by age twenty-six. (Which is exactly what Thurman did, taking almost no courses in religion at Morehouse, graduating from Rochester Theological Seminary in 1926, at age twenty-six.) What Black Christianity needed, Johnson wrote, above all, were learned ministers, ministers who knew how to think as well as talk, ministers up on the latest biblical scholarship. This meant for Johnson seeing Christianity as an evolving religion rather than as a set of fixed doctrinal obligations. To this end he sent Thurman an (unfortunately unnamed) "brief history of the People of Israel in the Old Testament," encouraging him "to cultivate the historical perspective." Above all, he advised Thurman to study: "Prepare! Prepare! This is the one and only word for you. You need have no fear about work; you will find plenty of work to do both while you are in school and afterwards."[66]

Thurman replied to Johnson shortly thereafter and agreed to follow Johnson's "thoughts of encouragement so tenderly encouched in your letter," noting that "never before had I arisen to the full consciousness of which must necessarily devolve upon men, if I must preach the Gospel."[67] He told Johnson what he was reading: several Baptist weeklies and two books, both published under YMCA auspices, fitting into what David Setran has characterized as the YMCA's "conservative social gospel," with its emphasis on replacing "bad men" with "good men" and on Christianity as an exercise in muscular character building.[68]

These early letters give us a last glimpse of Thurman as someone comfortable speaking the language of evangelicalism. With the instruction of Johnson and others, this aspect of his background was soon effaced. Despite Johnson's promotion of the "historical perspective" to Thurman, there is at least one account that suggests that he remained a biblical literalist through his years at Morehouse. A classmate, writing in 1937, tells that E. Franklin Frazier, the eminent sociologist and aggressive atheist with whom Thurman had a stormy relationship at Morehouse, regularly taunted Thurman about religion. He would "ridicule certain Scriptural stories with bitter sarcasm, and Howard Thurman would be moved to such a point that he would fold his arms, look up to the ceiling and sigh audibly, "at which point Frazier would 'turn up the heat' while Thurman would remain silent."[69] By 1924, when we have the earliest preserved writings from Thurman on religion, he is a full-fledged Protestant modernist, rejecting the Virgin Birth and other Christian dogmas. But when he was writing to Johnson, Thurman, like almost all eighteen-year-olds, was very much a work in progress, an evangelical Christian and ardent race man, parts of his worldview he would soon either discard, submerge, or transform.

3

"The Personification
of the Morehouse Ideal"

Since 1996 there has been an annual Parents' Parting Ceremony at Morehouse College. The evening before parents leave their freshmen sons on the campus, there is a service in the Martin Luther King, Jr. International Chapel. A chest that Thurman acquired in India is placed in front of the chapel. To the accompaniment of African drumming, parents write on a card of their hopes for their entering freshman. At the service parents affirm their love for their sons and how that love requires them to let them go and allow them to become men. The students thank the elders, those present and those absent, and promise to honor the family name. Outside the chapel there is a crypt, a tall white tower that contains the ashes of Thurman and Sue Bailey Thurman. After the service, two parents are selected to carry Thurman's chest into the crypt, where it remains overnight. One of the parents stated: "It's as if Howard Thurman's spirit will cover and guide all of these young men. Mr. Thurman's spiritual ashes will be released with another job well done."[1]

Thurman's spiritual ashes are everywhere on the Morehouse campus. From the time of his graduation, he has been lauded as the "personification of the Morehouse ideal."[2] He has been hailed, with King and longtime Morehouse president Benjamin Mays, as a member of the triumvirate that created the "Morehouse theology," a liberal Protestantism (in Thurman's case, a very liberal Protestantism) whose commandments were a commitment to social activism, the teachings of Jesus, race pride, and an ethics and politics of universal human inclusion.[3]

Morehouse was not Thurman's first choice. While in high school, Thurman wrote, "there awoke in me the desire to go North for my education," with a special "ache to go to Worcester Academy and Brown University. "Every year for three years I wrote to Wooster [sic] for a catalogue. When it came I dreamed myself there. But I did not make it."[4] Both schools had admitted a trickle of African American students in the past, but an Ivy League education was an extravagant dream for a poor Black student from the South. Still, Thurman "refused to believe that such opportunities were not for me." If Morehouse was what today we might call his "safe school," he knew how lucky he was, given his background and need for a complete scholarship, to be accepted by any four-year college. While his college education was to be in Georgia and not New England, he knew that he had not been "mistaken in my desire, in my dream." Thurman came to Morehouse already adamant to refuse anything less than the highest possible academic standards for himself and his classmates.[5]

Thurman's Morehouse roots were always important to him. He returned to his alma mater on many occasions, taught there (and at Morehouse's sister college, Spelman) from 1928 to 1932. He was a featured speaker at celebrations of the college's seventy-fifth anniversary in 1942, at its one-hundredth in 1967, and was a frequent visitor to the campus.[6] His undergraduate years at Morehouse permanently stamped Thurman. "I was profoundly affected by the sense of mission the college inculcated in us," he would write in his autobiography. "We understood that our job was to learn so that we could go back into our communities and teach others."[7] He never lost this sense of mission or his fondness for Morehouse or his classmates, but Thurman was not a notably sentimental person about his past, and old school ties never hindered him from coolly evaluating Morehouse's strengths and limitations. Thurman was a proud but wary Morehouse man, refusing to make any concessions or allowances because he was attending a Black college.

Morehouse men were a relatively new commodity in 1919, when Thurman entered the freshman class. It had only been in 1913 that the former Atlanta Baptist College acquired its new name, honoring Henry Lyman Morehouse (1834–1917), the longtime executive director of the American Baptist Home Mission Society, a man who is best remembered for coining the term "talented tenth," the elite cadre of college-educated African American men and women whom the white Morehouse founders and benefactors such as Morehouse hoped would become the natural leaders of Black America. The college had been founded as the Augusta Institute, in Augusta, Georgia, in 1867, by the American Baptist Home Mission Society, the mission arm of the Northern Baptist Church, to educate formerly enslaved persons and to train promising candidates for the ministry. In 1879 the school moved to Atlanta, becoming the Atlanta Baptist Seminary, and in 1897, in a name change that was more reflective of its aspirations than its accomplishments, the Atlanta

Baptist College.[8] With its new name in 1913, despite honoring a Baptist luminary, the college was advertising its wish to shed overt denominational identifications and its ambition to become the premier academically oriented men's college for African Americans in the Deep South.

Thurman admired the founders of Morehouse, Baptists from New England and New York State who came south to transform the freedmen into proud citizens and to purge from them any lingering traces of what it is no longer fashionable to speak of as an antebellum "slave mentality."[9] This was still taught in Thurman's day, and it was what he believed. Enslaved people had developed, Thurman told his Morehouse classmates in 1922, "a rather shiftless, desultory nature and almost no sense of responsibility for the future." This he blamed on Africa, where they had been "supplied with a cheap plenteous food and a hot climate," and it was compounded by their treatment in America, since it was the "southern white man" who had to "feed, to clothe, to care for" enslaved persons.[10] If Thurman soon left behind the more questionable aspects of this analysis, he continued to believe that to move from slavery to freedom had required an educational shock treatment, a ruthless purging of old ways of thinking, and a sudden plunge into a new icy-cold mentality. He stated in 1938, "Men cannot be slaves for three hundred years . . . without finally developing a way of looking out on a world that belongs essentially to the beaten and the chained."[11] In 1942, addressing his alma mater on its seventy-fifth anniversary, he stated that his admiration for his college's white founders was tempered by the knowledge that most of them did not believe that Blacks were their social or intellectual equals. Still, they gave their students self-confidence in their abilities and prepared the way for the day when the college would be staffed and administered by Blacks.[12]

By the time Thurman arrived at Morehouse in 1919, the transition to a Black leadership and faculty was largely complete. (However, it remained almost entirely beholden to northern philanthropic largess for its funding.) Since 1906, Morehouse had been run, tight as a drum, by its first Black president, John Hope. His was a carefully calibrated life. He had been born in Augusta, Georgia, in 1868, only a year after the Augusta Institute was created. He was the son of a white father and Black mother. Hope, like Mordecai Wyatt Johnson, was very light-skinned. After his father died when young Hope was eight, the executors of his father's will denied him and his mother the support that had been promised, and Hope struggled to obtain an education, eventually obtaining a bachelor's degree from Brown University in 1894. Hope thereafter commenced a career as an educator, becoming the first Black Atlanta Baptist College/Morehouse president at a time when Black college presidents (and even Black faculty) were uncommon at the "better" (that is, privately funded) Black colleges.[13] If the roots of Morehouse date back to the early years of Reconstruction, its dominant educational philosophy and political strategy emerged from its ruin. A frontal assault on white supremacy and privilege was impossible; the paramount concern was keeping itself healthy and intact; any progress toward racial equality would at best be incremental.

Hope's career exemplified the dilemmas of educated Blacks in the South in the early twentieth century. The twin goals of the fight for political equality and the need for educational self-betterment were not easily reconciled. To emphasize one overmuch was to put the other in jeopardy. Hope was, in the early 1900s, if not quite a radical, a militant racial egalitarian, a nationally known figure in the major anti-Washingtonian organizations, the Niagara Movement and its successor, the NAACP. He would always be a close associate of W. E. B. Du Bois, his ally in promoting academic coursework of the highest standing in Black colleges. And Hope, throughout his years at Morehouse, entertained, if in an increasingly wistful manner, ambitions for national Black leadership. Just as Hope was starting his tenure at Atlanta Baptist College, in September 1906, a vicious riot in Atlanta that took between twenty-four and forty-five Black lives along with causing staggering property losses, was a reminder of the horrible fragility of the African American situation in the city. It was the event that inspired Du Bois's "Litany of Atlanta": "Bewildered are we, and passion-tost, mad with the madness of a mobbed and mocked and murdered people."[14]

Hope agreed. But as Leroy Davis points out, the responsibilities of being a college president led Hope to moderate his politics, to seek accommodations with the wielders of power in white Atlanta.[15] He befriended Booker T. Washington in a largely successful effort to increase funding for the college. By 1919, Samuel Archer, a Black dean at Morehouse, wrote in a letter of "the progressive conservatism of President Hope."[16] This did not prevent Hope from describing, in private correspondence, the reaction of government authorities to the rioting of the "Red Summer" of 1919 as "flabby, helpless, impotent," or from attending that year, with Du Bois, the first Pan-African Conference in Paris.[17] Hope often emphasized that "Morehouse men were not expected to participate in any voluntary segregation."[18] But he also, to Du Bois's consternation, obtained a leadership role in the Commission on Interracial Cooperation (CIC), a white-dominated organization formed in the wake of the 1919 disturbances and committed to better race relations and an end to lynching, but not at the expense of changing, except superficially, the existing realities of Jim Crow.[19] Benjamin Mays wrote of Morehouse during Thurman's undergraduate years, "Though no one at Morehouse taught submission [to segregation], neither did anyone encourage Morehouse students by force to overthrow the system."[20]

Thurman recalled a meeting with the CIC and Hope concerning a forthcoming concert of the great African American concert tenor Roland Hayes. Hayes, a Georgia native, and later a good friend of Thurman, had gone north to make his career and wanted to appear in his home state. The authorities agreed to segregate a concert hall for his appearance vertically rather than horizontally, with the center aisle as the color line, rather than placing Blacks in the back of the hall or the galleries. Thurman was so "disgusted with this bit of racial legerdemain that [he] walked out of the meeting." Hope followed, put his hand on Thurman's shoulder, and told him: "Thurman, I know how you feel about what is going on in there, but you must remember that these are the best and most liberal men in the South. We must work with them. There *is* no one else."[21] Thurman understood Hope's dilemma, but it was also a reminder to him that any Black institution in a segregated society would have to compromise with its best intentions. He also understood why Hope would have written to Du Bois in 1924 that his role at Morehouse required such a fine-tuned act of balancing "that blowing one's brains out is a great sight easier than some of the things we have to do and stand."[22]

Morehouse tried to both protect and prepare its students for life outside of its greensward. It was a small, cloistered world. There were only forty students in Thurman's class. A dormitory, built a few years before Thurman's arrival, permitted all college students to live on campus rather than boarding with local families. As recently as 1915, Morehouse was still primarily functioning as an elementary and secondary school. Of its 277 students that year, 110 were in the elementary program, and about the same number were in the high school, leaving only 38 students doing college-level work, with another 18 in a ministerial program.[23] By 1919 the precollegiate programs had been closed.[24] Thurman and his classmates were together from sunup to well after sundown, carefully watched by the faculty (who in turn were intrusively supervised by Hope). Students were unable to leave the campus without permission. Benjamin Mays, for one, deeply resented Hope's charge to spy "on students for rule infractions," and then his using that information to suspend or expel them.[25]

Thurman knew the routine, one he had mastered at Florida Baptist Academy. Daily chapel service, often with additional prayer meetings in the evening. No cursing, smoking, misbehaving in class, playing cards, or (especially) unchaperoned visits to Morehouse's sister school, the all-female Spelman College. Hope did not hesitate to expel or suspend malefactors. Mordecai Wyatt Johnson, a 1911 graduate, had been suspended for a semester for card playing in his room. Football players learned to keep their expletives to themselves, however fiercely they were knocked to the turf.[26] Thurman did record one incident of insurgence on his part—he was disciplined after starting a cafeteria contretemps over the quality of the grits—but neither at college nor at any other point in his life did he have the temperament of a rule-breaking hell-raiser.[27]

At Morehouse, in the fall of 1919, it was, in a phrase that Warren Harding would soon make famous, back to normalcy. The Great War was over. No more maneuvers on the quad. No more careers detoured by military obligations. But a return to normalcy creates its own problems. There was a sense of delayed and unfinished business to attend to, with upperclassmen returning from the service, with their lives to get back on track. And it was back to normalcy in race relations as well, with the horrible events of the so-called Red Summer, with murderous riots in Chicago and more than three dozen cities, and the massacre of more than one hundred African Americans in Elaine, Arkansas, alone. Thurman's undergraduate years were shaped by the realization that the war, and the service of hundreds of thousands of African Americans in it, had brought no change in their subordinate status.[28]

But John Hope wanted Morehouse and Morehouse students to get on with the educational task at hand. He supervised Morehouse with an unrelenting and paternal scrutiny, imprinting his personality and style everywhere. Thurman described John Hope as "genteel, scholarly, decorous."[29] Others used less flattering descriptors: austere, stern, formal, tyrannical, and autocratic.[30] As Leroy Davis, the most thorough scholar of his career, has suggested, by the 1920s, Hope's autocratic and paternalistic style of management was wearing increasingly thin with both faculty and students.[31]

But Thurman and Hope had an intimate mentor/protégé friendship, one of unusual closeness and intimacy for a college president and an undergraduate. Thurman, writing in uplift-speech, told John Hope in June 1921 that his "trend of fundamentals is forward" and that his previous school year had been "pregnant with experiences sufficiently exacting to fit me for many of the battles of my early years." Thurman was then passing through another of his unspecified and undescribed crises. Hope, in response, appreciated the turmoil Thurman was passing through while suggesting that Thurman needed to become a bit less self-dramatizing. "You are mentally and spiritually endowed to feel things very keenly," he wrote, adding that Thurman also had the empathy to feel the crises of others. Hope told Thurman that he would spend his lifetime carrying heavy loads, and he could not let them crush him: "The burdens are heavy but it is the part of a man to bear burdens." As a minister, Hope suggested, a gloomy personality was not a vocational asset. He would have to become a professional inspirer, and he had to

Prize, student orator Emancipation Day, representative to National Y. M. C. A. Conference, Cincinnati, Ohio, Y. M. C. A. Cabinet, alternate debater, Othello, Program Committee Pi Gamma; Senior: first scholarship, president Y. M. C. A., president Atlanta Student Council, varsity debater, editor-in-chief Annual, summer session Columbia University (1922), valedictorian. Commencement speaker, class poem, assistant to the Dean.

Scholar-Christian-Man. Slow in speech, large in stature, with long dangling arms, "Dud" is a striking figure in any group. The personification of the Morehouse Ideal—a genuine christian. His big heart and massive brain have been the repository of many student problems, only to be solved and settled. Brainy and sympathetic he is our ideal of a minister, one who shall furnish us with a rational and practical christianity. Holder of the two highest offices of the class, president and editor-in-chief of Annual, varsity debater, winner of a different prize every year, president of Y. M. C. A., orator, writer of class poem, actor, student's unanimous choice to National Y. M. C. A. Conference, Cincinnati, Ohio, he has won the confidence and respect of entire school. His effect on other students as president of Atlanta Student Council—A. U., Morehouse, Morris Brown, Clark and Gammon—assistant in dean's office, honor student, valedictorian, commencement speaker, "Dud" is our most brilliant classmate. This annual, the creature of his hands, ably attests the literary ability of our friend and brother who soon leaves to win higher honors in Rochester Theological Seminary.

HOWARD WASHINGTON THURMAN
"Dud"

"*A spirit all compact of fire*
Not gross to sink but light and will aspire."
Born in Daytona, Fla., November 18, 1899; Florida Normal and Industrial Institute, 1919; Freshman: first scholarship, Edgar Allen Poe Short Story Prize, Athenaeum Literary Prize, Y. M. C. A. Cabinet, Glee Club, Pi Gamma, Chi Delta Sigma; Sophomore: second scholarship, Paxon Prize Oration, literary editor, Athenaeum, Y. M. C. A. Cabinet, class president, chaplain Pi Gamma, Chi Delta Sigma, Hamlet; Junior: first scholarship, Chamberlain Scripture Reading

Entry for Thurman in the 1923 Morehouse College yearbook

"develop good cheer and great hopefulness" to those seeking relief. He went on to discuss his own worries and those of his fellow Black college presidents about interference with their jobs from racist southern state governments.[32]

Hope imagined great things for Thurman and primed him for an academic career on the Morehouse faculty. In 1926 he asked Thurman to write his biography. Thurman demurred, claiming that he wasn't suited to that sort of writing project.[33] In the summer of 1931, when both men were traveling in Europe, at one of the lowest points in Thurman's life, after the death of his first wife, the two men met in London and "saw each other daily, went to the theatre, and discussed racial problems." When the first biography of Hope appeared in 1948, Thurman bitterly complained, "I am shocked and amazed that the biographer saw fit to give no place in the book to any facet of the very unique relationship which I had with Mr. Hope."[34]

Hope saw himself as in the business of making men. Manhood and its cognates were big words on the Morehouse campus. A 1918 advertisement for Morehouse in *The Crisis* touted it as "an institution famous for its emphasis on all sides of manly development. The only institution in the far south devoted solely to the education of Negro young men."[35] Thurman remembered that when he entered Morehouse, "a whole new career began because now I was intimately associated with men." No more crushes on female teachers as in high school. "My grandmother was strong and positive and that sort of thing, but now I am in a men's college with classmates, teachers. The whole climate [was] very different from anything I'd ever known before."[36] If Thurman's sense of his own masculinity was at times less than totally secure, he certainly tried to fit in at Morehouse.[37]

Of course at Morehouse manhood was not just about maleness. At a time when, as Thurman noted, the "indignity of being called 'boy,' or 'nigger' or 'uncle' was rampant, Hope always addressed Morehouse students as 'young gentlemen.' What this term of respect meant to our faltering egos can only be understood against the backdrop of the South of the 1920s," when "our manhood and that of our fathers was denied on all levels by white society."[38] (After growing up in a society in which whites often called Blacks only by their first names, Thurman would sometimes in the opening salutation of a letter address Black friends—never whites—by their last names only, such as "Dear King," as if this was a more personal greeting than their given name.)[39] What Hope tried to create at Morehouse, in Thurman's opinion, was a place in Georgia where "lynchings, burnings, unspeakable cruelties" were not "the fundamentals of existence" for the Black men at the college, and where their lives would not be "defined in less than human terms."[40] Toward the end of his life, Thurman would write, "As I look back on my own past I think that the most damaging result of prejudice and discrimination on my own soul was the constant temptation to charge all personal failures, other than those due directly to physical causes, to the handicaps created in the white world around me."[41] But this had to be balanced against the reality that, indeed, white prejudice and discrimination were the cause of many Black personal failures. The challenge was to acknowledge the intrusive power of white racism while denying it authority over one's life.

Thurman dealt with this tension and contradiction in the most significant surviving document of his undergraduate years, his 1922 Morehouse Emancipation Day oration, "Our Challenge." It is the speech of a young man still finding his way intellectually, very much reflecting the ideas of John Hope, of an orator wanting to impress his audience more through the force of his rhetoric than the cogency of his ideas. Still, in it Thurman was clearly working his way toward questions he would spend a lifetime pondering. It is a speech riven with sharp dichotomies. It opens with the contrast between physical slavery—"the frantic wail, the awe-inspiring groan of black men as they crouch and cower beneath their master's lash"—now in the past, and psychic slavery, still very much a reality. Thurman claims that "every black man in America" is still "chained and fettered" by a "psychic slavery" that is "so complete, our sleep so sound" that "though we are victims, we do not realize it."[42]

This psychic slavery takes several forms. It can be reflected in a "complacency" because "we have become intoxicated with our own progress." Alternatively, because of bad habits inherited from Africa and a leftover from slavery, it could be psychic slavery as "the thralldom" of ignorance and aimlessness, and living exclusively in the present rather than planning for the future. But the biggest form of psychic slavery was that "the masses of our people" grant the white man "the nature of a god," a god to be "honored, adored, feared, and obeyed." As a result, "our thoughts, our attitudes, our ideas and in many respects, our destinies, all, are being shaped and planned by those who love us not."[43]

What to do about it? Thurman suggests that "in our struggle for existence in the American civilization" the "salvation" of the Negro will be "our independency, our organization, our keen sense of responsibility for the future." The oration ends with Thurman calling on his Morehouse classmates, fellow "teachers and prophets for a new era," to "go forth wherever black men live and suffer," soaring ever-higher above "the sordid ruins of our hindrances," overcome and enter the "judgment hall of our own race consciousness." Thurman's prose, purple throughout, hurtles toward a Wagnerian climax that is as overripe as it is unclear: "Judgment fires" will "kindle" the "pillars that stay race prejudice" and "fire the entire civilized dome," and only then "will the car of Negro freedom, physical and psychic, rumble on forever, over the bleak and dismal loneliness of an exterminated slavery."[44]

What is clear is that Thurman really hadn't yet come to terms with his "white problem." In "Our Challenge," whites are foreboding specters, puppet masters of their Black marionettes. Thurman wants to build strong Black institutions that would be impervious to their influence, and with typical Morehouse talented-tenth elitism, assumes that his classmates and those similarly situated will be the natural leaders of the race. At the same time, he argues that the only way to overcome fear of whites is to treat them as equals, undeify them, and strip them of their aura and their power to control Black lives. But he does not address the question of whether the way forward will require more or less interaction with whites. If "Our Challenge," unlike later writings, is overt in its racial nationalism, it is also more frightened, more fearful than his later work. What he retained from "Our Challenge" was the conviction that freedom could never be granted by others, however benevolent.

One becomes free by claiming one's freedom. "No one can do this for us! We have been freed, now let us be free." This would have many echoes.[45]

Thurman thrived at Morehouse, a big man on campus in every way. The college yearbook, of which he was of course the editor, lists some of his accomplishments. He was valedictorian; winner of scholarships every year; class president; assistant to the dean; class representative to the YMCA; editor of the *Athenaeum,* chaplain for Pi Gamma and Chi Delta Sigma fraternities; member of the debating team; and winner of the Edgar Allan Poe Short Story Prize, Paxton Prize Oration, Pozon Prize Oration; and Chamberlain Scripture Reading Prize. He was in the glee club; acted in performances of *Hamlet* and *Othello;* and so on, and so on. His classmates voted him the best orator, the most dignified, the busiest, as well as being one of the class of '23's best eaters. (He was also in the running for the title of having the "biggest head" and for being the "most sanctimonious.") In the Class Poem (which he cowrote) he called Morehouse "our nursery, our fostering Mater." The yearbook encomiums culminated in a description of Thurman as "Scholar-Christian Man. Slow in speech, large of stature, with long dangling arms . . . the personification of the Morehouse Ideal. . . . His big heart and massive brain have been the repository of many student problems . . . our ideal of a minister, one who shall furnish us with a rational and practical Christianity . . . our most brilliant classmate." When the yearbook asked, "What does Morehouse need most?," one of the answers, along with a larger endowment, new campus buildings, a larger library, and better food in the dining hall, was, using Thurman's Morehouse nickname, "men like 'Dud.'"[46]

He achieved this, evidently, without being much of a hale and hearty fellow. He was never much of a joiner. When Hope finally allowed Morehouse students to join fraternities, Thurman was a prominent abstainer.[47] Thurman's abundant spiritual gifts were already apparent, as was his talent to help others make articulate and comprehensible their own spiritual and personal strivings. In 1922, a classmate, and later a distinguished Atlanta minister, wrote Thurman, perhaps with a touch of hyperbole, "I really believe that my success in life depends on my relation with you, God and myself alone being excepted."[48]

However, Thurman's coursework at Morehouse included only a single class in religion. He followed Mordecai Wyatt Johnson's advice to learn other about things as an undergraduate. Thurman, like so many bright young persons, soaked up knowledge like an epistemological sponge. He claimed that, along with classmate, James Nabritt Jr.—a future president of Howard University—he read every book in the rather small Morehouse College library.[49] He started thinking he would concentrate on English, but not caring for his instructors in that subject, "I shifted to economics, something that had no relevancy to this inner feeling, but something that my kind of quick mind for that sort of thing could do."[50]

The most revealing glimpse we have of Thurman as budding economist is a letter he wrote to John Hope in 1923 about his plans for a "Negro Scholarship Fund," to be funded entirely by African Americans, unlike other Black-oriented philanthropies that were underwritten by white benefactors. Thurman wanted the fund to aid "talented Negro men to pursue advanced courses" and then "return to Negro college or colleges as professors," thereby "arising the standard of said college" while bringing "the blessings of higher education within the reach of the average Negro youth." Thurman imagined himself as the director of the fund and went into detail about how he would use his business acumen to accrue interest on the principal until the fund reached $1 million. Nothing came of this, but under the aegis of the Howard Thurman Education Trust in the 1960s and 1970s, he would realize a similar philanthropic ambition.[51]

Economics for Thurman was an opportunity to strip the world of moralizing Christian pretense and gaze upon things as they actually were. This was knowledge that, in his view, had often been deliberately denied to African Americans. If economics, as taught at Morehouse by Lorimer Milton, was to some extent a study of how Blacks could succeed in business, sociology at the college was often the study of African Americans who were, in one way or another, failing. The two disciplines were overlapping, more so in Thurman's day than ours, and he took several courses in sociology and probably counted them as part of his economics concentration. If Blacks needed to become better at business, they also needed to learn of capitalism's great limitations. Both sorts of knowledge were liberating, in different ways. He would later write that "I majored in economics, but I could not be said to understand the modes of production until I was able to predict the effects of the application of economic principles on my own environment, that of a black man in America."[52] Thurman wanted the abstractions of economics to enter into his soul.

In his memoirs Thurman singled out two professors of sociology who had a huge impact on his intellectual and personal development. One is almost completely forgotten today. Garrie Ward Moore's promising career was cut short by his premature death at age thirty-one. Moore was a Florida native, a 1912 American Baptist College/Morehouse grad who became the first Morehouse graduate to have his degree validated at Columbia University. He went on to obtain a master's degree in sociology, writing a thesis on poverty among West Indian immigrants in New York City.[53] He thereafter returned to Morehouse, teaching sociology. He was the first African American probation officer in Fulton County (Atlanta), worked with the International YMCA in France during the war, and in 1920 became the founding director of the Atlanta School of Social Work (which was affiliated with Morehouse). Moore, a bachelor, lived on campus, and Thurman and his classmates spent considerable time chewing the fat with him in his quarters.[54]

Thurman certainly knew about Black poverty in Daytona (he didn't have to look any further than his own family), but nothing prepared him for the abjectness of the poverty he witnessed in Atlanta. Atlanta for Thurman was always a city polluted by white racism and Black hopelessness. In the early 1920s it was the home and headquarters of the revived Ku Klux Klan, then rapidly growing in numbers and strength. As the first director of the Atlanta School of Social Work, Moore was Thurman's guide to the area around Morehouse and its sister colleges, a teeming laboratory of African American social ills and problems. The campus was surrounded by squalor in slums such as Beaver's Slide and Hell's Half Acre, where its residents lived in hovels, without water mains or sewerage, regular garbage pickup, paved roads or sidewalks, or police protection (except perhaps for those paid off by the area's flourishing sex trade). For the remainder of his life, Beaver's Slide would remain for Thurman an epitome of Black despair, a place haunted by Black self-loathing.[55]

If Moore is today little remembered, his replacement was in the early stages of a career that would make him the most eminent African American sociologist of the first half of the twentieth century, E. Franklin Frazier. Frazier was a defiant atheist/agnostic, notoriously prickly, short-tempered, sharp-tongued, and frank to the point of rudeness. Frazier's agnosticism only began with God. It extended to most Black leaders, institutions, and philosophers. Thurman had never met a Black intellectual with Frazier's hair-trigger pugnaciousness and penchant for smashing icons. (The student editors of the 1923 Morehouse yearbook, affectionately or not, gave Frazier the sobriquet of "Karl Marx" and an accompanying tagline, "Who is Your Authority?")[56] Some of this certainly rubbed off; Thurman probably learned more from him than from any other instructor at Morehouse.

Frazier, a graduate of Howard and Clark Universities, came to Morehouse in 1922. He was not happy to be there, having to cross the "Styxian Potomac" to a land that "rests upon principles as truly out of harmony with civilization as slavery itself."[57] In a 1924 article he criticized the curriculum of Black colleges as providing "too much inspiration and too little information," producing "a sentimental rather than a rational attitude toward life."[58] As for the Black church, he had written in 1920 that it had "sold itself for money" and had become "a business for profits." The younger generation was rejecting the "peculiar Negro" ardor for Christianity, which had made them "meek" and "docile."[59] In the early 1920s Frazier was a political radical, championing what he called the "new school" of African American political thought of A. Philip Randolph, Cyril Briggs, Marcus Garvey, and other radicals, socialists, and nationalists who came to prominence in Harlem after World War I. The conservative politics of Booker T. Washington had "lost its place among the masses of colored people" because they were models "of cowardice and syco-phancy." With the wounds of the Red Summer of 1919 still unhealed, Frazier approvingly quoted sources stating that "no intelligent Negro is willing to lay down his life for the United States as it now exists." Rather than making the world safe for democracy, the Negro was now trying to make "America safe for himself."[60]

Thurman and Frazier did not have an easy time of things at Morehouse. Thurman had just attended summer school at Columbia University (of which more below) and now fancied himself an expert on "social theory," which was the subject of Frazier's class. Thurman chatted so incessantly that one day an exasperated Frazier told him: "Howard Thurman, if Dean Archer wanted you to teach this course, you would be standing where I am and I would be seated where you are. . . . From this day forward you are not to speak a word in this course, not even to answer 'present' when the roll is called."[61] Thurman did as he was told. In addition to teaching Thurman a valuable lesson in humil-ity, Frazier's course whetted an abiding interest in democratic socialism, and in social schemes such as workers' proft-sharing, consumer cooperatives, and other innovative ways to humanize or transform capitalism.

Frazier has often been caricatured as an arch-assimilationist, but what he wanted, above all, was an end to what he saw as the cozy and coy embrace of segregation by Black institutions and the Black middle class, which left Blacks with the worst of both worlds, limited intellectual horizons joined to a tem-porizing politics.[62] He wanted both better and stronger Black institutions: the "spiritual and intellectual emancipation of the Negro," he would write in 1924, "awaits the building of a Negro university, supported by Negroes" whose products would not be afraid to interact with whites as equals.[63] Thur-man relates in his autobiography that when students questioned Frazier on why he refused to sing the Morehouse alma mater on ceremonial occasions, he told them: "At the present, the only thing that Morehouse means to me is a job, nothing more. I am not a hypocrite."[64] Thurman was at once disturbed by and admired Frazier's utter honesty about the realities of life in a segregated institution, even one as self-hallowing as Morehouse.

Thurman learned a similar lesson about looking at Morehouse with a critical eye from Benjamin Mays, who perhaps is the individual most asso-ciated with the college over its long history and would spend almost three decades as its much-revered president. None of Thurman's professors at Morehouse would play a larger role in his life than Mays, his teacher in psychology and trigonometry. They became acquainted in 1921 and remained fast friends for the next sixty years. With their oft-entwined careers, they would emerge as their generation's twin giants of what Barbara Savage has called "southern Black liberal Protestantism." Their emphases differed; their goals did not.[65] Mays was, like Frazier, only six years older than Thurman—John Hope was doing an excellent job in recruiting the best young Black academic talent available—and like Hope, Mays, though born and raised in rural South Carolina, was a graduate of a northern liberal arts college, in his case, Bates College in Maine. After his 1920 graduation, he continued his education at the University of Chicago before Hope persuaded him to come to Atlanta.[66]

Mays and Thurman found they had a lot in common. Both were involved in the campus YMCA branch. (Thurman was the student president of the YMCA, making him the de facto "religious leader on campus.")[67] Thurman, by his senior year, had one of the two coveted spots on the debating team. Mays was the coach of the debating team, and Thurman was "an inter-collegiate debater of the first magnitude." If that year's debating topic—"Resolved: That the United States Should Subsidize Her Merchant Marine"—might strike contemporary readers as a bit arcane, it was an important issue in the 1920s as the United States adjusted to postwar realities, and it offered one more example of Thurman's interest in economic matters during his Morehouse years.[68] Mays and Thurman found in each other a kindred spirit: "Our free minds gravitated to each other like a magnet."[69]

Mays, like Hope and Frazier, was a strong believer in an academic meritocracy, training Black university students to think themselves the equal of their white counterparts. In a 1926 address, he lamented that the "number of Negroes developing a new psychology with regard to inter-racial affairs is still small." This new psychology meant, Mays said, in words similar to those of Thurman's "Our Challenge" oration, overcoming the perception that "the white man is a little god—to be honored, revered, and idolized; or to be feared and obeyed." It was time to reject "the white man's Christianity" and its social order, "the lynching; the unjust distribution of school funds, the discrimination in the courts and the injustices in the social and economic worlds." He urged those who heard him to "strive to be an agriculturalist, not a Negro agriculturalist . . . a doctor, not a Negro doctor. . . . Aspire to be great—not among Negroes, but among men."[70] Mays and Thurman would not be hyphenated. Unlike Hope, whose views on religion were relatively conventional, or Frazier, whose views were almost entirely dismissive, Mays's

Christianity, as outlined in his 1925 master's thesis at the University of Chicago, "Pagan Survivals in Christianity," had great similarities with Thurman's own emerging religious modernism, a Christianity that could speak to the rising mood of skepticism among young Blacks. In his thesis, Mays was also scathing in his condemnation of fundamentalism:

> Not many months ago, I heard a minister (supposed to be very intelligent) say that we can find in the Bible all the sciences, such as mathematics, astronomy, physics, chemistry, etc. Likewise, he said that all psychology and philosophy can be obtained from the Bible. It is too often true that in an effort to elevate the Bible in modern thought, many an expounder has resorted to this method, forgetting that the Bible primarily is a religious book, written for religious ends, and portrays the evolution of man's spiritual and ethical ideas in his quest for God and in his efforts to relate himself aright to God and man.[71]

From talks with Mays, Thurman developed a real hunger for studying philosophy.[72] For both men, philosophy was something broader and in some ways more basic than religion. At Morehouse, Thurman would complain, there were "only were only two courses in philosophy; one in logic and one in ethics, which was really a glorified Sunday school class that the president of the college taught to all seniors."[73] The reason why philosophy was not taught at Morehouse, Thurman became convinced, was because it was too powerful: "The shapers of our minds [that is, the white founders of colleges like Morehouse and some of their Black successors], with clear but limited insight into the nature of our struggle for survival and development of American life, particularly in the South, recognized the real possibility that to be disciplined in the origins and development of ideas would ultimately bring under critical judgment the society and our predicament in it. This, in turn, would contribute to our unease and restlessness, which would be disastrous, they felt, for us and our people."[74] A rigorous examination of the compromises and evasions on which Black higher education was built, especially the acceptance of segregation as a condition for its existence and toleration by the white structures of power, would expose its flaws and contradictions.[75]

Following a suggestion from Garrie Moore, he decided to study philosophy at Columbia University's Summer School. He calculated his costs down to the last penny: "Then I set about to win all the cash prizes to be awarded at Commencement. This would be a great step toward my goal. I won them all." Between the end of classes in May and the beginning of summer school in July, Thurman prepared by staying with a relative in Cleveland—an early venture north of the Mason-Dixon Line—doing chores in his spare time, otherwise sitting in a local library, reading its entire shelf of philosophy books, from the pre-Socratics to William James.[76] He then went to New York City, living with a friend in Harlem and keeping his expenses down to fifty-five cents per day.[77]

He took three courses at Columbia: two philosophy courses, and one on American government. The course on reflective thinking, Thurman always felt, was "perhaps the most significant single course I ever took."[78] It taught him "a basic methodological approach to problem solving in all fields of investigation" from simple decisions "through the most confused patterns of human behavior." He learned an "approach that I would use not only in my subsequent work as a counselor but also in thinking through the complex and complicated problems I would encounter in my personal life and as a social being. As a tool of the mind, there is no way by which the value of this course could can be measured or accessed."[79]

"Reflective thinking" was a favored term of John Dewey, and the course on it, and the Columbia philosophy department as a whole in the 1920s, was Deweyian to its core, as was the textbook used in the class, *An Introduction to Reflective Thinking*, cowritten by nine members of the Columbia philosophy department. It defines reflective thinking (quoting Dewey) as "active, persistent and careful consideration of any belief or supposed form of knowledge in the light of the grounds that support it and the further conclusions to which it tends."[80] The volume is a series of case studies, emphasizing philosophy and reflective thinking as a form of practical reason. The case studies range from investment strategies for stocks and bonds, to the theories of Copernicus and Darwin, the historical veracity of the Torah, to the question of individualism versus collectivism, and a variety of other social problems.

Thurman was taught that reflective thinking meant rejecting lazy habits of thought, eschewing unexamined a priori assumptions, and avoiding the leap to premature and hastily formed conclusions. For Dewey, in his 1910 book *How We Think,* another course text, reflective thinking was "always more or less troublesome because it involves overcoming the inertia that inclines one to accept suggestions at their face value; it involves willingness to endure a condition of mental unrest and disturbance. Reflective thinking, in short, means judgment suspended during further inquiry; and suspense is likely to be somewhat painful."[81] This was the sort of bold encouragement of doubting and skepticism that Thurman badly needed to hear. Dewey emphasized that reflective thinking was a creative and democratic process, part of his politics of progressive pragmatism. The final sentence of *How We Think* states that "genuine communication involves contagion; its name should not be taken in vain by terming communication that produces no community of thought and purpose" between the teacher (or preacher) and listener. For Thurman, "community" and "contagion" would always be closely linked ideas and processes. Thurman's truths, even the truths discovered by a mystic in solitary contemplation, were always shared, democratic, and necessarily contagious.[82]

Something that was contagious among young, progressive Christians in the early 1920s was pacifism. During his junior year at Morehouse, Thurman caught the bug from George "Shorty" Collins—Collins was six foot five inches—the southern field organizer for the Fellowship of Reconciliation (FOR). Founded during the war, it rapidly became the leading Christian pacifist organization in the United States and Europe. Thurman became a fervent convert. Collins would become the first white person he would ever call friend. As Thurman stated in his autobiography: "I had no particular interest in the peace movement per se. But in my encounter with the FOR, as exemplified in the life of one of its secretaries, Shorty Collins, I found a place to stand in my own spirit—a place so profoundly affirming that I was strengthened by a sense of immunity to the assaults of the white world of Atlanta, Georgia." Collins was "one of the few voices moving through the South, creating islands of fellowship across racial and cultural lines."[83] Pacifism was another of the lifelong commitments and passions he acquired at Morehouse. For Thurman pacifism was always less about militarism and overseas conflicts than addressing the violence that was inherent and implicit in almost every interaction between whites and Blacks in America. When Thurman graduated from Morehouse, he was listed as one of three class pacifists. He also probably was one of the fourteen members of his graduating class who considered themselves a socialist (along with twenty-two Republicans and one Bolshevik).[84] Pacifism and socialism, two related ways of making the world better, were for Thurman less fixed ideologies than entrance passes into a new vibrant community of like-minded souls.

Thurman's pacifism is discussed in more detail in later chapters. Let me end this account of Thurman's Morehouse years with an odd story, one that Thurman evidently told only once, recounted by his first biographer, Elizabeth Yates. He was back home from Morehouse for his summer vacation and stepped into a Daytona five-and-ten-cents store for a purchase. The white female clerk made "a remark to him that a Negro couldn't answer." Annoyed by his silence, the clerk told her manager that she had been insulted. He left and returned home. Later that afternoon he was sitting on his porch with his grandmother when he saw of a crowd of people gathering down the street. He thought it was a mob coming for him. In Yates's somewhat overwrought prose: "Howard put his head in his hands to shut out the threat and its horror.... Was there no way a man could defend himself? ... He could not let her

[Grandma Nancy] see that despite all he was learning in college, fear could still get its hold on him."[85]

The story has a happy ending. It wasn't a white mob but a group of his neighbors coming to congratulate him on his success in college. That Thurman couldn't tell the difference, even at a distance, between a white lynch mob and a congratulatory group of Black neighbors is an indication of how fearful he must have been of the consequences of suposedly sassing a white woman. It reveals that the life of fear that he knew he faced if he stayed in Daytona and the different life he was trying to make for himself. These two worlds, his two lives—were not that far apart. The two worlds came together when he graduated from Morehouse in 1923. He insisted that his shy, reticent mother travel to Atlanta for the ceremonies. She seemed overwhelmed, out of place, and uncomfortable amid all of the educated, middle-class Morehouse men and their families. When Thurman introduced her to John Hope, at first she seemed at a loss for words. But finally she spoke, telling him, "I just want to thank you for what you have done for my boy." Hope replied, "Oh no, it was done by you, long before he ever came here."[86]

This was no doubt true. It is also so that it was at Morehouse that Thurman's unique skills and abilities really began to be noticed. In 1936 Benjamin Mays wrote of Thurman's Morehouse years that there was no one at the college "who had a finer mind" and that he was also superior to most of his classmates in "human sympathies and social imagination." Thurman was "so interesting and stimulating that I associated with him at Morehouse more than I did many of the professors." He was a bit different. He "was less interested in social affairs than most students were," and the intensity and unconventionality of his religious beliefs were already evident. None of this interfered, Mays wrote, "with his general popularity because he possessed a mind and an integrity of character which they were forced to respect."[87] Morehouse sharpened Thurman's mind and honed his already well-developed sense of integrity. It gave Thurman the tools to understand what Morehouse could and could not provide him. It was an excellent education.

4

"The Sound of Rushing Water"

Rochester Theological Seminary

It was late at night, and it would be a long a wait for the next trolley. Thurman decided to walk back to his dorm at Rochester Theological Seminary (RTS). He had not been out carousing but teaching Bible study at the Colored Branch of Rochester's YWCA. Most of the students were domestic servants who attended the late class only after they were free from their daily chores. In Rochester, Thurman's life revolved around RTS's almost entirely (save himself) white student body and faculty. Thurman did his best, however, to stay close to Rochester's relatively small African American community, attending, when possible, the Black Baptist church and teaching the Bible class. Rochester at night was an unfamiliar city to Thurman, and, always attuned to the numinous quality of darkness and quiet, he listened to its distinctive sound as he walked down Main Street:

> There was almost no traffic. As I walked along, I became aware of what seemed to be the sound of rushing water. I realized that I had been hearing this rumbling for quite some time, but had only suddenly become aware of it. The next day I was talking about this with one of my professors who told me that for a certain distance under Main Street there was a part of the old canal. This was the sound of water that I had heard. The sound itself was continuous, but when there was the normal traffic in the daytime, the sound could not be heard. It was only when the surface noises had stopped that the sound came through. This is analogous to the mystic's witness of God within, whose Presence may not become manifest until the traffic of the surface life is somehow stilled.[1]

If Thurman saw the hidden river beneath his feet as an allegory of the mystic's quest for "centering down," perhaps we can also read it as a story about his years in Rochester, a city where he learned to listen to himself in new ways. The Rochester years were a time of remarkable personal and intellectual growth. Heretofore we have glimpsed Thurman in various waystations of his maturation. The man who left Rochester in 1926 was the person he would be until the end of his days.

As with Morehouse, Rochester Theological Seminary was not Thurman's first choice. Since high school, after reading an advertisement in a Baptist magazine, he had wanted to attend Newton Theological Institution, in Newton, Massachusetts, near Boston, one of the oldest and most distinguished religious seminaries in the country, but in 1923 it did not accept Black students. After he applied, he received what he described as a "very cordial letter" from its president, explaining its "no Negroes" policy, encouraging him to apply to Virginia Union, a Baptist seminary in Richmond, Virginia, where Thurman "would be able to secure the kind of training I would need to provide religious leadership for my people."[2] In 1979 the dean of what by then was called Andover Newton Theological School wrote Thurman, asking and apologizing about the episode. Thurman told his story, adding, "long ago I absorbed the violence of this rejection."[3] Thurman felt that he could best serve "his people" through obtaining the best possible theological education for himself, which he felt could not be found in a Black seminary. He applied to RTS, a school he knew accepted African Americans. One of his teachers at Morehouse, Charles Hubert, and his mentor Mordecai Wyatt Johnson were graduates. Thurman was accepted, though evidently his letter of acceptance made him feel that the school felt it was doing him a great favor, almost an act of charity, in permitting him to attend. Rather than Andover's "no Negroes" policy, RTS had a "two-at-most Negroes" policy (so they could room together). At first, Thurman had the distinct impression that his presence would be tolerated rather than truly welcomed. In any event Thurman knew RTS would be utterly unlike his previous places of education.[4]

Rochester Theological Seminary was founded in 1850 by German Baptists in the same year and by many of the same people who founded the University of Rochester. For many decades the seminary was dominated by Augustus Hopkins Strong, its president from 1872 to 1912, best known for his *Systematic Theology,* a weighty three-volume tome that was probably the most influential Protestant work of its kind produced in late nineteenth-century America. Strong was a bulwark of Baptist orthodoxy, despite a tentative rapprochement with both evolution and the Higher Criticism, concessions that came at the price of theological consistency.[5] Although Thurman never met

Strong, who died in 1921, his influence over the seminary lingered for many years, so much so that Thurman, supplying information to his first biographer, called his chief advisor at RTS, George Cross—who had been hired as Strong's successor—"Dr. Strong."[6]

Strong in his later years was wont to complain that the Social Gospel movement had undermined the belief in the divinity of Christ. For this, at RTS, he had only himself to blame, for in 1897 he hired Walter Rauschenbusch for the faculty. Over the next two decades, from his position in Rochester, Rauschenbusch became the most prominent figure in the Social Gospel movement, insisting that the social mission of Christianity was central to its message.[7] As with Strong, Thurman never met Rauschenbusch, who died in 1918, but his impact at RTS remained palpable during Thurman's years in residence, 1923 to 1926, and the school was a center for liberal Protestantism, devoted to the social mission of Christianity.[8] An account of American theological education published in 1924 described the recent history of RTS as making "a great break from the dogmatic to the scientific, from the theoretical to the practical, and from the ecclesic-centric to the social-centric point of view."[9]

In 1918, writing to Mordecau Wyatt Johnson, Thurman had been quite forthright about his future calling: "I want to be a minister of the Gospel."[10] Five years later, if still oriented in the same general direction, he was more equivocal about his subsequent plans. Although Thurman wanted to study in seminary and wanted to learn the techniques and vocabulary of modern religious thought to find a framework for his rather inchoate spiritual strivings, he was much less certain about his plans after graduation, as he would tell an interviewer in 1969:

> I didn't know if I wanted to become a minister, a preacher, but I knew that I wanted to understand man's story with reference to his quest for God. Because the one thing that had enabled me to keep from being destroyed by the violences of my environment, as a youngster growing up in Florida, was a deep religious sense I had that I, Howard Thurman was of infinite worth and that that worth was not contingent upon anything external to me. No judgment external to me could be definitive in working out how I felt inside of me. And this to me was the meaning of religion. It had nothing to do with church, as such.[11]

We do not quite know precisely what sort of religious beliefs he brought with him to Rochester, though he was definitely in transition toward thoroughgoing Protestant modernism. His college yearbook expressed confidence that Thurman would "furnish us with a rational and practical Christianity."[12]

By the time he graduated from RTS in 1926, the transition was complete: "At RTS I learned how to think creatively about religion without having the wings of my thought clipped by dogma and theology." At RTS Thurman learned, from a bevy of theologians, the unimportance of theology: "It was there I made the discovery, which to me was primary and first, that all dogma, all theologies are inventions of the mind. They are what the mind does in its effort to reduce religious experience to something that can be apprehended— comprehended." All theologies are "always a little out of date," ex post facto reconstructions of actual religious experience, and what was most important was the experience and not its explanation. Thurman's religion had always been based on intense, immediate experience. It was at RTS that he began to acquire the language to understand this experience, which he would later call his mysticism.[13]

There was something else Thurman had to learn at RTS. "When I entered seminary," he wrote in his autobiography, "I experienced the most radical period of adjustment of my life up to that moment. I was living for the first time in an entirely white world. The impact of this fact alone was staggering."[14] (Although it should be noted, as mentioned above, in Bible classes at the Colored Branch of the YWCA, on many Sundays, and during the summer, he left the white world behind.) Before Rochester, Thurman wrote in a memorable phrase, "it had never occurred to me that my magnetic field of ethical awareness applied to other than my own people."[15] Whatever the ethical or moral rule, white people were always within "the category of exception," that is, they were "tolerated as a vital part of the environment" but were "a world apart, in another universe of discourse."[16] Whites and Blacks felt no ethical obligations to one another, no responsibility to recognize their common humanity. Honesty and openness were casualties. For Blacks, whites were obstacles to be maneuvered around. They could be malign, indifferent, and sometimes even benign or friendly, but there was no expectation that the relationship would be truly honest or reciprocal or that you would treat a white person as you would a Black person, as someone whose feelings had to be understood and respected. But this created a dilemma if you found yourself in an entirely white world. A field of ethical awareness that does not extend beyond one's self is not a field of ethical awareness.

At RTS he had to at first room by himself. He felt that he would be judged by a different standard by his white classmates and would be either ostracized or patronized, that his education at Morehouse had been inferior to that of his white classmates, and that he was not their intellectual equal. But even as he realized his fears were unwarranted, he still felt his classmates had an "unyielding advantage." They "were at home in this world and I felt a stranger.

Whether they were gifted intellectually, or mediocre, the fact remained that the world belonged to them." Thurman felt that his "sense of alienation was reinforced by certain professors and visiting lecturers" who assumed that in his attitudes and in his Christianity he was "a person apart."[17] When he was elected class president for his senior year, the president of the seminary, Clarence Barbour, told him, "Don't let recognition on the part of white people go to your head."[18] A former classmate wrote him many years later: "Prexy Barbour [had an] inability to see life through your eyes."[19] Even as class president, he was sometimes reminded of his outsider status. One of his duties was to represent his class at the funeral of the school janitor, and to be an honorary pallbearer, only to be disinvited to perform that role at the request of the deceased man's family.[20]

Rochester's racial lessons were complex. Thurman was glad to be in a city, and in a part of the country, where the minatory rules of Jim Crow did not apply. But this new freedom brought its own complications. Without strict rules of racial separation and Black subordinance, every new interracial acquaintance and friendship had to follow its own improvised script. And Thurman was of course aware that the mere absence of segregation did not mean that he would always be treated as he wished. Thurman soon became an expert in navigating his newly expanded "magnetic field."

Thurman's first published article, "College and Color," was about the discrimination Blacks faced at majority-white institutions of higher learning. Some of it, perhaps most of it, came from his personal experiences. The article appeared in a student Christian journal in 1924, and it provides a collection of the slights, jibes, and awkward gaucheries that he and other Black students faced, such as sitting in a classroom surrounded by a cordon sanitaire of empty seats; professors telling "racially humiliating jokes"; or "blatant outbursts of 'white supremacy.'"[21] Thurman offered a taxonomy of campus attitudes. There were the "indifferent and thoughtless," such as his fellow students and instructors who made casual reference in front of him about "nigger heaven" (a common term at the time for the top balcony of a theater). There were those who made a show of tolerance, by an ostentatious acknowledgment, an overemphatic hello or good-bye, behind which "lies every emotion ranging from genuine hatred to total indifference." And there was the paternalist who thought he was doing his Black friend a favor by sheltering "an 'unfortunate,' just as a plantation owner defends a peon on his farm." In such cases, the underlying motives may be genuine, "but pity always weakens and embarrasses." There were those who loudly announced, "I have no prejudice," as a way of masking their ambivalence, or thinking that mere courtesy was somehow an exceptional gesture. And there were the openly hostile, the sort who "intentionally and maliciously brushes against the Negro student in the corridor, steps on his foot, makes wretchedly nasty statements about his race." Thurman stated that at least with the openly hostile students, "in their favor is their utter lack of hypocrisy," compared to the squishy insincerity of others. Through all of this, Thurman was acutely aware of the double standard. White students would not be called out for their behavior or, if they were, would be able to apologize. (As did the professor who spoke to him of "nigger heaven.") As for himself, he knew there was no margin for error. If he ever displayed bad manners, lost his temper, returned hostility with hostility, he would be marked. As a result, "there would never be a moment in his life when he could afford himself to be off guard."[22]

And if Thurman was no longer in the South, some of its most malevolent institutions had made their way north. Thurman, who never spoke of having a confrontation with the Ku Klux Klan in the South, had several encounters with the Klan in Rochester, which was then enjoying a resurgence in places far from the states of the old Confederacy. He was, as he would remain for his entire career, in demand as a preacher, and during his years at RTS, he made his way to many local congregations near Rochester. After finishing one sermon near the end of one spring semester, a man came up to Thurman and told him that he had attended almost every sermon he had preached that year and had been recording the details. Thurman knew at once that this man was a Klan member and was making a threat, warning him not to get out of line in his racial comments. On another occasion Thurman went to preach at a church in an area that was a Klan stronghold. After some discussion he kept the engagement but had to walk past a gauntlet of grim, tight-lipped, and probably armed (but apparently unhooded) Klansmen, standing shoulder to shoulder, as he walked to the sanctuary. Nothing happened, but when Thurman returned to Rochester, "I became so anguished that I lost my appetite and took to my bed until morning."[23]

And yet, despite racial incidents, minor and potentially major, Thurman thrived in Rochester, and ultimately, this was not despite but because of the racial climate. His room became a meeting place for bull sessions and chewing the fat.[24] Despite an unwritten rule at RTS against interracial roommates, and the efforts of the president of the seminary to prevent it, Thurman was invited by two white classmates to share a suite in his last two years. If his instructors sometimes showed little understanding of the particularities of what it meant to be Black in America in the 1920s, they treated him as a full equal in the classroom, where he soon proved his worth. Ignorance could be dispelled, as when at dinner, one young girl wondered if he could rub his blackness from his skin and was satisfied when he said he could not.[25]

Another repeatedly whispered, "Stop, Nigger, stop," in reference to the family's black cat. The girl's parents apologized for the cat on the table but not for its name. Still, he was eating dinner with white families and preaching in their churches, unlike the near impossibility of this in the South.[26] "College and Color," in addition to the varieties of racial hostility it catalogued, included one additional type, the white student who understood, or tried to understand, without preconceptions, persons "not bound by traditional attitudes or group complexes" but governed by "sympathetic understanding," whose friendship was "as invigorating as a refreshing shower in the midst of a tropical summer." Beautiful friendships of this sort soon became central to Thurman's life and thought.[27]

Thurman concluded his article "College and Color" by stating that what he did not want for Black college students was "special favors" or "special treatment." This would be "pauperizing." He merely wanted "all the privileges and freedom of regular matriculated students, no more, no less," and for African American students to be treated "as individuals" with whites "respecting their personalities," and to be dealt with as "students, not as *Negro* students."[28] At the same time, of course, when one of his seminary colleagues told him, "I never think of you, Howard, as a Negro," he did not take it as a compliment. "I am a human being, but also a Negro," he told his friend. If Thurman did not want "special treatment" for Blacks, he also wanted white students and faculty to remember that whites and Blacks lived in a society that was profoundly unequal.[29]

Thurman loved Rochester's commercial openness: "The city of Rochester looked fabulous to me. I enjoyed window shopping, looking at all kinds of beautiful things—chinaware, furniture, linens, clothing. There were several excellent restaurants that served foods deliciously foreign to my palate. Generally, I was not troubled by the question of race; I was never refused service or otherwise insulted in any of the stores." By saving money, he was able to go to the movies once a week and attend concerts and operatic performances at the newly opened Eastman Theater, open to him without Jim Crow seating arrangements. And the relative proximity to New York City allowed Thurman to cast his nets even wider and take excursions to the city for theater and ballet. On occasion, as a man willing to make sacrifices for culture, he slept on a bench at Grand Central Terminal overnight, waiting for the first train back to Rochester.[30]

Thurman's only major complaint about Rochester was that it "seemed to me to have the most consistently cold weather in the world." This is not surprising for a man who had only seen snow once before, and who at first lacked the most basic necessity for surviving a Rochester winter, a sturdy overcoat.

This he remedied through the offices of a welcoming Jewish haberdasher, Jack Schooler. They would remain in touch for decades, corresponding both about clothes and life in general. Schooler would be the first of many close Jewish friends, inaugurating a pattern of philo-Semitism, both for Jews and Judaism, that would persist throughout his life.[31]

Perhaps the difference between Rochester and the white South was less in individual racial attitudes than in the political centrality of race. Atlanta and Rochester were in the mid-1920s roughly comparable in population, cities of about three hundred thousand persons, but Atlanta was 45 percent Black to Rochester's 1 percent. Atlanta had a long history of bitter racial tensions and the active suppression of Blacks. Rochester, if by this point largely coasting on its abolitionist legacy, did not. The race question was not absent in upstate New York, as the revival of the Klan suggests, and as Rochester's Black population increased in the decades to come, so did the city's racial tensions. But in the 1920s, if Thurman never forgot or was allowed to forget about America's underlying racial realities, neither was he compelled to dwell on them. Thurman found in the cool, crisp atmosphere of Rochester a place where he could breathe freely. One of Thurman's favorite biblical quotations was from the Epistle to the Hebrews, describing Abraham setting out for a strange and distant place, a city "whose architect and builder is God" (11:10). In a sermon on this topic from 1953 Thurman described this city: "We are looking for something that will not deceive us. . . . [I]t will not be betrayed by our limitations but something that will never desert us." If Rochester was not the city of God, for Thurman it was a city of refuge.

Thurman's life in Rochester centered around RTS, which, at Alexander Street and East Avenue, was in the heart of the city.[32] Beyond the racial differences, RTS was wholly unlike any school he had previously attended. It lacked the "more personal and responsive ambiance of Morehouse College" and was far more formal. If at Morehouse some of his most influential instructors, like Frazier and Mays, were essentially his contemporaries, at RTS the professors were older, bearded, and carried themselves, Thurman noted, with a donnish mien. Each course began with the distribution of an extensive syllabus. Each class session began with prayer. First names were never used. The daily chapel service was "stylized in a manner outside of my experience."[33]

RTS also reflected the disparity in the resources available to elite white schools as compared to Morehouse. The size of the RTS library dwarfed the holdings at Morehouse, and Thurman, dazzled by its plenitude, would wander the stacks for hours, sampling book after book, as if unable to believe his good fortune. He took out books to read during the breaks between classes, others for the weekly trolley trip to the YWCA, and still others he left strategically strewn around his dorm room. The library was an entryway to a democracy of learning in which ideas would be judged by their strength and coherence, and nothing else.[34] Dave Voss, his RTS roommate, remembered Thurman's ferocious reading habits and recalled that Thurman was so impressed by Henry Adams's paean to medieval culture and Gothic architecture, *Mont-Saint-Michel and Chartres,* that he paid the munificent sum of fifteen dollars for a well-illustrated copy. Perhaps Adams's account of how the mystical and the practical were joined in twelfth- and thirteenth-century France struck a chord; Thurman would have a lifelong fascination with the great French cathedrals.[35] "The Gothic Arch," he would write many years later, "marks one of those awesome moments when God touches the mind, the imagination of man with the Shekinah of his presence."[36] However, not all of his interest in medievalism was quite so high-minded. Voss also remembered Thurman's having as a prize possession a volume entitled *Love Life of the Popes.*[37]

Thurman's curriculum at RTS included courses on the social basis of religion, the psychology of religion, Christian ethics and sociology, and Christianity in modern civilization.[38] This social orientation certainly represented the perspective of the faculty members who most influenced Thurman: advocates of historicist, experiential, antidogmatic Christianity. Thurman singled out three instructors in particular as being "profoundly influential": Henry Burke Robins, Conrad Henry Moehlman, and George Cross.[39] They had much in common. They were Baptists, all in their fifties or sixties. They had all studied at the University of Chicago, the Baptist-founded university that was a bastion of the historical Higher Criticism of the Bible. They had all been colleagues of Walter Rauschenbusch. There were differences in what they taught and believed, but they were close enough to help instill in Thurman a common, shared vision of a new, modern Christianity. Like most advocates of the Social Gospel (including the deceased Walter Rauschenbusch), they did not place the problems of African Americans in the center of their social vision, although some of his instructors expressed more concern than others about racial matters.[40] But Thurman had become an expert learner and judged his teachers by their strengths, not their weaknesses.

Thurman described Henry Burke Robins (1874–1942) as "silver-haired and somber, [he] let us listen to the springs of his own spiritual landscape. . . . [H]is course in the history of religion revealed a new world to me," communicating "the awe, the mystery, and the glory of the presence,"[41] and that "the spiritual experience of the human race was essentially one single experience."[42] When Thurman was planning his trip to India, Robins told him that Christianity did not have "any word for the under-privileged but 'sweet charity' and exhortations to be content with the lot into which they are born" and that a new message had to be crafted.[43]

Conrad Henry Moehlman (1879–1961) was a prolific writer on many subjects, an opponent of fundamentalism, and believed, as did Thurman, that institutional Christianity had "transformed the religion of Jesus into a theology," a secondhand theology that was only a religion "concerning Jesus."[44] Thurman wrote of Moehlman that he "introduced me . . . [to] the struggle for survival of the essential religion of Jesus."[45] Moehlman also believed, like Thurman, that the religion of Jesus required challenging the "three inherited unethical Christian attitudes [that] involve the American Indian, the Negro, and Judaism."[46]

The most important of Thurman's instructors at RTS was George Cross, his primary mentor. Born and raised in Canada, Cross had an active career as a minister before attending the University of Chicago for his doctoral work. In 1914 he replaced Augustus Strong as professor of systematic theology at RTS. (Strong was not pleased at the choice, calling Cross's hiring "the greatest calamity that has come to the seminary since its founding," and labeling Cross's theology as "agnostic, skeptical, and anti-Christian.")[47] Cross had a classroom personality that was both wry and stern.[48] Thurman was attracted to the steely, comprehensive power of his intellect, as "he dismantled the structures of orthodoxy with scrupulous scholarship," leaving Thurman "in turn fascinated and outraged by what seemed to me to be his supreme self-confidence."[49] Cross's religious modernism was thoroughgoing, but at times he seemed saddened at his obligation to demolish the grand theological edifices of the past.[50] Like Thurman, he placed great emphasis on the experiential dimensions of worship, arguing that "religion that is not a matter of subjective experience is not religion at all," and that "every man must be his own theologian, whatever the consequences."[51] Cross reinforced the Deweyian lessons taught at Thurman's 1922 Columbia summer course, and like Dewey saw experience as encompassing "the whole of our intellectual and volitional activities."[52] If Thurman admired Cross, there were considerable differences in their religious thinking. Cross, who believed that Christianity was "destined to displace all other religions" because "all that is truly worthful in them finds fulfillment in the Christian faith,"[53] had little genuine interest in other religious traditions. Cross was a systematic theologian, and the details of Cross's late-Hegelian Christian idealism held little interest for Thurman. Cross wrote little on politics or racial matters.[54] And yet from Cross and from the years at RTS Thurman absorbed a theology that was progressive, conscious of itself as boldly breaking with the past, and rooted in personal experience.

Thurman's three surviving student papers from his RTS years provide the clearest indication of his emerging religious thinking. The earliest student paper, "Virgin Birth," was probably written in the first half of 1924, most likely for a course on the history of Christianity taught by Henry Burke Robins. It represents a young man in the flush of a newly embraced modernism. (Then again, it was probably the last instance in which Thurman ever referred to Jesus as "the Son of God.") The paper argued that the idea of the virgin birth is wholly mythological, an idea "born in error" and perpetuated as a dogma of the church out of a misplaced need to honor the delusions of an earlier day. Thurman's paper was an exercise in armchair anthropology akin to James Frazer's *The Golden Bough* and similar works, picking and choosing examples from immense collections of ancient and non-Western folklore, with the assumption of a great, unbridgeable gap between the workings of the primitive mind, labile and gullible, and that of the modern, rational, scientific European and American mind of the early twentieth century.[55]

The student paper that provides the best glimpse of the future religious thinker is "Can It Truly Be Said That the Existence of a Supreme Spirit Is a Scientific Hypothesis?," written in a course with George Cross in the fall of 1925.[56] Drawing on the text he used at his 1922 Columbia University summer course on reflective thinking leavened by some Neo-Kantianism, Thurman argued that a good scientific hypothesis was "simple, inclusive, fruitful, and explanatory," an attempt to make sense of the "immediate facts of existence" which are ordinarily "confused, disorderly and complex." However, since no scientific hypothesis can be based on all possible facts, "any final belief as to the constitution of the universe cannot depend on scientific knowledge but must depend on faith," giving the example of atoms and electrons, which, according to a fairly widely held view at the time, could not be demonstrated to be real entities but were only useful hypotheses.[57]

In the most interesting part of the paper, he makes a distinction between religious belief and religious knowledge: "There are times when I am supremely conscious that I make contact with *somebody* and I know that I am not alone." When this happens, "with my total personality I do not only say 'I believe' but when I am most myself, I say 'I know.'" Thurman concluded, in a passage underlined for emphasis, when "we drop into ourselves to find the raison d'etre of our affirmation and we spend the rest of our lives seeking a verification which will cover the total range of all our experience." If Thurman's pragmatic notion of experience—"the validity of the faith that there is a supreme spirit is determined by whether or not it will stand the test of experience"—was drawn from William James (cited in the paper) and others, it was moving toward a personal mysticism that he did not yet have the vocabulary to adequately describe.[58]

Thurman's final paper at RTS, his graduation thesis for his bachelor of divinity (B.D.) degree, was by far the longest of his student papers and one of the most important and unusual of all his writings. It was on a topic to which he would never return in depth, but which would subtly underlie much of his mature writings: "The Basis of Sex Morality: An Inquiry into the Attitude toward Premarital Sexual Morality among Various People and an Analysis of Its True Basis," completed in April 1926.[59] The paper is a product of his discovery of and intellectual infatuation with the person who was probably the most significant influence on Thurman's thought during his RTS years, the South African novelist, feminist, pacifist, and social theorist Olive Schreiner (1855–1920).[60]

The paper is also the product of Thurman's extensive conference-hopping travels on the student Christian circuit, in a pattern he would follow until World War II. In the thesis, under the very 1920s Jazz Age heading "The Revolt of Youth," he wrote: "Last summer I spent more than twenty-five days in daily and intimate contact with several hundred young college men and women. We discussed everything from birth control to the planetary hypothesis."[61] One suspects that the discussions about birth control were livelier than those about Copernicus.

The previous September, he had been an invited guest at a ten-day retreat in Pawling, New York, in eastern Dutchess County. Thurman and about twenty-five other men and women stayed in an old hotel for about ten days in a conference sponsored by the Student Christian Movement—a combined program of the YMCA and the YWCA—for the upcoming generation of student movement leaders.[62] We do not know the identities of most of the participants at the Pawling retreat, but it seems reasonable to assume that if Thurman was not the one African American in attendance, he was one of a small handful. Having drawn the short straw, he was obliged to share his double bed with a fellow conference participant, Allan Hunter, a young Congregationalist minister, who arrived late. As Thurman related in his autobiography, "with frank simplicity he told me that although he had been unaware of harboring any racial prejudice until that moment, he also had never faced the prospect of sharing a bed with a Negro. Social relationships with Negroes were beyond the scope of his experience." And so, they talked. "We explored our souls together that night and helped each other exhume ghosts of racism each of us had considered forever buried. We talked until early light, and then we went to sleep. When we awoke, our lives were bound together in friendship and affection which the years have crowned with a shekinah that remains undimmed." There is something rapturous about Thurman's account of his night talking to Hunter, of a deep intimacy, a shedding of inhibitions, the glow that comes from releasing secrets, far in the night, when all the world, save you and one other person, are fast asleep.[63] Thurman and Hunter, later a prominent pacifist, would remain lifelong friends.

However, a lot of the conversations, at Pawling and elsewhere, as he traveled the student Christian circuit, were about sex. In his thesis he noted he was impressed by the "seriousness" of these discussions and the "almost flagrant disregard which they held for anything which savored of external authority. There was nothing more bitterly assailed than the present conventional attitude taken toward questions of sex. The hot spot was, 'Why is it wrong for me [as an unmarried person] to have sexual intercourse?'"[64] Thurman was discussing sex with white women: "I was impressed by the fact that the theological students from Union, Yale, Oberlin, and Rochester were raising the essentially same questions raised by undergraduates from Wellesley, Barnard, or Holyoke [three women's colleges]."[65] If Thurman could, in 1925, talk with white women about their sexual desires and sexual practices—and presumably, talk with them about his own feelings—he no doubt felt that, in the right circumstances, there was nothing that was out of bounds, even this most tabooed of topics, that stood in the way deeper interracial understanding.[66]

But at this memorable conference in Pawling, frank talk about neither sex nor race was the highlight for Thurman. In the evening the retreat participants shared favorite poetry, stories, or memories. Shorty Collins, the Fellowship of Reconciliation field representative who had befriended Thurman in Atlanta, read an allegory about a hunter who spent a lifetime looking for a giant bird that he saw, only once, and then only her reflection in a lake, "a vast white bird, with silver wings outstretched, sailing in the everlasting blue." The hunter spent the rest of his life restlessly and relentlessly searching for the bird. He never sighted the bird again. When the hunter was near death, he said: "I have sought, for long years I have labored, but I have not found her. I have not rested. I have not repined, and I have not seen her; now my strength is gone." He would be forgotten, but others will walk the path he blazed, climb the steps he had hewn from stone. "At the clumsy work they will laugh; when the stones roll they will curse me. But they will mount, and on *my* work, they will climb, and by *my* stair! They will find her, and through me! And no man liveth to himself, and no man dieth to himself."[67]

On hearing the allegory, Thurman had an instant intellectual coup de foudre. Thurman had been listening to Collins read "The Hunter" by Olive Schreiner, from one of her several books of allegories. "It seemed," he later wrote, "that all my life long I was being readied for such an encounter." His fascination with the writer whose "ideas have influenced my own thought at a very profound level" lasted a lifetime.[68] In short order, he read everything by Schreiner that he could lay his hands on, and her work formed the intellectual core of his thesis. In 1927 he and his wife named their daughter Olive in her honor. In 1973 he would realize an ambition of many decades and publish an anthology of her writings, *A Track to the Water's Edge*.[69]

Olive Schreiner was born in 1855 in Cape Colony, in what became South Africa, the daughter of missionary parents. Her best-remembered novel, *The Story of an African Farm* (1883), loosely autobiographical, was the first important novel about the "New Woman," the story of a restless overturner of society's constraints on women's lives and loves. Her book of allegories, *Dreams,* which included "The Hunter," was published in 1891, and allegories became a favorite genre. She spent most of her later life in England, where she became a well-known feminist and author of an important work of feminist theory, *Women and Labor* (1911).[70] She was also a pacifist and wrote extensively about this and many other topics, including the political situation in her native South Africa. With her close friend, the pioneering sexologist Havelock Ellis, she wrote extensively on the psychology, physical realities, and spiritual significance of human intimacy.

Thurman was attracted to Schreiner by her language, steeped in KJV cadences, a late-Victorian style of prose-poetry that was "making music I was attuned to hear," a type of writing he would very much make his own.[71] But most of the attraction was its message, which was resonantly spiritual but not explicitly Christian, even post-Christian. In some ways, "The Hunter" is a story Thurman had heard many times before. It is an allegorical tale of uplift, describing how we stand on the anonymous shoulders of those who came before us; how our individual quests are collective and shared, how we succeed through renunciation of the superfluous, and how every small increment ahead is part of a giant leap forward. But Schreiner took uplift away from the rock-hard racial realities of the post-Reconstruction South and constructed a metaphysic of striving, a quest that is its own goal and own justification, where the quest becomes the new religion, the basis of what one Schreiner scholar has called a "politics of yearning."[72] Reading her, Thurman would write, "it became possible for me to move from primary experience, to conceptualizing that experience, to a vision inclusive of all of life." Thurman called her appreciation of nature and life "metaphysical," whereas his own was "religious."[73]

One obstacle to Thurman's immersion in Schreiner's works was that he soon discovered that she was a white South African. On learning this, he tried to disavow the connection: "I became immediately suspicious and felt guilty that I was so affected by her. . . . I had to answer the critical question. How could a white woman born and reared in South Africa think as she thought and feel about man as she felt?" Although she was, for her time, forward-thinking about the future of South Africa's native peoples, they were never central to her politics. Thurman was even more upset when he discovered that Schreiner was not above using the word "nigger" as a neutral descriptor for native Africans.[74] But Schreiner was Thurman's casually racist white South African soulmate. He was able to look past their profound outward dissimilarities and find deep affinities. As a young child, much like Thurman, she had found more inspiration in nature rather than in conventional religion—she in the vastness of the veldt, he contemplating the immensity of the Atlantic. They both believed, in a similar way, in the aliveness of nature. Thurman's thesis is the first product of his encounter with Olive Schreiner. It was sweepingly, outspokenly, and in places, incandescently, feminist.[75]

"The Basis of Sex Morality" opened, like Thurman's paper "Virgin Birth," with a *Golden Bough*–esque ramble through the relevant anthropological literature, starting with preliterate societies. But unlike "Virgin Birth" and as Margaret Mead would famously argue two years later in *Coming of Age in Samoa,* Thurman found that many primitive societies had more reasonable attitudes toward sexual couplings than their more sophisticated successors: "In the Malay Archipelago intercourse between unmarried people is generally considered neither a crime nor a danger; and the same is perhaps even more generally the case among the uncivilized races of India and Indo-China."[76] However, these more sensible approaches were rejected by Judaism and then Christianity, and this aspect of the major monotheisms continued to dominate American sexual mores.

Thurman's argument became explicitly feminist when he argued that the prohibition against premarital sex was selective, enforced against women and not men, and only against middle-class and upper-class women, giving men the freedom to pursue their sexual urges with women outside of their class or race without the nice formality of respectable courtship rituals. Middle-class women became trapped in their marriages and were so bound by societal restrictions and conventions that they were made dependent on others, becoming what Thurman, following Schreiner, called the "parasitic woman." At the same time, other women often had their bodies directly exploited by men, either as prostitutes or subject to coercive sexual relations. Quoting a source with approval, Thurman argued that "the contemporary peculiarities of women are mainly determined by the existence of the Men's State," and modern feminists were in revolt against "the selfishness, injustice, and domination" of men and the society they created to perpetuate their ascendancy.[77]

It is in this context, in a short paragraph of three sentences, that race made its only appearance in the thesis, in a discussion of the antimiscegenation laws then on the books in twenty-nine states. They exposed "the girls in the minority group to the lustful ravages of men in the majority group."[78] But Thurman in his thesis, following Schreiner and his other sources, was primarily concerned with the situation of white, middle-class women.[79] It is possible that Thurman chose this topic because he felt (or was encouraged to feel) that he had to "prove" himself by writing on a non–African American topic. But another explanation is that in discovering feminism, he discovered a parallel to the experience of American Blacks, especially educated Blacks like himself. Women, too, were at once inside and outside the structures of white male dominance and had similar but different approach to their common enemies.

The feminist movement, Thurman argued, in revolt against male domination, was fighting for ideals: "Freedom, Independence, Labor, and Individuality."[80] This meant the right to education. Women had been "segregated and kept in ignorance so long" that their education was, at first, as much about proving they belonged as obtaining the education itself.[81] This meant the right to vote: "The disenfranchisement of women has been the most outstanding exercise of the male right. It meant that women were not the equals of men and that they were classified with children, with prisoners and with the insane."[82] It meant economic freedom, the right to choose their employment and earn equal salaries to men, and with this came the control over their bodies: "If she controls her body, then she feels she can do with it what she pleases."[83] The women's movement was a struggle against men, whom Thurman, quoting Tennyson, called "a Savage race, that Hoard, and sleep, and feed, and know not me."[84] His point seemed unmissable: where white women have gone, or have started to go, Black men and women must follow.

All of these trends for Thurman culminated in new attitudes toward sexual behavior. When a white female college student woman asked Thurman in 1925 whether the sex she was having with her boyfriend was immoral, his answer, in this thesis, was that "if unmarried adults" enjoy a "spiritual unity," it was acceptable, because "spiritual companionship is the relation of personalities as a whole," and only through sex can the "integral man" connect "to the integral woman." Thurman assumed that appropriate premarital sex would be monogamous, would be a transitional stage to marriage, and would be between a man and a woman. (Thurman cited in his bibliography some pioneering authors and texts on homosexuality, but this topic goes unmentioned in his text.)[85] The thesis was an attack on any society that would deny that a person's sexuality was a key aspect of their identity. Sexual relations, properly understood, were one of the highest forms of "respect for personality," and no society should try to prevent this. When "a normal individual has to stretch himself out of shape in order to be proper and acceptable to society, then the standards of society are such that the individual becomes immoral in conforming to them."[86] Thurman, citing Havelock Ellis and others, thought sex had to be demystified. "Sexual intercourse is one of the chief methods by which nature disposes of sexual energy," which he explained by a brief excursus into "Physiological Chemistry" and "Behavioral Psychology."[87] Thurman insisted that sexual energy was not limited to one part of the body but argued that it was diffusely present "throughout the human organism," and ultimately pervading all of lived reality, in ways that perhaps anticipated the fervid sexual theorizing of Wilhelm Reich.[88] But to demystify sex, to free it from the censoriousness and Comstockery that had long surrounded it, was to appreciate its true mysteries. With Schreiner, Thurman insisted that sexuality was a spiritual force and that, indeed "sex intercourse is the great sacrament of life."[89] By the spiritual and the sacramental quality of sex, Thurman didn't mean "any mysteriously supernatural qualities" but those qualities reflective of all the "higher mental and emotional processes which in human nature are gaining greater power."[90] Thurman saw sex as a tool of humanity willing itself to a more advanced state, closing his thesis by hoping that "we may dare to believe with Olive Schreiner that the history of sex with its great power and its beauty of holiness is still in its infancy."[91]

Over the next half century Thurman rarely returned to the themes of "The Basis of Sex Morality." Although he was an early supporter of the Equal Rights Amendment and mentioned it and Olive Schreiner in *Jesus and the Disinherited,* feminism was infrequently discussed in his later sermons or books.[92] The reason for this reticence is not clear—certainly he would have pared away at the extravagance of some of the language of the thesis—but there is no reason to think he changed his views in any significant way, and the thesis undergirded much of his later thought, and not merely about sexuality or feminism but also about what Thurman called in the thesis "respect for personality" and a self-knowledge that "the good life" is the "unified life, the undivided life, and it has no particular reference to social approval or disapproval other than what is normally included in the conception of the undivided life."[93]

With Schreiner, Thurman sought to demystify not only sexual relationships between men and women, but intimate, nonsexual friendships as well. Lurking behind Thurman's argument is a hint of the higher androgyny. Growing up, Thurman was always concerned that his life had been too dominated by women and that his masculinity was somehow and somewhat suspect. After reading Schreiner, Thurman seems to have regarded the male/female binary, like Black/white, as another of the invidious dichotomies promoted by orthodox Christianity to create a religion and social order comprised of winners and losers, superiors and inferiors.[94]

Perhaps Thurman's best-known catchphrase is, "Life holds a crown over my head that I'm always trying to grow tall enough to wear." It is derived from a Schreiner allegory.[95] He would say toward the end of his life that the phrase "sums up the meaning of my religious pilgrimage, my confidence in the integrity of the journey."[96] The phrase captures much that Thurman found appealing in Schreiner: a sense of evolution that was purposive, moving toward ever higher goals, ever transforming and remaking itself. But Schreiner's evolutionary philosophy did not rely on abstract forces to implement these changes; it required the crucial assist of activists, trying to work toward these goals with an unswerving doggedness. How this would operate perhaps could be found, based on the frequency with which he quoted it, in his favorite Schreiner allegory, "The New Mother," in which the new mother tells her child to seek the truth, not to accept the truths of parents or authorities as your truth, not to accept your old beliefs or truths if you find that they are not "founded on that which is," and be ready to "die poor, unknown, unloved, a failure—but shut your eyes to nothing that seems to them to be the truth."[97]

"The Basis of Sex Morality" was the culmination of his Rochester years. Writing about women was another way of extending his ever-enlarging "magnetic field of ethical awareness," recognizing that to understand Black oppression he had to recognize, and respond to, the oppression of others. In writing a thesis that owed so much to the views of Olive Schreiner, Thurman was also demonstrating that however much he learned about a progressive Social Gospel at RTS, he would, as in "The New Mother," follow his own truths wherever they led, to the borders of Christianity, and if necessary, beyond.

5

A New Prophet in Oberlin

"In Oberlin, Ohio, traditional home of prophets, has recently appeared a new prophet. He is the Reverend Howard Thurman, pastor of Mount Zion Baptist Church." This was the takeaway from Susan Hinman's March article "Howard Thurman—Prophet" in the *American Missionary,* a magazine with a predominantly white audience. It was the first extended article written about Thurman, and it was the first time he had been called a prophet in print. It would not be the last. By 1928 the legend of Howard Thurman and his remarkable spiritual gifts was quickly growing.[1]

The possibility of Thurman coming to Oberlin emerged sometime in the fall of 1925. One of his instructors at RTS, Conrad Moehlman, wrote that, of all the seniors, "thus far Thurman has made the deepest impression. He has the opportunity to go to Oberlin, Ohio, to a negro church of one hundred members or more."[2] Thurman got the job. On Sunday, 13 June 1926, Thurman preached his first sermon as minister of Mount Zion Baptist, a week after graduating from Rochester Theological Seminary. Between his graduation and his inauguration, he had been very busy. When Thurman arrived in Oberlin, he was a married man, still on his honeymoon. Two days earlier, on 11 June 1926, Howard Thurman had married Katie Laura Kelley in a small, early-morning ceremony at her home in La Grange, Georgia. Thurman remembered the "softness of the rising sun reflected in the mysterious beauty of her eyes."[3] Her wistful, dark eyes and radiant, delicate beauty leap out from her surviving photographs. Shortly after the ceremony, the young couple boarded a train and arrived in Oberlin the following day. With this rapid accumulation of new duties and responsibilities Thurman bid an emphatic farewell to what he called his "years in training."[4]

Katie Kelley was born in 1897 and graduated from Spelman Seminary in 1918.[5] She was a product of the Black middle class, the daughter of Morehouse and Spelman graduates. Her father, Charles H. Kelley Sr., was a successful schoolmaster in La Grange, Georgia, about sixty-five miles southwest of Atlanta. Katie followed her father into the teaching profession. She began her career as an elementary school teacher in Birmingham, Alabama, where she soon had charge of "fifty-five very active little folks."[6] But she wanted further education and a different sort of career. She left primary education for study at the University of Chicago, where in 1921 she took courses at the Divinity School. Kelley then returned to Atlanta, recruited by John Hope to study at the Atlanta School of Social Work, associated with Morehouse and Spelman. In Atlanta she also became the "Colored Educational Agent" for the Atlanta Anti-Tuberculosis Association. In this position, she investigated the sanitary conditions in Black households and neighborhoods. The work went beyond purely health-related matters and explored the broader questions of social services to Black neighborhoods and whether, in matters of sanitation or fair business practices, Black communities were being well served by white merchants. The position at the Atlanta Anti-Tuberculosis Society, she wrote Lucy Tapley, president of Spelman Seminary, in 1921, was "a remarkable chance to render service, and at the same time be in a position to help my people and help myself."[7] In 1925, after study at the New York School of Social Work, she took a position at the Morristown Neighborhood House Association, a settlement house in Morristown, New Jersey, a city in the northern part of the state.[8]

Thurman's roommate, Charles H. Kelley Jr., later a prominent radiologist in Washington, D.C., and professor at the Howard University School of Medicine, introduced Thurman to his sister. The Kelleys were a large and close-knit family, and Thurman was enveloped into their circle. They encouraged his ambitions and provided him with financial support.[9] The details of Howard and Katie's long-distance romance are unknown, but Thurman writes about his frequent visits to New York City during his years in Rochester, when Kelley was in northern New Jersey, and perhaps there were occasional dates in the city. One way or another, love found its way.[10]

Katie Kelley was an intelligent, educated, and ambitious young woman. But a shadow soon fell on her life and marriage. Shortly before she was married, she was diagnosed with tuberculosis, which through the 1920s exacted a higher annual death toll than cancer. Whether her antituberculosis work in

Atlanta led to her contracting the disease is impossible to say. In a terribly sad letter to her mentor, Spelman president Lucy Tapley, written in April 1927, one senses the strain her illness was placing on her and her husband: "This has been a year of many adjustments for me.—A leftover condition of my illness of two years ago has made it difficult to for me to become acclimated to the conditions in Oberlin. Thus it has been difficult for me to enter wholeheartedly into the new responsibilities of home-making and the pastorate." She was looking forward to warmer weather restoring her "old 'go'" and was "confident that the greatest struggle for my health is passed."[11]

Tuberculosis often cruelly toys with its victims, with apparent remissions only making the subsequent relapses all the more devastating. Her condition did improve. In October 1927 Katie Kelley gave birth to a daughter, Olive Kathleen. But the tuberculosis returned. The Thurmans made the decision that Katie needed to return to Georgia, where her family could look after her. Howard, starting in the fall of 1928, took a teaching position at Morehouse and Spelman to make this possible. But the progress of the disease was relentless. Katie Kelley died in December 1930, plunging Thurman into an extended period of deep mourning. It is a mostly opaque time in his life, largely shielded from the biographer's gaze, with little surviving correspondence. One senses that even fifty years on, when writing his autobiography, the marriage summoned emotions too painful and private to share, and he told us little about her or their marriage. Katie Kelley was only thirty-three when she died.

When Thurman arrived in Oberlin, not only was he a married man; he was an ordained Baptist minister. Ordination is a necessary formality for a would-be minister, and it appears that Thurman at first approached the process in this spirit, as a formality, like an annoyed driver having to spend a day at the Motor Vehicle Bureau getting a new license. But he found to his surprise that it became a genuine rite of passage to a new phase of his life.

His ordination was the culmination of a long process. The first requirement for being a good preacher is not the words but the voice to utter them. Thurman spent a good deal of time honing his instrument. In the summer after graduating high school, a cousin found him work in a bakery, ten hours a day, six days a week, eleven dollars per week, hot and unpleasant work anywhere, especially in the summertime oven that was Daytona Beach. The pay was decent, and Thurman decided to part with $1.25 a week for a half-hour weekly voice lesson. He was never much of a singer—but he learned much about breath control, proper use of the diaphragm, and similar techniques, which he always credited as helping him to be an effective public speaker.[12]

Mordecai Wyatt Johnson was one of the most noted Black orators of his age, and one whom Thurman from his high school years on emulated. John Hope was another noted public speaker. Hope required all Morehouse students to memorize and deliver an original speech every year, before the demanding and often highly critical audience of the student body and faculty. There was, Thurman wrote, a distinctive oratorical style that could identify the speaker as "one of John Hope's men."[13]

Thurman early on developed a distinctive preaching style. Although the first of the approximately eight hundred recorded sermons and lectures he would leave behind dates only to 1948, there are plentiful accounts of his preaching from earlier in his career. He delivered his sermons slowly and deliberately, always speaking in perfectly enunciated Standard English, avoiding any resemblance to the stereotype of the overheated or undereducated Black preacher. Indeed, for some listeners his diction could sound a bit fussy, like a posh English accent. This was to confuse Thurman's insistence on precision for affectation. In his speaking voice, as in so many other areas, Thurman refused to be pigeonholed or easily categorized. At the same time, Thurman was one of a long line of African American baritones whose deeply resonant speaking voices commanded attention because of their inherent power. His manner was at once elevated and intimate. His Morehouse economics professor, Lorimer Milton, spoke "with a slight hesitation" which "gave the listener a split second to race ahead and try to complete the word or sentence before Milton could. The result was that one's mind rarely strayed from Milton's lectures."[14] Thurman adopted a similar hesitation in his delivery, perhaps less to gather his thoughts than to invite his listeners to share in his thinking process. Thurman also admired the Scottish minister Hugh Black, the refined pastor at the very refined Fifth Avenue Presbyterian Church in midtown Manhattan. Thurman attended services there while in New York City for summer school in 1922.[15] One gathers what Thurman admired most in Black's preaching was his relaxed, learned, conversational style. For all he borrowed from his models, Thurman's preaching was distinctly his own; compared to his influences, he was more extemporaneous (he rarely preached from a written text), more personal and intimate (without being confessional), avoiding hectoring, didacticism, lecturing, or "preaching" to his audience, working hard to make his artful sermons seem as artless as possible. There would be other influences on his preaching style—notably the still, small voice of the Quakers—but by his college years he was well on his way to developing a unique pulpit presence.

Between his freshman and sophomore years at Morehouse he preached a trial sermon at his home church in Daytona, the Mount Bethel Baptist Church. Success afforded Thurman an informal license to preach at any

Baptist church (but not the authority to preside over the rites of baptism, marriage, or communion). His text was Psalm 32:8, "I will instruct thee and teach thee in the way thou shall go," an audacious text for a nineteen-year-old addressing his elders. Thurman went on too long, and the presiding minister, Dr. S. A. Owen (1886–1974), told him: "Brother Howard, I will pass on to you what was told to me when I preached my trial sermon many years ago. 'When you get through, sit down.'"[16] Despite Thurman's garrulity, the trial sermon went well. Shortly thereafter Owen left for a summer course at the University of Chicago, and Thurman filled in.[17]

Owen was succeeded by A. L. James. A native Floridian (1877–1968), James was five years old when his father was killed by a white mob in Madison County, the home country of Thurman's mother and grandmother. An Atlanta Baptist College/Morehouse grad, he then became a YMCA secretary in Europe during World War I and was called to the First Baptist Church in Roanoke, Virginia, in 1919, where he would remain for the rest of his long career. In 1924, and again in 1925, he invited Thurman to come to Roanoke as his assistant, but he told Thurman that he had no money for his salary and that he would have to convince the congregation that his presence was worth paying for. Thurman did his best to earn their trust and some pocket money, plunging into the life of the congregation, directing a summer Bible school for three hundred pupils, counseling parishioners, preaching, making pastoral visits, writing articles in the church newsletter, a bit of everything. (He also learned to drive a car, a skill he would put to sparing use over the next fifty years, out of concern, he would write, for the safety of others as well as himself.) And in his second summer in Roanoke, he was ordained.[18]

It proved an ordeal. The young demythologizer, wanting to rid Christianity of the virgin birth and other atavisms, saw the rite of ordination as ripe for similar treatment. He did not want to submit to what he regarded as superstition. The ordination committee wanted to put the young whippersnapper in his place. When quizzed on the Baptist catechism, on such topics as the Incarnation and the Resurrection, he provided equivocal answers. Thurman's view of the afterlife, one minister complained, sounded less a Christian heaven and more like William Cullen Bryant's "Thanatopsis," with its vision of the "pleasant dreams" of a quiet, uninterrupted, eternal, and nondenominational rest. Thurman was interrogated for four hours, and in the summer of 1925, the summer of the Scopes trial, Thurman felt that he was becoming another martyr for rationality.[19]

The ordination meeting reached its climax when one of the members of the committee asked Thurman, "When did God the father and the God the Son and God the Holy Spirit meet for the first time?" Thurman, tired and annoyed, answered, "I don't know, because I wasn't there." This provoked laughter, but the questioner looked sternly at Thurman, answering his own question: "It was at the baptism of our Lord. I pray that they may see fit to meet in your heart." After the interview, his interrogators approved Thurman's ordination, and James insisted, against Thurman's request, on including the ceremony of the laying on of hands. Although Thurman considered it another mythological relic, a magical healing touch, he relented. And when it came time, at the climax of the ordination ceremony for the ministers, as one by one—S. A. Owen had traveled from Memphis just to be there—the ministers placed their hands on his shoulders, he found it immensely moving, a revelation, a "moment of transcendent glory" when the "spirit descended like a dove." The epiphany reminded him that old mythologies had endured for a reason.[20]

It was during his years in Rochester that Thurman's preaching career really began. By the time he graduated, he had spoken "in almost every town in the area around Batavia and Rochester" and was increasingly in demand for farther-flung locations in New Jersey, Illinois, Iowa, and elsewhere. He usually spoke on special Sunday-evening services. Many of these congregations were white. None of Thurman's RTS-era sermons are extant, but some of the titles and a few newspaper summaries are. Some were on explicitly African American themes, such as "Thinking Black," several versions of "The Faith of the American Negro," "The Gift of the American Negro," and his first addresses of many on Negro spirituals.[21] In his early career there were many invitations to speak on racial topics. Often these came about when an audience was impressed by his general speaking ability, as when, after an address at the State Student Volunteer Conference in Ithaca, New York, in 1925 he had made such an "unusually fine impression in the modest yet forceful way in which he presented his theme" that he was asked by the First Baptist Church of Rochester "to give his views on the Race Question next Sunday evening at 7:30."[22] What did he say about race on such occasions? He was certainly capable of making strong and provocative statements, as in a 1925 article in which he condemned "certain governments that have raped the [African] continent and its people through these weary bloody years."[23] But it seems likely that most of his comments were similar to what he told an audience in Cedar Falls, Iowa, in October 1926 (shortly after his arrival in Oberlin), that "regard for the essential humanity of other races is a necessary part of Christian character."[24]

But what was most striking about Thurman's early sermons was how often he did not speak on specifically racial topics. His repertoire of topics included "The Temptations of Jesus" (a subject to which he would frequently return throughout his career), "Creative Idealism," "The Value of Silence," "The Christian Emphases," "Friendship," and "The Meaning of Faith."[25] By the time Thurman graduated from RTS in 1926, his pattern of public speaking and preaching was well developed. In these sermons he often warned against becoming too entwined in the false promises of 1920s American civilization. Why was it, he asked in a 1925 article, that "so often the biggest and most outstanding men and women on our campuses are not challenged by the faith which we profess to have?" Thurman diagnosed the problem as one of "the perils of immature piety," a holier-than-thou "use of words without an adequate experience or the assumption of an attitude that has little basis in fact." What college students wanted, Thurman argued, weren't mere words but the experience itself, an embrace of life rather than a retreat from it. Any notion of Christian service that "does not synthesize *all* of life around that ideal is barren." The problem with much of campus Christianity was that "we seem to *drag* God into everything rather than to find Him as a part and parcel of all experience."[26]

When Thurman tried to answer that perennial question of college students, "What Shall I Do With My Life?," a sermon he often preached in these years, his answer was to first recognize the "interdependence and unity of all life, all experience and all peoples," and then to develop "an attitude that demands giving of one's life at the place where that life can be best used and in the field in which the individual can enter with abiding enthusiasm."[27] This was also the theme in a sermon he delivered at the end of 1926, when he was a featured speaker at the National Student Conference of the Counsel of Christian Associations in Milwaukee, sponsored by the YMCA and YWCA, attended by 2,500 delegates. This was Thurman's most prestigious speaking engagement to date, with Thurman sharing the podium with the Nobel Prize–winning physicist Robert Millikan, a young Reinhold Niebuhr, and other stars of the liberal Protestant lecture circuit such as Kirby Page and Henry Sloan Coffin. Thurman, at twenty-six, was the youngest featured speaker. Somewhat surprisingly, Thurman was not the only African American speaker, an honor he shared with his mentor and future boss, Mordecai Wyatt Johnson (who had likely arranged for Thurman's appearance). Johnson spoke on "The Meaning of God's Universal Fatherhood in the Relations of the Races." Thurman spoke on the subject of "Finding God."[28]

In "Finding God" Thurman argued that one seeks and finds God through a commitment to one's life purpose. He gave examples of prominent creative artists who did this through dedication to their calling, such as the actor Walter Hampden, who had to play Hamlet "to keep a contract with his soul," or the tenor Roland Hayes (the only African American mentioned in the lecture), whose listeners know they are "in the presence of one who sings because he must."[29] This sense of calling could also be found through service to others, and he gives the example of an Indian from Calcutta, living in Oberlin, who found his purpose in life and God through helping poor boys in his neighborhood. One finds God, Thurman stated, through dedication to a cause: "I must have demands within myself for the kind of energy God releases, and that energy must be with reference to a need which calls it forth and will not let me rest until I find it." The process that begins by recognizing "a deep sense of moral and spiritual inadequacy" must lead to the discovery of the "essential kinship of all the creations of all the people in the world." And then the same sense of mission provides the courage to try to implement it, whatever the potential personal consequences, quoting one of his favorite poems: "I'd rather go down in the stirring fight / than drowse to death by the sheltered shore."[30] In this, Thurman outlined his spiritual mechanics for devotion to the cause of social transformation, a theme he would in decades to come return to again and again.

In Susan Hinman's article about Thurman, she talked to him about "Finding God." He told her that "perhaps this should not be mentioned, but I believe that this was the first time that a Negro has spoken before such an audience on any other question than that of race relations." When Hinman asked why it shouldn't be mentioned, Thurman gave an angry answer: "Because it is a thing of which anybody should be ashamed. It was even humiliating to me. You see for a Negro to address a white audience is a subject for apology and the only justification would be that he should have something about his race and its problems."[31] The following year, in the deepest South, he became the first African American to speak at the Women's College of Alabama, in Montgomery. Thurman spoke on "What Jesus Means to Me" after his representative made clear to those who invited him that he "would not be interested in talking on 'race,' because his field was religion and race enters into it only as an incidental matter."[32] We do not know what Thurman said on that occasion, but within a few days of the sermon, the young women at the college were quoting Thurman to their peers.[33] For the young women of the college to treat him as a human being, as an authority in his field of religion, perhaps to question some of their assumptions about Black people, was a real achievement. If it did not immediately change any of Alabama's oppressive racial realities, he thought it a necessary first step.

This was part of Thurman's presentation to white audiences from the beginning. Indeed, Hinman stated in her article that "I know nothing about Mr. Thurman's ancestry except that he is obviously of pure African lineage." Thurman was well aware that the darkness of his skin would "obviously" be the first thing that any white person would note about him. Hinman continued, no doubt thinking it a compliment that "this brilliant young Negro wishes to be judged as a man and not as a representative of his race." This was not so, of course. What he wanted from whites was a recognition that "Black" was as universal a category of personhood as "white." In her article Hinman presented Thurman as one who was neither bitter nor deferential toward whites. He welcomed white friendship, while cutting through their standard rationalizations about race relations. He told Hinman that when "he made up his mind to love my enemies, I found that I had been praying to a God that . . . sent his enemies to hell." But at the same time Thurman gave her "the severest criticism of the church that I have ever heard," she wrote, quoting Thurman: "It is the experience that in the situation of my own people, of any minority group, I cannot look to the church for help." He added that "Christianity as practiced on me" was difficult to reconcile with "the genius of the religion of Jesus."[34] Hinman's confusion over what it meant for Thurman to be Black, to be a person, or a Christian was just the sort of fruitful perplexity and unsettling of expectation Thurman hoped his presence would foster in white minds, whatever the sermon topic.

Like Susan Hinman, Thurman's mentor at RTS, George Cross, sensed the tension in Thurman between the race man and the prophet of universalism, and like Hinman, he didn't quite understand it or know how to respond. Thurman often referred to his last conversation with Cross, held just as he was graduating in the spring of 1926. (Cross died before the two men could get together again.)[35] The conversation, in Thurman's words, "astounded me." Cross told Thurman he had superior gifts and that he would be "able to make an original contribution to the spiritual life of our times." But he added that Thurman was "a very sensitive Negro man" who doubtless felt "under obligation to put all the weight of your mind and spirit at the disposal of the struggle of your people for full citizenship." He cautioned Thurman against what he called the "terrible waste" of devoting himself completely to "the race problem, however insistent in nature." Instead, Cross counseled, "give yourself to the timeless issues of the human spirit." Thurman did not respond, and Cross sensed his unease. "Perhaps," he continued, "I have no right to say this to you because as a white man I can never know what it is to be in your situation."[36]

Cross was correct. He didn't have the right to say what he said. Thurman's retrospective accounts clearly indicated that this was how he felt: "I wondered what kind of response could I make to this man who did not know that a man and his Black skin must face 'the timeless issues of the human spirit together.'" But sometimes it is necessary to say what is better left unsaid.

The conversation resonated with Thurman because Cross had identified a real tension and division within Thurman's understanding of his mission and ministry. He did have an extraordinary gift for addressing "timeless issues of the human spirit." But the "race problem" was equally urgent. Thurman would spend the rest of his life pondering how to bridge the gap between the perennial questions of religion and the more immediate needs of African Americans. He realized early that his God abhorred dichotomies.

Oberlin was a good place for Thurman's first ministerial position and first full-time job. It had a lot to offer: a relatively large and prosperous African American community, comprising 20 percent of the town's population in the 1920s. Mount Zion's membership when Thurman arrived was "small but substantial," with its members including many pillars of Oberlin's Black community. Thurman had to learn to speak to many audiences at once, the young and the old, the devout and the casual churchgoers, to attract newcomers and to retain the support of longtime members. Like many a young minister, he had to learn to control his impulse to show his congregation how smart he was, impart the latest scholarship, and avoid condescension. By his own description, "initially, the temptation was to try to educate and re-educate my congregation in the light of my own learning and my own process of understanding." When he tried to introduce James Moffat's new translation of the Bible—a translation so committed to the Documentary Hypothesis that it used different typefaces for the main J, E, P, and D strands of the Old Testament—many older members balked, especially those who saw the King James Version less as a translation than as the authoritative word of God. Thurman had several meetings with the congregation, examining different translations, winning over skeptics to the idea that neither the Hebrew Bible nor the New Testament was originally written in English.[37]

Thurman started the practice of having a series of sermons around a common theme, enabling him to be lightly and casually didactic. This was a technique he would use to the end of his career. The congregation approved, despite the fact that his first sermon series, on medical quackery, directly challenged some of his congregation's favored nostrums and home remedies. He opened the communion service, which in most Black Baptist churches was open only to members, to anyone wishing to partake in the ceremony. He organized various classes that met at the parsonage, on subjects such as contemporary politics, Black history, the study of selected books of the Bible, and one of Thurman's first efforts to explore the life of Jesus.[38]

Thurman soon found his congregation expanding beyond its Black Baptist base, no doubt through a combination of local appearances and favorable word of mouth. Within a few months of Thurman's arrival in Oberlin, Mordecai Wyatt Johnson wrote him that "a young white woman in Chicago was telling me Sunday night that the students in Oberlin are leaving the white churches to come and hear you preach. I am greatly thankful that you are able to understand the eager yearnings of the student mind and minister to them."[39] A few weeks later, an official from the Congregational Education Society wrote a colleague that Thurman was "a rather remarkable young man" and "a very unusual speaker. I am a little afraid myself that he is 'playing up' his particular mannerisms a little too hard, but he certainly makes a strong impression upon most young people and is an effective person, especially in college groups. I understand that he thinks he has more success in white colleges than in colored schools." I rather doubt Thurman thought this—I know of no statement by Thurman to that effect—but the fact that a white observer thought so is proof enough of his success with white audiences.[40] Thurman's Oberlin ministry was not limited to Blacks or whites—or, for that matter, to Christians. Asians, from India and China, attended his services. He felt deeply gratified when a Chinese Buddhist told him, "When I close my eyes and listen with my spirit I am in my Buddhist temple experiencing the renewing of my own spirit." On hearing this, Thurman felt that "the barriers were crumbling."[41]

Key to his success, no doubt, was his growing ability to share his deep inner spiritual life with the congregation and other audiences. This too was not easy. At first his public prayer struck Thurman as forced, reflecting an unease at sharing something so inward and personal. Thurman had to learn how, as unselfconsciously as possible, to "acquiesce to the demands of the spirit within" with others watching, and to become "one in the spirit of God" with the congregation. And as Thurman discovered his ability to pray in public, his concern with teaching lessened, and his sermons became largely devoted to "the meaning of our experience of our common quest and journey."[42]

One of the advantages of being a pastor in Oberlin was the proximity to the local college. Thurman was interested in advancing his education at Oberlin College, an institution of higher learning with a storied abolitionist past and a long commitment to African American education, a place where Black college graduates went to further and finish their education, including many old friends from Morehouse and Spelman. (Graduating just as Howard and Katie were arriving was Sue Bailey, completing her studies at the Oberlin Conservatory of Music.) Thurman flourished in the environment of Oberlin, taking classes, directing plays, growing the congregation, learning how to be a pastor.

Thurman arrived at Oberlin at a time when the college's commitment to the cause of Black equality and Black students had ebbed. The relation between the Black "town" and white "gown" was largely nonexistent. Blacks in Oberlin did not attend the college and had, in Thurman's words, "few examples to follow in terms of persons with higher education." Like far too many places in the North with similar legacies, Oberlin College by the 1920s had largely walked away from its commitment to African Americans. Black students comprised only about 3 percent of the student body and increasingly were segregated in their sleeping and dining arrangements, denied access to prestigious campus activities, and left off the rosters of athletic teams.[43]

Thurman arrived in Oberlin diffident about his future educational plans. He did register for a master of sacred theology (S.T.M.) degree, but as he wrote the dean of the Oberlin Divinity School, "the matter of the degree is secondary; if I can get the work that is the major consideration."[44] He wrote Johnson that he planned to spread out the work for the degree over several years, and "the thing I want now is improvement in techniques of research. I am weakest there—so is Rochester, by the way."[45] He never completed his S.T.M., which is not surprising because, as he wrote Johnson at about the same time, he had "definitely given up the notion of working for a Ph.D."[46] Certainly his thesis on "The Basis of Sex Morality" showed Thurman to be a competent researcher, but it was not the sort of scholarship he would pursue again. On a practical level, a Ph.D. probably wasn't necessary, since at the time a doctorate was still more of a rarity than a necessity for employment at a Black college, and there is no evidence that its lack was ever a professional impediment for Thurman. (Although he would invariably be called "Dr. Thurman" for much of his career, as far as I know he never corrected any misapprehensions that this was only an honorary title.)

Thurman's decision not to pursue a doctorate was a mysterious one, even to some extent to himself. Late in life he gave a number of possible explanations. He had questioned that "if I were to devote full-time to a doctoral program, academic strictures would gradually usurp the energy I wanted to nourish the inner regions of my spirit" and undermine his responsibility "to the guidance of the Voice in my heart."[47] He wanted to train his "mind to think, deeply and creatively" and worried that a life of scholarship might dull his creative edge. At the same time he also wondered if he had the necessary discipline for first-rate scholarship, and as he contemplated this he found himself once again in "the Valley of the Shadow of Failure into which I descended."[48] He worried if once saddled with a Ph.D., there was "the possibility of being cut off from the majority of my fellows and the appeal of arrogance over them I could not manage."[49] Or it might have been "that I anticipated the bitterness I'd feel, even with so high a degree when I was still a Black man in a white world."[50] In some way Thurman felt that pursuing a doctorate would upset a sensitive balance, perhaps between his intellect pursuits and spiritual wants, between his quest for personal autonomy and the expectations of others, between his vaulting academic ambitions and his need for racial solidarity. Forgoing a doctorate was, he knew at the time, a "radical choice," one that seemed "unbelievable" to him on some level, but something he knew he had to do.[51]

Nonetheless, he did pursue a course of study at Oberlin seminary. He studied briefly with Edward Increase Bosworth, with whose works he had been familiar since his teenager years.[52] He had a more extensive course of study with Kemper Fullerton (1865–1941), a professor of Old Testament, who encouraged Thurman to study at Oberlin. Fullerton, an unacknowledged influence on Thurman's thought, was a philo-Semite who emphasized the Jewishness of Jesus. He was a Zionist and a racial liberal who worried that "the southern attitude toward the negro is penetrating more and more into the North. A sectional point of view threatens to become a national one." He also thought that Oberlin College, "to save its own soul," had to renew its commitment to Black students, have classes on Black subjects, and he even ventured that "perhaps we should introduce some colored teachers into our faculty."[53] Thurman was excited to work with him. Together they studied the "suffering servant" in Isaiah (Isaiah 52:13–53:12) and Job. Their time together was "a great creative adventure for my mind and spirit; I have never since lost sight of the far-flung mystery and redemption of the sacrament of pain."[54]

The problem of pain, as the health of Katie Kelley worsened, was not an academic subject for Thurman. His mood in Oberlin, to the extent we can glimpse it, seems increasingly bleak. His lectures on medical quackery to his congregation were part of a broader feeling—one shared by many in the 1920s, of the essential shoddiness and fraudulence of American civilization. "I have a growing conviction that we are fed and clothed by a vast system built upon deceit and adulteration," he wrote to Mordecai Wyatt Johnson in 1927. "And it almost seems futile to talk about sincerity, about purity, about honesty when they are eating, seeing, reacting to a mighty array of lies." Americans were as cheap, flimsy, fake, and insubstantial as what they ate, wore, and purchased.[55]

Thurman was neither the first nor the last African American to wonder why Blacks were clamoring for entrance into a society as fundamentally flawed as the United States. The America of the 1920s, mammon-gorged, intoxicated, and soulless (or over-soulled by religious extremism) seemed to him particularly uninviting. Thurman was worried about the phenomenon of Black Babbitry. In 1928 he wrote of an unnamed professor of sociology at a prominent midwestern university who had told him, "The thing that you need to tell young Negroes is to get money." Thurman was not impressed. Why should Blacks adopt a creed that denies the sacredness of life, and assert that "human life is cheap" and all that matters is "economic power and control"? Blacks must affirm "the superiority of the human spirit to the domination of things," else they too would "embrace the religion of materialism," and this would mean "death, and that speedily."[56] African Americans had been relatively immune from the tyranny of things and the economic power they represented because, traditionally, they had little of either. This was changing in the 1920s. In "The Task of the Negro Ministry" (October 1928), Thurman argued that ministers had to "lay bare the awful truth that where the highest premium is placed upon the possession of things, human life is relatively cheapened. And when life is cheap, ideals languish and the souls of men slowly die."[57]

The challenge was neither to join this society on its terms nor leave it entirely. Nationalism or separatism never had any appeal to Thurman, whether Garveyism in the 1920s or its lateral descendants. For Thurman, the Black church was riven by the contradictions of American life. The church was at once "pretty largely apocalyptic," and, at the same time, deadened by a callow materialism, "a growing passion for building temples and towering structures" that "represent great spiritual waste." Echoing Nietzsche, Thurman wrote "people always build their temples to their dead Gods." And these two extremes, Thurman concluded, play off each other, leaving many Blacks at once very cynical about worldly success while seeking it uncritically. Black ministers had to steer congregants away from an "overemphasis on the other world" without getting sucked too deeply into the world they must live in. The solution was to insist that there was "no clear-cut cleavage between this world and the other world."[58] The alternative to a too-passive otherworldliness and a too-worldly shallowness for Thurman was a commitment to radical social transformation.

A skepticism of existing institutions of all kinds was central to Thurman's religious and political thinking in the 1920s and beyond. "There *seems* to be something about joining a church which deprives an individual to be exercised increasingly about being Christian," he wrote Johnson in 1927, noting that in Oberlin the best church members weren't members, or didn't seem to be, having "transcended" the church.[59] Thurman railed against the "artificial barrier between religion and life"—this would become one of his most frequently articulated beliefs—the false view that what was valuable in religion could be contained within the four walls of a church. The African American minister must "interpret life in terms of a creative expansive idealism," which requires embracing modern science and all this entails; remaining

"God-conscious," placing faith "in the contagion of the spirit of Jesus rather than in the building of organizations that perpetuate his spirit." New challenges call for new institutions and bursting asunder old ones.[60]

In 1927 he wrote Mordecai Wyatt Johnson, "I am going thru a veritable upheaval in my thinking—I do not know where I shall come out—and it hardly matters."[61] He does not give any more clues as to the nature of this upheaval, and it had a number of possible causes, among them the health of Katie Kelley, or perhaps the aftereffects of one of his periodic bouts of overwork. (Johnson evidently cautioned him about the necessity for a "limitation of intake," later a favorite Thurman sermon topic.)[62] Thurman was searching for a form of spiritual transcendence. Another term for this search might be mysticism, and though he had been called a mystic since his undergraduate days, his mysticism was underdeveloped and undertheorized. Compared to other aspects of his religious thinking, he had not really tried to understand mysticism as a historical, psychological, and spiritual phenomenon. This was about to change.

Thurman's deeper immersion into the mystical tradition started incidentally, out of boredom. Sometime in 1927 he was at a meeting on religious education at a town near Oberlin. Uninterested in the proceedings, he decided to leave early but saw a table of books for sale—ten cents each—as he was leaving. Never one to pass up a book sale, he purchased two books, one a biography of Mary Baker Eddy. He also purchased, because he liked the title, a short book titled *Finding the Trail of Life*. He sat down on the church steps, started reading it, and no doubt had a bolt of recognition at its compelling opening: "I am convinced, too, by my own life and wide observation of children that mystic experience is much more common than is usually supposed. . . . [Children] have more room for surprise and wonder. They are more sensitive to intimations, flashes, openings. The invisible impinges on their souls and they *feel* its reality as something quite wonderful." The author went on to say, "The trouble is that very few boys betray their deepest thoughts and musings, and when they get old enough to tell what was going on in their inside world, they have become too old to remember the details."[63] Your first God is your best God.

Sitting on the church steps, he read the entire book, about 150 pages. As with Olive Schreiner, he had found someone else who understood, who knew that lonely children found God outside of any catechism. *Finding the Trail of Life* was a spiritual autobiography of a Quaker boy in Maine in the latter third of the nineteenth century, of a boy who found God out of doors all about him, learned during adolescence to confine his God to the views of his elders, only later to learn that God "worked from within as a living creative energy."

What the author never lost was the importance of experiencing God. The book concludes: "There are no more important epics than those of the inner life. If a man can succeed in telling about the building of his soul, it is worth more than the telling of any other kind of tale." And the point of building one's soul, as the book's title implied, was to find God through finding the "trail of life."[64]

Thurman had never heard of the book's author, Rufus Jones, though given the prominence of Jones and his writings in the circles in which Thurman traveled, this is quite surprising. But he immediately determined, if possible, to study with him. Jones was one of the leading lights of liberal Protestant thought in the early twentieth century. Born in 1863, he attended Haverford College, a Quaker college near Philadelphia, then studied philosophy at Harvard with William James and Josiah Royce. From 1893 until 1934 he taught at Haverford, in the process writing fifty-seven books, probably thousands of articles on religious topics, and was at once a serious and respected scholar and a tireless popularizer of his religious ideals.[65]

Jones was the foremost American scholar of mysticism of his generation. The study of mysticism itself was a relatively new discipline, arising in the late nineteenth century among scholars of comparative religion who believed that there were characteristic "mystical" experiences in every religious tradition, representing a shared experiential understanding of the divine.[66] Jones translated—or perhaps the right word is "demystified"—ancient mystic traditions, with all of their weighty rigor, asceticism, and solitariness, making them accessible, as mysticism became something friendlier and more free-floating, what a later generation would call "spirituality." People are wrong to think that mysticism "is for saints and apostles, but not for common everyday people like ourselves," Jones wrote in 1922.[67]

Thurman knew that there were many obstacles to his plans to study with Jones. He had a full-time job in Oberlin. He had a sick wife and an infant daughter, Olive Kathleen, born 5 October 1927. He needed to support himself while studying at Haverford. He didn't know if Jones would accept him as a student. And he worried (with good reason) that Haverford did not admit Black students. All of these issues would be worked out.[68] The illness of his wife forced a relocation to Georgia, where his wife could be cared for by her family. Starting in the fall of 1928, Thurman was hired by his alma mater, Morehouse, and its sister school, Spelman, as a professor of religion. He applied for and received a grant from the National Council on Religion in Higher Education for six months of study with Jones. And despite the fact that Haverford, turning its back on its abolitionist founders, admitted no Black students from the late nineteenth century until 1947 (with the exception of a sole West Indian recruited for the cricket team), Jones agreed to accept Thurman as a special student.[69] In the spring of 1929, Thurman left Atlanta for six months of study with Jones at Haverford.[70]

At Haverford, Thurman had a weekly meeting with Jones and attended a regular seminar on the fourteenth-century German mystic Meister Eckhart. Douglas Steere, a classmate of Thurman's in the seminar, later a prominent Quaker theologian, wrote in 1975 that Eckhart's lesson that "you can only spend in good works what you have earned in contemplation" must have lodged deeply in "Howard's mind and spirit for it has been a theme song of his ever since."[71] Thurman would have an enduring admiration for the bold speculations of Eckhart, the medieval mystic revered by Jones, known for many centuries as the man "from whom God hid nothing."[72]

In addition to Eckhart, Thurman studied Spanish mystics such as St. Teresa and St. John of the Cross, French quietists such as Madame Guyon, and St. Francis of Assisi, on whom Thurman wrote a lengthy (though unfortunately lost) paper. He also attended the Wednesday meeting at the Haverford Meeting House, at which Jones often spoke. From this latter experience, Thurman acquired a Quaker sensibility and a deeper appreciation of the importance of silence, meditation, and spiritual spontaneity that would ever after be central to his understanding of worship.[73] One can perhaps exaggerate the influence Jones had on Thurman. Sue once wrote an exasperated letter to her husband complaining that "you were 40 leagues deep in mysticism long before . . . you met Jones. And it is not true that you are a product of Rufus's mind."[74] This is certainly true. But Jones helped Thurman shape a part of his religious experience that had largely been inchoate, not planted in the history or systematic study of mysticism. And as Thurman wrote to a future biographer of Jones about his time in Haverford:

> I can only say that the period that I spent guided by his mind and spirit in my reading and study marked the watershed of my whole life. It was he who first opened up to me the world of mystical religion as it has been witnessed in the literature of the faith.
>
> It was far more exciting than I have words to express to discover what I had sensed and experienced in my own spiritual journey was a part of the movement of God in the life of man through the ages. It was as if I was surrounded by a cloud of witnesses which gave to me a sense of belonging that the madness and terror to which I was exposed in America could not undermine.[75]

Central to Jones's understanding of mysticism (and subsequently to Thurman's) was the distinction between negation and affirmation mysticism.

Negation mystics were, for Jones, solitary and determined souls who sought "union with God, absorption in his being," living only "for the rare moment of ecstasy and beatific vision" when the "self ceased to be."[76] Opposed to this were "affirmation mystics," those who "find the revelation of God in the finite" and "who make *vision*, not the end of life, but the beginning." They know "God's will not merely in private inward bubblings, but in genuinely sharing in a wider spiritual order through which God is showing himself."[77] And for Jones this meant social involvement: addressing social ills, preventing or ending bloodshed or warfare, righting injustices. Jones found many of the best exemplars of affirmation mysticism in his own Quaker tradition, and for the three decades after its founding in 1918, he was a leader and guiding spirit of the American Friends Service Committee (AFSC), which was awarded the Nobel Peace Prize the year before Jones's death in 1948.

But if Thurman learned and borrowed much from Jones, there were important differences. Thurman wrote that Jones "did not have what may be normally recognized as ecstatic moments when he was taken out of himself and became one with some transcendent configuration or feeling tone or image or concept. . . . [H]is mysticism was pedestrian," and as a consequence his mysticism was "ethical" rather than experiential.[78] Jones's "mysticism for the masses" could at times seem bland, middlebrow, and somewhat complacent and institutional, a religion at home in the Philadelphia Main Line.[79] For Thurman, there was "a profound element of anarchy in all spiritually motivated behavior."[80] Jones was unambiguously a Christian mystic. For Thurman mysticism was as much a way out of, or a way around, the Christian tradition. Jones had little interest, and evidently little patience, for non-Christian sources of mysticism. When Thurman met Gandhi, there was a profound meeting of minds and souls. When Jones, a decade earlier, had met Gandhi, there was little more than strained condescension. Jones dismissed Gandhi as being "first, last, and always a Hindu." After giving Gandhi a failing grade for his unfamiliarity with the Quakers George Fox and John Woolman, he sniffed that Gandhi lacked both "universal interests" and a deep understanding of mysticism and saw him as clinging "to the outgrown superstition of his racial religion."[81] Thurman's mysticism was never limited to Christianity. From the outset his was directed toward non-Christian sources, from the Hinduism of Rabindranath Tagore and Kshitimohan Sen, to an interest in post-Christian thinkers like Olive Schreiner and Edward Carpenter, many of whom believed that all religions were fundamentally one.

Another difference between them was, as Thurman wrote, that Jones's "ethical emphasis" was on questions of "war and peace, the poverty and hunger of whole populations, and the issues arising from the conflict between nations," while he had "no witness for the less dramatic, less obvious sufferings of mankind."[82] For Jones, the less dramatic sufferings included burning domestic questions such as labor unrest and race relations, and this was a "blind spot" which Thurman found "very difficult to understand." Thurman wrote that during their time together he would now and then bring up racial matters, but Jones always moved the conversation toward abstractions about "the great creative expanse about the meeting of human need," thereby rendering "the specific issues of race with which I had been confronted all my life as strangely irrelevant." Thurman found Jones in this area "limping" and that it was "rationally unbelievable" that a man as ethical as Jones could tolerate segregation at his home institution. Still, he felt of Jones, "somehow he transcended race," and in his presence, "I did, too, temporarily," a feeling at once comfortable and uncomfortable. By the time he was studying with Jones, Thurman was all too familiar with liberal Protestantism's frequent lack of urgency or lack of understanding of African American realities. Thurman did not allow this blind spot in his mentor to become an obstacle to absorbing his lessons.[83]

One consequence of his study with Jones was that Thurman, ever after, would self-consciously identify himself and be identified as a mystic. He began to lecture on mysticism and to teach about it at Howard.[84] He had been called a mystic before. As early as his Morehouse days, Benjamin Mays would write that it was clear that Thurman possessed "more mysticism in his religion than the average person" and that, as a result, he was "considered queer" by some of his Morehouse classmates and instructors.[85] As Mays hints, being labeled a mystic was not always a compliment. When Lester Granger, the executive secretary of the National Urban League, wrote in 1941 that Thurman's lectures "frequently smack of mysticism," it was not intended as words of praise.[86] However, by the early 1930s Thurman was regularly identified as "the Negro mystic" or described as expressing "one of his characteristically mystic attitudes," and most comments about Thurman's mysticism were complimentary, if at times somewhat uncomprehending.[87]

Thurman rarely discussed his own mystical experiences. One exception is in a 1939 lecture when describes, in a poem, being on a hilltop at dusk when "awareness of self spread out till I and all / Around me run together / In one expansive, streaming, liquid quiet . . . God so near / I was radiant / With holy light."[88] However, he was usually more comfortable in discussing mysticism in general, or helping others on their own mystical or spiritual journeys, than talking about his own experiences.

In his first publication on mysticism—a short book review from 1934—he suggested that "perhaps there is no word in our language that has been as completely misunderstood and as freely interpreted as 'mysticism.'"[89] Over the course of the 1930s he tried to explain what he meant by mysticism, most significantly in the four-part lecture series "Mysticism and Social Change" he delivered at Eden Seminary near St. Louis in 1939.[90] For Thurman, mysticism was "a personal, private experience of Reality, of God. It is direct, immediate, and synthesis-achieving."[91] Thurman, while acknowledging that he had "lived a long time in the stream of the mystic's experience," disclaimed "having scaled the heights of rarefied illumination so vivid to the mystic in his moments of clarity." Mysticism for Thurman was "one of the truest lines of human thought," religion at its "most concentrated and exclusive form," though he added it was "*a* way to God and not *the* way to God."[92]

With the gathering political storms of the decade as a backdrop, he argued that this sort of personal, experiential connection to God was needed because people no longer have confidence in "their own abilities to live rationally and forcefully." Some turned to dictators to do their thinking and feeling for them. Others turned to "the formal experience of the religious life" but found only "uncertainty, priestcraft, compromise." Both were false idols, ceding power over one's soul to someone or something else. Instead, "each soul must learn to stand up in its own right and live" and find "that which speaks to the deepest needs of the spirit."[93] Mysticism for Thurman was an aid to rational thought, not its opponent.

He objected to accounts of mysticism that presumed that mystic union involved dissolving the individual in the greater glory of an infinite God. Instead, he suggested true mysticism was recognizing the infinite within each of us, "the point at which the infinite enters the finite," recognizing our own "uncreated element," a notion borrowed from Meister Eckhart.[94] For Thurman, mystic union involved not the negation but the enhancement of individual personality, and the recognition that "personality is something more than individuality—it is a fulfillment of individuality in community."[95] Mystics, Thurman acknowledged, do tend to traffic in unities, but Thurman was at pains to argue that unity did not mean uniformity or sameness. "The mystic experiences unity" with God, he wrote in 1939, but "not identity."[96]

In "Mysticism and Social Change" he expounded at considerable length on the social implications of mysticism. He started the lecture series by stating that because "it has been necessary for me to participate both passively and actively in what is known as the social struggle," his was a mysticism that had worldly consequences.[97] The mystic is "under obligation to achieve the good which in some profound sense is given in the moment of vision."[98] In affirmation mysticism, for Thurman, "the distinction between personal and social religion" becomes "artificial and unrealistic."[99] The affirmation mystic's vision of the good is connected to the social struggle, not primarily "because of any particular political or social theory" or because of "humanitarianism or humanism." Rather, the mystic is "interested in social action because society as he knows it to be ensnares the human spirit in a maze of particulars so that the One cannot be sensed nor the good realized."[100]

Is it fair to ask why Thurman felt he could in good conscience leave his infant daughter and seriously ill wife for a semester of study with Rufus Jones in Haverford? I am not sure. He certainly believed that Olive and Katie, with Katie's parents in La Grange, were in the best possible hands. It is also true that his study with Jones had been very difficult to arrange; it was something he felt he needed to do, and for personal and professional reasons, he felt it couldn't be delayed. We have no insight into Thurman's thinking about this. But if his time at Haverford provided a temporary respite from Thurman's "maze of particulars," there was no respite from worry. Perhaps the most important lesson he learned from Jones was that mysticism was not a cave, and that there is no escape from the circumstances and obligations of one's life. Affirmation mysticism seeks a mystic intensification and embrace of life in all of its aspects, from the mundane to the sublime, from exaltation to heartbreak. This is the mysticism Thurman brought back with him to Atlanta. It was a fitting conclusion to his formal education.

There is a story Thurman liked to tell. Reinhold Niebuhr, particularly in the 1930s and 1940s, was a close associate and frequent visitor to Thurman at Howard University. After one such occasion, they stayed up late having their "typical no-holds barred discussion about religion and our society and the rest of it." Niebuhr returned to Union Theological Seminary, and in his next class referred to this discussion. There was one Black student in the class. After the class he came up to Niebuhr and said: "I'm glad you mentioned that man. He is the great betrayer of us all. When this Thurman fellow came up out of Florida, and began to talk around, many of us who were much younger were sure that at last someone had come who would be our Moses. And what did he do? He turned mystic on us!"[101] At this point in telling the story, Thurman would laugh heartily. But one knows what the student was complaining about. Thurman was a different sort of Black leader and a different kind of fighter for African American equality. But a leader of and fighter for his people he undoubtedly was. And, as he would no doubt have pointed out, Moses was a mystic, too.

6

"A Technique of Survival for the Underprivileged"

A Return to Atlanta

Thurman had probably always seen the Oberlin position as a good place to start his career but no more. Certainly, almost from the time he arrived in Ohio, there were tantalizing vocational possibilities opening elsewhere. Perhaps he could replace Mordecai Wyatt Johnson in the pulpit of First Baptist Church, Charleston, West Virginia, or perhaps he could work with Johnson on the faculty of Howard University. He was invited to preach a trial sermon for the campus ministry at Tuskegee Institute, a sermon that greatly impressed George Washington Carver, though it is difficult to imagine Thurman flourishing in a college environment as conservative as Tuskegee's.[1] But when it came time to move on, there really was only one choice. Katie Kelley was ailing. She wanted to be near her family in La Grange. Thurman accepted a position in nearby Atlanta, starting in the fall of 1928, at his alma mater, Morehouse College, and its sister school, Spelman College. He would remain for four years, until the summer of 1932. Thurman's return to Atlanta was dominated by Katie Kelley's struggle with tuberculosis. She lost her fight in December 1930.

Katie's death and its aftermath plunged Thurman into a deep despair, probably unequaled in his life. Thurman's dark mood during his years in Atlanta was compounded by an array of other troubles and worries. He never really liked living in Atlanta. He loved his students at Morehouse and Spelman but did not like his boss or care for many aspects of his job. And then there were the broader causes of unhappiness not specific to his own circumstances. The Depression put much of America into an ill temper. There was little evidence that race relations in the United States were improving. The lessons the Great

War had taught on the evils of militarism, nationalism, and colonialism were going unheeded. But if Thurman's Atlanta years were doleful and lean, they were also thick with accomplishment, with important breakthroughs in his thought in a number of areas, all adding to his burgeoning national reputation. And they had a very happy ending: an appointment to the academic position he had always wanted, and a marriage to a woman, Sue Bailey, who would, in every way, be his life's partner.

Thurman had a joint appointment at Morehouse and Spelman, but his direct supervisor appears to have been Spelman's president, Florence Read, and not his old mentor John Hope. Thurman did not care for Read, who had been named president of Spelman in 1927, remaining in the position until 1951. Thurman's autobiography, *With Head and Heart*, is a volume notable for its lack of rancor and score settling. One of the few people Thurman criticized extensively in it is Florence Read. When she came to Spelman she was in her early forties. Read was a graduate of Mount Holyoke College and had for a number of years before coming to Atlanta worked for the Rockefeller Foundation on educational matters.[2]

Read was the last white president of Spelman, and Thurman, like many Black academics in the 1920s, thought that the era of white presidents of Black colleges should have come to an end. He also did not think she was qualified, possessed of only a bachelor's degree, and she once admitted to him that she did not think she had the qualifications to be a president of a white women's college.[3] Reed, with her background in educational philanthropy, was brought in as Spelman president at the behest of the Rockefeller family–sponsored General Education Board, a crucial conduit of funds to Atlanta's Black Baptist colleges.[4]

Reed's main mission in coming to Spelman, accomplished in 1929, was to establish "the association" between Spelman, Morehouse, and Atlanta University, reducing duplication and placing them under common authority, thereby diminishing the autonomy of Morehouse. Thurman resented this, and he also resented the reality that Read had become the dominant partner in her relation with the aging Morehouse president, John Hope. As related by Thurman, Hope "deeply regretted" the change: "I shall never forget his voice, or the sadness of his eyes. 'It may kill me,' he said, 'but I must do it. It will assure the future of Morehouse.'" Above all, Thurman resented the fact that Read wanted him to inform her of his Sunday travel and speaking schedule, though Thurman had no Sunday responsibilities at Spelman—it was the custom for Read to preside at chapel, with a local white minister offering the sermon. This would be a recurrent problem for Thurman, who prized his freedom to preach widely and opposed administrators, white and Black, who wanted their star minister to primarily stay home and preach in his own pulpit.[5]

Meanwhile, the Depression highlighted the economic and political powerlessness of African Americans, scapegoats for an economy gone bad. In Atlanta the Klan-like American Fascisti Order of the Black Shirts had paraded down Peachtree Street in 1930 carrying signs such as one that read, "niggers, back to the Cotton Fields—City Jobs are for White Folks!"[6] If Thurman had spent much time in the 1920s decrying the woes of conspicuous consumption and people who had too much and didn't know what to do with it, his politics in the 1930s revolved around the desperate challenges facing those who had too little.

But what remained the same for African Americans, whether in flush or hard times, was the constant threat of white violence. In June 1930, a Morehouse undergraduate, Dennis Hubert, was murdered, ushering in a reign of terror on the Morehouse campus. The house of the murdered man was burned to the ground. His uncle, Thurman's Morehouse colleague Charles Hubert, was kidnapped, though later released. Waiting for nightriders, Morehouse faculty, long guns at the ready—which as African Americans, they were not legally allowed to possess in Georgia—waited on porches.[7] (It is not clear if Thurman was among those armed with a shotgun, but when confronted with a similar situation in 1947, when he was in Pine Bluff, Arkansas, to deliver a commencement address at Arkansas Agricultural, Mechanical, and Normal College, the lifelong pacifist did pick up a gun and contemplated, if fired upon, "return[ing] the fire until I fell.")[8] In both instances, the nightriders did not materialize, but the turmoil at Morehouse led the usually rather mild-mannered John Hope to pose a rhetorical question that did not have an answer: "Must all the colored youth of Atlanta, of Georgia, forever go about in terror of their lives?"[9]

A version of Hope's question was raised again with new force when, the following March, nine young Black men were arrested in Scottsboro, Alabama, falsely accused of raping two white women. The case soon achieved worldwide infamy. Four years later, its stench had hardly dissipated, and Thurman and the Negro Delegation were often queried by Indians who wondered about the facts and significance of the Scottsboro case.[10] A few months after the Scottsboro incident another notorious episode of America's racial brutality attracted much attention and, for Thurman, involved a deeply personal loss. On 6 November 1931, Juliette Derricotte, dean of women students at Fisk University, was driving from Nashville when she and a student were both badly injured in a traffic accident, near Dalton, Georgia. She was refused admission at a local, whites-only hospital, and only many hours later an ambulance arrived to take Derricotte and her companion to a Black hospital in the nearest large city, Chattanooga, some thirty miles away, where she died the next day.[11]

Only thirty-four at the time of her death, Derricotte had already made a mark as one of the most remarkable women of her time. She had been a national secretary for the YWCA for many years, and while speaking on the "Y" circuit, she became friendly with Thurman, where their paths often crossed. As early as 1925 she praised his gifts as a preacher, and like Thurman she was a representative of a socially engaged, liberal Black Christianity.[12] A statement by African America YWCA officials after her death affirmed that she "captured . . . the voice of the Race student" and had the "intelligence and sincerity to give the problems of race and religion" the new perspectives they needed.[13] But as Marion Cuthbert lamented shortly after Derricotte's passing, in a moving recital of her accomplishments and of the lives she had touched and changed, in the eyes of the white South, after the accident, she was "only a nigger woman" who was dying.[14]

One of Derricotte's closest colleagues (and fellow YWCA national secretary) was Sue Bailey. Seven months after Derricotte's tragic death, Sue Bailey would marry Howard Thurman. She would later write that Derricotte, that "magnificent brown American," demonstrated that the "true lover of God must ever be challenged by the impossible," even perhaps paying "with physical death for the ultimate triumph of some heroic dream" to which they had given their "whole life."[15] Derricotte was an inspiration for the visit of the Negro Delegation. She had been a delegate to the 1928 meeting of the World Student Christian Federation held in Mysore, India, and later wrote that after India, "I am no longer free. . . . I ache with actual physical pain when I remember the struggles of all India today, religious, caste, social, economic."[16] Her deep empathy with the Indian people made such an impression that native Christian leaders started to clamor for more African American visitors.[17] When Howard and Sue were preparing for the India trip in 1935, Paul Hutchinson, editor of the liberal magazine *Christian Century,* somewhat snidely asked: "I should think it would give all connected with this project a good deal to think about when they remember that its forerunner was Miss Derricotte. Suppose the Indians begin to ask what became of her?"[18] Hutchinson needn't have worried. Both Howard and Sue saw their time in India as a means of furthering her legacy. When they returned from India, Sue Bailey Thurman started the Juliette Derricotte Scholarship Fund, which, before it was interrupted and ended by the war, sent several African American female undergraduates to India to study.[19]

An indication of both Thurman's closeness to Derricotte and his growing stature was that he was asked to deliver the eulogy at her well-attended funeral in her hometown of Athens, Georgia. All that survives of what he said on that occasion is a snippet: "There is work to be done and ghosts will drive us on. This is an unfinished world; she leaves an unfinished task. Driven by the power of her spirit we dedicate ourselves anew to the developing process which she had begun in an imperfect world. To this we set our hands in our time."[20] Her ghost would help drive the Thurmans to India. Ever afterward, these same ghosts would be one of Thurman's favorite catchphrases, invoked whenever he felt an audience was in urgent need of haunting.[21]

The keyword for Thurman during his return to Atlanta was survival. These were years saturated with thoughts of death, the reality of death, and mourning. In 1927 he had railed against what he saw as the dominant creed of American life: "No sin, no future life, no sacredness of life, nothing but the survival of the fittest and every man for himself."[22] Beyond his personal situation, the question of the hour was the continued survival of the weakest, those least able to defend themselves, those most likely to fail, the most exposed, the most vulnerable, those Thurman came to call the disinherited. The question of how members of any "despised circumscribed minority group" continued to survive and thrive spurred his thinking in any number of directions: on the African American past, present, and future; on pacifism and the power of the powerless; and on Jews, Jesus, and what it really meant to be a Christian.

Survival meant many things for Thurman. Physical survival, surely. No Black person in the South in the 1920s and early 1930s would have seen the quest for survival as purely metaphorical. As Thurman often cautioned during these years, the fact that Blacks were not real citizens meant that they could be attacked, assaulted, and sometimes murdered with impunity. During the Depression years it surely meant economic survival as well. And it was collective as well as personal survival, the determination that African Americans as African Americans could chart their individual and shared destinies as they wished. Survival for Thurman also had a spiritual quality. It was far more than just getting by, eking out an existence, merely surviving. Survival meant fashioning a creative response to one's environment, trying to shape it rather than merely being shaped by it. Perhaps the key anecdote for Thurman about Black survival in the South, one he often told, first in 1929, was the following:

A sense of helplessness and despair is apt to work its way into the very soul of such a stigmatized minority group [African Americans.] This helplessness expresses itself in many ways. I was going through a section of Atlanta known as Beaver's Slide [a slum area near Morehouse] when my attention was called to a deep baritone voice singing this refrain:

Been down so long—
Down don' worry me

A Negro man whose soul had given up the ghost in the struggle![23]

For Thurman, this was a song of resignation and defeat, not one of survival.

In one of the first sermons he gave at Spelman, in October 1928, he spoke about someone who did not give up the ghost, the patriarch Jacob. Alone and pursued in the desert, his past was filled with "tragedy, tragedy, tragedy, the thought of which would fill the soul with horror." His future was radically uncertain. And at this juncture, Jacob, exhausted, lay down in a field, a stone for a pillow, and, sleeping fitfully, had an extraordinary dream, "of a stairway set on the ground and its top reached up to the sky, and angels of God were going up and down on it." The dream formed the basis of the spiritual (to use Thurman's spelling) "We Are Climbin' Jacob's Ladder." For Thurman, Jacob was without "a redemptive element" in his "present situation," adding, "How true was this of the slaves!" Enslaved persons had been "driven and herded together like cattle, felled in their own blood if they resisted, these panic stricken souls found their present cruel and demoralizing" with a brutal past and prospects of an equally brutal future. The message of the spiritual for Thurman was that "there are no situations which are so depressing, so devoid of hope, that the human spirit cannot throw itself into a realm in which these conditions do not exist." Thurman cautioned about using one's dreams as an "escape mechanism," as a way of avoiding harsh realities. But the point of Jacob's ladder was not to climb to heaven or to avoid reality but, rather, to survive one's circumstances and not be trampled or destroyed by them. Its message was to affirm that "I am beaten and brutalized by power-maddened men, but I shall see to it that my experiences do not crush me." This was what Thurman meant by survival.[24]

Thurman's discussion of "We Are Climbin' Jacob's Ladder" was the first of five sermons he delivered the week of 15 October 1928 in the Spelman chapel on "The Message of the Spirituals."[25] The spirituals were a touchstone for Thurman, something he returned to again and again throughout his career, the subject of two of his most important books, *The Negro Spiritual Speaks of*

Life and Death (1947) and *Deep River* (1945; 1955), many articles, and count-less sermons.[26] But the essence of all of Thurman's writings on the subject can be found in this, his earliest surviving writings on the spirituals.

The spiritual is the only African American art form that Thurman wrote about at any length. They represented for him the first, and in many ways the most important, effort of Africans in America to make sense of and come to terms with their plight and the realities of their existence. If Thurman was exposed to spirituals from his earliest days, probably in fairly rough-hewn versions, he was more likely to take as his models the polished, quasi-classical arrangements pioneered by the Fisk Jubilee Singers. With their success, the Negro spiritual became the first genuine African American musical genre to become internationally popular.[27] But with their success came the inevitable white stereotyping and misunderstanding. James Weldon Johnson wrote in 1927 that the "chief effect of this slave music upon its white hearers was that they were touched and moved with deepest sympathy for the poor Negro," which Johnson dismissed as a mere "sentiment" instead of deeper interaction with the singers, their songs, or their plights.[28]

Johnson and Thurman were writing against a dominant interpretation of spirituals, both among white and Black commentators, that saw in them an African expression of patience and love; songs of resignation and not resistance; accepting suffering in this world in exchange for sweet chariots in the next. To sing spirituals was to be seen as performing Black docility.[29] By the 1920s newer Black musics—ragtime, jazz, and the blues—more indi-vidual and more aggressive, dealing with love, sex, loss, and all the earthier emotions—to many rendered spirituals both thematically and melodically passé. Thurman had first begun to seriously think about the meaning of spirituals when he was a senior at Morehouse. There was a chapel service, with several directors of the Rockefeller-led General Education Board in attendance. The custom was for the Morehouse student body to greet their benefactors by singing spirituals. But when the signal was given to sing, the students, by prearrangement, remained silent. The signal was given again, and again, yet no one sang. Morehouse president John Hope was furious and reprimanded the student body that evening. They were unrepentant. Thurman, one of the nonsingers, later wrote that the students had refused "to sing songs to delight and amuse white people. The songs are ours and a part of the source of our own inspiration transmitted to us by our fore-fathers."[30] Two years later, a similar situation at Howard University, when students refused to sing spirituals for white visitors, helped spark a stu-dent strike that led to the resignation of J. Stanley Durkee, Howard's last white president. There were other incidents in the 1920s over the place of spirituals at Fisk University and Hampton Institute. The "New Negro" did not sing spirituals.[31]

Except when they did. James Weldon Johnson's quote above is taken from his introduction to the *Second Book of Negro Spirituals,* published in 1927. Johnson's purpose was to rehabilitate the spiritual, insisting that it was a vital African American art form.[32] Much the same argument can be found in Thurman's future Howard colleague Alain Locke's essay on Negro spirituals in 1925, where he called them "the most characteristic product of the race genius yet in America."[33] Thurman wrote in 1975 that his writings on the subject were "addressed to a generation which tended to be ashamed of the Spirituals or who joined in the degrading or prostituting of the songs as part of conventional minstrelsy or naïve amusement exploited and capitalized by white entertainers."[34]

Thurman's defense of the spiritual paid little attention to their African origins because in his view, such arguments missed what he found most important about the spirituals. They were made in America and do not reflect the presence of Africa in the lives of enslaved peoples as much as Africa's absence. In an article on the spirituals from 1939, he wrote that "slavery stripped the African to the literal substance of himself, depriving him of those props on which men commonly depend—language, custom, and social solidarity. In addition to all of this he was a slave; without freedom of movement or of person."[35] Whether or not Thurman was correct in questioning the centrality of African influence on the spirituals—certainly the scholarly consensus in recent decades is against his position—one must remember his context.[36] At the time Thurman was writing, many self-proclaimed "experts" on the spirituals argued that the spirituals were African songs rather than slave songs and that therefore oppression did not account for either their origins or their meanings.[37] To emphasize the Africanness of the spiritual for Thurman was to open the door to reducing Black people to their supposed fixed and unchanging African essences, which he saw as at best limiting, reductive, restrictive, and, all too often in mainstream culture, either overtly racist or covertly patronizing.

The spirituals, for Thurman, were thoroughly American, put together from shards of African memories and melodies, brutal New World realities, and all somehow tied together by a new religion that had been foisted on them. Thurman's interest in his writings on the spirituals focused on their religious message, but by this he did not mean their surface Christianity. Indeed, he argued that the fact that enslaved persons adopted the religion of their masters was "amazing as well as ironical."[38] What they took from their masters was not theology but their Bible, filled with its miraculous and wonder-working stories. As he later wrote, "they were exposed to the Book, and the Book [was] far more important than the Church." They took the words and crafted them into hymns of survival. If "Jeremiah in his agonies, asked 'Is there no balm in Gilead, is no physician there?,'" enslaved peoples, wrote Thurman, "took the question mark . . . and transformed it into an exclamation point: "*There is* a balm in Gilead!"[39] The creators of the spirituals were practical people who used the Christian materials at hand, but they were not interested in doctrine or catechism. The message of the spirituals, Thurman would say in another context, was that "My meaning does not arise from your interpretation of my significance," and that "No judgment you impose upon me, no order of society into which you seem to have me regimented," can "sever my roots" from "my inner significance."[40]

Thurman elaborated on this in his other sermons on spirituals to Spelman students in 1928. "My Soul Is a Witness" was about conversion as self-acceptance. "Heab'n, Heab'n" was a study in spiritual hypocrisy—"Ev'rbody talkin' about Heab'n ain't goin' dere"—and how insincerity was an inevitable consequence of it: "People who live under social pressure as in a master-slave society and its posterity find it almost impossible to be honest with each other."[41] The final sermon from 1928 was on "Deep River," which he called the "most philosophical of all the spirituals." Rather than a meek acquiescence in fate, its message was, "Whatever my present situation may be, I can afford to be calm, self-possessed, because Eternity is on my side." A river may face "an abundance of obstructions and hindrances: it may be shifted many miles from its course, but nothing can permanently keep the river from its goal, the sea."[42] Thurman wrote of a Mississippi River that, perhaps deliberately on his part, is the opposite of the Mississippi of Black resignation, which in the famous words of the song by Jerome Kern and Oscar Hammerstein II "Ol' Man River" (1927), "don't plant taters . . . don't plant cotton" while "dem dat plants 'em / is soon forgotten."[43] Thurman's Mississippi remembered those who toiled on its banks. In a 1930 sermon on "Deep River" he stated that its message was that nature's greatest forces and human life are united rather than alienated from each other; great rivers like the Mississippi "take on the color and the content of everything they touch."[44] Inspired by the great rivers, enslaved people created the basis of their "ground of hope and self-respect," the means of survival.[45]

Thurman had been an active pacifist since joining the Fellowship of Reconciliation in the early 1920s. He looked at the world situation with a pacifist's dismay, writing in 1924 that "the horror of the recent war is still felt in our bones, and yet it seems as if mankind could not take to heart the most drastic lessons" from the war, and the response of established institutions, not least the church (very much including the Black church) was "a vast medley of confusion."[46] Thurman's initial article on pacifism, which was also his first writing to find a wide audience, "Peace Tactics and a Racial Minority," appeared in the December 1928 issue of the *World Tomorrow,* the leading pacifist journal in the United States, closely associated with the Fellowship of Reconciliation. Thurman reworked the piece for a collection of articles published in 1929 as *Pacifism in the Modern World* in an expanded form with a new title, "'Relaxation' and Race Conflict."[47] And as the first notable statement of a distinctive African American pacifism, it was perhaps the most important article he ever wrote, with its significance broader than a consideration of Thurman himself. It is a largely forgotten key to understanding the quest for Black freedom in twentieth-century America, an indirect inspiration to James Farmer, Bayard Rustin, Martin Luther King, Jr., and many, many others.

Pacifism in the 1920s was changing from the efforts of largely well-to-do men and women of goodwill striving to put an end to armed conflict to a consciously oppositional political lifestyle that, with Gandhi as the exemplar, had a much broader agenda than just opposing militarism.[48] This new approach was one reason why the popularity of antiwar positions approached ubiquity within Thurman's liberal Protestant milieu in the late 1920s and early 1930s.[49] *Pacifism in the Modern World* was a volume dedicated to the "new pacifism," which, in the words of the editors, "directly challenges imperialism, industrial autocracy, punishment as a basis for penology, race prejudice, indeed every phase of the existing social order which thwarts fellowship and love." Shorty Collins wrote on "Pacifism and Social Injustice," largely about labor disputes. Devere Allen wrote of "the New White Man," who has abandoned "imperialism and arrogant race consciousness," meeting on equal terms "the New Negro, the New Chinese, the new oppressed and submerged colored people anywhere." The new pacifism was opposed not only to militarism but to all forms of violence, explicit or implicit, foreign or domestic.[50]

Thurman, however, was the only "New Negro" (or for that matter, the only author from a racial minority) to contribute to *Pacifism in the Modern World.* He let readers know this in his opening sentence: "It is a very simple matter for people who form the dominant group in society to develop what they call a philosophy of pacifism that makes few, if any, demands upon their ethical obligations to minority groups with which they may be having contacts."[51] Pacifism, for the powerful, all too often "becomes a mere quietus to be put into the hands of the minority to keep them peaceful and controllable."[52] This assumption, that pacifism was a "mere quietus," an ideology for the meek and submissive, would long dog its African American advocates. Thurman's idea of pacifism had nothing to do with being "peaceful" or "pacific" and everything to do with developing techniques for the powerless to challenge their oppression, a way not of dissipating one's anger or rage but channeling, focusing, and transforming it.

Exploring Black hatred of whites was a main theme of "'Relaxation' and Race Conflict." Thurman wrote so often and so viscerally about Black rage that he was no doubt writing from experience, but here and elsewhere he rarely parted the veil to reveal his own emotions. In his essay on pacifism, when he observed that many educated Blacks were mired in "pessimism, bitterness, and tenseness," it sounds like something he had worked diligently to avoid. His chief concern about hatred, throughout his career, was how it distorted the hater. One response to white oppression was "the rather blind imitation of the dominant majority," that is, learning to "hate people so bitterly that one becomes like them," which for Thurman was a form of intellectual and social passing. It was a form of hatred of one's enemies that barely masked an intense self-hatred, and hatred and castigation of other Blacks for their supposed "inferiority." Thurman argued that those who felt this way were often "those who ride on top in a minority group," and who "may treat those below them, so to speak, as they are treated by the dominant majority."[53] At about the same time he argued that a problem with members of Black "society" is that their cultural pretensions often outweighed their economic foundations, and its members insisted on riding on top of a stagecoach— Thurman was a fan of westerns—where "they often tumbled to the ground, riding in discomfort for fear they would lose their seats" rather than mingling with the lesser folk inside the carriage.[54] Thurman's argument echoed (and maybe was was influenced by) his onetime Morehouse professor E. Franklin Frazier, who argued in 1929 that the Black middle class "has fatuously claimed kinship with the white bourgeois[e]." To Frazier's argument Thurman added his acute psychological insight that Black imitation of whites was a survival strategy, albeit a particularly insincere one.[55]

Whites were experts in the many modalities of controlling Blacks, direct and indirect, brutal and insinuating. Slavery, he argued, "would have been very difficult to maintain as a [system] if there had not been developed a stern, relentless will to dominate and control in minute detail," giving the example of his grandmother, who was trained from childhood to think that "the will of the mistress must be the desire of her heart."[56] This system of control required the elimination of the humanity of the enslaved person, and their reduction to "a *body*" and the belief that Blacks were basically automata, devoid of feeling, an attitude that Thurman noted, from personal experience, persisted to the current day.[57]

The problem with trying to dominate another group was that however complete the domination, it can never be complete enough to eradicate the fear that the subordinate group was forever poised to resist, and they were therefore vigorously policed for the tiniest spark of pushback. This, Thurman argued, was the situation Blacks faced: "The will of the dominant group is tense; it is increasingly concentrated on the domination and control of the minority group, utilizing all the machinery at its disposal to that end. Nothing is spared: the press, including the comic sheet and the highbrow journals; the church, including the pulpit, much that goes by the name of charity and many of the materials of religious education, and for the most part, the technique and the philosophy of education."[58]

For Thurman the only way forward was what he called "relaxation." Relaxation is probably connected to his studies of mysticism, the calm and detachment needed in anticipation of true transformation. It was the determination to keep one's inner core intact while acknowledging oppression's external reality and power, without accepting it, or letting it inside the core of one's personality. "I am of the opinion," wrote Thurman, "that it is possible for a member of a minority group to live a relaxed life in the midst of a majority group without the apparent or real loss of self-respect or manhood."[59] (In this, Thurman suggested, the "supposedly ignorant Negro," poor Blacks, can provide some pointers to middle-class strivers, who often tried too hard to find acceptance in a white society determined not to accept them.)

Relaxation was, he acknowledged, "agonizingly difficult" and "perhaps . . . impossible." But this was the task that Black pacifism had set for itself, one both personal and collective. The pacifist sensibility "springs out of a sense of the unity, the basic interrelation and the vast sacredness of all life. It has its roots in a primary self-estimate, a self-awareness from which it gets its key to the life around it. Hatred seems to spring out of a warped self-estimate."[60] Armed with a true self-estimate, one that was "indigenous" but not separatist, racial minorities can reach out to whites from a position of moral strength. Without this, all attempts to bring about a better society would be "dashed to pieces against an adamant wall," the wall that on one side was labeled "The Will to Dominate" and on the other "The Will to Hate the Man Who Tries to Dominate and Crush Me." (Walls for Thurman were always things to demolish and tear down.) Once demolished, the way would be "clear for the operation of the will to share joyfully in the common life—the will to love healingly and creatively."[61] In later writings he would elaborate in greater detail how this process might unfold, but "'Relaxation' and Race Conflict," published in the year Martin Luther King, Jr. was born, was a first blueprint for a Black-led nonviolent movement for civil rights that would recognize its own universality.

The more Thurman thought about the prospects of Black survival in the late 1920s and early 1930s, the more he turned his attention to what survival had meant to Jesus and his immediate followers. In his first year at Spelman, in the fall of 1928, he taught a course on "The Life of Christ." The course would explore "the mind of Jesus as found in the Gospels" based on a "scientifically historical and spiritual appreciation of the life of Jesus."[62] Thurman was a careful student of the latest New Testament scholarship that tried to place Jesus in his specific historical context. But Thurman's view of Jesus always had as much, if not more, to do with the realities in twentieth-century America as in first-century CE Palestine. As he later wrote in his autobiography, he and the young women in the class found themselves "on a personal quest for a sense of our own worth, using the life of Jesus as example. The racial climate was so oppressive and affected us all so intimately that analogies between His life as a Jew in a Roman world and our own was obvious." In a less formal way Thurman had similar discussions with men at Morehouse, at Saturday-night bull sessions: "Most often we came around to the central problems of self-realization as Black men in American society. . . . How can we immunize ourselves against the destructive aspects of the environment? How manage the carking fear of the white man's power and not be defeated by our own rage and hatred?"[63]

Thurman's discussions about Black rage and the religion of Jesus led to a series of talks he gave in the Atlanta area and elsewhere. In 1935 he published his first article on the subject, "Good News for the Underprivileged."[64] In 1948 he expanded this into a lecture series and the following year into his most popular and enduring book, *Jesus and the Disinherited*.[65] Thurman throughout his career approached Jesus "as religious subject rather than religious object," that is, Jesus as one who prayed to God rather than one prayed to as a God.[66] As early as 1928 he told an interviewer that what saved Jesus "was his consciousness of God. If we were as sure of God as Jesus was that would be our answer."[67] For Thurman Jesus was always the Master, but as he told a Methodist audience in 1937, he tended to pray to God and not Jesus, "and in my mind and my own experience, those two things are not necessarily identical."[68]

One of the main lessons Thurman drew from the era's New Testament scholarship was that to understand Jesus one must understand the historical context of Judaism in first-century CE Palestine. However, this literature often was quite unsympathetic to Jews, past and present, and saw Jesus as one who had challenged and risen above the parochial and rule-clotted religion of his birth.[69] This was not Thurman's view. He was unabashed in his philo-Semitism, identifying with the Jewish people and their plights in both the first and twentieth centuries. For Thurman, writing in 1943, Jews and African Americans were fellow "minority communities" aware, in different ways, of being outside the white Christian majority.[70] In 1935 Thurman wrote that there were three crucial facts about Jesus. First, "Jesus was a Jew." Second, "Jesus was a poor Jew." Third, Jesus, "underprivileged and to a great degree disinherited," was not a Roman citizen. What this meant was that Romans could treat him and other noncitizens with impunity, without consequences for their behavior: "If a Roman soldier kicked Jesus into a Galilean ravine, it was merely a Jew in a ravine. He could not appeal to Caesar."[71]

The earliest accounts of Thurman talking about the religion of Jesus survive in accounts in Black newspapers. In February 1932 the *Atlanta Daily World* reported that Thurman, addressing a standing-room-only, sitting-in-the-windowsills crowd, left it "spellbound and awed" with his "characteristic mysticism and philosophy," speaking on "The Kind of Religion the Negro Needs in Times Like These." It was a religion that received "much of its significance from the fact that its first exponent was a member of a despised circumscribed minority group" and that the religion of Jesus was "the spiritual survival economy of a minority group before it became a world religion."[72]

Spiritual survival required that the "despised minority" did not internalize their detestation by the majority group. Overt racism was usually easy to spot. Its subtler manifestations were becoming more insidious and more ubiquitous. Commercial media, in the movies, on the radio, and elsewhere, even when not blatant, spread a stereotyped message of Black inferiority and the incapacity of nonwhites to an ever-wider African American audience. In a December 1932 talk in Washington, D.C., "The Message of Jesus to Underprivileged People," he told the audience that that "the tragedy of the race is that the idea of being the world's underdog is sinking into his soul," a message in which "the press, magazines, schools and even the church" all "conspir[e] in one grand course to make us think that we are nothing."[73] Thurman paid particular attention to the world he knew best, the church. Mainstream Christianity's positive images were white, whereas the negative images were dark-skinned.[74] (The white whale in *Moby-Dick,* he suggested around this time, "is the only instance in American literature where white is a sign of evil.")[75] Is it any wonder, asked Thurman, that Black children wonder that with "God white, with all blond angels to serve him," and Satan Black and evil, "what chance do I have?"[76] Thurman had no interest in replacing a white God or white Jesus with a Black alternative, but as Paul Harvey has suggested, he wanted deracialize Christianity.[77] The question of the color of Jesus or God for Thurman was one of surpassing inconsequence, and he wanted others to feel the same way.[78]

How, then, should Blacks, "an underprivileged, disinherited, despised, and disorganized minority," respond to the assaults of the "ruthless majority"? Through the message of the religion of Jesus, which "started as a technique of survival to the underprivileged." Its message was, "You must love without cowardice or fear; you must be wary without hypocrisy and you must be full of peace without contentment."[79] In "Good News for the Underprivileged," Thurman expanded on his understanding of the religion of Jesus as a religion for those lacking effective citizenship. He contrasted Jesus, a Jew without citizenship, with Paul, a Jew who was a Roman citizen.[80] Invidious comparisons between Jesus and Paul, to the discredit of Paul, were a commonplace of liberal theology of the nineteenth and early twentieth centuries, in which Paul began the path by which Jesus' religion of the poor was transformed into the religion of the mighty and powerful.[81]

Thurman gave the Jesus/Paul comparison a distinctive African American twist.[82] He often related a conversation he had around 1920, when, home from college, he was reading the Bible to his unlettered grandmother. She had never allowed him to read, with few exceptions, from the Pauline epistles. Thurman had long ago learned that one did not question the commands of his formidable grandmother. Nonetheless, screwing up his courage, he asked her why she never wanted to hear passages from Paul. She told him that when she was in bondage her master regularly had a white minister preach to the slaves on Sunday mornings: "Always the white minister used as his text something from Paul. At least three or four times a year he used as his text: 'Slaves be obedient to them that are your masters. . . .' I promised my Maker that if I ever learned to read and freedom ever came, I would not read that part of the Bible." Ever since that day, Thurman had "been working on the problem her words presented."[83] Paul, though a Jew, equipped with his Roman citizenship, "could never escape the consciousness of his citizenship," and it was a "distinguishing mark setting him off from his group in no uncertain fashion." He was "of a minority but with majority privileges."[84]

For Thurman, citizenship was as much a religious as a social or legal status or category. If, as with Paul, it could sometimes dull one's empathy for those who lack it, it remained essential for a sense of self-worth. Only those without it know how important it is. Citizenship does not admit of degrees or gradations. Thurman rejected the idea that there was any such thing as second-class citizenship, and as Thurman wrote in 1940, "generally speaking the Negro is not a citizen."[85] Jesus and other Palestinian Jews were "not citizens of the Roman Empire and hence were denied the rights and privileges such citizenship guaranteed.

They were a captive group, but not enslaved." This was the condition of African Americans in the 1920s and 1930s: no longer enslaved but still captive.[86]

Religion does provide some of the same sense of personal safety as citizenship. In "Good News for the Underprivileged," Thurman wrote that religion had "a transcending basis of security which locates its center in the very nature of life." Or in "conventional religious terminology," it "assures the individual that he is a child of God." This sort of self-knowledge "makes for an inner-togetherness, carrying with it the moral obligation to keep itself intact."[87] This is how the religion of Jesus can give its adherents a sort of self-created, virtual citizenship for those who lack it. To be a citizen you first must act like one, and properly fortified with the religion of Jesus, one could "in complete confidence" know that the religion of Jesus "sends him forth to meet the enemy upon the highway; to embrace him as himself, understanding his limitations and using to the limit such discipline upon him as he has discovered to be helpful in releasing and purifying his own spirit."[88]

If there was a model for how this might work, Thurman would meet its exemplar a few months after the publication of "Good News for the Underprivileged." Mahatma Gandhi would describe it in his own way, with his own religious vocabulary. Faisal Devji has written that Gandhi's mission was "retrieving sovereignty from the state and generalizing it as a quality vested in individuals."[89] For Thurman, the message of the religion of Jesus was not specific to Christianity. It was the recognition, with Gandhi and others, that the first step to genuine citizenship for the oppressed was for every individual to claim and establish sovereignty over themselves.

Survival and healing take place on many levels. Thurman's first three years in Atlanta were dominated by Katie Kelley's illness and death and his mourning for her. After Katie's passing in December 1930, Thurman had primary responsibility for caring for his young daughter, Olive. It does not seem to have been a task for which he was particularly well-suited. Until Katie's death, Olive primarily stayed with her, often in her parents' home in LaGrange, Georgia. Afterward, Thurman was a single parent, though he recruited his mother and his sister Madaline to help in the cooking and child-rearing duties.[90] Within two weeks of Katie's death, he was on the road, speaking in his hometown of Daytona Beach in an Emancipation Day (1 January 1931) address at Bethune-Cookman College. Over the next six months, Thurman would speak in Washington, D.C., Nashville, Rochester, and Detroit, in what had become an annual appearance in a Lenten series during Holy Week—Detroit by this time was home to an active and ardent Howard Thurman fan club.[91]

That summer, Thurman took his first international trip, going to Europe, with Olive remaining with Madaline. He went to London. Initially he had problems finding a hotel that would accept Black guests; he eventually lodged in an area that catered to East Indians. He spent his time walking the streets of London, learning its geography "through the soles of my shoes."[92] (Perhaps he caught a glimpse of another visitor to London that summer, Mahatma Gandhi.) While in London, he spent some time with Morehouse president John Hope, and according to a 1948 biography of Hope, "the two men saw each other daily, went to the theatre, discussed racial problems."[93] Thurman paid visits to settlement houses and other similar institutions.[94] With Herbert King he traveled to Paris and Geneva, perhaps meeting with representatives of the World Student Christian Federation, headquartered in Geneva.[95]

However, by Thurman's own account he mainly stayed by himself. He spent a month as a paying guest on a Scottish sheep ranch, where his daily routine consisted of breakfast, tramping the moors, and, like a Brueghel peasant, eating his lunch while sprawled in the fields, taking an afternoon nap, an exercise in the healing power of enforced aimlessness.[96] He would write John Hope that "one thing I have learned from the long terrible illness through which I passed with Kate—The test of a man's life is to be found in the amount of pain he can absorb without spoiling his joy."[97] However, for several years after Katie's death, there seems to have been little joy in Thurman's life. Those close to him during these years remember that he was as melancholy a person as they had ever met, with a pervading gloom that was not helped because Katie Kelley's illness had engendered some ill will between Thurman and Katie's family.[98]

In the fall of 1931, one female visitor, admitted to Thurman's home in Atlanta, reported that all the shades were drawn tight. It was still a shuttered house of mourning. She opened his curtains and drew his blinds: "What happened was truly symbolic. It was time to let the light back into his life."[99] The bringer of light was Sue Bailey, a national secretary for the YWCA. In June 1932 she and Howard were wed. They both had made a name for themselves among the circles of Black liberal Christians, and she was, at the time of their marriage, at least as well-known as her husband. As she said many years later, she saw him "as a man, the likes of which would never come again."[100] Thurman for his part said of Sue that she "brought into our coming together a rare beauty of person, a clear and analytical mind, and a fresh enthusiasm of heart that only love could inspire."[101] In a short memorial tribute, written the year after his death, Sue wrote that one of the last things he said to her was: "It was wonderful that you did not come between me and my struggle. You did not stand in my way."[102] Together, they helped each find their own paths.

Susan Elvie Bailey was born in Pine Bluff, Arkansas, in 1903, and was raised in Dermott, Arkansas. Unlike Thurman, Sue Bailey was a product of the Black middle class, with parents who were highly literate and quite accomplished. Still, Sue, like Howard, was only two generations removed from slavery. Her grandmother Elvie had been born into slavery in Mississippi. Elvie's owner, a T. S. Ford, made her his concubine—he evidently purchased her for that purpose. Together they had three children. After Emancipation, Elvie Ford and her three children moved to Arkansas. Her youngest, Susie Ford, wanted an education and went to St. Louis to get it, eventually graduating from Sumner High School and Normal School, and by 1883 had settled in Pine Bluff, Arkansas, to begin her career as a schoolteacher. Shortly thereafter she married Isaac G. Bailey (1847–1914), a Baptist minister, educator, and, during Reconstruction, a member of the Arkansas legislature. His mother, Virginia, was a Cherokee who came to Arkansas during the Trail of Tears in the 1830s. His father, Perry Bailey, had been born into slavery on the Eastern Shore of Maryland, where, according to family legend, his relative was Frederick Bailey, who later adopted the name Frederick Douglass. In 1830 Perry Bailey was a founder of one of the first Black Baptist churches in Arkansas. Together Susie and I. G. Bailey had nine children, only three of whom lived to adulthood. Susie Elvie Bailey was their youngest. After her birth, the family moved to Dermott, Arkansas, where I. G. Bailey founded the Southeast Baptist Academy.[103]

After her father's death, Sue Bailey went to Washington, D.C., where she spent two years at Nannie Burroughs's National Training and Professional School for Women and Girls.[104] Burroughs, probably the most prominent woman in the National Baptist Convention, enforced strict discipline at her school, with twice-a-day prayer services, at which Bailey, her musical talents already evident, often played the piano. After two years there, and another at the Lucretia Mott School, also in Washington, she went to Atlanta to study at Spelman Seminary, where one of her roommates was Alberta Mayo, mother of Martin Luther King, Jr. In 1922, she entered Oberlin College, graduating in 1926 with a double degree in music—she was the first African American to graduate with a bachelor's degree from the music program—and liberal arts.[105]

Bailey then joined the staff of Hampton Institute as one of its few Black faculty members. The following year she was one of a handful of Hampton faculty members to support a student strike, in protest of efforts to segregate Hampton's auditorium, previously open to both races. Like many student strikes at Black colleges in the 1920s, it was also protesting the stifling paternalism present on many campuses.[106] Bailey, along with her good friend Louise Thompson, were fired for their efforts, and Bailey and Thompson (later a prominent Black Communist) made their way to New York City, where they moved in the circles of the Harlem Renaissance, with Langston Hughes, among others.[107] Bailey had been active in the YWCA in Hampton, reported to them on the Hampton troubles, and was hired in 1928 as one of its five African American national secretaries.[108]

Bailey's primary responsibility was to travel to Black college campuses for the Y and help to arrange conferences on the Student Christian Movement circuit. In June 1929, after helping to organize a YWCA conference in Atlanta, she was praised in the *Pittsburgh Courier* as combining "a most unusual array of personal and professional accomplishments which assert themselves in a charming personality, and much of the success of the conference is due to her vision of the students themselves, and her able selection of leaders."[109] One of the leaders Bailey often selected was Howard Thurman. They were together at a conference in January 1929, and again at the annual Kings Mountain Colored Student Conference in June of that year, where Thurman spoke on "The Deeper Meaning of the Negro Spirituals," and again in Atlanta the following March.[110]

Sue Bailey and Howard Thurman undoubtedly became reacquainted at these conferences, although they were old friends. She had been on the staff of the *Athenaeum* in 1920, the joint Morehouse-Spelman literary magazine, to which he was a contributor, but according to Bailey, they did not meet until the following year, after her graduation, when she stayed on at Spelman to complete courses needed for admission to Oberlin. Their friendship began when they started reading and critiquing letters the two of them were receiving from their respective beaus. In 1926, as Bailey was leaving Oberlin, Thurman and Katie Kelley were arriving. She met Kelley in an Oberlin dormitory: "I passed Katie in the stairwell, and we had a brief chat—we had never been alone together before. I think of that time often. What would we have said, if we had known we would share motherhood to our little daughter, Olive, in years to come?"[111]

Sometime in late 1931, when both Howard and Sue were sitting on a dais for a program at Spelman, he passed Sue a note asking her if she would join him for breakfast at his house the following day. She suspected she was invited to the event by persons unknown, who wanted to set them up. Although they had a long friendship, Sue felt that in their recent interactions Howard had been something of a blowhard, querulous and difficult to deal with, complaining about every engagement she arranged for him. Nonetheless, she agreed to the breakfast date, and the ploy to get them together, if that is what it was, worked. She opened his blinds, drank his muddy coffee, and a romance soon blossomed.[112]

In May 1932 their engagement was announced. The forthcoming wedding, the *Atlanta Daily World* opined, "will be an event of the early summer." If nothing else, the elaborate engagement dinner, a six-course meal with "allur-ing molds of ice cream in the form of pink wedding slippers" and even mono-grammed sugar cubes, announced that Thurman was now a member in good standing of the Black bourgeoisie. They were married on 12 June, appropri-ately enough during the annual Student Christian Movement gathering at Kings Mountain, Thurman's true spiritual home. Inclement weather forced the event indoors, along with the two hundred guests.[113]

Thurman announced that the ceremony would be divided into three parts. It opened, like so many of his sermons, with a few selected readings, includ-ing Langston Hughes's "The Negro Speaks of Rivers" and passages on love.[114] Then there were musical selections, sung by an interracial thirteen-person choir, with Thurman's best friend, the Rev. Herbert King, acquitting himself admirably in "Drink to Me with Only Thine Eyes." The final part of the cer-emony would be conducted in silence, another characteristic of Thurman's worship services. The bride and groom walked to the accompaniment of the wedding march from *Lohengrin* ("Here Comes the Bride") with little Olive, as the only bridesmaid, bestrewing their path with flower petals. Howard and Sue then knelt at an altar for an extended period of silence, he read two stanzas from Tennyson's "In Memoriam" (a favorite poet and poem), they recited their vows together—with Sue omitting the standard female obliga-tion to "obey"—and the presiding minister, Thurman's good friend the Rev. Clarence J. Gresham, pronounced them man and wife. Thus ended what one observer called "unquestionably the most unique rites in the annals of mod-ern matrimony."[115] In October 1933, their daughter, Anne Spencer Thurman, was born.[116] By February Sue proudly wrote to her mother that Anne, now weighing fifteen pounds, looked "like a pumpkin or tomato."[117]

The marriage of Howard and Sue lasted almost forty-nine years, until Thurman's death in April 1981. It was a marriage of opposites and a marriage of equals. Sue's relaxed and ingratiating extroversion poised against Howard's introversion and sometimes formidable spiritual intensity. He inspired, she befriended. Stories abound of young men and women, seeking direction in life, who found refuge in her abundant kindness. Howard and Sue supported each other's careers, even if Sue put hers on hold for a few years after her marriage and resumed it with a different trajectory. No marriage is without its tensions. But as Jean Burden suggested, it was the sort of union that even cynics about marriage envied.[118]

About two months after his wedding, in August 1932, Thurman preached in Plymouth Congregational Church in Washington, D.C., pastored by Her-bert King, on the topic "Barren or Fruitful." The sermon was so well received that members of the congregation paid to have it printed. It was Thurman's first published sermon. He contrasted two plants, the comparison taken from Jeremiah. First, "a desert scrub that never thrives; set in a salt[y] solitary place in the steppes," forever "undeveloped and underdeveloped, undernourished, and emaciated." Then, Jeremiah's "tree planted by the water," whose "leaves are always green." Thurman attributed the difference to being the sender and recipient of love. "When I love someone," he explained, "I seem to be at the center of all meanings and all values. Life takes on a new significance and I seem to have a quality of experience which is or which was the guarantee of all experience. Again, under the compulsion of love, I send my life forth to do and be things that nothing else is capable of inspiring." He had been barren; now he was fruitful, planted by the waters.[119]

7

In Black Athens

Howard University

In September 1926, the newly installed president of Howard University, Mordecai Wyatt Johnson, wrote to his protégé, wondering whether he had made the right move. The decision to leave his pulpit in Charleston, West Virginia, was accompanied by "some very great pain" on Johnson's part, and he thought it "remains to be seen if I shall be able to do a greater work here for the Master and his people." Johnson soon overcame his new-job jitters and would spend the next thirty-five years as Howard's supremely self-confident president. In the same letter, he wrote that it was "one of my hopes that some day I may have you here with me."[1] The following year Thurman returned the sentiment: "Me! I wish I was near you!"[2] For various reasons, especially the illness of Katie Kelley, this reunion had to be delayed. In the interim, however, Johnson ensured that Thurman would be an almost annual presence on the Howard campus and at Rankin Chapel.[3]

By the time Howard and Sue married in June 1932, they knew they would be setting up housekeeping in Washington, D.C. The acquisition of Thurman's services was part of Johnson's grand plan to make Howard University, as the subtitle of a 1941 history of the university put it, the "capstone of Negro education." Founded in 1869, Howard had always been unique among historically Black colleges and universities because of its federal charter and access to congressional funding. Johnson was Howard's first Black president, and he managed the trick of expanding its financial support from a Congress dominated by segregationists while increasing the university's outspokenness on racial matters.[4]

Thurman's new position was campus minister, presiding over Rankin Chapel, and professor of Christian theology in the School of Religion. Howard University would provide a physical home—as campus minister, he and his family lived in on-campus accommodations provided by the university—as well as a spiritual, political, and ideological base for twelve years, from 1932 to 1944. It was a remarkable time for Thurman. This would be the longest time he would spend in any position.[5] These might have been the most fulfilling years of his career, especially if we include the Indian sabbatical year of 1935–36. Thurman drew on Howard's unique resources: a steady stream of superior African American students, taught by the most distinguished Black university faculty in America. Howard University was at the center of things in the 1930s, as the importance of the federal government steadily increased during the Roosevelt years. If Thurman was not a member of so-called "Black Cabinet," many of his friends were, notably its unofficial leader, Mary McLeod Bethune. When Bethune founded the National Council of Negro Women in 1935, Sue Bailey Thurman was one of its leading figures and was the founding editor of its magazine, the *Aframerican Woman's Journal.* The combination of the large Black community in Washington and its nearness to the precincts of power made the city a natural home for many national Black organizations. Thurman was present at the creation of the slowly gathering force that became known as the civil rights movement, benefited from the ferment, and was one of its creators.

Thurman's arrival at Howard in 1932 was the culmination of fifteen years of friendship and the realization of a dream he and Johnson had long cherished of being able to work together. When Thurman came to Howard, he was dismissed in some circles as just another instance of Johnson's cronyism. The *Baltimore Afro-American* reported the rumor that "Rev. Mr. Thurman may have such outstanding qualifications as will prove a veritable investment to Howard University, but his appointment at present is being viewed as of the famous friendship variety."[6] Their "famous friendship" evolved over Thurman's years at Howard. Mentors and protégés have a different relationship than do bosses and subordinates. Thurman did not like being told how to do his work; Johnson had a notorious reputation for doing just that, or in the probably somewhat hyperbolic words of Rayford Logan, Howard University historian and Johnson critic, a reputation for telling "E. Franklin Frazier the kind of sociology to write" and "Abram Harris the kind of economics to study."[7] Johnson's tenure was characterized by extremely high degrees of internal faculty animosity, especially in the 1930s. Thurman was not in the anti-Johnson camp, but neither was he a sycophant, and at times their bonds were tested. Thurman was certainly disappointed when Howard's administration

Howard Thurman and Mordecai Wyatt Johnson
on the Howard University campus, ca. 1940

required him to take a sabbatical without pay for his year in India, which caused considerable financial hardship for his family. Thurman's active off-campus speaking schedule was another matter of contention between the two men. Logan records that when Johnson announced that the university "was not to be used as a basis of operations," Thurman told him that the remark was directed at him.[8]

Thurman always remained grateful for all that Johnson had done for him. In 1976, in a eulogy for Johnson commenting on their sixty-year friendship, Thurman stated that during his years at Howard, Johnson had given him "complete freedom to experiment" at services at Rankin Chapel. Further, "for me in my post, there was no censorship, no guidelines emanating from the office of the president, but rather participation in the full program of the chapel as often as his time and energies would permit."[9] He eulogized Johnson as a man who put his eloquence, the "naked energy" of his "creative thought and soaring imagination," at "the disposal of an entire people, *his people,* who for long weary years were victimized by a heritage of human slavery and in whom again and again the *tender roots* of a sense of their own worth were stunted and destroyed before they could blossom into the fruits of true manhood and womanhood."[10]

Johnson's motive in bringing Thurman to Washington, beyond friendship, was to improve the teaching of religion at Howard University. Although the Theological Department was founded in 1870, shortly after the university itself, and despite the fact that almost all of Howard's presidents (including Johnson) had been ordained ministers, it had, almost from the outset, been the university's "stepchild" or "poor cousin." When Thurman arrived, it was housed in a dilapidated building, one badly in need of a paint job, across the street from the main campus.[11] Unlike all the other divisions at the federally chartered university, the Theological Department was forced to make do on private donations, with a long-standing dispute between the Congregationalists and Presbyterians over which denomination would be the lead sponsor, "the complications of which," Logan wrote in his history, "are too tedious for extended discussion," and he was probably right.[12] But neither denomination supported the Theological Department with much munificence, and by the 1920s, as Thurman noted, northern denominational support of Black higher education had begun to dry up, at Howard and elsewhere.[13]

But in some ways, things were looking up. In 1932, as Thurman was arriving, the Theological Department was upgraded with a more prestigious title, the School of Religion. The following year it became solely a graduate school.[14] Johnson, from the time of his arrival at Howard, was committed to upgrading the teaching of religion on the campus, both institutionally and intellectually. In his inaugural presidential address, in 1927, Johnson argued that the "simple, unsophisticated, mystical religion of the Negro cannot continue to endure unless it is reinterpreted over and over to him by men who have a fundamental and far-reaching understanding of the significance of religion in its relation to the complexities of modern civilized life."[15] Thurman coming to Howard was a major step in this direction. And the position held other attractions for Thurman. Only months before arriving in Washington, Thurman had told an audience, "If I never run into a $3,000 a year position, I will nevertheless be hasty to thank God that I was able to get a college education."[16] Thurman was able to bust the $3,000 ceiling with an initial salary of $3,500 on arrival at Howard, though in general salaries at the School of Religion were below those of comparable positions elsewhere at Howard.[17]

The hiring of Benjamin Mays in 1934 as dean was another major addition to the faculty of the School of Religion. Mays came to Howard not for "the glories of the Howard University School of Religion, but the challenge to improve it."[18] This he accomplished, aiding in its transition to a graduate school, increasing the enrollment, improving the caliber of the faculty, and moving into a superior physical facility. He also acquired from the shuttered Auburn Theological Seminary a vastly enlarged library, with the School of Religion's library undergoing a thirtyfold increase from 1,443 to 46,527 available books. Mays's work as dean culminated, in 1939, with the accreditation of the School of Religion by the American Association of Theological Schools.[19] Although Mays and Thurman had been friends for many years, and their paths had crossed numerous times on the Y and Student Christian Movement circuit, the six years they were together at Morehouse deepened their friendship.[20] The two men shared drafts of forthcoming articles and writing assignments. When Mays left for the presidency of Morehouse in 1940, he wrote Thurman that the Howard years marked "a continuation of a friendship that began back in 1921" and expressed hope that "it will continue to grow with the years."[21] They created in the School of Religion a rigorous modernist curriculum, which they hoped would rouse students from their theological complacency. As James Farmer, who entered the School of Religion in 1938, observed, "bewilderment" was a key objective, or at least a frequent result: "Scriptures were subject to the scrutiny of biblical criticism. . . . One first-year seminarian came to class one morning red-eyed and falling asleep; he'd been up all night crying and praying for his professors' souls. Two others packed up and went home within the first month."[22] But for those who stuck it out, like Farmer, the Howard University School of Religion in the late 1930s and early 1940s offered its students a challenging brand of Christianity.

Thurman contributed to this in a number of ways. Although he was the professor of Christian theology, he apparently never taught a course on Christian theology, or on systematic theology of any kind. In 1939 he proposed to Johnson that his title be changed to professor of the history and philosophy of religion, a suggestion Johnson apparently passed on.[23] While at Howard he regularly taught courses on "Introduction to the Study of Religion," "History of Religion," "Introduction to the Psychology of Religion," "Modern Trends in World Religion," and "History of Mysticism," and special courses on some of his favorite mystics, past (Meister Eckhart) and present (Rufus Jones). All of these courses emphasized the commonality of all religions and the crucial importance of religion as "experience" rather than as dogma or a set of beliefs.[24]

Thurman was an inspiring teacher. If Thurman did not directly lecture on the news of the day, in his approach to religion current events he bridged the spiritual, the moral, and the political, and he encouraged others to do the same and to build on his insights. James Farmer wrote a master's thesis for Thurman—which, he proudly tells us, received an "A"—titled "The Relation between Religion and Racism with Special Reference to the American Scene."[25] In it, he argued that from the beginning of British settlement in North America, religion justified exploitation and racism, and New England Puritans distorted the notion of the elect and the damned to justify African slavery. At the same time, Farmer argued that religion, properly understood and harnessed, could become a prophetic, revolutionary force for social change. Thurman was very impressed and encouraged him to publish it, though his efforts to do so proved unsuccessful.[26] This was one of the many Thurman-inspired and -directed theses by Howard students in the School of Religion, such as James Russel Brown's 1935 master's thesis "An Examination of the Thesis That Christianity in Its Genesis Was a Technique for Survival for an Underprivileged Minority." As the title indicates, Brown's thesis examines in considerable depth Thurman's rooting of the religion of Jesus in the social and political realities of Roman Palestine.[27]

Thurman had a distinctive teaching method, one that relied less on textbooks than on fostering a dialogue. He would throw out an idea, such as the relation between the universal and particular, and challenge the students to work out its implications, sometimes with an extended dialogue with an individual student. James Farmer in his autobiography has a vivid description of Thurman in the late 1930s:

> When this extraordinary man walked into social ethics class, a silence born of awe reigned. It always seemed as if we had dragged him away from private meditation. He would look over the heads of those in class, into space, for what seemed minutes. Then he would open up, in his slow, laborious manner, with a provocative thesis, such as "When you young preachers fulminate about what you should do in any given situation, remember one thing: we are what we do—despite our reservations."
>
> He would wait for a response. My hand was usually up first with a question: Dr. Thurman, are you saying that if a soldier kills the enemy, he is a murderer, or at least a killer? Or if one accepts an assigned status of inferiority—let us say, sits in the balcony of a Jim Crow theater—he is inferior?[28]

Thurman rarely said more than an occasional "ah" as he pressed students to think more deeply about the question under discussion. Thurman's method was Socratic, undertaken as Socrates and Plato might have approved, helping individuals to find, through interior reflection and careful discussion, truths they already knew, truths hidden in the recesses of their soul. Or, in Farmer's words, "It was Thurman's belief that answers must come from within, from the bit of God in each of us."[29]

This approach to teaching worked equally well, if not better, in more intimate settings than a classroom, and these were often Thurman's preferred venues. "I have no great faith in the basic effectiveness of large public meetings," he wrote in 1937, "and would be quite happy to confine my discussion to smaller groups."[30] And the smallest possible group was an intense dyad of two. Throughout his career, Thurman was in demand as a mentor and advisor. Counseling is, of course, a core responsibility for all members of the clergy, but Thurman clearly had a special calling for it, less a matter of dispensing advice than assuming the role of a spiritual psychologist, helping others to find their inner voice, what he later called the "sound of the genuine," and to assist them in formulating and answering their own questions.[31] People began to look to Thurman for advice/inspiration/counsel early on, by his undergraduate years, and it continued throughout his life, leaving a trail of acolytes behind him.[32] One Howard student, the Rev. Samuel L. Gandy, wrote him in 1938 that "each and every day I run across someone who gives me a lift for the day by saying, 'So you are a student of the great Thurman?'" Although Gandy allowed he sometimes had to elbow other students for the privilege of prime sitting space, "the fellowship of those hours spent in meditation and small group discussions plus our own informal personal chats have meant much to me."[33]

Along with spiritual insights he was fully capable of dispensing very practical and sometimes harsh advice. He had learned, observing his grandmother Nancy, that a person could be "positive, strong and tender" and "tender as over against soft." She was "kind without being sentimental," and Thurman sometimes was similarly down-to-earth.[34] Thurman was no prude and expected people to take their responsibilities seriously. In 1938 he told his protégé, the Rev. Melvin Watson, aged twenty-eight, not to get isolated in his new job, to develop a record collection, and that while he knew he was in need of "really stimulating feminine companionship," gave him the good advice to avoid dating students on his campus, and not to "waste your time with a child, or someone who would consider you a good grab off the tree."[35] He could at times be quite harsh, reprimanding a student in 1940 who had failed to finish several chores Thurman had assigned to him: "What kind of man are you anyway? . . . You need not get sore because you are very sensitive and thin-skinned. You cannot make an impression on me by sulking. Take it on the chin because you deserve everything that I am saying."[36]

Most who came to Thurman seeking enlightenment of some sort did not leave disappointed. A description from a summer conference in 1941 (likely primarily involving white students) gives a sense of Thurman's impact as a provider of counsel:

> June—a summer conference of the Student Christian Movement—under a tree beside a lake or on the front steps of a tent or cabin. They have been there for two hours already and others who have appointments have been sensitive enough to let them alone, as though some inner voice spoke. In the end, the two (or three, four, or more) get up and slowly walk away and those who know feel the hand of God has touched another student's life through the voice and sensitive spirit of Howard Thurman.[37]

This frequent giving of himself could be both emotionally exhausting and quite time-consuming. In addition to his other duties, Thurman created a new undergraduate religious organization known as the Fellowship Council, which had as its purpose fostering student-teacher interaction and creating small study groups organized around particular topics or purposes (religion, relations between men and women, poetry, a group dedicated to reading the *Nation* magazine).[38] The Thurmans frequently opened their house to students, entertaining them for meals, which constituted a welcome breach in the usual social distance and chilliness that had heretofore characterized faculty-student relations at Howard.[39] For some, of special closeness to the Thurmans, admission to their ambit could feel like an informal adoption.[40] With all of this, as Thurman complained in his final annual report as dean of chapel, from June 1944 (when problems related to World War II likely led to an increasing call for his services): "The demands for counseling grow out of the Sunday services [and] is a continuous stream. All of this means that the Dean of the Chapel finds it impossible to get any one day of complete rest. He has no Sabbath, no day of rest!"[41]

But as important as his teaching and counseling were, his main responsibility at Howard was to Rankin Chapel and its services, first as campus minister, and after his return from India, as dean of chapel. When he arrived at Howard, Thurman completely redesigned the order of service at the chapel. He preached there on most Sundays during the school year and was responsible for seeing that it was operating properly on those Sundays when he was elsewhere. He brought in a range of guest speakers, from anywhere within "the Judeo-Christian tradition," including a number of rabbis.[42] He did not invite any white speakers from institutions that excluded or discriminated against African Americans.[43]

Thurman came to Howard at an interesting and difficult time for campus ministry. Howard had abolished mandatory chapel services in 1922, part of a wave of many leading colleges and universities making chapel attendance optional (though Howard was one of the first historically Black colleges or universities to do so).[44] Needless to say, without a steady supply of captive souls, attendance at chapel services plummeted. Beyond the lack of compulsion, one reason for the declining attendance at college religious services in the 1920s and 1930s was the lack of interest in religion itself, especially among those who thought themselves in the front van of the forward-thinking, many of whom had clustered at Howard. As Thurman asked when he was the featured speaker at Howard's Week of Prayer in 1930, "Is there anything inherent in religion, the church, or an education which must of necessity estrange an educated man from the church?"[45] Benjamin Mays, writing in 1940, argued that "no Negro college would have a lower percentage than Howard University when it comes to students' church membership."[46] Thurman, meaning this as a compliment, later called Howard "a very tremendous pagan university" and saw being dean of chapel as a great challenge, precisely because of the ferocious intelligence of so many of the learned despisers of religion on the Howard campus.[47]

Thurman tried in numerous ways to attract the skeptics, mockers, and uninterested. Mays noted that the services at Howard were "among the best to be found anywhere in the country," with superb music (something to which Thurman always paid close attention), well-planned, and relatively short (in and out in ninety minutes). Mays estimated that about five hundred persons attended on an average Sunday, largely filling the chapel. Thurman had in

Rankin Chapel, Howard University, in the early twentieth century

part rebuilt the services by attracting those outside the immediate Howard community. Half of the regular attendees, Mays estimated, were Howard students, the other half Howard faculty and persons from the outside community. Mays noted that this meant that no more than 15 percent of Howard students regularly attended services at Rankin Chapel.[48] If this was unfortunate, Thurman was delighted that he had been able to transform worship at Rankin Chapel into worship that people attended not out of a sense of leaden obligation but out of excitement.

By the time he arrived at Howard his preaching had acquired the aura of legend. Carlton Goodlett, an usher at Rankin Chapel, thought that the religiously skeptical student body at Howard was "electrified" by Thurman's sermons, and "students began coming to the chapel early Sunday mornings so they could get a seat." Another Howard student who testified to its power was Verna Dozier, a Washington, D.C., native and later a prominent Episcopal layperson. She attended Howard in the late 1930s and found Thurman to be a pulpit "poet" who "used language beautifully" and whose sermons frequently left Dozier "spellbound." She came to Howard as an agnostic, typical of a time when, as she wrote, "most intelligent Black people . . . questioned everything about traditional religion." Thurman opened her eyes to the possibility "that Christianity was not the only way to respond religiously" and that Jesus could be seen as a model for behavior rather than as a savior. Listening to Thurman talk about "new approaches to biblical criticism and new ideas of social justice" convinced her that a Christian faith could be intellectually respectable. She convinced her agnostic father to also become a regular at Thurman's Rankin Chapel services.[49]

Thurman had a not entirely justified reputation for delivering difficult sermons. "When Thurman occupied the university pulpit, Rankin Memorial Chapel was packed," wrote James Farmer: "Though few but theologians and philosophers comprehended what he was saying, everyone else thought that if only they had understood it would have been wonderful, so mesmerizing was his resonant voice and so captivating was the artistry of his delivery. Those who did grasp the meaning of his sermons were even more ecstatic."[50] If Thurman's sermons were difficult, it was not because their language was abstract, the subjects highly scholarly, or the vocabulary recondite, but because they required creative and intent listening. His sermons didn't emphasize or linger over the obvious, and he often made his points with subtlety and shades of meaning.

From models such as Mordecai Wyatt Johnson, an exemplar of sophisticated African American oratory, Thurman's sermons were built on the foundation of the careful use of educated English. "The basic requirements for effective speaking are two," Thurman would write in 1940: "First, a consciousness of having something to say, and second, the ability to use the English language clearly, intelligently, and correctly."[51] Evilio Grillo, an African American of Cuban descent who also attended Howard in the 1930s, wrote of Thurman that "he spoke with a transfixing eloquence. He had an awe-inspiring command of the English language. He was understood by most people, for his sermons expressed feeling eloquently, were lucid, and above all, were poetic. He managed always to involve his audiences as he wove, with his expressive face, piercing eyes, and gracefully moving arms and body. . . . He would struggle almost painfully as he introduced a theme, insisting that his auditors struggle with him for understanding. Once assured that the congregation was fully his, he poured forth with a waterfall of language, beautiful, ethereal, profoundly moving."[52] Grillo was one of many who felt that Thurman had a unique ability to make a listener feel that he was speaking directly to them, as if there was no one else present.

Thurman's sermons aspired to be prose poetry, and he used poetry extensively, often opening with a poem or poetic reading, such as an allegory of Olive Schreiner.[53] As he explained, "I quote poetry in my addresses often because a good poem summarizes very often effectively in short compass what it would take many prosaic utterances to do."[54] In 1976 the novelist Ralph Ellison, wishing to make the case that "elegance turns up in every aspect of Afro-American culture," provided a number of examples from high and popular culture, from Jimmy Rushing singing the blues to Joe Louis deftly delivering an uppercut. At the head of his list of examples of African American elegance, Ellison placed "a sermon of Howard Thurman."[55]

At the same time, Thurman was wary of making his sermons too elegant. He preached extemporaneously in part to impart a sense of spontaneous roughness to his message.[56] He was given the advice as a young preacher not to work over his material "till you have taken all the life out of [it] with polish" and to remember that "truth is rugged." There was a temptation, which he tried to avoid, "to let the beautiful turn of phrase divorce itself from the movement of the spirit that generates the word."[57] At the same time, in his own way, every sermon was a performance. As Evilio Grillo observed, "While he projected himself as the deeply spiritual man that he was, his every sermon was also an exercise in virtuoso theater."[58] Thurman had a lifelong interest in the stage, as audience member and occasional actor and director.[59] In 1927 in Oberlin a Black theater troupe put on a play by a recent graduate of the college in a performance that, according to the *Pittsburgh Courier,* was "creditable to the director, Howard Thurman."[60] In December 1931 he directed a production of *Macbeth* at Morehouse College.[61] Thurman's stage presence was obvious enough to observers to make him a candidate to play the lead in the 1948 Broadway adaption of Alan Paton's famous novel *Cry, the Beloved Country.*[62]

Like any actor, Thurman fed off his connection to his audience, addressing them, seeking their approbation, wanting tangible evidence that he was making a connection, and worried when he felt he was not.[63] This required a subtle reading of his listeners; his sermon style did not encourage audience interjections, the raising of right hands, or shouts of amen. When he started to deliver short sermons on television in the late 1950s, Thurman worried whether he could preach without an audience present.[64] Thurman's theatricality abhorred staginess, overemphatic presentations, and flamboyance. It was a theater of subtleties and interiorities rather than melodrama. Its ultimate purpose was to get his listeners to think about themselves and to create a mood in which personal spiritual exploration could flourish.

To avoid the didactic and the prosaic, and to reach his listeners on a level where rational argument merges with intuition, Thurman's Howard services sometimes directly incorporated aspects of theater or performance. He put on plays and dramatic presentations in Rankin Chapel, such as T. S. Eliot's *Murder in the Cathedral,* dramatic readings from Kahlil Gibran's *The Prophet,* or a play based on the life of St. Francis.[65] At times, Thurman led special services consisting entirely of him reading passages from the Bible, such as favorite psalms with a quiet organ accompaniment in the background, ending with the audience sitting in silence for five minutes at the end of the service.[66] He was an early champion of liturgical dance. One such program from the late 1930s was constructed around "Praise—Thanksgiving—Contrition—Faith," in Thurman's words "four of the universal moods of the human spirit that were present wherever men worshipped their God," in which a young white dancer improvised to these themes in the chapel.[67]

A similar motivation was behind Thurman's annual "living Madonna" series, in which, during the Christmas season, he would present tableaux of famous Renaissance paintings of the Madonna image, accompanied by settings of the Ave Maria, with participants' skin color ranging from "albino white to burnt umber."[68] The tableaux added a bit of High Church ceremonial and some white faces to the proceedings in Rankin Chapel, but Thurman's point was less sacramental than archetypal, showcasing that the sacredness of the mother-child relationship was not limited to one religion. As he wrote in 1938: "The Madonna and Child is not the exclusive possession of any race or any faith. . . . It affirms the constancy of the notion that life is dynamic and alive and that death as a final consummation of life is an illusion. . . . The stirring of the child in the womb is the perennial sign of man's attack on bigotry, blindness, prejudice, greed, hate, and all the host of diseases that make of man's life a nightmare and a holocaust."[69]

Thurman's sermonic style, with its pregnant pauses and extended silences, was influenced by his contact with Quaker culture during his study with Rufus Jones, when he regularly attended the Germantown Pennsylvania Friends Meeting.[70] At the heart of the complexities of Thurman's sermonic style is the familiar mystic paradox of the need to use words to express the ineffable. As he wrote in 1939: "It is strikingly significant to me that when meanings become vast and communication between the human spirits has to do with the deepest understandings, speech, vocal speech is singularly inadequate."[71] Not all of Thurman's listeners followed him into every nuance of his sermons, and few would have claimed to fully grasp the depths of his mysticism. Nonetheless, most who heard Thurman understood enough. As a 1939 encomium from *The Crisis* put it: "There are many people who will cancel everything to go hear Howard Thurman speak; his language is beautiful, his ideals and point of view intriguing. Most of all, people are overwhelmed by his silences, and marvel how eloquent he can be without ever shouting or 'orating' and his ability to get to rock bottom issues."[72]

When James Farmer first walked on its campus, and spied some of the greatest Black scholars of the age walking across its quad in the flesh, he knew he had arrived at "Howard University, the Black Athens." The 1930s was Howard's Periclean apex. The university's luminaries included the poet Sterling Brown, philosopher Alain Locke, sociologist E. Franklin Frazier, political scientist Ralph Bunche, economist Abram Harris Jr., Charles H. Houston, dean of the law school, and historians Rayford Logan and Charles H. Wesley. The list of academic stars in Howard's firmament could easily be extended. But above all for Farmer there was "the incomparable Howard Thurman. Mystic, poet, philosopher, preacher."[73]

Thurman wrote in his autobiography that he was "caught up in Mordecai Johnson's vision to create the first real community of Black scholars, to build an authentic university dedicated primarily to the education of Black youth." He added, somewhat skeptically: "For many years this was regarded as a pretension, and, in some important ways, it was a creative mixture of fact and fiction."[74] The "fact" of Howard in the 1930s was that, as Thurman later remembered, it was "our only great university, the best minds in the whole Negro world were there."[75] Few disagreed, and by general consensus, it was the greatest accumulation of stellar African American intellectual power in one institution before or since. And the "fiction" was that Howard remained a segregated institution in a segregated America, and segregated institutions, even if in some aspects superior to their white counterparts, were still not, in basic ways, equal to them.

These were practical questions, not merely sociological abstractions. In 1938, a prospective divinity student, Roy Norris, was torn over the question of whether to attend the Howard University School of Religion or the Yale Divinity School for his graduate work. He wrote Thurman for advice. After warning him about New England's cold weather—"almost every year some Negro student dies of tuberculosis"—he offered a frank comparison between the two schools:

> You will get some things at Yale which you cannot get here. We may just as well be honest about it. There is a better theological library immediately available to you, larger faculty, larger contacts with more able students who will give your mind the exercise and discipline that it needs. Again, I doubt whether there is as much inspiration for you, a Negro, at Yale, as there is at Howard. Then, inasmuch as all the academic contacts you have had have been in a Negro college it may be to your advantage to spend some time in a white institution. You will get at Howard a good course, restricted because of our faculties, but comprehensive, and you will not have to be bothered with the questions of race and the like.[76]

Norris went to Yale.[77]

Howard University's golden age was built on a contradiction. Bright Black students like Norris, and like Thurman before him, could attend white colleges and graduate schools (though often subject to an informal quota). But by an unwritten rule, no African American could be hired by one of these schools as permanent faculty. Howard's golden age was a testimony not only to Johnson's ability as a faculty builder but to the reality that African Americans academics, however glittering their resumes, had no place in mainstream higher education. And this reality was made all the more bitter to individuals like Thurman and many of his Howard peers who had excelled during their student years at white institutions. If in India those Thurman met often misheard Howard as Harvard and thought he taught at the latter, no African American would ever make that mistake.[78] Howard University was intended by its mostly white creators to be an adequate college for African Americans and no more, not a "great Negro university," much less a rival to the great white institutions of higher learning with their vastly greater endowments, facilities, libraries, and salaries.

No one was more aware of this paradox, and the paradox that was at the heart of Johnson's tenure at Howard, than Johnson himself. In 1928 he had said that "Negroes must do a contradictory thing. They must work with all

Howard Thurman and Sue Bailey Thurman with
Howard University students, ca. 1940

their might against segregation, and at the same time strengthen their so-called segregated institutions as if they expected them to last forever. They must insist that the doors of Harvard and Yale be kept open to Negroes and at the same time build up Howard and Lincoln as if there was no Harvard and Yale."[79] A decade later, addressing the NAACP, Johnson offered another version of this chiasmus, criticizing "the philosophy of working out our future within a segregated sphere" as "dangerous and illusory." Instead, he would "support segregated institutions just as long as it was necessary to keep up the fight for the complete integration of the Negro in American life."[80] Or, as succinctly stated in historian Carter G. Woodson's influential *The Miseducation of the Negro* (1931), "our minds must become sufficiently developed to use segregation to kill segregation."[81] Thurman wholeheartedly agreed.

One problem with segregated education was that often it prepared students for a world that did not exist, a world without segregation, where Black graduates would be judged by their ability. In 1929 Thurman stated that "the philosophy and technique of education which are the tools of the educated Negro are alike the tools of the educated white man. They are to be used by people who stand in society as keepers of the established order."[82] But Black colleges were allowed to exist to promote an "established order" that was not theirs, that they could not control, that was inimical to their best interests, and that everyone knew on some level was evil and had to be overturned. As Thurman put it in 1935, addressing the Richmond NAACP, "whatever the high fa-lu-tin theories of education," he had "the skills, the methodology and the sociology of those who control society, but the day I set foot out of college I found I was educated to take part in the control of society but being an underprivileged man, I had to conform to the rules set up by those who control society."[83]

There was little even the best-intentioned Black educators could do about this, especially in the South. "Any institution of learning that varies notice-ably from that fundamental position [upholding the racial status quo] cannot hope to live."[84] And so, the "price that the institution must pay for survival in society is to leave, for subsequent generations, its framework."[85] But it no longer sufficed by the 1930s for Black colleges to merely perpetuate them-selves, with the hope of better days ahead, and in many ways, mere perpet-uation had become a hindrance to the furthering of Black political aims.[86] The situation was particularly acute, or especially familiar to Thurman, for African Americans with advanced education. Thurman wrote in a 1929 essay of the need to address the sense of overwhelming frustration felt by Black col-lege graduates in the face of the plight that "drives a brilliant Negro holding two degrees from one of the dominant group's best symbol of 'education' to become a dining-car waiter."[87] For African Americans, the knowledge gained by advanced education often was not power but just a more enlightened (and more cynical) knowledge of their own powerlessness.

But the problem was more general, and neither of the two main options was palatable: either preparing Black students to lower their horizons to adjust to the limited opportunities available to them; or inspiring them to try to realize their ambitions as if the barriers set against them did not exist. What was needed was a basic rethinking of the purpose of education. Thurman's progressive pedagogy, like his modernist religious views, argued that for too long, education had been a conservative institution, upholding the status and positions of the rich and powerful, primarily committed to imprinting new generations with old truths and insisting that they follow them obediently.[88] As he wrote in 1929, the purpose of education was "to make people at home in the world so that they may live fully and creatively. It aims to put at their disposal a technique of mastery over themselves and over their environment, as far as possible."[89] As for segregation, the lesson to teach students was to neither adjust to it nor succumb to it.

Black colleges had to eliminate their often suffocating sense of privilege for both students and faculty, the conviction that they were the natural leaders of the race, and that their job was both to differentiate themselves as much as possible from the Black masses and serve as their unquestioned leaders. If present trends continued, he said in 1938, "the average [Black] college student will look upon the mass of Negroes in the same critical, hostile manner that people on the outside regard them."[90] He told the graduating class of Tennessee A&I in 1938, "I have never in my life seen an educated Negro who was not discouraged unless I am looking at someone this morning."[91] The alternative to this sort of discouragement was "to relate everything you learn to the needs of the masses, of which you are a part, and if that is not done, then what use is it?"[92] This was because "the fate of the least privileged was tied up fundamentally with the most privileged and most advantaged."[93] Or, in other words, the notion of "privilege" or "advantage" for any group of African Americans was an illusion fostered by segregation. And by shattering that illusion, they gain mastery over their real situation, and the confidence to try to transform it, to create an educational program "coordinated and unified on the basis of a creative synthesis which will enable the members of the college community to work out their own destiny."[94]

At Howard, Thurman sided with students in battles against stifling conventions on such issues as the right to chew gum and wear lipstick to more urgent personal matters, to the demands for a student council. He supported the creation of a faculty union.[95] All of this was part of his effort to upend the hierarchical presuppositions and tendency to autocratic leadership that had long dominated many Black colleges. In 1940, as a cochair of the short-lived Fellowship of Religious Workers in Negro Colleges and Universities, he called for an exposure of "tyranny, despotism, and corruption" at Black colleges so that the "possibility of real democracy at work in a specific community" could be demonstrated.[96] Thurman described the larger goal of Black colleges to a crowd in Madras in 1935: "The fundamental purpose of Negro education is to give the Negro not only a training in the skill and technique of civilization, but, of far more importance, it is to give him a certain social attitude which can be injected into American society, so that it will become increasingly impossible to have separate schools for whites. The Negro attack is directed against segregated institutions of the present day."[97] Thurman's goal, like that of Mordecai Wyatt Johnson, was to turn segregated historically Black colleges into antisegregation machines. What this meant, precisely, for the future of Black colleges was unclear, but there was no alternative.

Intellectual pendulums swing. Thurman's skepticism and ambivalence toward existing Black institutions was a dominant current among Black intellectuals in the interwar years, with the most intense island of anti-institutionalism located at Howard itself, a reaction against the era of Black institution building associated with Booker T. Washington and his peers.[98] (The pendulum would swing back the other way in the 1960s, another era of Black institution building.) Thurman's Howard colleague E. Franklin Frazier, as we have seen, was a caustic critic of middle-class Black institutions. Howard economist Abram Harris Jr. and Thurman's good friend, the political scientist Ralph Bunche, also offered sharp critiques of separate Black institutions from a distinctly left-of-center, non-Communist Marxist perspective. Bunche thought the average race leader was "ordinarily very allergic to democracy—he prefers to play the role of the aristocrat, or the dictator or tyrant."[99] Thinking that the 10 percent of the American population, and a politically and economically disempowered 10 percent at that, could solve its problems without the cooperation, on some level, of the other 90 percent, was to Bunche, delusional and self-defeating.

When it came to religion, as we have seen, Thurman was largely an institution of one, a mystic always suspicious of the deadening effects of organized Christianity. Writing Mordecai Wyatt Johnson in 1927, he called for "seek[ing] how we may release to the full our greatest spiritual powers, that there may be such a swell of spiritual energy that existing systems will be upset from sheer dynamic."[100] Benjamin Mays, probably Thurman's closest colleague at Howard, may not have shared his anarcho-mysticism, but he was an acute critic of the institutions of the Black church. In 1933, the year before Mays joined the Howard faculty as dean of the School of Religion, he published (with Joseph Nicholson) *The Negro's Church,* a pioneering study of African American religious denominations.[101]

The book offered a systematic review of all aspects of the Black church, urban and rural, north and south. It was for the most part a searing indictment of its shortcomings. "The analysis," Mays and Nicholson conclude, "reveals that the status of the Negro church is in part the result of the failure of American Christianity in the realm of race-relations; that the church's program, except in rare instances, is static, non-progressive, and fails to challenge the loyalty of many of the most critically-minded Negroes; that the vast majority of its pastors are poorly trained theologically; that more than half of the sermons analyzed are abstract, and imbued with a magical conception of religion; that in church schools less than one-tenth of the teachers are college graduates."[102] Thurman no doubt agreed with every word of the indictment. (He was cited in Mays's acknowledgments.)[103] He wrote a short review of the book for the *Intercollegian,* a magazine of the Student Christian Movement. Thurman was not an inspired writer of book reviews; most of them were brief and rather perfunctory, adequate summaries of the book in question and little more, but this review finds Thurman at his most animated. The book reveals "a pathetic picture." Black churches "seem to be lacking in almost everything except vitality. What a criminal indictment they are to the American white man's religion in whose midst they were established and subsequently developed! The story is an eloquent dramatization of the tragedy of the segregated church." He concluded: "To preach the Kingdom of God from a segregated pulpit is one of the profoundest kinds of atheism."[104]

This did not mean, either for Mays or Thurman, turning their back on the Black church any more than it meant turning their backs on Black colleges. The Black church was their home, and it was the home of millions of African Americans; it was something that they owned, that was theirs, that could not be taken away from them. It was a place, within its walls, however physically and politically circumscribed, that Blacks were largely free to say, feel, and be what they wanted to be.[105] But this was not enough. Strengthening the Black church, or any other Black institution, if not joined to an assault on segregation, was ultimately a dead end. The inadequacy of Black institutions was a function of their separateness. For Thurman, the beauty and truth of religion was that, in a segregated church on a segregated campus in a segregated city, for an hour on Sunday, one could glimpse what might be possible. Thurman described in his autobiography that Rankin Chapel on Sunday morning had become, despite the fact that those attending services were still overwhelmingly African American, "a time and a place where race, sex, culture, material belongings, and earlier religious orientation became undifferentiated in the presence of God."[106] The challenge was to create new vessels, new spaces, new institutions, even a new America, where the meaning of Christianity was not contradicted by its setting and location.

8

Delivering the Message of Nonviolence

Lessons from India

After Thurman returned from India in April 1936, one of the first places he visited was Atlanta. While there, he had dinner with his old friends Martin Luther King, Sr., and Alberta Williams King. With seven-year-old Martin Luther King, Jr., presumably in earshot, he talked of his adventures in India and his meeting with Gandhi. Thurman told this story to the historian Vincent Harding, and both men thought there was some deeper significance to this meeting, something stronger than coincidence. If indeed, as Gandhi told Thurman, "it may be through the Negroes that the unadulterated message of non-violence will be delivered to the world," Thurman wasted no time in passing on the message to the person who would be most responsible for fulfilling it. (If nothing else, the story demonstrates that the younger King knew Thurman from his earliest days.)[1]

Two decades before King burst into political prominence, Thurman was one of the prime deliverers of the message of African American nonviolence. There were many who were listening. In August 1942 Thurman was interviewed by a reporter from the *Pittsburgh Courier*. Thurman was in a feisty mood. He was angry that Churchill had recently rearrested Gandhi and the leaders of the Congress Party in India. "The imperialist stubbornness of Britain" had reduced their claims to be fighting for democracy "to a moral absurdity." Try as they might, in their usual brutal fashion, the British will not be able to lock up the "spirit of present day India" however many jails they build. The reporter took the measure of the "modest, stocky black man, with resonant voice and smiling countenance" before him. He had, he told his readers, "probably moved more cynical men and intellectual women than any other speaker

158

of his generation." This man was a mystic, "but a mystic with a practical turn of mind" who understood politics and economics. The reporter, Peter Dana, suggested that Thurman was "one of the few black men in this country around whom a great, conscious movement of Negroes could be built, not unlike the great Indian movement with which Gandhi and Nehru are associated."[2]

History took another path, and neither Thurman's talents nor temperament were suited for the role of lead strategist and tactician for a national political movement. But in the years after his return from India, in the late 1930s and early 1940s, when his advocacy for nonviolence was at its freshest and most ardent, he was being heard. After his return to the United States Thurman would spend several years crossing the continent from Canada's Maritime provinces to California trying to explain, to himself and his audience, "What We May Learn from India," to borrow a frequent lecture title.[3] He was a prime shaper of a distinctive, radical African American interpretation of Gandhian nonviolence, placed into a broadly Christian framework, one that Martin Luther King, Jr., when he was old enough, and many others, would inherit.

Returning home after a long trip abroad can be an anticlimax, particularly when it takes a month to get home. So it apparently was for the Thurmans and the Carrolls, who at the end of the Pilgrimage of Friendship retraced their steps from Colombo, Ceylon, back to New York City. And while they wrote extensively about the outward journey, about the return trip they were silent. (A highlight of the return for Howard and Sue must have been reuniting with their two young daughters, Olive and Anne, in Geneva.) When Thurman was again on American soil, in April 1936, he was the possessor of a new title from Howard University, dean of chapel.[4] But one suspects that Thurman would have preferred some back salary rather than a new prestigious title. Thurman had been obliged to travel to India on an unpaid sabbatical; the payment he received from the American Student Christian Federation did not make up the difference. As his mother, Alice Sams, wrote him in June 1936, "I know you got broke on your India trip."[5]

One of Thurman's understandings with the American Student Christian Federation that sponsored the India trip had been that he would speak extensively about it upon his return, though Thurman generally did not require much coaxing to hit the lecture circuit. He traveled more or less continually, picking up an honorarium of from fifty to seventy-five dollars per engagement.[6] By the fall, when he had to resume teaching and preaching duties at Howard, Thurman was sick in body and perhaps a little sick in mind. He wrote A. Ralla Ram, the Indian sponsor of the Negro Pilgrimage, in November 1936 that since returning to the United States in April he had traveled some fifteen thousand miles.[7] By late summer there were reports that Thurman was suffering from a "nervous collapse," and while this is an imprecise phrase that could cover a range of psychological conditions, it seems clear that he was physically and mentally exhausted.[8] His mother, sensing something was not quite right, told him, "I want you to rest your braines and mind as much as you can."[9]

And yet, despite his exhaustion, little could keep Thurman from his appointed rounds of preaching and lecturing. This required extensive work in planning his sprawling itineraries. Thurman had something of a romance with train travel. (He rarely drove himself and detested flying.) He enjoyed the freedom from obligation and from other persons, in being beyond the reach of phone calls and importuning disturbances, and having ample down time to prepare and ready himself for his next engagement. When nothing else was pressing, he was likely to catch up on the latest mystery novel or just doze off, rocked by the gentle rhythm of the rails.[10]

As much as Thurman liked traveling by train, he was acutely aware that as a Black man in the middle decades of the twentieth century, a potential cloud hovered over every trip. Certainly, in the Deep South he was sometimes obliged to travel in Jim Crow cars, and elsewhere the rules governing the separation of the races on interstate train travel were maddeningly varied and complex, with numerous regional differences, and often inconsistently applied. Thurman wrote little about this, though he confided to his first biographer, Elizabeth Yates, that the myriad rudenesses and discourtesies meted out to him in the course of his travels were "where I die daily."[11] In the 1940s, going from St. Louis to Cheyenne, Wyoming, there was the little girl who pointed to Thurman and silenced the dining car by blurting out, "Mama, there's a zigaboo sitting down." The chief steward, who had never met Thurman before, came up to Thurman, shook his hand, welcomed him to the car, and the tension was relieved.[12] Or the time an older woman, on a trip from Chicago to Memphis, complaining to the conductor and all of her fellow passengers, "What is *that* doing in this car?" The conductor tried to defuse the situation by replying, "*That* has a ticket," but Thurman felt the atmosphere shifting from "common indifference to positive resentment of my presence."[13] I suspect incidents such as these only spurred his determination to travel by rail. Every trip in which he was treated with respect, had a good night's sleep in a Pullman compartment, or ate in the dining car without disturbance was a test and victory for American democracy. He was a stand-in for every Black American, including the millions who didn't have the wherewithal or professional standing to do the same.

Between his return from India and his move to San Francisco in 1944 were probably Thurman's most busily itinerating years. In addition to purely financial concerns, Thurman needed to travel extensively to get his message out because he was still primarily a speaker, not a writer. He published little that was widely accessible before the late 1940s. If he was not, as a somewhat overeffusive protégé wrote him in 1938, "one of the most talked about men in the country," he was certainly becoming better known.[14] But his lack of publications is one reason his impact in the 1930s has been largely overlooked. During the interwar years, the summer circuits of the YMCA and YWCA were still flourishing, the inheritors of a long tradition of liberal Christian and Chautauqua lectures, before radio and other electronic media marginalized them as a primary source of information.[15] Thurman spent his summers speaking at myriad churches, college chapels, conferences, and institutes and was an active speaker throughout the year.

During these years, Thurman spoke extensively to both white and Black audiences. There were likely very few events at which the racial mix was relatively equal, and those probably were limited to self-consciously "interracial" gatherings. The bigger events and conferences on the summer Y circuit were predominantly attended by whites, though there was a Black Y circuit as well, such as the Y summer retreat at Kings Mountain, North Carolina, where Thurman made an annual appearance. Probably, in the course of the year, he made more relatively local appearances in the Washington-Baltimore area at Black venues (not including his regular preaching at Rankin Chapel), though there was no lack of national Black organizations that sought out Thurman as a speaker. If I were to hazard a guess, one made without the benefit of a quantitative analysis, I would suggest that the ratio of Black to white venues in his talks during these years was relatively even, perhaps with a slight Black preponderance.

Thurman wanted to touch all minds and spread what he often referred to as his "contagion" as widely as possible. At times the appeal of Thurman to whites was explicitly racial; the novelty of hearing a Black man articulate their inner needs in a way they would not have thought possible. In 1932, Earl Alcorn heard Thurman speak in California and thought that his words had "the ability to put a finger directly upon the sore spots of life in such a manner that they would begin healing at once." It "was an experience which later I knew I had secretly hoped for, yet wondered if it ever would come." But that its inspiration should be "from one of not only another race, but another color than myself,—How small the world is, and how tremendous is the drive of Life, after all!"[16]

Thurman's ability to cross the racial divide without embarrassing himself impressed many Black observers. In August 1939 there was a laudatory article by G. James Fleming on Thurman in *The Crisis*, "Preacher at Large to Universities," calling him Black America's "interracial minister plenipoten-tiary," noting that Thurman's "flock," though "starting with his own people . . . includes men and women of all races and colors and all nationalities." The article notes with pride that he had spoken in the chapels of more than one hundred white colleges, at many of which, the author, apologizing for the hoariness of the cliché, said he had been "the first Negro" or "the only Negro." Wherever he went, the article continued, this "philosopher, mystic, inter-preter, student, preacher and very human person all in one" "wins friends for the Negro race" and for a "'broader vitalizing democracy' in America."[17]

The article in *The Crisis* assured its readers that he remained "every inch a Negro" and in no way scraped and bowed before white audiences by telling them what they wanted to hear. Like many observers of Thurman at the time, Fleming noted a combination of the lofty and the visceral in his preaching, his ability, while dwelling "on the mountaintop" to "call a spade a spade." While "he is never hateful, he often takes up the cudgels for his race and can be mil-itant and caustic."[18] Another observer, Lester Granger, the executive secretary of the National Urban League, wrote that Thurman was "in great demand by student groups of both races." He worried that his style was at times too "flow-ery," though added that "every now and then he throws his mysticism away and delivers his audience a hard sock on its intellectual solar plexus."[19]

As enthusiastic as whites were to hear Thurman throughout his career and perhaps especially during the interwar years, his base and his primary audience were always his fellow African Americans. The Black press reported on his comings and goings, and sometimes reported on and summarized his speeches and sermons. He had fan clubs; there was a Howard Thurman Club in Detroit in the 1930s.[20] In 1933 his associate Frank Wilson suggested that Thurman be given leave from Howard to visit selected Black colleges and have extended sessions speaking to students and faculty because he was uniquely qualified to speak "deep down beneath the superficialities of the present socio-economic scene" and provide an alternative to "the strategies of pure rationality or ruthless violence." Thurman's message, thought Wilson, could speak to those usually indifferent to religion, those who thought that religion and politics were two utterly separate spheres, to the many "crushed by the weight of tragic circumstances" and the oblivious few "who have the illusion of being untouched by the rush of events in a heartless and largely impersonal society."[21] Before Black audiences he certainly was more overt in speaking about racial matters and asserting a racial bond with the audience, sometimes talking about why, "if Negroes were honest, they couldn't survive" in white America.[22] But before all audiences his purpose was rarely an airing of grievances or suggestions of a concrete political strategy; rather, he spoke of the need for personal spiritual reflection and how this can and should lead to a new social awareness.

In his article on Thurman, Fleming stated that Thurman did not limit himself to one topic or one line of inquiry, but "sooner or later, those who come into contact with him try to find out what is his solution for the problem of race, want to know what is his prescription for interracial amity."[23] Yet if white audiences wanted to know what Thurman thought about this, he rarely told them directly. As early as 1928 he told an interviewer, "I never accept any calls to speak on race relations."[24] Although there were occasional exceptions, this became a fairly hard-and-fast rule. When in 1934 he was invited to speak on racial matters at Haverford College, a college that he knew, because of his time studying there with Rufus Jones, did not regularly admit Black students, he replied: "I am not a sociologist and am not qualified to make a scientific presentation of all that is involved. I know what I think and what I feel and why I think it. To express this is to waste my time and other people's time. Very few people change their racial attitudes on the basis of an address regardless of how powerful it may be."[25] He wrote to a representative of Berea College in Kentucky in 1936 that "only under most exceptional circumstances do I permit myself to speak on the Negro in public address," explaining that his "major reason for doing so in addition to my inabilities is my complete lack of confidence in that kind of thing as a method for deepening interracial understanding."[26] Some Blacks were impressed that Thurman resisted the urge to speak about race before whites. In 1938, after a sermon at the University of Chicago's Rockefeller Chapel, he received a letter from a National Urban League official, William Ashby, who, after acknowledging the seriousness and ever-present reality of the race question, told Thurman: "I have observed over and over again that when our ministers are fortunate enough to appear before audiences such as was yours, they invariably seek to bring in some aspect of the race problem. Indeed, too often they go into ravings and rantings and excoriations which are very harmful." Thurman replied that "it has been a long time since I have received a letter with which I was more complete accord." He added: "My training and main interest are in the field of religion. I do not accept invitations to discuss the race question; not because I do not think that the race question needs to be discussed, but I am determined to make my contribution along the lines of my preparation and my chosen field of activity." For him to do otherwise would reduce him to a mere "propagandist."[27]

If Thurman did not want to be a propagandist, this was despite his belief, as he wrote in early 1935, that "the struggle between Negroes and white people in this country becomes more terrible every day."[28] During these years racial slights often left him in a state of furious indignation, whether directed at Jim Crow restrooms in Washington department stores or toward an insurance company physician who had subjected him to "humiliation."[29] He especially raged against the racial hypocrisies of organized Christianity. When he learned that he had been advertised as a featured speaker at the segregated Blue Ridge, North Carolina, YMCA summer conference—from which Blacks were usually barred—he denounced it as a "colossal fraud."[30] For Black speakers to appear at the conference would involve a "gratuitous compromise" and performing "unnecessary acts of spiritual degradation."[31] Although he was firmly committed to Christian interracial efforts, he acknowledged that he and his students found it at times "extremely difficult to keep up an interest on the part of our students in any religious adventure that involves American white people because of the extreme tensions that are present in our environment."[32] In early 1937 he would write a letter complaining of the "stupid white mind."[33] No doubt he was even more frank in speaking to his closest Black friends.

But Thurman did not see using his anger to provoke his listeners as part of his ministry. Black anger displayed before whites usually engendered one of two reactions, feelings of guilt or reactive anger at being called out, and Thurman thought that both emotions were unhelpful. His first task was to get a white audience to view him as a real person, and not simply as an incarnated stereotype. This he thought he accomplished in part simply by showing up. As he wrote in 1940, because he was "definitely Negroid in type," any "address that I give to a predominantly white audience has more bearing on race relations than my words."[34] His second task was to demonstrate to white audiences that the realities and ramifications of being Black in America were likely not reducible to whatever amelioration might be afforded by their understandings of the "Negro problem" and to introduce them to a deeper and broader reality. In his sermons, he wrote in 1937, his "point of interest is religion interpreted against the background of my life and the life of my group in America. I am very much interested in some of the problems that arise in the experience of people who attempt to be Christian in a society that is essentially un-Christian."[35]

All of this was intended to work toward the ultimate goal of connecting to his listeners on a personal and not conventionally political level. He wrote toward the end of his life that "in preaching the greatest source of illustration is my own life, my own reaction to something I have read, seen, or experienced. It is my witness that I must share."[36] To do this he wished to emphasize what he had in common with his audience, and how they faced the same questions, had the same doubts and weaknesses, and had similar spiritual needs. Thurman was a man of multiple identities, and the one identity he could not share with a white audience was his race. He did not wish to tell them what it meant to be Black, even if he thought it possible. He wanted to use his own life as a mirror to help his listeners better understand themselves. He had discovered that "more than campaigns or propaganda, however efficacious in creating the climate of social change, my gifts moved in the direction of the individual and what could be done by the individual in his world, in his home, on his street."[37]

And this was, for Thurman, not an avoidance of political commitments but, rather, rooting them in the deepest and most substantial part of oneself, and not as shallow or fleeting reflections of the headline causes of the moment. Thurman's own politics were clear. In a 1938 sermon he spoke of the "thousands and thousands of defenseless men, women, and children" being killed in aerial bombardments in Spain, China, and India and the lives of "sharecroppers in Mississippi and Arkansas." We think, "what a nightmare life must be for those who live always on the threshold of some thing of terror." But Thurman cautioned that "the temptation is to stop with our being outraged," and if not careful, "we will discover that in our outcry and in our anxious indignation we have merely sublimated our impulses to help," and it becomes "less and less likely that we shall go beyond outrage and beyond crying out loud."[38] "Crying out loud" was not a substitute for real politics. Thurman could not tell anyone what cause to fight for. They would have to discover their own commitments. Thurman could only aid in their process of self-discovery. At the same time, he was convinced that the examined life would necessarily remove the complacencies that most people invoked to survive and endure in a radically imperfect world and would lead to life-altering commitments to realizing a better, more just society.

One additional reason that Thurman did not emphasize race when speaking before white audiences is that he believed that a narrow focus on racial issues was counterproductive and that discussion of the betterment of the condition of Black Americans could not focus on the situation of African Americans alone and had to be considered within the context of the array of pressing economic issues that confronted all Americans in the 1930s. Thurman had been close to the Socialist Party since his Morehouse days. If by the 1930s the Party had lost much of its former influence, it retained the support of many individuals like Thurman. As Joseph Kip Kosek has written, "The Socialist Party offered a way for Christian pacifists to maintain their political and economic radicalism without having to swallow the contradictions they saw in Communism."[39] Thurman undertook an extensive study of socialism in the early 1930s, knew many active in the Socialist Party, and envied those who could be more active in Socialist Party politics than himself, writing to a white friend running for Congress as a Socialist in 1936: "I am very glad that you are carrying out your convictions relative to the way religion works in political affairs of man. I only wish that I myself were located in a community where that sort of activity would be possible for me."[40] (Washington, D.C., residents in the 1930s remained almost completely disenfranchised.) When Thurman invited Francis A. Henson, an official with both the YMCA and the Socialist Party, to speak at Howard in 1934, he encouraged him to speak on "the spiritual significance that may be found in the search for a better and more clean-smelling world."[41]

Thurman remained active as a pacifist. In 1934 he agreed to be a field representative of the Fellowship of Reconciliation (FOR) and to make appearances on its behalf.[42] An advisor to FOR, especially on racial matters, he urged the organization to be more active in the South, to go beyond anodyne appeals to racial "harmony and reconciliation" and directly engage "the Negro masses," so pacifism could lose its reputation as a "high brow" movement, irrelevant to the daily concerns of average Black people.[43] By 1935, even before Thurman went to India, his reputation as an expert on the techniques of satyagraha preceded him.[44] In the mid-1930s he was an active supporter of the Delta Cooperative Farm in Hillhouse, Mississippi, a project of the interracial Southern Tenant Farmers' Union and the Socialist Party, working closely with its promoters, Socialist Party stalwart Sherwood Eddy and Howard "Buck" Kester, a white minister who was a fearless investigator of racial incidents, and a leader of the interracial Fellowship of Southern Churchmen, another organization in which Thurman was involved.[45]

Thurman saw interracial cooperation as crucial, though he always approached questions of the economy and peace from his vantage as a Black American. He was on a first-name basis with most of the important Black leaders of the day, among them Walter White, Roy Wilkins, and his fellow Floridians James Weldon Johnson and A. Philip Randolph.[46] In 1936, at Randolph's request, Thurman presided over a Washington meeting of support for the International Brotherhood of Sleeping Car Porters, and when, in the late 1930s, Randolph was president of the left-leaning National Negro Congress, Thurman was active in that organization as well.[47] Another acquaintance was W. E. B. Du Bois, who knew Thurman well enough to invite him to participate in the Second Amenia Conference in 1933, an attempt to reorient Black politics toward economic issues. Thurman did not attend, probably because of other speaking commitments.[48] Du Bois also invited Thurman to participate in his never-to-be-published "Encyclopedia of the American Negro," an offer Thurman enthusiastically accepted, volunteering to write the article on the "Christian Religion and the Negro," promising Du Bois that his article "would not be along conventional lines but it would be genuine and authoritative."[49]

If there was one person closest to Thurman in his political views in the 1930s, it likely was his Howard colleague Ralph Bunche, whose politics at the time were socialist, with some Trotskyist leanings. Bunche did attend the Amenia Conference in 1933 and became one of the leaders of a movement of Black intellectuals who thought that traditional civil rights organizations, notably the NAACP, had spent too much time ineffectively fighting for political or legal demands, and not enough time organizing around economic issues and, in particular, fighting for the creation of a vibrant, interracial union movement, and that Black organizing solely for Black self-improvement was a dead end. Thurman's sympathies were in the same direction.[50]

In September 1934 Thurman wrote Bunche, agreeing with his lacerating attack on the early stages of Roosevelt's recovery schemes: "Just a note to thank you for the excellent analysis which you gave of the New Deal."[51] An early distrust of Roosevelt and the New Deal was very common among members of FOR; a 1932 poll indicated that only 3 percent supported FDR.[52] In 1935, Bunche would organize a conference at Howard on "The Position of the Negro in Our National Economy," and he wrote extensively on the New Deal's failures. For Bunche, it was an example of "state capitalism," an alliance of "middle-class political power and the economic power of big business" closer to fascism than socialism. Thurman likely agreed as well with Bunche that the New Deal was serving "to crystallize those abuses and oppressions which the exploited Negro citizenry of America have long suffered under laissez-faire capitalism, and for the same reasons as in the past."[53]

But over the course of the decade, Thurman (and Bunche) came to look at the achievements of the Roosevelt administration in increasingly positive terms, and his initial skepticism would later turn to something close to adulation, bolstered by a bevy of good friends working to expand government services for Blacks in New Deal agencies, among them Mary McLeod Bethune.[54] In his autobiography he wrote: "The New Deal, the dynamism of the Roosevelts, the upheaval deep within the inner processes of the federal government, gave deeper stirrings to my own mind and emotions."[55] Surely one of the proudest moments of his life occurred in May 1944, when on the eve of leaving for San Francisco, Eleanor Roosevelt was the featured speaker at a testimonial dinner in his honor.[56]

If the New Deal was one question faced by the progressive Black Left in the 1930s, another was the challenge of Communism, which experienced an unprecedented surge of popularity during the decade.[57] The active role the

Communist Party and its affiliates played in the Scottsboro case helped make the Communist cause respectable among African Americans, and support for it remained strong throughout the decade. Communists and those in the Communist circle were plentiful in Thurman's circle, from Howard colleagues such as Doxey Wilkerson, to the writer Langston Hughes, and Sue Bailey Thurman's close friend Louise Thompson.[58] Both Hughes and Thompson were participants in a famous trip to the Soviet Union by prominent African Americans in 1932, and Thompson, later Louise Thompson Patterson, became one of the most prominent Black women in the Communist Party.[59] Howard, through Sue, came to know Hughes, and he befriended Thompson as well, presiding at her mother's funeral in Harlem in 1933.[60]

Thurman, like many African Americans at the time, was fascinated by the social and economic experiment of the Soviet Union, and the (supposed) outlawing of racism and anti-Semitism within its borders. In 1934 he invited Frederick Hecker, a former Methodist minister, now a dedicated Communist, to speak at Rankin Chapel.[61] In *Religion and Communism* (1933) Hecker argued that, although there was tolerance of all religions in the Soviet Union, Communism had made older forms of religion obsolete; the future Communist society would be "the most favorable environment for the development of a spiritual culture never dreamed of by prophets, sages, or poets."[62] Thurman found Hecker's book, written by one "who comes to Communism steeped in the piety of Methodism," a "rare and scintillating" combination.[63] (Hecker's enthusiasm for the Soviet Union proved to be tragically short-lived. In April 1938, he was arrested by Stalin's secret police and murdered in a Soviet prison several months later.)[64] Thurman was hardly alone among his contemporaries in being insufficiently critical or curious about the real conditions in the Soviet Union. Mordecai Wyatt Johnson got into considerable hot water for his 1933 Howard commencement address in which he praised the Soviet Union as an alternative to the failure of traditional religion and Western political and economic institutions.[65]

Thurman's most puzzling statement on Communism in the decade—puzzling because there is nothing else in his work that resembles it—was a 1937 article in the *Richmond News-Leader* (a white newspaper) with the headline, "Claims Communism Is Help to Church." The short notice quoted Thurman as saying, "Communism, far from being a destructive element to the Christian church, is actually aiding the present day program." The article concluded that "the nationally known lecturer and preacher does not see communism as a threat but holds that: 'The reds have a very refining influence on the white and Negro church in America.' Dr. Thurman dismissed the 'Moscow scare' and seriously stated that the present program of the Communists in America should be of great value to the organized church."[66] We do not know the context for this quote, or if he was quoted accurately in the article. It is not clear to what the "Moscow scare" refers, but probably to the Great Purge, then enjoying a brief hiatus between major show trials. But if this is at all an accurate reflection of Thurman's view, it was an all-too-typical view at the time, holding that the value of the new society being wrought in the Soviet Union outweighed its rougher edges, amounting to a willed ignorance about the true nature of Stalin's regime.[67]

But as a whole, Thurman's response to the new importance of the Communist Party and Communism on the American Left was more complex than the *Richmond News-Leader* article indicates. He was alternatively wary and appreciative. If there were aspects of the Communist Party and the Soviet Union he admired, especially their commitment to social and economic justice, its supposed outlawing of racism and anti-Semitism, there were many things about Communism he actively distrusted, among them its dogmatic atheism, its dogmatism in general, and its commitment to revolutionary violence.[68] Nonetheless, in the 1930s the Communist alternative was definitely a goad to his thinking. The Communists were trying to make the world a better place; the Christians were just talking about it. Thurman in his autobiography related a conversation he had in India with the prominent Methodist bishop E. Stanley Jones, a particular bête noire. When Jones asked him if he had read his recent book, *Christ's Alternative to Communism,* Thurman told him he had made a very good case for Communism and a weak case for Christianity.[69]

Thurman's time in India intensified his socialism, pacifism, anti-imperialism, and general radicalism. In 1937 Thurman wrote to Max Yergan, the first Black American to work as a YMCA official in South Africa, who had broken very publicly with organized Christianity and moved toward an identification with Communism: "Since we saw you last, we have been to India and we have seen for ourselves. The only thing that I can say in passing is that I did not know what it was to wrestle with hate until my experiences in that country. I may add I am not thinking of anything directed at me as a person but the complete futility that is present in the mind when one sees what Imperialism truly involves."[70] Surely, an astonishing statement. How could a Black man born and raised in the maw of the harshest years of the Jim Crow South not have known what it meant to wrestle with hate before he went to India?

How can Thurman's comment to Yergan be explained? Was it, perhaps, his brief experience of "white privilege" in India, being treated as a Euro-American rather than as a native? Seeing servants "everywhere degraded" reminded Thurman "a great deal of the land of the free and the home of the brave."[71] Or perhaps it was that South Asia seemed like almost a Platonic ideal of white supremacy, where numerically insignificant numbers of foreign whites controlled a vast, dark-skinned dominion, where the gulf between the rich and poor was, possibly, vaster than anything with which he was familiar in the United States, as was the unbridgeable social gulf between the rulers and the ruled, without even a pretense of living in a society with mutual and shared obligations. The rulers and the ruled did not, for the most part, quite literally, speak the same language, nor did they practice the same religion, or have any sense of being members of a shared polity.

Thurman's time in India put him in touch with his deepest and angriest feelings about race. Writing to a correspondent in the summer of 1937, a few months after his return to the United States, he stated that he was "convinced from my experience, my reading, and my reflection, that there is a deeply lying effort on the part of the white race as a whole to hold the darker races in subjection, if not complete servitude."[72] Thurman is probably using "lying" here to mean "foundational" rather than "deceitful," but both meanings fit his purposes. There was, for Thurman, a basic dishonesty about the ways whites exercised their power to control darker-skinned peoples, a reluctance to frankly confront their own role in its preservation.

As with his domestic politics, Thurman was no doubt influenced by his Howard colleagues and the so-called "Howard school" of international relations that tied imperialism to the subjugation of darker-skinned persons. Alain Locke, Rayford Logan, Merze Tate, Ralph Bunche, and other Howard colleagues were prominent figures in this effort.[73] Bunche's fieldwork in Africa in the 1920s and early 1930s was the basis of his pathbreaking study *A World View of Race,* which identified the basis of colonialism as the unfounded belief in Black inferiority, which "furnishes a rational justification for our coveted doctrines of blind nationalism, imperialism, and the cruel exploitation of millions of our fellow-man."[74] In a 1935 article Thurman complained that the member nations of the League of Nations were practicing "virtue on helpless Liberia" by investigating allegations of slave labor conditions in its rubber plantations rather than investigating their own imperialist crimes, or discrimination within their own borders. The peace that Western nations sought was the peace "between the powerful and the powerless," giving as an example the way the United States threw its weight around in the Americas, treating other nations as so many cantankerous schoolboys needing chastisement: "If nations get too obstreperous, send in the marines."[75]

This was the hard imperialism of invasion and domination. There was also the soft imperialism of ridicule, condescension, and the deliberate dissemination of misinformation, keeping subordinate peoples shackled in ignorance and, often, reinforcing a sense of their inferiority. Thurman had railed against negative stereotypes of Blacks in the American press in the 1930s, though he and Sue were, if anything, more outraged by the treatment of American Blacks in the Indian press. Thurman, in a journal he kept during his stay in Ceylon, recorded his impressions of his first interview by the press shortly after his arrival in Asia. He knew before arriving that discussions of Indian independence were forbidden, along with anything else that might "offend the white man lest our journey be cut off before it started."[76] In his first exchange with reporters on the tour he noted that "they wanted to know about Negroes who had achieved things in life—I mentioned several but true to the mentality of the white world they did only mention Booker T & [George Washington] Carver."[77] Reporters also wanted to ask the Negro Delegation about the boxer Joe Louis, probably the African American with the greatest degree of worldwide fame at the time of Thurman's trip to India. But Howard and Sue were greatly annoyed by the efforts of the Indian press to reduce Louis to a stereotype in articles that, for example, focused on his alleged gluttony and reported that "true to his race he turns to the garish with gaudy-colored shirts, vivid neckties, and yellow colored shoes."[78] This was, Sue argued in an article published shortly after her return from India, evidence that American Negroes and the Indians alike were victims "of the most careful, astute, invidious systems of modern propaganda that modern imperialism has yet perfected. . . . It militates against us when we are in our beds asleep. The sun never sets on the end of its operations."[79] Howard wrote in 1937 that many Indian people had been "so completely victimized by anti-Negro propaganda that their minds were made up about us long before we came on the scene."[80] In partial response, Sue's Juliette Derricotte Memorial Scholarship Fund sent Black female college students to India to counteract the misinformation before the program was discontinued because of the war.[81]

After his time in India, Thurman, looked at the political situation in America with new eyes and, perhaps somewhat surprisingly, found new grounds for hope.[82] The British ruled India from the presumption of their absolute superiority to their subjects and displayed a cold stiff-upper-lip paternalism when dealing with the "lesser breeds" with a ruthless frankness that dispensed with the need for hypocrisy.[83] The British had perfected the art of ruling through dividing, using Hindu-Muslim tensions, the caste system, and the princely states to maintain control, using India's diversity to convince native Indians that they had little in common with one another. Thurman paid particular attention to the persons of mixed race who formed a distinct mulatto class and filled the lower tiers of the colonial service in India. The Anglo-Indians, often embarrassed by their native roots, generally identified with their British ancestors.[84]

American racism, by contrast, was too voluble, too violent, too consumed by its own hatreds to be in control of itself. "The brutality of the Britisher seems to me to be deliberate, mature, reflective, while the brutality of the American strikes me as being adolescent and immature," Thurman wrote. American racism was not as clever. The "one-drop rule" had the perverse consequence, from the perspective of the oppressor, of uniting all persons of African ancestry rather than dividing them by pigment and income. The failure of white Americans, during and after slavery, to promote a separate mulatto case, said Thurman, "from the point of view of white supremacy and control in America was the master blunder in strategy.[85] American Blacks might be a conquered people, but they were not, at least to the extent of the South Asians, a divided one.

On his return to the United States, Thurman worried that American racism was getting more like the British version and gaining in cunning. The white American was "rapidly becoming more mature and reflective in his brutality." The example he gave was what he thought was the growing preference for lighter-skinned Blacks over their darker brothers and sisters in mainstream culture and employment. This was one of the very few times that the jet-black Thurman spoke on this sensitive subject. Lighter skin was often a marker of class and Black respectability, and now, he felt, whites were beginning to exploit this. His worry was that the United States would, like India and South Africa, try to rule its nonwhite peoples through instituting and legalizing invidious gradations of blackness and nonwhiteness.[86] This filled him with "complete despair."[87]

Thurman called for Blacks to resist pressures to divide themselves over trivial differences. At Morehouse College in the fall of 1936, Thurman told the students that "we rise and fall by our attachment or our detachment from the masses" and urged "the college-educated group to show its solidarity with the under-privileged masses."[88] But Black unity wasn't enough. White America wasn't going anywhere. The British in India had the option of leaving and would eventually do so. Thurman once related a story of his time on an Indian railroad coach when an Indian porter, humiliated by an inadequate tip from a British colonel, threw the coin in the colonel's face. A fracas ensued, and the porter jumped off the train and ran alongside it, "pouring out expletives which I could not understand but I could feel. All the way to his destination, the colonel kept muttering to himself; the only thing that I could hear was a repetition of the phrase, 'it's time for me to retire and leave this blank country.' The force of the revolution was at work."[89]

The British could and would slink away from what they had wrought in India. But in America neither whites nor Blacks had an exit. In the United

States, the Negro, "along with the American white man, is a foreigner in a land stolen from the American Indian. They are both, the American Negro and the American white man, trying to become a nation on foreign soil." That is to say, neither whites nor Blacks could claim priority in terms of their tenure on the land, and no one had any choice but to create American society together.[90] This could be accomplished only if all Americans, of whatever race or ethnicity, recognized that they shared a country, a country that had to be organized along democratic lines "before which undemocratic practices can be condemned as antithetical and immoral." And most shared a religion, "in the light of which unbrotherly practices can be properly classified as sinful and unchristian."[91] If Thurman had his grave doubts about democracy and Christianity as it was practiced in America, the reality was that most whites and Blacks at least paid lip service to the same religious and political principles. And however hypocritically and inconsistently these principles were treated by some of those who professed them, they were a potential portal to a moral "common ground." "In America," Thurman wrote in 1934, Christianity "had its greatest opportunity since its beginning, because it started on the ground floor with one of the most audacious political experiments in the history of the world. Its present state of impotency is a [sad] commentary upon the use to which it has been put."[92]

If Thurman's views on American democracy bears a resemblance to what Gunnar Myrdal would call in his landmark study of 1944, *An American Dilemma,* the "American Creed," it probably was not an accident. Myrdal largely borrowed the idea from one of his chief research associates, Ralph Bunche.[93] But if Thurman and Bunche helped to formulate the idea of an American creed, they would not have agreed with Myrdal that "the Creed is gradually realizing itself" or that "in principle the Negro problem was settled long ago."[94] The democratic ideal, as Thurman liked to call it, was a yardstick to measure how far America had fallen short of its highest aspirations. It was not self-actualizing. Still, it was better than what India had, where there was no "Indian creed," no pretense of shared democratic principles, and where the evils of race and racial oppression were even more blatant and more intolerable than what Thurman experienced in the United States. And yet in India there was a way of trying to address these problems, which, if translated to an American context, might prove that Christianity wasn't quite yet finished as a vehicle of social and spiritual change. This was the path of radical nonviolence.

The culminating statement of Thurman's religious and political views in the 1930s was the lecture series "The Significance of Jesus," six related sermons on Jesus and Christianity, socialism and capitalism, and the theory, theology, and practice of radical nonviolence. He delivered the lectures for the Student Christian Movement of Canada at Lake Couchiching, about ninety miles north of Toronto, in September 1937. Thurman prepared the lectures carefully. After his bout of exhaustion in the fall of 1936 he promised his physician to take things easier the following summer, and he was still "having a difficult time restoring myself from last year's tremendous experience in India" the following year.[95] He did cut back on his engagements, but one he kept was the Lake Couchiching invitation. His ample time off allowed Thurman to write out the lectures in advance, contrary to his usual practice, and he wanted them to consist of "precisely what I want to say and the way I want to say it."[96] It was the first of his writings he attempted to publish as a book, and if the project was nixed by obtuse New York City editors, fortunately Thurman allowed a small mimeographed edition, distributed only to those who attended the lecture series, to be published.[97] "The Significance of Jesus" remains Thurman's fullest response to the challenge of Mahatma Gandhi.

The first lecture, "Jesus, The Man of Insight," was an expansion on his previous writings on the life of Jesus, but unlike his earlier essays on the topic, the essay was not a comparison of Jesus and Paul. Rather, it set Jesus in the context of his immediate Jewish contemporaries. Thurman's biblical scholarship is inevitably somewhat shopworn some eighty years on, but what is most important is his analysis of what he would call, in a talk the following year, "The Hope of the Disinherited."[98] For Thurman, the key fact to know about the Palestine of Jesus' day was that it was a colony, under the boot of a ruthless imperialist overlord. As he would tell the graduates of Tennessee A&I the following year, the essence of imperialism is people "being ground into so much powder."[99] The colonized were acutely aware of this and desperately wanted to avoid this fate. There was "one overmastering problem that the underprivileged always face," he told the audience in Ontario, "their attitude to their master, their oppressor."[100]

The dilemma faced by the oppressed is that, usually, there is no obvious way to end their oppression: compromise can be degrading or deracinating; overt resistance can be futile or suicidal; and muddling through just preserves the unacceptable status quo. Thurman discussed five religious factions in Palestine. There were the Sadducees, upper-class Jews, comfortable with Rome, for whom "any disturbance of the established order meant upsetting their position," persons who "loved Israel, but loved their comforts and luxuries more." Then there were the Pharisees, upholders of the law, who maintained that "if the Jews were to remain a race, they would have to protect themselves from the Hellenistic influences by which they were surrounded" by cutting themselves off, as much as possible, from the dominant Roman power, "no contact, except in the most formal matters, no respect for the Roman dog," and who "fought off every attempt at innovation." (In the light of contemporary scholarship, all very questionable assertions.)[101]

Then there were the Zealots, who believed in "violent revolt," who thought that the Romans had "built their empire on violence, bloodshed, refined brutality; and it was the only thing that they respected." The Zealots were "religious patriots who were fighting and dying for their country," who "loved liberty better than life." There were the Essenes, whom he saw, in those pre–Dead Sea Scrolls days, as peaceful, life-negating mystics, who had opted out of "problems incident to the national life of the Jew." They were escapists, "feeling perhaps, that if one withdrew from the filth and struggle and anxiety incident" to "commerce, fame, and honour," there would be, in "that act of withdrawal and consecration," a spirit released that "would shake the very foundations of that which was evil and iniquitous."[102]

And finally, there was a fifth option, the alternative of Jesus. He taught the truth that "all men are the children of God, and as such must live under his Divine scrutiny." Jesus was not just a "harmonizer" trying to be "all things to all men," trying to reconcile various factions. Instead he sought "a single purpose" that judged all people alike: "This is true of the Roman, the slave, the Pharisee, Sadducee, Zealot, Essene—all men. There is no escape." Splitting and dividing humanity into contending factions, nations, or races was an exercise in bad faith, an effort to avoid affirming the common humanity of all.[103]

Thurman's discussion of first-century Palestine did not draw explicit parallels to contemporary affairs, but it is difficult not to see the account as a parable of sorts for contemporary Black politics, which was very much at a crossroads in the late 1930s. The goal, an end to white supremacy, was agreed to by all. But the way to get there was unclear, and it was easy to make a good case that any of the proposed alternatives—seeking inclusion, seeking separation, working within the system, working to overthrow the system—were more likely to fail than succeed. The path of Jesus—a radical, encompassing, inclusivity—was no easier, but it held out the promise of a lasting solution, which the other options did not. When Thurman wrote the following year that Jesus "refused to be made into a political leader and resisted the pressure to become a merely popular Jew," he might have been thinking about his own role, and his own resistance to becoming a political leader because of, and not in spite of, the desperate need of African Americans for dramatic political change.[104]

Thurman made the scope of the political challenge clear in the next two lectures in the "Significance of Jesus" series. The second lecture, "The Temptations of Jesus," is his interpretation of the confrontation between Jesus and the devil in the wilderness.[105] Thurman's Satan is a sociologist and political scientist. The devil tells Jesus that God didn't create everything; rather, "I made the relationships between men," all of the worldly muck of structures and institutions that hold people in thrall. Thurman, as the devil's advocate, explained: "Many men have found that they were caught in a framework of relationships evil in design, and their very good deeds themselves have developed into instrumentalities for evil." Thurman cited the progressive muckraker Lincoln Steffens for the proposition that most reformers failed to realize their objectives because they focused on individuals, and individual morality, rather than on deep structural changes: "It is not enough to save the souls of men, the relationships that exist between men must be saved also."[106] That is because, as he said elsewhere in "The Significance of Jesus" series, the struggle was not against individuals, because they were "puppets in the hand of an invisible power." Eliminate one, and a replacement will quickly be found. Instead, the struggle was against "invisible powers, invisible networks, intimacies, of which the individual is but an agent."[107] To focus only on changing or saving individual souls and to concentrate on individuals was to reveal "one of the potent fallacies of Orthodox religion, namely, that the world can be made good if all the men in the world become good men—after the souls of men are saved, the society in which they function will be a good society."[108] Thurman's emphasis on self-reflection and meditation always carried a caveat—in the end, the world is not about you, or your state of spiritual knowledge or refinement. To save the relationships between people, society and its institutions must be transformed. He also took a swipe at "the basic fallacy in certain types of social radicalism" such as Marxism, criticizing the opposite position, that "after relationships between men are saved, then the individual men will become instruments of positive weal." The two processes of transformation, personal and social, must be coordinated.

In so saying, Thurman was reflecting the influence of Reinhold Niebuhr, his close friend. Niebuhr is best remembered for *Moral Man and Immoral Society* (1932), a blunderbuss he discharged at the advocates of the Social Gospel, whom he accused of naively trying to change society by converting souls and reforming morality, individual by individual, rather than taking on the task of changing society's structures as a whole.[109] Thurman agreed, writing in 1935 that "the Kingdom of God will never come by a moral appeal to people who must always live in an immoral society."[110] The two men frequently crossed paths on the Christian lecture circuit, and Thurman and "Reini" were frequent correspondents.[111] At Thurman's invitation, Niebuhr preached at both Morehouse and at Howard, where he spoke almost every year during the 1930s.[112]

Niebuhr has been criticized for the lack of urgency in his attitudes toward the civil rights movement in the 1950s.[113] Whatever the truth of this for his later career, in the 1930s his outrage at the condition of Black America helped stoke his fiery theology, and there is little doubt that his friendship with African American religious thinkers such as Thurman shaped the evolution of his thought. In 1932, the year *Moral Man and Immoral Society* appeared, Niebuhr, with Thurman giving the benediction, gave a rousing commencement address at ceremonies for Morehouse and Spelman graduates. He cautioned the graduates against "aping middle class white life," urging them to avoid "the rut of bourgeois existence." Instead the graduates needed to ask, "what can I do to emancipate my people" as their "life theme" and thereby "emancipate" themselves. But Niebuhr cautioned the graduates that this would be a fierce fight. He doubted whether "the majority group of white people will ever be unselfish" because "power makes selfishness." Indeed, "instead of the ethical idealism that most our Christian brethren have in dreaming of worlds where all men are brothers, we should have political realism, social intelligence and moral good will." Indeed, "preaching two sermons and saying nice made up phrases will not establish human brotherhood. It takes more than words. Individual man is nice and sweet in his own particular realm. But the devils of hatred, greed, and racial outrages arise from collective man. And these devils cannot be drawn out by man."[114] As Niebuhr wrote in *Moral Man and Immoral Society,* using a phrase that Thurman would soon make his own, patient negotiation from a position of inferiority was a losing strategy: "But will a disinherited group, such as the Negroes for instance, ever win full justice in society in this fashion? Will not even its most minimum demands seem exorbitant to the dominant whites[?]"[115]

Thurman and Niebuhr are often placed on different sides of the liberal Protestant divide of the middle decades of the twentieth century; Thurman was the mystic Gandhian pacifist, the loosey-goosey therapeutic seeker of "self-realization," whereas Niebuhr was the hard-edged, neo-orthodox cold warrior, expert in the varieties of human sinfulness, calling out radical evil.[116] These contrasts are overdrawn. Both men, in their own ways, were reacting against the limitations of the Social Gospel. And both men realized the need to develop novel forms of religiously based social protest that challenged and changed the basic structures of society.

Thurman knew, on a deeper level than Niebuhr, that in no arena had the Social Gospel been more limited than the status of African Americans, on which Thurman had heard a surfeit of well-intentioned, ineffectual words. What was needed was a way to harness Christianity as a spur to collective social action, to create a Christianity that wasn't interested only in saving souls or inculcating moral goodness but was also concerned with a transformation of society.[117] But for Thurman, like Niebuhr, the process began not by the writing of manifestos but by the rooting out of personal sinfulness, by living one's life constantly, self-questioningly, "under the conscious judgment of God," to "purify our hearts and live our individual lives under the divine scrutiny."[118]

The third lecture in "The Significance of Jesus" series, on "Jesus and Love," laid out Thurman's plan for social transformation.[119] For Thurman, self-love, an activity having as its purpose "the maintenance and furtherance of one's life" above all other ethical ideals, is the root of "all imperialism," "all exploitation," the "fundamental passion that urges the individual to guarantee and perpetuate himself, his family, his group or class," and the basis of private property.[120] To maximize the reach of one's self-love, and to ensure its perpetuation and continuity, one must control others. The businessman finds "that which he depends on as a guarantee of his economic survival becomes an extension of himself. It becomes his private property, and any individual who threatens to disturb his security threatens his life." Thurman gave the example of police and hired thugs in labor sit-down strikes and demonstrations. He concluded that "property becomes sacred only when it has already become private, and when property becomes sacred, personality becomes secular."[121]

For many Christians the response to the existence of private property and the disparities in wealth is to give to charity through "sharing his excess, his surplus." This is insufficient.[122] Because understanding the true love of Jesus "will lead an individual to put himself squarely against the possession of all personal property and to recognize it as a thing for evil in the world and to work in all ways for legislation and public opinion that would make private property impossible."[123] He predicted that that "time will come in society only when the security of the individual is guaranteed by all individuals" and when "certain attitudes that are now considered exceptional and belonging only to a minister's sermon would be day by day life in the world." This would be a world in which "the imperialistic will of persons" would be relaxed, and "it would not be necessary for a man to accumulate possessions."[124] Quoting one of Gandhi's favorite catchphrases, he stated that "he who has more than he needs is a thief."[125] He emphasized, however, that Gandhi was not talking about mere personal asceticism, but the elimination of the surplus consumption of society as a whole. If this ever happens, Thurman predicted that "the basic economic needs of the persons will be located in the collective will of the body politic," and our lives, grounded in acts of love, would be "a wide series of gratuitous deeds of unasked-for kindness."[126] Although he would occasionally return to this utopian vision, he would never again ground it in the elimination of private property.[127]

In the last two parts of "The Significance of Jesus," Thurman provided a schematic of the tactics needed to realize his vision of a better society.[128] He would, over the course of the late 1930s, make similar arguments in numerous sermons, laying out a three-step program of how individuals and groups could (and must) get involved in the task of social transformation.[129]

In "The Cross of Jesus," Thurman argued that no "man can live in a society of which he does not approve without some measure of compromise." The first responsibility of the good person is to reduce their area of compromise, keeping it "away from the centre of one's conviction," something a Black man navigating realities in the Jim Crow South would experience daily, such as submitting oneself to its indignities only when absolutely necessary, for example when there is no alternative to taking segregated public transportation.[130] As he would state in St. Louis a few months later, it was all too easy to "find ourselves putting the *imprimatur* of our character on the bad things that do not seem so bad." Nonetheless, "as an individual I share the guilt of my society— of my class in society. Therefore, I must exhaust all possible means, and this is important, that do not conflict with my ends, for defeating the kingdom of evil." (That is, as a pacifist, one must not employ violence or hate.)[131]

Once one makes the decision to practice active nonviolence, the first level is moral suasion, with protests that are "an attempt to awaken individuals to some kind of consciousness of what they are doing." (Like Gandhi, Thurman at this stage in his career paid little attention to the usual methods of democratic participation, such as voting, because he thought them either unavailable or unavailing.) The effectiveness of moral suasion is limited "by the amount of moral atrophy that has taken place in a man." It requires "hooks on which to hang it," and if the other party "has taken out all the screws," there is no internal conscience to latch onto. If someone becomes so confused that they are unable "to distinguish between the bad and the good," moral suasion is apt to fail.[132] As he stated in 1939, "preaching to such persons, in my opinion, is apt to be a waste of time and is a blind alley."[133] One must then ratchet up one's witness. More drastic forms of pressure might be necessary: "To wait for moral pressure to do its perfect work may be too late. The oppressed may be annihilated meanwhile."[134]

Rather than waiting for moral suasion to work, the next step was what Thurman called "shock" or the "shock method," the function of which "is to tear men free of their alignments in the kingdom of evil," freeing them by giving them "a sense of acute insecurity," through "organizing a boycott, by organizing widespread non-cooperation, by engineering non-violent strikes."[135] The shock method is necessary because those with power "do not voluntarily, my friends, relinquish their hold on their place without being uprooted," and only by trying to "tear men free from their alignments to the evil way, to free them so that they may be given an immediate sense of acute insecurity" that prompts "volcanic eruption from within."[136] Speaking in Ohio before the National Assembly of Student Christian Associations in early 1938, he stated that when this happens, "for one breathless moment or for one breathless week he becomes the brother in experience with the insecure and weak; and while he is in that condition it may be that the spirit of God can take advantage of the looseness of his situation and effect another combination before he settles down again."[137]

The shock treatment, and protests like it, were a form of coercion. On this he probably agreed with his friend Niebuhr.[138] At the least, as its very name implied, the shock method was unpleasant, something better to give than receive. But he disagreed with his friend that the difference between violent and nonviolent coercion was a relatively unimportant distinction. Nonviolent coercion can lead to lasting transformations for all involved. The victories won by violent coercion can be sustained only by the perpetual policing of the coerced. It is true that nonviolent efforts at forcing a change in the basic institutions of society were likely to be met with violence: "Resistance to any efforts pointing toward community among the masses is the inevitable reaction of the controllers of society. By threats, coercion, overt violence, depending on the desperateness of the situation, they will seek to hold the masses in a state of depersonalized individualism."[139] But advocates of nonviolence cannot respond in kind. Hate for Thurman was "a form of annihilation of self and others—in short, suicide. Violence is animal and atheistic because it denies the unity of life and defeats its maintenance and furthermore on its highest levels."[140]

If the shock method fails to achieve its intended result, and if those in power respond with violence, there is always one remaining option, the highest form of nonviolence, what Gandhi told Thurman was the practice of "self-immolation," using one's life as an ultimate witness against evil. Thurman did not think practitioners of radical nonviolence should deliberately seek out personal suffering, but neither should they try to avoid it. It is, Thurman wrote, "better to be killed than to kill," and "when society closes in on an individual and he is forced to compromise his life it is better to die."[141] When one "has exhausted all of the strategies that are permitted to me," it "becomes necessary for me to register, with all of my passionate endeavor, my complete disapproval of an evil world."[142] This was what Jesus did, "without morbidity, without a martyr-complex."[143] To take up the cause of social justice and equality without compromise was to "enter immediate candidacy for martyrdom on a cross on the hill outside the city wall."[144] Any cause worth fighting for had to be one worth dying for. This, for Thurman, was the message of the life and death of Jesus.

While heading down this path is clearly a profoundly individual choice, it cannot be taken alone. Radical nonviolence can never be the work of a single individual. Evil can only be effectively fought collectively, with comrades. It is true that, as Thurman noted, Jesus, like all of us, ultimately faced his death by himself.[145] But Jesus faced his death within the context of his followers, disciples, apostles—his small fraternity of similarly thinking individuals. Jesus needed his apostles, Thurman argued, less to perpetuate his views than to "have another-than-self reference which will be a social echo of the voice of God. Standing within this group he projects himself into a world in which the common assumptions are radically opposed to his teachings." Without a "group footing" Jesus might have been "pushed away from his moorings and destroyed."[146] Even lone martyrs need to draw on the courage and bravery of others. He told the National Assembly of Student Christian Associations in 1938 of the tasks that need to be accomplished through "a sustained relationship with an inner group of like-minded and like-dedicated people."[147] These small groups of utterly dedicated persons will be small knots of dissenters who through their moral force change the world. Thurman, a few years later, would call them "apostles of sensitiveness," the advance guard of the civil rights movement.[148]

An interesting question is the extent to which Thurman's conception of radical nonviolence drew on earlier models and theories. It is not easy to answer, because Thurman made little reference to the existing literature on nonviolence in his writings on the subject in the 1930s or thereafter, save for some general references to Gandhi. It is certainly reasonable to suppose some familiarity with earlier works, such as Richard Gregg's influential *The Power of Nonviolence* (1934), with an introduction by Thurman's mentor Rufus Jones, though there is no direct evidence of this.[149] He was a reader of the leading pacifist journal, the *World Tomorrow,* until its demise in 1934, and no doubt he read its successor journal, the *Christian Century,* and continued to read and befriend its leading lights, such as Kirby Page and Sherwood Eddy.[150] Thurman's emphasis on the importance of small groups of committed activists had echoes in the existing literature.[151] If Thurman had no single model, much of his argument would have been familiar to contemporary pacifists. What made Thurman's treatment of pacifism distinctive was his emphasis on the religious implications of the broader strategy of nonviolence rather than on the tactical details. A few months before delivering "The Significance of Jesus," he told his listeners that "happy is the man who has become the captive of a great commitment," and he advised them to select "some cause, some great purpose, identify yourself with some overwhelming need; give yourself to it in abiding enthusiasm and in complete devotion." Make it something "that looms before you as of more importance than the fact of life or death, something that becomes for you the call of God."[152]

Thurman did not tell others what cause to choose, but he left little doubt in the minds of his listeners that without the sort of dedication to a cause that he was describing, their spiritual journeys would be incomplete. Thurman had relatively little to say about race in his talks on radical nonviolence in the late 1930s. He did not ignore the topic entirely, but it was not his focus. (No doubt one reason for this was that most of the surviving versions of his talks on nonviolence were delivered before white audiences.) But whether or not he explicitly spoke of it, it was clear to all who heard Thurman speak, white or Black, that this dark-skinned man thought radical nonviolence had a part to play in changing the status of Blacks in American society.[153]

At the end of 1937, a few months after delivering "The Significance of Jesus," he was in St. Louis, giving an address before the National Methodist Student Conference.[154] His message was much the same. St. Louis was, of course, a segregated city, though the conference organizers had made an agreement with the hotel that Blacks could attend the conference but would not be allowed to eat or lodge there. Thurman was unaware of his limited access, and though, unknown to him, he had been granted a dispensation for breakfast—Jim Crow in practice was never more insidious than when it allowed temporary "exceptions"—when he tried to order lunch, he was told that he would not be served.[155] He left the premises, spent the day with a "very very terrible headache," found a Black restaurant, and then returned to the hotel to fulfill his obligations and deliver a talk on "The Sources of Power of Christian Action."[156] He started by relating the events of the day, adding: "The time will come when you are in the same position as the men who made this commitment [to exclude Blacks from eating at the hotel] on your behalf. When the time comes I want you to remember this experience."[157] At the end of the talk he took a few questions from the audience. One student asked, "How can we put moral approval on that which we know to be immoral?" Thurman's answer was blunt: "I do not know how we do it; I only know that we do." The more secure we feel, the more "we tend to be immoral and irreligious" and convince ourselves that evil "is not as bad as it seems." In the end, "I am what I do, including my reservations."[158] We are judged by our actions and not by our good intentions.[159]

When he finished his talk in St. Louis, he left the hotel, met a former student for dinner, and went to the train station. He had arranged for a berth in a Pullman car that would take him, in the morning, to Ohio for another conference. (Thurman's speaking schedules were nothing if not ambitious.) Although the train was not due to leave before midnight, Thurman was asleep in his berth by nine thirty. When the organizer of the conference wrote him to apologize for the incident, Thurman responded that the episode "dramatized all over again that in matters affecting race relations absolutely nothing can be taken for granted. It is for this reason that confidence and trust is so difficult to obtain between Negroes and white people. The framework of the relationships is so completely without high ethical quality that even the most simple ethical advances challenge the entire society."[160]

Thurman awoke, one hopes refreshed and headache-free, at Miami University in Oxford, Ohio, where he was to address the National Assembly of Student Christians. One of his addresses, "Christian, Who Calls Me Christian?," once again drew on "Significance of Jesus" material. He spoke of "the freedom of mind that comes with a great commitment." It leads to an "orderly recklessness of action" that "robs a man of the fear of death." This path is reserved, Thurman boldly states, "for fanatics," for it requires a degree of fanaticism to confront "the kingdom of evil." To be able to overcome one's doubts, hesitations, and misgivings is an infinite task, one that requires "an infinite power" to "address itself to an infinite need." But if one can feel this, perhaps, one can become, and feel oneself becoming, however briefly, "a central part of the purpose of life." And if you can't do this, and "do not know what that means, in terms of the power necessary for the transformation of life and of systems," then Thurman asks—"Christian, Who Calls Me Christian?"[161]

Thurman's talks at Miami University in Ohio were a great success. Shorty Collins, who had recruited him into the Fellowship of Reconciliation some fifteen years before and had not seen him in a number of years, saluted him: "You are one of the prophets of the day."[162] He was not alone in seeing Thurman as a prophet. Allan Hunter had plans to include Thurman in a book he was writing on contemporary Christian prophets.[163] Another acquaintance, Harold "Pete" Ingalls, also present at the Oxford, Ohio, conference, left the following reminiscence: "Oxford—the 1937 National Assembly of Student Christian Associations. Thirteen hundred of us from all over the map in hushed silence as we reached out for his words and sought contact with his soul. 'Christian, Who Calls Me Christian?' was the topic, and many of us went away wondering just why anyone should call us Christian."[164] The coming of the most violent event in human history would soon give Thurman a chance to put his vision of nonviolence to the test.

9

Footsteps of a War,
Footprints of a Dream

On 24 November 1941, Thurman wrote to a correspondent, Christine Harrington:

> It is true that we are in a terrible moment in the history of mankind but I do not think you should permit yourself to become discouraged because this is not the end of everything but it is the beginning of something new in the world. You have fortunately been born at a time when the world was experiencing great upheaval, when old things were disappearing and new things were not quite born. Such periods are dominated by pessimism and skepticism. You must know that the world is very young and that man is even younger than the world. The world is not finished completely but is in the process of being made. Nations reap what they sow even as individuals reap what they sow. Our civilization cannot go on the way it has been going: exploiting, violating values, wasting raw materials, keeping three-fourths of the mankind in economic bondage as a result—so upheaval, destruction, all these things are atonements for social, political and economic sin and injustice. Under such circumstances the innocent suffer with the guilty but so is life. The moral law of God is working itself out and the human race passing through this refining process, will be purged and purified and the dream for which we all seek shall come to pass.[1]

Thurman certainly was right about the terribleness of the moment. The day he wrote the letter was poised about midway between the Babi Yar massacre of 29–30 September 1941, when Einsatzgruppe C murdered more than thirty thousand Jews from Kiev in two days, and the Wannsee Conference of 20 January 1942, when Nazi officials approved the plans for the extermination of the remainder of European Jewry. He wrote to Harrington just two days before a Japanese carrier task force slipped its mooring in Tankan Bay, in the Kurile Islands, on a rendezvous with Pearl Harbor. As bad as things were, they were about to get far worse. When Thurman wrote Harrington that at such times, "the innocent suffer with the guilty but so is life," he wasn't being callous, just describing what happens in wartime. Innocence is trampled.

For Thurman the war's major cause was the brutality of European imperialism. He had said in June 1940, as Hitler's forces were entering Paris: "If nations for hundreds of years can build their empires out of the blood and vitality of millions of defenseless and so-called backward peoples, if they can exploit and abuse and torture human life and squander their resources until there is nothing left but a mockery of decency and self-respect—if nations can do this as they have done in Europe for several centuries and not themselves be bathed in the blood they themselves have caused to flow upon the earth, then the moral order itself is an illusion."[2] By emphasizing imperialism as the ultimate cause of the war—a very common argument at the time, especially among pacifists—he was perhaps trying to depersonalize the war, and perhaps to some extent de-Hitlerize it, make it less about the evil of one man than the evil of a system, in many countries, building for centuries, that finally had turned on itself in a bloody comeuppance.

Thurman's comment that old things "were disappearing and new things were not quite born" perhaps echoes the Italian Marxist Antonio Gramsci's famous remark in his *Prison Notebooks* that "the crisis consists precisely in the fact that the old is dying and the new cannot be born. In this interregnum a great variety of morbid symptoms appear."[3] Surely all great wars are times of interregnum, periods of unclear transition from the antebellum to the postbellum, times of "pessimism and skepticism," pregnant with topsy-turvy possibility, sometimes welcomed, sometimes feared. When Thurman wrote Harrington that the war was a "refining process," he was invoking the stern and minatory Hebrew prophet Malachi: "But who shall abide the day of his coming? . . . For he is like refiner's fire."[4] Like Malachi, like Gramsci, like Yeats writing of the "terrible beauty" of the 1916 Irish rebellion, Thurman was acquainted with the fruitful oxymorons of war and revolution. As he told Christine Harrington, this was not a time for pessimism, but for courage.

World War II began for Thurman with one of its earliest intimations. In 1935, as he was sailing toward India, his party headed toward one of the first armed conflicts arising from the long unraveling of the fragile post–World War I settlement, the Second Italo-Ethiopian War. He wrote the English pacifist Muriel

Lester in September 1935, "As you doubtless know the Mediterranean may be a war zone by the end of the month," lamenting that "we have moved few steps ahead of where we were in 1914."[5] They made a port of call in Djibouti, in French Somaliland, in early October, almost to the day when troops massed in neighboring Italian Somaliland (now largely in Eritrea), invaded Ethiopia.[6]

Thurman's acute sense of the connection between the war crisis and imperialism was one widely shared by many African Americans. In July 1937, Juanita Harris, a Howard undergraduate, wrote Thurman about the recent outbreak of hostilities between Japan and China and said that she would be glad to see Japan conquer China, because "if she does not the white man will," and Japan had "foresight enough" to play the white man's game, and as a "Negro she wanted to see the darker Races become as strong as possible." Thurman responded that he was "inclined to agree with your position relative to Japan," though he added that he was opposed to imperialism "whether the imperialist be Black, yellow, white, or any other color," and that the facts of the invasion indicated that Japan's attack was an act of imperialist aggression. Nonetheless, his "sympathy is with China, while my pride is with Japan," although "as a pacifist, I am opposed to the whole sordid struggle that is going between China and Japan."[7]

Thurman's somewhat fancy footwork on display in his answer to Juanita Harris is indicative of a larger problem for Thurman and for the pacifist ideal in general in the late 1930s. What had seemed obvious almost beyond the need for justification in the early 1920s—that all wars and all violence are evil, and all combatants share equally the responsibility for the moral stench of warfare—seemed a lot less obvious in the late 1930s, in Asia, and especially with the rise of Adolf Hitler. As another world war seemed ever-likelier, the pacifist cause was unable to staunch the flow of defectors from its ranks, and even some of the most dedicated pacifists wondered how to respond to a murderous tyranny, seemingly oblivious to all of the tools of radical nonviolence. It was a time that the historian Joseph Kip Kosek called the "dark night of the pacifist soul."[8]

It is not easy tracing the precise evolution of Thurman's thought on the war in the late 1930s and early 1940s because of his usual hesitance to speak in public or write at length or in depth about current political developments. But when, in the fall of 1940, he agreed to become one of three executive vice chairmen of the Fellowship of Reconciliation (FOR), the most significant political commitment of his entire career, he was presumably in general agreement with its antiwar stance.[9] The previous fall FOR had issued a pamphlet by Thurman's colleague Kirby Page, *How to Keep America out of War.* The pamphlet contained the following Q&A:[10]

Should not the United States help the other democracies to destroy the totalitarian dictatorships?

This is not a war between democracy and totalitarianism, but a death grapple between rival imperialisms, with oppressor arrayed against oppressor. Hitler caused the war but the allies caused Hitler.

Other pacifist friends of Thurman active in FOR expressed similar sentiments in more strident language. "If I can't love Hitler, I can't love at all," said A. J. Muste in the summer of 1940 (a statement, writes Kosek, of either "pure saintliness or pure foolishness"). John Haynes Holmes, who equated "Nazi barbarism" with "British-American imperialism," thought that a victory for either side would be a disaster.[11]

A March 1939 letter by Allan H. Hunter, an uncompromising pacifist, gives some secondhand evidence of Thurman's views as the European war crisis moved toward its climax. Hunter recalled a recent occasion when Thurman had been preaching in Hunter's Los Angeles church: "Often we recall what you said to Connie, the girl engaged to a communist who kept pushing you after church in the manse on the issue of what a Jew should do about the Nazis. What you suggested there,—that one can somehow maintain one's spirit on the third level of refusing to hate,—lingers with us."[12] The meaning of the "third level" is not clear, but it perhaps is the third stage of nonviolent resistance, self-sacrifice. If Thurman was giving this sort of advice to Jews confronting the Nazis—his response to Hunter is not extant—it echoes Gandhi's very controversial advice to German Jews after the November 1938 Kristallnacht pogrom, that "suffering undergone voluntarily will bring . . . an inner strength and joy."[13] Faisal Devji has argued that Gandhi's understanding of Nazism was not naïve but, rather, reflected his utterly unsentimental understanding of nonviolence; sometimes many will have to die to uphold the principle of life, and in the broader cosmic and karmic balance, weighed out over many generations, there is no such thing as fruitless or wasted self-sacrifice for nonviolence.[14] Perhaps Thurman felt somewhat similarly, but I would like to think that Thurman's conception of nonviolence, rooted in the gritty African American realities of slavery, night riding, and lynching, was too concerned with the importance of "survival" to countenance something so extravagantly suicidal as Gandhi's advice.

One of Thurman's clearest statements of his pacifist convictions, early in the conflict, was a February 1940 sermon in Syracuse, New York, on "The Quest for Peace," delivered at a time when the "world was rolling in darkness." It appeared that world events were making the case that violence works, is "very efficient" and "very effective," and that the best response to violence is counterviolence, and the best response to the enemy's hatred was hating the enemy back. This was an ancient belief: "Civilization after civilization, groups after groups, individuals after individuals have tried to thro all the long weary centuries to bring about peace by inspiring hatred . . . it cannot be done." The "inner relentless logic of social behavior organized as it is can lead to only one place and that is to death and more death and more deadly death." While the options of those who believe in peace were "very few," one must choose those things for which "I shall stand and those things against which I shall struggle with all of my passion and endeavor." And one must choose life, and shun death, quoting Edna St. Vincent Millay's poem "Conscientious Objector": "I shall die but that is all I shall do for death / I am not on death's payroll." "Are you," he asked his audience, "are you?"[15]

However, as Thurman would write a few years later, in July 1944: "I am a Pacifist, but I am also a human being. I am not an absolutist because I do not have the wisdom to be that."[16] His was not a pacifism that treated non-pacifists as warmongers or thought that pacifism held all the answers to the world's problems. Thurman remained friends with many who left the pacifist fold, such as the Smith College chaplain Ralph Harlow. When Harlow heard a FOR leader state that it didn't matter whether Britain or Germany won the war, he "recognized then that I was not a pacifist any longer. For me it *did* matter, very much."[17] Others such as Herbert King or Benjamin Mays had never been active in the pacifist movement.[18] Thurman also remained on good terms with Reinhold Niebuhr, subsequent to his very public abandonment of pacifism and his becoming, in these years, one of the country's most prominent voices for military intervention. After Niebuhr's visit to Howard University in early 1941, Thurman asked Niebuhr to write an article on "the balance sheet of democracy" for the *Journal of Negro Education,* saying that he was "the best man to do [this] particular thing," knowing that he would call for support of Britain's war effort.[19]

Thurman's pacifism was predicated on the rights and prerogatives of the individual conscience. He strongly supported the right of draft-eligible men not to participate in the war if it violated their deepest beliefs. Although Thurman generally kept his distance from Black denominational affairs, he worked closely with the National Baptist Convention in 1940, encouraging them to officially support conscientious-objector status, a matter Thurman thought of "transcendent importance."[20] He himself, in his early forties, became eligible for the draft during the war, and he quietly registered as a conscientious objector rather than taking the ministerial deferment available to him.[21] He worked closely with conscientious objectors, such as his protégé James Farmer and other young Black peace activists, including William

Worthy (later a well-known and controversial journalist) and Bill Sutherland (later a leader in the fight against South African apartheid in the United States and in Africa). Sutherland wrote Thurman in 1941, reminding him "of a night long ago at Bates College, when I kept you up until one o'clock philosophizing and such." Sutherland was writing Thurman for advice on whether to be imprisoned rather than register for the draft. He did not register and spent four years in federal penitentiaries.[22]

Thurman's brand of pacifism reflected his own personality and his disinclination to be provocative for the sake of provocation. It also reflected his keen sense that Black Americans faced a different reality than white Americans. If Thurman insisted on the rights of would-be conscientious objectors, he was equally vehement in defending the rights of Black soldiers who either wanted to serve or were drafted into the service. Thurman made this clear in his letter to A. J. Muste on 16 September 1940, in which he agreed to serve as vice chairman of the Fellowship of Reconciliation. Weighing heavily on Thurman was the passage, four days earlier, of the Selective Service Act of 1940, which instituted the first peacetime draft in American history, requiring all men aged twenty-one to thirty-six to register for the draft. Thurman had been worried about this possibility for months and was distraught that, despite the continuing protests of civil rights organizations, Black men would be drafted into a segregated, Jim Crow military. Besides accepting the position with FOR, he also wrote to Muste:

> The crisis that is upon us simply deepens my responsibilities here in the university and elsewhere. Negro men and women need so much more counseling during these times than ordinarily. The complications of our social order make it very difficult to keep clear of critical conflicts. For instance, I am sure that the thousands of Negro men who will be taken into camp should not be deserted by other Negroes like me. Often our very presence will stay the hands of brutality and cruelty on the part of white men who are in positions of authority over them and whose normally weak scruples as to treatment are almost thoroughly routed by the customary moral disintegration opened by war. And yet I know that war is not only futile but is thoroughly and completely evil and diabolical. What my duty is as a Christian is sometimes very obscure.[23]

Thurman told Muste, using a military term, that he would not "desert" Black men in the military. This meant that he would not criticize either their decision to enlist or accept their draft status. And it further meant that he would not, except in the most general way, criticize the war effort. (How could you effectively counsel persons who knew that you thought their war service was abetting evil?) As much as a pacifist could, Thurman supported the war, doing everything in his power to support Blacks in the military. Given the general mobilization, this had suddenly become a key civil rights issue.[24]

Throughout the war, as he wrote in his annual report at Howard in June 1943: "My correspondence with men in the camps is voluminous. I have tried to maintain personal contact with all of the fellows who advised me as to their mailing address."[25] To one former student, the first Black chaplain in the navy, Thurman praised the trailblazing "magnificent job" that he was doing, confident that he was setting a standard that many would emulate.[26] To M. C. Merriweather, another former student, chaplain, and the only commissioned African American officer in his segregated unit, the 366th Infantry Regiment, Thurman wrote in early 1943 of his "unique responsibility," expressing hope that he would be able help Black soldiers to "go through this experience without complete moral and spiritual bankruptcy."[27] Two years later, Merriweather and his regiment had been posted overseas and had seen combat in North Africa and Italy. By January 1945 the regiment now had a number of Black officers, many of them from Howard. "You can never know the extent to which you have influenced the thinking of the men who know you and have heard you speak," Merriweather wrote to Thurman, "and the esteem in which you are held by them."[28]

In addition to keeping up the spirits of his former students serving in various capacities in the military, he defended the achievements of Black soldiers to skeptical whites. To a correspondent in April 1942 who had questioned African American military valor, Thurman wrote, "I regret it is necessary for me to categorically deny the statement of your friend, relative to the emotional stability of Negro men under fire at the front," informing her as well about the prevalence of commissioned and noncommissioned officers in the army and saying in closing: "Little by little, the significance of Negroes for the armed forces on sea, in the air and on land is being realized, and I dare say before the war is over they will be in all of the armed forces. It is the only democratic thing to do."[29] In 1943 he praised the work of a white woman in Kansas who started a USO post for Black soldiers, writing, "You are working away to make a breathing space possible for soldiers who have no power at the moment to help themselves," and adding, "Even now we can win the military victory on the battlefield of the world, and lose the war at home."[30]

Thurman's ambivalences about the war were fully on display in one of the most unusual and seemingly anomalous publications in Thurman's entire output, the April 1940 lecture "A 'Native Son' Speaks."[31] Delivered before the Chicago Roundtable of the National Conference of Christians and Jews, it was an overtly political and sociological lecture on a racial topic, with religion playing a relatively small role in the contents. It appeared, obscurely, in the *Advocate,* a Chicago Jewish weekly newspaper, and was never republished by Thurman. I do not know why Thurman chose this audience to break his long-standing rule against speaking on race and politics before white audiences, but he did, with the urgency of the times perhaps being a motivation. The oddity of the essay begins with its published title, which was definitely not Thurman's—he had called his lecture "The Negro in the City." If there is something grotesque in linking the self-possessed, hyperarticulate Thurman with Bigger Thomas, the brooding, mumbling antihero of Richard Wright's *Native Son,* recently published to much mainstream acclaim, perhaps there was something in the essay, with its invocation of Black urban rage, that frightened the editors of the *Advocate.*[32] But the essay as a whole was hopeful, discussing unfinished business from the last war and setting a possible social agenda for the war and postwar likely to come.

The essay stated its main point early on: "The fundamental thesis of my paper is that the Negro in the northern city is not a citizen and his position is a perpetual threat and constant disgrace to democracy. Responsibility for this rests on the shoulders of those who control schools, churches, and the state."[33] (Thurman was speaking in a northern city, and perhaps the proposition that Blacks in the South were not citizens was too obvious to require stating.) Although in the South Blacks were "always a victim," in the North Blacks suffered from a lack of a sense of place and community, and their lives were uprooted" and "depersonalized." In northern cities the newest European immigrants soon learned even before they learned English that they had a higher social standing than local Blacks. Christianity utterly failed Black migrants, whether it was established Black churches in the North snobbishly excluding southern newcomers or white Christians discovering that they were "much more kindly disposed to the Negro while he lived in the south than [they were] toward him as a neighbor in the north. It was eas[ier] to love the Negro at a distance than to welcome him as a brother."[34]

There had been one recent exception to this. During the previous war "the Negro became aware to some degree of his citizenship." Those running the nation realized they needed Black support for the war effort, both from Black soldiers and civilians. For one "breathless, swirling moment" the Negro was meant to feel "that he counted—that the future of democracy was dependent upon him" and he became "conscious of being part and parcel of the very core of the nation."[35] (As we have seen, those who felt this way included the young Thurman, who spent the summer of 1918 tenting on the campgrounds of Howard University in concert with other young Black prospective officers.)

None of this availed Thurman or the other Blacks who served or thought of serving, since when the war ended, white America "sought to place the Negro back in his anonymity" with the deadly riots of the Red Summer of 1919. But Blacks fought back. "This rioting was a sign of life, of an awakening citizenship"—an unusual statement from a pacifist. In a striking metaphor, he compared this to an account he read of an unorthodox Canadian physician who supposedly enjoyed success in manipulating unresponsive limbs back to life and feeling. Thurman quoted the father of a young patient: "When our daughter first came, the doctor could do anything to her foot and she would not feel it, so today when I heard her scream, I said, thank God, life is in the foot at last."[36] Pain, rage, anger were all signs of Black life. Thurman understood Black rage. Speaking of the hatreds of the oppressed a few months earlier, he stated that "hate is often a profoundly significant weapon of individuals who are weak, for groups that are weak, when individuals and groups find themselves caught or trapped by . . . power or injustice, hate often crystallizes personally and makes possible . . . defiance to be flung at the people which would destroy the final spasm of human spirit."[37]

But if Thurman empathized with Black rage, he did not think it productive, individually or collectively. In the last paragraph of "A 'Native Son' Speaks," Thurman briefly outlined a way forward to remove Blacks from the "periphery of national life" and confer on them "persona or personhood." One way to achieve this was by the creation of interracial labor unions, "churches, schools, governing boards of all kinds." Left unstated in the short essay was whether 1940 and the years ahead would be years of moving toward effective Black citizenship or a return to the howls of Black rage. Thurman would continue to be outspoken. As he wrote the following March to Marshall Talley, a leading figure in the National Baptist Convention: "We must keep on working, and must keep on blasting. In my opinion we have compromised and soft-pedalled so long that the truth always seems radical and terrifying."[38]

And then, after two years on the sidelines, America entered the war. For Thurman the war, he wrote in 1945, was "total, devastating, terrifying," when "whole wide world is as midnight," a global silence of "desolation, plague, and hunger" broken only by the "Frankensteinian wail of [dive] bombers."[39] Even on the home front in the United States, far from any active war theater, Thurman found the impact to be overwhelming, and in its own way, just as terrifying. The war was ubiquitous, inescapable, and omnipresent. The actual coming of the war only heightened Thurman's ambivalence. The positive side of the war was the excitement of living in the midst of people whipped into a state of temporary unity. He told an audience at Morehouse in 1942 (with the teenage Martin Luther King, Jr., almost certainly in the audience) that despite the insistence of the American Red Cross to store "white blood" and "Black blood" separately, "all life is one" and that the current crisis was in part caused by the fact that "we have stubbornly constructed political units, little political worlds, islands . . . at the expense of the personal organismic union that guarantees the significance of life."[40] The quest for organismic union was reaching into and reshaping every aspect of public and private life, from where people lived and worked to how people slept—as Thurman noted, the United States was on permanent daylight savings time, commonly called "wartime"—for the duration.[41] "It is a simple observation that conditions of total war cause a profoundly radical shift in the generally prevailing culture pattern."[42]

For those, like Thurman, who had been waiting for such a "profound radical shift" in the "culture pattern" his entire life, he would take it, despite its martial auspices. "The state [has] taken over," Thurman wrote in early 1945, and Americans are now "state centered." Indeed, "all national life is now increasingly organized around the achieving of a vast national objective—victory for the United Nations [that is, the Allied Powers]. Almost every detail of the common life is affected."[43] The war, as Thurman noted, led to a vast increase in the size, scope, and superintending powers of the federal government, with the national debt increasing fivefold, to $250 billion during the war years.[44] Pacifists usually oppose big central governments, especially their propensity to engorge and enlarge themselves during wartime—as Randolph Bourne had famously said, "War is the health of the State."[45] But for African Americans, so long at the mercy of racist state and local governments, a large, intrusive national government was a necessary, if by no means sufficient, condition for the fight for racial equality.

One consequence of the war, Thurman argued, was that "the deadly monotony of ordinary living is blasted out of the doldrums." This spoke to a deep psychological need: "We want to feel that we are engaged in a total enterprise that is meaningful. There must be a sense of something at stake in the day's experience." If not, "life grows dingy on our sleeve."[46] This, Thurman argued, is why people find war or its aura so attractive (so long as they are not on its receiving end): "It is not because there is no memory of what war has cost the human race, it is not because men are deceived into thinking that war is a lark, a holiday—men know that war is a cruel, evil, nasty, business. But when war comes, something is at last at stake in the day's living."[47] The home front was transformed: "It becomes critically important what everybody does. No one is exempt. Everybody and everything counts." It was true that "one of the most tragic commentaries on modern life" was that people "often need war to rouse them into a sense of action and importance."[48] People can be roused by evil causes: "Hitler has succeeded in making a great part of the German people understand what commitment to a cause is."[49] But, Thurman argued, the German example showed that if there are not good causes, people will dedicate themselves to bad ones: "Can the human race afford to feel enthusiasm, readiness to die, to sacrifice personal aims for a cause that is not the highest possible?"[50]

Thurman was one of a long line of antimilitarists and pacifists who found that there was something similar in the commitment of a radical pacifist and the life or death vows of a soldier.[51] America during the war was a fruitful place for making commitments, thought Thurman: "Something is in the air—things are happening. . . . Something is at stake! A new kind of civic responsibility appears sired by new and awful responsibilities." One type of commitment mattered to Thurman above all others: "The ordinary individual counts in a strange new way. His country cares about what he does—all secondary and tertiary citizens become citizens first class."[52] The war, he wrote in "The Will to Segregation" (1943), has "caused the average Negro to become aware of counting civically in a new way."[53] But if Uncle Sam wanted Black bodies, it was not clear if this new bestowal of citizenship was transactional and temporary, merely for the duration of the war, or something more lasting. One reason why it was so important for Thurman to keep up correspondence with Howard students in uniform was that most of them were unable to resolve the contradictions of fighting and dying for a country whose "ideals . . . to them are either unreal or hypocritical."[54] Although the war was being touted as a war for democracy, Thurman felt that the democratic ideals of the Allies, and the support of them, were largely a chimera. A particular bête noire was the Atlantic Charter, agreed to in August 1941 by President Roosevelt and Prime Minister Churchill, a statement, issued six months before America entered the war, that was already looking forward to the postwar world. It was filled with high-minded statements such as promising to "respect the rights of all peoples to choose the form of government under which they live."[55] But these promises were largely empty. Churchill soon made it clear that this did not apply to British colonies, and especially to India, and the United States, albeit reluctantly, did not challenge Churchill's presumption.[56] If the independence movement in India can be quashed, he argued, "then freedom of men everywhere can be throttled."[57]

Neither did the Atlantic Charter address the meaning of democracy in the United States. "Mere slogans are completely meaningless," Thurman wrote.[58]

Indeed, if Thurman hoped that the war would somehow improve the condition of racial minorities, the available evidence indicated that the reverse was happening. Thurman suggested that part of the problem was that advances toward racial equality were often hesitant and halting, but its opposition was adamant and determined. It took the threat of a massive march on Washington by A. Philip Randolph to get the Roosevelt administration to agree, in July 1941, to establish the Fair Employment Practices Commission to investigate discriminatory practices among defense contractors, but its enforcement powers were weak, and discrimination remained widespread. This did not prevent African Americans from starting to work for defense contractors in ever-larger numbers. From 1943 to 1945 their percentage increased from 3 percent to 8 percent of the defense workforce, and the number of Blacks working for the federal government tripled.[59] But as Blacks moved en masse for war work in Detroit, San Francisco, and elsewhere, they often found only inadequate housing and other social services, along with white hostility and flaring tensions. In the single year of 1943, forty-seven cities recorded 242 violent interracial incidents, large and small, from pushing episodes on busses and streetcars, to massive rioting and loss of life in Harlem and Detroit in the summer of 1943.[60] And beyond actual incidents, there was growing white fear of Black restlessness. Thurman would write about the wartime rumors of so-called "Eleanor Clubs," organized by Black maids against their white employers, the fear of what he described as "secret revolutionary organizations of Negroes, sponsored by Mrs. Roosevelt."[61] In 1943 he wrote that for many whites, after Pearl Harbor, the fact that Japan's "'daring' to attack a white race," was an excuse to release "the expression of the prejudices against nonwhite peoples just under the surface of the American consciousness."[62] To a correspondent in the fall of 1942, he confided: "Grave indeed, is my concern as I watch the mounting tension all over the country. I have traveled some thirteen or fourteen thousand miles since early June, and the picture is the same everywhere—sporadic outbursts of violence, meanness, murder, bloodshed, and a great paralysis in the presence of it all."[63]

But rather than paralysis, Thurman the pacifist who found the war both dreadful and inspiring, the racial optimist grown weary of empty talk of "democracy," made a commitment that reflected his spiritual values, a leap of faith, one that had very real practical consequences for himself and his family. They would join the tens of millions of Americans uprooted during wartime. He decided in the midst of the war and in many ways because of the war, to become copastor of a tiny, fledgling interracial church in San Francisco, a move he always referred to as his "bold adventure." In every person's life, he would say in 1957, there is a "great moment" when one's life "is exposed to confirmation, to validation, to a radical demand. One does not ever quite know when such a moment emerges."[64] In the fall of 1943, Thurman's "great moment" arrived.[65]

In February 1936 the Negro Delegation was in Peshawar in February 1936, then in British India, now in Pakistan, then and now on the border with Afghanistan. They were spending a morning of sightseeing, going to the nearby Khyber Pass, the fabled crossing in the rugged Hindu Kush mountains, a passageway between Afghanistan and South Asia.[66] The Khyber Pass was a place where the veneer of British imperialism was thin, and the layers of Indian history were deep:[67] "We stood looking at a distance into Afghanistan, while to our right, and close at hand, passed a camel train bringing goods and ideas to the bazaars of North India. Here was the gateway through which Roman[68] and Mogul conquerors had come bringing with them goods, new concepts, and the violence of armed might. All that we had seen and felt in India seemed to be brought miraculously into focus."[69] What Thurman called his "moment of vision" at the Khyber Pass (and what has come to be called the "Khyber Pass epiphany") was an example of his affirmation mysticism, a moment of utter clarity that propelled Thurman not into reverie but to action in the real world.[70]

Thurman glimpsed at the Khyber Pass what he found most vital in India: a gateway to the country's multiethnic and multireligious character, without (the temporary overlordship of the British aside) a single, dominant ethnicity, religion, or even skin color, with all of the (usually) fruitful tensions and harmonies this brings: "We saw clearly what we must do somehow when we returned to America. We knew that we must test whether a religious fellowship could be developed in America that was capable of cutting across all racial barriers, with a carry-over into the common life, a fellowship that would alter the behavior patterns of those involved."[71] This would be an "intercredal, interracial, and intercultural" church, one that would at once celebrate difference, while through a "deepening of an experience of the living God" render those differences ultimately "superficial and trivial" and pioneer a new way of living together.[72]

If the setting for the Khyber Pass epiphany was as exotic and romantic as any Hollywood fantasy-adventure, its inspiration was far closer to home, an account of a new church in Philadelphia. Thurman had read an article while touring India, about an interracial church service in Philadelphia, the Fellowship Church. It sparked his imagination.[73] The first meeting had been held in October 1935, with Mordecai Wyatt Johnson as the featured speaker.[74] On his return to the United States, teaching at a segregated university in a segregated city, it was difficult for him to find ways to realize his vision and try to "find out if experiences of spiritual unity among people could be more compelling than the experiences that divide them."[75] But even at Howard University, Thurman thought there were ways to create religious services where spiritual unities outweighed intellectual or credal differences, such as meditation or dance services, in an effort to jar loose dogmatic religious sensibilities and open them to new possibilities.[76]

But in the end, the only effective way to create interracial worship was to create new institutions not defined or limited by mainstream American Christianity, in which every congregation was, by common stipulation, either "white," or "Black" (or otherwise "nonwhite"). Thurman evidently tried to find or create a situation in which founding an interracial congregation would be possible in some large eastern city.[77] Nothing came of these efforts. The leading figure behind the Fellowship Church in Philadelphia that had so impressed Thurman was Marjorie Penney, a secretary of the American Friends Service Committee.[78] Thurman had just returned to the United States from India when, in April 1936, he received a letter from Penney and her "Young People's Interracial Fellowship" inviting Thurman to be a guest preacher the following year. Attendance at the early meetings of the church averaged about six hundred (80 percent African American).[79] Thurman, in response, wrote Penney, "Is it not interesting that a Christian church of this type is not a monstrosity?"[80] Thurman probably first spoke at the church in 1938; he would do so again in 1940 and 1942.[81]

Thurman's only problem with the Fellowship Church of Philadelphia was that it wasn't really a church. It was more of a floating, interracially themed religious meeting held on every third Sunday of the month, not always in the same location, not a genuine congregation or religious community. Nonetheless, his appearances at the Philadelphia church services gave him ideas. Marjorie Penney wrote him in October 1942: "Believe me, if and when the Fellowship Church becomes more than a series of services, we shall be seriously thinking of what you said regarding your interest it."[82] Fellowship House, which opened in Philadelphia in 1941, wasn't quite a church either— it was more like a civil rights–oriented settlement house—but it gave Penney's idea more institutional permanence. It attracted some big names. In 1945, Frank Sinatra, skinny and ardently liberal, spoke there, telling the audience: "I don't want my children to grow up in a world in which hate against people of other races and creeds exists."[83] Even more epochally, in the spring of 1950, when a second-year student at nearby Crozer Seminary attended a meeting at Fellowship House, with a lecture by Mordecai Wyatt Johnson, it marked the first time that Martin Luther King, Jr., remembered being exposed to the teachings of Gandhi and the principles of satyagraha.[84]

Fellowship Church and Fellowship House in Philadelphia were among the first manifestations of what would be a small but gathering trend in the late 1930s and 1940s, the intentionally interracial church. From the earliest days of African American Christianity, Blacks and whites often worshipped together, although, as had been the case for Thurman's grandmother Nancy Ambrose, often as slave and slave master.[85] Emancipation largely, though not entirely, sundered interracial worship.[86] Thurman had respect for denominations that maintained interracial worship. They were often on the far fringe of respectability, such as the Pentecostal, Holiness, and Adventist sects that were more interested in spreading salvation to all comers than in maintaining the social and racial proprieties. Thurman was not always an admirer of the Roman Catholic Church, and like many liberal Protestants, he sometimes worried about its hierarchical structures, and he could on occasion claim that it "is in some rather significant ways authoritarian."[87] Nonetheless he admired its pretension and at times its practice of treating Christianity as a universal apostolic faith.[88] Thurman found that "much may be learned from such religious groups as Jehovah's Witnesses, the Seventh-Day Adventists, the Salvation Army, or even the Roman Catholic Church" in comparison to mainstream Protestantism in their openness to racial minorities, but this was racial openness and interracialism largely by inadvertence and married to dogmatic Christianities that he found unacceptable.[89]

Conscious interracialism in American Christianity did not really get under way until after World War I. In the early 1920s the Federal Council of Churches started to promote "Race Relations Sundays," generally advocating a wan and unenergetic interracialism, which largely consisted of pulpit exchanges and general exhortations to racial benevolence.[90] Like the southern Council on Interracial Cooperation, founded in 1919, which helped popularize the term "interracial," all too often Christian interracialism promoted a brand of racial cooperation that fell short of a direct challenge to segregation. As Marion Cuthbert argued in 1933, "for some people the inter-racial experience has become one so inept, so futile, and so sentimental that they have become nauseated."[91] If Thurman was not nauseated by it, he was often leery of interracialism's pretensions. In contrast to church groups "trying by slow processes of education and cultivation to bring about reconciliation and harmony," the time was ripe, he wrote in 1936, for an interracialism with more "guts."[92]

There were a few examples of intentional interracial churches dating back to the 1920s.[93] But it was not until the war years that the idea of interracial church gathered strength and moved beyond its somewhat tentative embrace of genuine equality. Some, like the Fellowship Church in Philadelphia and the Fellowship Church (Interracial) in Pasadena, California, used the term "church" rather loosely to describe a monthly interracial meeting.[94] Other churches were genuine congregations, such as the short-lived Congregation of His People, organized in Detroit in 1942 and close to the Communist Party, which advertised itself as an "inter-racial congregation" dedicated to the elimination of the "the evils of racism, anti-Semitism, [and] oppression," and uniting "the peoples of the world,"[95] or the All Peoples Christian Church in Los Angeles.[96]

The interracial church movement was furthered by the development of a smattering of interracial Gandhian cooperatives during the war years. Gandhi had told Thurman that the ultimate goal of ahimsa is that "your life must be a living sermon."[97] For many Gandhian acolytes, the only real way to demonstrate a commitment to interracialism was by living an interracial life. These small, ephemeral interracial urban communes—or, as they were often called with a nod to Gandhi's living arrangements, ashrams—were located in Black neighborhoods, catalyzed in part by the wartime housing shortage, and spoke to the need to merge the personal, the spiritual, and the political. The best-known example was the Harlem Ashram, founded in 1940 by the white Christian pacifist Jay Holmes Smith. Its members lived simply and collectively and dedicated themselves to their spiritual callings and to assisting the local Black and Puerto Rican communities.[98] James Farmer lived there briefly, not caring for either the food or its general asceticism. (Its meals, he complained, were "an inducement for fasting.")[99] There was a Newark Ashram in existence from 1940 to 1943, whose members, before both were incarcerated for draft resistance, included Dave Dellinger, later a prominent opponent of the war in Vietnam, and the African American pacifist Bill Sutherland, a Thurman protégé.[100] And when a group of women formed an urban pacifist commune in San Francisco in 1943, they put into motion a chain of events that would have a decisive influence on Thurman's life.

Meanwhile, Thurman was doing what he could to further the interests of FOR, and as its highest-ranking Black official, he was often called upon for African American troubleshooting. In March 1941 A. J. Muste asked Thurman to go to Detroit, to see if he could soothe tensions between Blacks and whites during a UAW (United Auto Workers) organizing campaign at a Ford plant, worried that "there is going to be terrible trouble if the situation gets out of hand" (which is what happened, culminating in June 1943 in Detroit's sanguinary anti-Black pogrom). Thurman wrote Muste that Blacks "have been exploited in so many ways that it is hard for them to believe in anybody under any circumstances. Least of all, any group bearing a union label." He nonetheless agreed to consult with FOR representatives in Detroit on an upcoming visit.[101] In February 1943 Muste wanted Thurman to make an appearance at a FOR event at a Harlem church: "I don't want to make myself an absolute pest, but that is what you get for being Howard Thurman," he wrote, adding that Thurman would be "indispensable for the meeting."[102]

Probably Thurman's greatest service to FOR during the war years was his recommendation in December 1939 that it hire James Farmer as a field operative concentrating on civil rights and African American matters. Farmer was hired by the Fellowship as a part-time organizer shortly thereafter and joined full-time after graduating from Howard in 1941. On the national staff of FOR, Farmer agitated for the Fellowship to create a civil rights program. An article, "The Race Logic of Pacifism," published in the FOR journal in February 1942, argued that the war had exacerbated racial tensions and that African Americans were "increasingly outraged" and "more actively indignant" about their circumstances. He used Thurmanesque language to argue that pacifists should refuse "to participate in, and cooperate with, all those social practices which wreak havoc with personality and despoil the human community."[103] "I think it is a very good thing," Thurman wrote to longtime FOR official John Swomley in 1941, "to have Jimmie Farmer working as [race] relation secretary."[104]

Farmer was one of a growing number of pacifists who thought that in the midst of a generally popular war, pacifists, without dropping their witness against war, could most effectively demonstrate the relevance and efficacy of nonviolence by directing it against the violence of segregation. In Chicago, in May 1942, Farmer and a small group of like-minded pacifists organized one of the first civil rights sit-in demonstrations, when twenty-eight persons, in small interracial groups, occupied all the available seats in Jack Spratt's Restaurant. The manager called the police, and when the police came and told the manager that those participating in the sit-in were not breaking any law, the protestors were victorious. This was one of the first actions of the Committee (later the Congress) of Racial Equality, better known as CORE, the first organization to wed the tactics of Gandhian nonviolence to the fight against Jim Crow.[105] Although CORE started as a project of FOR, it soon became independent. Some in FOR were leery of even the hint of relying on armed coercion (such as the police who upheld the law in favor of the protesters), or felt that disturbing the peace over civil rights was a bit outside of FOR's ambit. For his part, Farmer and other leaders of CORE, while committed to pacifism, did not want to limit or inhibit the participation of nonpacifists in nonviolent civil rights protests.[106]

Thurman was a mentor and inspiration to CORE from its earliest days, giving behind-the-scenes advice to Farmer and other CORE leaders.[107] When civil rights firebrand Pauli Murray and some associates attempted a similar sit-in demonstration at a Washington restaurant in 1944, Thurman gave his support, counsel, and ran interference with Mordecai Wyatt Johnson.[108] Murray would become a good friend of the Thurmans. In 1943 Farmer asked Thurman about the advisability of A. Philip Randolph's proposal for a "broad national campaign based on non-violent civil disobedience" in which African Americans would refuse to obey any law that "violated their basic citizenship rights." Thurman replied that "nonviolent civil disobedience is a technique that presupposes . . . a profound spiritual conviction, which by its very nature is devoid of either ill-will, contempt, or cowardice." He approved of Randolph's idea (which was never implemented) as "a very good thing provided it is built upon a definite discipline so that the masses of people will not be inspired by fear, revenge or hate."[109]

This avoidance of revenge and hate was, Thurman knew, particularly difficult for African Americans. In September 1942, he wrote that "for many years Negroes for various reasons have tended to be far too docile. Their docility has been confused with an alleged meekness and cowardice. Of course, this overall picture is not true, but so deep is the resentment of many Negroes to this overall picture that the technique of non-violent action is regarded by them as being an expression of cowardice."[110] African American nonviolence had to be utterly fearless and brave so as to "maintain in non-violent *action* an increment of courage that would be disassociated from the so called 'hat in hand attitude.'"[111] Practitioners of nonviolence had to learn the very difficult lesson of how to respond nonviolently to the violence that effective nonviolence begets. Thurman sometimes told the Buddhist tale of a story of a cobra that was persuaded by a holy man not to attack a village, at which point the villagers started to torment the cobra, pulling its tail. The cobra complained to the holy man, who replied, "I told you not to bite the people, but I did not tell you not to *hiss* at them."[112]

Thurman, still more of a lecturer and speaker than a writer, had been prodded for several years by the editors of FOR's journal *Fellowship* to write something for the magazine: "As a general rule we do not carry on our Editors' list anyone who does not contribute anything in the course of a year. However, we feel that you are the exception that proves the rule—at least for the present."[113] A year and a half after this compliment and veiled threat, in the summer of 1943, Thurman finally earned his place on the masthead with his article "The Will to Segregation."[114] In it, Thurman gathered and summarized all of his evolving thinking on radical nonviolence and the wartime realities of African American life.

He had been writing for years about segregation as something unnatural, something that could only be imposed and enforced with continuous and relentless effort, an act of will, the "American technique for the control of the Negro minority." Segregation was not just a political or social act. It was an attack on nature, on the natural order, an attack on God. "Racial and class prejudice is directly a denial of God who is the Father of life," he wrote around this time, at once "antireligious, anti-God, anti-Christian."[115] It was also a denial of the structure of the universe and of life itself, which, in Thurman's physics and metaphysics, abhorred separateness and artificial divisions. As he would write a few years later, "The cosmos is the kind of order that sustains and supports life and its potentials, varied as they may be," and therefore the cosmos (and God, which for Thurman were not easy to separate) "demands that the relationships between men and between man and God be one of harmony, integration, wholeness, all that we mean by love."[116] All of this informed the political struggle against segregation, which was "contrary to the dream of democracy in this life of ours."[117]

Thurman argued in "The Will to Segregation" that the war "has caused the average Negro to become aware of counting civically in a new way."[118] It no doubt was a rare positive appreciation of the social impact of the war in the pages of the journal of the Fellowship of Reconciliation, though he acknowledged that it was unfortunate that it took a war "to give the Negro a fresh sense of significance and power." But perhaps the central paradox of the war for Thurman was that while pacifists would never choose to use a monstrous war to advance their social agenda, as long as the war had been thrust upon pacifists, they, without denying their antiwar creed, needed to use the profound perturbations the war caused for their own benefit. As he wrote a former student in late 1942, who was then serving in the army, "It is a cruel fate that only by mass threat can goodwill and decency seem to have a chance in the world."[119]

In "The Will to Segregation" Thurman detailed all of the social, psychological, and spiritual harms segregation created for the segregated and the segregators. Segregation always requires violence, explicit and implicit, and can only exist between "peoples that are relatively weak and relatively strong." The ultimate fear of the weak is that they will be subject to random violence and "dying under circumstances that degrade and debase; dying like a dog in an alley, or a rat in the gutter." For the strong, segregation creates a "false sense of superiority" while becoming "a seed-bed of all kinds of fears and superstitions with reference to Negroes." Segregation breeds different but closely entwined fears in the minds of the powerless and the powerful.[120]

African Americans were beginning to demand real civic equality. It was a coming of age, as Thurman argued, in a metaphor of sexual potency, as "when the first full bloom of manhood possesses the mind and the body." But in the nature of American politics, with African Americans representing a largely powerless tenth of the population, they could only advance their interests slowly and tentatively, with internal divisions and wobbly allies. Social and political progress for African Americans was slow and tentative; the counter-reaction was swift, forceful, and implacable. This progress was in some ways only making the situation of African Americans as a whole less safe and more precarious. Those who supported this backlash, wrote Thurman, thought "Negroes do not know what to do with their new sense of significance. They are flippant, arrogant, bigoted, overbearing. Therefore, they must be curbed, held in check so that when the war is over they may quickly drop back into their prewar secondary citizen status." As a result, despite some real but still modest advances in their civic status, the Negro was "caught in the grip of a deeper frustration and restlessness than he has ever known."[121]

For Thurman, the way out of this dilemma was radical nonviolence. He provided an account of the steps of nonviolent resistance, similar to programs he had previously outlined, starting with moral suasion and culminating in "some form of shock" administered by "men [who] are spiritually prepared to apply Christian idealism to un-ideal and un-Christian situations." With a nod to CORE and similar efforts, Thurman stated that "examples of these techniques are being developed by FOR groups and others in different parts of the world even now."[122]

Not all of his readers were convinced. A former student asked Thurman the following: "Do you limit 'the exercise of some form of shock' to 'organizing a boycott, or widespread non-cooperation, or the like'? If their purpose 'is to tear men free from their alignments to the evil way' are they strong enough to do it? Does not evil like a rock become so deeply set that dynamite is needed to loosen it? I wonder."[123] This was indeed the question. Whether nonviolence was sufficient to the task was impossible to say. All that Thurman knew was that there was no other way and that to oppose the will to segregation "required great discipline of mind, emotion, and body" to prevent the release of forces "that would do complete violence to one's ideals and one purpose. All must be done with the full consciousness of the Divine Scrutiny."[124]

Thurman, like Gandhi, tended to think that the practice of radical nonviolence, at least in the beginning, would have to be limited to a spiritual elite, to a James Farmer or a Pauli Murray, a small band who would show the way for others to follow. However, he appreciated that segregation was an affront to God and that Christianity needed to be taught, catechized, and broadcast as widely as possible, especially in the civic institution most concerned with the relation between God and humanity. In "The Will to Segregation" he argued that there needed to be a "radical internal reorganization of policy and structural change" in the church. It was long overdue for "the resources of mind and spirit that are already in the church" to "begin working formally and informally on the radical changes that are necessary if the church is to become Christian."[125] (If it could not do this, he wrote the following year, Christianity "is doomed to become merely an esoteric sect stripped of all power and redemption.")[126] This transformation would not happen quickly. Dealing with the most difficult issue first, Thurman acknowledged that this "may not mean that there will be no congregations that are all Negro, or that are all white" but that individuals will have "a sense of alternatives," which for Thurman was always the true meaning of freedom.[127]

Thurman concluded his comments on the future of the church by offering it a sharp challenge: "How dare we undertake to teach reverence to children when we ourselves do not believe in reverence for life in general or life in particular as a valid concept in our kind of world?" More specifically, he wondered how we can speak of "the brotherhood of man" when "we over and over again" give "the sanction of our religion and the weight of our practice to those subtle anti-Christian practices expressed in segregated churches and even in segregated graveyards!" Why try to desegregate restaurants, roller rinks, or shipyards when churches remain exempt from similar calls? "Can we expect more of the state, of the body politic, of industry, than we expect of the church? How can we teach love from behind the great walls of separateness?"[128]

A. J. Muste, the editor of *Fellowship,* was perhaps thinking of this passage on October 8, some two months after "The Will to Segregation" appeared, when he wrote Thurman, again using Thurman as a liaison to Black Christians and Black pacifists: "Note the portion of this letter from Alfred Fisk, one of our very strong and capable people in the San Francisco Bay area, relative to a co-pastor from an interracial church. I have written Alfred that you would be the person most likely to have suggestions if the man they are hoping to get cannot make it. Will you think about this, and let Fisk have your suggestions? Fisk is tops for a project as this."[129]

The nucleus of this project began several months earlier when the Gandhian collective in San Francisco wanted to transform their cooperative into a church. The women, in Thurman's words, "wanted to live in the midst of the densely populated Negro area brought into being by the demands on industry. They sought to share a common life with Negroes and help them with their individual and collective needs."[130] They started to hold meetings with the local residents: story times and games for the children, and simple worship services for the adults. At some point, they thought of placing their worship services on a more permanent and established basis and contacted the Fellowship of Reconciliation, which put them in touch with Alfred Fisk.[131]

We do not know as much as we would like about these young women: how many they were or even—save for one, Hope Foote—their names.[132] Presumably they were all white, college-educated women—one, Thurman tells us, was a graduate of Mt. Holyoke—from comfortable middle-class backgrounds. They were inspired by the English pacifist Muriel Lester, who had helped arrange the meeting between Gandhi and the Negro Delegation.[133] We have no documentation from the women themselves, only secondhand accounts by Thurman and especially Fisk (who came to intensely dislike them). They were known as the "Sakai Group," named after the owner of the house in which they resided. Like all of the wartime pacifist cooperatives, the Sakai Group proved ephemeral and disbanded as a cooperative even before Thurman arrived in San Francisco. But in Fellowship Church they helped create a lasting legacy.

Thurman responded to Muste's initial letter promptly and wrote Fisk as well. After hearing from him, Fisk wrote Thurman directly, explaining the situation in San Francisco in more detail. Fisk was planning on becoming the copastor of the fledging venture. The Presbyterian Church had provided the building and two hundred dollars per month. With Lincolnian prepositions, he explained to Thurman that he didn't want the new church "to be in any sense run by whites 'for' Negroes. It should be *of* and *by* and *for* both groups."[134] The church would practice a true equality—in the choir, the board, the Sunday school. The copastors would have "absolutely equal status" and would preach on alternative Sundays. Given the limited amount of funding and a salary of only one hundred dollars per month, Fisk was looking for "a young man as high caliber as possible," perhaps a student finishing his work in seminary or a recent graduate who could supplement his work "at the Negro center here."[135]

Thurman's first thought was Herbert King, who needed a job. King had recently gone through a traumatic firing/resignation from the YMCA, where he had been a national student secretary since 1936, with special responsibility for Black colleges.[136] Even before the letters from Muste and Fisk, Thurman had been making inquiries for King.[137] King's firing had been for Thurman an object lesson in the perils of interracialism. Thurman thought the efforts against King were "a very despicable piece of skullduggery."[138] Thurman had written his protégé Melvin "Monk" Watson, as the storm over King was breaking, that "the assumption that the Negro and white movement are one, as you know and I know, is an illusion. In the last analysis, the movement reflects the societal patterns in which the movement functions."[139] Thurman was adamant that at least the appearance, and likely the reality, of racism was behind the decision to remove King and that the white leadership of the YMCA "felt it unwise to have too many Negro secretaries going around."[140]

Thurman said that if King was not treated fairly, "we shall no longer cooperate with the Student [Christian] Movement, and shall spread this affirmation within the Negro constituency as far as possible."[141] Thurman was as good as his word, and though the YMCA or the Student Christian Movement had in many ways been his lifeblood since his teenage years, after the firing of King his involvement with both organizations ebbed considerably.

Thurman wrote Fisk recommending King for the position. King subsequently turned Fisk down, largely because of its paltry salary.[142] Nonetheless, Thurman added that he himself was "quite excited over the prospects of the venture and wish very much it were possible for me to take some time out and help you in the early days of the work. It seems to me the most significant single step that institutional Christianity is taking in the direction of a really new order for America."[143] Fisk, who had heard Thurman speak in the Bay Area the previous summer—the two men had briefly met—read past Thurman's initial hesitance and sensed a deeper interest, writing back a few days later, with a real sales pitch: "If I could believe in miracles, I would dare to hope that the suggestion of you yourself coming to San Francisco might really be realized. Certainly nothing could be more wonderful!" Laying out an image of building a "socially integrated community," Fisk, raising his plea several notches, concluded by asking, "Shall I say that the destiny of San Francisco hangs in your hands?" Or even, in a subsequent letter, "San Francisco, so it seems to me now, is doomed if you do not come!"[144] Whatever the truth of these pleas, Thurman did not need the hard sell. By mid-November he was determined to take a sabbatical from Howard and go to San Francisco. The moment to fulfill the vision at the Khyber Pass had arrived. From the time he first heard of the San Francisco venture, it had "kindled in my mind the *possibility* that this may be *the* opportunity toward which my life has been moving."[145]

There were, of course, myriad practical considerations standing in the way of Thurman going to San Francisco, even for a temporary one-year position. The salary was meager and would involve a huge salary cut from $4,100 to $2,400, on which Howard was expected to support a family of four and provide assistance to his mother.[146] His wife and two daughters might have had their own ideas about wanting to uproot themselves and move to San Francisco. And he needed permission from Howard University, stretched thin by the war, for a leave of absence. Thurman and Fisk tried to address these and other matters. Sue Bailey Thurman was initially not in favor of the move. She had developed a career in Washington, working closely with Mary McLeod Bethune at the National Council of Negro Women, and was serving as the editor of its magazine, the *Aframerican Woman's Journal*. She told an interviewer late in life that at first she "hated leaving her work in Washington, DC, to come to San Francisco."[147] But Sue was soon reconciled to the move. The two daughters, Olive and Anne, agreed to it as well.[148]

The question of finances was trickier. When Thurman spoke about it with Mordecai Wyatt Johnson, he was sympathetic and understood the importance of the new church and Thurman's urgency and excitement about it but told him that it would have to be as an unpaid sabbatical and wondered: "How on earth can you support your family on two hundred dollars a month? How will you manage? How will you live?" Thurman, echoing what his mother had told him in 1910 when he was worried that Halley's Comet would incinerate the Earth, gave Johnson "a pious answer, but one I believed utterly: 'All I know is, God will take care of me'"[149] If "there is any validity in our claim that God sustains His kingdom in the world," he wrote Fisk afterward, they had to assume the "risks involved in our bold venture and we must be prepared to take our share of them."[150]

Fisk worked hard to make the San Francisco situation financially possible for Thurman, agreeing to forego any compensation himself.[151] This proved unnecessary. Fisk, a Presbyterian minister, had persuaded the Presbyterians to take an interest in the project and successfully petitioned the War Emergency Board of the Presbyterian Church—everything that occurred in America in 1943 and 1944 was a war emergency—to up their contribution to $3,600 annually—$2,400 for Thurman; $1,200 for Fisk, who retained his position as a professor of philosophy; along with rent-free living quarters for the Thurmans in the small building that was the first home of the new church.[152] Thurman's salary would increase over the years, and it was supplemented by an annual East Coast speaking tour in January and February.

The move to San Francisco involved other sorts of sacrifices, among them a headlong dive into pursuits he had long largely managed to avoid, especially fundraising and administration. Thurman would spend considerable time over the next few years reaching out for financial support for the church: meeting wealthy individuals, writing letters, preparing grant proposals. And he would also spend much of his time in committee meetings at the church, soothing frayed tensions, offering sage advice, and in general trying to untrouble the waters. There were the inherent sacrifices involved in moving three thousand miles and exchanging one of the most prestigious religious positions in Black higher education to pastor a fledgling and minute church, in a city that, unlike Washington, was far from the center of Black American life. Thurman wrote Fisk in March 1944 that his announcement, early in the year, of his move to San Francisco, "came as a distinct shock to the student body as a whole and to many of the faculty. Serious pressures are already being exerted in an effort to force a reconsideration but to no avail."[153] Others complained to Thurman that he "would be denying myself the ever-increasing opportunity to develop my career beyond the campus, at a time when my creative powers were beginning to peak."[154] There was particular concern that Thurman was cutting himself off from his crucial job of training and mentoring a rising generation of Black divinity students and that, rather than preaching in a university chapel with an average Sunday attendance of about five hundred, he would be ministering to a congregation that, at its first services, had about sixty persons in attendance, only one-third of them African American.

Thurman was willing to walk away from much to go to San Francisco. In the midst of his deliberations about the position, in December 1943, in one of his many letters to Howard students in the service, he wrote Pvt. William Gardner that the "will of God" is to be distinguished from "mere desire, or whim" and was instead to be found "in the core of a man's yearning." He distinguished between fate and destiny. One's fate is imposed, externally, outside of one's control. One's destiny "is determined by what he does with his fate."[155] Thurman had been living within the confines and constraints of his fate, the accidents of his birth and upbringing, since his earliest days. The San Francisco church was an opportunity to seek and claim his destiny.

The move to San Francisco was also, on a less exalted level, an opportunity to change his job. To what extent "push" as well as "pull" elements factored into his decision to become copastor of Fellowship Church is difficult to say, but it seems safe to assume that he was open to the possibility of moving on. If generally satisfied at Howard, he had occasional problems with Mordecai Wyatt Johnson's imperious ways, sparring with him over his schedule and other matters.[156] There were limits at Howard as to what he could say and do. In the fall of 1942, Jay Holmes Smith, founder of the Harlem Ashram, led a fourteen-person "interracial pilgrimage" from New York City to Washington protesting racial discrimination, with public meetings in cities along the way. In response to Smith's request for a meeting at Howard, Thurman wrote: "After conferring officially with the administration, it seems best that Howard University should not be identified with the Pilgrimage in any way. As a public institution it must safeguard its public relations in every reasonable way. If I were minister of a local church, I could do with pleasure the things I cannot do with the Chapel, which is a part of the university."[157]

Thurman had been wooed many times before. In 1936 he was offered the presidency of Shaw University, a historically Black college in Raleigh, North Carolina.[158] Two years later, when Samuel Archer was retiring from Morehouse, he begged Thurman to succeed him. Thurman, who greatly admired Archer, told him that "he has no ambition to become the president of Morehouse College."[159] Nonetheless, the position that in 1940 went to Benjamin

Mays had probably been Thurman's for the asking.[160] (Before Mays finally took the position, the two men engaged in a bout of "after you; no, after you" politesse.) The same year, the aging Nathan W. Collier, president of Florida Normal and Industrial Institute—Thurman's former high school, which was making the transition to a four-year college—urged Thurman to succeed him, suggesting, really insisting, that he was uniquely qualified to save the "one-half million Negro youth in Florida" currently melting "under the strains of rag-time music, rushing pell-mell into the jaws of hell through the doors of Florida's jungles of ball rooms and jooks."[161] Thurman politely demurred.[162]

Then, in 1941, Thurman preached a trial sermon at Olivet Baptist Church in Chicago, one of the largest Black Baptist churches in the country, with approximately ten thousand members. He wrote a member of the church's search committee in February 1941 that, though satisfied with his position at Howard, he was prepared "to consider prayerfully and with as much judg-ment as is available to me, the challenge and opportunity a fine church like Olivet offers."[163] The trial sermon went well. Thurman wrote that he "took a text that belongs to the 'war horses' and the 'whoopers' but I wanted to appeal to the minds of the people, being confident that the feelings would take care of themselves. This, I think, was demonstrated on Sunday."[164] Things were so advanced that the false rumor was circulating that he had been called to Olivet.[165] Instead of Thurman, the position went to a man who was in almost every way Thurman's polar opposite, J. H. Jackson, best remembered as per-haps the most prominent and most flamboyantly vituperative Black conser-vative opponent of Martin Luther King, Jr.

One senses that by the early 1940s Thurman was, if not eager, certainly ready to move from Howard if the right position came along. He had written with regard to the Olivet position, "I cannot refrain from exposing myself to the possibility of another kind of opportunity where problems are different and the responsibilities [are] of a more varied type."[166] He turned down the university presidencies in part because he was not interested in the fundrais-ing and administrative duties they entailed and because the positions would have greatly curtailed his ability to work as a minister. All of the positions he considered, the college presidencies and Olivet, would have been more secure, more remunerative, and more prestigious than the San Francisco church. But they shared the following drawback: they were all securely within the Black religious and academic world and would have reinforced one of Jim Crow's barriers that, as of 1944, remained well-nigh impregnable—the custom that Black ministers could pastor only Black congregations and that Black academics could teach only at Black colleges, regardless of their accom-plishments. And in all of these positions he would have been entering an existing institution, and he would have had to accept the burden of their history. Going to San Francisco gave him the opportunity to break free of many barriers and create a church that was neither Black nor white, something that was radically new.

When Thurman arrived in San Francisco he briefly kept a journal, in which he noted that Alfred Fisk, after meeting the Thurmans at the conclusion of a rather exhausting five-day transcontinental train trip undertaken in wartime conditions, immediately took Thurman to a series of meetings: "Everything we did could have waited until the next day. This is the kind of zeal Alfred Fisk has." In 1943 Alfred Fisk was thirty-eight years old, five years younger than Thurman (he only lived to be fifty-four). Thurman described him as a "highly nervous and tense individual with a deep sense of mission and a profound sincerity."[167] A Presbyterian minister, a professor of philosophy, his involvement with the church project arose out of what Thurman called his "deep desire to extend the experience of brotherhood to all people."[168] Two of Fisk's colleagues said of him in a memorial tribute that "he was as near as being a personification of the Kantian man of duty as anyone we have known."[169] Zealous Kantians do not always make for easy collaborators. Fisk could be brisk and brusque and seems to have had a talent for making enemies. But it was he, more than anyone else, who brought the idea of Fellowship Church into reality.[170]

In wanting to create an interracial church, the Sakai Group and Fisk were motivated by general pacifist and humanitarian impulses, and they were also responding to very specific circumstances in San Francisco. The Great Migration of Blacks from the South, which began in the East during World War I, only commenced in northern California on a large scale during World War II, largely fueled by the expansion of defense contracting in the Bay Area. San Francisco, a city of some 630,000 persons in 1940, had a Black population in that year of fewer than 5,000. By 1945, the Black population had increased to about 32,000 persons. As the distinguished Black sociologist Horace Cayton wrote in September 1943, "That's a lot of Negroes" for San Francisco "to digest in such a short length of time."[171] When Sue Bailey Thurman visited San Francisco in 1942, she found Blacks were "scattered all over the city." When she moved there, two years later, there were large Black neighborhoods.[172]

In San Francisco, as in other large West Coast cities during the war, the new Black migration was superimposed on the tragedy of the Japanese expulsions and internments. As in many cities, the former Japantown, already conveniently reserved for non-Caucasians, became a largely African American neighborhood. The Sakai Group, as mentioned above, received their name from the owner of the house in which they set up cooperative housekeeping, now in an internment camp. When Thurman arrived in San Francisco in 1944, as he later wrote, it was "not infrequent that one saw billboard caricatures of the Japanese: grotesque faces, huge buck teeth, large dark-rimmed thick-lensed eyeglasses." The point and effect were to "read the Japanese out of the human race" and to create "an open season for their potential extermination."[173] The Japanese internments had been an important issue to Thurman while he was still in Washington, and he paid visits in 1942 and 1943 to internment camps.[174] (FOR and other pacifist organizations were among the few voices raised on behalf of the internees during the war.) The first home of Fellowship Church was San Francisco's former Japanese Presbyterian church. The absent, interned Japanese were a hovering, haunting presence during the early days of Fellowship Church. As the war ended, they would become important members of the church.

The wartime surge in San Francisco's Black population created a number of social dislocations. The Black neighborhood in the city rapidly became badly overcrowded. Alfred Cleage, who would become the assistant minister to Fellowship Church in early 1944, wrote that "twenty thousand Negroes were crowded into make-shift rooming houses and apartment houses which had accommodated about eight thousand Japanese."[175] Joseph James, the chairman of San Francisco's NAACP branch and a founding member of Fellowship Church, wrote in 1945: "Caucasian San Francisco turned the machinery at hand [formal and informal means of discrimination] for the subjugation of the Oriental and applied it to the Negro."[176]

Old-line Black San Franciscans did not necessarily treat the newcomers much better. Langston Hughes in the spring of 1944 wrote that established Black San Francisco treated the newcomers as "cotton-patch Negroes" and were "almost as prejudiced against the new dark arrivals from the South as are reactionary white folks."[177] Nathan Huggins remembered from his childhood "what a small community" and how "self-satisfied" Black San Francisco was in 1940, with its "black bourgeoisie of redcaps, porters, waiters, the occasional civil service employee, and the one or two professionals," and "how ambivalent everyone was about the wave of blacks from the South, brought in to man the new jobs in the war industries." As a result, "racial tensions rose" along with incidents of police brutality.[178] The fear of racial violence in San Francisco in 1943 and 1944 was palpable and felt on all sides of the racial divide. In May 1944 the Black sociologist Charles S. Johnson published *The Negro War Worker in San Francisco*. It detailed a long catalogue of social woes: widespread discrimination in housing, schools, employment, recreational opportunities, social services, places of worship, all contributing to a general sense that San Francisco was a "race relations test tube."[179]

After the Detroit and Harlem riots in the summer of 1943, Francis Biddle, the U.S. attorney general, speculated that San Francisco might well be next.[180] He was not alone. Albert Cleage, who arrived in San Francisco in February 1944, found the city to be "suffering from a bad case of riot-jitters. Everywhere people seemed to be waiting for the signal which was to begin the fire-works. Both Negroes and whites are frightened and angry in the presence of something they couldn't understand."[181] For Alfred Fisk, addressing these circumstances was one of the major, if not the major, reason for his involvement with the church project: "New Negroes [are] pouring into this area in the tens of thousands; tensions rising to the breaking point; the outbreak of violence in minor instances with more general rioting only averted by a hair's breadth."[182]

There were a number of responses to what Horace Cayton called the "tension area" of wartime San Francisco. Charles Johnson's report on Negro war workers was intended to stimulate conventional social service organizations to better understand and respond to the crisis. There was a vigorous response by some CIO unions to fight discrimination in the defense industry. There were pacifist efforts at addressing the situation through specific acts of nonviolent protest. Bayard Rustin spent some time in San Francisco in the fall of 1943 organizing nonviolent protests under the aegis of CORE against segregated facilities, with Fisk and other future members of Fellowship Church, including members of the Sakai Group, participating. Virginia Scardigli, later a secretary of Fellowship Church, wrote Thurman in October 1943 that "she had been working like a beaver in a Race Relations Workshop led by Bayard Rustin" and that later in the day she would be part of a group of four persons trying to desegregate a local skating rink.[183] All of these efforts, along with a deep religious commitment to creative interracialism, provided an impetus for the creation of Fellowship Church.

In early February 1944 the announcement that Thurman was planning to come to San Francisco was widely covered in the Black press.[184] Meanwhile, Fisk had the daunting task of getting the new church off the ground, with an array of mundane and not so mundane tasks, such as meeting with members, organizing its structures, conducting services, exploring fundraising possibilities, finding a new home for the church, and in general dealing with the inevitable crises that occur when efforts are made to implement dreams from scratch. To keep Thurman abreast of these and other developments, Fisk wrote Thurman copious and frank letters, informing him of recent developments, asking his opinion on various matters, and not, infrequently, letting off steam, with Thurman responding as best he could. It is an irony that we are better informed about Fisk and Thurman's interactions about Fellowship Church for these first months than we are for the period after July 1944, when Thurman and Fisk could speak daily and directly and left no permanent record of their conversations.[185] Even before the congregation had decided on a permanent name—the initial name was the Neighborhood Church— or many of the other necessary particulars had been determined, the church started holding regular services.[186] The first was on 12 December 1943, with sixty-six persons attending, about one-third of them African American. The following Sunday, thirty-six persons braved a storm to attend.[187] It was a rainy winter in San Francisco. Fisk wrote Thurman in late January that the weather had kept down the average attendance to about forty persons.[188] In addition to those intending to be regular members, church activities attracted the interested and the curious. About eighty persons attended the Lincoln Birthday dinner, equally divided between whites and Blacks.[189]

Everyone knew from the outset that the first home of the church was a stopgap. The former Japanese Presbyterian church had a tiny sanctuary that could hold only about one hundred persons comfortably.[190] Fisk spent much of the spring searching out possible new homes for the church, striking out repeatedly. Some alternatives, like the nearby Booker T. Washington Community Service Center, used for dances on Saturday, was "not a worshipful room."[191] Other alternatives were too expensive, like a white Baptist church and a Lutheran church, both of which had congregations that wanted to get out of the increasingly Black neighborhood. A local synagogue, Seventh-Day Adventist Church, and Quaker meetinghouse were unavailable for various reasons. Several white fraternal organizations did not want to rent their space to an interracial venture. The question of where Fellowship Church would move was unsettled when Thurman arrived in July.[192]

There was other pressing business that required the attention of Fisk and Thurman. Some members of the church were unhappy with its affiliation with the Presbyterian Church, wanting to be completely independent. Fisk, Presbyterian to his core, was affronted by this, writing Thurman that "in a real sense I do not think that we have any right to discuss it."[193] The Sakai Group disagreed with Fisk on this and, evidently, on most other issues.[194] Unfortunately, we only have Fisk's side of his growing controversy with the Sakai Group, but Fisk's Christianity was more formal and traditional than what the members of the Sakai Group and some others in the church found comfortable. In June 1944, when the Sakai Group dissolved, Fisk was positively gleeful.[195] In his responses to Fisk on this issue, Thurman politely sympathized with Fisk's troubles but said little of substance. One senses that though he was wary of their factional tendencies, Thurman was in basic sympathy with the Sakai Group's perspective on the future direction of Fellowship Church.

However, the biggest controversy that Fisk had in the opening months of the church did not involve the Sakai Group. It was a confrontation between Fisk and the temporary Black copastor, Albert B. Cleage Jr., who served in Fellowship Church for about five months, from February 1944 through June, until shortly before Thurman's arrival. It was a dramatic demonstration of the potential perils of interracialism. Cleage, born in Detroit in 1911, a 1943 graduate of the Oberlin Graduate School of Theology, was suggested as a potential assistant pastor when Fisk was dissatisfied with the initial interim Black candidate.[196] Cleage, unhappy with his role as an assistant minister in a Black Congregationalist church in Lexington, Kentucky, leapt at the chance to come to San Francisco.[197] Before Fisk met Cleage, his praise of him, via testimonials of others, was so effusive that Thurman reconsidered his plans, suggesting that if Cleage would be such a good fit for the congregation, perhaps it would be better if he stayed in Washington.[198]

But when Cleage arrived in San Francisco, relations between him and Fisk soon soured. Fisk thought that he did not take his pastoral duties seriously, and he was troubled by Cleage's "very blunt, tactless way of dealing with other folk." Fisk was even more offended by one duty he did take seriously, preaching his every-other-week sermon. He found Cleage's sermons were "brilliant from an intellectual point of view" but "completely unreligious and very defeatist" in their message, "ethical, rather than religious."[199] Cleage, writing many years later, was equally unimpressed by Fisk's efforts. Fisk "talked of the glorious fellowship washed in the blood of the Lamb; I talked about hell on the alternate Sundays. He felt upset about my preaching, but he didn't want to raise racial tensions in his heaven."[200] An activity that Cleage did organize for the church, a forum in May on discrimination in Bay Area shipyards, brought the relations between the two men to the breaking point. Discriminatory practices by AFL craft unions were opposed by CIO unions, many of which in the wartime Bay Area had close ties with the Communist Party.[201] Though Fisk opposed the Jim Crow "auxiliary locals," he complained that Fisk had "so overloaded" the forum with Communists that Cleage "gave our church the reputation of being a communist organization, and it was investigated by the FBI."[202] It was probably at this forum that Cleage (according to Fisk) announced "from the pulpit that the church was a futile institution and that men might well leave it and join the C.I.O," letting it be known that he considered "such an interracial institution as our[s] futile."[203]

In the aftermath of the forum, there was talk of firing Cleage. This did not happen, but rumors that he had been let go circulated in the Black community.[204] Fisk wrote Thurman after the forum that Cleage "is said to stand for Negro 'nationalism'—which I really doubt, but he certainly has a defeatist outlook."[205] Cleage was indeed a Negro nationalist and would become, by the 1960s, one of the most prominent promoters of Black religious nationalism in the country, achieving national recognition for his Detroit ministry in the 1960s at the Church of the Black Madonna. In the mid-1940s, however, his Black nationalism was more Marxist than separatist, and after his own fashion he supported the idea of Fellowship Church.[206] For Cleage, interracialism was not about racial harmony or amelioration but, rather, about advancing the cause of Black liberation with white allies. In late 1944 he wrote an article about Fellowship Church with complimentary things to say about the church (along with a few knocks against an unnamed Fisk) but concluded that "a Christian church must be even more than a place where Negroes and whites worship together, or it will inevitably become less."[207] By the late 1960s Cleage told a biographer, speaking of Fellowship Church, that an "interracial church is a monstrosity and an impossibility."[208]

Thurman never would meet Cleage, who left San Francisco shortly before his arrival. Cleage's dispute with Fisk had left Thurman "uneasy in my spirit," and he was glad that Fisk had not fired Cleage, which would have been seen as evidence that an interracial church "simply cannot work." Thurman probably wished that Cleage had been less of a firebrand, and Fisk more sensitive to a proud, outspoken Black man. When Thurman was asked to evaluate Cleage in the fall of 1944, after stressing that he had never met him, he wrote that Cleage was "a deeply religious man with a full social problem orientation. He believes, it seems, in making this fact clearly known at all times." Cleage was deeply critical of organized Christianity and the ways "in which the Church has given its approval again and again to race and social discrimination within its fellowship" and its silence "in the presence of some of the gross injustices in the social order." As a result of his outspokenness, it "is easy to see that the persons who come in contact with him will feel very strongly one way or the other about him."[209] If they had met, Thurman probably would have felt both ways. The Fisk-Cleage controversy was a reminder to Thurman, if he needed one, of how easy it was for interracial cooperation to collapse in grievance, petulance, and misunderstanding.

Despite Thurman's attention to the events in San Francisco, his voluminous and detailed correspondence with Fisk, and the usual enveloping complications of a big move, most of Thurman's focus was necessarily elsewhere. In the first half of 1944 his schedule was unusually crowded, perhaps out of an interest in cramming as much as possible into his remaining few months on the East Coast. By moving to San Francisco, Thurman was leaving not only Howard but also the eastern United States at a time when, before easy air travel, the distance between the coasts was greater than it is now. (Not that air travel was an option for Thurman, anyway, who was at best an extremely reluctant flyer.) He spent the first few months of the year maintaining his teaching schedule and other obligations at Howard, traversing his circuit, visiting familiar places, and meeting with old friends. In the first half of the year he spoke in Detroit; Madison, Wisconsin; Poughkeepsie, New York; Providence, Rhode Island; and he made two trips apiece to Massachusetts, North Carolina, and Chicago; and three separate visits to Pennsylvania. At Howard, during his final year, in addition to his regular preaching turn at Rankin Chapel, he preached the Founder's Day and baccalaureate sermons, and several special "twilight hours" services. He supervised a play depicting the life of a disciple of St. Francis of Assisi; for Religious Emphasis Week, he brought in speakers to discuss Hinduism, Buddhism, and other Eastern religions; and he continued his work organizing campus events and counseling students.[210]

Thurman was proud of his increasing fame, especially outside the Black world. In May, in Chicago for a week of sermons sponsored by the Church Federation of Greater Chicago, he was quite pleased by the attention he was receiving, writing his mother that he saw "on the elevated platform a big sign 4 feet high with my name written advertising the fact that I shall be preaching there all the week. There are 150 of those big announcements at as many platforms throughout the entire city," adding to his pious mother, "I pray that God will give me the strength and the wisdom to do His Purpose in all these things."[211]

But some old problems remained. He demanded that the sponsoring organization push for accommodations for him in a downtown Chicago hotel, almost all of which had previously been off-limits to Black guests: "The hotels should be advised that quite clearly I am a Negro, that my complexion is dark, so that there should be no question to what they are doing."[212] (He had exerted similar pressure, successfully, on the Detroit Council of Churches to desegregate downtown hotels in that city the previous year.)[213] In the end there was a compromise solution, one not entirely satisfactory to him. An official from the Chicago organization had to accompany him to the registration desk. Thurman in these years was inhabiting a twilight world, speaking to a white America that admired him and wanted him to speak to them on the most personal and intimate spiritual matters but in certain fundamental ways did not treat him as a full equal.

Thurman was slowly beginning to write more. He had seven publications in the first half of 1944.[214] That January he published a brief article titled "The White Problem," which was one of a number of articles that appeared in the wake of Gunnar Myrdal's greatly influential *An American Dilemma: The*

Negro Problem and Modern Democracy,[215] suggesting that Negroes were not the race with the "problem."[216] At the end of the year his first book appeared, the privately published *The Greatest of These.*[217] It included his longest and most ambitious prose poem, "The Great Incarnate Words," which contained Thurman's first use of the image of the hellhound:

> Fear, the great companion of the poor,
> The creeping, slinking Hound ever on the trail of the
> Bedeviled seekers for surcease from oppression and wrong[218]

The highpoint of Thurman's last months in Washington surely was the testimonial dinner the Washington Council of Churches held for him on 30 May at the Universalist National Memorial Church. It was sponsored by Coleman Jennings, a retired philanthropist and an active Episcopalian, who had become and would remain one of Thurman's closest friends and sometime financial supporter. The guest of honor was Eleanor Roosevelt. She made a few comments at the dinner and wrote briefly about Thurman and Fellowship Church in her syndicated column "My Day," certainly the most widely circulated acknowledgment the new venture had yet achieved. From the Khyber Pass to a dais in the nation's capital with the First Lady, it was a time when Thurman unburdened himself of the weight of the past, and all seemed possible.[219]

10

In the Queen of Cities

Building Community in San Francisco

Howard and Sue Thurman arrived in San Francisco on Wednesday, 12 July 1944. As on many a summer's day in the city, the weather was cool and foggy, and the Thurmans, after a five-day train trip across the continent during wartime without adequate sleeping accommodations, were "tired and quite weary."[1] If Thurman was annoyed by Alfred Fisk immediately hurrying him off to meetings, he and the family quickly adjusted to their new surroundings and soon were having "a gay time in this queen of cities."[2] Falling in love with San Francisco was (and is) easy. It would remain their home for the remainder of their lives, despite their twelve-year hiatus in Boston from 1953 to 1965.

Their first home, connected to the former Japanese Presbyterian church, "was ghastly for everyone. We had to fight not only congestion and dirt, but rats."[3] But the fight with rats aside, the Thurman family soon found themselves caught up in their new lives. Sue, by October 1944, was on the board of directors of the integrated Central YWCA in San Francisco and head of its World Fellowship Committee and on the board of directors for the International Institute of San Francisco, which was helping to prepare for the imminent return of the Japanese to the city.[4] She would, in the next few years, publish a series of meditations and a history of early Black settlement in San Francisco.[5] Olive spent the year at San Francisco State College, preparatory to entering Vassar in the fall of 1945. Anne was attending the Frederick Burke Elementary School, an experimental school attached to San Francisco State College. Thurman's calendar was full too. He and Sue were active in many organizations "because it is necessary for doors to open for the 20,000 Negroes who have become an integral part of the city."[6] He was working with the local Conference of Christians and Jews, the San Francisco Council of Churches, and the American Civil Liberties Union in addition to "addressing numerous groups on a daily schedule."[7] Although he largely confined his speaking engagements to the Bay Area, he did find time to go to remote Belden, California, in the northern part of the state, to conduct a two-day retreat in August for conscientious objectors confined at a Civilian Public Service Camp.[8]

At his first meeting of the board of trustees, he encountered a variety of opinions about Fellowship Church. In his journal (which he kept for a few weeks after his arrival) he recorded some of their responses. One man wanted to worship "in a place that was not bound by racial or class barriers." A Norwegian immigrant who "suffered so much as a foreigner and stranger as a young child" developed an early sympathy with Black Americans. One woman had worked closely with Blacks since her experience with the Red Cross during World War I. Some were attracted to the church because of their previous acquaintance or admiration for Thurman. Others were interested in Fellowship Church because it seemed like a good fit after years of wandering "around trying to find a church that was generally friendly."[9]

Although he appreciated the board's answers and their honesty in expressing them, Thurman's initial impression was that he "found very little evidence that there was a clear cut notion as to what we are trying to do in this corner." There were, from his perspective, several looming problems facing Fellowship Church. There were questions about the location of the church and whether it should remain in San Francisco's Black neighborhood. Thurman was dubious. Others were under "the general impression that this is a church of Pacifist[s]." (Given its connections to the Fellowship of Reconciliation, that was an easy impression to form.) Thurman wanted the church's commitment to peace to be found "in the quality of life that emanates from the place rather than from pronouncements of one kind or another."[10] Other concerns included the "interest in the church on the part of local political social radicals," by which Thurman meant local Communists and their effort to involve the church in their activities. As Thurman knew from the fracas over the shipyard forum, this was very much a live issue. Another issue was the connection to the Presbyterian Church, which Thurman saw as necessary but restrictive. He felt that the Presbyterians were treating Fellowship Church as a mere branch of a larger franchise, to be ordered about by its management.[11]

All of these questions would have to be dealt with, fairly quickly, by Thurman, Fisk, and the members of the church. But first Thurman wanted to impress upon those participating in the Fellowship Church experiment its importance, its broader significance, its uniqueness, and that it was not simply a local church but the first footstep of a national reckoning with racial inequality. On 23 July he preached his first sermon. Its theme was the "tragic sense of life," the reality that "man's highest dreams are always undergirded by the possibility of the lack of attainment. What we see we are not quite able to achieve. The margin of error never disappears."[12] In this regard he spoke of *Moby-Dick,* his favorite novel, and read an excerpt from Lewis Mumford's study of Melville. In the excerpt Mumford argued that the novel expressed "the tragic sense of life which has always attended the highest triumphs of the race, at the moments of completest mastery and fulfillment. When that sense is lacking, life shrivels into small prudences and weak pleasures and petty gains."[13] Thurman had modestly outrageous ambitions for the tiny new church, and he wanted its members to embark on the voyage with him, with all of its thrill and all of its uncertainty.

For Thurman, the first order of business was to create a statement of purpose for the church. Although he disliked formal creeds, he felt that Fellowship Church required some form of explanation, both for its participants and for interested onlookers. From Thurman's perspective, a formal Commitment was needed because there was "no organic relatedness within the weekly congregation," which was only a "fellowship, a very loose fellowship at that." In Thurman's view, the church, because of its newness and unprecedented nature, was "without status," for some observers "just a bit up the ladder from the storefront churches that had begun springing up all over the area" with the difference that it was a storefront church at which "apparently self-respecting white people were always in attendance."[14]

Most of those in the Fellowship Church circle opposed Thurman's idea of a formal Commitment: "The general reaction was—Don't do it. If you do, you will splinter the group. No one would be satisfied. So long as you do not write anything out there will be no problem. Besides, in matters of religious belief we are likely to be as far apart as we are together in what we are doing." Nonetheless Thurman was convinced that without a written "platform on which to stand, all authentic growth would be cut off."[15] There are several differing accounts by Thurman of how the Commitment was drafted, but it was prepared and approved by the board by August 1944.[16] For the remainder of the summer, with Fisk away on vacation, Thurman preached for four straight weeks on the ideas behind the Commitment.[17]

It opened with the pledge, "I desire to have a part in the unfolding of the idea of Christian fellowship through the union of men and women of varying national, cultural, and racial heritage, in church communion." It went on to pledge to seek "a vital interpretation of the highest manifestation of

God—Jesus Christ—in all my relationships." The final sentence promised to try to find "the strength of corporate worship" through "membership in the Fellowship Church of San Francisco." There would be two further versions of the Commitment, one adopted in 1945, the third in 1948 or 1949 (it remains in use today). The two revisions moved the Commitment away from an explicitly Christian pledge; "the idea of Christian fellowship" was replaced by "understanding all men as sons of God." "Jesus Christ" was replaced in the second version by "Jesus of Nazareth" and in the third by "Jesus of Nazareth and other great religious leaders," changes that brought both praise and criticism.[18]

The Commitment was an announcement and presentation of Fellowship Church to the wider world. What is perhaps most important from Thurman's perspective is that the Commitment was entirely about the church, and not about any external political obligations. The Commitment does not speak of racial discrimination, integration, interracialism, or the need for social justice. Written primarily by pacifists in the midst of the largest war in human history, it says nothing pro or contra about the war, militarism, or any related issue. It was about, precisely, "the strength of corporate worship" in one tiny, self-selected group of individuals who decided to come together to form and build a new kind of church.[19]

Another way to demonstrate the institutional solidity of the new church was to have a formal inauguration to announce its creation, with all possible attendant pomp and publicity. Fisk and Thurman tried to arrange an event in one of the local Presbyterian churches, but this "proved embarrassing," probably because San Francisco's Presbyterians had reservations about hosting a large mixed-race event. The event was held at the First Unitarian Church on 8 October 1944, with an impressive array of religious personages on hand to offer their blessings and support: an Episcopal bishop, Presbyterian officials, a rabbi, Black church leaders, a Chinese Christian lay leader, and the leader of a kindred experiment in interracial religion located across the bay in Berkeley, the South Berkeley Congregational Church.[20] Joseph James, the head of the San Francisco chapter of the NAACP, a shipyard worker, and a founding member of Fellowship Church, sang at the event. A professionally trained concert singer, his voice and interpretation reminded Thurman of the African American tenor Roland Hayes. Thurman spoke on the theme of "A Vital Religion in the Modern World," arguing that the unifying power of religion did not "violate the contexts of meanings by which religion, in particular instances, may be defined," in what amounted for him to a "confession of my religious faith."[21] For Thurman, the "cold, unblurred facts of history" were that until the October inauguration "there were no 'members' as such, there being no organized church." And in the first months after his arrival in July 1944, "the group was only in the process of becoming a church." Only a week after the 8 October inauguration, at the next Sunday service, did prospective members sign the Commitment, and the new church finally had members.[22]

Of the problems that confronted the new church, none was more urgent than the question of its location. Its first home, the once and future home of the Japanese Presbyterian church, was not only too small, it was unprepossessing and in any event would have to be vacated when the war and the Japanese internment ended.[23] As we have seen, though Fisk put much time and legwork into finding a new building for the church, the issue was unresolved when Thurman arrived in San Francisco. This was not just a matter of finding a better abode. Thurman insisted that the new church site be located outside of what was rapidly becoming San Francisco's Black neighborhood.[24]

For Thurman, the matter was complex, but the decision was clear: "I knew if we did not move, we would become a Negro church in a relatively short time or entirely disappear."[25] He was told "again and again" that "the church must be located in the heart of the Negro district." For Thurman this did not make any sense: "Is the idea that in some ways the church is to bring into its walls the Negroes off the street of the neighborhood?" If this happened, Thurman felt, it would be perceived as a Black church, and it would be "merely repeating the pattern of Protestants and will be fought to the end by the Negro churches in the area."[26] Whites would not come to an interracial church in a Black neighborhood in sufficient numbers, and the church would cease to be, in any significant way, "interracial." High-minded sentiments would confront the hard realities of urban racial sociology, and the high-minded sentiments would lose. For Thurman it did not "matter what the intent and purpose of an institution is in its dedication to brotherhood, if it is a geographically segregated district, and if it accepts as its assignment the meeting of the needs of the people in that district, such an institution in time will become like the district—segregated."[27]

However, given that for many, if not most, members of the church working with those in the local Black community was much of their rationale for their involvement, it is not surprising that Thurman's suggestion provoked, in his words, "almost unanimous resistance." To move the church would mean "running away from the social problems of separateness," placing the church "above the struggle" and therefore being unable to contribute anything to the self-respect of those who lived in the Black neighborhood. Thurman was attacked as a recent refugee from the academic ivory tower, out of touch and out of "sympathy with the plight and predicament of the masses of my fellows." The church needed to stay where there was the greatest need, which was where it currently was, and if it had to move, it needed to stay in the immediate vicinity.[28]

The argument between Thurman and the other church members was rooted in a philosophical and psychological divide that was, as he acknowledged, probably too wide to "be met by argument."[29] It was a disagreement about the nature of interracialism and integration, and a disagreement about the basis of white and Black interaction and cooperation. For Thurman, like almost all Blacks raised in the South during the Jim Crow era, segregation was less about separating whites and Blacks than about limiting what Blacks could do and the spaces into which they could freely enter. The rules were asymmetrical. For Thurman, integration and interracialism were as much about where it occurred as about the act of exclusion.

An integrated church in a Black neighborhood had one meaning; an integrated church in a white neighborhood had another. As he had written in "The Will to Segregation," because segregation is always a matter of the strong imposing their will on the weak, "the strong may separate themselves from the weak, but because the initiative remains in their hands they are ever at liberty to shuttle back and forth between proscribed areas." He gave the example of train travel: "White passengers move at will from one section to the other, but the passengers in the Jim Crow car sometimes experience difficulties in even passing through the other coaches."[30] Thurman often told the story of his return to Daytona Beach with his daughters around 1940 and preventing them from entering a whites-only playground, and then having to address "the inescapable moment of truth that every Black parent in America must face sooner or later." He told Olive and Anne that it required the entire weighty apparatus of the State of Florida, using its unshakable "will to segregation," to prevent "two little Black girls from swinging in those swings. That is how important you are!" It was a message that he had no doubt often told himself as a young man, that his importance was demonstrated by the lengths that white America went to bar him from its spaces.[31] For Thurman, an integrated church in a Black neighborhood raised the specter of high-minded religious slumming. Even if it could work, it would prove very little.

Thurman won the argument. In the fall of 1944 Fellowship Church moved to the former Filipino Methodist Church of San Francisco, in a swap of sanctuaries effected by the Methodist and Presbyterian denominations. It was only slightly to the east of Van Ness Avenue, which had become the informal dividing line between white and Black San Francisco. The distance to the racial boundary was less important than the fact of its location: "It is irrelevant that we were less than two blocks from the 'other side of the

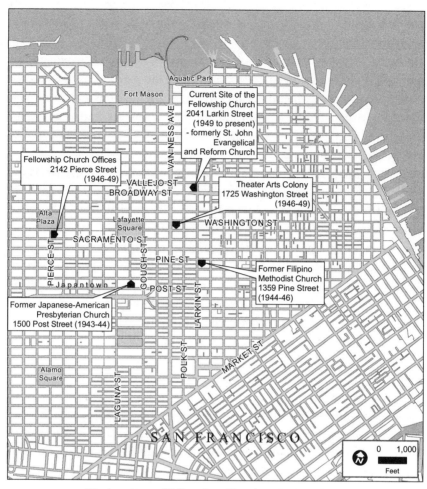

The locations of Fellowship Church in San Francisco

tracks.' Moving outside of the ghetto gave to our beginning a freedom and a challenge which would never have been had we remained."[32]

A closely related question to the location of Fellowship Church, and one that was even more momentous for its future, was its relation to the Presbyterian Church. The issue had been debated since the earliest meetings about the church, a debate that, Thurman later wrote, "very nearly destroyed the church even before it was formally organized."[33] Fisk was adamant that the church retain its Presbyterian ties. Thurman was much less certain, though he obviously recognized that since the San Francisco Presbytery had provided the church, and the Presbyterian Church was paying his salary, the connection was in the short run essential. As he wrote in his history of the church, the Presbyterian yoke was not unduly burdensome, other than an obligation to write a monthly letter to Presbyterian officials about the progress of the church.[34]

The Presbyterian Church did not demand that Fellowship Church identify itself as a Presbyterian project. And Thurman thought the connection useful, as a bridge to organized Christianity, and it dispelled what he described as the common reaction to the church: "It's a fly by night group supported by the lunatic fringe of the community, and it can't possibly survive; and the man who came out from Washington is just out for a lark. Everybody's anxious to come out to California for the weather anyway."[35]

However, if Thurman appreciated the Presbyterian support, he saw no reason why other denominations might not also support the project. He tried to get the American Baptist Convention to provide funds, without success.[36] And Thurman was always suspicious of the broader motives of the Presbyterians, confiding in his journal shortly after his arrival in San Francisco that "the Pres. church expects to exercise the same control as it does over other Pres. Churches that are not self-supporting."[37] Thurman and the Presbyterians saw Fellowship Church through very different lenses. For Thurman, it was simply the most important experiment in lived Christianity taking place in the United States, and the church authorities should be "in some sense humbled by the magnitude of the opportunity" to support it.[38] The primary interest of the Presbyterian Church was to create a mission church in San Francisco to address the practical and spiritual needs of the city's burgeoning Black community.[39]

Thurman from the outset was certain that the delivery of social services to the Black community was not the purpose of Fellowship Church. If defined as a mission church, it would be seen as (and would likely become) a Black church, one that was at best only incidentally interracial. When Thurman thought that the venerable Rosenwald Foundation, especially noted for building schools for Blacks in the South, might be involved in the church, he offered a strong negative to Fisk in early 1944: "Mrs. Thurman and I have talked the matter through very carefully and we are agreed that it would be very unfortunate if our coming out there was subsidized by the Rosenwald Foundation, or any of the uplift foundations with which we are acquainted."[40] Uplift, for Thurman, was the opposite of integration. If Fellowship Church became, or became perceived as, a mission church—a church sponsored by a largely white denomination as a mission to a Black neighborhood—it would, in the minds of Blacks, simply recapitulate "the deadly disease of condescension," an illness that "has dogged the vitality and health of the Christian enterprise." If perceived to be a mission church, it would become "a dumping ground for do-gooders who would get an uplift once a week by coming into the Negro community and helping a struggling interracial activity. I wanted people to come because of the contribution it makes to their lives."[41] (And perhaps Blacks would have seen the church's Black minister as mere window dressing for the white denomination that was really calling the shots.) The Presbyterian Church, Thurman wrote in 1947, had tried to turn Fellowship Church into an unwitting agent of racial separation.[42] As Thurman emphasized in italics in his history of Fellowship Church, "*if a man feels sorry for you, he can very easily absolve himself from dealing with you in any sense as an equal,*" and helpfulness becomes "twisted into a form of patronage under which human dignity cannot exist."[43] (In an interview later in life he remembered when, for several years as a young boy, he had been clothed out of his school's "missionary barrel" in which there were discarded garments sent down to Daytona from New England. He felt a "deep resentment about this" and thought that one of the goals of Fellowship Church was to "learn how the necessities of people could be relieved and their dignity held intact.")[44]

From the Presbyterian perspective, its Board of National Missions was under the impression that "while this work was to be interracial in character . . . the primary function was to serve the immediate community in which the project was located." Moreover, a Presbyterian official concluded that from all reports, Fellowship Church had, by August 1945, made "little impression upon the immediate community within whose bounds the Fellowship Church has been located." He concluded that "unfortunately, your objective in the establishment of the Fellowship Church" and that of the Presbyterian Church "were not one and the same objective." Thurman could not have agreed more.[45]

By February 1945, the church already was having serious discussions about its future, and Thurman informed his Presbyterian contacts that "some kind of interdenominational structure" was likely, and that the church was exploring "the prospects of us becoming self-sustaining."[46] By that summer, it was time for a general membership meeting on this subject, and a letter was sent to all the members of Fellowship Church who had signed the Commitment, asking them if they wanted (1) to become a regular Presbyterian congregation, (2) to continue the current relationship of some connection to the Presbyterian Church, or (3) to become fully independent. Presumably Thurman kept his own counsel during the debate, a "vast fog of conversation" generated by the church's current members, but it was likely that few had doubts about Thurman's position. Almost everyone agreed with him—the vote was overwhelmingly in favor of becoming an independent congregation, cutting loose the Presbyterian connection (and its attendant funding).[47] "Suddenly we were on our own without a roof over our heads, with no organized backing," and this caused "a moment of panic—quiet, muted, glowing panic."[48] (Since the Presbyterian Church was providing support for Fellowship Church at its current location, they quickly had to find a new home for the church.)[49] Christianity, Thurman often complained, was "adjectival." There was no such thing as a mere church: "It has to be some kind of church—Methodist, Baptist, Congregational, or what not."[50] For Thurman, Fellowship Church would espouse a Christianity, a religion, without the adjectives.

There were costs to the decisions to leave its original neighborhood and to cut ties with the Presbyterian Church. Fellowship Church was thereafter fated to remain a relatively small church, and it never became a real political or social force in the Black community. Thurman argued that while the church was not a "worker's church," neither was it a "white-collar" church, dominated by professionals, but it seems fair to say that its membership was predominantly middle class.[51] Without the Presbyterian connection, it was chronically strapped for funds, its high ambitions often tethered by its short purse strings. And it meant that the roiling social problems of Black San Franciscans would only be indirectly addressed by the church. Legitimate questions were raised at the time, and can be raised today, as to whether Thurman made the right decision, whether he gave up too much to create and maintain an interracial church. Thurman himself never had any doubts. He wrote friends back at Howard a few months after the decisions were made that Fellowship Church was "no longer an 'experiment' or a 'venture.'"[52]

Two other changes happened to Fellowship Church in short order. Thurman had to resolve his status. He had come out to San Francisco in July 1944 on a one-year leave of absence from Howard. In 1945 it was renewed for a second year. It would not be renewed for a third, and by early 1946 Thurman was faced with a very difficult decision. His preferred solution would have been to split his time between Fellowship Church and Howard University, using his time at Howard to, among other things, groom assistant ministers for the church.[53] He tried to interest President Johnson in the plan, but in April 1946 Johnson wrote Thurman that all wartime leaves were canceled and that, if he wanted to retain his Howard affiliation, he needed to return for the full 1946–47 academic year.[54] Thurman decided to resign his position at Howard, writing that he did so "with emotional lacerations and a deep sense of personal loss."[55] Many, like Benjamin Mays, were shocked to hear that Thurman had severed his ties to Howard, but Thurman was convinced that in having to choose between "two things, both of which must be right," he had opted for the one "more completely in line with oughtness than the other."[56] After the painful decision, there was catharsis. He wrote shortly after his resignation that "it goes without saying that this was the most crucial decision of my life, because it means burning bridges behind and sailing forth in the open independence of the sea."[57] Whatever feeling he had had that the San

Francisco position was just temporary, that his real life was elsewhere, was over. As he wrote another friend, "I feel a deep urgency and an exhilaration in the choice."[58]

A few months later, Alfred Fisk resigned his position as copastor of Fellowship Church. This was probably not much of a surprise to Thurman. After the decision to sever the Presbyterian connection, Fisk had written in September 1945 to Presbyterian officials in the denomination's Philadelphia headquarters that he deeply regretted the move and that it meant "that my own relation to this church will terminate in the near future."[59] In addition, his relationship with many of the members of the church had frequently been strained, and he had been accused, by various parties, "of trying to impose my ideas on a church that did not want them." The previous year had been a "battleground of such conflict I long to resolve it and find some way to relieve the tension." The primary reason Fisk gave to Thurman for leaving was a lack of a Sunday school for his son, but his resignation was a culmination of accumulated grievances.[60]

Perhaps Fisk's most important consideration was simply that, after two years, Thurman's leadership and his charismatic presence made Fisk superfluous. Thurman's reaction to the resignation is unknown, but he probably felt it was inevitable. He had written a friend in 1945 that the copastorate was more symbolic than practical, since it was difficult to have two equal sources of authority in a single organization, concluding that "the church should outgrow the copastor arrangement as soon as possible. Obviously, such an arrangement is artificial."[61] The parting between Fisk and Thurman seems to have been amicable, though there is no indication that they remained in close contact.[62] But by the fall of 1946, Fellowship Church was Thurman's church.

Without Fisk or the Presbyterians, Thurman proceeded to, as democratically as possible, shape Fellowship Church in his own image. The church's raison d'être, its calling card, was its interracialism, and this had to be carefully maintained. On one level it was a matter of raw numbers. In 1949 the church had about 285 members, 60 percent of whom were white.[63] Two years later, the church had 345 members; a little more than half were white, 40 percent were African American, and 10 percent were Asian.[64]

But interracialism in an institution like Fellowship Church was far more complicated than its gross percentages. The church faced the fundamental paradox of all intentional interracial institutions—the path to "color blindness," creating a situation in which a concern about racial balances can be relaxed, requires, at first, a phase of acute color vigilance. Responsibilities and authority must be distributed fairly. Attention must be paid to perceptions as well as realities. The tendency for white dominance even in (or especially in) interracial settings had to be addressed firmly but without creating hard feelings. Thurman was uncertain if the Black members of the church would remain if the church had a white minister.[65] Virginia Scardigli, the church secretary, wrote in 1947 that "in the early days we made a special effort to get a 'mixed bouquet' in all our groups and committees in order to demonstrate the interracial aspect. That is not done now."[66] This is too sweeping a statement; these matters were still taken very seriously (certainly by Thurman) for years thereafter. He became alarmed that the choir, perhaps seen as a traditional African American role in a church, had become "4/5ths Negro." He spoke to the (white) choral director and "insisted that she work at restoring a more authentic inter-racial balance to the choir."[67] This was done. Thurman felt that maintaining "an authentic inter-racial institution in our kind of multi-racial society takes a special kind of ability, sensitiveness, and program."[68]

One issue at the time that called for particular sensitivity was the per-ception that intimacy in worship was a waystation to physical intimacy. "The question of intermarriage," he wrote in his history of Fellowship Church, "is the fact, or the red herring, that provides the final roadblock to realistic con-siderations of integration."[69] As part of his ministry he officiated at interra-cial marriages and sometimes tried to calm the nerves and fears of friends and family who thought that such unions were destined to fail.[70] Thurman related a conversation he had with a fellow minister who told him, somewhat facetiously, "Well, old man, all you need is one significant intermarriage in Fellowship Church, and that'll be the end of the dream."[71] He thought he was being jocular; Thurman didn't think it was funny. He rejected the contention that an interracial church was a "breeding ground" for interracial marriages but acknowledged that it made their possibility more likely. This was fine. To take any other position was to somehow justify "the long agony of shame in the South from the days of slavery to now."[72]

The church employed several ways of trying to create an "authentic inter-racial institution." One crucial way was through what was then called "inter-cultural education" and what we now label "multiculturalism" or "diversity training." There was no better place for this than San Francisco, a city with an extraordinary racial and ethnic mix, with (as an early church brochure put it) "sixty-three national and cultural background groups."[73] It was very important for the Thurmans to get beyond the Black-white dyad that domi-nated most American discussions of race. As another brochure boasted, the church was located in a city that "in a very real sense . . . is the crossroads of the world" and for a home of Fellowship Church, "no better spot could have been selected."[74] Intercultural education was for the Thurmans one of the most important tasks of the church. Sue was in charge of its extensive inter-cultural programs.[75] There were special programs for children, at summer school and during the year. Special funding was raised for an Intercultural Workshop.[76] The program included visits to different ethnic and religious communities in the city and offered arts and crafts and other activities along similar lines.[77] For adults there was an Intercultural Concert Series and an Intercultural Library of several hundred volumes. Young adults had their own intercultural program, described in a 1947 brochure, capturing the church's interracial ideal:

> An open fire cracked and popped. Hearthside rays glanced from an East Indian reflected to the intense faces—the faces of young people in dis-cussion—all young Americans—a Negro sailor from Chicago, a Nisei girl, a native San Franciscan, a Caucasian from a southern state, a Filipino youth leader. . . . Questions, answers, opinions flew back and forth. Sud-denly the mugs of cocoa appeared, the discussion drew to a close. . . . The whole group joined in laughter, song, and fun.[78]

Intercultural programs of this sort had become increasingly popular in the 1930s and 1940s.[79] Their main goal was to explore cultural difference without reducing difference to stereotypes.[80] The challenge—recognizing individual complexity while respecting group identity—was a tall order, as was the effort to not use white American middle-class culture, circa 1945, as the invariable standard by which to judge other people or peoples. As a 1947 publication of Fellowship Church queried: "Can a Church operate a junior intercultural workshop which does not develop a 'missionary' or 'settlement' attitude in the children about themselves or the people they are acquainted with?"[81] Revers-ing the missionary impulse, bringing other cultures and peoples to American Protestantism rather than the reverse, was a quest close to Thurman's heart.

One frequent criticism of intercultural programs then, or multicultural programs now, is that they can amount to an evasion of politics, or a failure to recognize that some ethnicities were more unequal than others.[82] This was not so for Fellowship Church, where there was no sense that the recognition of the "cultural equality" or "diversity" was in any way a substitute for the fight for genuine political equality. The church's basic, distinctly left-of-center political commitments were probably too widely shared and too fervently believed to require constant reinforcement or reiteration. Still, Thurman did his best to keep the message of the church from becoming too overtly political or ideological. Thurman was in many ways a deeply political person, but his complicated sense of politics required a clear separation between the spheres of religion and that of social agitation and change, such that the purity of the former vouchsafed the legitimacy of the latter. Only when they were distinct could they function together, without one dominating the other.

For Thurman, politics had to remain away from the church's core. As he told *Time* magazine in 1948: "Our hardest job has been to keep our church from becoming a social whip. The radicals bear down, say that we are not in there fighting. Others want us to become an organization, a placement bureau, a mission that gives people jobs and gives away shoes. We are a religious group. It is important that we give strength to people working on interracial problems, but the interracial character of our own group is becoming the least significant part of it. . . . We have remained a church."[83] Jean Burden wrote in 1953 that a few persons in the congregation "have tried to pressure him [Thurman] into endorsing their own political beliefs" and noted that "one woman walked out on one of his sermons because she felt he wasn't meeting the social issue squarely." As Thurman told Burden at the time: "People are always trying to tie a label on me. I'm nothing."[84]

What was crucial to Thurman? As he wrote a friend in 1948: "I wish you might visit the church sometime and have the sense of wholeness that comes from participating in the fellowship of God as a human spirit without age, sex, race, or denomination. There is something cleansing about ridding oneself of barriers that separate one from one's fellows."[85] Fellowship Church existed to raze spiritual walls. When it happened, the experience amounted to what Thurman called a "common faith," which did not mean "one creed, one doctrine, one dogma, one church" but "a pulse beat that is so fontal, that is so basic to all of the movements of life" that, as he said of the worship in the church in a 1952 service: "*This is a universe! This is a universe!*"[86]

Thurman used many techniques to create this feeling. He brought his distinctive views about worship with him from Rankin Chapel. In San Francisco he held regular experimental services featuring liturgical dance and created a Liturgical Dance Choir to lead the dance services. "It is the genius of the dance," Thurman would write in his history of Fellowship Church, "to effect by movement in space a synthesis of body, mind, and spirit."[87] As Thurman intoned appropriate readings, such as from Rabindranath Tagore's *Gitanjili,* dancers improvised, in Martha Graham modern dance style, to recordings of medieval and Renaissance music, or choreographic re-creations of the visionary drawings of William Blake, or dances to opera.[88]

As at Howard, Thurman led a Christmas vesper service based on re-creations of Renaissance paintings of the Madonna figure. Unlike at Howard, though, where the racial diversity had to be imported, the congregation could itself supply much of the needed variety to populate the tableaux, one of which included persons of "American Indian, Caucasian, Negro, Filipino, Korean,

Chinese, Italian, French, Armenian" descent.[89] There were special music services as well, such as a vesper service devoted to the "music and liturgy of the synagogue."[90] There were art exhibits, often by church members such as Peggy Strong, an artist who encouraged Thurman to take up painting, which became a hobby for the remainder of his years.[91] (His specialty was paintings of penguins—birds that carried their distinctive white-and-black coloration with dignity.) Another genre of art at the church would be the occasional "color motion picture service," often a nature film, with poetic commentary by Thurman.[92] Choric speaking, or choirs declaiming in unison, was another innovation, as were dramatic presentations during worship services. In 1949, the church hosted a Religious Arts Festival, which included a performance of Sophocles's *Antigone* and a performance of the spiritual-based oratorio *The Ordering of Moses* by the African American composer R. Nathaniel Dett. The church also had a choir that practiced the delicate art of hand-bell ringing.[93]

Music was always very important to Thurman, with classical music, hymn tunes, and spirituals at the core of his musical tastes. He evinced little interest in Black musical genres more recent than spirituals, such as jazz, blues, or gospel (or at least they make little appearance in his writings.) His favorite composer was Beethoven, and he was especially drawn to the hushed secrets of the late quartets. "If I could share the mystery of the lonely giant Beethoven," he once wrote, "I would have the clue to my own solitariness."[94] One of Thurman's most astute students, James Earl Massey, compared Thurman's sermonic style to late Beethoven, with its sudden starts and stops, its syncopations and suspensions, "almost forcing one to become introspective." It seems unlikely that Thurman consciously modeled himself on Beethoven, but both men were masters of a style that often conveyed a casual, almost conversational profundity.[95]

Thurman was proud of his recruitment of a first-rate choral director, Corrine Williams, for the church.[96] Williams was one-fifth of the Fellowship Quintet, a group in addition to Williams, a white woman, consisted of men of Dutch, Mexican, Chinese, and African American backgrounds.[97] The Fellowship Quintet appeared professionally at events in the Bay Area and elsewhere on the West Coast and made recordings. It was, for Thurman, "an ambulatory example of the basic concept upon which our church was built."[98] A highlight for the Fellowship Quintet was a 1949 trip to Paris to perform at a UNESCO convention, with other engagements at the Sorbonne and in London.[99] There were criticisms that the church was too "highbrow," and there is no doubt that Thurman's services could be very refined. Music had a liturgical function for Thurman, and perhaps, as one observer commented, the high quality of the church's music was "to accomplish without ritual the same kind of dignity and

The Thurman family, late 1940s, at home in San Francisco. *From left:* Olive
Thurman, Howard Thurman, Sue Bailey Thurman, Anne Spencer Thurman

decorum that exist in the Catholic and Episcopal churches."[100] It was a ceremonial call to inwardness rather than to outward observance. What Thurman
said of the dance can be extended to his view of all arts as vehicles for worship:
"Modern man, too often beset by sins and anxiety, desperately needs experiences that make for wholeness, for synthesis, for validation," for the "integrat-
ing moment."[101]

Thurman was also deeply attracted to the least ritualized of all forms of
Christian worship, the Quaker meeting; without music, formal sermon, liturgy, or structures, the meeting was simply an immersion in collective solitude. He had been introduced to Quaker worship while studying with Rufus
Jones at Haverford College in 1929. As he told the Fellowship Church congregation in 1951, at his first-ever Quaker meeting he sat in a plain room, and
at first, "nobody said a word . . . just silence." As he described the experience:
"I was just Howard Thurman. And then . . . I don't know when it happened,
how it happened, but sometime in that hour I passed over the invisible line
and became one with all the Quakers. I wasn't Howard Thurman anymore;
I was a human spirit, involved in a creative moment with other spirits, in the
presence of God."[102] At another Quaker meeting, after an extended period of
silence, a verse of scripture that he was about to quote was suddenly recited by

another participant, and "it seemed that all in that room were sharing deeply in the same kind of transcending experience which greatly confirmed and sustained us all but was at the same time much, much more than any one of us, in and of himself."[103]

Thurman tried to bring this feeling to Fellowship Church. As he wrote, "The most significant result in the Fellowship Church communion is not the participation in the fellowship by a cross section of people, but rather it is quality of the individual's religious experience achieved through worship and the effect of that experience on daily behavior."[104] For Thurman, the "most important part of the service is the period of meditation preceding the sermon." In 1948 he introduced a half-hour meditation service, before the regular service, devoted to "the deepening of one's private devotional life in fellowship together." Breaking somewhat from the Quaker pattern, soft organ music was played during the meditation period. As a "pump primer," Thurman started to prepare short mimeographed meditations for each service. At the end of the meditation service, Thurman would summarize in two or three sentences reflections on his own meditation and then withdraw, with the main service beginning after a five-minute break.[105] Thurman would eventually publish five volumes of these meditations. The church also developed a meditation room, filled with religious texts and artifacts from many different religious traditions.

What was an average Sunday morning like at Fellowship Church? Jean Burden has a vivid recollection of a first visit, sometime in the early 1950s: "I looked around at the congregation as it slowly filled the pews. About half were Black, the other half divided between white, Oriental, and a smattering of East Indians in saris and turbans." Those in attendance were "alert for a personal religious experience." The organist played a Bach fugue, the choir began to process and sing: "At the end of the line walked a stocky black bear of a man in academic robes, singing the processional in a hearty, off-key baritone. . . . When the sermon began, I studied him. . . . Merriment lurked in those murky depths of eyes, but when the light dimmed they were sad. His long hands, pale palmed, were constantly moving, clutching his closely cropped head, pointing dramatically to the ceiling, leveling them at us in gestures of appeal or exasperation. Then I was caught up in his voice and the poetry of his words, and Howard Thurman the man became Howard Thurman the spellbinder."[106]

Starting in 1948, we know much more about Thurman's sermons because many of them were recorded. Taking advantage of what then was a new technology, only recently introduced commercially, and with the largest of a benefactor, Fellowship Church acquired the ability to tape-record sermons.[107] Thurman, who always felt that his most effective means of communication was through his largely extemporaneous sermons, and whose previous sermons were almost all lost to the ether, was delighted. He soon started holding regular midweek study sessions with interested members of the congregation at which the sermon was replayed and analyzed and discussed by Thurman and the study group.[108]

Thurman's sermons were rarely topical, certain extraordinary events excepted.[109] As Jean Burden observed in 1953 in the church, "There are no sermons on the racial problem, on politics, on bigotry" as such, but almost every sermon, in one way or another, addressed what Thurman felt to be "the mainspring of social ills," inequality, separation, and spiritual apathy rather than their particular manifestations.[110] Thurman did not, save for Holy Week and Christmas, tie his sermons to the liturgical year. Nor, with a few exceptions, did he tie his sermons to particular Biblical prooftexts.[111] Thurman often presented his sermons in a topically related series, providing a sense of continuity and anticipation and giving Thurman an ability to explore a given topic in its many facets or to deepen, with appropriate variations, a given line of thought. The topic of a sermon series could be quite specific, such as "The Message of the Hebrew Prophets," or more general, such as "Man and the Moral Struggle."[112] In the spring and summer of 1953 he delivered his final sermon series at Fellowship Church, thirteen sermons on major figures in the history of mysticism. In the final sermon in the series, he quoted Virgil's last words in Dante's *Divine Comedy,* as Dante went up to the empyrean: "This is as far as we can go—as far as I can go. From now on you are on your own."[113] The summer of 1953 was a time for both Thurman and the members of Fellowship Church to ponder what had they accomplished together and what they would, henceforth, have to achieve separately.

Thurman had little doubt that when he moved to San Francisco, his new job was of the utmost national importance, a "revolutionary idea," because "the kind of church we are building has never been built in the United States before."[114] Thurman tried "to give the widest possible spread to the knowledge concerning the venture because it will help a climate in which this sort of thing can take place effectively in other parts of the country."[115] When he was in negotiations to leave Howard University in the spring of 1946, he wrote that "it seems clear to me that for the next 10 or 15 years I should give my life to the Fellowship Church Movement in this country," telling Mordecai Wyatt Johnson at about the same time that "ultimately, I hope to give all my time to developing the ideas of Fellowship Church in various parts of America."[116]

Thurman worked extensively to publicize the church. He wrote articles about it within months of his arrival and spoke about it extensively on his tours, paying special attention to calls from other cities from ministers who wanted to start something similar to Fellowship Church.[117] He would eventually develop a monthly, and subsequently a quarterly, magazine, the *Growing Edge*—long one of Thurman's favorite phrases—for the church that would further spread the message. In the early 1950s it had more than nine hundred subscribers, probably including Martin Luther King, Jr., who definitely was a reader of the magazine.[118] Every issue contained a recent sermon by Thurman.[119]

The *Growing Edge* was one way to keep in contact with the "national associates" or "at-large" members of Fellowship Church.[120] They were central in Thurman's vision of the church from the outset, giving a small church in San Francisco a national presence and ambit. By the early 1950s there were about 1,200 national associates.[121] One of the first, something Thurman was always quite proud of, was Eleanor Roosevelt.[122] Other national associates included Benjamin Mays, Mary McLeod Bethune, Ralph Bunche, and Mordecai Wyatt Johnson.[123] Another was the South African novelist Alan Paton, who dedicated his most famous novel, *Cry, The Beloved Country,* to two members of Fellowship Church for their extraordinary help in getting it published. After attending a service, "the spirit of the church impressed Mr. Paton so deeply" that he wanted "to speak to the church." His lecture, an early account of the evils of apartheid, was published in the *Growing Edge.*[124]

National associates of the church were crucial benefactors and fundraisers, the most deep-pocketed of whom formed a special group called Friends of Fellowship Church. They funded the *Growing Edge* and, most importantly, provided the subvention that allowed Fellowship Church, after wandering to three unsatisfactory places in its first half decade, to purchase, in 1949, its permanent home. This was located at 2041 Larkin Street, in a North San Francisco neighborhood whose residents were then primarily Italian and Chinese. Formerly it had been St. John's Evangelical and Reformed Church, built in the late nineteenth century, where at one time Gustav Niebuhr, Reinhold's father, had served as minister. The building could safely accommodate five hundred persons in the sanctuary, with room downstairs to accommodate an overflow. Obtaining it had been an adventure. Thurman and the church found that "no commercial institution would lend us the money despite individual collateral of property holders, because primarily as an interracial institution it [*sic*] was the feeling that we had no future."[125] National members Emily and Arthur Crosby chaired the Friends of Fellowship Church, raised the funds, around forty thousand dollars, needed to purchase the church, and then lent them to the church, interest-free. With the help of other wealthy national members, the church was able to pay back the loan in only three years.[126] Thurman did not envision this as the final home for the church and dreamed of a new home, built for the congregation, with a theater and other amenities, and a sanctuary, designed by him, that would, in stone and wood, depict "the natural evolution of man's worship of God," connecting the worshippers to the omni-religious drama of "the deepest yearnings of the human spirit to come to itself in its Creator."[127]

To start to realize these ambitions, after purchasing the building on Larkin Street, Thurman's national ambitions for the church increased. He had spent his first six years at Fellowship Church wanting "to make the case for this kind of fellowship at the level of the grassroots before anything else was attempted."[128] Now he wanted to bring the church to a national audience, and in 1951 had a series of "public dinners for the purpose of giving wide exposure to our idea and experience" the following spring.[129] The most impressive event was a dinner sponsored by the New York Committee for Support of the Fellowship Church that raised almost three thousand dollars, with many Black and white notables in attendance, and Broadway star John Raitt providing the entertainment.[130] Articles on the church in *Time* magazine, the *Christian Century,* and the *Atlantic* helped broadcast Thurman's dreams.[131] Interviewed in early 1953 for the article in the *Atlantic,* he stated that "what we are fumbling towards now" at Fellowship Church "tomorrow will be the way of life for everybody."[132] "Sue and I," he wrote in his autobiography, "were totally involved in our work, our community; we were comfortably settled, for life."[133] Yet by the time he spoke to the *Atlantic* he had already made the decision to leave Fellowship Church to accept a position as dean of chapel and professor of spiritual disciplines and resources at Boston University's School of Theology. It was a surprising decision for many, at least as unexpected, if not more so, than his decision, a decade earlier, to leave Howard University and come to San Francisco.

If there were successes at Fellowship Church, there were also problems, tensions, and incompatibilities. From the beginning, Thurman's national ambitions for Fellowship Church clashed with those who wanted to keep it a local, neighborhood church. The national associates were important in the church, but early plans to use them as nuclei of their own independent churches in their home cities never materialized, and as Thurman acknowledged, the associate members had "of necessity, an informal relationship to the church," and it was "never quite possible to involve them in the overall activity of the church in a consistently creative and effective manner."[134] On the other hand, the national associates paid most of the bills, and the local church members were both grateful and somewhat resentful of their role. When Thurman left the ministry of the church in 1953, its national apparatus collapsed in fairly short order.

By 1953 it was clear that what Thurman sometimes called the "Fellowship Church Movement" was not growing rapidly.[135] There had been a brief surge of intentional interracial congregations founded during and in the immediate aftermath of World War II and interest in what was called "the emergence of the interracial church" as a small but growing trend in American Christianity.[136] But after this initial flurry, few other congregations organized themselves along explicitly interracial lines. In the end, as Mark Wild has suggested, Fellowship Church was "widely admired but rarely imitated."[137]

Part of this slow growth was a consequence of contradictions inherent in the idea of a Fellowship Church Movement. Thurman's goal was not to create a string of integrated churches; it was to integrate the American church. As Homer Jack wrote of the early interracial churches, they were trying to create "a pattern by which it will seem natural and practical for existing churches more nearly to adopt this interracial ideal."[138] Although Thurman worked to promote other interracial congregations, he was adamant that he did not want other Fellowship Churches: "To multiply ourselves on the basis of program and commitment and thereby become another denomination" would be a mistake. To "make this a new sect" would be just one more attempt to overcome the divisions in Christianity by adding to them.[139] The more successful the idea of interracial churches becomes, the less the need for intentionally interracial churches. As Thurman wrote in 1945: "It seems to me that if an established church is in a community that wishes to become an open church it should do so without dramatizing the fact. If this is done, the development would be normal and the assimilation of the various minorities would be a relaxed process."[140]

But the larger problem was that interracialism in American worship remained an anomaly. Most white churches remained white, Black churches remained Black, all at best nominally interracial. Without a concerted effort to have an interracial congregation, most African Americans and other racial minorities would continue to feel unwelcome at white churches. And as Thurman noted in 1959, the racial geography of the postwar American city, with whites leaving in large numbers, had made the creation of interracial congregations more difficult.[141] And most Blacks remained skeptical of interracial churches, as if they were surrendering their most precious possessions. As Thurman wrote in 1950, the social situation "of the Negro in this country is so rugged that for the most part despite whatever confidence he might have in me as a person he has looked with the greatest suspicion upon the validity of this kind of enterprise. He is slow to believe because his faith has been so prostituted and exploited."[142] In 1950 Benjamin Mays made the bold prediction that a half century hence "there will be no Negro church in the year 2000 and there will be no white churches. There will only exist Christian churches." It was a sentiment echoed by Thurman (and, subsequently, by Martin Luther King, Jr.), if not with the same confidence or specificity.[143] In truth, as Thurman, Mays, and King no doubt always knew, the Black church had little to fear from the interracial church movement. In many ways, the interracial church movement had plateaued by the early 1950s.

In his frankest moments, Thurman would acknowledge there was a certain artificial, aspirational quality to the race relations at the church. In 1951 he contemplated having his younger daughter, Anne, spend a few weeks at Fisk University in Nashville to learn the lesson that America was "still a bitter place for a sensitive Negro man or woman," and "it would be tragic if she is not emotionally equipped to deal with the vicissitudes of American life that have not been informed by the idealism of Fellowship Church." One "of the peculiar costs of the kind of undertaking in which Mrs. Thurman and I are engaged is that unless we plan it carefully, our younger daughter will find it difficult to develop a sense of group roots," and Thurman wanted to toughen her, so to be better able to deflect "the poison arrows of a socially sick environment that expresses itself in gross and refined hostilities."[144]

There were other, more personal factors related to his career and his personal priorities that likely contributed to his decision to leave Fellowship Church. It is no doubt true, as Thurman said in 1953 of the turbulence in church affairs, that "life cannot continue to be life when there are no tensions. . . . We are very alive here."[145] That said, he wearied of his role as day-to-day manager and umpire of the church affairs, refereeing squabbles, trying to prevent the endemic factionalism of church members from becoming too disruptive. These had only increased over time. Fundraising was never congenial to him. Many old friends, like Mary McLeod Bethune, writing in 1951 after her first visit to the church, wondered about the wisdom of him putting so much of his time and energies into this often all-consuming task: "I pray that it is going to be possible, Howard, for you to concentrate your efforts upon the very distinctive work of the Church, and someone else will take care of the fund-raising."[146] Every year he took off a month in the winter to make a speaking tour in the East, often piling on multiple speaking engagements in churches, schools, and colleges daily, using "all of my physical resources not only to raise money for the church but also to secure enough funds to supplement my salary to make ends meet."[147] This schedule was, by his own admission, a "man-killer. It is far more than any sane man should undertake."[148]

Another, subtler, problem was that Thurman had become so identified with Fellowship Church that it became difficult to know where Thurman ended and the church began. Because his sermons and his bearing were such compelling explorations of his own spirituality, "many of our members, at first, believed with my belief until they were able to believe with their own belief."[149] Though he wanted those who heard him "to have a sense of God rather than a sense of Thurman," for many, the latter was an indispensable first step to the former, and some never got beyond that first step. He was "constantly harassed" by outsiders referring to church members as "Thurman followers."[150] In 1951, an article on the church in the *Christian Century* posed the following questions: "What is the future of this church? Is that future bound up with Dr. Thurman, so that this experiment in right human relations will end when he gives up its leadership? Opinions differ within the congregation."[151] Thurman was uncertain himself. At one meeting of the church board he was shocked when a proposal was made for the church to take out a life insurance policy on his life. For Thurman "it seemed incredible" that "our survival as a religious fellowship could possibly be dependent upon any human individual."[152] But this is perhaps what happens when, as he acknowledged, the church was being made such a reflection of his religious, political, and even his aesthetic judgments that "in a sense I 'called' the membership, whereas usually the membership calls its minister." As he wrote, "perhaps no sentiment occurred more in my own private prayer life than that my ego would not come between the people and God."[153] This was one prayer that God did not, and perhaps could not, always answer.

But likely Thurman's greatest dissatisfaction with Fellowship Church was the lack of teaching opportunities and the lack of regular contact with Black graduate students and seminarians. For the sixteen years prior to his coming to San Francisco, in Washington and Atlanta, Thurman had combined the roles of pastor and teacher. In San Francisco he was largely limited to the role of pastor. He continued to do some college teaching while at Fellowship Church. He taught so successfully at the University of Iowa in the 1946 summer session that they offered him a tenured position in the School of Religion.[154] This would have made him one of the first African American tenured professors at a major university, but he turned it down.[155] Weighing against it was Iowa's nearly all-white student body. He wrote a correspondent that he would have "prefer[red] teaching in one of our own schools [that is, a HBCU] if I am to remain in teaching."[156] He would write at the end of 1950 of an impending visit to Morgan College in Baltimore and the "keen anticipation" of once again "living in the thought world of Negro students."[157] Fellowship Church could never satisfy his interest in teaching African American students.

Still, there seems to have been little urgency on Thurman's part to leave Fellowship Church. As late as October 1952, answering an inquiry about a possible pastoral position in Chicago, he was adamant that "my commitment and satisfaction in the work here are of such that I would have no interest in considering any change."[158] But Boston University soon convinced him otherwise. Thurman had known the university's president, Harold Case, since the mid-1930s, when he was a Methodist minister in Kansas. In 1937, as described in chapter 8, Thurman, speaking at a Methodist conference in St. Louis, had been barred from eating in the hotel's dining room. When, later that evening, still furious, he arrived at the train station for the Pullman berth that was to take him to his next speaking engagement, waiting for him at the station were Harold and Phyllis Case. They told him that "our main purpose for meeting you here is to say that if the time ever comes when we can take some firm, even dramatic action to show that the incident that happened here is not our desire or in keeping with the true genius of the Methodist Church, I want you to know that you can depend on us to do it."[159] By 1953 the time had come.

In July 1952 Walter Muelder, dean of the School of Theology, wrote Thurman asking if he had "given any thought to the possibility of returning to academic life? Could I possibly interest you in considering a position here at Boston University School of Theology? I think you have a great deal to give to theological students in many ways."[160] Thurman's response was guarded, but he expressed some interest.[161] The campaign to lure Thurman to Boston continued with a December phone conversation with Case, after which he allowed that the idea of the move "was significantly challenging to me," the attractive possibilities had to be balanced against the deep responsibility he felt to the church members and to "the hundreds of little people scattered all over the United States, whose hopes have been revived because of our survival up to this time."[162] In early January 1953, when both Case and Thurman were in Los Angeles for a conference, Case evidently upped the ante, offering Thurman the deanship of the university chapel (the position he had held at Howard), a tenured professorship of Spiritual Disciplines and Resources, and an offer to take "leadership of religion in the life of Boston University."[163] The agreement to come to Boston was consummated during Thurman's previously planned speaking tour in Massachusetts. On 9 March, Thurman wrote a letter to the board and members of Fellowship Church, stating that he was accepting the offer and would be moving to Boston in the fall.[164]

Many in the church were crestfallen on hearing the news. Coleman Jennings wrote Thurman congratulating him on the rightness of the new position but added that he knew that "this does not reduce the pain. I have a full realization of what that will be, the pathetic look from the eyes of those who will have to face life without you, the haunting question of how your years of work will stand up in your absence."[165] Some members of Fellowship Church were openly hostile. Joseph Van Pelt, a member of the Fellowship Quintet, wrote, "Personally, I feel tremendously let down by your leaving, and keep asking myself if it would have made any difference had the progress of Fellowship Church been more rapid and dramatic, but I think not." "Howard Thurman the man" was revealed as a lesser and different person than "Reverend Thurman" the Sunday preacher, and Van Pelt told him that "I have used you as the very cornerstone of my faith, and now I must clear away the debris and start again."[166] Some tried to satisfy themselves that Fellowship Church's loss would be humanity's gain: "We will miss you but we feel that you will do a greater work; with the youth coming out of Boston University it will establish that fellowship all over the world."[167] An interested observer, from the Buddhist Church of San Francisco, saw the move in terms of karmic uplift: "In this incarnation you have been born into the Negro Race, being the One selected to lift that race higher in the estimation of mankind as a whole. You accomplished this with your wonderful work at the Fellowship Church but the Divine Law knows when certain work is finished. Now, with your latest appointment, you elevate the entire Negro Race still higher."[168] But, if in the aftermath of the decision Thurman was "emotionally raw because of what it means to think of leaving here," he saw it as necessary and probably delayed too long the severing of apron strings.[169] He wrote that "after a series of various kinds of meetings, we are all slowly reconciled to the fact that one of the surest ways for the church to find its own feet is for me to be out of the picture for a while." After a year's absence, "there will be rather strong indications of the stamina or lack of stamina of the church."[170]

Surely no man has ever loved a church as much as Thurman loved Fellowship Church. As he wrote as he was preparing to leave for Boston: "I have given nine . . . very productive years to the launching of this church. Into it has gone the kind of sustained work unlike anything I have ever given to any commitment. This church is as much of my life as any dream or its projection could possibly be."[171] As he wrote in his history of Fellowship Church, there "is a perpetual dilemma which constantly faces any creative movement of the spirit: If the movement is to last, it must somehow be caught and embodied in concrete manifestation. And yet when it is embodied in a concrete form like an organization or institution, the vitality tends to disintegrate."[172] If the idea of Fellowship Church were to survive, it had to be as a "kind of freemasonry, spreading all over the world," something operating outside of, or alongside, existing institutions.[173]

Thurman in the late 1940s was fond of quoting the abysmal statistic that less than one-tenth of 1 percent of Protestant churches had any significant racial mixing. If the numbers are now somewhat better, the "freemasonry" of Fellowship Church is one of the reasons why. So, too, if the sort of ser-vices Thurman championed—Christian, but explicitly interreligious, with extended periods of meditation—no longer seem so exotic within liberal Protestantism, or within liberal religious practices of any description, surely Thurman and Fellowship Church played a significant role in this.[174] Fellow-ship Church would be, over his long professional life, the summit of Howard Thurman's career, the position he was most fond of, most proud of, and he was sure that it would be his most enduring legacy. But all things come to an end. Thurman never abandoned his dream of Fellowship Church or forgot what he called the "inspiringly heartbreaking privilege" of leading the church for a decade, but by the spring of 1953 it was time to move on.[175]

11
Against the Hounds of Hell

In March 1941 Thurman sent a letter to an editor. "The first sentence in the manuscript which you sent me is as follows: 'Men and women who deal with the materials of religious experience and who undertake to guide the development of the religious life, must themselves become increasingly suave, clever, oily, hypocrites.'" However, he told the editor, this omitted a few words from his original draft: "Men and women [who] deal with the materials of religious experience and who undertake to guide the development of the religious life, must themselves become increasingly righteous and holy, or else they become suave, clever, oily, hypocrites."[1] Writing for publication can have its pitfalls, but Thurman was now doing this more frequently. Among the other accomplishments of the Fellowship Church years was that he finally found his voice as a writer. No longer an author of occasional and fugitive articles, he was now the author of books, seven of which were published from 1944 to 1953, including, in 1949, *Jesus and the Disinherited*.[2]

Thurman had long thought himself a better and more effective speaker and preacher than writer, and that in the best of circumstances, his written words lacked the beating heart, warm breath, and physical presence of their author. But by the middle of the twentieth century, if he wanted to reach a wide audience, he knew that it was not enough to utter his words; he needed to publish them. Thurman states that "until I came to San Francisco I had very little interest in writing."[3] This is pardonable authorial exaggeration. He had published more than thirty articles, sermons, book reviews, and other writings prior to July 1944. It is true, however, that most of his articles were published in relatively obscure venues and were not widely circulated. Prior to the mid-1940s those seeking Thurman's words in print would have had to be quite diligent searchers.[4]

Thurman's relative invisibility in print was not entirely due to a lack of effort on his part. He had tried in 1938 to publish "The Significance of Jesus" series as a book, going so far as to try to recruit Rufus Jones as a reference.[5] He submitted it to Scribner's, only to have its religion editor turn down the manuscript: "Of course, the subject has been worked over frequently by so many people. When one speaks, presentation from the platform makes a great deal of difference, and of course a writer is not able to place emphasis in the way a speaker can."[6] Leaving aside the question of why Scribner's religion editor thought that books about Jesus were somewhat passé, this rejection must have stung. It spoke to Thurman's worry that he was a better speaker and preacher than writer, and that on the page his words were flat and unemphatic.[7] This rejection seems to have tempered his enthusiasm for writing, and he made relatively little effort to publish his works for the next few years.

It is not entirely clear why Thurman emerged as an author in San Francisco. He certainly felt the need to publicize Fellowship Church, which he did every time his name was in print. He finally found encouraging editors and publishers. But one also detects a new confidence in Thurman, a new urgency to weigh in on the pressing issues of the day; spiritual, social, and political. (And probably, within mainstream publishing, there was a new willingness to seek out and promote African American authors.) At the end of 1944 Thurman published his first book, *The Greatest of These,* a series of prose-poems used as meditations at services at Howard University. The volume was privately published by Eucalyptus Press, associated with Mills College, across the bay in Oakland.[8] A review of it opened: "Howard Thurman is one those uniquely gifted spirits of our time about whom we may say: 'Why doesn't he publish more? We never see anything from his hand.'"[9] The reviewer would have been gratified to know that once Thurman started writing books, there would be little stopping him. He published almost a book a year for the next two decades. Eucalyptus Press also published his second book, *Deep River,* a series of reflections on Negro spirituals, and issued his first volume of meditations in 1947.[10]

In 1947 Thurman was invited to give his most prestigious lecture to date, the Ingersoll Lecture at Harvard University. These were lectures dedicated to exploring aspects of the "Immortality of Man," and Thurman's *The Negro Spiritual Speaks of Life and Death* explored "the immortality of life, defying the judgment of the degrading environment which spawned them," rather than individual immortality.[11] (The latter is a subject on which, whatever his private views, he wrote little.) The choice of the topic, given Thurman's long-standing interest in the significance of the spirituals, might seem obvious, but it was not. He was afraid that speaking of spirituals before a predominantly white audience at Harvard would only give credence to the "pervasive notion that black scholars were incapable of reflective thought on any matters other than those that bore directly on their own struggle for survival in American society. . . . I chose to examine the Negro spiritual again in spite of this prevailing opinion and not because of it."[12] This dilemma was at the heart of so much of Thurman's thinking: the need to affirm his racial identity without being limited or confined by it. Thurman usually found ways to confront this, as he did at Harvard. A Thurman fan who attended the lecture—probably an African American graduate student—reported to him that "you really 'knocked them out' at your lecture. You really impressed Harvard and, believe me. Harvard is hard to impress."[13] The lecture impressed someone else as well, since it was published later in the year by Harper and Brothers, Thurman's first book issued by a commercial press, and one with national circulation.[14] Harper's would remain Thurman's primary publisher for the next three decades, and over that time, it would publish fifteen of his books. Thurman became a star on Harper's roster of prominent liberal Protestant authors and would develop a close friendship with several editors at the publishing house.[15]

In San Francisco Thurman discovered that his voice in print could be almost as powerful as his voice from the pulpit. If politics was rarely in the foreground of his writing during these years, it always formed part of its broader context, and during these years that context was rapidly changing. There were the changing fortunes of the United States as World War II gave way to the Cold War: the Soviet Union went from ally to enemy, and the country emerged as the world's hegemon. And, with a drumbeat getting ever louder and more insistent, there was the demand for racial equality, which, for the first time since the end of Reconstruction, was forcing itself into the center of American politics, a place it has yet to relinquish. These new realities had to be connected to the experiment in religious and social values he was leading at Fellowship Church, and Thurman wanted to tell these stories and to spread his message as widely as possible.

Fellowship Church was conceived in wartime, but it had its real birth in the first years of the war's aftermath. Thurman's early letters from the West detail a swirl of war-related activity, of friends passing through San Francisco from Howard, on the way to or returning from overseas military assignments.[16] But by mid-1945, Thurman and Fellowship Church, like the rest of America, were confronting an end of wartime conditions and the vexed question of the shape of postwar America.

One welcome, if bittersweet, consequence of the approach of victory in San Francisco was that by late 1944, the Japanese internment camps began to close, and former Japanese residents of San Francisco started to trickle back into the city, trying to restart their interrupted lives. Fellowship Church, at first located in a one-time Japanese neighborhood, made a special effort to welcome the returnees, holding a dinner in February 1945 for twenty-four Japanese Americans, who were the guests of honor at a dinner with 130 Fellowship Church members and friends.[17] Japanese Americans became a crucial part of the church. In March 1945, answering an urgent need of Thurman's, the church hired Ayoka Murota, recently returned from the camps, as its first secretary. A few months later, Thurman was sitting in his office, holding her hand "from 8:30 in the morning until 2:00 in the afternoon while the tidings of Hiroshima were coming across the air. Her aunts, her uncles, her nephews were all there. Now and then, the grip of my hand would tighten on hers, or the grip of her hand would tighten in mine. There were no words for words were raspy noises, unuttered in the discipline that would make manifest what was stirring in our hearts."[18]

By the end of the year, Dave Tatsuno, president of the San Francisco chapter of the Japanese American Citizens League (and director of an award-winning film about his experience in internment) was on the church's board of trustees.[19] Hugh Macbeth, an African American lawyer from Los Angeles who was deeply involved in the struggle for Japanese American rights and was president of the United Races of America, was the guest speaker on a Sunday morning in June 1945.[20] In 1947 and 1948, John Yamashita, a Nisei Methodist minister, served as an assistant minister.[21] The congregation also had a number of Filipino members, who faced their own postwar problems as the independence of the Philippines in 1946 changed the immigration status of many of them.[22]

The sudden death of President Roosevelt in April 1945 became, for many, another way to mark the looming end of wartime America. Thurman was hardly alone in having traveled a long way with Roosevelt since 1932, with his one-time skepticism transformed into a deep admiration. His passing was mourned in a special service at Fellowship Church. (One suspects little was said about Roosevelt's Japanese internment policy.) As it happened, Hjalmar Petersen, a former governor of Minnesota, by then an official of the Office of Defense Transportation, attended the service and wrote about his impressions of Fellowship Church, noting that "members and visitors at this church include white and colored people, Chinese and Japanese Americans, and others." Thurman read a poem written by a congregant in Roosevelt's memory and mentioned that Eleanor Roosevelt was a great supporter of

Fellowship Church and "the president's conscience." In his sermon, according to Petersen, "Dr. Thurman dwelt eloquently on fate and destiny." After polio struck, said Thurman, "for two years Mr. Roosevelt labored to overcome fate, to gradually move his toes, and to be able, with the assistance of a cane, to stand. There was destiny for a man of such indomitable will power and courage, and in a democracy such as ours, Dr. Thurman added, we all have a personal responsibility for our country's fate."[23] For Thurman, Roosevelt's handicap was a reminder that one's fate, the cards one is dealt by life, does not determine how the cards are played.

If one wanted a vantage to view the emerging postwar order in the spring of 1945, there was no better place on the planet to be than San Francisco, the site, from 25 April to 26 June, of the United Nations Conference on International Organization (UNICO), a conference of the countries of the United Nations (that is, the Allied powers) organized to create a successor organization to the League of Nations. Fifty nations participated in the conference (if one counts, as UNICO did at Stalin's insistence, the Belarussian and Ukrainian Soviet Socialist Republics as independent nations), in addition to the many nongovernmental organizations and thousands of representatives of the press. Despite all else that was taking place elsewhere during these two extremely news-crammed months, San Francisco had the attention of the world, and Thurman and Fellowship Church knew it.[24]

Visiting speakers crowded the preaching schedule at Fellowship Church during the conference. Howard University president Mordecai Wyatt Johnson spoke at the Sunday service on 29 April. A week later, the church sponsored W. E. B. Du Bois in a public lecture at the First Congregational Church on "World Peace and the Darker Peoples," with an audience of more than seven hundred persons.[25] On 11 May, the church held a reception for the Black press present at the UNICO conference with more than 125 in attendance.[26] C. L. Simpson, the vice president of Liberia, spoke at the church on 27 May.[27] All of this helped generate publicity for Fellowship Church. Du Bois later wrote in the *Chicago Defender* that "in San Francisco Howard Thurman is co-pastor of a church which holds meetings of a high order of intelligence and is well-attended."[28] Ralph Matthews, reporting on the UNICO conference for the *Baltimore Afro-American,* wrote about the church that June, reassuring his readers that while "Dr. Thurman, working with a white pastor, is operating a church in which the race question has been abolished," its "members are not cultists, fanatics, or screwballs—just plain everyday substantial citizens," proving wrong "the divisionists" who "have carefully perpetuated the idea in America that if white and colored work together politically, economically, or in religion they are members of the lunatic fringe."[29]

Thurman was surely happy to receive the diagnosis of nonlunacy for his church, though without question the most effective booster of Fellowship Church in the Black press during the UNICO spring was Sue Bailey Thurman, who wrote four nationally circulated articles for the *Chicago Defender,* providing what was called the "distaff perspective" for the *Defender's* readers.[30] She attended the conference not only as a reporter but as a representative of the National Council of Negro Women (NCNW), whose president, Mary McLeod Bethune, called for the new organization to commit to "the abolition of colonialism, ultimate independence for dependent areas," and to "vouchsafe human rights irrespective of race, color, sex, or creed."[31] The Black press paid much attention to the three countries represented in San Francisco that had Black governments—Haiti, Liberia, and Ethiopia—and to the nonvoting delegates of nonwhite peoples present at the conference, representatives of the Dutch East Indies (subsequently Indonesia), India, the Gold Coast (subsequently Ghana), Nigeria, and Britain's Caribbean colonies.[32]

The conference was, from the African American perspective, at best a mixed bag. At its opening, the *Chicago Defender* could headline an article, "Color Line Absent at Frisco, Du Bois Finds," reporting on the presence at the opening plenary session of "all languages and shades of color."[33] Yet at its close, Du Bois was quoted as saying the decision at the conference to leave the existing colonial structure basically intact had "disenfranchised 750,000,000 persons living in colonies and made no provision for their representation in the new world order."[34] The UN Charter did condemn racial discrimination but on a level of generality and impreciseness to ensure, in part at the behest of the United States, that the apparatus of colonialism and Jim Crow would remain unchallenged and unvexed. This reality was underlined by the decision of the new U.S. president, Harry S. Truman, about a week after the UNICO conference ended, to name James F. Byrnes, the stalwart and die-hard South Carolina segregationist, as secretary of state (who was, under the law then in effect, in an administration without a vice president, next in the line of presidential succession).

On the other hand, in one of her articles Sue Bailey Thurman quoted her old acquaintance Ralph Bunche, in attendance as a representative of the State Department. This was, Sue noted, a new level of authority for an African American at a conference of this sort, a wielder of power rather than its mere supplicant. Bunche praised the participation of the "various groups who had interpreted the voice of the Negro to the world at large in San Francisco," noting that "all Negroes may mark this as an epochal event, for in no conference of the past has he taken such an active part."[35] This was no doubt true, but it was a very low bar to hurdle, and it didn't prevent Walter White, executive secretary of the NAACP, not prone to radical outbursts, to dismiss the African American presence at the conference as mere "window dressing."[36]

Thurman certainly agreed with Du Bois and other critics, saying that "the ghost of unrepresented people hangs over the San Francisco conference."[37] Nonetheless, there is little doubt that he was a big booster of the idea of the United Nations. In years to come he would be a strong supporter of "world government" organizations.[38] An article from 1945, "The Inner Life and World-Mindedness," without mentioning the United Nations directly, was Thurman's meditation on the events that transpired that spring in San Francisco. Like many, Thurman's starting point was the awesome level of destructiveness unleashed in the just-concluded war. "With the new tools of destruction in our hands," such as the V-2 rocket, the B-29, and the atomic bomb, "something radical must take place in the basic interpretation which we give to the inclusive meaning of life." A "profound revolution" without "palliative measures" was necessary, as "the push of scientific advance has made the world into a neighborhood." This had only heightened the tension between the individual and the "inner life" and "world-mindedness."[39]

Humanity, in the wake of the war, argued Thurman, faced a "mandatory revolution" of redefining what it meant to be human. This required a sense of how all human lives were interconnected, and the very real consequences of this: "The seeds of death are inherent in any form of private fulfillment which by its very realizability destroys the unfolding of the life of one's neighbor." He gave "economic imperialism" as an example and explained how "great world economic power[s]" built their "prestige, honor, and culture" upon the fact that their wealth was "sustained and guaranteed by the careful and scientific exploitation of other peoples and other lands." But for the great powers to relax their "imperialistic will" would require "an entirely radical undertaking down to the most insignificant detail."[40] For Thurman, what was perhaps most important in the foundation of the United Nations was the idea of uniting. He hoped for new steps toward uniting "man and the animal kingdom," the unity of "scientific truth, ethical truth, [and] religious truth," and, ultimately, the recognition of the unity of all life.[41]

If unity was one of Thurman's animating postwar principles, equality was another. He was reminded of this during the UNICO conference when he read Henry A. Myers's recent book *Are Men Equal? An Inquiry into the Meaning of American Democracy*.[42] On 28 May 1945 Thurman wrote a letter to Myers, calling the book the "most stimulating and creative interpretation of democracy that I have ever read."[43] Like many at the time, Myers regarded the just-concluded war as a struggle between democracy and fascism, a fight to the death between two world systems: "The two chief patterns for a world-wide society are the old imperial dream, revived by Fascism and National Socialism, of stability founded on the firm rule of a superior people, and the egalitarian dream of a world community of peoples, organized on the principle of equal rights and duties."[44] The essence of democracy for Myers was the principle of radical equality, and the rejection of inequality and superiority. What particularly interested Thurman was Myers's claim that real equality could not be reduced to mere legal equality or even social equality. Real equality exists as a consequence of each person's "ultimate value," or as Myers expressed it in a phrase that Thurman would soon make his own, "the idea of equality has its source in the private man's sense of his own infinite worth," for "all immortal souls are equally precious in the eyes of God."[45]

For Thurman, to realize the "infinite worth" of every person was an essentially political task, but it was one that had little to do with conventional politics. Like most Blacks raised in the South in his era, he did not grow up in a tradition of political participation—he voted for president for either the first or second time in 1944.[46] If electoral politics were important, for Thurman, as for Gandhi, the core political act did not involve voting but encouraging small groups of dedicated individuals, standing outside the traditional levers of power, to acts of protest. These people were, in what would be one of his favorite catchphrases of the 1940s and 1950s, the "apostles of sensitiveness." In his first sermon at Fellowship Church he told the congregation that the "apostles of sensitiveness" must understand that love is not only an emotion but a rational discipline. It must "be [the] wisdom for the planners and designers and operators of society."[47] He would make use of the phrase repeatedly in the next few years, delivering a lecture, "Apostles of Sensitiveness," that was subsequently published by the Interracial Fellowship of New York at the Cathedral of St. John the Divine in 1946.[48] His third book, published in 1947, was entitled *Meditations for the Apostles of Sensitiveness.*[49]

African Americans of Thurman's generation were fully aware of the perils of sensitivity. "You are a very sensitive Negro man," is how Thurman remembered what George Cross, his advisor at Rochester Theological Seminary, told him in their final conversation, and it doesn't seem that Thurman thought this a compliment.[50] As Thurman wrote in 1943, both oversensitivity and undersensitivity created problems: "For the sensitive, it [segregation] means a constant, persistent resentment that is apt so to disease the personality that mental health is critically attacked." On the other hand: "For the less sensitive there is ever the possibility of the acceptance of segregation, with its concomitant conscious admission of inferiority, of humiliation, of despair."[51] The sensitive person needs skin thin enough to be regularly pricked by the injustices of the world but skin thick enough not to be crushed by them and, above all, the ability not to focus on their own situation to the exclusion of the plights of others.

Moreover, "minority groups are in a unique position to be apostles of sensitiveness keeping alive the true genius of the democratic challenge" because minorities, canaries in the mineshaft of democracy, were apt to be the first to feel "the breakdown of the democratic ideals in the body politic."[52] That said, Thurman did not limit the apostles of sensitiveness to racial minorities. They were the small groups of individuals who were actively trying to implement a new democratic vision of America: the members of Fellowship Church; his friends like James Farmer and Virginia Scardigli, who were trying, in small integrated groups, to desegregate restaurants and skating rinks; in efforts like the 1947 Journey of Reconciliation, an attempt to challenge the color line on interstate bus lines.[53] They must have a "keen sense of alternatives," a passionate belief that, all the evidence to the contrary aside, things can be other than they are and challenge those who think "the present exhausts the possibilities of life." They were those who knew that a belief, whether in God or a social ideal, was "a thing upon which a man stakes his life and practice."[54] The apostles of sensitiveness were those "who with rare courage and scintillating insight will dare to define practically and efficiently the American way of life so that it will not as now do violence to the democratic way of life."[55]

Optimism was always a virtue for Thurman. One of the essential characteristics of the apostles of sensitiveness, he wrote in 1946, was having "a sense of the future," whereas the "guardians of the status quo . . . deny the future."[56] But postwar optimism had to be balanced against the memory of the wreck and carnage through which the world had just passed. He wrote in 1945 that the apostles of sensitiveness "must intensify their concerns and their efforts that during this dark age, the flickering torch may be unquenched that it may light the way through the long post war dawn that is to come," with the possibility "that they [will] look out upon the destruction of much for which they stand."[57] Like many, Thurman was unsure if the future betokened a "dark age" or a new dawn and thought it prudent to prepare for both. The forces of reaction may have been vanquished abroad, but they were still alive and well at home, and African Americans were acutely aware of how their hopes for equal citizenship during World War I vanished in the postwar fires of the Red Summer. Thurman's worries about these matters prompted one of the most urgently and directly political articles of his entire career, "The Fascist Masquerade" (1946).[58]

Few fears were as pervasive among left-liberals as the war drew to a close as the worries about a resurgent domestic fascism. In April 1944, the standard-bearer for the progressive Left, Vice President Henry A. Wallace (a few months before Roosevelt unceremoniously dropped him from the 1944 ticket) argued in the *New York Times* that there were several million American fascists, defining a fascist as one whose "lust for money or power is combined with such an intolerance toward those of other parties, races, classes, regions, or nations as to make him ruthless in his use of deceit or violence to obtain his ends," singling out anti–New Deal industrialists, the right-wing press, and "the KKK type of demagog[ue]" as the most likely culprits. Part of the insidiousness of domestic fascists was that they disguised their actual views or used front organizations to spread their propaganda. They claimed to be patriots but were isolationists who sought to maintain "Anglo-Saxon imperialism" and looked toward "war with Russia." Their talk of democracy was a ruse. "The final objective toward which all of their deceit is directed" was to gain political power in order to "keep the common man in eternal subjection." After victory over the Nazis, the next great antifascist fight would be "within the United States itself."[59]

In August 1945 Thurman was invited to write an essay in a collection on "the Christian rediscovery of resistance and resource." But rather than the worldwide coverage the editor wanted, Thurman chose to focus on a single topic, what he in the essay called "the basis of fascism as it has developed in America during the past decade."[60] This muckraking exposé of obscure right-wing organizations was indeed, as he wrote a friend at the time, a venture "into a brand new field of creative expression" and a new commitment to summon the spiritual force of organized Christianity to engage in the nitty-gritty of practical politics.[61]

Thurman devoted the opening section of "The Fascist Masquerade" to an effort to define the slippery notion of fascism, a term about which "there is a medley of confusion" and that has become a "'catchall' to describe individuals or movements with whom we are in disagreement," a statement just as true in the third decade of the twenty-first century as when Thurman wrote it. Thurman considered three definitions—including one from the horse's mouth himself, Benito Mussolini—before arriving at his own. Under fascism, the state was "supreme in its complete control and direction of economic life," the individual was subordinate to the state, and fascism "is committed to a fundamental inequality among men," a doctrine "from which there flows a bloody stream of racism and terror."[62]

Thurman argued that American fascism "crystallizes moods, attitudes and fears that are already in solution" as a part of a long-standing vigilante and racist tradition. American fascism was likely to take forms that lacked "any formal ideological recognition of the existence of classical fascism, either as a political or economic doctrine."[63] Although Thurman doesn't discuss the early history of fascism in the United States, one problem with the search for an American fascism, a search that began shortly after the term entered the political vocabulary in the early 1920s, was the scarcity of self-proclaimed American fascists, and the political insignificance of those who claimed the title.[64] In lieu of acknowledged fascists, those labeled American fascists were usually right-wing populists such as Huey Long or Father Coughlin, or anti–New Deal plutocrats such as the Du Ponts and the funders of the Liberty League. This was the approach of many on the left, including the Communist Party, which by the mid-1930s, in pursuit of the Popular Front, was redefining itself less as "anticapitalist" than as "antifascist."[65] The belief that when fascism came to America it would eschew the fascist label and take the form of exaggerated Americanism was a commonplace at the time. W. E. B. Du Bois wrote in 1940 that "you may even expect it [an American fascist movement] to deny its fascist character and foreign inspiration; yet it will embrace all the fascist fundamentals expressed in the natural idiom of local politics."[66] Thurman called this the "fascist masquerade," this disguising of true purposes and motivations, doing so in the name of a supposedly authentic Christianity and Americanism.[67]

If American fascism was sometimes hard to find, few doubted, especially African Americans, that if there was an American fascism, it was headquartered somewhere below the Mason-Dixon Line. In 1939, Mordecai Wyatt Johnson was quoted as saying, "Fascism [is] replacing Christianity" as the religion of the white South.[68] That same year the *Chicago Defender* criticized the newly released film *Gone with the Wind* as not only "un-American" and "subversive" but argued that its message "is fascism."[69] New York City's Adam Clayton Powell Jr. wrote in 1938, "We are members of a race that has known fascism in one form or another since 1619."[70] Even President Roosevelt called the South fascist, though on different grounds, arguing that the economic system of the South, still in the control of a handful of powerful men, was basically feudal, and "there is little difference between the feudal system and the fascist system."[71]

Thurman discussed three fascist organizations, all of them southern. Two are now quite obscure. The one significant contribution to American history of the vilely racist, anti-Semitic, and antilabor Christian American Association, founded in Houston, Texas, in 1936, was to popularize the term "right to work" and play an important role in the passage of the nation's first right-to-work laws (prohibiting the closed shop and union shop) in Arkansas and Florida in 1944.[72] For Thurman, the Christian American Association was "fascist because it is concerned with the control of production by a select few in whom all powers are resident and who in turn can determine arbitrarily the priority of privilege." That was the basis of their attack on collective bargaining, while "the appeal to racial and religious prejudice is the masquerade."[73] Like many left-liberals at the time, Thurman saw fascism as the effort of big businesses to retain their hold on power in times of stress and challenge by manipulating the fears of the white working class. Thurman thought the Christian American Association name perfect for its mission.

Thurman also discussed the even more obscure and short-lived Nationalist Party, which, in the words of its founder, former North Carolina U.S. senator Robert R. Reynolds, was intended to offer an alternative to the Democratic Party, which had been "first taken over by the New Deal, which was in turn taken over by the Communists, reds, and pinks; internationalists and interventionists, together with the CIO political action committee."[74] Much better-known is the third organization Thurman treated in the essay, the Ku Klux Klan. The Klan had been denounced as an American fascist organization as early as 1922.[75] What the three organizations had in common, for Thurman, was a middle-class or lower-middle-class fury against an America changing beyond their control.[76] Using the cloak of "true Christianity" or "true Americanism," fascism allowed "for a legitimatizing of sadistic and demonical impulses of which, under normal circumstances, they might be ashamed."[77]

The final part of the essay turned to "the challenge to the church." In Thurman's view, in the growth and nurturance of a native American fascism, no institution was more culpable than Christianity as it was commonly practiced and understood. For Thurman it was no accident that Christianity had become so deeply implicated in the defense of inequality. It is inherent in the most basic of Christian teachings, "the very categories of 'the saved' and 'the sinners,'" the invidious dichotomizing of humanity into two separate and unequal halves. It was no defense to say this is a false view of Christianity. That merely "etches more clearly than ever that the Church has done a wretched job in making clear what the Teaching is" and has allowed "various hate-inspired groups" "to establish squatter's rights" on its message. Christianity "is irrevocably committed to a revolutionary ethic, but it tends to implement the ethic by means that are short of that which is revolutionary." It does not take its most fundamental beliefs with the seriousness they demand and asks far too little of its adherents. Fascism, on the other hand, tried to implement a reactionary ethic by revolutionary means: "The Church must be as revolutionary in practice as it is in the genius of the ethic to which it is dedicated."[78] The failure of American Christianity has meant its toleration of the fetid swamp of racist ideas that nurtured a growing American fascism.

To read "The Fascist Masquerade" today is to confront a paradox. It is at once exaggerated and overblown, and at the same time, extremely searching and prescient. There was not a significant fascist underground in America in the 1940s. Thurman's argument followed a long line of left-liberal works written during and shortly after the war that exaggerated the domestic threat of fascism, Nazism, fifth columnists, and other far-right movements, and the role of big industrialists in directing these movements.[79] The emphasis in the essay on subversion or "masquerade" is typical of what has been called the "Brown Scare," the emphasis on right-wing crypto-fascist secret penetration of American institutions. In many ways, and with grim ironies, it was a dress rehearsal for the much better-remembered and much more effective Red Scare, with the tables turned, and many of the same arguments that had been used against alleged fascists now used against Communists, real or alleged.[80] In the following statement from "The Fascist Masquerade," Thurman sounds, disturbingly, a lot like J. Edgar Hoover scaremongering about the "masters of deceit": "Totalitarianism is a threat to, and the enemy of, liberty ever—it makes no difference whether the totalitarianism is benign or wicked, its power inevitably works toward the absolute and it cannot survive with any competitor. Watch out for the signs in your community, whatever may be the banner or the masquerade."[81]

Yet at the same time, Thurman's worries about domestic fascism were entirely justified and on-target. The groups he identified, and the ideology they represented, would have a decisive impact on the politics of postwar America, with an influence that far exceeded their numbers. The three southern groups identified by Thurman were in the forefront of a postwar reaction against labor, civil rights, and the legacy of the New Deal.[82] The brainchild of the Christian American Association, right-to-work laws, would, in 1947 with the passage of the Taft-Hartley Act, go from the "fascist" fringe to the mainstream, and no single piece of legislation would prove as influential in curtailing the legacy of the New Deal and limiting the strength of unions, especially in the South. The Christian American Association and the Nationalist Party were two of the first cracks in the solidly Democratic South that would lead to the Dixiecrats in 1948 and, eventually, to a solidly Republican white South. These organizations would do all in their power to delay, obstruct, evade, and harass the success of the civil rights movement, the rights of organized labor, and the other components of Thurman's egalitarian political agenda. In the "massive resistance" of the white South, it was fascist-like organizations, closely connected with the Klan, such as the White Citizens' Councils, rather than so-called southern "moderates," that dominated the debate.[83] As Thurman suggested, the fascist masquerade is forever protean and shape-shifting, taking on different names and guises, without ever changing its fundamental mission, forever hiding behind its "Christian" and "American" facade. So it remains in America today. "The Fascist Masquerade" is one of the few times in his career when Thurman outlined, concretely and with details, the political basis of his religious beliefs. It is a pity that he did not do so more often.

One warning "The Fascist Masquerade" offered, quoting another source, was that "indiscriminate pinning of the label 'Red' on people and proposals which one opposes is a common political device. It is a favorite trick of native as well of foreign fascists."[84] In 1945 Thurman warned that newly fledged apostles of sensitiveness must "resist every attempt to place false and misleading labels upon them such as *red, subversive, divisive.*"[85] But this was precisely the problem that those on the liberal-left faced in the late 1940s and early 1950s. The Popular Front assumptions of "The Fascist Masquerade" were vanishing. By 1949 Thurman recognized that "the fear of Axis fascism has been somewhat displaced by the fear of Russian communism."[86] But unlike fascism, which Thurman wholeheartedly condemned, when it came to Communism he wanted a nuance that was increasingly politically impermissible. "I realize that any public statement about the Communist development," he said in 1948, "at once classes the individual as either a baiter of that which is Red or a believer of that which is Red, so that we find ourselves tongue tied."[87]

If Thurman was sympathetic to many aspects of the political stances of the Communist Party, particularly on civil rights matters, Thurman went out of his way to ensure that Fellowship Church steered clear of any entanglements with the Communist Party and its affiliated California Labor School, despite the wishes of some in the congregation.[88] He kept his distance from organizations with Communist ties, such as the Civil Rights Congress, of which he said in 1952 that though he agreed with its goals, he did "not work through a channel merely because its goals are those towards which my own beliefs operate," but "if I select the channel through which to work, then I seek to satisfy the demands of my own mind about what its purposes, its methods, its supports are," and he shared the suspicion that it might be "some kind of 'front' organization."[89]

At the same time, the politics of Fellowship Church (and Thurman's politics) remained, if non-Communist, very left of center. There was considerable support in the church for Henry Wallace, the former vice president who campaigned for president in 1948 on the Progressive Party ticket, with considerable Communist support. (Thurman approved of the decision to keep the church formally neutral when a church usher chose not to wear a "Wallace for President" button while directing people to their seats.)[90] In 1948 an assistant minister delivered a well-received sermon on "the integrity of the man, Karl

Marx," and there were reports that FBI agents were regular attendees at services.[91] The church had a lecture series that regularly featured left-wing speakers, including, shortly before his 1953 deportation from the United States, the independent Black Trotskyist and historian C. L. R. James.[92]

The Community Relations Committee was involved in many causes, from trying to establish a California version of the Fair Employment Practices Commission (it failed), to helping Japanese Americans regain property stolen from them during internment, and to the fight against restrictive housing covenants.[93] The church was also active in the fight against loyalty oaths and other anti-Communist measures adopted by the State of California in 1950.[94] The following year Thurman gave a series of sermons on "The Meaning of Loyalty," an effort to rehabilitate the notion of loyalty from the murk of "are-you-now-or-have-you-ever-been" questions, maintaining that when the state attempted to compel loyalty "to some organizational structure, some party, some individuals, some office," then the state moved "into the centrality of the position which, in my definition of loyalty, only God should occupy."[95]

The controversy over loyalty oaths was just one manifestation of a ferocious and increasingly indiscriminate anti-Communism that was dominating American politics, and Thurman was horrified by what he saw as a new pervading national evil. Nowhere is this clearer than in a comment in a sermon he gave at Fellowship Church in June 1953, two days after the execution of Julius and Ethel Rosenberg.[96] Thurman rarely responded to political events so quickly and so viscerally, and there were few times in his career that he expressed himself with such bleak desolation: "There is great confusion and despair, disorder, because we have been part of something which makes naked the spirit and the mind of man. We have visited death on two human beings, whose deed, by the judgment of the court, merited death." Thurman likely thought the Rosenbergs innocent of the charges against them.[97] However, the evidentiary debate interested him less than the national clamor for their destruction: "What shall we say to God today, in our own land, in our own country—what can we say to Him? Can we say to Him that we were afraid and our fears mounted and mounted until at last, in our desperation, we act without compassion and with vengeance?" Some sins against God, Thurman seemed to suggest, can never be forgiven or pardoned:

> Can we say to Him that we are guilty of so much grossness and callousness and insensitiveness and brutality that our hearts have become weary in so much anguish and hardened themselves in quiet defense against disintegration? Can he understand what it means in all the ways that petrifies the spirit? And clogs all the inlets? From that which renews and

restores the hearts of man? What can we say to God today as we sit in the shadows nursing our fears and clutching the hands of two orphaned children? What can we say to God? What CAN we say?[98]

At the same time Thurman adjusted his language to the rhetoric of the Cold War. The economic radicalism of the 1930s was largely gone. By the 1950s he spoke less of fascism (a term closely tied to the Popular Front) and more about tyranny and totalitarianism. He became more extravagant in his praises of the idea of American democracy, often speaking of its divine inspiration. Some of these changes can be observed in his 1955 address at Washington University in St. Louis, "Freedom under God." (Thurman's title itself has a Cold War flavor, the phrase "under God" having been added to the Pledge of Allegiance only the year before):

> It is my conviction that our nation is involved in the far-flung purpose of God to establish a world community of friendly men living beneath a friendly sky. Think of our startling history at this point just for a moment! It is not chauvinistic to affirm that our total life as a nation has been a schooling in the meaning of human freedom against a time when the only thing that saves the collective life of man is a dynamic faith in the worth of the individual and the freedom which it inspires. Our national life was launched in a revolution against tyranny with its corresponding assertion of human dignity. Our emergence as a nation is a judgment against all dictatorships.[99]

If Thurman was adopting a measure of Cold War prudence by 1955, it was probably warranted. A few weeks after delivering "Freedom under God," the Cincinnati Bureau of the FBI received a complaint that Thurman had in May 1954 delivered an address that was "radical" and was full of "Communistic implications" and suggested that Thurman was "traveling around the country speaking in behalf of Communism." Thurman's name had come to the attention of the FBI as early as 1942, when, according to an informant, he had signed a petition on behalf of the Citizens' Committee to Free Earl Browder, the general secretary of the Communist Party, USA, who had been imprisoned for a passport violation. (A typical Popular Front organization, the Citizens' Committee included many prominent non-Communist supporters.) There were several other "subversive" affiliations alleged in the files.[100]

The malevolent and paranoid aspersions of the FBI's Cincinnati informant aside, any "Communistic implications" in Thurman's talks (other than a support for racial equality) were in the eye of the beholder. There was nothing artificial or feigned in his patriotism or his love for the "magnificent stirring lines" of the Declaration of Independence.[101] He was, he said in 1958, a believer in "manifest destiny of some sort," that America exists for a purpose, and that "it is not an accident that we in our land are here."[102] But Thurman's patriotism, like that of many African Americans, was based not on what America was, or is, but on what the "possibility of a freedom under God is, the crown that He holds steadily over our heads with the hope that as a nation we grow tall enough to wear it."[103] He had little good to say about America's current state. There were none of the complacencies in his thinking and writing that one sometimes associates with the term "Cold War liberal." When he delivered sermons on that popular 1950s topic, the American Dream, he claimed that while the United States was perhaps better suited than any other country to create a democracy not based on wealth, status, or privilege but, rather, on the infinite worth of every person, it instead seemed to dedicate itself to the "cult of inequality," the belief that a stable society requires a clear demarcation between the rulers and the ruled.[104] The ideal of American democracy was a yardstick to measure how far its reality had fallen short, not an excuse to engage in one-upmanship with the Soviet Union. The evils of American life, its militarism and racism, and western colonialism remained his chief political causes.[105] He remained a pacifist, though unlike in the aftermath of the previous war, pacifism was an ideology without much of a constituency. But it pointed the way to a very different kind of radical politics. There are few things more remarkable and unexpected about 1950s America than that, amid the hypermilitarization of the Cold War, a new transforming political movement would emerge under the ideological aegis of radical nonviolence. And few had more to do with this than Howard Thurman.

Radical nonviolence as a solution for the plight of African Americans was the theme of Thurman's most influential and most significant book, *Jesus and the Disinherited,* published in 1949. Rooted in the grittier realities of Black life in America, it has a different feel from his other books.[106] In many ways, *Jesus and the Disinherited* was Thurman's first book, the first written as such rather than a compilation of poems, sermons, or essays. It has a quality of a release of emotions and thoughts long pent up, almost tumbling out, one after another. Although the book had a very long gestation—Thurman had been thinking and writing about these issues for two decades—it was also very much a book of the late 1940s, written with a sense of urgency, with a feeling that the diffuse demands by Blacks for full equality in American life were sharpening, gaining focus and strength, and could no longer be denied. It was surely, as the title indicates, a book with a religious theme, but it had little to do with Thurman's many explorations of personal religious experience or mysticism.

In 1938, Alice Sams, Thurman's mother, told him to "remember you were born in the south."[107] *Jesus and the Disinherited* honored Alice's request. A book of Black southern memory, both Thurman's memories and those of others, it was an account of how African Americans, like his beloved backyard oak tree, buffeted, battered, but not breaking in the storm, came to understand and creatively respond to the realities of their social and political oppression.

Besides Thurman, the person most responsible for *Jesus and the Disinherited* was Karl E. Downs. In January 1948 Downs, president of Samuel Huston College in Austin, Texas, invited him to deliver the initial Mary L. Smith Memorial Lectures at the college that April. (The college was named after an Iowa Methodist and not the antebellum Texas politician with a differently spelled last name.) The lectures came with a generous five-hundred-dollar honorarium, and the series, created to increase the visibility of leading Black religious thinkers, promised to provide an assist in getting the lectures into print.[108]

Downs and Thurman were mutual admirers. In his autobiography, Thurman calls Downs "a young acquaintance of mine, a brilliant Black Methodist-Episcopal Minister."[109] Downs's only book, *Meet the Negro* (1943), amounted to a vibrant call for a new kind of Black citizenship. It opens: "America is deeply concerned about the 'Negro Problem,' and it is pitifully blind to the 'Negro possibility.'" What Black America wanted from whites was their "cooperation and understanding," not their "pity and sympathy."[110] Thurman had dedicated his life to this principle, and Downs had some very complimentary things to say about him. Thurman was the "fairest in the constellation of popular student speakers of this generation." Audiences were "overwhelmed by his silences and are spellbound at how eloquent he can be without shouting or orating and yet getting at the core of issues."[111]

One month after inviting Thurman to give the lectures, Downs, aged thirty-five, died of a kidney ailment. He never heard Thurman's lectures or read the book based on them. One of Downs's young admirers would later write that "Karl Downs died a victim of racism," killed by a botched operation after which he was left to die in a colored ward in an Austin hospital rather than receiving the emergency attention he needed. He also suggested that that Downs, "in ability and dedication," ranked with "Roy Wilkins, Whitney Young, and Dr. Martin Luther King, Jr." and said that had he lived, he would have had a comparable career.[112] The admirer was one Jack Roosevelt Robinson. Downs had been a father figure to the young Jackie Robinson growing up in Pasadena, and Robinson always credited Downs with saving him from becoming a "full-fledged juvenile delinquent," with helping him to come to terms with the racism he faced daily and giving him the confidence to confront and overcome it. The contrasting fates of Karl Downs and Jackie Robinson, then starting his second season with the Brooklyn Dodgers—Thurman was always a big baseball fan—lurk somewhere in the background of *Jesus and the Disinherited*.[113]

When Downs wrote Thurman in January 1948, he knew he was not giving Thurman much time for an April lecture series and thought he might have something in hand, nearly ready.[114] Thurman did. He proposed speaking on "The Religion of Jesus and the Disinherited." Thurman had been speaking of the "religion of Jesus" as a survival technique for the disinherited since the late 1920s. He had suggested the topic for a 1939 lecture series but then spoke on another topic, "Mysticism and Social Change."[115] A decade later, there was no doubt as to the topic.

Thurman delivered the lectures from 11 to 16 April. Although he generally spoke extemporaneously, for important lecture series such as this, he would sometimes write out his texts. This time, the words did not come easily. He wrote his amanuensis (who had the thankless task of turning Thurman's chicken-scratched handwriting into a typescript): "I am sending under separate cover trial and tribulation number two. I don't like this lecture because it is very difficult to have to put into words this sort of thing. The next two will be equally difficult."[116] But if Thurman wasn't satisfied with the lectures, his audience was. And Thurman enjoyed Texas, despite its location in a "still a beknighted [*sic*] part of the world," and was "happy over signs of creative ferment."[117] He described the lectures in glowing terms:

> They were given with a deep sense of freedom and inspiration. After I got there I decided that I would not read them from manuscript, but rather deliver them from the outline in my mind. It was a dangerous thing to do, but a very effective one. At the end of each lecture I had to take two or three bows and when the final lecture came there was the kind of ovation the like of which I have experienced only once before in my life. While the applause was going on a student arose to read a resolution from the student body requesting the administration to invite me to return next year to give the lectures. At the end of that the whole audience stood spontaneously and sang "God be with you until we meet again."[118]

After Thurman delivered the lectures, the next step was to get them published. It is not clear if the Methodist publishing house, Abingdon-Cokesbury Press, had the right of first refusal for the lectures, though Thurman thought they did.[119] In any event, Abingdon-Cokesbury was the first press to look at the lectures, and they agreed to publish them. Thurman had originally thought (and hoped) the press would not be interested in his manuscript because "of the southern bias in that organization" and was disappointed by their decision.[120] It was a testy and tense editorial process. The press made a number of requests of Thurman, which he agreed to with reluctance. Perhaps, as an author relatively new to the rough-and-tumble ways of commercial publishing, he was taken aback by the volume of editorial suggestions. Thurman described the editorial bloodletting in his autobiography:

> Problems surrounding the publishing of *Jesus and the Disinherited* were many and various. The editor had returned the manuscript, the pages covered with red ink—suggestions, criticisms, rephrasings. I was unaccustomed to this. Every comment, question, or criticism I took as a personal affront. My conference with the editor in New York was even more disconcerting. Ever critical, this man seemed nevertheless detached and indifferent. He was positive about nothing save the fact that the book could not be published without the suggested changes. At the end of our conference he returned the manuscript to me for revision and expressed his interest in its publication only after the changes were made. Eventually, we worked through our differences by compromise and capitulation.[121]

There is no reason to doubt Thurman's account of the editorial process (though there is relatively little trace of it in the extant correspondence).[122] But perhaps "southern bias" was a large part of the problem. Thurman worked closely with editor in chief Nolan B. Harmon, a native of Mississippi and a fourth-generation Methodist minister. On 12 April 1963, Good Friday, Harmon, then a Methodist bishop for northern Alabama, was one of eight Birmingham religious leaders (seven ministers and a rabbi) who issued a statement calling for the ongoing civil rights demonstrations in Birmingham to cease and for Black leaders to end their protests and seek redress through legal means and "observe the principles of law and order and common sense." In response, on 16 April, Martin Luther King, Jr., wrote, on the scraps of paper available to him in his cell, his famous "Letter from Birmingham Jail." A careful student has called Harmon's racial thinking "inconsistent and bewildered," at once paternalistic and calling for basic rights for Blacks, defending the status quo while criticizing segregation. (He had preached to his congregations in the 1920s urging them to set a good example for Blacks because they were childlike and often imitated the "dominant" race.) Racial change, Harmon believed, would come about only through "the slow, slow, slow processes of time."[123] Whether or not the ideological divergences between Thurman and Harmon entered into the editorial tension is not clear. But whatever happened, Thurman was satisfied with the final result. As he wrote Harmon at the end of the process, the manuscript "has to stand because it says precisely what I want to say."[124]

Jesus and the Disinherited was not Thurman's first choice for the title. He preferred the title of his lecture series "The Religion of Jesus and the Disinherited."[125] Abingdon-Cokesbury thought the title too long and lacking in pith. Thurman didn't much care for their suggestion, "Jesus and the Disinherited." This collapsed the distinction, crucial for Thurman's argument, between organized Christianity and the "religion of Jesus."[126] He made a counterproposal. Call the book "The Hounds of Hell." The editors refused to publish the book under that title, which they thought "suggest[ed] a murder mystery of the Sherlock Holmes type," and Thurman, not having much of a choice, relented.[127] But as he makes clear throughout *Jesus and the Disinherited,* if the religion of Jesus is the answer, the hounds of hell are the problem: "Whenever his [Jesus'] spirit appears, the oppressed gather fresh courage; for he announced the good news that fear, hypocrisy, and hatred, the three hounds of hell that track the trail of the disinherited, need have no dominion over them."[128]

The disinherited, Thurman announced in the book's opening sentence, are the "people who stand with their backs against the wall," lacking in security, in resources, and above all, alternatives.[129] They are, Thurman added, typically preached to by people who do not understand their plight. He "could count on the fingers of one hand the number of times I have heard a sermon on the meaning of religion, of Christianity," that was really addressed to them. This is because the message of Christianity is "muffled, confused, and vague" and offers advice and counsel from a vantage of superiority and comfort rather than true solidarity.[130] "It ill behooves the man who is not forced to live in a ghetto," Thurman wrote, "to tell those who must how to transcend its limitations."[131] Only the disinherited have the standing to advise the disinherited. Indeed, one of the subtly revolutionary aspects of *Jesus and the Disinherited* is that it is written for the disinherited. It is not about hand-wringing over the "Negro problem," or how those in power can aid or assist the downtrodden. Indeed, it largely ignores the vantage and perspective of elites. Thurman argued that the disinherited will have to be the main actors in the quest for their own souls, for their place in society, and, ultimately, for the fate of society itself. Those in power needed to recognize this, acknowledge this, and make way.

Thurman started to make this argument by an examination of the religion of Jesus. The key to understanding Jesus, as he had argued previously in the 1930s in such works as "The Significance of Jesus" and "Good News for the Underprivileged," was that Jesus was not a citizen of the Roman Empire and lacked the security of citizenship: "If a Roman soldier pushed Jesus into a ditch, he could not appeal to Caesar; he would just be another Jew in the ditch."[132] A life of such "stark insecurity" is a breeder of "complete civil and moral nihilism and psychic anarchy." Only those who have lived "day by day without a sense of security" can understand this.[133] The disinherited, with no legal system to protect them, were always afraid of confrontations with authority, with the ever-present dangers of escalation. Their "values are interpreted in terms of their bearing upon the one major concern of all activity—not being killed. . . . *Not to be killed* becomes the great end, and morality takes its meaning from that center."[134] This is a much deeper fear than the mere fear of death and dying; it is fear of being murdered, dying randomly and unnaturally, of having a death without meaning.

In the central three chapters of *Jesus and the Disinherited,* Thurman discusses the three "hounds of hell": fear, deception, and hatred, and how the religion of Jesus can keep them at bay. Fear, he argues, is a safety device, like pain, telling an individual what not to do and where not to go. But when fear becomes a basis for avoiding all confrontation with hostile authority, then fear, which served originally as a "kind of protective mechanism for the weak, finally becomes death for the self. . . . In the absence of all hope, ambition dies, and the very self is weakened, corroded."[135] The answer to fear is for the disinherited person to recognize that no one can take from them the basic "integrity" of their life. And those who learn this, those who know this, "are unconquerable."[136] They are unconquerable because they know that the worst that can happen to them is death, being killed by their oppressors, and they have learned that "death cannot possibly be the worst thing in the world."[137]

Deception Thurman calls "perhaps the oldest of all the techniques by which the weak have protected themselves against the strong."[138] Children dealing with parents or teachers learn this lesson early. Women, too: "Olive Schreiner spent much of her energy attacking this form of deception by which the moral life of women was bound."[139] Enslaved persons became experts in "puttin' on massa" as a survival technique. Emancipation changed little. Often deception of white folks was the only way to get by, and Blacks as a matter of course learned never to disclose their true feelings to whites. But for Thurman, deception as a way of life carries with it a very stiff price: "A man who habitually lies becomes a lie, and it is increasingly impossible for him to know when he is lying and when he is not. . . . [T]he penalty of deception is to *become* a deception."[140]

Living within a system as complex as Jim Crow, which combined law and "custom" and at once could be unyielding and harsh, inconsistent, and paternal, it was easy for both whites and Blacks to think and feel that by not quite playing by the rules they had somehow evaded its sanctions, when in the end, this sort of deception strengthens the system: "For the most part the relationship between the weak and the strong . . . is characterized by a facile use of the mood of 'the exception.' It is easy to say of a particular individual, 'He is different,' or 'He is exceptional' and to imply that the general rule or the general attitude does not apply."[141] The only alternative to deception and hypocrisy is sincerity. It is a dangerous strategy for the disinherited, with a potentially high cost in "life, limb, or security."[142] But it is the only way to burst the bonds of oppression: "In the face of an overwhelming sincerity on the part of the disinherited, the dominant are caught with no defense," without their usual prerogative or presumption of impregnability.[143] The master-slave dialectic is rent. Evils are confronted, not circumvented; one becomes an example, an instance, rather than an exception. In this context Thurman quotes Gandhi for the only time in the book: "Speak the truth, without fear and without exception, and see everyone whose work is related to your purpose. You are in God's work, so need not fear man's scorn. If they listen to your requests and grant them, you will be satisfied. If they reject them, then you must make their rejection your strength."[144]

Hate is the third of Thurman's hounds of hell. For the disinherited, hatred, like fear and deception, has some initial utility. It is a "device by which an individual seeks to protect himself against moral disintegration," establishing "a dimension of self-realization hammered out of the raw materials of injustice."[145] But its usefulness is limited. The hater becomes dominated by efforts at revenge or, more often, impotent desires for revenge. It tends to be "blind and nondiscriminating," liable to be discharged erratically. One cannot sustain the initial "white heat" of hatred, and if it originally seemed "positive and dynamic," sustained hatred dries "up the springs of creative thought in the life of the hater," who focuses on the "negative aspects of his environment," while the tie to the object of his hate, often unvanquished and even more inescapable, grows ever-stronger. Hatred starves "the urgent need of the personality for creative expression."[146] In the end, hatred for Thurman was another mechanism by which the disinherited reinforce their own powerlessness.

Diagnosing a problem is usually easier than providing solutions. The final chapter of *Jesus and the Disinherited,* on love, was the most difficult for Thurman to write, and he rewrote it several times before he was satisfied with it. Nolan Harmon wrote him in May 1948: "I should also tell you that we feel that your last chapter on 'Love' is not quite as strong nor convincing as the others are."[147] The chapter is, perhaps, too short and too schematic to do all the work it needs to do. Thurman stated in the beginning of the book that he belonged to "a generation that finds very little that is meaningful or intelligent in the teaching of the Church concerning Jesus Christ" because it seems "to be a betrayal of the Negro into the hands of his enemies by focusing his attention upon heaven, forgiveness, love, and the like." This teaching has to be "put into a context that will show its strength and vitality rather than its weakness and failure."[148] This is the challenge he set himself in this final chapter, explaining the "strength and vitality" in the Christian injunction to "love thy enemy."

There are, says Thurman, different classes of enemies. There are acquaintances and former friends with whom you have had a personal dispute. Then there are the enemies within one's own group, those "who are willing to put their special knowledge at the disposal of the dominant group to facilitate the tightening of the chains." Thurman cites Roman tax gatherers in Judea, declining to provide more recent examples but stating, "In every ghetto, in every dwelling place of the disinherited throughout the ages, these persons have appeared." One must love them, out of respect for their persons, "but to love them does not mean to condone their way of life."[149] Thurman suggests a love that encourages them to betray their initial betrayal.

And then, for the disinherited, there is the hardest kind of love, loving one's true enemies, one's oppressors, for the Jews to love Romans, for African Americans to love the implementors and facilitators of white supremacy. For this sort of love, the oppressors must be separated from one another, disaggregated, treated as individuals. The power of oppression in part reflects its anonymous quality. The oppressors must be lifted "out of the general classification of enemy" and "emerge as a person." But this can only happen if the Jew and the Roman can meet outside of their own "social context."[150] The enemy must be isolated from his usual supports. Blacks can view whites "in the context of a common humanity." These interactions have to "be rooted in concrete experience," people meeting one-on-one or in small groups: "No amount of good feeling for people in general, no amount of simple desiring, is an adequate substitute."[151] Radical nonviolence, with its armamentarium of tactics, is one way to begin this process. Another way is meeting in a truly neutral site, bracketed at least temporarily from the usual social hierarchies, such as, he suggests, an interracial church.[152]

Thurman, late in life, contemplated writing a book about Jesus and the "'inherited,' the advantaged, the rich and the powerful."[153] Unfortunately, the book remained unwritten, but he was often asked about the book's message to white America. Janella Smith, the wife of a minister, wrote Thurman in 1956. She told Thurman that she and her husband were members of the "privileged" class, "the 'strong,' and in no way can we fully understand the position of the 'disinherited.'" Certainly white Americans, she asked, were confronting their own fears, deceptions, and hates and were also were in dire need of having to learn how to love their enemies? She suggested if "perhaps the main purpose of your book was not so much to console and educate the disinherited as it was to arouse people in my position."[154]

If this was not Thurman's intention, he definitely wanted readers such as Janella Smith. He replied that that the first task of most white Americans was to dispel their ignorance and fear of, and lack of personal connections to, Black America (Thurman suggested she befriend the wife of a local Black minister, doing so in a "normal" and "natural" way.)[155] The first step toward true equality was not whites trying to "help" Blacks but endeavoring to seriously and creatively interact and learn from them—rather than what usually passed for "understanding" Blacks—and then beginning to free themselves from their "white necessity" (a more elegant and searching term for what is now commonly called "whiteness" or "white privilege") and mingling their "desires with all the rest of the desperate people of all the ages."[156]

The book sets out an even more arduous task for the disinherited, to initiate the task of reconciliation with and love of their enemies. This kind of love cannot be reduced to a feeling or emotion. It is a process: "What one discovers in even a single experience in which barriers have been removed may become useful in building an over-all technique for loving one's enemy. There cannot be too great an insistence on the point that we are dealing here with a discipline, a method, a technique, as over against some form of wishful thinking or simple desiring."[157] It is a love that requires, he wrote in 1952, a "heart that is as warm as fire" and "a brain that is as cold as ice."[158] To either give or receive this kind of love is always painful. Forgiveness, Thurman writes, can never be entirely satisfactory or rationally explicable: "Can the mouse forgive the cat for eating him?"[159] There is always the danger, as he would write late in life, that the sharing of love "with avowed enemies" can be "a weak copout."[160] One must always be on guard against self-deception or premature pretensions to saintliness. But it must be tried. Thurman would state, a few years later, in the concluding paragraph of *Disciplines of the Spirit:* "The experience of love is either a necessity or luxury. If it be a luxury, it is expendable; if it be a necessity, then to deny it is to perish."[161]

Thurman's final point is that loving one's enemy is not really about one's enemy, or even about love in any conventional sense. As Gandhi had told him, love of one's enemy is an affirmation of a unity of life that transcends life's flux and apparent transience. Vincent Harding has suggested that *Jesus and the Disinherited* is about a "quest for a liberating spirituality, a way of exploring and experiencing those crucial life points when personal and societal transformation are creatively joined."[162] Loving one's enemy is freeing.

Toward the end of his short book, Thurman quotes the words of a spiritual, one that would be immortalized by one of its first readers:

Free at last, free at last
Thank God Almighty, I'm free at last.[163]

If there is music in *Jesus and the Disinherited,* however, until its final pages it is not the uplifting sound of the spirituals. It is a darker, more unsettled music, in a minor key. When reading *Jesus and the Disinherited,* one specific song comes to mind. It is hard not to think of Robert Johnson's haunting blues song "Hellhound on My Trail" (1937). This famous recording has the following opening stanza:

I gotta keep movin (2×)
Blues fallin down like hail (4×)
And the days keeps on worryin me
There's a hellhound on my trail
Hellhound on my trail (2×)

Thurman's taste in music ran to Beethoven and Brahms, not the Delta blues, and there is no evidence from his papers that he was familiar with Robert Johnson's recording. Yet for all of the differences between these two men, they both grew up poor and Black in the Jim Crow South of the early twentieth century. They both knew the psychological toll of oppression, how it could lead to an amorality in which neither self-respect nor respect for others can thrive. Johnson and Thurman would have understood each other's hellhounds.[164]

The braying hound, from the slave patrols to the prison camps and chain gangs, were indelible symbols of white supremacy. (Is there anything more redolent of Jim Crow's last stand than Bull Connor's attack dogs in Birmingham?) Johnson used the fairly common blues image of the hellhound to craft a blues that speaks of rootlessness, isolation, and instability, an ode to the feeling of disinheritance. Whether or not, as has sometimes been suggested, "Hellhound on My Trail" epitomizes the entire genre of the blues, discussions of the song, like so much of the broader debate about the blues, often centers on whether the blues is a music of personal resignation or of resistance.[165] The same dichotomy is central to *Jesus and the Disinherited.* Thurman suggests that "it may be argued that even nonresistance is a form of resistance, for it may be regarded as an appositive [that is, a closely proximate] dimension of resistance. Resistance may be overt action, or it may be merely mental and moral attitude."[166] Perhaps he said this with more clarity two decades earlier, writing about another Black musical genre, the spirituals, whose message he characterized as follows: "I am beaten and brutalized by power-maddened men, but I shall see to it that my experiences and my environment do not crush me."[167]

Thurman certainly acknowledged the immense damage wrought by segregation and white supremacy and its often shattering impact on Black lives and Black psyches. *Jesus and the Disinherited* is suffused with the language of contemporary psychology, with ego stabilization, self-realization, persona, personality, and the like. But *Jesus and the Disinherited* is not an example of the so-called "damaged psyche" school of midcentury psychologizers of Black mentality.[168] To acknowledge the damage of segregation was, for Thurman, to state the obvious. Segregation could ruin lives and destroy psychological stability. He did not sentimentalize or minimize the consequences of oppression, but neither did he sensationalize or pathologize it. While Thurman borrowed much from contemporary psychology and sociology, *Jesus and the Disinherited* is a work of spiritual reflection, and he rejected any hint of environmental or social determinism, elsewhere rejecting "all those jugglers of man's destiny," like "the unconscious," one's "social heritage," or "social behavior pattern," those external forces that so crowd a person "that he has no moment that he can call his own and be free."[169]

In *Jesus and the Disinherited* no psyche is damaged beyond repair, no life shattered beyond recovery, no one has to be comfortable in their abjectness, unlike the blues singer Thurman once heard in Beaver Slide singing, "Been down so long / Down don't worry me."[170] The book is a handbook for overcoming the handicaps imposed by white supremacy. Thurman argued that anyone can do this, regardless of the level of oppression. It is normal for the oppressed and disinherited "to develop a deep sense of insecurity." When this happens, "it provides the basic material for what the psychologist calls an inferiority complex. It is quite possible for a man to have no sense of personal inferiority as such, but at the same time be dogged by a sense of social inferiority."[171] Social powerlessness often feels like psychological damage to those on the receiving end and has often been misdiagnosed as such by outside social commentators.

To Thurman, "awareness of being a child of God" can overcome this powerlessness and lift an individual "to a place of pre-eminence that belongs to God and God alone" and can find "a new courage, fearlessness, and power." Thurman had seen this "happen again and again." He knew "communities that were completely barren, with no apparent growing edge, without any point to provide light for the disadvantaged," yet he had seen "children grow up without fear."[172] But in a damaged society, it was hard to keep healthy psyches intact since the aim of segregation was to keep the subordinate class circumscribed, limiting an individual's "ability to actualize potentials."[173] The "overwhelming criminality of segregation," Thurman wrote in 1956, was "a denial of alternatives. It freezes status, movement, position; it strips the victim of options. It is true that the human spirit again and again survives under a system of segregation because the sense of alternatives keeps actively at work pushing, always pushing against the wall."[174] When you stop believing in the possibility of alternatives, the segregationists have won. Only those, he says in the closing words of the chapter on "Love," who can place themselves "at the disposal of the Spirit" with the requisite "dedication and discipline" can live "in the chaos of the present [with] the high destiny of a son of God."[175]

By April 1949, *Jesus and the Disinherited* was in print. It did not make much of an initial splash. There were several brief, mostly positive scholarly reviews. One noted that Thurman "writes, as he speaks, with beauty and strength," and another that the little book "bristles with insights." One reviewer questioned if the religion of Jesus was really a "'technique of survival for the oppressed' and whether Jesus was so largely concerned with the circumstances of oppression at the hands of Rome."[176] Fellowship Church member Aubrey Burns, who had closely followed the book's progress, lauded it in the *Southwestern Review* as a book that should be read by "every literate member of every minority group" as well as by "every literate mind of the majority group."[177] There were notices in a number of Black newspapers, including two in the *Chicago Defender.* "Charley Cherokee" said of Thurman in May 1949 that he was "a profound man who speaks slowly, each word weighed with idea-seed," and suggested that his new book "can't be read in a hurry. It's best read when quiet of surroundings and spirit permit introspection and it has to be read piecemeal and digested."[178] In the same newspaper, the next month, Gertrude Martin called it "a thought provoking and deeply perceptive book," one in which Thurman had simply and succinctly "stated the spiritual problems of the Negro today in clear, stark terms." She hoped it would "reach a wide range of readers" and "give Christians of all colors pause."[179] Not all early readers were so complimentary. A Black minister from North Carolina wrote Thurman to complain his book denied that "Jesus Christ is God" and wondered if his purpose in the book was to try "to undermine the faith of God's people in his precious word." Thurman thanked the minister for his response but reminded him that Jesus told his flock, "judge not that ye not be judged."[180] That was about it for contemporary notices of the book.

Two early readers stand out. By 1949 Howard's mother, Alice, was nearing the end of her journey, with less than a year to live, and still residing in the old family home in Daytona Beach. After Thurman sent her a copy of the book in May 1949, Alice wrote Howard a letter. In her rough prose and unsteady hand, she proclaimed her love of her son and her love of God, two constants that had nurtured him from his earliest childhood: "My dear Son I thank god And you for the book It A great book I have only read A little my eyes Are not so good And I can t read to much It came the lass of lass week But It is A great book. I wonder where you got so much knowlege from God only Could give It to you I Am verry thankful to God for permiting me to be you mother."[181]

About a month later, she would suffer a serious stroke. Howard and Sue felt there was no alternative but to move Alice to San Francisco. For Alice, San Francisco was not only a move to the other side of the continent; it was a trip to a different universe. She was not well enough to attend church services, and she was unused to, and uncomfortable with, whites coming and going from the Thurmans' apartment. Her condition worsened. Thurman's family physician (and prominent Black newspaper publisher and political power broker) Dr. Carleton Goodlett had admitting privileges at one of the best hospitals in the area. But almost all the staff were white. Alice Sams was dying, and she didn't want prying white eyes or helping white hands to witness it. Like her son, she did not want white pity. She said as much to him, as he related in his autobiography:

> Howard, you've got to take me home.
> I said, "Mamma, you need to be here."
> No, if I've got to die, I want to die at home. Everybody here at the hospital is a Buckra [a somewhat derogatory southern Black term for white people.] The first chance they get, you don't know what they will do to you. I'm scared to go to sleep at night, and you just have to take me out of this place.[182]

Dying is intimate. One's final days are not the time to break and challenge a lifetime of fear, deception, and hatred. Her son brought her home, and she soon after died, peacefully.

If Nolan Harmon, the future Methodist bishop, castigated in Martin Luther King, Jr.'s "Letter from Birmingham Jail," was perhaps the first reader of *Jesus and the Disinherited,* another early reader was King himself. In the fall of 1949 he was a second-year student at Crozer Seminary. He quoted extensively from *Jesus and the Disinherited* in a student paper from the fall of 1949 (without attribution, as was his unfortunate habit) on the message of the slave preacher, who told his flock: "You—you are not niggers. You—you are not slaves. You are God's children." This, argued King (once again closely paraphrasing Thurman), "established for them a true ground of personal dignity. The awareness of being a child of God tends to stabilize the ego and bring new courage."[183] If King dated the beginning of his formal introduction to Gandhi's teachings to a lecture delivered by Mordecai Wyatt Johnson in 1950, he was already, by the fall of 1949, attuned to the potential spiritual and political power of radical Christian nonviolence. In 1966 King wrote Thurman that he "found all of your books most inspiring and one of my most abiding means of meditation."[184] His favorite was *Jesus and the Disinherited,* a companion on many of his travels.[185]

If King admired the book, it was not because *Jesus and the Disinherited* was falsely sanguine. Thurman had written that the God of the disinherited was "no weak, mushy Pollyanna . . . no shallow optimism here but a vast faith that reaches through all the dimensions of human life."[186] Neither did King think the book's emphasis on the psychological health of the personality was in any way a "therapeutic" exercise in evading political struggle; it was a way of inwardness and introspection that led outward, toward political involvement, making it possible, rendering it necessary. *Jesus and the Disinherited* marks the full emergence of Howard Thurman as a writer, and it stands at the pinnacle, if not of his entire career, then certainly for the Fellowship Church years. With Martin Luther King, Jr., his little book had found its ideal reader. But it was also written for Alice Sams. And, if they cared to read it carefully and thoughtfully enough, it was written for the Nolan Harmons of the world as well.

12

Disciplines and Resources

At Boston University

In the spring of 1953, when Thurman agreed to come to Boston University's School of Theology as the dean of chapel and professor of spiritual disciplines and resources, it seemed to him to be a near-ideal situation, a combination of the most attractive features of Howard University and Fellowship Church. As at Howard, he would again be teaching divinity students at an institution that, as much as any mainstream theological school in the country, had an excellent reputation for teaching African American students. He also had promises from university president Harold Case that he would be able to create a "religious fellowship" that would closely resemble the one he was leaving behind at Fellowship Church.[1]

He would be a pathbreaker. He would be the first tenured Black professor at BU (and, a fortiori, the first Black dean). No figurehead, his responsibilities would extend to coordinating "all religious affairs at the university, assisting the deans and student councils of the several colleges and schools in planning programs and assemblies of religious nature and be the adviser to numerous interfaith, interdenominational and denominational organizations on campus." Thurman wrote the Fellowship Church trustees that for "one of America's great universities" to give this level of responsibility to a Black academic was a "completely unprecedented step in American education," one that made "a limitless contribution to intergroup relations at this fateful moment in the history of America and the world."[2] Thurman felt that he had one more job in him, and this was it: "I am 52 years old, which means that according to the classical American timetable, I have 13 years of active work." (He was as good as his word, BU would be his last full-time employer, and he stuck to the timetable, retiring in 1965, aged sixty-five.) His age gave him "no sense of urgency, but it does point up the fact that if my life is to be spent to the fullest advantage on behalf of what seems to me to be the great hope for mankind, it is important to work on its behalf where there is the maximum possibility of contagion."[3]

Nonetheless, the decision to move to Boston was wrenching, and he had deep regrets about what he was leaving behind. It is true that in some ways it was an easier move than Howard and Sue's last move, in 1944, when Olive and Anne had been minors. Olive remained behind in California, where she would eventually marry the Chinese American actor Victor Wong, begin a family, and pursue a varied career as a theater director, fashion designer, and librarian. (Olive and Victor made pseudonymous appearances as beat generation hipsters in Jack Kerouac's final novel, *Big Sur.*)[4] Anne came to BU to finish her undergraduate degree and would later get a degree from the Boston University School of Law.[5] Probably Thurman's greatest personal regret was leaving his sister Madaline in California, whose bouts of severe depression sometimes required her hospitalization.[6]

Beyond the situation of his immediate family, Thurman felt great sadness in leaving Fellowship Church. In his early years in Boston he made a real attempt to remain deeply involved in its affairs while trying to respect the positions and prerogatives of his successors. This became less urgent over time, but Thurman, who persuaded a reluctant Harper and Brothers to publish *Footprints of a Dream: The Story of the Church for the Fellowship of All Peoples,* remained attached to the congregation he left behind.[7]

There was also trepidation about where he was going. Thurman did not like Boston, which in his experience lived up to its unenviable reputation as one of the most unfriendly northern cities for African Americans. He wrote in his autobiography, without giving any specifics, that he "suffered very unpleasant racial experiences in Boston during an earlier period, and I did not want to expose them [his family] to a climate I myself did not trust. Would they be subject to insults and discrimination as I had been?"[8] (As a baseball fan, Thurman was no doubt aware that the Boston Red Sox, six years after Jackie Robinson's debut with the Brooklyn Dodgers, had yet to hire a Black player. They would finally, in 1959, become the last major league team to break the color line.) Throughout his twelve years in Boston, he was a visitor. San Francisco remained his home.

Lastly, there were problems specifically associated with Boston University. He would be returning to what he called, somewhat euphemistically, "the controlled academic environment we had left in Washington."[9] He did not relish once again placing himself in a situation in which a college president

Thurman at Boston University, ca. 1955

had the power to approve, disapprove, or curtail his actions. One of the best parts of the San Francisco years for Thurman had been the ability to be his own boss, constrained only by the usually pliant church board of trustees. This would not be the case in Boston. And he knew that his superiors and peers on the faculty would all be white. Fellowship Church was an interracial institution that he largely created. At BU he would be a Black man trying to fit into an academic hierarchy that prior to his arrival had been entirely white. He was worried that he was being set up, despite President Case's good intentions. The situation at Marsh Chapel was "nearly moribund," and if he were to fail in turning the situation around, "one more door might be closed against black Americans." Case would get credit from those who "said that it took a great deal of courage on the part of the administration to put a Negro in this place," whereas he would be blamed for the failure.[10] One dean was sure that after his first year in Boston, "one of two things would happen: either the chapel would be empty on Sunday, or it would be full of Negroes from Roxbury [a Boston neighborhood]."[11]

Thurman's appointment was well received by the members of the School of Theology, some of whom had been calling for the appointment for many years.[12] The distinguished theologian Edgar Brightman was a national associate of Fellowship Church and had written Thurman in 1946 that the church was "one of the most important projects in American religion."[13] Brightman unfortunately passed away just as Thurman's appointment was announced, but not before conveying his gratification at the news to a colleague.[14] Faculty member and longtime civil rights activist Allan Knight Chalmers wrote Thurman after hearing the news of his appointment, "No words can quite express my joy in your coming to Boston."[15]

However, within the university there had been, as Thurman wrote in his autobiography, "much opposition to my appointment and ministry both on racial and theological grounds." There was an unnamed "greatly revered retired administrator" at Boston University who later told him, abashed, after he changed his mind, that he had done "everything I could to oppose your coming."[16] It was, Thurman felt, to Case's "everlasting credit" that he never revealed to Thurman "even a hint of the pressure to which he was subjected."[17] Although Thurman had been a frequent visitor to BU, he felt, once he arrived, that "as a black man, I was automatically an outsider. There were occasional rude reminders of this. A stare, a derogatory comment just loud enough to be overheard, a deliberate discourtesy."[18]

Thurman was joining a university that was in the first flush of postwar expansion, moving to a sprawling urban campus unfurling along Boston's Commonwealth Avenue. Almost since its founding in 1869 as the Methodist General Biblical Institute (then located in Concord, New Hampshire), Boston University and its School of Theology had been a flagship for American Methodism. (This provided one nonracial reason for opposition to hiring Thurman, who became the first non-Methodist dean of chapel.) In a city chockablock with eminent institutions of higher education, by the 1950s BU had elbowed its way to a position of prominence.[19] If Harold Case, like all of his Boston University presidential predecessors, was a Methodist minister, he was presiding over a university whose religious character was rapidly changing. The student body of the university was no longer primarily Methodist, and, indeed, BU was no longer a majority-Protestant institution. By the early 1950s probably no more than about 40 percent of the students were Protestant, the rest divided primarily between Jews and Roman Catholics.[20] Still, until Case became president, non-Protestant religions had had little expression at the university. It was only in 1952 that the first Catholic mass on the campus was celebrated, and Hillel House, for Jewish students, opened the following year. Not too surprisingly, nowhere on campus was the Methodist dominance more prevalent than in the School of Theology. In 1945, the faculty was entirely Methodist, all of whom, with one exception, were School of

Theology alumni. Broadening the faculty was one of Case's main goals, and Thurman's was one of the most visible appointments yet.[21]

There were other burgeoning diversities afoot. Starting in the early 1950s, the university was beginning to enroll a substantial number of Black students.[22] Nowhere was this truer than in the School of Theology, one of the largest divinity schools in the country with more than four hundred men and women enrolled in its programs. It had a vibrant international component, with students from more than twenty-five countries, many from non-Western areas. And no doubt of crucial importance to Thurman, it had a distinguished record of educating and graduating African Americans. It awarded its first Ph.D. to an African American, J. W. E. Bowen, as early as 1887.[23] In the 1950s, about half of all religious studies doctorates awarded to African Americans in the United States were earned at BU and the School of Theology.[24]

By coming to the School of Theology, Thurman was not only joining a faculty, he was joining a religious philosophy. BU was the home of "Boston personalism." This has been described as the "most coherent school of American liberal theology."[25] When Thurman came to the School of Theology, Boston personalism was well into its third generation, handed down and transformed since the days of Borden Parker Bowne (1847–1910), who taught at Boston University from 1876 until his death. In the years just prior to Thurman's arrival, the most prominent exponent of personalism was the philosophy professor Edgar S. Brightman. Dean Walter Muelder and others carried on in a reinterpreted personalist tradition.

For Brightman, personalism was "the thesis that the universe is a society of persons under the leadership of a Supreme Creative Person who gives meaning and immanent cooperation to all that is finite."[26] Rather than trying to narrowly define it, it is perhaps easier to think of personalism as a school of thought that incorporated many trends within twentieth-century liberal Protestantism: a more or less idealistic metaphysics via a diluted Hegelianism or Kantianism, accompanied by a pluralistic and nondogmatic theology. Personalists rejected both agnosticism and atheism as well as Niebuhrian neo-orthodoxy. Personalism meant both a sense of contemplative awe before the divine personality and a recognition of the need to maximize persons and personality in the social order.

Personalism was socially and theological progressive. The dean of the School of Theology, Walter Muelder was an outspoken activist for many causes, among them, international peace, organized labor, freedom of speech, and civil rights. For these and other political commitments, Muelder and the School of Theology earned a place, in the words of a *Reader's Digest* article in February 1950, on "Methodism's Pink Fringe." (Among the proofs adduced in the article for Muelder "giving aid and comfort to Communists" was his insistence on the religious importance of "racial brotherhood.")[27] Racial justice was a key concern of Boston personalism.[28]

Thurman never identified as a personalist or wrote about personalism, which is not terribly surprising since he rarely wrote about formal theology. However, there is no reason to think that he had any profound disagreement with its basic tenets. While in seminary in the 1920s, if not exposed to Boston personalism, he had been taught its Rochester variant. Thurman's professor Conrad Moehlman summarized the entire history of Christianity as the struggle between "authoritarianism" and "personalism." For George Cross, personality unified all the disparate parts of the human religious experience. It gave "meaning and worth to everything with which we have to do," and while as individuals we can only imperfectly realize our personality, it is only because we aspire to its realization "that we are content to live at all," leading to the conclusion that "*God is Personality.*"[29] As early as 1924 Thurman decried "any attitude . . . which strangles personality and inhibits its highest growth and development" as a "crime against God."[30] The following year he listed as a paramount obligation of the Christian the recognition of "the sacredness of human personality."[31] The recognition, protection, and enhancement of personality would long be a key aspect of Thurman's thought.[32] Thurman was fully formed theologically when, at age fifty-three, he joined the faculty at Boston University. (The same cannot be said for the young Martin Luther King, Jr., whose immersion in Boston personalism was undoubtedly more profound.)[33] To the extent that personalism was the common coin of the liberal Protestant realm in which Thurman spent his adult life, he was a personalist; to the extent that personalism required membership in a distinct theological guild, he was not.

Thurman's decision to accept the Boston position was big news. The Black press was full of praise. The *New York Amsterdam News,* to give one example, lauded his appointment as befitting "one of the most beloved Christian ministers—a minister's minister—known as scholar, philosopher, poet, preacher and ambassador between diverse peoples."[34] The *New York Times,* for the first time, acknowledged Thurman with more than a passing reference, even including his photograph.[35] In April 1953, *Life* magazine hailed Thurman as one of a dozen "Great Preachers" who were bringing "America back to the churches." He was the only African American in the group, which also included Norman Vincent Peale, Fulton J. Sheen, and Billy Graham.[36] For the rest of his life, biographical accounts of Thurman would invariably include this recognition from *Life,* sometimes with a bit of encomium inflation (as on the dust jacket

From left: Boston University president Harold Case, Howard
Thurman, Sue Bailey Thurman, and George Makechnie, ca. 1955

copy for his autobiography), expanding from one of America's great preachers,
circa 1953, to one of the great preachers of the century. The most notewor-
thy product of this flood of publicity was a five-thousand-word article that
appeared in the *Atlantic* in October 1953, just as he was beginning his time
in Boston, by Jean Burden, simply titled "Howard Thurman," which was the
best overview of Thurman's life and ministry yet to appear.[37] When Thurman
arrived in Boston, Case ordered reprints of the article to be sent to all Boston University alumni.[38] Burden would become, over the last three decades of
Thurman's life, one of his closest and most intimate friends.

One of Case's immediate reasons for hiring Thurman was to revive Sunday services at the university. Regular attendees before Thurman's arrival
consisted solely of a "few professors and elderly residents of the Bay State
Road area."[39] Thurman had been encouraged to create at Marsh Chapel, a
"community church at the university, membership of which would come
from the university family and the community of Boston. This would be a
non-creedal, non-sectarian, interracial, interfaith and intercultural religious
fellowship."[40] This community church would be similar to the one he had
created in San Francisco but would draw from a community that was even
more diverse. It might, he hoped, "touch at every step of the way hundreds of

young people who themselves will be going to the ends of the earth to take up their responsibilities as members of communities. Conceivably, this means the widest possible dissemination of the ideas in which I believe, in the very nature of the operation itself."[41]

From the outset, Thurman refashioned the chapel service to his liking, dropping the Lord's Prayer, the Affirmation of Faith, and the Act of Common Prayer from the service. In their place was an extended "Period of Meditation." Many of the traditional Christian and Methodist trappings of the service were removed. Thurman had come to take an active dislike to much of the standard Christian service and its accompanying iconography. "Even to this day," he wrote in 1959, "I find that whenever I see the cross, my mind and my spirit must do a double take, because the thing that flashes instinctively in my mind is that of the burning cross of the Klan."[42] Although his first sermon, on 20 September 1953, was on a traditional Christian theme, the temptations of Jesus, any regular worshipper at Marsh Chapel would have found much that was unfamiliar. In the program for this first service he tried to explain what he wished to accomplish:

This Sunday morning worship service is so designed as to address itself to the deepest needs and aspirations of the human spirit. In so doing it does not seek to undermine whatever may be the religious context which gives meaning and richness to your particular life; but rather to deepen the authentic lines along which your quest for spiritual reality has led you. It is our hope that you will come to regard the Chapel not only as a place of stimulation, challenge, and dedication, but also as a symbol of the intent of the University to recognize religion as fundamental to the human enterprise.[43]

Thurman soon gained an attentive and growing audience. F. Thomas Trotter, who was the Protestant chaplain at Boston University at the time of Thurman's arrival, recalled: "When Howard arrived, the tempo picked up. Marsh Chapel became a church."[44] Thurman soon had a regular congregation of about 225, which increased to about 300 by his last full year as active minister (1961–62), and he often filled the 500-seat chapel to capacity.[45] The congregation was generally about two-thirds white and one-third African-American and international students.[46] He brought to Marsh Chapel the techniques that he had used in San Francisco, an emphasis on nonsectarian services and meditation; excellent music; liturgical dance, and other nontraditional worship practices. One of the dancers, Beth Ruhde, later wrote, "Thurman drew us into a creative circle where our individual differences were expressed, appreciated, and used to unite us."[47]

At the heart of almost every service was Thurman the charismatic preacher. Hubert E. Jones, a graduate student of BU, remembered: "With my mind's eye I can see him in the pulpit of Marsh Chapel. He was an immense presence—awesome, not just in preaching, but in a way that would lead one into personal meditation."[48] For another regular attendee, Joan Diver, Thurman spoke "in a thunderous roar or a barely audible whisper," and she recalled that using "his full range of voice he would repeatedly urge each of us gathered to seek, find, and affirm our innermost 'center.'"[49] Barbara Jordan, a student at the BU School of Law from 1956 to 1959 and later a notable civil rights leader and congresswoman from Texas, wrote: "I went to Chapel practically every Sunday. The minister there, Howard Thurman, was outstanding. . . . His sermons were focused upon the present time that all of us were having difficulty coming to grips with. . . . I saved every chapel program. [They] contained a message that was always something moving and meaningful."[50]

The Marsh Chapel services were broadcast weekly over the radio, and Thurman's message found a larger audience than his immediate auditors. In 1956 a radio listener, Henry Bollman, having just heard Thurman's sermon, wrote him conveying his "appreciation of [Thurman's] profound understanding of the meaning of God's peace." A student of Hinduism, Bollman wrote, "Until I heard you today, I have never heard a Christian preacher who could be put on the same level of spiritual understanding as the great Swamis of India."[51] From 1958 until he left Boston in the summer of 1965, Thurman also appeared weekly on a local television program, *We Believe,* to which he provided a fifteen-minute meditation every Friday morning.[52] Thurman was at first uncomfortable with the thought of being on television and speaking without an audience: "I was sure that it would not be possible for me to do this because I need so much in my own public addresses and speaking the feel of the minds of the people to whom I am speaking."[53] He soon adjusted, though, speaking to the technical crew in the studio and buoyed by his virtual audience, who sent him letters and sometimes greeted him on the street.

Besides his responsibilities at Marsh Chapel and teaching duties at the School of Theology (discussed below), Howard, along with Sue, participated in a wide range of activities at the university. Sue had a special connection with the large number of international students and formed the International Student Hostess Committee, with monthly birthday parties; and she was instrumental in having the university construct an international student building to address their needs.[54] The Thurmans also entertained extensively in the apartment provided for the dean of chapel at 184 Bay Street, near the "center" of the elongated Commonwealth Ave. urban campus. In the 1955–56 academic year alone, eight hundred persons enjoyed their at-home hospitality, in gatherings ranging from six to sixty-five (the monthly reception for the chapel choir), with the Thurmans providing refreshments or meals for the visitors.[55] They had an open-door policy at their residence for those in need of friendship and nurturance. At Christmas, they opened their home to students who stayed on campus over the break and served a festive breakfast, with Thurman, whose love of cooking was inherited from his mother, preparing his special chicken stew, described by one sated eater as being "loaded with meat and vegetables, with spices and seasonings sprinkled as only his fertile imagination could concoct."[56]

In addition to his preaching and teaching assignments, he was, Harold Case wrote in 1957, the university's "senior religious officer," with far-reaching responsibilities beyond those associated with Marsh Chapel and the School of Theology.[57] He spoke widely at other BU organizations and campus groups. He also counseled students, faculty, and persons from the "wider university community."[58] After his first year at the university, he estimated that he met with an average of eleven persons a week, in sessions sometimes lasting over an hour.[59] The need for his counseling services, he wrote in 1955, "has been in excess of the time and the availability of the Dean of the Chapel." Nonetheless, and aware of his tendency to overwork himself, he was happy to be in demand. The success of the Sunday services had led to "an increased demand . . . from individuals throughout the university [for counseling.] This is very gratifying."[60] In his first years at BU, Thurman was largely contented with his position. He had expanded the scope of his ministry, reaching a larger and more diverse audience.

One of those who attended services at Marsh Chapel during Thurman's first year in Boston was a young man completing his doctorate in the philosophy of religion, Martin Luther King, Jr. Thurman's most complete discussion of his relations with King in Boston comes from a 1975 lecture:

> I suppose I am one of the few members of the faculty of the Graduate School of Theology at Boston University that while he was there had no influence on his life. The only primary contact that we had was watching the World Series around my television set. But I knew him all my life. His father and I were in college together. His mother and Mrs. Thurman for one year, her last year, were roommates. So that my life from one point of view is one which has been a part of the general and specific context in which he lived and thought and worked. [61]

A few pedantic annotations: King was a graduate student in the Boston University Department of Philosophy, not the School of Theology, though he took a number of courses with members of the School of Theology. King entered BU in the fall of 1951, and by the fall of 1953 he had finished his coursework and was preparing his dissertation, so it's not surprising that he didn't take any courses with Thurman. The two men were baseball fans, and according to one account, sometimes bet each other when their favorite teams played.[62] One suspects, however, that all bets were off when they watched the still lily-white New York Yankees beat the Brooklyn Dodgers in six games in October 1953, no doubt with both men rooting in vain for Jackie Robinson and Roy Campanella. Martin Luther King, Sr., was one month younger than Thurman, born in Decembers 1899. But he did not begin his collegiate studies until he was in his late twenties, graduating from Morehouse in 1930, while Thurman was teaching at the college as an instructor. Whether the elder King took courses from Thurman is not clear, but they knew each other, and Thurman probably heard of the birth of his son shortly after it occurred in January 1929. Sue Bailey, not yet married to Howard, probably heard about the birth at about the same time. A decade earlier, in 1920–21, she had been the roommate of King's mother, Alberta Williams King, at Spelman Seminary. The Thurmans moved away from Atlanta in 1932, but they remained friendly with the Kings and occasionally visited them. As the younger King grew to manhood, he learned about Thurman as a Morehouse campus legend, and there were occasions when Thurman and King the younger almost certainly met.[63] As we have seen, King was familiar with Fellowship Church and was an early reader of *Jesus and the Disinherited* before either man had any connection to Boston University.

The one year both Thurman and King were at BU, King attended some services led by Thurman at Marsh Chapel. King's roommate that year, Philip Lenud, told a researcher that King sometimes heard Thurman preach, listening carefully, and shaking "his head in amazement at Thurman's deep wisdom."[64] Coretta Scott King told Walter Fluker that her husband heard Thurman preach at BU and that he and his fellow Black graduate students would sometimes, with affection, imitate and mock Thurman's distinctive slow and deliberate preaching style. Comparing the itineraries of both men during the 1953–54 academic year, there were nineteen Sundays when King was in Boston and Thurman was preaching at Marsh Chapel.[65] Some of what Thurman said made a lasting impression. On at least eight occasions between 1953 and 1959, King made use of sermon material from Thurman, in addition to three additional allusions in King's first sermon collection, *Strength to Love* (1963).[66] Thurman had indeed always been "a part of the general and specific context" of King's life, before, during, and after their paths crossed at Boston University.[67]

It is, however, hard not to conclude that while both were in Boston, Thurman thought King was something of a lightweight. In the same brief reminiscence of King from 1975, no doubt with some irony, he noted that as a young man King was always "tonsorially correct" and that there "wasn't anything about his presence that made me feel sorry for him and wish that he had shined his shoes, or that he had on a clean shirt in order to help his cause."[68] This sounds like the prejudice of the ungainly and unflashy intellectual against persons of impeccable external polish, harboring the suspicion (or perhaps the hope) that beneath the immaculate exterior lay little of real substance. King also impressed him as "a very healthy, robust, Christologically speaking, orthodox Catholic priest"—not, for Thurman, terms of high praise.[69] Perhaps Thurman found King a bit too glib, a preacher's kid for whom everything had come too easily, in comparison to his own more impoverished upbringing. In a memorial tribute to King, he observed that he had not been "born in a situation which was essentially underprivileged. He was provided all of his life with the simple basic reassurances of a kind of, quote, 'middle-class security.' He was given the best possible education. His life was one in which it may have been very difficult for him to have identified himself with all kinds of people under all kinds of circumstances."[70] But Thurman added, King's genius was precisely his ability to overcome what he called this "handicap."

In December 1954 Thurman was asked about the suitability of King for the position of dean of chapel at Dillard University in New Orleans. He responded that King had "made a good record here in the university and I understand that he is a good preacher. I do not know anything about his experience with students. But, of course, a man has to start some time. Sue has had some conversations with King and is very much impressed with him." (She had attempted to recruit King as a potential assistant summer pastor at Fellowship Church.)[71] Thurman went on to recommend another Black divinity student at Boston University, Major Jones, for the position.[72] Given that King had already taken up, as of the fall of 1954, his position at Dexter Avenue Baptist Church—something of which Thurman was evidently unaware—it seems unlikely that a more enthusiastic recommendation by Thurman would have irrevocably changed the course of history and kept King, a year later, from the rendezvous with Rosa Parks, the Montgomery Bus Boycott, and his destiny.[73]

Whatever Thurman's biases, there were depths to King that Thurman, and perhaps King himself, had yet to discover during his student years. This would change with the bus boycott. If his life had been relatively untroubled, with a predetermined trajectory toward a prestigious pulpit or prominent teaching position, it no longer would be. On 5 December 1955, after a stormy meeting, King was chosen as head of the Montgomery Improvement Association for what was (originally) a one-day boycott of the city's busses, though not without considerable opposition to this relatively unknown newcomer to the Montgomery civil rights struggle. He went from the meeting to address an overflow crowd at Holt Street Baptist Church, with little time to prepare his speech. After reviewing the events of the last few days, he concluded by telling his audience about the importance of loving one's enemies and how the boycott would be an example of this: "We, the disinherited of this land, we who have been oppressed so long, are tired of going through the long night of captivity. And now we are reaching out for the daybreak of freedom and justice and equality."[74] Martin Luther King, Jr., entered into history paraphrasing the language and thought of Howard Thurman.

If Thurman was an influence on King, King and the ferment he came to epitomize regularly challenged Thurman in the 1950s. Thurman had long written about the necessary connection between personal spiritual exploration and social change, and as the civil rights struggle became more heated, Thurman considered both halves of the equation with more urgency, pondering anew the mystery of the transmutation of spiritual energy into political and social change. This was the main question he considered in the first book he completed in Boston, *The Creative Encounter: An Interpretation of Religion and the Social Witness,* initially delivered as a series of four lectures at Ohio Wesleyan University in March 1954, published later that year.[75] This was his second book that was not a collection of shorter writings. It opens with the assertion that "modern American man tends to be ashamed of his feelings. To feel deeply is to seem emotional, sentimental, weak. The rumor abounds that feelings are vapid, vague, escape hatches for the human spirit."[76] In contrast to what he saw as the facile objectivity of 1950s America, Thurman posed as an alternative the need for an "authentic religious experience," one in which "the individual himself is totally involved."[77] The volume is dedicated to exploring "how to feel, and at the same be intellectually self-respecting."[78]

Americans, he argued, "are surrounded by a climate of fear; fear of communism; fear of democracy; fear of one another; fear of tomorrow," an apt comment to make at the height of the McCarthy hearings in the spring of 1954.[79] This climate of fear resulted in isolated, frightened, and narrow lives: "Man builds his little shelter, he raises his little wall; man builds his little altar, he worships his little God; man organizes the resources of his life, he defends his little barrier, all to no avail!" Americans, he concluded, are frightened of themselves, frightened of what they would discover if they really explored themselves spiritually. They would find their "human spirit stripped to the literal substance of itself before God," come to regard the unity of humanity as more compelling than artificial divisions and distinctions, and act on this knowledge in their private and public lives. This alternative, if only glimpsed "dimly now in the churning confusion and chaos of our tempestuous times," was becoming ever-clearer.[80]

Two months later, on 16 May 1954, Thurman's Sunday sermon at Marsh Chapel was titled "Be Not Overcome by Evil." One of the typical ways to be overcome by evil, Thurman suggested, is by granting it too much dominion: "I am overcome by evil when I permit the factors or the elements in my environment, the situation, however you wish to say it, by which I am surrounded . . . make me [scale] down the ideals to which I am committed because as I look at the facts of my life and I do not now see that my ideals have any chance for fulfillment . . . and I may be tempted to say of my ideals that they are of no significance."[81]

Perhaps in planning this sermon, Thurman was thinking of the looming U.S. Supreme Court decision on school desegregation. The next day the Court handed down their unanimous decision in *Brown v. Board of Education*. America, for once, had not forced its Black citizens to scale down their ideals. Asked for his reaction by the *Chicago Defender,* Thurman's friend Horace Mann Bond, president of Lincoln University in Pennsylvania, allowed himself a few halleluiahs and hosannas: "Mine Eyes Have Seen the Glory of the Coming of the Lord!" Others hoped, like Benjamin Mays, that the white "South will adjust" and that there "will be no violence and no revolution down South."[82] Still others, like Mary McLeod Bethune, were not so sure.[83] Thurman probably shared some version of all of these emotions.

Thurman's first extant comment on *Brown* came at a commencement address a month later delivered at Bennett College in Greensboro, North Carolina, where he emphasized that implementing the extraordinary decision would require exemplary moral courage on all sides: "We are called upon to do what no other world has ever been called to do before—to confirm, to underscore, to initiate, a kind of human relations in which the heart is the precipitation of friendly men under a friendly sky."[84] He hoped that whites could be persuaded to do the right thing. His faith in the efficacy of persuasion was of long standing. "The conversion of white people to human brotherhood must be done one at a time," he had told a conference of Black college officials in 1943.[85] This remained his hope. Speaking to a Black audience in 1955, while acknowledging that legal and political victories had made "an opening wedge," he said that the "consolidation of our advances" would require reaching out to the unpersuaded through "face to face contacts among individuals, forums, letters to the editor and small sincere committees thrashing out problems around a table. These are the tiny investments which add up to tremendous dividends in the long run."[86]

Thurman placed particular hope in white ministers taking the lead in changing white southern hearts and minds. In a May 1957 article, "The Christian Minister and the Desegregation Decision," he provided a blueprint for this call to conscience. He wanted white ministers to declare racial prejudice not merely as "wrong, bad, unrighteous, and even unjust," but a sin. They must declare racial discrimination inimical to "the purification of the life, the redemption of the spirit, the salvation of the soul. . . . *Social* responsibility would be the inevitable result flowing from his experience of *personal* redemption."[87] Their eyes would be opened to "the question of segregation, of police brutality inflicted upon Negroes, the great inequalities in opportunities, the general social pattern of discrimination." They would read C. Vann Woodward's recently published *The Strange Career of Jim Crow.* The white minister, humbled by his ignorance, would discover that he "doesn't know anything about the life of the Negro who lives in his community. Until this happened, he thought he did." He would establish real friendships with local Black ministers, speak to his congregation about his new insights, and then "confront, sympathetically but firmly, a member of his congregation active in a White Citizens' Council."[88]

Alas, Thurman's hope that white Christian ministers, when faced with new post-*Brown* realities, would start to avow the religion of Jesus went largely unrealized. (Martin Luther King, Jr., had similar misplaced hopes.)[89] White ministers in the South who were too outspoken in their support for civil rights all too often found themselves looking for another position. The civil rights revolution, rather than dislodging white moderates from their zone of comfort and ambiguity, all too often reinforced their wariness of rapid social change.

If Thurman hoped for the best after *Brown,* he girded himself for the backlash. On 9 October 1955, as an introduction to a Marsh Chapel sermon on the subject of "Love Your Enemies," he spoke about the recent, brutal murder of the teenager Emmett Till in Mississippi, concluding, "Sleep well, Emmett Till; you will be remembered as long as men have tongues to cry out against evil."[90] The sermon went on to answer the question it only implicitly raised—can you love the murderers of Emmett Till? Thurman's answer was uncompromising: "A man cannot love his enemy until he is able to restore his enemy to good standing in the human race." And this will not happen until "he is able to get him outside a context that binds and defines him."[91]

A few weeks later, addressing a Boston chapter of an African American sorority of professional women, Thurman discussed the foulness that had enveloped the white South as they engaged in "massive resistance" against the *Brown* decision:

The world is divided between two spheres of influence and two competing ways of life. At home we have not yet learned how to live together as free citizens, but must expose to the world the spectacle of the state of Georgia blacklisting Negro teachers for belonging to an organization whose only purpose is to insist that the Constitution of the United States be obeyed, the state of Mississippi refusing to prosecute the kidnappers and murderers of Emmett Till—the state of South Carolina from which Rev. J. H. Delaine had to flee from injustice—the state of Florida where trade unionists cannot meet to discuss union business without being fired upon.[92]

He complained after the Little Rock crisis that President Eisenhower, in a position of "a vast moral and spiritual responsibility . . . again and again acts with utter ambivalence, at a time when he needs to act with utter unity."[93] In 1957 in an address to the all-Black Palmetto Educational Association of South Carolina, Thurman advised that Blacks in the state needed "the strength to be free and endure the burden of freedom." Those "not willing to take the responsibilities of freedom must be willing to become the slaves of others." This, the 6,700 members of the Palmetto Educational Association, threatened with the loss of their jobs for civil rights activism, knew all too well.[94]

The late 1950s were a perplexing time for the civil rights revolution. The early post-*Brown* hope of quick victories had dissipated; Thurman wrote in 1957 that "for the next fifteen years, the issues growing out of the Supreme Court's decision will be before the courts."[95] Jim Crow was beginning to totter but was far from toppled; the era of mass direct action was still a few years away. Thurman during these years became a life member of the NAACP and defended it against accusations that it was "infiltrated by subversion or Communism."[96] The crisis brought Thurman and King closer. Several mutual acquaintances wrote King early during the bus boycott, suggesting that he consult with Thurman. Lillian Smith, the veteran civil rights activist and novelist, wrote King on 10 March 1956, suggesting that Thurman "could be of help, perhaps, to you. He is truly a great man; warm, deeply religious."[97] Four days later, Homer Jack, a prominent pacifist and Unitarian minister, wrote King that he recently had "a good talk with Howard Thurman about your protest" and also suggested he speak with him.[98] On the same day in 1956, Thurman, with an impending visit to Tuskegee, Alabama, on his schedule, wrote King: "I would like very much to sit down and have two or three hours talk with you and one or two of your close associates. I prefer doing it in private at Tuskegee. Would you be interested in such a possibility and, if so, would it be possible for you to drive over to Tuskegee any time of Saturday afternoon,

March 24?" This and later attempts to meet did not prove feasible.[99] About this time, Thurman sent King a copy of *Deep River* and inscribed it with one of his favorite sayings, "The test of life is often found in the amount of pain we can absorb without spoiling our joy."[100]

When Thurman and King finally did get together, it was not under the best of circumstances. On 20 September 1958, King was signing copies of his recently published book *Stride toward Freedom* in a Harlem department store when a deranged African American woman stabbed and seriously wounded him. (Had the stab wound been an inch in a different direction, it would likely have been fatal.) Thurman related what happened next:

> Many times through the years I have had strange visitations in which there emerges at the center of my consciousness a face, a sense of urgency, a vibrant sensation regarding some particular person. On a certain Friday afternoon, Martin emerged in my consciousness and would not leave. When I came home I said to Sue, "Tomorrow morning I am going down to New York to see Martin. I am not sure why, but I must talk to him personally if the doctors will permit."[101]

Thurman went down to Harlem Hospital, likely on the weekend of 28–29 September. He was able to see King and told him not to rush his recovery, to give his body and spirit time to heal. The two men did not discuss in depth "the progress, success, or failure of the movement itself." Instead they discussed King's relation to the civil rights movement, which had "become an organism with a life of its own to which he must relate in fresh or extraordinary ways or be swallowed up by it."[102] King's first public statement after the stabbing, released on 30 September (presumably only a day or two after his extended conversation with Thurman) certainly contains echoes of Gandhi's comment to Thurman in their meeting in Bardoli: "I am now convinced that if the Negro holds fast to the spirit of non-violence, our struggle and example will challenge and help redeem, not only America but the world."[103]

In a letter written to Thurman about five weeks after their meeting, King thanked Thurman for suggesting he use his convalescence as a time for spiritual reflection: "I am following your advice on the question 'where do I go from here.'"[104] The fall of 1958 was for King, as his biographer Taylor Branch has written, "a period of relative stillness unique to his entire adult life" with a greatly reduced number of public engagements.[105] King wrote, "After I recovered from this near-fatal encounter and was finally released by my doctors, it occurred to me that it might be better to get in the trip to India before plunging too deeply once again into the sea of the southern segregation struggle."[106]

King traveled to India from 2 February to 10 March 1959, following a path taken by Thurman, traveling to the homeland of radical nonviolence, searching for sources of spiritual strength.

Probably at no time in his career was spiritual exploration more central to Thurman's ministry than in the 1950s. Throughout the decade he attracted a number of acolytes and disciples. For many, finding Thurman was a life-changing experience. As Karl Downs had written earlier, "volumes of letters" were written to him, many with a similar theme: "Your message ruined me, I will never be the same again. I must devote my all time to the meaningful things of life."[107] Thurman received one such letter in 1956 from a young African American minister, and much like Thurman's own first letter to Mordecai Wyatt Johnson, it had taken months of mental preparation to put pen to paper: "This is not my first letter to you but it is the first letter to you that you have had the occasion to read. I turned over in my mind, for many years, the desire to write to you and tell you what a blessing you have been through your writing and speaking."[108] The letter to Thurman, from James Earl Massey, was seven years in gestation. He had first heard Thurman preach in 1949 in his hometown of Detroit:

> I was moved by his preaching, very deeply moved, partly because hearing it all validated my own spiritual quest and findings in a way that no other preacher's words or pulpit approach had ever done, and partly because of the realization of divine presence I experienced in connection with his witness. As I listened, I understood his witness, and experienced God in my spirit, I sensed then and there that Dr. Howard Thurman and I were inwardly kin. . . . [He] did not preach like most of the African American preachers I had heard. There was no stormy struggle in his manner, no loud blaring of his words; his was rather a soft-spoken, assured and assuring witness, a statement that seemed to me more like an "inside word" about some treasured truth and not an outside attempt to break into the truth. His style seemed so uniquely at one with his subject. Thurman helped me to experience spoken truth more vividly than any preacher I had ever heard before.[109]

In 1956, after reading all of Thurman's available books and hearing him preach whenever possible, Massey, then a Church of God minister in an urban Detroit congregation, finally mustered enough courage to write to him.[110] They became good friends, and Massey would have a distinguished career as dean of chapel at Tuskegee University and dean of the School of Theology at Anderson University in Anderson, Indiana. He would also become the author of some of the earliest serious scholarly considerations of Thurman as a religious thinker.[111]

Thurman's ability, in Downs's words, to "ignite" his listeners was at its most intense among his students at Boston University, who had the opportunity to study with him on a regular basis.[112] BU became for Thurman a workshop of the spirit. Thurman spread his message to all who were open to listen, whatever their racial background. The realities at BU were, as Thurman no doubt knew before coming to Boston, that though the university had a number of Black and international students, most of those attending were white. (And though BU was thoroughly coeducational, most of the students at the School of Theology were male.) Some years his classes lacked any Black students. This certainly bothered Thurman on some level, and in the next phase of his career he took steps to remedy or compensate for this and have more direct contact with young African Americans, especially those aspiring for the ministry. But there is no evidence that Thurman felt, in any way, that his time teaching at BU was lessened because of this.

When Thurman was hired at Boston University, he was given two main responsibilities, dean of chapel and a position with a unique academic title— professor of spiritual disciplines and resources—and a unique charge: teaching others how to augment their capacity for spirituality. He was perhaps the first person at a major American seminary to be given this task, and he struggled with the assignment: "I had no idea how to teach such a course because, to my way of thinking, the life of the spirit and the meaning of religious experience are intensely personal. . . . [I]t was not the sort of thing one talked about. . . . The fundamental aim of the course, as I saw it, was to help men and women who were going into the ministry to acquaint themselves with their own inner life. I felt that the idea could be caught, but I did not think it could be taught."[113]

Thurman probably protested too much. He had, in one way or another, been teaching "spiritual disciplines and resources" for decades. As one of the major shapers of modern ideas of spirituality, he knew what he wanted to impart to his students, how to help them "acquaint themselves with their own inner life" in a way not limited by denomination, religion, or even any preconceived notion of religious experience. Every year he taught at BU he offered a two-semester course on spiritual disciplines and resources. Within a few weeks of the first class, he knew he had created something special: "Twice each week the forty-six students spend one-half hour of the class meditating around a central theme. Then they write a page giving glimpses of their inner stirrings. This is the most exciting experiment I have ever conducted."[114]

Commemoration of the 175th anniversary of the death of Phillis Wheatley at Boston University. (*From left:* Meta Warrick Fuller, sculptor; Howard Thurman; Sue Bailey Thurman; Beth Ballard, secretary of Marsh Chapel; Alzada Man Hayes, wife of Roland Hayes; Roland Hayes, tenor; Georgia Douglass Johnson, poet

The course had a reading list of writings about mysticism, primarily approached from a Christian perspective, as students read authors such as the Quaker mystic Douglas Steere—a classmate of his at Haverford with Rufus Jones—Søren Kierkegaard, Simone Weil, Evelyn Underhill, and D. T. Suzuki, a popularizer of Zen Buddhism. The second semester was a "study of suffering, tragedy, and love as the disciplines of the spirit through which an individual may be ushered into the Presence of God."[115] But what made the course unique were its frequent experiments in practical mysticism, extended periods of silence, and spontaneous reactions to a single meaning-laden word or image.[116]

The course had a number of "laboratory" sessions, which regularly met for an hour and a half at six thirty in the morning. In one session from 1955, students were asked to read Psalm 139 (Thurman's favorite) every day for a week at home. The class started with Thurman reading the psalm, with each member of the class instructed to "open his mind to the music of the words, to the general atmosphere which listening to the psalm generated in the mind" without paying attention to its meaning or ideas. Thurman then played a piece of slow, meditative music for twenty-five minutes, such as excerpts from Richard

Wagner's quasi-Christian opera *Parsifal*.[117] Each member of the class was then asked to select "a sentence, a phrase, a word, or an idea to which individual attention could be given for purposes of reflection, thought, meditation, or prayer" and to silently contemplate this for forty minutes. The session ended at eight o'clock, with the final verse of the psalm ("see if there be any wicked way in me, and lead me in the way everlasting") read as a benediction.[118] In 1963 Thurman published *Disciplines of the Spirit*, which was dedicated "to the students in my course on Spiritual Disciplines and Resources, 1953–1962." The contents of the volume were "winnowed out of the collective quest in which several generations of students and I have engaged."[119] All of the techniques were used to "clear away whatever may block our awareness of that which is God in us."[120]

Probably none of Thurman's students at Boston University worked more assiduously to reach this goal than Zalman Schachter, who in the 1970s changed his name to Zalman Schachter-Shalomi ("of peace"). Among those who accounted themselves among Thurman's spiritual disciples, none traveled a farther distance, or had a bigger impact as a religious thinker and teacher, than Reb Zalman. Born in Poland in 1923 and raised in Vienna, he had received a traditional Hasidic education, and after Austria's *Anschluss* to Nazi Germany, lived in Belgium and France. In 1941 he came to the United States, escaping from Vichy France. He became a disciple of the sixth Lubavitcher rebbe, Yosef Yitzhak Schneersohn, and in 1947 was ordained in the Lubavitch rabbinic seminary in Brooklyn. Thereafter he served in several Chabad Lubavitch positions and by 1955 was rabbi to an orthodox congregation in New Bedford, Massachusetts. Schachter-Shalomi was a restless soul who found Chabad's orthodoxy too confining. By the mid-1950s, he wanted to broaden his knowledge of religious psychology and get a job at a Hillel organization on a college campus, but this required a master's degree, and he decided to attend Boston University primarily because it was the only local college that would accept his unaccredited Lubavitcher schmicah (rabbinic ordination) for his matriculation.[121]

How he met Thurman was a story Schachter-Shalomi told many times. New Bedford is about sixty miles from Boston, and he arrived at Marsh Chapel for his classes early in the morning, not yet having said Schacharit, the morning prayers recited daily by observant Jews. Uncomfortable using any of the chapel rooms because of their Christian symbols and iconography, he started to daven in a small storage room. After a few mornings, a middle-aged Black man, whom Schachter-Shalomi thought might be the janitor, came up to him and said: "I've seen you here several times. Wouldn't you like to say your prayers in the small chapel?," which was downstairs from the main chapel. Schachter-Shalomi didn't want to offend the man and tell him he couldn't pray in a room with a crucifix, and said nothing. The man again suggested that he try praying in the small chapel next time he was on campus. When he arrived, the portable crucifix had been removed from the altar in the small chapel, two candles were lit, and the Bible on the lectern was open to Psalm 139. (After praying, Schachter returned the cross to the altar and opened the Bible to Psalm 100, the psalm of thanks.)[122]

Schachter-Shalomi enrolled in Thurman's spiritual disciplines and resources class but then had second thoughts; perhaps the instructor would try to convert him, and in any event, what could a Christian minister teach him about Jewish spiritual resources? When he came to address his concerns with the instructor, he was surprised to see the same Black man who had given him advice about his morning prayers. Schachter-Shalomi related his doubts. "Finally, Howard Thurman looked right at me and said, 'Don't you believe in the Ruach Hakodesh [the holy spirit]?'" and went to a record player in his office and put on a recording of Max Bruch's setting for cello and orchestra of the famous Kol Nidre chant. For Schachter-Shalomi, hearing "a non-Jew speak these Hebrew words so eloquently shattered my composure."[123]

He left Thurman's office without speaking but stayed in the course and proved to be an apt student. He was introduced to the classics of Christian mysticism for the first time, particularly remembering the Spanish mystics St. Theresa and St. John of the Cross, and St. Ignatius Loyola's *Spiritual Exercises*. He understood Thurman's experiments in responding to specific words, to musical moods. The purpose of this exercise was to "translate an experience of one sense to another . . . we would read a psalm several times and then listen to a beautiful meditative Bach composition—in order to 'hear' the psalm's meaning in the sounds of the music. In this way, we refined and became better able to experience the divine around us."[124] He would write that "in the exchanges with Dean Thurman and the other members of the class, I learned an important lesson which is still at the center of my thinking: Judaism and all the other western religions are suffering from having become oververbalized and underexperienced," and that "someone else's description of ecstasy or spiritual one-ness is not enough. I wanted to have the experience myself, and I'd like to make it possible for other people to have it too."[125] Schachter-Shalomi told me that he learned from the course that "some goyim are really wonderful souls," adding that he knew that Thurman had learned a similar lesson about white people. For Schachter-Shalomi, Thurman "wasn't interested in getting souls to Christ, but, like Jesus, he wanted to get souls to God."[126] Thurman was his "Black rebbe."[127]

Schachter-Shalomi graduated from the School of Theology with a master's degree in 1956. The following year he obtained a position as rabbi of a Conservative synagogue in Winnipeg and head of the Hillel Foundation at the University of Manitoba. In 1958 he published the first of his many books, *The First Step:*

A Primer of a Jew's Spiritual Life. It was heavily indebted to Thurman's course, opening with the statement, "This manual intends to give you practical information on spiritual discipline and resources." Many of the approaches to meditation in the manual were also borrowed from Thurman. Schachter-Shalomi acknowledges that his readers might feel that "some of the ideas and techniques given are taken from non-Jewish sources," though he insists that everything in the manual reflects "classic Jewish mysticism" and Chabad [Lubavitch] Hasidism.[128] When he sent a copy to Thurman, Thurman was so impressed that he immediately ordered a dozen copies: "Please know how exciting it is to me, personally, that you are making available to your students the spiritual insights which are not only their heritage but which they must honor the right to experience." For Thurman the "right to experience" was a fundamental liberty. He subsequently incorporated Schachter-Shalomi's book into his course.[129]

In February 1963, Thurman traveled to Winnipeg and the University of Manitoba to give a lecture series on "The Quests of the Human Spirit." Spending time with his friend was for Thurman a highlight of the trip, especially their visit to a nearby Trappist monastery—Schachter-Shalomi, always the spiritual adventurer, had become interested in the Essenes and monasticism, and had befriended the local monks. Thurman and Schachter-Shalomi met the head of training for the monastery (with the vow of silence temporarily lifted) and discussed the question of spiritual training of novices, and attended the services for vespers and complines. Thurman described the final prayers:

So, we went around and sat in the chapel in stalls in the rear while the Trappist monks had their ceremony up in the front part near the altar. When this was over, about, oh, maybe two-thirds of the way, something happened. I don't know how I can say this to you. But there came a moment while one of the chants was being sung, when it seemed as if I was moved out of my little, my little "this," and it was such a stirring thing. It seemed as if I was stripped to something very elemental in me, and I was not, it is the sort of thing that happens sometimes in prayer, when you are not you and you are not your problem, but you are sort of laid bare, just the palpitation of your essential self reduced to what is literal and irreducible in you in the presence of God. And when this happened, my eyes left the breviary, and I turned to him as he turned to me; our eyes met, this Orthodox Jewish rabbi and I. And our eyes met and held. And then as we turned away, I to go back to my breviary, the man, the Trappist monk who was leading the prayer, turned away from the altar in time for his eyes to meet our eyes.[130]

At this point, wrote Thurman, "somewhere in the march of the moments, the Conservative[131] Jewish Rabbi, the gentile preacher, and the Trappist monks became children of Life, finding their way into their Father's house." In the end there was silence, in which "every heart found its own place of rest and peace—a tranquility beyond forms, contexts, and altars."[132] This was as close to Thurman's spiritual ideal as he would ever achieve, a coming together of three quite distinct religious traditions, not merging, not effacing their differences, but joined in a search for the one and universal God.

Schachter-Shalomi would in the late 1960s be a primary founder of the Neo-Hasidic Havurah, or Jewish renewal movement, an effort to respiritualize the practice of Judaism, and was one of the most important figures in American Judaism in the second half of the twentieth century, creating a Judaism that drew on Hasidism and the Kabbalah and tried to reinvigorate ecstatic worship with singing, dancing, personal prayer, meditation, silence, and an openness to other religious traditions.[133] When I arranged an interview with Schachter-Shalomi in 2012, he was in declining health, his time carefully guarded by those close to him. But he insisted on talking to me: "I always have time to speak about Howard Thurman."[134]

Another Thurman student who had a major impact on the course of late twentieth-century religion was Walter N. Pahnke. Pahnke would, with Thurman's backing and guidance, help pioneer perhaps the most controversial arena of midcentury spiritual exploration. Born in the Chicago area in 1931, he was a 1952 graduate of Carleton College and a 1956 graduate of Harvard Medical School, with a concentration in psychiatry.[135] While pursuing his medical degree, he started attending services at Marsh Chapel and soon became a committed Thurmanite. Beth Ruhde remembers that Pahnke "used to pick me up on Sunday mornings by the church in which I worked and frenetically sped us on his motorcycle to Marsh Chapel in order to arrive two minutes early for quiet contemplation."[136]

For Pahnke, Thurman's services provided "a spiritual uplift by a creative encounter with the 'deepest needs and aspirations' of my own human spirit. I have felt as close to God there as when I have been all alone in a quiet forest of towering and whispering pines by the shores of a sky-blue mountain lake with majestic mountains and glaciers all around."[137] Pahnke audited Thurman's "Spiritual Disciplines and Resources" course in 1955–56—Zalman Schachter-Shalomi was a classmate—and after a year spent interning in various medical positions, he returned to Boston in the fall of 1957, planning to study at Harvard Divinity School. He was especially excited about an intense independent study course with Thurman, writing him that summer, hoping that it might open "new horizons and vistas" as they explored "the interrelationships between medicine and religion."[138]

Thurman's views on the relation between medicine and religion were quite complex. He had long believed that the body was a "community in itself" with resources undreamed of, or at least undiscovered, by conventional medicine.[139] He also had, dating back at least to the 1930s, an interest in the occult. In 1937 he wrote of an interest in the occult-oriented Rosicrucian society.[140] He had a kindred interest in faith healers, clairvoyants, spiritualists, and other proponents of alternative realities that he rarely discussed in public.[141] He discussed these subjects with Pahnke, including their mutual fascination with the famous seer Edgar Cayce.[142] Thurman wrote in 1960 to a woman working in an organization dedicated to Cayce's legacy: "You are in a very fortunate position to be able to study at first-hand the primary documents which deal with a long neglected aspect of human experience. I am sure that you will find it not only rewarding but helpful in your own self-realization."[143]

Thurman and Pahnke also discussed what was in the 1950s one of the most exciting frontiers of the body-mind barrier, psychedelic drugs such as psilocybin, mescaline, and LSD. (Until 1967, these substances were legal.) Their remarkable properties led some, most notably Aldous Huxley in his widely discussed *The Doors of Perception* (1954), an account of his mescaline experiences, to argue that psychedelic drugs had a phenomenological similarity to the mystic experience, allowing one "to be shaken out of the ruts of ordinary perception, to be shown for a few timeless hours the inner and outer world."[144] By 1959, Thurman was familiar with this literature, very likely through Pahnke, and he was sharing his excitement about the spiritual potential of psychedelics with his friends. Coleman Jennings returned to him in late 1959 "the copy of the fascinating articles about the marvels of LSD. It is something I would like to follow up on, for it seems to have limitless possibilities."[145] At some point, Pahnke's path crossed that of Timothy Leary (1920–1996), who joined the Harvard Psychology Department in 1959, where he would spend four turbulent years before his dismissal in 1963 for his promiscuous distribution of psychedelic substances, thereby laying the foundation for becoming—in Thurman's sarcastic words—the "patron saint" of the drug-saturated corner of the counterculture.[146] In 1960 Leary, with Richard Alpert (who later achieved his own countercultural fame as Baba Ram Dass), created the Harvard Psilocybin Project to test the therapeutic and spiritual properties of psilocybin and other psychedelics, in prisons, with artists, and in other diverse settings. By the beginning of 1962, Leary had gathered around him, in his words, an "informal group of ministers, theologians, academic hustlers, and religious psychologists in the Harvard environment [that] began meeting at least once a month" to discuss psychedelic drugs and their possible spiritual significance. Pahnke was a key figure in this group, and with their shared interests, Leary and Pahnke decided to collaborate on what would become notorious as Leary's last major psychedelic test while employed by Harvard, the Good Friday Experiment.[147]

Pahnke thought that the spiritual potential of psychedelics could be best tested among persons with a predisposition to religious experiences (such as divinity students), in a setting that might prompt such responses (such as a church or chapel) and during an observance at which personal spiritual reflection was appropriate or expected (as on Good Friday). This experiment would be the subject of his 1963 dissertation, "Drugs and Mysticism: An Analysis of the Relationship between Psychedelic Drugs and the Mystical Consciousness."[148] Pahnke got Thurman to agree to host the experiment in Robinson Chapel, downstairs from the main sanctuary, when no other space was available.[149] Obtaining the psilocybin for the experiment proved difficult, since by 1962, Harvard was curtailing Leary's access. Leary legally obtained it, only the night before, from a psychiatrist in Worcester, Massachusetts. On the morning of Good Friday in 1962, the twenty men in the experiment—divinity students from Andover-Newton Seminary and Harvard Divinity School, none of whom had previously taken hallucinogens—along with ten trained guides, gathered in the basement chapel within Marsh Chapel.[150] The study participants were given crushed powder in envelopes around 10:00 am. In the double-blind experiment, half were given 30 milligrams of psilocybin. The other half were given nicotinic acid. Shortly before noon, Thurman addressed the participants and then went upstairs to conduct the Good Friday service. The service was piped in, the basement chapel was locked and guarded, and there was no contact between the study participants and the worshippers at the main Good Friday service in Marsh Chapel. Thurman's Good Friday services were unlike any he gave in the course of the year. It was one of his few services tied to the liturgical calendar. It was in effect a lengthy meditation service, over two hours, without a sermon. The service in 1962, like Thurman's other Good Friday services, retold the life of Jesus, intoned the Seven Last Words to soft organ music and with Thurman reading from the Gospels and other selected texts. After a soloist sang the spiritual "Were You There When They Crucified My Lord?" the service slowly drew to a close.[151]

The response of the participants to the Good Friday Experiment varied widely. For those who had been given the placebo, there was little reaction. For some of the takers of psilocybin, there were adverse reactions. One participant imagined he was a fish; another, who thought he was a snake, started writhing on the floor.[152] Others remember reactions of paranoia on being prevented from leaving the ground-floor chapel area. After Thurman told the congregation that "you have to tell people that there is a man on the cross," one man somehow bolted from the chapel, ran outside to Commonwealth Avenue to spread the word, and had to be restrained.[153]

On the other hand, there were many positive reactions within the psilocybin group. Some remembered Thurman's readings as being "enormously powerful." On hearing Thurman's recitation of the Edna St. Vincent Millay poem "Conscientious Objector," beginning, "I shall die / but that is all I shall do for Death," decided that indeed, he had "died" and that his ego had "to die in order to live in freedom. I had to die in order to become who I could be. I did make a choice, in that willingness to die."[154] Another remembered kneeling to pray and "entering into the fullness of all being."[155] Also given psilocybin was Huston Smith, later a well-known professor of philosophy and religious studies. He remembered the Good Friday Experiment as one of the central religious moments of his life, his first direct personal encounter with God.[156] In his dissertation, largely based on the detailed reports and questionnaires the participants filled out, Pahnke concluded that the subjects who received psilocybin "experienced phenomena which were indistinguishable from, if not identical with, certain categories defined by our typology of mysticism."[157] The Good Friday Experiment soon became a legend and has since been reconsidered and re-created.[158]

Thurman never wrote about the Good Friday Experiment. He probably was somewhat embarrassed when news about it became public. The following year, when the *Reporter* magazine, in one of the first lengthy articles about Leary, "The Hallucinogenic Drug Cult," lauded the "the miracle of Marsh Chapel," Thurman (it would seem, without much cause) decried the article's description of events as "a gross distortion of fact."[159] Leary wrote Thurman in October 1962, inviting him to a meeting of his group on "experimental mysticism" and mentioning Pahnke, adding, "As you know the Good Friday experiment has turned out to be a ringing success—spiritually (for the subjects) and scientifically."[160] Whether Thurman attended any meeting of Leary's group seems doubtful. In any event their interactions ended when Leary left Harvard in 1963. But he remained in close contact with Pahnke, who would write extensively on the subject of psychedelics and spirituality until his untimely death, in an accident, in 1971.[161]

Thurman probably remained a skeptic in the matter of chemical mysticism, telling Luther Smith there were easier and less expensive ways to encounter God.[162] There is no evidence that he ever experimented with psychedelic substances himself. But whatever Thurman's thoughts on their efficacy, the Good Friday Experiment is best viewed as Walter Pahnke's effort to extend

Thurman's teachings on religious experience into a new, challenging, and controversial realm. Leary has hogged most of the attention about the experiment, but from the outset, the entire project was Pahnke's, from its planning and execution to the subsequent scholarly description. Unfortunately, Pahnke's careful, sober, and scientific evaluation of psychedelics has been crowded out of the popular discussion of the Good Friday Experiment by Leary and his subsequent shambolic career.[163] In his effort to understand, explain, and expand the scope of mystical experience and make it more widely available and graspable, Pahnke was a true disciple of Howard Thurman. In their own and different ways, Martin Luther King, Jr., Zalman Schachter-Shalomi, and Walter Pahnke were each leaders of revolutions in 1950s and 1960s America. Each understood their task as a spiritual discipline, and for each of them, Thurman was a mentor and guide who helped them find their own path.

Thurman certainly had his share of successes and triumphs at Boston University. Nonetheless, running through his time there was an undercurrent of disappointment, frustration, and bitterness. His most cherished project and highest ambition for BU never got beyond the planning stages, dashed by doubters and naysayers. He had wanted to create a religious fellowship at Marsh Chapel, along the lines of that at Fellowship Church, a group of persons united in a common commitment to worshipping together. In his first annual report as dean of Marsh Chapel, in June 1954, he wrote that he was working on plans "for establishing some kind of religious fellowship in connection with the chapel" and that he hoped the details would be ready by the end of the summer.[164] But this proved unduly optimistic. In April 1956 he was still trying to formulate a framework for a Boston University Chapel Fellowship and to fashion a statement akin to the Fellowship Church Commitment: "There must be some simple, comprehensive agreement, a covenant or commitment to which the individual who wished to be a part formally of the society would accept as the things on which he personally agreed to. Work out some statement, not a creed, that will bind us together."[165] Thurman wanted to keep it as simple as possible; while maintaining "a Christian orientation and inspiration, . . . organizational[ly] [it] has to be kept close to zero. The barest minimum necessary to provide a framework for the spirit."[166]

This effort ended in failure, and by the following year Thurman was convinced that "the plan to organize the Chapel, either as a church or as a formal fellowship, has complications which at the moment seem insurmountable." Therefore, he had "abandoned any plans which point directly to formalizing the religious experience which is a growing thing in connection with the ministry of Marsh Chapel."[167] But Thurman's most ambitious effort to create a Boston University Chapel Fellowship was yet to come. In the fall of 1959, a "Committee of Inquiry and Proposal" was formed; its members included Dean Walter Muelder, several students, and members of the outside community. Chaired by George A. Warmer, vice president for university affairs and a one-time Methodist minister, the committee tried to shape a proposal for a chapel fellowship.[168]

In the fall of 1960, a "Statement of Affirmation" was drafted by the committee, which carefully, if precariously, balanced clashing theological visions.[169] It opened by asserting that the Boston University Chapel Fellowship is "a community of worshippers of God" that addresses "itself to the deepest needs and aspirations of the human spirit. In doing so it does not seek to undermine whatever maybe the religious context which gives meaning and richness to one's particular life, but rather to deepen the authentic lines along which the quest for spiritual reality has led one."[170] This is pure Thurman, but other aspects of the statement reveal various concessions to more traditional understandings of Christianity, such as defining God as "Maker and Ruler of all things" (Thurman's God was perhaps a maker but not a ruler).[171] While "God has not left himself without specific witness in all cultures and all faiths," the Boston University Chapel Fellowship affirmed that "we believe in Jesus Christ and in his specific witness of God in our culture and our faith" (leaving the precise Christological status of Jesus indeterminate).[172] The services described in the Statement of Affirmation also reflect a certain bifurcation of purpose. They would be "rooted in the Protestant tradition of the university while experiments continue to find ways to become more increasingly inclusive of the total community within and without the university." It included an affirmation of the Holy Spirit, the Bible (as a source "containing insights useful for our faith and practice"), the Kingdom of God, "life everlasting," and "the inescapable necessity for social responsibility," before concluding in what was the cardinal dogma in Thurman's personal creed: "We believe that experiences of spiritual unity wherever they occur, are more compelling than the creeds, the ways of life and the ideologies that divide men."[173]

The proposal for the Chapel Fellowship had already been submitted to the board of trustees in the spring of 1960.[174] The "Statement of Affirmation and Statement of Governing Body Structure" from October 1960 indicates that it had been approved by the president of Boston University and the board of trustees and was beginning to solicit for potential members. There is no evidence that the Boston University Chapel Fellowship ever got beyond this preliminary stage. In any event, by June 1961, in his annual report, Thurman wrote that the proposal had been submitted "to the Trustees of the University and was rejected by them."[175] With the final rejection of the chapel fellowship proposal, Thurman determined to leave Boston University as soon as was practicable. In his autobiography, he wrote, "It was not long after this that my term of tenure at the university closed and I resigned the position as dean of the chapel and became university minister-at-large," sharply curtailing his involvement with the chapel and university affairs.[176]

Although he did not formally retire until 1965, after the spring of 1962 Thurman relinquished his two main responsibilities at Boston University; day-to-day and week-to-week responsibility for the chapel and its services, and his teaching responsibilities at the School of Theology. In his autobiography he attributed the loosening of his ties to the university to his desire to avoid an abrupt departure and a repeat of the "profound emotional upheaval" that had accompanied the decision to come to Boston, and to avoid "the psychic pains of withdrawal both for myself and those who felt dependent on my ministry" by a gradual and extended leave-taking.[177] This might have been one of Thurman's considerations, though in truth his effective departure from Boston University was both rushed and acrimonious. As was often the case in his autobiography, when it came to discussing or revealing his anger, he was less than candid.

According to Thurman, there were several main reasons for the decision of the board of trustees to disallow the chapel fellowship. Thurman wanted the fellowship to be autonomous. But there was worry that an organization calling itself the "Boston University Chapel Fellowship" would be a reflection of the wider university and therefore could or should not be autonomous. There was concern that a chapel fellowship was simply inappropriate in a university setting, serving an inherently ephemeral student body. Moreover, since BU was a commuter university, most churchgoing faculty attended their local churches. Since the services were open to the public, and many of the regulars attended primarily to hear Thurman, it was entirely possible that many members of the proposed Boston University Chapel Fellowship would have no connection to Boston University.[178]

Concerns over the future development of the chapel fellowship might have been reduced if Thurman had been a more conventional Christian. As the religious life at Boston University began in the postwar years to expand beyond its Methodist roots into a version of Will Herberg's famous 1950s triad, Protestant/Catholic/Jew, Thurman only with extreme reluctance fit himself into the role of the official campus Protestant.[179] As he stated in his first annual report, "in many people's minds, the chapel is the formal representative of Protestant Christianity on the campus," and they felt that "the ministry of the chapel should become the official Protestant mouthpiece and hold its own on equal footing with the Jewish and the Catholic positions."

However, as Thurman clearly stated, "The present Dean of the Chapel has no interest in that alternative." Instead, he was determined to create the chapel as "a center for religious worship in the heart of the university to which any and all members of the university may come for spiritual renewal."[180]

Thurman's relations with the official Protestant organizations on campus were frequently strained. In his annual report for the 1955–56 academic year, he complained of the "obvious discourtesies extended to him" by the Protestant chaplain on campus, Dr. William Overholt, the one time they met, and he was "ambivalent in regard to the measure of responsibility he should carry for the development of the Student Christian Association."[181] Their relationship, if never warm, improved, but they were never close. After the chapel fellowship was rejected, plans were made for a new Protestant ministry on campus, which seemed to have as one of its purposes to rein in Thurman's free-floating spirituality, as in a proposal sent to him in July 1961 that stated, "The Dean of the Chapel, as principal administrative officer for the religious life of the campus, shall serve as chairman of the Council for the Protestant ministry."[182]

There are two ways to look at this controversy. Thurman's services at Marsh Chapel, even after his careful pruning, were always, as he acknowledged, rooted in his and Boston University's Protestant origins more than in any alternative religious tradition such as Catholicism or Judaism, to say nothing of religious traditions more exotic in the America of 1960. Many of his sermon series ("Jesus and the Disinherited"; "The Religion of Jesus"; "The Temptations of Jesus") were explicitly Christian. It seems that many Protestants and non-Protestants wondered why Thurman was so insistent on disavowing his Protestant roots, and it seems likely that there were those in the university hierarchy who viewed Thurman's views on the chapel as more of a personal affectation than a comprehensible religious belief.

In truth, it was difficult to make those not sympathetic to Thurman's religious position understand what he was trying to achieve, an experiment in "how to provide an experience of spiritual growth for people whose approach to God and religious meaning may be radically different."[183] For Thurman there was ultimately "one faith" that could be shared by persons of different denominations and religions. Worship was about providing a sort of spiritual additive to the worshipper, spicing up and intensifying whatever the individual brought to the service. This is a hard concept to grasp, though this vision of liberal worship has more support in the third decade of the twenty-first century than in 1960, when Thurman's notion of worship must have seemed, for many, simply eccentric. It is easy to assent, in general, to Thurman's belief that the experiences of spiritual unity are more compelling than their divisions. It is more of a challenge to put this into practice in the context of a specific worship service and find a way to appeal to both those who wanted a specifically Christian service and those who did not.

As contention over the chapel fellowship grew heated, there likely was another, largely subterranean, dynamic at work. Thurman was acutely aware that all the people he was dealing with were white, and whatever their liberal veneer, their history of working with Blacks as full equals was limited. In these situations, Thurman's sensitivity to slights, to anything that smacked of being ordered or told what to do, was acute. In 1953, when he was on the verge of accepting the Boston University position, he had, according to his autobiography, told Case that "if I come, I think all of you will have a brand-new experience; you will have to learn to work in tandem with a Black man," and promised that "there will be times when this will cause you discomfort."[184] The discomfort was mutual. If the leadership of Boston University had little experience in working with a Black man as a true equal, neither did Thurman have prior experience in a working situation in which all of his colleagues and supervisors were white.

As had been the case at Howard with Mordecai Wyatt Johnson, a working relationship of boss and subordinate took some of the bloom off of his friendship with Harold Case. In July 1956, when Thurman was on vacation, Case sent Thurman's secretary a letter about procedures to be followed in the chapel, with hints of financial impropriety over the handling of the weekly collection.[185] When Thurman received the letter, he was furious that it had been sent to his secretary (who was white, though this didn't come up in the letter). That Case did not check with him before writing to his secretary "behind my back" about the allegations pained him deeply: "I interpret it to say that you have little confidence in my ability to function as Dean of the Chapel and that it was therefore necessary for you to take things into your hands and handle them from your office. If this is the way you want it then you do not need my services as Dean of the Chapel."[186]

The following year, when Case criticized Thurman for missing two meetings, he replied that he "resent[ed] with every fiber of my being, the implication in your letter that I am neglecting my responsibilities as Dean of the Chapel" and that "in order for me to cause no further embarrassment to you as President, of the University, I am willing in all good conscience to resign from the faculty of the University and from my post as the Dean of Marsh Chapel."[187] Whether or not there was a racial subtext to these disputes with Case, or over the fate of the chapel fellowship, Thurman probably thought there was, or at least he could never be sure that there wasn't. He certainly felt that in some ways, throughout his time in Boston, he was shortchanging African Americans and that, perhaps, he was shortchanging himself. As he wrote in 1963, "During my nine years in residence as Dean of the Chapel, I was acutely aware of the fact that only a minor part of my availability could be put at the disposal of the Negro Community."[188]

By the fall of 1962, Thurman, though still officially dean of chapel, had entered into a period of extended leave, which he called his "Wider Ministry," with few on-campus responsibilities. Thurman didn't expect his replacement as dean of chapel until his formal retirement. However, Case and the board of trustees evidently had a different understanding, and a replacement was named in the fall of 1962. He was unhappy with the procedure, unhappy with the way the appointment was publicized, implying that he had already retired, and unhappy with the choice, Robert Hamill, who had been chaplain at the University of Wisconsin-Madison.[189]

Hamill was a liberal Methodist but lacked Thurman's commitment to an interreligious service, and he revised the order of service, restoring the Lord's Prayer and other standard elements of Methodist worship. Thurman refused to preach under the new order of service.[190] Dean George Makechnie, who had regularly worshipped in Marsh Chapel since Thurman's arrival, complained to Case that the new order of service was inappropriate "for a university chapel in a community so pluralistic in character as Boston University" and that the new service was "not one with which my own spirit and that of my family can find union."[191] When, in April 1963, Thurman finally attended a service under Hamill's leadership, he described it in a letter to Case as "a traditional orthodox trinitarian Protestant Christian service of worship." Thurman wrote, "Now the campus has the three Faiths functioning in spiritual isolation, with the university Chapel deeply committed to one as over against the other two." He despaired that "in the public worship of God we are back where we were in the 18th century."[192]

When Thurman finally did retire, in 1965, the dean of the School of Theology, Walter Muelder, offered a few comments on Thurman's tenure at Boston University: "I may note in passing that it is no secret to historians and sociologists of the church that mystical devotion is a very dangerous phenomenon. Mysticism is generally verging on heresy and the mystic is seldom an organization man. Those who avoid the securities of mediated grace, whether in doctrine or sacrament or institution—and insist on speaking in public—give uneasy hours to the ecclesiastical bureaucrat."[193] If Thurman's mysticism, or disdain for the outer forms of religion and particularly those of Protestant Christianity, was one of the causes of tension during his years at Boston University, so too were personality clashes, fights with the administrative hierarchy, the great pull of demands on his time and attention, and the plight of a very proud Black man working exclusively with white colleagues, knowing or feeling that the very novelty of his appointment meant that he would be judged as much by the color of his skin as by his accomplishments or failures, and his perpetual uncertainty as to when and whether principled objections to his proposals carried a hidden undertone of racial bias.

Of all of Thurman's major jobs, the one he liked least was Boston University.[194] It is a bitter irony that this lifelong supporter of interracialism did not find his one experience working within a white institution to be very satisfactory. His comments on his work at Boston often convey a sense of exasperation and exhaustion. In 1956 he wrote Case that when he arrived, he "found a situation completely demoralized with all kinds of hostilities and conflicts. With God's help and much [*illegible*] I have worked quietly, slowly building a spirit of fellowship and understanding within the Chapel itself. Many things have been put in my way."[195] Three years later, when requesting a sabbatical, he wrote Case that the main reason for time off was that "our souls are weary and in defense of our own integrity of mind and spirit we must get away from the intense pressure of the University, not only for rest and renewal but also for taking a long look at what we are about here."[196] It also seems that some of his colleagues didn't quite get what Thurman was about because he did not write formal theology or treatises or have a doctorate, and they viewed him as a preacher, a spiritual advisor, and not as the important religious thinker that he undoubtedly was. (A book-length history of the School of Theology, published in 1968, allots Thurman all of three sentences.)[197] In 1978 Thurman was finishing drafting his autobiography. He wrote his editor that he was making "real progress . . . in wrapping up the manuscript," and, alluding to difficulties he encountered at Boston University, he stated, "I've found a way to get out of Boston without doing violence to the dead!"[198] By 1978 Case was deceased, as were some of the other people he had worked with at BU. One would sorely like to know what he had left out. The years at Boston University were at once rewarding and upsetting, a triumph and a failure. By 1962 he wanted and needed to get away.

In 1969 he told an interviewer that during the Boston years he would "come home at 3 o'clock, just dead, because there's nothing more exhausting than just sitting down, listening, and pouring your soul out that way, and I'd come home. And I'd say to Mrs. Thurman, 'I'm going to take a two-hour vacation.' I'd change my clothes, so my nervous system would get the message also, and then I would walk across the Commons and go over to Jordan Marsh's department store and ride the escalators—up and down, you know, for maybe a half hour, 35 minutes."[199] An escalator, forever going up and coming down. An apt metaphor, perhaps, for Thurman's Boston years.

13

"The Stillness of Absolute Motion"

The Wider Ministry

In 1955, in a Boston address, Thurman quoted the Declaration of Independence. Governments derive "their just powers from the consent of the governed," and when "any form of Government becomes destructive of these ends, it is the Right of the People to alter and abolish it." He wasn't giving a history lesson; he was speaking of current events: "It is this urge toward liberty and equality that explains the revolution now taking place among the peoples of Asia and Africa to throw off colonial rule and become equal partners in the community of nations."[1] Thurman had never doubted that all peoples had the right to "alter and abolish" their existing structures of imposed colonial governance. He had seen how the British, despite the best efforts of Gandhi and others, kept all of South Asia tightly manacled. The times were changing. India, Pakistan, Burma, and Ceylon were now independent nations; elsewhere colonialism was slowly losing its grip. But it had been two decades since the visit of the Negro Delegation, and Thurman had not made an overseas trip since. It was time to visit the nonwhite world again. The Thurmans had many motives for traveling; a pent-up wanderlust; a desire for a break and a change of scenery; wanting to have some extended time alone together. For Howard, one shouldn't underestimate the call of simple lassitude. He wrote in 1957 that he wanted "to take a slow boat" to Europe so that "much of the time will be spent on board ship" sitting in a deck chair and watching the sea.[2]

But above all Howard and Sue wished to witness and experience "the revolution now taking place among the peoples of Asia and Africa" with their own eyes and ears. It took a few years to arrange the necessary time off, but in

March 1960 the Thurmans embarked on a round-the-world journey from San Francisco, taking them through Asia, Africa (Egypt), and Europe, not returning to the United States until that September. The trip was a success, and the Thurmans wanted to do it again. Three years later, in the fall of 1963, they went on another round-the-world trip, this time in the other direction, leaving from New York, visiting Africa, Asia, Australia, and the Pacific Islands. In all, on their two journeys they visited more than twenty nations on four continents. The Thurmans spent well over a year on these two journeys, at a time when both the African American and African freedom struggles were at their most intense.

By the late 1950s, as we saw in the previous chapter, Thurman had grown tired and weary of Boston University. Before departing overseas on his sabbatical, he began his leave in the part of the world he knew best. In January 1960, he left for a tour of several historically Black colleges. With the United Negro College Fund (UNCF) paying their way, Howard and Sue visited Hampton Institute, Bennett College (a women's college in Greensboro, North Carolina), and Tuskegee Institute. Very unusually, during his visit he gave no public lectures or sermons. He was there solely to listen to students. After its conclusion, Thurman wrote to William J. Trent, head of the UNCF, that "the experience on the campuses exceeded all possible expectations as far as the Thurmans are concerned. We returned to Boston completely exhausted but profoundly exhilarated," and that "there is nothing that we could have done that could have been more significant on the campuses for us, and we hope for those we encountered, than this kind of journey." (Unfortunately for future biographers, Thurman added: "There is no time to write a re-action letter to you and I am not sure that that would be wise anyway. When I see you we can talk.")[3]

What Thurman experienced, almost surely, was the spirit of revolution, of a generation of students at historically Black colleges who were operating "within a context of segregation in a manner that will release the mind for a creative attack on the fact of segregation."[4] Although Thurman's "contagion" was not directly the catalyst, two weeks after his visit to Greensboro, students at neighboring North Carolina A&T (soon joined by students from Bennett) decided to sit-in at a Woolworth's luncheon counter, practicing nonviolence, steeling themselves against threats, insults, and physical intimidation. The demonstrations marked the beginning of the second phase of the civil rights movement, moving it into a higher gear, one that would not end until the legal framework of Jim Crow had been smashed forever.

A few weeks after his visit to Tuskegee, Thurman received a letter from a young political scientist there, Charles V. Hamilton, who would, later in the decade, with Stokely Carmichael, write an essential Black nationalist manifesto, *Black Power.*[5] Hamilton thanked Thurman for the "impetus and stimulation you provided when you visited my class in American National Government." Since his visit, students had begun to take an active role in protests unknown since the founding of the college by Booker T. Washington: "A mass civil rights rally was held on campus three weekends ago. The focus was a strong civil rights bill with effective voting provisions."[6] They challenged the dominant civil rights organization in the city, the Tuskegee Civic Association, to take a stance of greater militancy. His students, he wrote Thurman, "are learning more political science than I could possibly convey in lectures." In 1963, Thurman praised the upsurge in protests, "the 'boycott,' the 'sit-ins,' 'walk-ins,' 'pray-ins,'" as "collective device[s]" all "designed to awaken conscience and an awareness of the evil of a violent system, and to make available the experience of the collective destiny in which all people in the system, the advantaged and the disadvantaged, are participating."[7]

After visiting historically Black colleges in the South, the Thurmans prepared for their extended international tour and were out of the country from March to September, sailing from San Francisco to Yokohama. Although they were unable (save their time in Egypt) to visit Africa, they did spend extended time in Asia, visiting Japan, Hong Kong, Thailand, Singapore, Malaya, Ceylon, Egypt, and Lebanon, before making their way, via Greece, Italy, and France, to England and Scotland. In Edinburgh, courtesy of Coleman Jennings, the Thurmans had an apartment to themselves for a period of extended quiet, a time for "recollection and creative writing."[8] Traveling at the end of the era of oceangoing vessels, the reluctant-to-fly Thurman was able to complete his global circumnavigation with his feet (mostly) firmly planted on the ground or on the deck, quietly absorbing "the rhythm of the steamer and the diapason of the sea."[9] He had been obliged to fly from Manila to Bangkok, however, and at the end of the trip, a dockworkers strike in Britain forced Thurman to fly home before the beginning of the fall semester, complaining (largely in jest, I think) that he "did not believe that I would ever consent to that kind of violation of human decency but in order to get back to begin my work on September 17th I had to fly."[10]

Although Thurman did a bit of speaking and preaching on the tour, including a shipboard service, celebrating Palm Sunday in Tokyo, an address at the American University in Beirut, and—a special highlight and honor for him—presiding over a Sunday service at the famous London church St. Martin-in-the-Fields—the Thurmans were primarily traveling as tourists.[11] After the trip, the Thurmans wrote that it had been their privilege "to spend long evenings in good talk, among groups crossing all lines, with local and foreign 'nationals,' and visiting international friends closely associated, brooding together over the grave condition of a 'sick' world, probing deeply for solutions in lighted hearts and minds."[12]

Thurman was fascinated by nations recently freed from colonial control. In the Philippines, the Thurmans met many who shared "deeply in the journey of that nation from the status of a ward of America, to subsequently being captives of the Japanese, to all the full-blown glory and responsibility of national freedom." In Egypt he found it arresting "to see the enormity of the task of finding a way to [communicate] between peoples who are finding their roots watered afresh by a rebirth of an ancient faith. It is a faith with vast overtones of nationalism. Here also are people of the West with all the burden of the guilt of a necessitous imperialism." He discussed the situation of mainland China with refugees in Hong Kong, and of Israel and Palestine with Palestinian refugees in Lebanon, and with Belgians who wondered whether there was any atonement possible for the atrocities committed in their name by King Leopold II in the soon to be independent Belgian Congo. In Japan he connected with determined pacifists, "opposed to anything that might portend a future Hiroshima for themselves, or mankind anywhere."[13]

He returned to Boston in late 1960 convinced that "there can be no peace in the world as long as you have hunger, desperation, poverty, and insecurity among so large a number of people." He recognized that the new nations were gaining their independence in the context of a "competition between ideologies and ways of life between East and West," and that as long as there are desperate people, they "are ripe to be exploited" if "to them it is a means to an out."[14] He cautioned against thinking that this problem had easy solutions or that somehow the United States (or the Soviet Union) had the answers, citing a favorite Zulu adage, "Full belly child says to empty belly child, 'Be of good cheer.'"[15] The full-bellied nations of the West could not presume to lecture the empty-bellied people of Asia and Africa on the superiority of their democratic institutions. Instead, Americans needed to use their values to work for the "redemption of the stomachs of people" and address the gaping economic inequalities left by the detritus of colonialism. Thurman cautioned that "whatever moral, spiritual, and political leadership we will be able to give to the world will be hampered by, or helped by, what we do in our own country in the areas of anti-Semitism, anti-Negroism, and the other anti-isms that contradict the philosophy of our way of life."[16]

Thurman was overwhelmed by the emotions his travels provoked: "I wish I were five hundred people with an experience such as I have had," rather "than just being one person who puts his pants on, one leg at a time, like everybody else." But if he felt that "he did not have a sense of being able to do much about" the problems he saw, he also told himself that he "will never become discouraged" because "it doesn't matter how high the odds are, because the things that work for bigotry and discrimination—all of these things—life is against and cannot abide." Imperialism had been a prison, a forced confinement, for the two-thirds of the world's population of non-European descent, and "wherever a man is in prison, God is in prison," and "God cannot be what God is destined to be." He returned to the United States determined not to be anyone's jailer, and "to do everything I can not to be one to keep the key in the lock of the prison house."[17]

The Thurmans' 1960 sabbatical is best viewed as a dress rehearsal of sorts for the next phase of their lives. Howard and Sue appreciated the freedom it provided, the ability to make their own schedules, to be accountable only to themselves, to spend time with the people who most needed their attention. As he wrote a Boston University administrator in 1961, "The only way in good conscience that I can keep from feeling that the gifts of God that is in me is not being exploited by the University [sic], is the reassurance that it is available to be shared beyond the boundaries of Marsh Chapel and particularly to be shared with Negroes who live and work and suffer in American society."[18] During the 1961–62 academic year, Thurman and Boston University agreed that, unofficially, his duties would come to an end in the spring of 1962, though officially he would remain on the faculty until the spring of 1965. The reasons for this arrangement are not entirely clear—perhaps to allow Thurman to retire at sixty-five—and there were confusions on both sides (certainly on Thurman's part) as to what this entailed. As early as 1944 Thurman had written of his "wider ministry," and this is what he called the next phase of his career, starting in the fall of 1962.[19] As he wrote Boice Gross in April 1962, by September he would be "free of all responsibility to Boston University as Dean of the Chapel and as Professor of Spiritual Disciplines [and Resources.]" His time would be exclusively his own, and he would be under no obligation "to refer to the University for veto or certification of any act or function which I may wish to perform or undertake."[20]

Thurman had to largely fund his incipient Wider Ministry himself. Increasingly, the Thurmans would depend on wealthy white benefactors, primarily from California (such as Gross, a well-connected lawyer) for their livelihood, supplemented by numerous speaking and teaching engagements. In the spring of 1964, Robert Hamill, Thurman's successor, officially became dean of chapel, and Thurman acquired a new title, minister-at-large.[21] When Rabbi Zalman Schachter-Shalomi heard this, he responded: "I am greatly pleased with one thing. I've finally found out what you are. You have been, all the time, a minister at large, and no matter how wonderful and flexible the institution was, it could not quite contain you. I suppose this is what is meant to be in the image of one's Maker, whom the heavens can't contain."[22]

Thurman had a troubled exit from Boston University. As early as May 1962, Thurman was complaining to President Case that "it is as if I had already left the campus," and that fall he had to vacate his old office in Marsh Chapel and grumbled that he was relocated to one that was five elevatorless flights up.[23] The Thurmans were also forced to vacate their apartment at 184 Bay Street, and their forced relocation was not a pleasant experience (too rushed for the Thurmans; too drawn out for university authorities).[24] Although every step of Thurman leaving Boston University seemed to generate ill will, there were compensations, and moving away from the immediate environs of BU had its advantages. By November 1962, Howard and Sue had relocated to an apartment near the Boston Common. As Thurman wrote a friend shortly after the move, "It is the first time in 30 years that we have a sense of being private citizens."[25]

After their move the Thurmans "felt ourselves to be part of the city itself, and particularly its past, in which our history as a people was involved."[26] Both Thurmans had a long-standing interest in African American history and especially in some of its greatest figures such as Frederick Douglass and Harriet Tubman.[27] Sue Bailey Thurman had been a guiding light in establishing the archives program of the National Council of Negro Women in the 1940s and had published a book on the early history of Black California.[28] In Boston, she published a guide to places of African American and abolitionist interest in the city, and, with the well-known historian Nathan Huggins, she founded the American Negro History Museum.[29] Thurman had written James N. Nabrit Jr., his Morehouse College classmate and Mordecai Wyatt Johnson's successor as president of Howard University, in April 1962 that "I think that one of the needful things, as our young people storm the gates on the Frontiers of Freedom, is some sense of history that will enable them to share responsibly in laying out the new city."[30] He suggested that the university take the lead in establishing an African American history museum and archives in Washington, some six decades before, in 2016, one finally opened.

During Thurman's first year of the Wider Ministry, he had to sort through two hundred speaking invitations. (This sort of inundation was typical throughout his mature ministry, and it kept him and his beleaguered secretaries very busy.) In his annual report he noted that he gave "primary consideration to those which would provide the best opportunity for experiences of unity across [racial, ethnic, or religious] lines," with a special emphasis on Black institutions in the South.[31] But not all of his efforts at racial unity involved African Americans.

One special event took place with his visit to the Federation of Saskatchewan Indians in October 1962. Thurman had had, until 1962, little to say about North American Indians, though his sense of personal connection to them dates to his earliest years. He believed his grandmother was of partial Seminole ancestry, though this seems unlikely.[32] He wrote in his autobiography that "among the scattered fragments of my earliest memories are the inscrutable faces of the Seminoles—one sitting very still under an oak tree, another passing by silently on a country road."[33] They were a people even more dispossessed and disinherited than African Americans.

An old friend invited Thurman to address a meeting of Saskatchewan Indians, a group that, like African Americans, was standing at a crossroads.[34] It was only in 1960 that all Canadian First Peoples living on reserves had been granted Canadian citizenship, a move generally welcomed, though some worried that it would lead to assimilation and a dilution of their heritage and sense of cohesion. Thurman asked those he spoke to whether they considered themselves Indians or Canadians first, and he received the three possible answers (one, or the other, or both). After listening to their stories, Thurman concluded that "a reserve is segregation in its most erosive form." The reserves may have started as a form of protection, but "what was at one time a haven of refuge has now become almost a tomb. On a reserve, the Indian can be easily forgotten, and the collective guilt that would otherwise be a torment can be absorbed by provincial charity. To be relegated behind high psychic walls is the easiest way to be forgotten. The function of the ghetto is to provide drainage for guilt that a tender social conscience generates." This is, and had been, "a reflection of what has been for so long a prevailing Anglo-Saxon attitude toward the darker people[s]." The reserves were Jim Crow squared.[35] There was "slowly emerging a new sense of self-respect and dignity which had not been in evidence for generations in the communal life of the Indian reservation." This was heartening, but after writing of the treatment of Afro-Canadians, he concluded the situation of the Saskatchewan Indians is "a story as old as human misery. It is what the Indians speak of in their recommendations to the Canadian government. It is a story of the native people of South Africa and those who would give them courage and hope; the story of Mississippi, and the tragedy of the ghetto of Warsaw."[36]

In his addresses to the organization, Thurman tried to offer his solidarity and his insights. But probably most important to him was less what he said but how he said it. A fair number of those present were not fluent or could not readily comprehend English, speaking only Cree or some other Indigenous language. Most of the conference had been conducted with interpreters, but Thurman decided to forego them when he spoke about the need for dignity, about his own life, and about the possible American Indian descent of his grandmother. He described what happened next, one of those precious moments for Thurman when words were separated from their surface meanings:

> I wanted to see whether it would be possible to have a sense of unity, of meaning that could transcend even the limitations of vocabulary. So for ten minutes I talked, and you know the feeling, well, if you don't do well, when your words go up and they hit a wall and bounce back meeting other words that are coming and they dissolve out there somewhere and nobody gets anything. And then, suddenly, I don't know what happened, but the wall disappeared! And I had the physical sensation of flowing into those men and their flowing into me. And I knew now that a quality of being was shared that transcended all of the words and all of the vocabularies.[37]

Afterward, Thurman was asked by some attending the conference to make a final, unscheduled, address the following day. After he delivered it, those who heard it came up to him, one by one, grasping his hand, touching his shoulder, looking into his eyes, nobody saying a word. Few things were more sacred to Thurman than the ministry of silence.

Of all the events during the first year of his Wider Ministry, none had greater meaning for him than the celebration of Howard Thurman Day in his hometown of Daytona Beach on 25 May 1963.[38] This evolved out of an invitation to speak at the graduation exercises that year at Bethune-Cookman College, after which the college president and the city fathers arranged for a grander reception. After receiving a formal invitation to be the city's guest of honor, Thurman wrote the college's president, Richard V. Moore, that "your letter unhinged me. I did not believe the time would ever come when I would be the guest of honor of both Bethune-Cookman College and the City of Daytona Beach. The thought of this makes my head spin with memories that are too hot for paper."[39]

The event, on a typically warm and sun-drenched Florida summer's day, came off without a hitch. Thurman was met at the train station by a brass band and a contingent that included the mayor, who read the Howard Thurman Day proclamation, awarded for "his achievements as an educator and theologian in the field of education and religion, his forthright stand on the principles of equality and justice," and so on. A parade, with four marching bands, processed from the train station to the Bethune-Cookman campus, which was close to the Thurmans' old family home, the route lined with well-wishers waving placards reading, "Welcome Home, Dr. Howard Thurman" and "Local Boy Makes Good—Welcome!" He was particularly moved by the large number of young people either marching or cheering on the sidelines: "This is the future." There was a dinner in the evening, with 150 in attendance, equally divided between Blacks and whites. The highlight of the dinner was seeing Julia Green, who had been Thurman's kindergarten teacher almost sixty years before.[40]

Thurman found Howard Thurman Day immensely moving, writing Moore that, "Words are not made that are capable of saying precisely the height and the depth of my joy because of the fabulous weekend of May 25th" and writing the mayor that the event "demonstrated that where men of good will are willing to back their interests with sustained endeavor, all kinds of glorious possibilities for the fulfillment of a democratic society are obtainable."[41] But as he wrote in his annual report, this had to be contrasted to his early memories: "I was born and reared in Daytona Beach. The first fifteen years of my life were spent there. It was in that small Florida town that I was introduced to the terror and trauma of being born a Negro. During the years since, and after much living and experiencing, scar tissue marks the places where the early blows made their mark and the searing pain invaded body and spirit."[42]

Things were different in Daytona Beach on Howard Thurman Day, but not all that different. On 25 May 1963 desegregation in the city was very much a work in progress. The busses had been desegregated in 1956, but most public and private facilities in the city continued to operate on a Jim Crow basis. It was not until after the passage of the Civil Rights Act in 1964 that Blacks in Daytona Beach could "enjoy the beach, eat at most restaurants, and stay in most hotels and motels."[43] The one-third Black city elected its first African American to public office in the twentieth century in 1965; there was no comprehensive desegregation of its schools until 1970. As a Daytona Beach businessman told a reporter in the fall of 1963, perhaps thinking of events such as Howard Thurman Day, even though civic leaders praised the city's progress, "in reality Northeast Florida is still cracker country."[44] As the city celebrated Howard Thurman Day, local activists were planning a series of protests against segregated lunch counters, movie theaters, and cafeterias, demonstrations that lasted for several weeks and were noted in national newspapers.[45]

Although he was undoubtedly aware of the partial nature of desegregation in Daytona Beach, Thurman nowhere discussed this. Did he feel that he was being, on some level, taken advantage of by Daytona Beach's white leaders or worry that he was potentially distracting or retarding the continuing fight for civil equality in the city? He probably thought the advantages of providing Black Daytona with a flesh-and-blood role model, one of their own who had not let white Daytona Beach trample his dreams, coming home crowned in civic glory, while encouraging white Daytonans to fulfill their obligations to the city's Black residents, made Howard Thurman Day worthwhile. In any event, he no doubt thought that though in May 1963 Daytona Beach was still in midtransition, the civil rights revolution was unstoppable, whatever he said or did not say.

There was a lot of talk of revolution in 1963, not least by Thurman himself. Howard Thurman Day and all of his activities in the Wider Ministry took on "a new dimension in the light of the profound social revolution that is taking place particularly in the United States, one which involves the future of the relationships between black and white citizens of the land."[46] For Thurman, writing some years earlier, revolution and religion, with their mingling of individual and social experience, had much in common. Every religious person "stands in immediate candidacy to be a revolutionary, and every revolutionary in the last analysis draws upon the same springs of vitality and strength and energy that is the ground and the fulfillment of religion."[47] That spring and summer, for Thurman, the experience of religion and revolution were merging, both convulsively and harmoniously. That July he wrote that America was "in the throes of a mighty revolution."[48] In September, unusually demotic, he wrote of the "nitty-gritty of the revolution in which we are engaged."[49] Any successful revolution draws on a spirit of collective indignation and exhilaration, and the shared sense of power one gets from being a part of something much larger than oneself. Gregory Downs has described a revolution as what happens when, over a hectic and compressed period of time, "otherwise cautious women and men" are able to "transform their sense of the possible in a sequential metamorphosis of common sense," when the impossible suddenly becomes the probable.[50] Thurman was breathing and inhaling this spirit of revolution in Black America in the summer of 1963.

He would write that same year that "perhaps the most significant thing that has happened in the last few stirring years of the vast struggle for civil rights in the South and the North has been the dramatic loss of fear on the part of the masses of Negroes," with "the sense of direct, conscious, and collective participation in a joint destiny," generating "a strange and wonderful courage"[51] Thurman gave the example of a female undergraduate in an Atlanta lunch counter sit-in, shoved up against a wall and roughly manhandled by a police officer, quoting her thoughts: "It was my very first direct encounter with real violence. . . . I was not prepared for the stark panic that moved through me. This passed quickly and in its place I felt an intense and angry violence—but something in me held. I looked him in the face until I felt his fear and sensed his own anguish. Then I thought, now quite calmly, how desperate a man must be to behave this way to a defenseless girl. And a strange peace came over me and I knew now that violence could be taken, and that I could take it and triumph over it."[52] It was, thought Thurman, the calm of a commitment more important than life or death, a feeling of being "totally encompassed, totally alive," something akin to a collective mystic experience, a shared, fleeting glimpse of the "deep spiritual awareness that one's life is in vital touch with the Source of Being that holds and makes secure against all that destroys and lays waste."[53] Black America had learned how to overcome.

Thurman had helped to bring the message of Gandhi to an American audience and had mentored and inspired King, James Farmer, Pauli Murray, James Lawson, and countless others involved in the civil rights struggle. In 1960 *Fellowship* (the magazine of the Fellowship of Reconciliation) reprinted his prescient 1943 outline for a nonviolent revolution, "The Will to Segregation."[54] Those who followed Thurman closely would have read or heard his comments on the civil rights struggle and known how crucial and important it was to him. But not many did so. Thurman's lifelong aversion to attracting attention to himself did not change during this era. For most observers, Thurman remained on the sidelines. One of the most seemingly perplexing aspects of Thurman's career is that he did not participate in any of the major civil rights campaigns in the early 1960s. There are no photographs of him marching, arms locked, with Martin Luther King, Jr.; no impassioned speeches delivered in bombed-out churches; no letters to posterity written while incarcerated. In 1965, in the course of an otherwise laudatory review of Thurman's career, P. L. Prattis, in the *Pittsburgh Courier*, closed by asking a rather pointed question: "Not much has been heard of Dr. Thurman as an 'accomplice' in the so-called Negro Revolution. Is he a part of it?" Prattis decided that "indeed he is, if all who win respect for the Negro in the mass are part of it. His has been a way, a method, of winning new friends and respect for his people."[55]

This was nice of Prattis to say, but I suspect Thurman would have seen this defense as an evasion and a cop-out. In a time of social revolution, making a good impression on white people was not enough. One had to advance the cause of transformative change. By the mid-1960s Thurman was writing, for a wide audience, on the civil rights crisis. He was a member of the statewide Massachusetts Commission Against Discrimination during the early 1960s.[56] Still, he was not a marcher or demonstrator. Yet those who knew him well would echo the comments of Benjamin Mays: "Howard did not have to march to prove his freedom as a free man."[57] Or the comment of the Rev. Otis Moss, a Thurman disciple and admirer, who said that though Howard Thurman "did not march from Selma to Montgomery, or on many of the other marches, [he] participated on the level that shaped the philosophy or creates the march—without that, people don't know what to do before the march, while they march, or after they march."[58] If Thurman would have been too modest to accept so much credit, it is probably close to how he viewed things. But for better or worse, Thurman's participation in the civil rights revolution was not widely known.

There were critics of Thurman's seeming wishing to remain above the fray. In 1961, near the end of his long life, W. E. B. Du Bois complained in a letter that "what Howard Thurman really believes I have never been able to find out."[59] In 1978 an unnamed woman asked Thurman after a lecture whether his emphasis "on mysticism, with very little discussion of social action," was a "luxury for a very small elite in this world—mostly for middle class people."[60]

Thurman never felt he needed to explain his actions, and he would have said that he was involved in the movement in many ways, especially as counselor and spiritual advisor. And he was right. We are left not with a criticism, but a question: Why didn't Thurman, at the crest of a social revolution that he as much as anyone had helped create, practice what he had so often preached? No one knew better than he did the Gandhian injunction of the importance of visibility, not staying on the sidelines, of taking personal risks for one's beliefs. The answer is likely as much psychological as political; he felt that he couldn't march, for personal reasons that probably ran deeper than he was comfortable discussing. Thurman was not, as he would later tell Lerone Bennett, "a movement man" and never had been.[61] Perhaps he felt that calling attention to himself would be an act of vanity and distract attention from the younger generation of Black leaders, the men and women who had actually put their bodies on the line for the revolution. (As he wrote Jesse Jackson in 1973, who wanted him to be a featured speaker in a Chicago rally: "All of my life I have shunned publicity and the limelight.")[62] Perhaps he felt that involvement was precluded by his own spiritual disciplines or that the public voices of the movement required a fiercer message than he was comfortable delivering. We do not know.

There was one exception to his policy of noninvolvement in major civil rights protests. On a hot August day in 1963, he joined Frank Wilson and hundreds of thousands of others for the March on Washington. For decades he had been close with many of the speakers that day, including King, A. Philip Randolph, Ralph Bunche, and Adam Clayton Powell Jr., and by all rights, he should have been among them. Instead, he was intent and indeed joyful in his anonymity. There is always in revolution, Thurman had written some years before, "this sense of collective destiny, a sense of the me-too-ness with reference to other people"[63] Thurman described the March on Washington to a young expatriate African American journalist living in Denmark a few days later, writing of the event as if all of American history, certainly all of African American history, had arrived at its fulcrum:

You should have been in Washington on August 28. Nothing like has ever happened in the history of our country. I was one of 200,000 people sharing a moment that contained all time and all experience, when everything was moving and everything was standing still, a moment that had in it the stillness of absolute motion. From where I sat I could look at the face of Abraham Lincoln deep within the shadow of the Memorial but with his countenance illumined by a floodlight, while at the same time experiencing the 4½ hours of speeches and music and overtones. For me, personally, every 20 yards I ran into someone out of my past; going in one instance as far back as 40 years. America was present in Washington on the 28th, white and black, young and old, Protestant, Catholic, Jew, free-wheeler, male and female, conservative, middle-of-the-roader, labor leaders and workers, the schooled and the unschooled, the halt, the lame, the hale and the seeing—it was the gut of America spilling out along Constitution Avenue, congealing itself again as far as the eye can see from the portals of the Lincoln Memorial.[64]

The next month Thurman mused to himself that the previous "year has been full. I have done so much more than I dreamed and it has borne in [illegible] me quite deeply. The response to the words and ideas that have come through me has been beyond my more extravagant hopes or ideas. God is achieving a new result in me—what? I do not know. There is a kind of fire burning in me but I am not able to comprehend it. There never has been a time in my life when I was more alive in my mind and spirit. It is as if I am being readied for a fuller life than I have ever known." He added, rather morbidly, that this remarkable sense of fulfillment was perhaps "a mere prelude to my earth[ly] leave-taking."[65] But this would have to wait, there were more immediately pressing things to attend to. He wrote this in his stateroom, contemplating his first extended trip to Africa. This would be the greatest event of the Wider Ministry. He had been thinking about Africa for many decades. "You are an African with the pure blood of a thousand generations of noble blood in your veins—Long before they [white Americans] and their forebears were on the earth—your forebears were rulers in the greatest continent on earth": so Thurman wrote in 1932 to Balama Jaberi Mukasa, a Ugandan student at Morehouse College, who was having problems during his time in Atlanta.[66] In his autobiography, he wrote of his lifelong connection to Africa, and of his often "unarticulated identification with the African people," associating the continent with strong individuals like his grandmother and enslaved forebears, and rejecting any notion of African inferiority.[67] As early as 1925 he rebuked in print the imperial powers "that have raped the continent and its people through so many weary bloody years."[68] His friendship at Howard University with William Leo Hansberry, one of the first professors of African history at an American university, stirred Thurman's "vague longing" for a visit to Africa.[69]

However, Thurman had some ambivalence toward Africa. If he resolved to visit the continent after being inspired by Hansberry, he also knew that "he could not go until I was ready for the journey" out of some hesitation for "destroying the African mystery that had become part of my adult being."[70] Indeed, in 1963, somewhat contradicting the account in his autobiography, he wrote in his journal that "for a long time I had no ripe desire to go to Africa. It is hard to analyze it—only that it is true. Sue kept before me the necessity of the Pilgrimage. She insisted that I needed it for my own fulfillment and rounding out. I did not see this nor feel it. Days and weeks passed—then my heart began to stir and I made the first move of assent." His motives were complex, unsurprising for something he had contemplated for decades. But by 1963 one of his chief motives was simply avoiding embarrassment: "It is hardly possible not to have been to Africa without seeming to be uninformed as a Negro. No longer will I have to say upon inquiring 'No, unfortunately, I have never been to Africa.'"[71]

Boston University's African studies program, created in 1953, was one of the first such programs in the United States, and it was one of the factors contributing to Thurman's decision to come to Boston. (Like many area studies programs at the time, it had close connections to the State Department and the CIA.)[72] In 1962 Dr. K. Onwuka Dike, one of Africa's leading historians and educators, was awarded an honorary degree at Boston University's commencement ceremonies.[73] Dike was the chief administrator at the University of Ibadan, Nigeria's first Western university, then in the process of severing its ties to its parent institution, University College, London.[74] Thurman spoke to Dike at the commencement, and after some correspondence over the next few months, an arrangement was worked out. Thurman would teach at the University of Ibadan's department of religious studies for eight weeks in the fall of 1963.[75]

Thurman's time in Africa has considerable intrinsic interest; it is heightened because it is one of the few times in his life that he kept a journal, with a running account of his impressions and observations. Written for an audience of one, it is filled with sharp evaluations of others and penetrating comments about himself, all offered with a candor rare in Thurman's public writings, sermons, or even private correspondence. The journal opens on 19 September, with Thurman in his cabin, dockside in New York harbor, aboard the SS *France,* bound for London. Sue was not present. She flew to Nigeria a few weeks later. He was not in a good mood, anticipating an impending disaster:

"I have had a rare experience in the discipline of frustration. All things seem to converge to make my journey to Africa ill fated."[76] If he was looking for untoward auspices, an unhappy portent was the very recent loss of almost all of his cash, some three hundred dollars, whether by carelessness or pickpocket, on the way to the pier.[77]

His mood was buoyed by the gathering in his stateroom wishing him bon voyage. One of his financial benefactors, Esther Byrne, was present.[78] So too was his longtime secretary, Sydna Altschuler. Frank Wilson, a former college president and Presbyterian official was also there. Thurman called him "the oldest friend I have," noting that "of all the men I know he is the only one who gives me a feeling that he loves me in a robust and entirely masculine way."[79] His two daughters were there as well.

But all the good spirits could not dissipate his general gloom. He writes of a misdeed he had committed "in a vain and thoughtless manner." The nature of the offense, the person offended, and its place and time are not clear but it "was a terrible moment when I separated myself from the context of my life."[80] There was more self-reproach. Of Olive, he writes that "all the days surrounding her birth and early life I was preoccupied with the fight of her mother for life. I was not free in my mind to be a father as I was with Anne. The fact that her care had to be committed to others gave me from the beginning a kind of false start." Her turbulent early childhood "gave to me a sense of failure or guilt or remorse that for many years clung to me like a kind of sickness. I suppose that what I mean is that I was always trying to redeem something in my relations with her."[81] With Anne, to whom he was closer, he had "a strange kind of love and understanding," and he appreciated her "clear unmuddled mind that functions like a sharp tool in the hands of an expert—when she wants to." "She will be a remarkable woman in her maturity," he concluded. Perhaps most interestingly, Thurman mused on the fact he had no sons: "There are times when I find myself wishing that she [Anne] was a boy or a son. But this is only a passing flash of terrible illumination of some hidden region of my unconscious. . . . But as I grow older I have a strange yearning to pass on to a male the idiom of my spirit."[82]

But after his friends and family left, Thurman was alone. He wrote in his journal of the people he met on his way. There were, not surprisingly, many conversations about religion. He got annoyed when people felt free, or obliged, to unload on Thurman "whatever the person thinks of religion or whatever he has experienced with or in religion he assumes to be characteristic of me and my interest," complaining that this happens to him "all the time, everywhere."[83] He befriended a Black man from Boston who had converted to Islam, and they had many interesting conversations, though

Thurman considered him a "zealot." After another round of the Islam versus Christianity question with some other African Muslims, Thurman wearied of the disputations: "It seems to me that the strength of a man's position is immeasurably weakened by contenting himself to attack the 'weak' points in another's position. Let a man's faith make its own case, let it commend itself by its own inherent worth. It may be that what a man is surest of he does not feel under any necessity to prove."[84]

He had some pointed conversations with Christians as well, becoming upset when a young Nigerian Oxford-trained lawyer "went into a kind of ecstasy over the preaching of Billy Graham."[85] He was worried that once he arrived in Ibadan, he would find himself having to work with men "all of whom are trained in formal traditional Protestantism," and "long ago I have defected from that tradition, if indeed I was ever a part of it." As in India, a quarter century earlier, he was concerned that Christians would find his approach to religion insufficiently missionary in its inspiration, while in the eyes of Muslims "I shall be regarded as a propagandist for making converts to Christianity."[86]

For all that, he very much enjoyed his traveling companions. "I am overwhelmed by the friendliness of the Africans," who, on his voyage from London to Nigeria, included Anglican bishops, members of local parliaments, lawyers, Oxbridge graduates, and the like—an impressive lot.[87] Thurman evidently felt a bit intimidated: "I am not a scholar. My own chosen field of religion has not challenged me to scholarship."[88] They were also fluent in multiple languages, at least their native tongue and English, and often French as well. Thurman, with a typical lament of the monoglot, confided in his journal that "through neglect and a kind of bad start I did not or have not perfected a reading or speaking knowledge" of any foreign language. And Thurman had doubts about his English as well, writing of African English that he found "it difficult to follow the accent—it is not quite British nor is it like any other I know except possibly S. Carolina 'Geechee.'"[89] He was "deeply conscious of the fact that I am an outsider and my status is not clear." He worried that he was trying too hard to ingratiate himself with his fellow passengers, and that they saw through the artificiality of his efforts. In all, "somehow, I feel defensive or something," and he was worried that his time in Africa might be "the first great failure of my life time."[90]

Whatever his doubts and whatever his expectations, the time had come for Thurman to confront the reality of Africa. He had spent several days in London, went to Liverpool, and then boarded the SS *Apapa* for the voyage to Nigeria. There were rough seas on the voyage, and for the first few days sailing down the African coast, the coastline was occluded by clouds. The weather broke, the sky was clear, the moonlight brilliant, and when the ship was anchored off Bathurst, Gambia's capital, Africa suddenly came into view. As he wrote in his autobiography: "For the first time in my life, I beheld the west coast of Africa. I wept, or rather, I shed tears without weeping."[91] He knew that the Gambia River had been one of the main arteries of the slave trade, a route taken by as many as three million Africans transported from the Senegambian region to the Americas, including many to the port of Charleston, the likely disembarkation point for Thurman's African ancestors. Countless souls had their last look at their homeland from his current vantage. As he looked on the waves he saw "the full moon and the ghosts of my forefathers rise and fall with the undulating waves." He started to write. What did they think, what were their "inchoate mutterings locked tight within the circle of their hearts" while chained in "the deep, heavy darkness of the foul smelling hold of the ship."[92]

The Middle Passage, for Thurman, was for those enslaved a catastrophe so overwhelming and enveloping that it shattered their pasts. He wrote in his journal: "Nothing anywhere in all the myths, in all the stories, in all the ancient memory of the race, had given hint of this torturous convulsion. There were no gods to hear, no magic spell of witch doctor to summon; even one's companion in chains muttered his quivering misery in a tongue unknown and a sound unfamiliar." What then: "O my fathers what was it like to be stripped of all supports of life save the beating of the heart and the ebb and flow of fetid air in the lungs? How to find the courage to live, then?" Perhaps a faith that nothing, even a lifetime of enslavement and the enslavement of one's descendants, lasts forever. And perhaps in the 1960s, in Africa and America, that faith could be redeemed: "In the darkness did you hear the silent feet of your children beating a melody of freedom to words which you would never know, in a land in which your bones would be warmed again in the depths of the cold earth in which you will sleep, unknown, unrealized and alone?"[93]

Thurman was proud of his meditation, which he soon published separately as "On Viewing the Coast of Africa" and reprinted the text in his autobiography.[94] If the meditation emphasized the sundering of roots and ancient connections, Thurman was in Africa to reestablish them. The following day, when actually setting foot on the continent, he visited the soon-to-be independent colony of Gambia. It was a holiday in Bathurst, the day that Gambia gained complete internal self-governance from Britain.[95] He was pleased to see Black customs officials as he disembarked but noted that whites retained the ultimate authority. The town was very British; the people weren't. "How long," he asked, "would it take these people to possess the land in which they were born" and to overcome the "prostitution of the invader." The next port of call was Freetown, the capital of Sierra Leone, an independent nation since 1961. He found it "a bewitching city," crowded with activity: "There are people everywhere, literally hundreds of little children are to be seen everywhere. Almost every other woman seen in the streets has a baby attached to her back." He visited a madrassa, consisting of "two large rooms of school children—all under 12 years old. There was what seemed to me to be bedlam—every child was reading aloud." He visited Fourah Bay College, the oldest Western-style institution of higher learning in West Africa, founded in 1826. He was pleased by the attention paid to education in Sierra Leone.[96]

Finally, Thurman arrived at Lagos, Nigeria's largest city and, at the time of his visit, its capital. He was met by an old friend, Asa Davis,[97] an African American historian teaching at the University of Ibadan, who had been assigned to escort Thurman to the city about seventy miles to the north, Nigeria's third-largest with a population of about 650,000 (population ca. 2020 about 2.25 million). His quarters were in the Ford Flats, faculty housing built by the Ford Foundation. A crucial context to Thurman's time in Nigeria, one that indeed made it possible, though little discussed by him in his journal, was the growing importance of Nigeria to the U.S. government and prominent international foundations as a plum in the Cold War in Africa.

Nigeria was being groomed as the Western alternative to its near neighbor, Ghana, and its charismatic (and increasingly dictatorial and Soviet-leaning) leader Kwame Nkrumah.[98] (Ghana was a cynosure for African American activists in the early 1960s, a place to go for the young and hip, like Maya Angelou, and for the old and venerated, like W. E. B. Du Bois, who died in Ghana, a Ghanaian citizen, a month before Thurman left for Nigeria.)[99] Britain was in retreat in West Africa, and the United States took up the slack, and Nigeria became, in the words of one scholar, "America's African model." Thurman would meet many Americans in Nigeria working, in one capacity or another, for the U.S. government.[100] But in neither Ghana nor Nigeria would the hopes and promises of the early 1960s have a happy ending.

When in Ibadan, Thurman met in a very short time a wide variety of people; white Americans, African Americans, Africans, and others. A Chinese Canadian faculty wife told Thurman that it was "bad form" not to have a cook, a steward who does all the household chores, and a "baby sitter": "Mrs. X kept saying to me—I am useless. I want my home back. There is nothing left for me to do for my husband but to sleep with him." Here were echoes of Olive Schreiner's notion of "the parasitic woman" that he had written of many decades before.[101] The most famous Ibadan faculty member he met was Wole Soyinka, then twenty-nine years old, near the beginning of a career that would be capped, in 1986, with the Nobel Prize for literature, the first African to be so honored. Thurman commented that "he has written several plays and seems to be quite a poet. We hit it off at once because he is quick, sensitive with a kind of sure humor. We are to get together."[102]

During his time in Nigeria, few topics interested Thurman more than the vexed and complex ways in which Africans and African Americans navigated their differences and similarities. He wondered if it was true that, as he often heard, "Nigerians do not like Amer. Negroes and vice versa." Many Nigerians on the faculty had spent time in the United States, often at historically Black colleges. One woman complained that Black Americans at a college where her husband had taught were unfriendly. A biochemist who had taught at Brown and had had a very unpleasant run-in with the Providence police told him, "When I found myself on Nigerian soil, I breathed free air for the first time since I left." Thurman was ambivalent about such remarks: "If the events are told with some understanding of the American scene I help them document it. If it is told in a spirit that says we have had no such experience and I do not see how Amer. Negroes stand it—then I react with some measure of hostility because such an attitude is false and unreal," rejecting any aspersions that African Americans were docile or complicit in their oppression. Even so: "I accept it better from a Nigerian or other African but from a European—NO!"[103]

Thurman taught a course on the philosophy of religion and was somewhat annoyed at himself at tempering his opinions, not wanting to offend his colleagues and students, whom he thought more conventionally Christian. He was fascinated by African Christianity and the ways in which it blended traditional African religious practices with their Christian beliefs. He was deeply moved by a "low Anglican" church in an indigenous African denomination that had broken away from missionary control: "There is a time, when people are called forward for blessings—all women with babies, old people, visitors—usually the Nigerians dance up to the altar to the accompaniment of drums and at the altar there is the laying on of hands and a prayer." In all, his experience with African Christianity reminded him of the situation of the Black church after Emancipation, when the divisions and separation between white and Black denominations were still being sorted out, and when official, doctrinal Christianity had to share the hearts of its worshippers with older, less formal practices rooted, consciously or not, in Africa.[104]

One of the highlights of Thurman's time in Ibadan were several public lectures. The most memorable was on the "Negro Revolution in America." The lecture hall was filled to capacity. Thurman was aware that "there were many American [faces?]—Negroes and whites" in the audience, who wanted to hear what he was going to say and how he was going to say it, and to judge whether he made a "'correct' impression." He provided an overview of African American history, starting with the first shipload of Africans brought to British North America in Jamestown in 1619, and concluding with King and the Southern Christian Leadership Conference, James Farmer and CORE, and the new militants in the Student Nonviolent Coordinating Committee (SNCC). He closed by speaking of the three unrealized goals of the Negro Revolution; the destruction of segregation, voting rights, and full access to the resources of society.[105]

There were questions. One person asked why he hadn't spoken of the influence of African independence on the civil rights movement. He had intended to do so and apologized for the oversight. Another question was from E. U. Essien-Udom, a native Nigerian who had spent many years in the United States, where he had written what was one of the first (and still one of the best) books on the Nation of Islam, *Black Nationalism: A Search for Identity in America*.[106] Currently chair of the political science department at the University of Ibadan, he wanted to know why Thurman had said nothing about the Nation of Islam in his talk and, according to Thurman, was "sharp and brittle in what he had to say accusing me of doing the omission deliberately." Thurman "replied as dispassionately as I could even though I smarted under the attack." He agreed that the Nation of Islam had made "an important contribution to the social struggle and revolution by giving *heart* to many of the people who felt that they did not count." But he insisted in his journal that "any movement that insisted upon separateness either within America or as a colonization scheme somewhere else was doomed" and that "I refuse to permit anyone to challenge my right of home or birth. I deeply regard myself as a birth-right American." He viewed the Nation of Islam as "part of the subtle propaganda [which] is to make the Negro feel that he is an alien in the land of his birth and in which his sweat and blood have laid the foundation upon which the country is built."[107]

If Thurman was lecturing about divisions in the United States, he was learning about the discords in Nigerian society. Nigeria, in 1963, was a riven and fragile country, throbbing with internal tensions. "Slowly I am trying to put together the political structure of the country," Thurman wrote in his journal, trying to "get some clear notion of what is meant by the Nigerian Federation." It was a tall order. Nigeria was a country that (to oversimplify) was divided into three ill-fitting parts, the Muslim North; the West, dominated by the Yoruba people; and the East, in which the Igbo (commonly spelled Ibo in the 1960s) were predominant. Ibadan was in the western, predominantly Yoruba region of Nigeria. This made for a turbulent and centripetal politics in a perpetually divided country. Thurman had to go no further than the University of Ibadan itself to see how this was playing out: "While the University is predominantly Yoruba it is presided over by an Ibo. This has many complications which I do not understand."[108]

Some Nigerians he spoke to yearned for a strongman, like Nkrumah, to rule the country with an iron hand. Thurman had a searching conversation about the Nigerian situation with Victor Babaremilekun Adetokunboh Fani-Kayode, the deputy prime minister of the Western Region of Nigeria, a leading Yoruba politician. When Thurman asked Fani-Kayode about the future of Nigeria, "he looked deep into my eyes for a minute—held them there with face immobile—lighted a cigarette—then he said 'You may know. I am no good at prophecy." He proceeded to tick off Nigeria's main problems, such as the gulf between the rich and poor, unemployment, and regionalism, concluding, "some day these people in each region will find a voice and that voice will be the same for each region—and when that happens, there will be blood shed—and God help us all. Bloodshed. I do not see any other way to purge the country of the evils that are destroying it."[109]

The bloodshed would come, soon, and it would be far more sanguinary than almost anyone imagined. On 15 January 1966, a group of mostly Igbo army officers overthrew the government and its Muslim leaders in a violent coup. Six months later, on 28 July, there was an equally violent countercoup, led by Muslim and Yoruba officers. This led to the disastrous Biafran Civil War, in which eastern Nigeria, dominated by the Igbos, tried to secede from Nigeria, a rebellion that was violently suppressed at the cost of a million lives. For most of the next three decades, Nigeria would be ruled by a series of military dictatorships. The United States' efforts to showcase the country as a shining example of a pro-Western democracy largely came to an end. It is sobering to learn how many of the Nigerians Thurman met during his stay were either murdered, imprisoned, or endured long years of exile during and after the events of 1966.

Thurman's time in Nigeria was short, only seven weeks. A few weeks into his stay, Sue arrived. Just as they were beginning to learn about the country, it was time to leave. On 18 November he was in formal dress as the representative of Boston University, participating in the installation of a chancellor and vice chancellor for the University of Ibadan, on the occasion of its formal independence from the University of London. The Nigerian prime minister, Alhaji Sir Abubakar Tafawa Balewa, was installed as the chancellor (an honorary position in the British university system). Thurman was impressed by his bearing and his "simple but very impressive address." He would be murdered in the first coup in 1966. On the same occasion, Thurman met Joseph

Palmer II, the U.S. ambassador to Nigeria. The two would meet again several days later, under very different circumstances.[110]

The next day, the Thurmans paid a visit to the Olowo of the Kingdom of Owo, approximately 140 miles to the east of Ibadan. The Kingdom of Owo was one of many Yoruba states that had lost their sovereignty under the British but retained, under colonial rule and after independence, some of their former status.[111] The Olowo, in 1963 Sir Olateur Olabegi II—knighted by Queen Elizabeth in 1960—was a male heir of the previous Olowo, in a chain of succession that in Owo oral tradition dated back to as far as the twelfth century. In 1963, the Olowo was still a person of means and importance in local affairs, a minister in the regional government, with a number of local villagers under his control. He appointed local chiefs, who served at his pleasure, with approximately two hundred thousand persons in his dominion. The Olowo's afin, his palace, was the largest in Yorubaland, with more than one hundred rooms on 108 acres of land. Thurman described it as "a large rambling structure sitting back from the main street with what had been once upon a time a large and beautiful entrance. It is run down and reveals the ghosts of a long passed elegance." Thurman thought "the Olowo seemed to be very aware that he was functioning [in] the last phase of a dying system. All around were indications of silent decay."[112]

Thurman was fascinated by the polygamy practiced by the Olowo, who had twelve wives and approximately thirty-five children. Each wife had her own house, part of the palace, and lived with her children, whom she was responsible for nurturing and feeding. The Olowo was responsible for their education. There were, needless to say, "all kinds of jealousies . . . among the wives." But what Thurman found fascinating about the situation was that each wife had to earn her own living, and this tended to make them independent entrepreneurs. It was unfortunate that, when European and American Christianity first came to Nigeria, "the missionary preached salvation by one wife rather than salvation by faith. It was an effort to impose a western morality as a necessity for salvation and the two things are not compatible." If only they had focused instead on Jesus, then there might have been "a real integration of Jesus into Nigerian religious cultures."[113]

In Owo, and in Nigeria, Thurman gained a new appreciation of African religious cultures and of the communities they nurtured. Throughout his time in Africa he was aware of how Nigerian Christians had incorporated their ancestors into their worship. There was nothing in the United States like the Kingdom of Owo, a last glimmer of the glorious kingdoms of West Africa, with an unbroken, unenslaved history dating back centuries. It was an African community of a very different sort than the Waycross neighborhood of Daytona of his youth. He would write in his journal that the Olowo's extended family "is like the famed [banyan] tree in India. There is the main trunk with the giant branches extending in all directions, each of the branches begins to send wandering extensions of itself towards the earth."[114] But in the Western world, "modern man has no community of which he is a part." Writing in the journal, he was "sure that I am on the track of a really great idea" and that he could "develop it into a really top book. It will be different from anything I have ever written before. In a sense it will be the philosophical and theological basis of the Fellowship Church idea."[115] In Africa the idea of an extended community, in time and space, became more tangible than anything he had experienced in the United States. Thurman had begun to write about community more extensively in the early 1960s, shortly before leaving for Africa, and his need to write about the subject was strengthened by his time in Africa. In some fashion, these African insights made their way into Thurman's grandest philosophical essay, published in 1971 as *The Search for Common Ground: An Inquiry into the Basis of Man's Experience of Community.*

And then it was November 22, 1963. The Thurmans were enjoying their visit with the Olowo when, in the early evening, the phone rang with the shattering news from Dallas. The news was garbled. The first report that Thurman heard was that not only President Kennedy but also Vice President Lyndon Johnson and Attorney General Robert Kennedy had been murdered. Thurman was shocked but not surprised: "Immediately I thought that at long last all law and order had broken down and that our country was in revolution. Strangely enough this did not occur to me as an improbability. For a long time I have felt that unless there was some radical changes to take place in the social fabric of our country, law and order would break down." Like many, he thought the assassination of the president was somehow connected to white southern defiance of the Supreme Court's civil rights rulings and the "slow wearing away of regard for authority," leading to "general national disorder," so ferocious that "it would take national martial law to restore order."[116]

Thurman was still dealing with his reactions to the assassination when, on the following day, he was invited by U.S. ambassador Palmer to deliver the eulogy at a memorial service at the embassy in Lagos. The Thurmans were met on their return to Ibadan on Sunday morning and then driven to the embassy in Lagos. Thurman arrived at the embassy late that morning, had several meetings about the upcoming service and only about two hours to prepare his remarks. Once he started to write and express his own "personal feeling and thought" about the tragedy, the words flowed easily.[117]

Most Nigerians shared Thurman's initial sense (which proved not to be accurate) that Kennedy's murder was somehow connected to a reaction to the civil rights movement and revealed America to be the racist country they had always known it to be. Benjamin Nnamdi "Zik" Azikiwe, president of Nigeria (head of state, not head of government), who had been educated at Howard and Lincoln Universities, sent a telegram to President Johnson stating that the assassination proved that among many Americans there was a "deep-seated hatred of the black man as a human being" and that the newly independent states of Africa needed to reconsider their ties.[118] University of Ibadan Vice Chancellor Dike told Thurman in their final meeting, about a week after the assassination, that "of course the president was killed because he had taken a courageous stand for the black man" and that "in America life is held as cheap—there is killing all over the place," mentioning the murder of Medgar Evers and the recent Birmingham church bombing.[119]

Thurman, in his eulogy, did not offer any speculation as to the actors or motives for Kennedy's assassination. (Lee Harvey Oswald was murdered at the same hour that Thurman spoke.) But he made the focus of his eulogy Kennedy's somewhat belated commitment to civil rights. Thurman, living in Boston after 1953, certainly had a good vantage to view the rise of the Massachusetts senator, but he was not particularly impressed with a senatorial career marked by a strident anti-Communism and a general invisibility on civil rights issues. His attitudes began to change in the 1960 campaign with Kennedy's forceful support for the separation of church and state, and thereafter, he "did seem to fuse with what to him was the destiny of America." He mused in his journal that assassination represented something "deep in the psyche of America that rejected its destiny" or perhaps a "symbol of the extent to which that destiny had been betrayed" and also a sign of "some deep awareness that we cannot escape our destiny?"[120]

Thurman's eulogy, which spoke of Kennedy's "aurora of destiny," was all about personal, collective, and national destiny. There is no reason to doubt that Thurman was genuinely saddened by Kennedy's shocking murder, but his focus was less on what the president had accomplished and more on the tasks remaining. Thurman allowed that there had been, on his part and that of many others, some "impatience as to the speed with which his leadership affirmed itself" on the Black revolution, but there was never any doubt that he had become, in the last months of his presidency, the "voice of the American conscience in the matter of the civil rights of its citizens, particularly of the 20 million American Negroes and other so-called minorities in the land" and had been "acting out of the center of an informed heart and a conviction as to the true spirit and meaning of democracy and the American dream." But now, echoing the words of Lincoln at Gettysburg and in his Second Inaugural Address, Thurman spoke of the tasks ahead: "The unfinished work, the outlines of which he has vouchsafed to us in his living, may we carry on and may what we leave undone be the sacred work of those who in their turn shall follow us."[121]

Thurman spoke to about nine hundred persons who had gathered on the lawn of the American embassy, including Nigerian cabinet officials and members of the diplomatic corps, many in tears. He remembered that "the Russian Ambassador took my hand, held it and with his eyes burrowed deep into my eyes—said not a word and passed on." Thurman was proud of the eulogy, tried to circulate it to members of the slain president's family, and saw it into print.[122] The Thurmans and Ambassador Palmer became good friends, and he invited them to spend a few days at his residence before leaving the country. The next year Palmer would become chief of the Foreign Service in the State Department—one indication, perhaps, of the importance of Nigeria in American foreign policy at the time—and in his new position he and Thurman would work to recruit more African Americans for the Foreign Service and find them better postings.[123]

On 2 December 1963, the Thurmans left Lagos. Thurman, the reluctant flyer, had no choice but to fly to London and from there board a plane for Tel Aviv.[124] Visiting Israel had long been a cherished dream. He had wanted to visit the country in 1960, as a part of his round-the-world trip, but discovered the ongoing Arab boycott of Israel made it impossible for the Thurmans to include Egypt, Lebanon, and Israel on the same trip. (The boycott was still in effect in 1963, as it would be, in its most direct form, until Egypt's peace treaty with Israel in 1979.) This time, Howard and Sue entered the country and spent two weeks there.[125]

His first comment in his journal after arriving in Israel was that "Israel is an unhappy land." He does not seem to have enjoyed his time there. Efforts to arrange a meeting with the great Jewish sage Martin Buber proved unsuccessful.[126] He was dismayed by the emphatic secularism of most Israelis. A physician told him, when queried about his beliefs: "I am a materialist. I have no time for the illusions of religion and its cant. I leave that to those who have nothing else to do or to think about." At the same time, when he saw Hasidim and ultra-Orthodox Jews in Jerusalem, they were very different from free spirits like Zalman Schachter-Shalomi: "We saw the men in their long Black [*Jewish?*] coats—the beards, side burns and zealot countenances—but it was all grim and foreboding. I wanted to flee away—this seemed like a rearguard holding the rear lines a vast RETREAT covering a rout." (As was all too common at the time, Thurman's Israel journal has nothing to say about Israel's Palestinian population.)[127]

On their trip to Jerusalem, the Thurmans were limited to visiting West Jerusalem, the part of the city that, from the end of the Arab-Israeli War of 1948 through the Six-Day War of 1967, was controlled by Israel. East Jerusalem, controlled by Jordan, contained almost all of the iconic landmarks, including the Old City. All they could see of East Jerusalem was a no-man's land of barbed wire and checkpoints. This probably led to the complaint in his journal that "there was nothing to remind me of what through all the years I had come to think of Jerusalem." He would add in his autobiography that he "was in quest of a spirit that seemed to evade me on every hand."[128] After a visit to Marc Chagall's stained glass murals of Jacob and his twelve sons in Hadassah Hospital he felt that there was "nothing here that gave me a[s a] Gentile any awareness of the great spiritual heritage of Israel." While acknowledging that he came to Israel with his own Christian biases, and like many responded to the wealth of its biblical place-names, he wrote in his autobiography that he felt a "great gulf that separated me from the present place and the symbolism of what that place meant in the history of my own life and tradition. I do not desire to see it again."[129]

Rabbi Roland Gittelsohn, reading Thurman's account of his time in Israel in *With Head and Heart,* wrote to him: "I wonder if you were not looking for an idealized, almost childish kind of Jerusalem which you remembered from your early lessons in Christianity."[130] It was a fair criticism, and Thurman said much the same in his autobiography, preferring the "long-time security of *my* Jerusalem, which does not exist in any place or any time but which is a part of the fluid area of my own living experience."[131] At the same time, perhaps Thurman was reacting to the sadness he intuited beneath the typical Israeli bravado, in a country that was more garrisoned, more militantly secular, and more hidebound in its religious orthodoxy than he expected, born of having to deal with the shattering weight of the recent Jewish past while trying to confront its difficult present and future. From Thurman's perspective what had been lost was a creative interaction with the matchless religious heritage of the Jewish people.

Israel was not the end of the trip. The Thurmans, in mid-January, were still about two months out from a return to the United States. After going to Naples to avoid the Arab boycott, they boarded the SS *Oransay,* and then, passing through the Suez Canal, they took a leisurely cruise across the South Pacific. There is no complete itinerary of the trip, but they stopped in Fiji; Sydney, Australia; and Hawaii, where Thurman gave several lectures, before returning to San Francisco in late February or early March.[132] There is very little documentation of this part of the trip, but the Thurmans must have enjoyed it, because in 1970 they took a very similar and better-documented cruise in the South Pacific.

What were Thurman's overall impressions of his time overseas? One reason for wanting to travel in Asia and Africa, as he told an audience in Boston in June 1964, was that "in America we seem to have lost sight of what the real condition of mankind is." He told his Boston audience that he "had seen in the last four years [in] Hong Kong, Manila, Bombay, Cairo, Japan—hunger, poverty, deprivation." He wrote of his time in Nigeria that "I could not sleep one night as I kept going over in my mind the fact that in a city the size of Ibadan, nearly a million people, there were *two* dentists—that one young pediatrician working in a government hospital said he saw every day more than 350 babies—that for thousands of youngsters who had escaped the diseases of children there was no future of work and meaning to fashion their hopes and their dreams."[133] In Japan and elsewhere he saw the lingering effects of the last war, of how cities had been "ripped open like a ripe melon by bombs and the ruthless march of armies." It raised thoughts of the atrocities of that war, horrors that "we are unable to even imagine," the "six million human beings like us being put in gas ovens; of children being buried alive," along with resonances of atrocities closer to home: "American Indians had been almost completely emasculated and all their ancient values destroyed; that American Negroes had been exploited, raped, and systematically often suppressed." There was no bottom to the pit of human suffering: "All these thoughts moved through the forest of my mind like a huge crawling python."[134]

These dark musings aside, Thurman added, "yet I was unwilling even in my thoughts to abandon hope of my country."[135] And one reason for this hope was his pride that "the darker races of mankind" were taking advantage of their new freedoms, and he basked in their courage. They could now "move on earth" freely and enjoy the freedom to expand "a sense of local residence" so that the traveler, physically or mentally, "can live in his place and move over the earth, enlarging his sense of local residence giving to the places he touches a bit of the glory that he has found in the place that he calls his home."[136] As Thurman would write a few years later, this was part of "the vast undertaking of man's becoming at home in his world," something that had long been denied to the "darker races of mankind."[137] Thurman's ministry could be stretched no wider.

Thurman summed up his travels by reading from a poem, "Ithaca," by the master Greek poet Constantine V. Cavafy, writing of the voyage of Odysseus, a long, meandering passage of dangerous self-exploration, one that took a lifetime to prepare for, a journey not to be wasted on the young:

Setting out on the voyage to Ithaca
You must pray that the way be long
Full of adventures and experiences.
. . . .
But do not hurry the journey at all.
Better it should last many years,
Be quite old when you anchor at the island.[138]

But perhaps Thurman described his years of travel even more eloquently in his own words, when he said of the rapt crowd gathered at the Lincoln Memorial for the March on Washington, that it was a privilege to be moving with the "stillness of absolute motion."

14

Common Ground? Coming Aground?

"The Cataclysms of the Civil Rights Revolution"

When the Thurmans returned to Boston in April 1964 after seven months of globe-trotting it must have been an odd homecoming. Howard had no significant responsibilities at Boston University, although he still had an office and secretarial help, and occasionally (very occasionally) preached at Marsh Chapel. He continued to give weekly television broadcasts on the *We Believe* program. They now lived in the city. Sue was involved in her activities in promoting the African American history of Boston. Howard busied himself with his writing. But they were essentially marking time and waiting for Howard's official retirement in the spring of 1965. Afterward they would be moving back to their true home, San Francisco. Meanwhile they watched the news, of which there was plenty, and continued to monitor what Thurman would call "the cataclysms of the civil rights revolution in which we are engulfed."[1]

Thurman spent much of his last year in Boston writing what would be one of his most overtly political books, *The Luminous Darkness,* subtitled *A Personal Interpretation of the Anatomy of Segregation and the Ground of Hope,* published in the fall of 1965.[2] Thurman had long wanted to publish an updated version of *Jesus and the Disinherited,* and if *The Luminous Darkness* isn't quite that, it represents his fullest response to how the situation of Black America had changed over the previous fifteen years. As was usually the case for Thurman, even in his more political writings, he shied away from discussions of conventional politics. *The Luminous Darkness* was not a history of the civil rights movement or a sketch of its leading events or figures but an account that focused on individual and social psychology. Thurman wrote in the book about the need for jobs—he calls for what came to be called affirmative action, political representation, the urban crisis, and of course for the end of legal segregation and its informal penumbras. But it was, as the subtitle indicated, a study of the psychology of segregation. "It is clear for the Negro," Thurman states at the beginning of the book, that "the fundamental issue involved in the experience of segregation is the attack it makes on his dignity and integrity."[3]

For Thurman, the "immoral exercise of [the] power of the strong over the weak" was the essence of segregation, and as he reflected on during his Daytona boyhood, this bred "amorality" on all sides, with its "cold, hard, minute, and devastating" understanding of the other," the "kind of understanding one gives an enemy." Now, the prospect existed for both greater harmony and greater discord, very possibly both at the same time.[4] Compared to fifteen years before, when Thurman wrote *Jesus and the Disinherited*, genuine Black equality seemed both more tangible and less abstract, and at the same time somehow more elusive and slippery. For whites, the challenge of the civil rights revolution was to recognize that when dealing with Blacks, you are "dealing with citizens. There are no degrees in citizenship; a person cannot be almost a citizen but not quite. He is a citizen or he is not a citizen." Whites cannot bestow citizenship. It "is not a prerogative that any group within society has the right or the capability of conferring upon other individuals or groups in society." Blacks must claim their citizenship and cannot use ill treatment as an excuse to cast it aside: "Once an American feels that America is not his homeland, he has given up his right to claim the fruits of citizenship. This right must be maintained at all costs because if it is lost in the spirit of Negroes, then the door to citizenship closes within his own heart. It would mean that the external denial of citizenship as expressed in segregation becomes internalized and all is lost." For all Americans, Thurman writes, "we become persons by an other-than-self reference which is other persons. We become human in a human situation."[5] Neither whites nor Blacks had much experience in treating each other as fully human.

The path to citizenship for Thurman was the path of nonviolence. When he attended the March on Washington in August 1963, what impressed him most was not the milling crowds, the music, or the oratory, but "a small group of young people who represented student nonviolent groups, fresh from the jails and violences of the South." This was a "call to sacrifice, the sense of participation in a collective destiny that involves the total nation," much as he had seen taking place during World War II.[6] It had forced hardened segregationists into a last-ditch struggle for a fading racial hierarchy: "The use of electric cattle prods, the turning of the full driving stream of water for fighting fires upon little children, defenseless girls, the dynamiting of a church resulting in the deaths of little children . . . these are the deeds of men with their backs against the wall, they are at *war*." What a striking turnabout from *Jesus and the Disinherited!* It was now Jim Crow's defenders with their backs against the wall because "the active fear in the Negro, one of the foundation stones providing uneasy stability for segregation, is rapidly disappearing."[7] The protests were forcing white moderates to do what they had long tried to avoid after *Brown*, to unequivocally take sides: "The southern white liberal could no longer work for improvement of conditions and relations between the two groups without taking a side either *for* the decision or *against* the decision."[8] Many, though not all, no longer able to waffle, came down against the decision, unwilling to disturb their comfortable social hierarchies.

African Americans were faced with a choice between nonviolence and something grittier, more visceral and immediate. Thurman recognized that the white-hot emotions of the civil rights revolution could not always be channeled into peaceful and irenic courses, and if he deplored violence, he was deeply sympathetic to the civil disturbances beginning to occur in Black neighborhoods in northern cities. Blacks who had been "depersonalized, pickled, and preserved in and by hate" discovered that what had been inert now became "uncongealed, fluid, dynamic" directed at forces that "stood squarely in the way of their individual and collective self-realization." There was the local merchant "able to fatten himself on their poverty and hunger," the race leaders who spoke much but did little, and especially "the ever-present policeman who seemed always the guardian at the gate to hold them back."[9]

If this rowdy self-realization differed from the prayerful reflection he had taught at Boston University, it commanded and demanded attention from many who had habitually averted their eyes.[10] It was welcome because "things that have been smoldering are moving into the open" where they can be dealt with.[11] He was deeply worried, and rightly so, that one consequence of Black violence was that white America would feel their "responsibility" and debt to Black Americans paid, and with the end of legal segregation, they could once again live comfortably with their consciences and build new walls to separate themselves from Black America. Thurman often told the story of the dog he had at Howard University, Bearimore, who saw his task as barking at the paperboy making his afternoon rounds, but only from behind the safety of a picket fence. One snowy winter's day, as Bearimore charged the paperboy, snow drifts took him over the fence, and, writes Thurman, "he yelped as if he had been struck; I ran to the rescue. But the only rescue he needed was from the shock of face-to-face confrontation."[12] For all the manifold evils of segregation, it provided a protection of sorts to those immured within its walls. Any routine, however blinkered, had the comforts of familiarity. And like Bearimore, it was easier to spend a lifetime thinking about what it would be like to catch the paperboy than to have to deal with the reality and consequences of catching him.

Thurman was not surprised that white America was building new walls. What distressed him no end was that Black America was doing the same. In *The Luminous Darkness* he wrote of a minister he invited to preach at Rankin Chapel who told the congregation, "I want Negro policemen, I want Negro jails, if I am to be hanged, I want a Negro gallows."[13] For Thurman this sort of attitude was understandable, and he recognized that Black institutions provide "the ego structure to withstand the shattering impact of rejection" by white America. But it remains a way that "the human spirit accommodate[s] itself to desolation," without addressing the underlying cause. The Black church often played a similar role. It was for Thurman, a "great irony" that the Black church was in the forefront of the freedom struggle because, some notable exceptions aside, it had backed into its revolutionary role. It had "not become a civil rights rallying center because of its religious ethical teaching as such." Its importance came because it was the one institution unambiguously under Black control, but it had to be prodded into civil rights activism by forces outside itself, and Thurman worried that the church, and large sections of Black America as a whole, might revert to its former complacency and false sense of security by valuing their separation from white America more than the fight for equality.[14]

The title of the book, *The Luminous Darkness,* Thurman tells us, came from the phenomenon experienced by a scuba diver passing into deeper water, not illumined by sunlight. At first there is only darkness, but as the diver's eyes adjust, the darkness becomes luminous. If there is a bit of a mystic paradox in the title, it reflects Thurman's views of America's racial realities in 1965. The country was, at last, diving ever more deeply into the heart of its far-too-long-unobserved racial realities. As the eyes of the nation adjusted, people had to learn not to be afraid of what they saw or not to worry if, as of yet, they saw nothing clearly. To God, wrote Thurman, quoting his favorite psalm, "the darkness and the light are both alike."

Thurman in *The Luminous Darkness* was anticipating a day of shadows such as 9 March 1965, when Martin Luther King, Jr., John Lewis, and the protestors in Selma, Alabama, were violently halted in their march as they crossed the Edmund Pettis Bridge, in the episode that became known as "Bloody Sunday." Hours after the march, in Selma, Jim Reeb was attacked and suffered a fatal blow to the head. Thurman knew Reeb, a Unitarian Universalist minister from Boston who had gone down to Selma after King made a plea for clergy to join the march. They had spoken several years earlier, when Reeb was determined to "give his life to the inner city and in particular to working on the problem of integration" and thought that Thurman, with his experience with Fellowship Church, would be "the one person who can help him to resolve his own problem." After their conversation, Reeb relocated to Boston and, in Thurman's words, "chose to give his life to live and work among people whose dwelling place is on the razor's edge of marginal subsistence, for whom no one speaks and whose desperation is known intimately only of God."[15]

Thurman did not know Viola Liuzzo, a woman from Detroit who was murdered on 25 March after the completion of the Selma to Montgomery march, though he offered eulogies and memorial tributes to both Reeb and Liuzzo soon after their deaths: "Who spoke for us on that tragic night in Selma, Alabama? And in which voice?" After the deaths of Reeb and Liuzzo, "how may we make atonement? You must find your answer even as I find mine." He quoted a line of Hermann Hagedorn that he had often used before in tragic circumstances: "But we who live must do a harder thing than dying is. For we must think, and ghosts shall drive us on."[16]

After Selma, and after the summer of 1965, marked by the passage of the Voting Rights Act and the rioting in Watts, the civil rights movement was moving in new directions. In July 1966 Thurman resigned from the Advisory Committee of the Congress of Racial Equality (CORE), an organization he had been involved with, through James Farmer, from its inception in 1942. Once the most interracial of major civil rights organizations, by 1966 it had taken a sharply nationalist turn. Friends were writing Thurman about possible anti-Semitism in some of its leaflets. In June 1966 CORE endorsed the new and controversial slogan "Black Power." Thurman resigned from the Advisory Committee, he wrote, because the decision had been made without asking the committee's advice. CORE's director of public relations, Don Smith, explained to Thurman that Black Power was a "new dimension in the quest for freedom and equality of Black Americans" but was being "deliberately misrepresented by evil, guilty or fearful people." It sought only to "end the syndrome of powerlessness of Black Americans—by their own effort." In response, Thurman said he did not want to get into an argument but that "everything that you have said about Black Power is an old story to me" and that "the road is a long one and there are no authorities or road maps."[17]

One reason for the rise of Black Power was that the main alternative, integration, seemed to be withering in the face of a fierce backlash by its white opponents and a sense from African Americans that what white and Black liberals favored would still leave African Americans several leagues short of full citizenship. Neither nonviolence nor interracial cooperation had proven to be sufficiently fruitful strategies for Black advancement. Nonviolence, for many, had lost its spiritual aura, was increasingly reduced to a mere tactic, and one of questionable effectiveness. (Prominent pacifist and antiwar activist Dave Dellinger, taking aim at one of the cardinal tenets of Thurman's understanding of Gandhi, stated in 1964 that it was no longer possible to "justify the presumption" that "the goal of non-violence is to convert our opponent.")[18] Thurman had long worried that segregation and discrimination in the North might prove a more elusive foe than the overt racism of Jim Crow, and as the civil rights movement broadened out of the South, there were many who came to the same conclusion.[19]

Self-doubts entered even the firmest supporters of nonviolence and integration, such as James Farmer, who, several months before Thurman, had left the top executive position at CORE over worries about its nationalist turn. In his 1965 book *Freedom, When?* Farmer stated that while "much of 'integration' remains valid for us and, in our view, for America," he had growing doubts. Farmer was not (or perhaps was no longer) a "rabid integrationist" because he did not believe "that *all* Negro separation was inherently inferior" and would prefer to call himself and those who agreed with him "desegregationists" and that the civil rights movement would benefit "as Negroes and whites come to realize that desegregation and not total integration, total assimilation, is our goal."[20] "Integration" had suddenly become a word that Black activists, even fervid advocates such as Farmer, were learning to avoid.

Thurman still embraced the term in one of his most urgently political essays, "Desegregation, Integration, and the Beloved Community." It has an odd history. He wrote it in September 1966 for a forthcoming Festschrift for Benjamin Mays. But the volume failed to appear on time, and Thurman waited for its publication. And waited. Impatient at first, he soon forgot about the essay. The delay stretched from years to decades, until finally, in 2009, a small publishing house issued the Mays Festschrift, although Thurman and many of the contributors were long deceased.[21] It is a pity that the essay intended for the America of Lyndon Johnson did not appear in print until the presidency of Barack Obama and unfortunate that Thurman did not try harder for its more timely appearance. Still, the essay has lost little of its relevance.

In 1966 legal Jim Crow was fading, Thurman argued, but white supremacy was not. It remained "ingrained in the structure of our society" and was "guaranteed by economic, political, social, and religious sanctions." That is why "the attack on segregation in order to be meaningful and effective has to involve revolution, social upheaval."[22] The reality was that, twelve years after *Brown,* public education remained largely segregated, and "the collective will to segregation remains basically intact."[23] Thurman was skeptical that Black voting rights would be enough to change this "because, left to itself, the voting right supports the established structure."[24] More concerted activism was needed, especially in the North, where the "Negro ghetto" was "the hard core of *experienced* segregation," and as long as they persisted, Blacks would be treated by the white majority at best "through gesture[s] of economic benevolence" rather than as something of real concern to their own lives and interests.[25]

What Black people needed "during the period of the revolution" was "an entirely new and radical power base," though Thurman quickly added that he was "not referring to the current unreflective slogan: Black Power."[26] Black power must lead toward inclusive citizenship and integration, and not away from it. If "integration" is a term that entered America's racial vocabulary in the 1930s, first popularized by African American intellectuals and journalists, "desegregation" is a more recent term, not in wide use before the early 1950s; it reflected the need by Black social scientists to have an intermediate term that described a situation neither fully segregated nor fully integrated. Like many commentators during the civil rights era, Thurman distinguished between the two terms.[27] Desegregation was segregation's negation, but it was not segregation's opposite. It was just a first step, akin to what Thurman calls "token integration," when "one or more non-white persons become a part of a larger white group." This was often confused with serious integration. Integration will come only when "the pattern of segregation" is "disturbed by revolutionary forces" and the economic structures and social realities of segregation, in the ghettos and elsewhere, are overturned. This higher level of integration, which had as its goal "to unify, to combine, to become whole, to become one," cannot be achieved through "the superficial and mechanical juggling of different kinds of belonging,"[28] but instead was "grounded in the many sided aspects of the common life."[29] Integration was much more than mere race mixing. It was the realization of the equality of infinite worth. Indeed, integration could not be directly sought at all but only arrived at: "Integration can never be achieved as an end in itself but must emerge as an experience after the fact of coming together."[30] Fellowship Church was one, very partial, attempt to move in this direction. It was not integrated by its racial percentages and ratios but only when its members were able to "participate meaningfully in the various phases of their living."[31]

Integration of this sort could lead to the creation of the "beloved community," a term first used by Josiah Royce and widely popularized by Martin Luther King, Jr.[32] The term "beloved community," Thurman acknowledged, "has a soft and sentimental ring," conjuring images of "tranquility, peace, and the utter absence of struggle and of all things that irritate and disturb."[33] (It was not a common phrase in Thurman's writing, probably for this reason.)[34] In the beloved community there will be "disagreements and conflicts" aplenty. What there will not be are "hard or critical lines of conformity yield-ing a glow of sameness over the private or collective landscape," submerging the possibility for real individual and group expression.[35] This is Thurman's utopia, one in which coercion of all types has been replaced with a blend-ing and merging of various forms of individual and collective creativity.[36] By 1966 it was becoming ever-clearer to Thurman that the civil rights revolution would stop far short of realizing this "dream of the race" that "has moved in and out on the horizon of human strivings like some fleeting ghost." It was perhaps unrealizable.[37] But the alternative was staring "at each other across stormy seas, our eyes gleaming with the burning frenzy of our unhappy and exhausted spirits."[38] Thurman was offering few predictions or promises.

On 16 May 1965, Thurman preached his last sermon at Marsh Chapel.[39] On 19 May 1965, Boston University gave Thurman a testimonial dinner on the eve of his retirement. Many close friends and associates attended. President Case presided, Dean Muelder spoke, and the featured speaker was Joseph Palmer, director of the U.S. Foreign Service, whom Thurman had met in Nigeria in 1963.[40] On 1 July, his retirement became official.

On 29 May, he gave his last television program in the *We Believe* series, on which he had been appearing regularly since 1959. Regular watchers were devastated. One wrote Thurman that when she tried to watch his final pro-gram her house lost power, and she quickly "managed to get myself invited to a neighbor's house in order not to miss your program."[41] Another *We Believe* fan wrote Thurman that "I felt absolutely sunk when you told us this was your last broadcast" for the broadcasts had helped her to understand that not "theology and dogmas" but "the capacity of listening" was the basic spiritual experience, adding (as did many *We Believe* fans) that "this is the first letter I have ever written to anyone on TV."[42]

As Howard and Sue's days in Boston dwindled, their new lives in San Fran-cisco beckoned. Howard would never again have a permanent ministerial or academic position, or someone to report to or answer to. But if anything, by cutting his institutional obligations to Boston University, his retirement years saw an increase in his schedule of preaching and teaching, a schedule he maintained, with only a few interruptions, until the last months of his life. Retirement for the Thurmans, as for many couples, meant having to get by on a reduced income. In 1963 Howard wrote a benefactor that he had $15,000 in savings and was expecting a postretirement income of about $4,800 including his social security, and estimated that he needed an income of about $6,000 "so that Sue and I can move gracefully into the twilight."[43] (An annual family income of about $6,000 to $7,000 in 1963 qualified one for middle-class status.) Thurman wrote Coretta Scott King in 1974 that "since my retirement," he had to get by on a "greatly reduced income."[44] Thurman had a pension from Boston University and had been careful with his finances. For many years he had relied on his former Morehouse instructor and subsequently successful Atlanta banker Lorimer Milton to direct his modest investment in securities.[45] In addition, he continued to earn honoraria for his speaking and teaching engagements.[46]

Thurman was never a wealthy man and probably never really wanted to be one, but he had long harbored dreams of being a philanthropist. As we have seen, while still an undergraduate at Morehouse, he proposed to John Hope the creation of a Negro Scholarship Fund, with the funds to be raised by "soliciting [regular] contributions from among my people."[47] While nothing came of this, it did little to still his philanthropic impulses. At Howard, Fellowship Church, and Boston University, circumstances and funds permitting, he provided assistance to needy African American students. In October 1960, Thurman wrote Lloyd M. Smith, a Los Angeles lawyer, telling him that in recent years "an increasing number of individuals have privileged me by putting varying sums of money at my disposal to be given to people," and at least two persons had made "arrangements in their wills for some considerable money to be dispensed by me." In addition, Thurman wanted to make portions of his own income available for the same purpose. Thurman was using the Marsh Chapel discretionary fund for this but was contemplating his retirement and asked Smith for help in establishing the "Howard Thurman Trust Fund" under the laws of California to aid students of religion and human relations and "to make emergency grants to individuals whose life has fallen upon evil times."[48]

The Trust, soon to be renamed the Howard Thurman Educational Trust (HTET), was chartered on 1 July 1961.[49] It started very modestly, with Howard and Sue providing the initial one-hundred-dollar contribution to the fund, with the two of them as the original trustees, along with Gene K. Walker, a San Francisco businessman who had been chairman of the board of trustees of Fellowship Church.[50] By June 1965 the Trust had disbursed about six thousand dollars since its founding and had about the same amount on hand. "We have discovered," he wrote at this time, "that a little money wisely placed can achieve infinite results."[51] Gifts totaling about ten thousand dollars were given him upon his retirement from Boston University. These funds were transferred to the Trust and gave it some impetus.[52] The first task of the Trust upon the return of the Thurmans to San Francisco was providing them with a place to live and work. It leased the building on 2020 Stockton Street that doubled as the Thurman's home and the Trust's offices.[53] It would be their home (and, after Howard's death, Sue's home) for the remainder of their lives.

In June 1965, just before he left Boston, Thurman wrote Frank Wilson that the Trust would primarily have two purposes: "1) The broadening and deepening of the cultural life and historic sense of young Negroes studying in our schools [that is, HBCUs] in the South and 2) Aiding in strategic, crucial ways toward developing an indigenous Christianity."[54] The latter was largely focused on Nigeria and developed on contacts Thurman had made during his stay there in 1963, though this was curtailed in the wake of Nigerian political instability after 1966.

The Trust also supported Howard and Sue's interest in African American history. The Trust helped exhibit Robert Witt Ames's seven-hundred-pound bas-relief sculpture *Freedom Now,* which told the history of African Americans and their struggles for equality in America in thirty carvings, from the Middle Passage to the recent civil rights martyrs James Chaney, Andrew Goodman, and Michael Schwerner; a life-size quilt of Frederick Douglass, and other Black history projects.[55] It also maintained Sue Bailey Thurman's International Rooms, primarily located in historically Black colleges in the South, consisting of collections of dolls dressed in a wide variety of Native costumes.[56] (There was interest on Thurman's part in extending the work of the Trust to another nonwhite group of special interest to him, American Indians, though this remained a small aspect of the Trust's work.)[57]

In all of these ways, as Thurman wrote (in the third person) in 1971, "the concept which inspired the formation of the Trust was to provide a structure for the continuous unfolding of the spirit and ideals that shaped the life of the man for whom the Trust is named." This spirit was "essentially religious" but not limited to the truths of any one religion; rather, the goal was to further the ideal that "all human life is bound together by ties that transcend race, culture and religions."[58] For the last fifteen years of his life, the Howard Thurman Educational Trust became the main vehicle for his message and its wider dissemination. It functioned as a philanthropy for causes dear to Thurman, and it was a platform for the study and dissemination of his words, works, and ideas.[59]

Returning to San Francisco for Thurman also meant confronting his relation with the Church for the Fellowship of All Peoples without the luxury of an intervening continent. Fellowship Church was in 1965 a very different institution than it had been in 1953: it was smaller, more local, no longer imagining itself in the van of a great national movement. *The Growing Edge* had ceased publication shortly after Thurman left, and most outside funding and attention for the church had withered away as well. The church remained committed to interracialism and interreligious comity, but questions of its identity, post-Thurman, had roiled an increasingly divided congregation. The two issues—the need to establish a sense of purpose and debilitating factionalism—were in Thurman's mind closely related. As he wrote in 1960: "What the Church needs desperately is a *sense of Cause*. Something has to be at *stake*. Where this is not present the people must take it out on each other in ways that are positive and destructive rather than positive and constructive."[60]

Both Thurman and Fellowship Church had moved on, but to some extent both sides were unwilling to acknowledge this. As minister-at-large, he still enjoyed an outsized influence in the church, consulting and weighing in on staffing questions and other matters, both officially and often unofficially, as a stream of gossipy letters sent to him from members of one faction or another sharing their grievances indicates.[61] In addition, almost every summer during the Boston years, the Thurmans returned to California, and at Fellowship Church, he was the featured attraction, preaching on almost every available Sunday and often leading retreats for the congregation.[62]

Thurman's appearances at the church created problems. Writing to the chairman of the board of trustees in March 1958, he said there was something "vulgar" about the crowding into the sanctuary of Fellowship Church to hear him preach, often by persons who had not attended the church since the previous summer, while regular members were "crowded out and pushed aside." Regarding his summer visits, "when I zoom in like a comet visiting the solar system, and zoom out again," he felt "a lot of little pieces must be picked up and painfully cemented together when I leave."[63] By the end of the decade, he had decided that he had to curtail his preaching at the church and had come to the conclusion that his presence and seeking national support had been harmful to the church in other ways as well, writing in 1959 that outside fundraising "has crippled us through the years. I am sure that there would have been far more cohesiveness in our congregation if the ownership of our present building had been the result of real sacrifice on the part of the people, but, as you recall, instead the entire cost of the building was paid for by persons who were not local members of the congregation."[64]

Thurman felt he needed a Black successor because, as he wrote Benjamin Mays on the eve of his departure to Boston, "we are not far enough out of the woods in our society for any considerable number of non-Caucasians to cast their lot with confidence in an enterprise led predominantly by a Caucasian," adding that his "remark comes out of ten years on the firing line."[65] But his next two successors were white. (Part of the problem, as Thurman noted, was that talented Black ministers could find more substantial and better-paying pulpits elsewhere, and few potential candidates had Thurman's ability to supplement the fairly modest salary by raking in speaking honoraria.)[66] Despite his comments to Mays, Thurman had strongly recommended to the Fellowship Church board that he be succeeded, at least on a temporary basis, by the Rev. Dryden Phelps, a white minister who had been working at the church as the assistant minister.[67] (Thurman did suggest a regular monthly preaching rotation that also included an African American and Mexican American minister.)[68]

Phelps was seen by Thurman as a temporary solution. Already over sixty years of age in 1953, Phelps had recently returned to the United States on a permanent basis after spending over three decades as a missionary in China. He had left after the 1949 revolution, but his sympathetic comments about the new realities—"God is working alongside these Communists"—led to the State Department confiscating his passport and his being drummed out of the American Baptist Foreign Mission Society.[69] (The fact that Fellowship Church hired him speaks volumes about its Cold War politics.) Phelps was accomplished but, one gathers, given an impossible act to follow, perhaps a bit stolid and dull, if only by comparison. Complaints about his lack of inspiration and his administrative competence reached Thurman in Boston.[70] After two years, Phelps and Fellowship Church parted ways. (However, rather than realizing Thurman's fears that under white leadership Blacks would depart, the opposite occurred, with the percentage of Blacks increasing and Thurman "profoundly disturbed" by this development. According to one estimate, in 1958, 65 percent of the regular attendees were African American.)[71]

In 1955, Fellowship Church hired Francis Geddes as Thurman's permanent replacement. Geddes, thirty-two years old at the time, a graduate of Stanford University and Yale Divinity School, had worked in Fellowship Church as assistant minister and director of the Intercultural Workshop.[72] Thurman wrote Geddes that he did "not want you to feel in any sense under the pressure of my shadow," whether it be "the desire to do things somewhat after my manner" or "just the reverse of that." Thurman suggested that it might be wise for him not to preach at Fellowship Church the following summer—though he did—so as not to "unwittingly handicap the birth of new spirit and life." Geddes's task was one that "will require that you heal many wounds, lift many spirits, and joy many hearts."[73]

But although Thurman wrote in 1958 that Geddes accommodated his continuing role in the church with "unbelievable graciousness," by the following year the relation between the two men had become increasingly awkward.[74] Geddes comes off second-best in his epistolary war with Thurman, and we should not judge his long career, whose active commitment to civil rights included marching with King in the 1960s, on the basis of this intemperate correspondence. Both men were responding to, from opposite positions, the anxiety that Thurman's profound influence on Fellowship Church had left in its wake.

Geddes wrote Thurman in late 1959 that Thurman's remaining active in the church came "at a cost . . . to me and to the independence of the church." He offered the obvious analogy: "There are many ways in which you have and are helping the church. There are many ways in which a parent can help his teen age adolescent, many things that can be done for the youngster, but sometimes the 'help' can be a hindrance to the development of necessary independence and self-sufficiency."[75] Thurman largely agreed with Geddes, replying that he would ask the board of trustees to change his status from minister-at-large to minister emeritus and that with this "designation my relationship to the Church will be merely that of any member-at-large."[76] Thurman's abjuration only deepened the tensions within the church, with the pro-Thurman faction accusing Geddes and his supporters of forcing Thurman to reduce his involvement, and Geddes responding that the church's Commitment was "not the 39 Articles" and that some members "judge everything by the standards and experience of the years 1944–53 and are unhappy when things change."[77]

The dispute between Thurman and Geddes was certainly about bruised feelings. But it also touched on serious questions about the church's future. Was the interracialism of the church something already achieved or something to work toward? What, ultimately, did the fact that a group of middle-class persons from different racial backgrounds could come together for worship in one moderately sized church in San Francisco mean for the future of race relations in the United States? Geddes argued the church needed a new direction because "the fact that an integrated church can work and maintain itself has been demonstrated." Thurman was dumbfounded and responded in rare fury. He wondered "what on earth that sentence means?," adding that as long "as America is prejudice ridden, as long as there is as much sheer religious, class and racial prejudice with basic discrimination, as there is even in our beloved San Francisco, such a demonstration has to be continuous." Thurman went on to argue that "Fellowship Church has not been able to maintain even an authentic interracial character or quality. At this point the Jungle Growth of our society has closed in upon it. At the present time the church lags behind the tradition. There can be no escape from the past by an attitude of hostility toward the past." Thurman did not want to make the church into a mere "instrument in group therapy."[78]

For Thurman, Geddes's vision for the church had no "sense of crisis and collapse in the midst of which comfortable middle-class Americans are trying to find answers of resolution." Thurman went on to state that discrimination in San Francisco, in his experience, was worse in 1960 than it had been in 1944. What Geddes was suggesting, Thurman added in a stinging rebuke, was "what white Protestant ministers in Alabama, Georgia etc. north or south have been saying since Reconstruction." Fellowship Church, Thurman was saying in effect, had been founded in an effort to overcome the "will to segregation," and this was no time to declare victory in the battle.[79]

Thurman stayed away from Fellowship Church for the remainder of Geddes's tenure, which ended in 1963. But the impact of the fight lingered. In 1964 he wrote that "one of the poisonous bits of propaganda under the regime of Francis Geddes was the rumor that I kept the church from settling down with him in anticipation of the time when I would return and become the pastor. It was aided and abetted by certain delusions of grandeur which many people had with reference to the almighty significance of the Fellowship Church."[80] When Thurman returned to San Francisco he had no interest in playing any significant role in the church. He wrote the board of trustees, during a crisis over the future of the church in 1970, that "since my return to San Francisco 5 years ago, I have, with great care and with a real sense of self-denial, refrained from the simplest forms of participation in the life of the church, for fear that my continuous presence would tend to make a break with the past difficult if not impossible." Nonetheless there were those "who have said that despite this effort on my part, my very presence keeps alive a shackling past and renders enthusiastic grappling with the present half-hearted and inadequate." This Thurman rejected as an "alibi." He was blunt. Fellowship Church was "sick," not "meeting the needs either of the community or its membership," was "rife with internal strife," and was not, "at this time, either a center of worship or the center of program."[81] Four years later, during another crisis, he resigned his status as minister emeritus, stating the "dilemma created by my dual position as minister-emeritus and local member" could no longer be reconciled.[82] Thurman continued to attend services at Fellowship Church when he was in San Francisco and otherwise unoccupied on Sunday mornings, but toward the end of his life, even his physical presence at services declined and not only because of his increasing infirmity.

If Thurman was disappointed in what became of Fellowship Church, he never disowned the dream that gave it birth. In November 1980 he preached one of his by now quite infrequent sermons at the church on the occasion of the thirty-sixth anniversary of its founding. It had a title he had used many times before, "The Growing Edge," and it included, as had many sermons throughout his career, a reading from Olive Schreiner. The sermon reviewed the history of the church and discussed some of its current problems, adding, "I don't want to say all of these things to depress you, but what I am saying is the miracle is, in our society, that a remnant of this church has survived." He was uncertain whether "it is possible, and I am dead in earnest ladies and gentlemen, whether it is possible to develop a caring, sensitive, loving community in a world organized on violence and brutality and hate. . . . The burden of proof is on our weary shoulders. The day is long and the night is very hard." The efforts to create and keep Fellowship Church alive had been very difficult, but the fight had been worth it: "So, while we have a chance, let's try again and again and again." These are the last words from the last sermon he would ever preach at Fellowship Church, and almost certainly the last words of the several thousand sermons Thurman preached in his lifetime. Five months later he was dead.[83]

The anniversary celebration had been for Thurman one of the days that justified the existence of Fellowship Church. Another was probably the saddest Sunday in its history, 7 April 1968, the Sunday after the assassination of Martin Luther King, Jr. That morning, Thurman spoke at the pulpit. He wrote a protégé, who would soon be coming to San Francisco as an interim minister, about it: "I would venture to say that nowhere else in the United States on that Sunday could there be found 500 or more people assembled who had such a deep sense of original community. Despite the monumental disaster of the assassination, Negro and white people were together as one family with no self-consciousness or sensitivity due to the vicissitude of the current mood. This, my dear young friend, was the harvest from the planting of other years in Fellowship Church."[84]

On Thursday, 4 April, news of the murder of Martin Luther King, Jr., in Memphis was announced around 7:00 p.m. Central Standard Time. Thurman, in San Francisco, would have heard the shocking announcement in late afternoon. The death of King was a tragedy for Thurman on many levels. It was a personal loss. He and Sue knew King well; they knew his wife, his parents, and their children; they all were a part of his milieu. King had embodied and realized many of his ideals, in a very dramatic, public, and world-shaking way that would have been impossible for Thurman. His death was a tragedy for nonviolence, for civil rights, for America, for the hope that religion could be a force for unity and not division. King's assassination was an attempt to murder all of Thurman's most fervently held and cherished beliefs.

Thurman was perhaps fortunate that he wasn't obliged to remain alone with his thoughts after the news broke. KPFK, Los Angeles's left-of-center noncommercial radio station, contacted him to record a statement about King. He was given two hours to write it, and the station played it many times over the next several days and also quickly shared it with other radio stations—a friend in Boston heard Thurman's comments the following day. Subsequently, Thurman circulated his comments.[85] He was interviewed on San Francisco radio station LSFO on Sunday evening.[86] Earlier in the day, on

Sunday, 7 April, he presided at the service at Fellowship Church mentioned above. It opened with a litany, with responsive reading between Thurman and the congregation, focusing on King's children, emphasizing the personal, family aspects of his murder. He reminded those crowded into Fellowship Church that "it is so easy to forget that what you experienced in the light is no longer true because you are in the darkness. What you experienced in the light remains true and you must hold this until the light breaks again."[87]

What Thurman repeatedly said in the days after his murder was that King's greatest achievement had not been "his amazing charismatic power" or "his peculiar and challenging courage with its power to transform the fear-ridden Black men and women with a strange new valor" but that "he spoke from within the context of his religious experience, giving voice to an ethical insight which sprang out of his profound brooding over the meaning of his Judeo-Christian heritage." And this insight was that "discrimination, segregation, brutality, all these terrifying things" were not only wrong but were mortal sins and by his insistence on this "he gave organized religion no hiding place."[88] Thurman had been saying this for decades; King forced the entire world to take notice.

King also made liberal America, white and Black, put their bodies where their words were: "What we have lacked in America, for a long time," in terms of the social struggle "has been an authentic voice of ethical and moral awareness and responsibility that was not maudlin and sentimental."[89] For Thurman, King made his very existence a challenge to America: "If Martin had been an apostle of nonviolence without adding nonviolent direct action[,] then at the center of his nonviolence would have been a kind of sticky piety. But at the center of his nonviolence was always the insistence upon confrontation, upon facing with all of his passionate endeavor the total implication of this way of life and to do it with confidence."[90] He never allowed nonviolence to become a mere "technique" or a formula, for "a man can project love as a technique and not love" or speak of "non-violence and he himself be a man of violence." King insisted on testing his profession of nonviolence with direct action, so it did not "degenerate" into "a manipulating ethic."[91] Both the defenders and detractors of nonviolence often failed to understand this. For Blacks and whites alike, "something deep within us rejects nonviolent direct action as a dependable procedure for effecting social change. And yet, against this rejection something always struggles, pushing, pushing, always pushing with another imperative, another demand. It was King's fact that gave to this rejection flesh and blood, courage and vision, hope and enthusiasm."[92] For an apostle of nonviolence to die a violent death was at once a consummation of its ideal and perhaps also its refutation.

In the days after King's death Thurman had an almost biblical sense of divine judgment and wrath, warning of the likely consequences for America of its waywardness and backsliding. He closed his King sermon to Fellowship Church with a stern prophetic injunction: "Do not make God repent that he ever gave us the chance to live."[93] He told the interviewer on the San Francisco radio station after King's death, "I feel that once again American society has almost a split second in which to change the course of history." When his interviewer asked him if this sudden course correction was possible, he responded that we have the resources, "human and psychological, spiritual, material." He was less certain of whether Americans had "the will to do it."[94]

Thurman's belief in nonviolence was not so absolute as to not want to take strategic advantage of violence, or chaos, in the pursuit of a higher order. He hoped, as he had with similar episodes of Black violence, that while King's death "has released a great deal of activated heat, I think it also releases a great deal of activated concern and informed social grace." King's murder was a disaster, but "the sense of disaster can be a sense of creative disaster. And the little people whose voices have not been heard can whisper and be heard in this lull."[95] But he soon changed his mind. In that notorious year of disasters, 1968, it was hard to maintain that the concatenation of catastrophes was in any way creative. Frank Wilson wrote Thurman after King's murder, suggesting that "the sickness in the soul of America is revealed in one tragic symptom after another. What shall we do to be saved? Or is this sickness unto death?"[96] Thurman was leaning toward the second option when he replied to Wilson shortly after the murder of Robert Kennedy: "Two assassinations within a period of six months have left the country naked, frantic, and despairing. We do not know what to do about the tremendous hostilities and hatreds that have been generated by so many years of mal-living. . . . Whether the violence itself arises out of a great hatred or hostility or whether it is a desperate act of self-defense seems to have no bearing on the logic of the violent act itself. The only thing that violence knows to do is to perpetuate itself."[97]

In December of that year, in an unpublished preface for the reissued *The Negro Spiritual Speaks of Life and Death*, Thurman reached the nadir of his despair. What the contemporary situation revealed was "a vast amalgam of bitterness and hatred which no one dared to acknowledge," an anger that "was more than the emotions could absorb or the reasons tolerate." The result was a "polarization of Black and white" as "two ugly monoliths animated and charged with a terrible life of its own," which were "ruthless, bitter, destructive, blind to good and evil, each moving in its own relentless way." In "the maelstrom of the present social upheaval" Thurman found few silver linings.[98] In 1970, in a private journal, he wrote that Black Americans were "losing our compassion," that is, "the quality to feel with another and this is different from feeling *for* another." When one does this, "I place myself at his disposal and this means I trust him not to undertake my destruction. If in his desperation this is what he does then I must protect him and myself from catastrophe."[99] However, King's assassination underlined the growing sense of many Black Americans that this catastrophe was happening and that they would do better to save themselves than engage in a likely fruitless effort to save white America from its self-destruction.

In the late 1960s the divisions of white and Black, left and right, were often being exacerbated by the divisions between the young and the old, the endlessly discussed "generation gap." Living in San Francisco near the Haight-Ashbury and Castro districts, Thurman had a front-row seat to the theater of political and lifestyle changes that were shaping this sharp generational demarcation. He found it both exciting and perhaps somewhat scary. (He would say that in a very secular time, "of all the cities in America I think San Francisco is the most secular.")[100] If the "Summer of Love" could well have been a phrase promoted by Thurman, he was one San Franciscan who definitely did not wear a flower in his hair. That said, Thurman approached the generational problem with a good deal of humility, for, as he wrote in January 1969, "whatever we say about the behavior of the youth of our time must be said with a profound sense of guilt because in some very important way long before they were able to fail us, we failed them."[101]

The generational divide was the main topic in early 1969 during an interview in a Seattle television station. When the interviewer, Roberta Byrd Barr, asked him, "How do you reconcile yourself to this time?," he answered, "It is not very easy and not very hard, because I believe that a man has to honor the seasons through which he lives and to be current with himself, and therefore, I do not try to be what I should have been when I was twenty, at sixty-eight." Thurman felt he had to support the young generation of Blacks making their own way and stand back, and for him this "deepens the agony that I feel, because I can see the logic of . . . some of the things that are being done—which logic they cannot see. For if they could see it, it would cut the nerve-center of their activity, and that would be terrible." Even if they made mistakes, the younger generation "represent[s] the growing edge, and everything that I or anyone else can do to keep that alive and persistent and creative—I think we're under an obligation to do it, or else there's no future."[102]

In a follow-up interview, Thurman spoke to a group of eight Black college students (all male) who peppered him with tough questions. If most interviewers of Thurman tended toward the reverential, these men did not. They pushed Thurman to speak about political change, wanted to tie him down to concrete positions, and were generally impatient with his emphasis on personal spirituality. How was he, one asked, "attacking the problem of people's oppression and unfreedom in this society? What are you doing to attack that?" They wanted him to go beyond the "peace-love-God" stuff and wondered if he believed in a "wait-and-see, the unity of people with their God will take place and we'll all be together and all love at some point in the future" kind of religion. Did he believe in such things as "patience, tolerance, a priori faith in an ultimate salvation" that "de-emphasize assertive action?" Thurman replied that this wasn't how he defined his "religious idiom," which was that he and all people were persons "of infinite worth," a "worth that was not "contingent upon any social or political or economic classification."[103]

His interviewers were not satisfied with this answer. One stated, "You sort of rap about, sort of like a universal man concept," and they asked him, "Like can you break it down to me 'as a Black man' rather than just a man?" One stated that Thurman underestimated the power of white supremacy: "The white man controls the world in terms of life and death matters," and "he can just push a button," and then so much "for your ideals of cutting across the cultural and racial lines." Still another thought that because Thurman had "gotten up on the hill," he couldn't relate to ordinary Blacks. Yet another questioned his notion of "infinite worth": "How is this persona supposed to develop? Does it just sort of 'poof?'" They all wanted Thurman to explain how to make the transition from his sense of infinite worth to concrete social action.[104]

Thurman did his best to answer: "I certainly did not mean to convey the idea that I am postponing any sort of creative or sane or hale or healthy human relations to some far-off time in the future. But what I did say, what my thought indicates, is that we are involved in a many-sided struggle for which, in my thought, there is no simple, pat, automatic answer; that the problems are therefore very complex, and I think that they call for a wide range of attacks, rather than a particular solution that can be brought into play at any given moment in time." He was pressed on the need for immediate social change: "Yes, I agree. I agree . . . I think that I cannot wait for the complete end or collapse of the culture, or the civilization, or the system. So that it seems to me that I have got to use every political and economic and social instrument in my world." Thurman was then asked the Malcolm X question: Does this mean "by any means necessary?" Thurman replied: "I may be willing to go that far. My own limitation, and of this I speak quite frankly . . . I don't want to find myself using an instrument, the integrity of which I feel I can't quite trust, because of the way that instrument has victimized me." He could not "participate in the destruction of the system, until I begin something that is, to use my language, socially redemptive for me. It seems to me I just have to start somewhere, and I've got to start where I am."[105]

There might not have been a complete meeting of the minds at the interview, though afterward many of the students who had spoken with Thurman came away impressed. He was "a very heavy dude—very heavy, you know," and "a very mystical man," perhaps from "a long line of, maybe, voodoo doctors, and I'm saying this really in a real fine sense. He was really exciting." Another student said that what Thurman was really saying was when bad things happen, "what are you going to have to sustain you? And I think he talked a little bit about something that's philosophical, something that's mystical, something that's almost religious, that would sustain us." When Thurman started to talk, one man thought, "He's yesterday, but he certainly isn't today." But after a while he decided that "Dr. Thurman is sort of a man of the times." Perhaps he had made a partial convert or two, but Thurman knew that whatever he said, he would be viewed as an old man at a time when young African Americans were to a large extent uninterested in hearing wisdom from their elders. He would tell them, nonetheless.[106]

In the months after King's death, Thurman considered several writing projects. There was talk of Thurman writing a book on King, perhaps a biography.[107] He again considered an updated version of *Jesus and the Disinherited*.[108] He combined these ideas, and more, into what was to become his most ambitious book, *The Search for Common Ground: An Inquiry into the Basis of Man's Experience of Community*.[109] In 1971, when the book was completed, he said that it was "an expression of his concern about the way in which so many blacks were reacting to the King assassination by 'separating themselves behind self-imposed walls.'"[110] Although King is only discussed in the final pages of the book, he is a presence throughout, the embodiment of the ideal of community. King, for Thurman, "shot across the heavens like Halley's comet, making a mighty radiance in the light of which ancient dwellers in darkness could find their way to brotherhood."[111] Comets, to their ancient viewers, were signs in the heavens, and Thurman, who had vivid memories of the passage of Halley's Comet in 1910, also saw King's brief life as a harbinger: "Here at last was a man who affirmed the oneness of black and white under a transcendent unity, for whom community meant the profoundest sharing in the common life."[112]

However, King and the movement and struggle he represented occupy only the concluding section of *The Search for Common Ground*. The book takes a roundabout path to get there. Most of the book is concerned, instead, with Thurman's understanding of the idea of community. He is often, and rightly, seen as a preeminent theorist of community, largely on the basis of *The Search for Common Ground*.[113] It is nonetheless striking how late in his career that community becomes an explicit category in his thought. Before the mid-1950s, explicit references to "community" are fairly sporadic, and it was only in the early 1960s that he began to write extensively on the subject.[114] His first extended account of community is in February 1961 in the Mendelhall Lectures, four talks at DePauw University in Indiana, on the subject of "Community and the Will of God."[115] In a 1963 sermon, "Community and the Unity of Life," he indicated that he would publish something on this topic later that year, but nothing was forthcoming.[116] All of these sermons provide early versions of the arguments in *The Search for Common Ground*. On 10 December 1965, Thurman signed a contract with Harper and Row for a book to be titled "Man, Cobra, and Cosmos," that almost certainly was intended to be a study of community.[117]

Community, as Thurman understood it, above all, represented order, a living, natural, and divine ordering. It was not to be confused with the daily tumult of human interaction and intrusion. Thurman was a man who always guarded and prized his privacy and, indeed, believed that loneliness and isolation were an essential component of faith.[118] In 1961 he complained: "We have made an idol of togetherness which takes the form of a muted mass hysteria. Togetherness in this sense is the watchword of our times. It seems that it is more and more a substitute for God. In the great collective huddle, we are desolate, lonely, and frightened." Togetherness was the antithesis of community. Indeed, "there is within reach of every man not only a defense against the Grand Invasion but also the energy for transforming it into community."[119]

If Thurman didn't always use the term, the centrality of the idea of community had been part of Thurman's vision of the world from his early childhood. As he wrote in *The Search for Common Ground,* he had from early childhood "a tendency—even more, an inner demand—for 'whole-making,' a feel for a completion in and of things, for inclusive consummation."[120] This sort of "whole-making" was impossible among humans in Jim Crow Daytona, and Thurman sought it in nature. The natural world was the entrance to the real meaning of community, of which human attempts at community were at best a pale and inadequate facsimile. Thurman's favorite catchphrase, "the growing edge," refers to the regenerative ability of living cells, which demonstrated that "no expression of life exhausts life" and the unquenchable "upward reach of life."[121]

In 1944, perhaps for the first time, in "The Cosmic Guarantee in the Judeo-Christian Message," Thurman offered what would become a signature aphorism, a cryptic tautology, the "utterly astounding fact" that "life is alive."

Life, Thurman further explained, is "even more alive than any particular manifestation of life." Thurman's purpose was clear. If "the cosmos is the kind of order that sustains and supports life and its potentials," then it "sustains and supports the demands that the relationships between men and between man and God be one of harmony, integration, wholeness, all that we mean by love." If "life is alive," then life is indivisible. Segregation equals death.[122]

In the 1960s Thurman made explicit what had always been contained in his idea of "life": life is community. (And since "life" and God were largely interchangeable for Thurman, God was community, too.) In his 1961 lectures on "Community and the Will of God," he argued that the aliveness of life means that life is "goal-seeking," "purposive" and "directive" and that "life is synonymous with vitality."[123] Thurman gave considerable evidence for this proposition, drawing on naturalists, biologists, and other sources. The same arguments can be found in *The Search for Common Ground*. Cells cluster together, he explained, for various purposes: to fight disease, to communicate, to warn, to repair, and, above all, to collaborate. When the body is functioning properly, wholeness is maintained; equilibrium is restored. The human body is a community of communities: "If any part of the body loses its sense of community and thus strikes out on a course of independent, non-communal behavior . . . it becomes 'mal' or sick or out of harmony."[124] There may come a time, Thurman speculated in 1964, "when the stuff of human relations will manifest the same kind of order and harmony that the body has already learned."[125] Thurman did not limit this sense of vital community to individual organisms. There is a "common consciousness" in higher animals such as rattlesnakes, crows, dogs, gorillas, communicating both within and between species. Even trees have the ability to communicate. Some humans have cultivated this common consciousness and have developed a kind of extrasensory "kinship with all life."[126] Indeed, if "directiveness and creativeness are inherent in life," Thurman speculated, it might be possible to get beyond "the wall, barrier, or context" that separates one form of life, one species, from another, perhaps by means that were currently unacknowledged by contemporary science.[127]

Thurman understood "life" in its broadest possible sense. *The Search for Common Ground* opens with a poem by Robinson Jeffers that states, "there is not an atom in all the universes / but feels every other atom."[128] For Thurman "there is no unambiguous signpost marking in time and space at which the inanimate becomes the animate."[129] We are part of a "dynamic, living universe that breathes with elemental vitality. It is true, quite literally, that the earth itself breathes."[130] If Thurman never used the word "hylozoism"—the technical term for the position that all matter is in some sense alive—he was part of a long tradition of philosophical biological vitalism that held, in the words of one of its ablest chroniclers, that life has agency, "an intrinsic capacity to act in the world, to do things in a way that is neither predetermined nor random."[131] From this perspective, biology cannot be reduced to mechanical explanations: God is not a mere watchmaker; nature does not speak in the passive voice.[132] Thurman drew on many sources for this worldview, from Scholastic philosophers to Gandhi and Albert Schweitzer.[133] However, the most important influence on his evolutionary and biological thinking was Olive Schreiner. She rejected social Darwinism without rejecting Lamarckian evolutionism and believed that humanity and all of nature was evolving toward a higher destiny.[134] As Thurman wrote in "Community and the Will of God": "It was Olive Schreiner who suggested, many years ago, that one of the reasons why men cannot implement effectively any notion of respect for human personality is due to the fact that this excludes so much of life. And that men cannot have respect for human personality if they do not have a fundamental respect for all of life." And when humans respect this kinship, they discover that community was part of "the givenness of existence."[135]

But if community can be found in structures of the physical and natural world, it also adheres in the deepest roots of our common human culture. In *The Search for Common Ground* Thurman, in addition to his discussion of biology, explores creation myths, from Genesis to those of the Hopi in the American Southwest and the Apapocuva in Brazil.[136] Almost all creation stories share common features. They imply intent, a creative force, if not a creator. They start from the position of an original, primordial unity. "The collective memory of humanity" is an original situation that is "orderly, whole, completed, integrated, in fine, a climate of community." But all creation stories look back in sadness since the creation myth is invariably told with "an acute awareness of the absence of this," explaining how this order fell apart.[137]

But if our mythologies often begin in a postlapsarian lament for lost community, they also yearn for its restoration, and Thurman then turns his attention to the other end of the human voyage, in a study of utopian visions, what he calls "the search for the prophet's dream."[138] He discusses Plato's *Republic,* Thomas More's *Utopia,* and, above all, the Hebrew prophets who called the Israelites to form a holy community, as examples of utopian thinking. Thurman cites the famous prophecy of Isaiah that the "wolf shall dwell with the lamb" as an example of how "community shall be a literal fact in the fulfillment of life at every level."[139] The prophets insisted that "over against all of the discontinuity of any age or period, there is an unyielding continuity, the reality of the aliveness of life."[140]

Thurman then turns to human community in present-day America. Some have argued, with some reason, that Thurman's view of community was naïve, that, in the words of Victor Anderson, it "breeds an optimism about the possibility of human reconciliation that is hard to sustain in light of . . . the threat of mass urban and rural nihilism, and the often tragic qualities of daily life."[141] Perhaps. Thurman acknowledged that his conception of life and community might "easily fall into the category of wishful thinking," a "mirage, a delusion," or even might be "the fantasy of a mind unable to deal with the realities of its literal experience."[142] But Thurman's hopefulness had to be lived in a fallen world, and perhaps, as he wrote of the spirituals, he sought "a deep optimism arising out of the pessimism of life."[143] A man born and raised in Jim Crow Florida needed no lessons from later generations on the worst that was possible in human nature. But it was his conviction that cynicism, alienation, and isolation were self-defeating and self-negating luxuries that those with their backs against the wall could not afford. He wrote in *The Search for Common Ground* that, for many years, "I have had to wrestle with many spiritual crises growing out of what seemed to be the contradictory demands of love and hate, of vengeance and mercy, and of retaliation and reconciliation. In all of these experiences there is a part of me that seeks ever for harmony, for community, for unity and creative synthesis in conflicting relations; and an equally articulate urgency within me for withdrawal, for separateness, for isolation, and for aggression."[144] Thurman's optimism embraced, rather than tried to explain away, life's complexities and contradictions.

Reconciliations are always hard-won and always a work in progress, and certainly in post-King America Thurman found scant evidence that the idea of community was advancing, and much to suggest that it was regressing. Thurman provides a litany of examples: environmental, social, and political disorder, and "the immoral war in Vietnam."[145] The touchstone of community is the family, and "the family unit is a part of a larger social unit in an ever-widening circle of belonging." But in America Thurman found a "collapse of the family structure . . . as a sense of belonging and support."[146] He saw this decline as particularly pronounced among African Americans, as always the most vulnerable group in American society.[147]

Thurman in *The Search for Common Ground* does not limit the scope of his argument to African Americans. He includes other racial minorities, such as "Mexican-Latin Americans" and all those living in "the so-called Third World," and he writes movingly about the dispossession of American Indians and the destruction of their community, a history that it is "a long, slow, anguished dying" that is "worse than death."[148] But his argument is primarily addressed to his fellow African Americans. As in *The Luminous Darkness,* he was not too surprised that whites had retreated from the idea of a "common ground." What distressed him greatly was that Blacks, in increasing numbers, had no use for it either. The new Black sense of community was one formed "*of* the rejection of the white community rather than being rejected *by* the white community."[149] And as a consequence, "the antiblack hatemongers have become legitimized and, in many cases . . . violence and brutality against Negroes have been given moral and social sanction . . . [and] the will to segregate that is inherent in the structure in American society is more and more stripped of its disguises and making itself felt without its customary facades."[150]

White America had never really addressed the root cause of Black rage: "The residue that accumulated in the collective and individual psyche of the black man from the awful sense, *that always, under any and all circumstances, his life was utterly at the mercy of the white world, is the most important, single clue to the phenomena of the present,*" a hurt so deep that "the *bodies* of Negroes remember."[151] And for the first time, the younger generation of African Americans were expressing this rage, unfiltered and unconstrained, what Thurman had many years before called "the screaming of the disinherited," making sure that they would be heard, not caring how their message was received.[152] Thurman and those of his generation were "angered by their anger, even though secretly we marvel at the courage of their anger," expressing openly what their elders felt they could not.[153] And those of the older generation of African Americans understood why so much of the anger was directed at them: "They turn and rend us because we have sought to nourish them with the sense of our failure."[154]

But if Thurman tried to be understanding and sympathetic, he was also hurt by the "profoundly angry black man, hard and unyielding."[155] Thurman catalogued, in very personal terms, and with unusual public harshness, his displeasures with the new turn toward Black separatism, and the conviction that "only within fixed boundaries, *self-determined*—and that is the key word— that the goals of community could be experienced, achieved, or realized."[156] There was an upsurge in vulgarity—"the trade mark of many who had freed themselves of the contamination of the white society." As "Black is beautiful" and Blackness became "a metaphysic," those who seemed to question it in any way were deemed "Uncle Toms" or "traitors" to the new order, which was defended "with the strident insistence that any notion of inclusiveness was merest illusion, and the term 'brainwashed' was applied to anyone with a contrary point of view." There was a rejection of the "traditional tools" of education, such as reading and writing, in favor of "uprooting and replanting," which demanded that every Black institution be either razed or remade in this new image.[157] Those trying to "build community as a closed entity within the large society" were not only "suicidal" but displaying "the sheerest stupidity." Whites, who had tried for three centuries to isolate Black Americans, found that "what they were unable to accomplish after three hundred years is now being done for them without having to lift a finger."[158] In a rejection of King, "violence became the watchword" of the new ideal of community.[159]

But if Thurman was angered by Black anger, he reserved his greatest ire for white anger at Black anger. If Blacks were now rejecting white society, white American certainly had it coming. Indeed, in the current circumstances, "the new sense of community within self-determined boundaries seems the most realistic and immediately practical solution to a cruel and otherwise seemingly insoluble problem."[160] That said, it was his considered judgment that the "present solution is a stopgap," a "halt in the line of march toward full community," a "time of bivouac on a promontory overlooking the entire landscape of American society."[161] Eventually, "the liquid fires of Martin Luther King's dream," the words and voice of a new prophet, will again sweep "all before it in one grand surge of beatific glory." The new prophet will teach that "community cannot feed for long on itself; it can only flourish where always the boundaries are giving way to the coming of others from beyond them."[162]

Thurman's statement that "community cannot feed for long on itself" is Thurman at his most eloquent, a succinct summary of his entire social philosophy. But those who had read *The Search for Common Ground* from the beginning would have recognized that in saying this, Thurman was not just offering a metaphor or a striking observation. It was, in some ways, for Thurman, a simple biological fact. "Community" too, properly understood, was a living entity. It was alive. In *The Luminous Darkness* he had written: "The burden of being Black and the burden of being white is so heavy that it is rare in our society to express oneself as a human being," and to be human "the individual must have a sense of kinship to life that transcends and goes beyond the immediate kinship of family or the organic kinship that binds him ethnically, 'racially,' or nationally. . . . [H]e belongs to the whole kingdom of life that includes all that lives and perhaps, also, all that has ever lived . . . to be a human being, then, is to be essentially alive in a living world."[163]

This was the common ground. The common ground was not a place of compromises, for tentative, tepid reconciliations, for resigned settlings for only half a loaf, where dreams are thwarted by dull, implacable necessity. It is a place of self-realization, where life is truly alive, where humans will relearn the meaning of community as something liberating, not confining. Thurman told George Makechnie after completing the book that he was "struck with the feeling that here I had set down in rather formal terms what reveals itself as my lifelong working paper."[164] *The Search for Common Ground* was at once his most personal book, in some ways even more so than his autobiography, and at the same time his most comprehensive, his most successful attempt to put down, in one place, his entire worldview.

Thurman's conception of the common ground, and the audacious mystical political ecology that undergirded it, had been a part of his thinking for decades. But he felt the need to articulate it at a time when his own vision of progress had been shattered by an assassin's bullet and by a civil rights revolution that had stalled and fissured, seemingly unable to hold its own against the teeming and gathering forces of the counterrevolution, now a movement seemingly coming aground. *The Search for Common Ground* was the alternative to despair. If humanity's move toward community was too fickle, there were other resources to draw upon, other communities, found out-of-doors, or observed through the microscope or telescope, to admire and emulate. The late science writer Stephen Jay Gould once wrote he had "a somewhat cynical rule of thumb in judging arguments about nature that also have overt social implications: when such claims imbue nature with just those properties that make us feel good or fuel our prejudices, be doubly suspicious."[165] It is a good rule, and when Thurman was in a skeptical mood he expressed similar sentiments.[166] Nonetheless, and without passing judgment on his biological speculations, I would add only that Thurman knew the odds African Americans and other disinherited peoples faced in overcoming segregation and its lingering, inertial vestiges and the vast task in trying to fight the entrenched will to maintain artificial human divisions and inequalities. Those who would dare challenge this needed not only God to be on their side but also to enlist as allies everything that breathes and grows, every planet revolving around every star, and every atom in the universe.

15

With Head and Heart

At the very beginning of the 1970s, in January and February, Howard and Sue took their last foreign trip, a two-month cruise. The era of the ocean liner was rapidly coming to an end, but the Thurmans booked passage on a ship still plying the South Pacific. They had sailed through this part of the world on their return from Africa, and they wanted a second look. The trip was accompanied by a number of moral quandaries, as Thurman recorded in a journal he kept for its duration. How could they justify taking a voyage of this sort "at this moment of such grave tensions?" How in "light of such great human need" in the world could they "possibly justify this form of luxury and all the indulgences that it represents?" Given the financial need even within his own family, "how could such an investment be rationalized?" One way to do so was to acknowledge that the trip was a gift to the Thurmans from their wealthy benefactors, who were picking up most of the costs. But if this made financing the trip possible, it only increased his guilt over its auspices. Others were paying for Thurman to get some much-needed R&R, with the expectation that he would be rejuvenated and resume his career as the great Howard Thurman. Once he accepted their money, there was an implied "commitment to the future in terms of work and service." But what if he just wanted to take their money? After a lifetime of "reaping and sowing," what if he wanted to do neither and just lie fallow? But he knew that this was impossible. However they got to where they were, whether on the ship's passage or on life's journey, he concluded, "at any rate, here we are."[1]

There are hints that Thurman had recently been out of sorts, in a depressed mood, perhaps brought on by stress and overwork.[2] For many decades he had viewed long ocean voyages as the perfect restorative, with perhaps some remembrances of childhood reveries on Daytona Beach. The time in the South Pacific did the trick: "At last I am beginning to feel a bit rested. It is the first complete rest that I have had in nearly 40 years. I had no idea what boundless fatigue I had accumulated." He added, "The sea is so healing and slowly something way down deep inside of me is stirring—so much of life comes back into a wonderful luminous perspective."[3] He wrote Rabbi Dudley Weinberg that on the trip he had been collecting decades of overdue "back rent."[4]

On the voyage, Thurman took the injunction to strip himself down to his bare essentials literally, writing Weinberg: "Can you imagine what it's like, Dudley, to walk into your cabin at eleven o'clock in the morning and hear your bed say to you, 'Where in the world have you been? I'm tired [of] waiting.' I had no idea what it would be like to go to bed, minus all clothes of any kind, two or three times a day."[5] This was evidently one of Thurman's favorite means of relaxation, a sort of Quaker nudism of the spirit. Edward Kaplan remembers Thurman telling his class at Amherst College that it was his custom, particularly if he had been in preaching and intense interaction with others, that "at the end of the day I take off my clothes lie down on my bed and let the day drain out of me."[6]

Howard and Sue took special care to ensure their privacy on their journey, knowing that "the matter of the racial character of American Society" did not stop at the boundary of its territorial waters. They assumed that they were likely to be the only African Americans on the cruise. There was a strong possibility that their fellow passengers "would be but an intricate reflection of the social climate of American & Western culture," responding to them with some combination of hostility and awkwardness, with the result that the Thurmans would be constantly reminded of their Blackness. If so, the danger of "the whole purpose of our going being undermined" was considerable. They asked for and received their own table and then worried about how this would be perceived. They wanted to "keep the initiative in our hands as to the extent of our interest in socializing" but would have to do so "without being defiant, sensitive, aggressive or reticent." After almost a half century of being a promoter of interracial harmony, Thurman was still delicately navigating his way through white America and, when confiding in his journal, still annoyed at the effort it required and the toll it exacted: "We are free to be as available or as withdrawn as we wish—which is normal for the white passengers but for non-white, particularly, black, must be worked out."[7]

All of Thurman's extended overseas trips were voyages into the netherworld of imperialism and its aftermath. After they boarded the SS *President Wilson* in San Francisco, the next port of call, after Hawaii, was Tahiti. With visions of Gauguin in his head, he found that the Tahitians "seemed gay and carefree but it struck me as being more a cliché than a reality." They had perfected the art of appearing to be what white tourists wanted them to be. This made Thurman very uncomfortable: "It is strange how I could not resist the feeling of guilt to be one among the tourists. . . . This has come over me many times in my travels—a sense of shame to be classified with American white society and regarded in the same way. Sometimes I have wanted to shout, I am with them by necessity but I am not one of them." Seeing a life-size poster of Martin Luther King, Jr., in a local Roman Catholic church brightened his mood.[8]

In the South Pacific, the Thurmans were traveling through the last large area on the planet to undergo decolonization. Many of the destinations they visited—Tahiti, Fiji, American Samoa, the Territory of Papua and New Guinea, Hong Kong, and Guam—were (and in some cases still are) colonial possessions. Imperialism was much on his mind. When he was in Fiji, set to become independent later in 1970, he noted that "British imperialism seems subtle, behind the scenes, very class conscious and steeped in Anglo Saxon notions of superiority. There was an air of arrogance even among the British children we encountered in the streets. I was glad to leave." He noted correctly that the British legacy would be a hornet's nest in the form of the substantial East Indian population they imported in the late nineteenth century to work the sugar plantations, washing their hands of the violent ethnic and political fights to follow between the Indians and those of native Fijian ethnicity.[9]

American Samoa, he concluded "is American Imperialism" superimposed on a Native population. He complained that his tour guide, a Samoan who had spent time in Los Angeles, "was glib, smart-alec, quick in repartee—in other words exhibiting the most reprehensible aspects of our culture." The indigenous Samoans "did not seem sad or happy but resigned." He found Western imperialism to have a deadening impact on the indigenous cultures he saw, from the "terrible decayed teeth" among the Tahitians, to the general imperialist rot encountered everywhere. His thoughts turned to his first encounter with European colonialism: "I am more confused about the religious significance of Christianity in the world than I was 35 years ago when the issue was first raised for me in India."[10]

In the South Pacific, Thurman had much time for what he called "brooding." He worried that Blacks in America were being "overtaken by a vast tidal wave of anger and our joy is dying" and that "we stand on the threshold of a deep inner collapse." Joy had existed previously because of the ability to process the hate and hostility endemic in white America without being poisoned by it. This was changing: "We [Black Americans] are internalizing the hostility and the hate by which we have been surrounded for so many years. Something in the soul has gone sour. Apparently, we have reached the point of zero in what can be absorbed without saturation." These unsettling thoughts aside, Thurman's time in the South Pacific was deeply restorative. "I am coming to the end of the journey. . . . Sue and I have enjoyed each other fully. There has been time for much long and solid talk. It has been an unheralded delight to . . . savor each other's thoughts and to get perspective on our journey through the years. The years have been good."[11]

The 1970s would be the last full decade of Thurman's life. As one ages, old friends depart: "One by [one] the leaves fall from the trees and the cycle ends, to begin again. This is the story of life and this is the fate of man."[12] So Thurman wrote Coleman Jennings in 1966, after the passing of Herbert King, who had been his closest friend in the 1930s and 1940s, a friendship of the deepest intimacy. For reasons that are not clear, there was a cooling off in the 1940s, though by the 1960s their close friendship was reestablished, with much of the jocularity he reserved for his closest African Americans friends, addressing King as "Dear Brother of the Fallen Order of the Sons of Ham."[13] By the 1960s, King was teaching at the McCormick Theological Seminary in Chicago. Thurman, Frank Wilson, and King formed a triumvirate, getting together when their schedules and travels allowed, with their last meeting probably in Chicago in April 1966.[14] Three months later Herbert King was dead. Howard could not make it to Chicago for the funeral; Sue attended. Shortly thereafter he wrote about King's passing: "It seems incredible that those who walk the way with you for so long a time disappear in the mist. There is a strange necessity in the human spirit that cannot accept this as final."[15]

However, in his final decades, Thurman was lucky enough to make a number of new friends to supplement his losses, speaking to the many facets of his personality. One of the closest relationships over the last three decades of Thurman's life was with the poet and writer Jean Burden.[16] His letters to her offered a view of the most personal and private parts of his life, a glimpse that he gave few others. Burden, living in Southern California, had been invited, around 1950, to attend a service at Fellowship Church. She became an immediate convert.[17] Burden's article on Thurman, appearing in the *Atlantic* in October 1953, was the best and most insightful treatment of Thurman yet to appear.[18] Like many whites drawn to Thurman, Burden was a spiritual seeker, dissatisfied with conventional Christianity, an explorer of Zen Buddhism, Theosophy, and other esoteric religious traditions.[19] Thurman gave Burden "the greatest gift one can give anyone," release from "self-hate" and "self-doubt," a gift he gave many.[20] Although Thurman and Burden never lived in close proximity (facilitating the flow of their correspondence), "in all the unspoken regions unlit by day," Burden wrote, "we were in the same place." It was an epistolary friendship in which the correspondence often took on the quality of a platonic love affair: "I need to feel that I am inside your coat pocket," she wrote him in 1974, "where you can reach down and give me a squeeze once in a while. . . . My tears are stormier than the gentle rain."[21]

Burden, writing a tribute following Thurman's death, asked the following question: "Did anyone ever think of his color after being in his presence more than thirty seconds? He could have been purple or polka dotted for all any of us cared. Though I do not mean by that his blackness was not vital to everything he did. It was. But in another sense, he transcended color as he transcended so much else."[22] Almost everyone who knew Thurman said something similar. After his death, Jesse Jackson, a great admirer, said Thurman was "black, but he did not wear his blackness as a garment. . . . He did not have to work at being black, he was black without effort; and so, he focused beyond ethnicity on that which is ethical."[23] Both Burden and Jackson understood Thurman well. But what might have seemed effortless to those who met Thurman later in life was surely the product of decades of dogged determination to be at once fully Black, fully American, and fully human, and a refusal to define himself through the dichotomies that governed American race relations. He never ignored America's racial realities, but he rejected their stability, their finality, their dominion over the lives of those on either side of the divide. To many living through the racial chaos of the times, and to many African Americans, Thurman's solution seemed be an anomaly, or even an impossibility. The 1970s were, in many ways, Thurman's most challenging decade, a time that put one of his most cherished aphorisms—"the contradictions of life are never final"—to the test.[24] Black America as a whole spent the 1970s defining and debating the universalities and particularities of their racial identity and their status as Americans, and what it meant to be citizens of a country that could both create and destroy a Martin Luther King, Jr. Thurman was very much a part of this searching.

One person who shared many of Thurman's views on these matters was Whitney Young Jr., the leader of the National Urban League, who had transformed that somewhat somnolent concern into a militant civil rights organization. In the 1960s, Young and Thurman became close. "How I wish I could sit down for a whole evening," Thurman wrote Young in 1966, "and think with you about things old and new."[25] The admiration only increased when other civil rights leaders, such as James Farmer and King, passed from the scene. Thurman was shocked by Young's sudden death in 1971 and was one of his eulogists. Thurman told the large crowd assembled at Riverside Church in Upper Manhattan that Young was utterly unsentimental about the power relationships in American society and knew that "American life is largely controlled and dominated by white society," and more specifically a narrow elite within it who "have in their hands the power of veto and certification" over the economic well-being of the vast majority of Americans, "poor and dependent," many of whom "may be designated as among the Wretched of the earth."[26] This invocation of the Internationale or Frantz Fanon was not a call to revolution but for radical equality, in all spheres of life—in economic and political life, and in recognition and realization of the "infinite worth" of every individual. In this quest, speaking for the powerless to the powerful, Young called for justice, not charity. He "was a bridge between; he was not a beggar."[27]

Young's funeral at Riverside Church brought together, at least for one sad afternoon, a remarkably diverse crowd, everyone from U.S. Attorney General (and soon to be convicted Watergate co-conspirator) John Mitchell to fiery Black nationalists like Amiri Baraka, who was a pallbearer.[28] Thurman stated he could "think of no other occasion which, by choice, would bring together the very rich and the poor, the black separatist and the white segregationist, those who had abandoned all hope for the internal reordering of society on the basis of equality of opportunity and privilege, and those who were dedicated to an orderly reshuffling of priorities which would give maximum participation to all in the fruits of a good society."[29] But this common ground never really existed, just politely gathered for an instant to honor the memory of a great man before everyone went their separate ways.

For John Mitchell and his boss, Richard Nixon, the main reason to eulogize Young was to rhetorically bury Black radicalism and dichotomize a supposedly safe and unthreatening Young with the scary alternative. Thurman was in a similar position, a potential African American great white hope: calm and not angry, an advocate of reconciliation and integration, not separation or armed revolution. Thurman never accepted that dichotomy and would not let himself be played that way. This did not mean, as we have seen, that he minced his words when it came to Black separatism. At times his attitudes could be surprisingly rigid. When he heard of a suggestion in 1967 from the eminent rabbi Abraham Joshua Heschel "about the urgency for a publication by Negroes about Negroes," Thurman thought that would be "turning the clock back" and was "fearful at this moment in American history of that which would tend to isolate us from the current of American life and struggle."[30]

He felt the same way about ongoing efforts to establish Black caucuses or groups within mainstream denominations. In May 1968, Black members of the Unitarian Universalist denomination called for the creation of a Black

Affairs Council, one that would be supported financially by the denomination but would otherwise be entirely independent of denominational control. Thurman disapproved. A partial solution, he suggested, would be for the Unitarian Universalists to hire more Black clergy.[31] In April and May 1969, James Forman, a former leader in the Student Nonviolent Coordinating Committee (SNCC), issued his "Black Manifesto," a call for white Christians and Jews to pay $500 million in reparations, declaring "war on the white Christian churches and synagogues" and a willingness to fight for his demands "by whatever means necessary."[32] This included attention-grabbing disruptions of services at the wealthy and liberal Riverside Church in New York City and a takeover of the New York City headquarters of the Presbyterian Church. Thurman wrote Frank Wilson, a prominent Black Presbyterian official: "Of course, who am I to compete with the prophet of the 21st Century, Foreman [sic]. I understand that he turned the Presbyterians every way but loose. His cohorts invaded headquarters while he himself was 'manifestoing' on the floor of the General Assembly. Seriously, Frank, I wish I could talk to you about all of this. I have ideas, man."[33]

However, Thurman's response to the nationalist and separatist turn in Black politics and culture was multisided. Perhaps complete consistency was impossible. As Beth Ruhde, a close student of Thurman, observed, he often explored polarization and opposites before attempting synthesis and integration.[34] Without relinquishing his profound distaste for any form of Black separatism, he never ceased wanting to remain connected to the dominant currents of African American opinion. Any criticisms needed to be offered as a sympathetic insider, not as an outside scold. Thurman never lacked an abundance of racial pride, and if wearing it on one's sleeve was the new style, he could adjust, after his own fashion. He spoke at the conventions of the racially militant National Committee of Black Churchmen, he preached on the subject of Black Pentecost and other "Black" topics. In his writing and preaching he slowly but steadily made the transition away from using "Negro" in his writing and speeches. Regardless of how Thurman saw himself, others had no difficulty in viewing Thurman from a Black liberation or Afrocentric perspective. In 1974, Irvin Stuart Moxley wrote the first dissertation on Thurman, "An Examination of the Mysticism of Howard Thurman and Its Relevance to Black Liberation." He wrote Thurman the year of its completion that "your words have always been meaningful to my Blackness, and I know you will continue to give men that revolutionary strength to be free and free others."[35]

Perhaps no one more epitomized the nationalist turn in Black religious and political life than the person many saw as King's successor, Jesse Jackson. At a commencement address at Howard University in 1970 he told the assembled,

"It's Nation Time!," and when the audience stood and shouted "right on!" he raised one hand in a Black Power salute and the other in a V sign.[36] The same year he was claiming that integration was a "systematic plan to destroy blacks."[37] And yet, Jackson was an ardent disciple of Thurman. Their bond was intense. When they were together, Jackson, according to his close associates, "literally sat at the master's feet."[38] Thurman was, for Jackson, "a teacher of teachers, a leader of leaders, a preacher of preachers."[39] Jackson has claimed that his familiar catchphrase, "I am Somebody," which he first used during the Poor People's Campaign in Washington, D.C., in June 1968, was inspired by his reading of *Jesus and the Disinherited*.[40] After Thurman's death, Jackson said he taught that "if your spirit is disciplined and determined, and your will is cultivated, that is more than enough." This, said Jackson, was the "philosophical presupposition" of the entire civil rights movement.[41]

Another Black intellectual who combined a sharp critique of integration with a deep admiration of Thurman was the controversial legal theorist Derrick A. Bell Jr. (He argued that the U.S. Supreme Court in 1954 should not have overturned *Plessy* but instead mandated that separate institutions be truly equal.) Despite their political differences, Bell cited Thurman favorably in his books, was a trustee for the Howard Thurman Educational Trust, and wrote him congratulatory letters after his public appearances. According to a man who knew both, the Rev. Paul Smith, the two "spent quality time together," and "Bell honed his skills as a brilliant law professor through his conversations with Howard Thurman." When Bell was dying, he asked Smith to read to him from Thurman's writings on the spirituals.[42]

Bell was not the only African American integration skeptic close to and influenced by Thurman. These included several of the most important Black writers of African American history during the civil rights era. Vincent Harding (1931–2014) combined the careers of an academic historian, lay religious thinker, and political activist. He followed a similar trajectory to Jackson, apprenticing with King in the Southern Christian Leadership Conference (SCLC)—he drafted King's famous address opposing the war in Vietnam delivered at Riverside Church on 4 April 1967—and, like Jackson, was an early embracer of the rhetoric of Black Power.[43] Harding became one of the most prominent African American religious intellectuals of his generation, a pioneer in what came to be called "Black theology." In 1967, he caustically rejected the recent civil rights past when "nonviolence was our watchword and integration our heavenly city" as so much "smugness" and "sentimental yearning" for a unity that never really existed.[44] In 1970, as director of the nationalist-oriented, Atlanta-based, Institute of the Black World, he dismissed the idea of integration, asking who "wants to integrate with cancer?"[45]

Vincent Harding adored Howard Thurman. Harding came to San Francisco as often as he could. When they were together, there was "listening, understanding, admonishing when necessary, sharing silence, surrounding and undergirding me with prayers. . . . Indeed, it may be that he was the wisest and most compassionate man I have ever known . . . [a] mentor and father-in-the-faith."[46] Harding recalled "how carefully and sympathetically he questioned me about the Black Power/Black Identity movement."[47] Harding's masterwork was his militant, nationalist-inspired history of Black resistance to slavery, *There Is a River* (1981).[48] Thurman helped him find a publisher, and his *Deep River* was the source of its title and inspiration for its theme, "a narrative, analytical, and celebrative history of the freedom struggle of black people in this country," with its "long, continuous movement, flowing like a river."[49] The book appeared shortly after Thurman's death. On the top of the dedication page, it reads:

To the memory of Howard Thurman
Father in the faith,
Companion in the way,
Dauntless and peaceable warrior
For a world of love, justice, and truth.[50]

But by the time *There Is a River* appeared, Harding was evolving as a historian, in no small part due to Thurman's influence. The following year, asked for the major influences on his historical writing, he touted Thurman as "one of those older Black men who constantly lived ahead of their time. . . . [He] cannot easily be labeled. He was theologian, mystic, visionary, pastor, and concerned citizen-creator of a new, multiracial American reality."[51] Moving away from African American history as such, in the 1980s and 1990s he was a pioneer in what came to be called multicultural history. When asked about this shift in 1997, he answered that he hadn't changed, but now emphasized the inherent potential for all peoples to benefit from the Black struggle for freedom: "Black people were in a sense breathing in the fragrance of what democratic development could do for us and the nation."[52]

Lerone Bennett's *Before the Mayflower*, first published in 1962, with many subsequent editions, was probably the most widely read overview of African American history published during the civil rights era. Bennett (1928–2018) had similar views to Harding, and as the longtime senior editor of *Ebony* magazine, he popularized the phrase "Black Power" and used his editorial perch to broadly disseminate his distinctive brand of nationalist-influenced Black history and politics.[53] He was active in Harding's Institute of the Black World, and in addresses there in the late 1960s, he called for quasi-revolutionary and autonomous structures of Black governance in America's cities. He sharply castigated those in the Black community who, in his opinion, had failed to rise to the "challenge of Blackness."[54]

Thurman, in Bennett's view, was up to the challenge. Bennett was a great admirer of Thurman. Both Morehouse graduates, they first met in the 1950s.[55] By 1968 Thurman was sending Bennett his latest books and sermon recordings, and Bennett, in turn, was giving him updates on "the blazing sense of togetherness" in "the Black Consciousness Movement."[56] A decade later, in 1978, in a lengthy article in *Ebony,* "Howard Thurman: 20th Century Holy Man," Bennett offered his readers a moving account of his life and his lifework. Probably no article about Thurman in his lifetime reached more African American readers. It opened describing Thurman as a "shy, retiring, God-intoxicated theologian," some of whose admirers say that he "is a saint or, at the least, the nearest thing to a saint we are likely to see in the 20th century." Thurman demurred over his canonization, but for Bennett, Thurman was "a Black world soul" who was rooted in the "universality of his own idiom."[57] It was, he wrote in a eulogy, "an honor to live in the same world with this man."[58]

A third historian in Thurman's ambit was Nathan I. Huggins (1927–1989). Few persons, outside of their daughters, were ever as close to the Thurmans. His was a life of remarkable achievement punctuated by tragedy. He was born in Chicago in 1927 to an African American father and a Jewish mother. By the time he was fourteen, he and his sister were parentless and living in the Bay Area. At some point their paths crossed that of the Thurmans, who opened their home to them. With their encouragement, Huggins, a high school dropout, attended the University of California at Berkeley, where he studied history and then went to Harvard for his doctorate. (By which time, the Thurmans, living in Boston, were again in close proximity.) He went on to an illustrious career as a professional historian that culminated in 1980 when he was named the first W. E. B. Du Bois Professor of History and Afro-American Studies and director of the W. E. B. Du Bois Institute for Afro-American Research at Harvard University. He also served, for many years, as vice chairman of the Howard Thurman Educational Trust. He died much too soon. In Huggins's 1989 obituary, his survivors were listed as his wife and "his adoptive mother, Sue Bailey Thurman of San Francisco."[59] Thurman himself, of course, was by then deceased, but he had written Huggins in 1964 that their relationship was that "between a father and his son."[60] It was a spiritual, if not a legal adoption.[61]

Unlike Harding and Bennett, Huggins shared Thurman's broadly integrationist views and historical sensibility, an awed appreciation of the African American pursuit of what Huggins called the "transcendence of tyranny" in the face of near-impossible odds, an attitude that suffuses his history of slavery, *Black Odyssey: The African American Ordeal in Slavery,* published in 1977. Its final words praise Thurman for bringing "slave religion into serious discussion for the first time," noting that his works have "often been the starting point for recent historians."[62] In 1971, Huggins, sounding much like Thurman, called for a vibrant African American history, but not "historical emotionalism" or history "obliterated by strong feelings of black rage and white guilt."[63] These he compared to "biting on an aching tooth, sucking pleasure from the pain of it."[64] Huggins insisted that Black history was inseparable from American history in general. "What is remarkable about much that is called black culture," he wrote, "is its Americanness; and conversely, much of what is considered most uniquely American is essentially Afro-American."[65]

How to explain Thurman's influence on so many African American historians, thinkers, and leaders in the 1970s? To all who came to him, he was a spiritual mentor, more interested in the person and their spiritual life than their politics. Jesse Jackson said of Thurman that he was a "spirit doctor" who "cherished stripping people with penetrating questions" with "a kind of spiritual laser-beam." ("Who are you?," he asked Jackson. "I know you're famous and all, but *who are you?*")[66] At the same time, Thurman's appeal transcended ideology and is one more example of the truism that students of African American thought need to avoid the clumsy pigeonholing and sorting of complex political stances into broad and mutually exclusive categories as integrationist, assimilationist, nationalist, or separatist.

Thurman was an acute historical thinker, and for the historians who came into contact with him, *Jesus and the Disinherited* was a model of creative Black history writing. Despite its mere 112 pages, there is an epic quality to Thurman's short book, a history unburdened with facts or dates, a history that both generalizes and personalizes its subjects, and places the pain and beauty of the quest for self-knowledge of enslaved people and their descendants at the center of the American story, and was emulated and expanded upon by Harding, Bennett, Huggins, and others.

Thurman, when angered, could sound as irate as any 1960s or 1970s radical complaining about the treatment of Blacks in standard histories. In 1971 he complained to Lerone Bennett that the history of the Southern Christian Leadership Conference was "being told, for the most part, by white camp followers who kept diaries and who will become the official historians of what took place," and that this was a "vast catastrophe," and he wanted Bennett to address this.[67] But at the same time, one of the messages of *Jesus and the Disinherited* was that the history of African Americans was as universal in its significance as that of Jews in first-century CE Palestine. Black historians had to tell this story in their own way, but they couldn't hoard it. When Bennett insisted that Black history "must be interpreted both in terms of its particularity and universality," he was echoing Howard Thurman.[68]

Questions of universality and particularity were at the core of Thurman's response to the growing interest of African Americans in Black identity. When called to talk about it, he would do so in his own way. He never treated Blackness as a metaphysical or religious category. In 1972 he was asked to deliver a sermon on the subject of "Black Pentecost" to a Black audience in Roxbury, Massachusetts.[69] He spoke of the Pentecost event, the gathering of the followers of Jesus, "from every nation under heaven," experiencing the descent of the Holy Spirit. For Thurman, the key fact of the Pentecost event was that "every man heard the Word in his own tongue."[70] An individual can only hear a message, even one from the heavens, from within the context of their own lives. So if Blacks hear a Black message, that doesn't mean that others will experience it in the same way. Pentecost "could be green experience, it could be red experience, it could be white experience." But Thurman was there to speak about Black Pentecost, and he spoke about his enslaved grandmother and his life experiences. The ultimate message of Black Pentecost, he told his listeners in Roxbury, was that it could not be exclusively Black, and starting from experience that was parochial or sectarian, from "the tiny cell in which" Blacks have been confined, it was "possible for that kind of experience to supply enough energy to support a universal morality, a universal brotherhood." In a similar vein, in the late 1970s he claimed that "the outcome of every sectarian religion or point of view is inclusive rather than exclusive. Black revolutionaries are no longer considering separatism as viable."[71]

Thurman found a similar stumbling from particularity to universality in the history of the United States, restated with great eloquence in a sermon he delivered in the bicentennial year of 1976, "America in Search of a Soul."[72] It bursts with providentialism and American exceptionalism: "Don't be upset by what seems to be a doctrine of manifest destiny," he warned his listeners at one point. Don't be bothered by that." America was the product of a motley agglomeration of peoples, forcibly thrown together in a foreign land, wrested from its Native inhabitants, "a fertile land, a benevolent and beneficent land," the enslaved and their enslavers, the American Indians and their expropriators, the weak and the strong, all pursuing, often ruthlessly, their self-interest. Yet this human patchwork created a nation whose ideals were so extravagantly exalted it would take centuries to realize. "It was as if the Creator of existence wanted to discover whether or not a certain ideal could be realized in time and space," an experiment in whether "somewhere on the planet there would be a primary unit of human beings" who would learn to cross "lines of race, of color, of creed, or background, of enforced or restricted neighborhoods" or shatter itself trying.[73]

For Thurman, freedom was the process whereby "standing in my place where I am, I can so act in that place as to influence, order, alter, or change the future." It begins by the taking of "responsibility for how . . . I must react to the forces that impinge upon my life, forces that are not responsive to my will, my desire, my ambition, my dream, my hope—forces that don't know that I'm here."[74] Liberty, on the other hand, was dispensed by the state: "It can be given, it can be taken away." Those without liberty cannot easily exercise their freedom. But freedom was not "the exercise of option." It was rather "the sense of option, the sense of alternatives which only I can effect." And no one, unless you let them, can take this away. He related the story of when as a boy, to impress his older sister, he stepped on a small snake, and although the snake couldn't move forward, it continued to wiggle, thereby keeping "alive the sense of option."[75] This for Thurman was the meaning of the American dream for the disinherited in America, stepped upon, under a heavy boot, nonetheless still trying to wiggle, writhe, and squirm their way forward. Like perhaps Thurman's grandmother, Nancy Ambrose. She was born into slavery and lived her long life in an America in which she never really had her liberty. But never, for a moment, did she lose her sense of freedom.

Thurman in the 1970s continued to encourage and disseminate the values and issues most important to him, the advancement of African Americans and their concerns, and the universality of his religious vision. The Howard Thurman Educational Trust (HTET) became an increasingly important vehicle for this, especially in its reorientation to more specifically promote Thurman and his works. This had not been Howard and Sue's original intention. Nonetheless, as a Trust document from May 1980 stated, "Although Dr. Thurman has never sought to be the center of attention," it was "inevitable that his words nevertheless form the core of the Trust's work."[76] It is certainly true that the common bond for those involved in the Trust was a shared admiration for the works of Howard Thurman, and it was not too surprising that the Trust, by the mid-1970s, was devoting increasing attention and resources to getting out the message about its tutelary spirit.

The Trust, through Thurman, was in possession of his burgeoning collection of recorded sermons, lectures, addresses, and eulogies that he had been accumulating since 1949. Thurman had tried some dissemination of his recorded remarks on long-playing records and occasional transcriptions of them since his days at Fellowship Church, but these tended to be relatively small-scale operations. In the late 1960s the new technology of the cassette tape made it possible for the first time to inexpensively disseminate recorded texts. By 1977 more than eight hundred different meditations, sermons, and lectures were available from the Trust.[77] A full set of the tapes was stored in a fireproof vault in downtown San Francisco. Thurman considered the cassette recordings in the Trust offices his "technological immortality."[78] The distribution of the tapes led to the establishment of what became known as listening rooms, where individuals or groups could come to listen to tapes or simply have a quiet place for personal reflection. The first listening room was at the San Francisco headquarters of the Trust. Their numbers rapidly increased, and by 1980 there were about thirty listening rooms, primarily in the United States, at historically Black colleges, Boston University, the Cathedral of St. John the Divine, and other locations in the United States and overseas, including a listening-room project in apartheid-era Capetown.[79] After Thurman's death in 1981, the listening rooms began to cease operations. The idea of the listening room survives in the online "Virtual Listening Room" of the Howard and Sue Bailey Thurman Collections at Boston University, making Thurman's recorded sermons freely available to all.[80]

If the listening rooms provided the Trust with one form of outreach, in-depth seminars with the rising Black generation of scholars, ministers, and thinkers offered another. The Trust in 1980 stated that while it "never planned it this way" and there was "never any promotion of inspirational seminars at the San Francisco headquarters," the "requests kept coming in, and finally a series of seminars came to life." After starting in early 1975, by November 1980 eleven seminars had been held at the Trust headquarters. Luther E. Smith Jr., a young scholar at Eden Theological Seminary who would write his dissertation on Thurman and become a leader in the first generation of Thurman scholars, was the key figure in the development of the seminars. In a letter to two colleagues, he summarized Thurman's thoughts about the upcoming "sessions for spiritual renewal." Thurman felt the seminars could be held "without 'the blowing of trumpets'; that is, we do not need to try to tell the world that we have initiated a great work."[81] This was done in part to avoid "cut throat competition" for seminar slots. Although the letter did not make this explicit, participation would be limited to African Americans, who would consider "the grounds and the meaning of religious experience." The seminars would "examine the bearing of these elements on the life and the fulfillment of those of us whose roots are in the Black community. The general direction of our discussion will be along the lines of my statement in 'Jesus and the Disinherited.'"[82]

By August 1980, there had been eighty-one seminar participants, with many divinity students, ministers, and teachers attending.[83] One seminar was reserved exclusively for therapists, social workers, and those in "behavioral professions." There is no available breakdown of participants by sex; one seminar in March 1980 had six men and four women.[84] As word of the seminars spread, those wishing to attend wrote to Thurman or the Trust expressing their interest. If accepted, they usually were expected to pay for their own travel, meals, and, sometimes, lodging. The seminars lasted from three to five days, and the main activity was listening to tapes selected by Thurman and then, with Thurman present, discussing the tape. (Thurman used tapes because he wanted to share in the experience and be challenged rather than assume the role of preacher or leader.) In at least one seminar, Thurman began by reading, in his slow, deliberate voice, the entire Gospel of Mark.[85] Participants were expected to keep a log or diary and to share their reactions with the other members. Thurman was very pleased by the first seminar, writing shortly afterward, "I think we are in the presence of a whole new development of the ministry."[86] From the beginning he was worried about his energy, but he continued to throw himself into the work.[87] In his last years, he found the seminars increasingly enervating, writing in October 1979 of "the psychic violence of working so intensively for seven hours a day—five days in succession," but the seminars were too important for him to cut back or curtail.[88]

Many of the participants found the seminars revelatory. Paul Smith, who attended the first seminar, wrote Thurman afterward that his "life was changed, refreshed and disturbed by this encounter." He continued: "When the spirit was in command you heard some of my cries. I have a better understanding of *me;* I feel closer to God and I am not ashamed of what I am in His presence. I have a better feeling for other human beings. I have not arrived, but I am on my journey."[89] Morrison Smith wrote Thurman that while "much of my understanding about my Christian faith has been shaken to its very roots," his "mind has been stretched beyond its former boundaries," and "a new door is opening up to me; I will be patient and wait for it to open fully."[90] Walter Fluker, who attended the seminar in late 1979, felt it was "life-changing in every sense of the word. It was one of the very few experiences in my life where I felt I was totally engaged and understood." Fluker added that "some of us, including myself, begged to stay in San Francisco with him. I remember that he thought our petitions to remain were so humorous that he actually spat out his coffee unable to refrain from his hearty laughter."[91] Many of the participants in the seminars became lifetime keepers of the Thurman flame and leaders of the first generations of Thurman scholars, among them Luther Smith, Walter Fluker, and Mozella Mitchell. The seminars were one of the most rewarding activities of Thurman's last years; through them, he changed many lives and created many disciples.

Thurman teaching, ca. 1975

If the seminars provided a handful of persons an intense experience with Thurman, televised interviews provided for outreach on a vastly larger scale. Thurman became a favorite subject for interviewers, a wise elder discussing his life while dispensing his insights. Of the several late interviews, the most popular was *A Conversation with Howard Thurman,* which primarily covered Thurman's early life and upbringing. Edited and produced by the BBC, its two segments—each slightly longer than fifty minutes—were shown on British television in March 1977 and subsequently, in condensed form, on PBS in early 1978.[92]

All of these activities—the televised interviews, the listening rooms, the work of the Trust—helped Thurman to become better known, though he would never be as well-known as his significance warranted. But for several decades he had been a member of that odd class of semi-celebrity who were "widely known for not being sufficiently famous." He already had one of the marks of fame, a biography, Elizabeth Yates's *Howard Thurman: Portrait of a Practical Dreamer,* published in 1964. Yates was a prolific and prize-winning author, best known for her books for young adults.[93] A resident of New Hampshire, she became an occasional attendee at Thurman's Marsh Chapel services and fell under his spell. Thurman agreed to her proposal, and over the summer of 1963 Yates interviewed him extensively.[94] The interviews form the bulk of the book, and it hews so closely to Thurman's own narration of his life that, as one reader told him, "Your biography . . . should be titled 'autobiography,' except somebody else wrote it."[95] This was Yates's intention, as she wrote Thurman: "The book is really your speaking and thinking as heartily as I could catch it, follow it, transcribe it, get it into my notes, and then transcribe my notes."[96] Thurman read the entire manuscript before publication, was enthusiastic about the book, and worked with the publisher and one of his usual benefactors to make copies available to white and Black schools in the South and for young Black men studying for the ministry.[97] Yates did a credible job, but the book was hardly the last word on its subject. Thurman wrote to Luther Smith in 1974, who was then contemplating writing a dissertation on Thurman, that while Yates told "a good story as a story," the biography did "not go into depth except when she is quoting," adding that a successful study of his life "would have to be both factual and creative."[98] Let those words be a challenge to anyone presuming to write a life of Howard Thurman. But before future biographers had their chance, Thurman wrote his own life story.

Thurman had long used his life experiences to make broader points in his sermons and writings. In 1959 he devoted the first chapter of his history of Fellowship Church to relating his life story, going back to his early days in Daytona.[99] Writing the autobiography would be the last and the longest writing project of his life. When *With Head and Heart* was published in October 1979, at 270 pages it was almost twice the length of any of his previous books. Thurman knew that its writing would be taxing. It took several years of his life, including several breaks or informal "sabbaticals" from outside obligations. Without his knowledge, some admirers established a fund to replace some of the income he lost.[100] His daughter, Anne Thurman, worked closely with him throughout and was in many ways a coauthor of the volume.[101] Writing of the autobiography to Jean Burden in 1976, as the project was getting under way, he expressed the hope that "my health will just give me enough time to complete this. If not, there is no complaint."[102]

For Thurman, one reason to write his autobiography was to demonstrate, to himself and others, that his life had been a coherent whole. As he told an interviewer in 1980, he was "convinced of the unity of life and that . . . in living my life I am making a single statement even though I live it in terms of particular moments, incidents. So that if today I had a motion picture reel that had recorded the story of my life from my birth up to this present moment, and if I unwound it backwards, I would see that every single moment, every single step was an unfolding of the same basic, fundamental idiom."[103] If Thurman hoped that he would "discover" his idiom, his "red thread," in the course of writing his life story, he knew a key dimension would be "the inner story of the unfolding of my own spirit as it grappled with the realities of my life as a black man growing up in American society," over the first three-quarters of the twentieth century.[104]

There is a different tone to the autobiography than in his previous books, more informal and relaxed, chattier, at times almost garrulous, a quality perhaps attributable to Thurman's decision to first tape-record his memories before putting pen to paper, trying for greater spontaneity. He changed publishers for the autobiography. After three decades with Harper and Row, which since 1947 had published fifteen of Thurman's books, he switched to Harcourt Brace Jovanovich. William Jovanovich, the chief executive of the firm, also served as Thurman's editor.[105] They began to work together early in 1976, and that July, Thurman signed a contract for an advance of fifteen thousand dollars.[106] While it was unusual for the chief executive of one of the nation's largest publishing firms to personally edit the work of an author, Thurman and Jovanovich had an unusually close relationship. They had been introduced by Daniel Collins, the West Coast director of Harcourt Brace Jovanovich and a founding member of Fellowship Church.[107] By 1976 Thurman had known Jovanovich for several years and insisted that "I will not and cannot write this book without his personal editorial help."[108] Jovanovich was in return a great admirer of Thurman, writing to him in 1978, "There's a lot we must talk about, serious and unserious, and it is what my soul needs, a good talk with Howard Thurman, wondering about the typicalities of living."[109]

After *With Head and Heart* was published in the fall of 1979, Thurman heard from many old friends, such as Jack Schooler, the Rochester haberdasher who had outfitted him a half century before, and who was surprised and honored to be mentioned in Thurman's book.[110] It received considerable publicity. An ad in the *New York Times Book Review* called it "an inspiring chronicle of America's racial and religious coming of age."[111] Vernon Jordan, president of the Urban League (who had provided a blurb for the book), praised it in his syndicated radio commentary, saying that *With Head and Heart* "moved me as few books have."[112] Many provided similar encomia. Rev. Otis Moss Sr., who had taken part in one of Thurman's seminars, wrote him: "Reading your Autobiography is like meeting a pilgrim of truth on his way to the city who shares some of the most profound moments of his journey. Thank God for the pilgrim and his journey."[113] Those unknown to Thurman were often similarly enthusiastic: "It is 6:30 A.M. and I have just completed *With Head and Heart.* I am breathing deeply and there is a surge throughout the body and spirit. Praise God, Praise God!"[114]

Yet praise was far from universal. His old high school teacher, Ethel Simons Meads, wrote him, hoping that he was "paying no attention to any disparaging criticism of your magnificent book."[115] She had probably read some of the reviews. The first one, released in September from *Kirkus Reviews,* was a sign of things to come. Calling *With Head and Heart* "tamely edifying memoirs by the noted black preacher and author," the reviewer complained of an autobiography that was "lethally predictable," containing "no dramatic struggle, contradiction, doubt, etc." and having little to say about "the whole civil rights era and its aftermath."[116] Doris Grumbach's January 1980 review in the *New York Times* reached a far wider audience. Grumbach wrote of Thurman's "formal, colorless prose" and the book's "plodding narrative," which she found both "flat" and "featureless." Ignoring Thurman's twenty-one previously published books, she complained that *With Head and Heart* was written "with the painful earnestness that often characterizes the inexperienced writer." She also held Thurman to an absurdly high standard: "One needs only to go back to Frederick Douglass's superb account of *his* life to see what is missing here." She did acknowledge, with some condescension, that *With Head and Heart* was "edifying, even uplifting in the old-fashioned sense of self-improvement stories" and that the volume's limitations "cannot entirely obscure the shining example of his life."[117]

Benita Eisler in the liberal magazine the *Nation* lambasted not only Thurman's prose but also his moral character. The autobiography was "self-congratulatory," a volume "made to order for the *Reader's Digest*'s 'Most Inspirational Character.'" She saw Thurman as a sycophant who decided early in life that "white philanthropy was the key to success" and whose actions were directed by his "keen sense of social standing" and indifference to poor Blacks. Eisler considerably exaggerated the importance of white philanthropy in his early life, and her review badly distorted Thurman's career, falsely stating that Thurman was invited to Fellowship Church by "several liberal San Francisco millionaires" and that he funded the HTET from "the profits from his bestselling sermons." In her sharpest attack she accused Thurman of being indifferent to the civil rights movement and of only including a memorial tribute to King and other civil rights martyrs at the behest of Jovanovich (a claim for which there is no evidence). She concluded that "rarely have . . . lives and deaths so harshly condemned their eulogist."[118]

Thurman claimed not to have read the reviews.[119] This was not so. He had read and been wounded by them. Someone who understood the hurt was Benjamin Mays, who wrote Thurman that Grumbach's review "was not fair" and "missed the point." Much more questionably, Mays added, no doubt judging Grumbach and Eisler by their Ashkenazi Jewish–sounding last names, that Thurman shouldn't "worry about the storm that the Autobiography created among certain groups of Jews in the East."[120] (Although Grumbach and Eisler were of Jewish backgrounds, both were using names acquired through marriage, and Grumbach was a practicing Episcopalian.) If Mays's anti-Semitic outburst was deeply out of character, it is no doubt a reflection of how outraged he was by the reviews.[121]

While the reviews were harsh and in some ways quite unfair, their criticisms did speak to certain limitations of *With Head and Heart,* as well as to ways it could have been read as old-fashioned by the late 1970s. Thurman's young friend Ed Kaplan, later a distinguished professor of French and religious studies, admired the autobiography but wrote Thurman that he felt "you were writing in a very restrained fashion. Each time an explosive emotion would be evoked, you seemed to lead into it, and then foreclose the description." *With Head and Heart* is not an angry book; Thurman did not write it to settle scores. Unlike many Black autobiographies, it did not include visceral accounts of his own experience with white racial violence in all of its brutality and savagery. It was a reticent book; he did not expose aspects or parts of his life he did not want exposed. Kaplan suggested that Thurman's description of his mother—"There was about her a deep inner sadness, which, as a boy, I could not understand. It was not gloom, but a quiet overcast of feeling"—could equally apply to Thurman himself. Kaplan asked: "What is the clue to your sadness and the way in which you transmute it into a deep confidence tinged with a tragic sense of your fragility? What is this melancholy?"[122] These were astute observations and excellent questions, but Thurman's autobiography provided only oblique answers.

At the same time, *With Head and Heart* was a worldly book. Thurman was proud of the remarkable and unlikely success he had enjoyed in his life and wrote of his triumphs. He had defeated racism by getting an education, advancing in the Black academic hierarchy, and then, in midcareer, going beyond it. This is the story he wished to tell, with its Washingtonian overtones; up from postslavery Florida in turn-of-the-twentieth-century America; up from poverty, up from obscurity and marginality to a life as a respected national figure. Like many autobiographers, Thurman is most vivid when relating his younger, formative years. It was not a memoir of the civil rights movement, which I suspect is what its reviewers most wanted to read. Perhaps Thurman's greatest challenge in writing his autobiography was trying to explain why he personally remained on the sidelines of the civil rights movement, even though he was inspired by and was an inspiration for it.

One reader who did understand Thurman was Richard Newman, a supremely knowledgeable scholar of African American religious history. Thurman would write Newman after reading his review that "of all the reviews that have come to my attention, yours seems to be most insightful and sensitive."[123] Newman found Thurman to be "unique in American religion"; a "pioneer in transcending boundaries of race, class, nation, culture and religion"; and "a mystic in the midst of American religious activism." Newman wrote: "The dialectic between these political realities and the spiritual reality discovered by Thurman on his true, inner journey constitutes the real substance of his autobiography." Thurman's spirituality, as reflected in *With Head and Heart,* "is a product of his radical self-understanding and his realization that the truth he found in himself is universal."[124]

With Head and Heart was published in the fall of 1979 into a world that was very different from the one he had been born into eighty years earlier. Like most men nearing eighty years of age, Thurman's values and tastes had been formed decades before, and he was disinclined to follow the latest fashions: no beard or goatee, no Afro, no dashiki. He did not use the profane vernacular to "tell it like it is," and, to judge from his sermons and writings, he had little interest in contemporary African American writing or music. And yet in some ways Thurman was a good fit for the new politics and new sensibility of the 1960s and 1970s. He was a mystic and seeker of "whole-making" in an era that honored mysticism and holism; an advocate of centering down in a culture whose idea of religion increasingly saw individual meditation as perhaps the highest form of religious expression; a spiritual quester for an era of religious searchers, a nature mystic at a time when many were looking for God out of doors.[125] "To me," Thurman wrote a correspondent in 1977, "the only God you will ever find is the God who will become real to you as you seek answers. To worship any other God is to worship an idol."[126] In what has become perhaps his best-known quotation, he advised the author Gil Bailie: "Don't ask yourself what the world needs. Ask yourself what makes you come alive, and go do that, because what the world needs is people who have come alive."[127] (To me, Bailie's quote, even if he correctly remembered the exact words Thurman used, does not strike me as truly representative of his thought—Thurman, the practitioner of affirmation mysticism, was always asking people to be concerned with what the world needs but would have wanted people to approach the task of repairing the world joyfully rather than as a leaden, imposed obligation. Choose some cause, he said in 1937, "some great purpose, identify yourself with some overwhelming need; give yourself to it in abiding enthusiasm and in complete devotion."[128] Or perhaps he was telling Bailie, as he suggested in *Deep Is the Hunger:* "The crux of the problem is not merely that we desire the right and find it difficult to achieve it, but that it is also true that, again and again, we do not desire *to desire* the right."[129])

Thurman certainly thought that one thing the world needed was peace, and this remained an urgent issue for him. "What is in violence that is so bewitching?" he asked in 1970. Perhaps, he suggested, one answer is that its "illusion . . . makes a man feel temporarily that he is omnipotent" and "can veto or certify another human being's life," and satisfy the "ancient hungers to control, to dominate, to master."[130] He continued to believe that any society built upon violent coercion, which included all societies past and present, was built on a flaw that was at the root of all of the inequalities of wealth, race, and gender. If in the later years of his life his relation to formal pacifist organizations became somewhat attenuated, he remained, to the end of his days, within the broad pacifist penumbra and connected to the Fellowship of Reconciliation.[131] In the 1950s and 1960s he was an active member of the United World Federalists, an organization that called for effective world government.[132] By 1961 he was on the masthead of SANE (Committee for a Sane Nuclear Policy), a liberal, antiwar (but nonpacifist) organization that demanded an end to the nuclear arms race, and contributed a short essay, "Two Options" (extinction or survival), to a volume titled *God and the H-Bomb*.[133]

Although Thurman remained very concerned about nuclear weapons, the antiwar issue of the hour was the debacle of the American military involvement in Vietnam, the only issue, in the 1960s and 1970s, that rivaled race and civil rights in its ability to cleave and roil Americans. If for some old colleagues, like A. J. Muste, opposition to the war provided the opportunity for a very public last hurrah, Thurman said relatively little about it in his sermons and writings. In March 1965, just as regular U.S. troops were introduced into the war, in a television broadcast he asked: "What can we say to our soldiers in Vietnam? For what freedom, what freedom, do they fight, suffer, and die? What can we say to them?"[134] He signed petitions in 1965 and 1967 sponsored by SANE calling for President Johnson to open negotiations with North Vietnam.[135] (This position, amid the fervid antiwar politics of the time, was considered fairly mainstream.) In *The Search for Common Ground,* albeit largely in passing, he criticized "the immoral war in Vietnam."[136] His strongest comments on the war occurred in his private correspondence: "We are caught in the agonizing grip of the kind of madness that seems to afflict nations and civilizations that have grown fat and secure in their power."[137]

If the Vietnam War was a severe challenge to the geopolitical assumptions of the Cold War, domestically there were equally sharp confrontations to the prevailing norms about gender and sexual identity. Thurman was once again a quiet advocate for radical change. Feminism, the radical feminism of Olive Schreiner, had been a foundation of his thinking since the 1920s, though he wrote little about it in the intervening decades, save a defense of the Equal Rights Amendment in *Jesus and the Disinherited*.[138] This reflected his general disinclination to speak on political issues, but the depth of his support and belief in gender equality can be gauged by his close association with some of the country's leading Black feminists, among them Mary McLeod Bethune, Pauli Murray, and of course his wife, Sue Bailey Thurman, a former national secretary of the YWCA, editor of the *Aframerican Women's Journal,* a leader of the National Council of Negro Women, and a delegate to the first Inter-American Congress of Women in Guatemala in 1947, among her other commitments to women's and feminist causes.[139] In 1973, after more than three decades of trying, Thurman finally published an anthology of Olive Schreiner's writings, which includes generous selections of her feminist writings.[140]

Thurman never made the transition to using gender-neutral language in his writing. (By the time he was writing his autobiography in the late 1970s, this had become a serious issue, one he discussed extensively with his daughter Anne, but in the end he felt more comfortable with his familiar pronouns, probably just reflecting the habits of a lifetime rather than any ideological concerns.)[141] At the same time, Thurman had long been a supporter of enhanced roles for women in the clergy, and in his final months in 1980 he gave his unstinting support for a project to eliminate barriers to women in theological education.[142] He wrote that he was "very mindful of the unique barriers facing women who feel called to ministry," because of the "unwillingness on the part of some to acknowledge the fact that God does not discriminate in favor of men or against women." Thurman thought it critical that women "do not approach ministry defensively and apologetically," and he pledged his cooperation to help "the witness of God to blossom in the mind and the life of women."[143]

By the late 1970s, the question of gay and lesbian identity became a very public issue, perhaps nowhere more so than in Thurman's hometown of San Francisco. It was a subject on which he had written little or nothing, even in his bachelor of divinity thesis titled "The Basis of Sex Morality," where he wrote that sex was a "private act between two individuals" and "not a social act *per se.*"[144] (In the thesis he did cite early defenders of same-sex relations such as Havelock Ellis and Edward Carpenter.)[145] In an unfortunate episode, a 1978 lecture at San Francisco's First Unitarian Church, Thurman offhandedly suggested that one of the similarities between contemporary America and ancient Rome in the early decades of the empire was a "phenomenal increase particularly of homosexuality between boys and men."[146] A Unitarian Universalist minister in the audience wrote Thurman an angry letter accusing him of being prejudiced and "guilty of perpetuating discrimination and segregation." In an equally angry response by Thurman, he denied the accusations and stated that he did not regard himself "as a judge of the mores, the sexual behavior patterns of my fellows."[147]

Thurman's remarks probably referred to male pederasty rather than same-sex relations in general, though he should have chosen his words more carefully, and it probably would have been best if he had avoided the questionable comparison entirely. But the comment did not reflect his true attitudes, or his close, nonjudgmental friendships with many gays and lesbians over the decades.[148] In 1973 John Pfleiderer, after being forced from the Methodist ministry because of his openness about his sexual orientation, came to San Francisco to start a ministry for gay men.[149] He met with Thurman, and they discussed Pfleiderer's "dream of a church which could include all people— regardless of race, religious convictions, or sexual orientation. You told me of Fellowship Church and of your dream come true."[150] After some difficult years, in 1979 he was called to a United Church of Christ pulpit and wrote Thurman: "My brother, you helped me more than you can ever know. Your financial help was greatly appreciated, but much more important, you held me, cried with me, and gave me the encouragement I needed to hold on!" Thurman replied: "What a perfect fulfillment of my hope and my prayer for you. . . . I am grateful to God for this fresh manifestation of His concern for His children."[151]

Environmentalism was another social concern that blossomed in the 1970s and was another longtime concern of Thurman's. As early as his 1938, his lecture "Man and the World of Nature" was an environmentalist tract avant le lettre.[152] In 1965, in a sermon delivered to a prominent Fifth Avenue Manhattan congregation that made the pages of the *New York Times,* he argued that in the assault on nature, humanity was only attacking itself. Humans could not continue to "poison the atmosphere, pollute the streams, denude the hills without affecting the psyche deep within. The pain is felt in the collective organism and expresses itself in the emotional aberrations that take the form of mental disturbances of one kind or another."[153] In 1970, just before the first Earth Day, Thurman wrote that "one day nature will revolt & man will discover that he cannot destroy and plunder without being destroyed himself and all his kind."[154]

Thurman's environmentalism, as we have seen in *The Search for Common Ground,* had mystic overtones. He might not have regularly consulted his horoscope, but he stated in 1965: "Man is part of this living universe. The old astrologers had something of truth in their position. When they talked about the relationship between the movement of the heavenly bodies and the psyche they were dealing with a crucial aspect of reality."[155] In the 1970s, quasi-occult views of nature were newly fashionable. Thurman was interested in William Irvin Thompson's effort to link humanity and nature in heralding the emergence of a "planetary culture" and consciousness.[156] In 1979 he wrote to Guy Murchie, complimenting him on his book *The Seven Mysteries of Life*, which argued that the earth and the universe were superorganisms and that conventional boundaries, between individual living things, between species, between life and nonlife, and between astronomical bodies and the vast distances of space, were largely arbitrary. Thurman told Murchie, "In all of my reading and studying, I have not found a book that placed before my mind, observations and analysis of the world, a nature that confirmed in minutest detail, my own philosophic and spiritual insights."[157]

Much of Thurman's mystical musings and thoughts about nature has an affinity with the capacious 1970s religious category known as New Age thinking.[158] There has been some debate as to whether Thurman is properly placed within its ranks.[159] One's answer depends in part in whether the label of New Age is viewed as a compliment or a slur. Certainly, for some of the characteristics of the New Age—an emphasis on the religious significance of spirituality, meditation, mysticism, and do-your-own-thingism—Thurman was in some ways a New Age precursor. Beneath his usual sobriety, it is easy to miss Thurman's streak of gentle anarchism and unconventionality, in which there were no religious rules one could not transgress. Although Thurman and Henry Miller, the controversial author of many a ribald sexual coming-of-age narrative such as the long-banned *Tropic of Cancer*, might seem like an odd couple, Edward Kaplan, who knew both men, did not think so and urged them to get together. Miller, living in Big Sur, wrote to his northern California neighbor in 1966: "Dear Dr. Thurman: Our friend Ed Kaplan reminds me that one day before either of us passes away we must meet. I'm no Christian, I hope you know. But we will surely find a meeting ground. Sincerely, Henry Miller."[160] It does not seem that the two ever met, but if they did, they would have had much to talk about, as both were animated by a similar drive for personal freedom, for freedom of expression, and for throwing off the traces of external constraint.

Some of Thurman's disciples were unambiguously practitioners of New Age religiosity. In the 1970s, Zalman Schachter-Shalomi emerged as the leader of the Havurah, or Jewish Renewal movement, explicitly taking its inspiration from New Age sources.[161] Both Sam Keen, who studied with Thurman in the 1950s and was an author of popular books on New Age spirituality, and Mozella Mitchell, who studied with Thurman in the late 1970s, described Thurman as a shaman, that archetypal New Age prophetic category.[162] For Thurman, a Christian was "a person who has entered into fellowship with Jesus and to whom his spirit or the spirit that was in him is an active agent in the individual's life," and there is no reason to doubt that, by his definition, he always remained a Christian.[163] At the same time, he had always been interested in non-Christian and post-Christian spriritualities. He told Jean Burden in the 1970s: "My own attitude becomes increasingly nonsectarian—neither Buddhist, Christian, Hindu, or whatever. . . . They call me a Unitarian. They're always trying to put a label on me. I'm *nothing*."[164] In 1978 he wondered if it was "too far to hazard a guess that the period through which we are passing now is one which either is preparing the way for a new dimension of the meaning of religion, or a new religion? I don't know, it worries me sometime in my sleep because I don't want to miss it."[165] Thurman compared America in 1978 to first-century CE Rome, with its plethora of new mystery religions, the declining respect for the old gods, and the sense of dislocation as Rome's imperial ambitions wrenched people away from identification with their traditions, a society whose spiritual needs were not being met.[166] Perhaps New Age religiosity was part of the answer, much as some religious seekers in Roman society turned to the latest mystery religion from the East, Christianity.

At the same time, if one sees New Age religion as an excuse for febrile pseudomysticism and excessive navel-gazing, Thurman belongs in another category. Thurman's mysticism was always linked to the need for radical social change and, in particular, to his engagement with the travail and promise of the history of Black America. Personal religious experience had to be connected to the imperatives and complexities of history. Moreover, Thurman's spirituality was always nonprescriptive, helping others on their path, not providing rules or structures. He was a mystic, but a mystic who did not indulge in lengthy, deadening descriptions of what he saw when he was enlightened. He knew that any spiritual regimen, even one as open as his own, was liable to be routinized into a formula or dogma. He wanted others to be open to the universe of spiritual options and alternatives and not to believe as he did. He was, in the words of Sam Keen, "no guru, no answer man."[167]

If the 1970s saw the dawning of the Age of Aquarius, it also saw the sunset of the long era of the New Deal order and the slow ebbing, in American life and politics, of a set of liberal racially, socially, and economically egalitarian values that had been important to Thurman's thinking for a half century. The 1970s saw Blacks begin to solidify some of the gains of the civil rights movement, fighting all the while against a gathering backlash that would culminate, a few months before Thurman's death, in the election of Ronald Reagan as president, ushering in a new conservative era in American history. This long-term trend, of course, would not have been obvious to Thurman at the time, but he knew that, as always, America's worst and best impulses were engaged in a perpetual tug of war, with no ultimate victory and no ultimate defeat. If community was Thurman's ideal in the latest years of his life, by the 1970s "community" had become a byword for racial divisiveness, a fighting word that cleaved America, claimed in different ways by white and Black America.

Perhaps nowhere were the perils of "community values" or "community control" more evident than in Thurman's former home of Boston, where in the early 1970s fights over school busing, between the white working-class neighborhoods of South Boston, the Black neighborhoods of Roxbury, and the well-to-do areas of Back Bay Boston, flared into violence and unwanted national attention. The era's definitive account of Boston's time of troubles was J. Anthony Lukas's Pulitzer Prize–winning book *Common Ground*.[168] Lukas's book concentrated on three Boston families, one of which was that of Joan Diver, the daughter of Thurman's good friend (and fellow Boston University dean) George Makechnie. Through Diver, Thurman is a guiding spirit of the book, starting with its title, which is explicitly drawn from *The Search for Common Ground*. In 1976, doing research for the book, Lukas met Thurman in San Francisco. Thurman told him that his lifework was as a witness against "all that fragments and shatters," against an America in the 1970s whose citizens "seemed ready to abandon their search for a unitary society and to huddle in little ghettoes of the spirit, proclaiming their irreconcilability."[169] In that same year, 1976, Thurman was asked in the BBC interview whether he was "pessimistic or optimistic or fatalistic about this great struggle between the races across the world?"[170] Thurman knew enough not to give a straight answer.

Thurman always had reasonably good health. He was somewhat stocky for his five-foot, ten-inch frame, and doctors sometimes advised to lose some weight, exercise more, and watch his blood pressure. A nagging injury to his right wrist bothered him for many decades.[171] But in the 1970s there were several serious health crises. There was a swollen hip and leg that hobbled him for several months in 1974.[172] There was an incidence of cancer, probably in 1976.[173] There were other health problems as well. He took more extended breaks from his work. By 1980 his health had clearly diminished. He wrote Jovanovich in April 1980 that "for the past months I have been deviled by an old demonic asthma with bronchial congestion. Even now breathing is a chore" causing "psychic panic." Thurman wrote that he would return to editing an anthology of his writings when "I can get through a few hours without coughing and fighting for air."[174] (The anthology would be completed by his daughter Anne after his death.)[175] At around the same time he wrote that his "health has been a bit uncertain for three or four years";[176] he told another that "in recent years" his "own energies have decreased without any apparent reduction in demands" on his time.[177]

His last extended trip outside San Francisco came in May 1980, when he traveled to Atlanta to deliver the baccalaureate sermon at Spelman. (He flew, because even if he could find accommodations on America's rapidly contracting passenger rail network, he was no longer up to its multiday rigors.) At Spelman, he urged the women to find the something within that "listens for the sound of the genuine in yourself" and "listens for the sound of the genuine in other people."[178] While in Atlanta he met with many old friends, including Benjamin Mays, with whom he had his last visit. Thurman's last public appearance was probably the anniversary sermon he gave at Fellowship Church at the end of October.[179]

Thurman's respiratory condition sharply deteriorated thereafter, and his physician ordered him to enter the hospital for a period of complete rest. In addition to serious asthma, Thurman was hospitalized for a ruptured appendix early in 1981.[180] Although he had a recurrence of his cancer, his final illness was the product of his persistent bronchial problems and his general physical deterioration.[181] By one account, in his last year he "was more than once near or beyond the point of clinical death."[182] Thurman once said, "I don't think a person who is sick can ever die until somewhere in his organism a decision is made, a conclusion is arrived at which says that all of me, the totality of my organism is at last contained in the event."[183] Death came on 10 April 1981.

In an unpublished chapter of his autobiography he wrote about his death: "I am at ease knowing that nobody like me ever lived before. I am at ease because there is a nonspatial and nontemporal dimension of my personality that has to do with life and is not bound by death. I function freely outside an interval of time in which I happen to be living at the moment: I can hark back thirty years, or project thirty years, leaping to the past, leaping to the future. I can be aware of my dying right up to zero. Part of me will be watching Howard Thurman, the time binder and space binder, being delivered from a particular time and a particular space. I shall be a participant in my dying as I have been in my living."[184]

In one of his last interviews he was asked about the relation between life and death. Thurman replied that it was just another dualism and that "life is against all dualisms; that ultimately all dualisms exhaust themselves, and therefore when I, in my journey, when I make these separations, I'm dealing with the unrealities of my reality."[185] Sam Keen wrote of meeting with Thurman a week before his death and remembers Thurman asking: "Why was I born a *black* man and you a *white* man? What, in the universal way of things, required me to be this particular person that I am?" Thurman whispered to Keen, "Why should the ultimate secret of my life be kept from me?"[186] As he passed in and out of consciousness he continued to ponder life's dualities:

Thurman with Jesse Jackson, ca. 1975

"Why is there black and white, why is there male and female?"[187] Perhaps, in the end, he found his answer. In a conversation with Sue days before he died, after a near-death experience, he told her that "he encountered the 'particular' man and the 'universal' man within himself and wrestled them to earth, until he won the consent of both—to Life, to Death, and back to Life."[188]

His funeral service was held on 16 April at the First Unitarian Church in San Francisco, where some thirty-seven years earlier, he had celebrated the founding of his proudest creation, Fellowship Church. There were some spirituals, some Bach, and much of his other favorite music. Frank Wilson presided at the service; the Rev. Marvin Chandler, executive director of the HTET, read the 139th Psalm and delivered a eulogy. Two rabbis, Saul White and Alvin Fine, spoke, as did Jesse Jackson, William Jovanovich, Vernon Jordan, and Hugh Gloster, president of Morehouse College, and several others.[189]

Benjamin Mays couldn't make the trip from Atlanta but recorded his comments for the service. A few months earlier he had written, in a response to a nomination of Thurman for the first class of so-called MacArthur Foundation "genius grants"—Thurman's death rendered the nomination moot—that his old friend had spent his life "searching after the truth," and "he will never stop searching until he dies."[190] (And not then, if Thurman had anything to say about it.) A month after his death Mays, as Morehouse president emeritus, devoted the annual college baccalaureate sermon to Thurman's legacy, and the college glee club sang settings of some of Thurman's poems.[191] Mays said that Thurman was "born free—free as the wind that blows and free as the birds that fly," and that he walked, wrote, and spoke like a free man, and together they resolved not "to let the white man's world destroy us." As one who could not and would not be a slave, Mays placed Thurman in the company of Moses, Denmark Vesey, Nat Turner, Harriet Tubman, Frederick Douglass, both Booker T. Washington and W. E. B. Du Bois, St. Francis of Assisi, and the Africans, their names erased and forgotten, who, rather than face enslavement in America, chose freedom and death by drowning themselves in the Atlantic Ocean.[192] The great boxer Joe Louis died two days after Thurman. Several columnists linked the two men. Vernon Jordan wrote that they "stood for an entire body of black achievement, and as inspiration to countless black people who drew sustenance from the deeds of one and the message of the other."[193] Thurman would have been flattered by the comparison.[194] It is as good way as any to remember Thurman; a Joe Louis of the inner presence, a Joe Louis of African American nonviolence.

The institutions Thurman tried to build have crumbled or faded. The Howard Thurman Educational Trust slowly ceased operations in the years after his passing. Fellowship Church endures, though in reduced circumstances. Perhaps this is as it should be. It is the nature of all institutions, he once said, "whether church, state, school, whatever—to deal impersonally with the problems in which persons are caught."[195] This has not hampered the slow spreading of his thinking and message. The first Thurman scholars were primarily his students or those who knew him and fell under his spell.[196] They have been followed by several new generations of Thurman students. Through 2020 there have been at least forty dissertations and at least thirty publications on Thurman, among them monographs, self-help books, films, musical settings of his verse, a five-volume documentary edition of his papers, and a children's book.[197] There have been towers and sculptures dedicated to Thurman. The continued interest in his work will be his lasting monument.[198]

Is Howard Thurman still relevant? For many seeking to know God, to find their spiritual bearings in a confusing world, he remains an unparalleled cartographer of the soul. "Howard Thurman," wrote Nathan Huggins, "taught infinity," explored boundlessness in a bounded world, emancipation in a world that is still not free.[199] We live in a different political world than the one he inhabited. At the same time, none of the questions that most exercised him have lost their salience. We still wonder if the powerful social glue that is religion is a force that can unite as well as divide. We still need to quiet the noise of our lives to hear the cries of the disinherited. We still need to create an America capacious enough for Thurman's belief in the "equality of infinite worth" to include all within its borders. Vincent Harding wrote of the widening of "Thurman's community of the wall," to include groups both unmentioned and perhaps unanticipated by Thurman. Perhaps he would say that all of us now must live with our backs against the wall, in peril of losing the priceless inheritance of our water, land, and sky.[200]

More than one person close to Thurman came away with the impression that the world was somehow revolving around this quiet man. For Lerone Bennett, Thurman was both a "black man" and a "world soul," a Black man "totally, passionately, creatively engaged in a quest for common ground beyond race, beyond creed, beyond labels."[201] Gil Bailie, a Roman Catholic, wrote Thurman in 1978 of the Catholic belief that "what ultimately determines the fate of the world is the number (never more than a relative handful) of genuinely centered human beings alive at the time." Bailie honored Thurman "for choosing to be a visible example" of "such centered people."[202] From a different religious tradition, Rabbi Alan Fine described Thurman in much the same way, calling him one of the Lamed Vav Tzadikim (thirty-six righteous people). Fine wrote, "According to an ancient rabbinic legend there are in the world, at any given time, thirty-six wise and righteous persons gifted with special spiritual powers that enable them to perceive the Divine Presence with clear insight and understanding." For Fine, Thurman was "one of those thirty-six spiritual prodigies who keep human faith alive at all times."[203]

I don't know if these notions have a secular equivalent, but I do think that Howard Thurman was one of the unacknowledged persons around whom twentieth-century America revolved, one of its quiet pillars, his willed inconspicuousness out of all proportion to his importance. Standing in the way of a broader recognition of Thurman's significance, and not only for white Americans, was the challenge of his distinctive brand of subversive Black universality. Thurman always understood that there was a sub rosa quality to his thinking, resistant to being blared and better suited to dissemination through what he called his "freemasonry."[204] Perhaps, perhaps, America is now ready to listen to him more intently. However, what Lerone Bennett said of Thurman in 1987 undoubtedly remains true, that "perhaps his greatest influence was exercised through the good offices of the men and women who studied in the 'Thurman University' and went on to occupy major positions in American institutions. As a result, men, women and little children, who never heard his name are his debtors and his disciples."[205] The "Thurman University" is a university still more invisible than visible, with countless graduates unaware of their attendance.

Thurman experienced the American century's heights and depths, knowing that, to paraphrase his beloved Psalm 139, God was present when America tried to ascend to the heavens, and present when it made its bed in hell. In his democratic vision, all people were infinitely equal; in his world, boundaries were just lines drawn on a map and religious creeds just words written in a book; in his universe, everything was alive, connected, and filled with divine sparks. He wanted us to hear the small, urgent voices within, and to listen to the clamor of the disinherited without. He was not cowed or intimidated by the vicious contradictions of American life, which he tried to understand and change but neither minimized nor excused. Those touched by his message must continue to oppose humanity's most tenacious and implacable foe, our voluntary imprisonment within our fears, our lies, and our hatreds. Let us take up Howard Thurman's battle against the hounds of hell.

Notes

Abbreviations

HT   Howard Thurman

HTC Howard Thurman Collection, Howard Gotlieb Archival Research Center, Boston University.

PHWT *The Papers of Howard Washington Thurman.* Edited by Walter Earl Fluker. Vols. 1–5. Columbia: University of South Carolina Press, 2009–19.

WHAH Howard Thurman. *With Head and Heart: The Autobiography of Howard Thurman.* New York: Harcourt Brace Jovanovich, 1979.

Introduction

1. For a longer account of Thurman's journey to India, going into more detail than is possible here, see *PHWT,* 1:80–339; and Quinton Dixie and Peter Eisenstadt, *Visions of a Better World: Howard Thurman's Pilgrimage to India and the Origins of African American Nonviolence* (Boston: Beacon, 2011), 65–151.

2. The Negro Delegation traveled throughout British India (including what is now Pakistan and Bangladesh), Ceylon, and Burma, but the journey was invariably called the "India trip" by Thurman and others associated with it, and I follow that convention. All place-names and territorial divisions are referred to by the names current in 1935 and 1936.

3. The main source for Gandhi's meeting with the Negro Delegation is "With Our Negro Guests," published in *Harijan,* Gandhi's weekly English-language magazine, in March 1936, and reprinted in *PHWT,* 1:332–39. This is supplemented by Thurman's many accounts of the meeting, including "Mahatma Gandhi" (1 February 1948), in *PHWT,* 3:255–62; "The Quest for Peace" (24 July 1949), Folder 33, Box 11, HTC; "Men Who Have Walked with God: Mahatma Gandhi" (1 October 1950), Folder 65, Box 11, HTC; and "Men Who Have Walked with God: Mahatma Gandhi" (7 June 1953), Folder 91, Box 11, HTC; and *WHAH,* 130–35.

4. *WHAH,* 131–32.

5. "The Faith of the American Negro: Prof. Howard Thurman's Address," *The Hindu* (Madras), 19 November 1935, in *PHWT,* 1:305–6.

6. "Education and Social Stability," *Madras Mail,* 4 December 1935; W. E. B. Du Bois, *Black Reconstruction in America* (1935; repr., New York: Athenaeum, 1992), 349–52.

7. For Thurman and Bunche, see HT to Ralph Bunche, 9 November 1934, in *PHWT*, 1:216–17. For the importance of interracial unionism for Thurman, see HT, "A 'Native Son' Speaks" (1940), in *PHWT*, 2:251.

8. "Education and Social Stability," *Madras Mail*, 4 December 1935.

9. Mahatma Gandhi, "Gandhi Denied He Opposes Intermarriage," *Baltimore Afro-American*, 16 June 1934. See Sudarshan Kapur, *Raising up a Prophet: The African American Encounter with Gandhi* (Boston: Beacon, 1992), 77–79.

10. Thurman had been questioned by an American missionary in Lahore who argued that Arabs, not Christians, bore the main responsibility for the Atlantic slave trade (see Henry W. Luce to HT, 12 February 1936, in *PHWT*, 1:325–27; and *WHAH*, 123–24).

11. HT, "India Report" (10 February 1938), in *PHWT*, 2:138.

12. Richard Brent Turner, *Islam in the African American Experience* (Bloomington: Indiana University Press, 1997), 47–90.

13. Review of "The Negro's Church" (1933), in *PHWT*, 1:173; HT, "India Report," in *PHWT*, 2:138; *WHAH*, 132.

14. "Ji," in Hindi, is a mark of respect and usually added to the end of the name.

15. HT, "India Report," in *PHWT*, 2:139.

16. For an account of Gandhi's often dismissive attitude toward Black South Africans, see Joseph Lelyveld, *Great Soul: Mahatma Gandhi and His Struggle with India* (New York: Knopf, 2011), 57–77.

17. See Kipton E. Jensen, *Howard Thurman: Philosophy, Civil Rights, and the Search for Common Ground* (Columbia: University of South Carolina Press, 2019), 11–23.

18. *PHWT*, 1:335–36.

19. Gandhi angered many leaders of the untouchables during these years with his insistence that they be counted as Hindus in the 1935 religious census rather than placed in their own religious category. For Thurman's account of B. R. Ambedkar, the leader of India's Dalits (a term he preferred to Gandhi's Harijan) and a fierce opponent of Gandhi, see HT, "Mahatma Gandhi" (1 February 1949), in *PHWT*, 3:260. For Thurman's agnosticism about the caste system, see HT, "India Report," in *PHWT*, 2:146–47.

20. Augustine Ralla Ram to Frank T. Wilson, 28 June 1934, in *PHWT*, 1:193–95; Winnifred Wygal to Betty Harrington, 14 August 1934, Howard Thurman Papers Project Files. For the Negro Delegation as singers of spirituals, see Dixie and Eisenstadt, *Visions of a Better World*, 75–77; and *PHWT*, 1:286–87.

21. Augustine Ralla Ram to Frank T. Wilson, 28 June 1934, in *PHWT*, 1:193–95.

22. HT, "The Message of the Spirituals" (October 1928), in *PHWT*, 1:126–39. The Negro Delegation spoke about or sang spirituals at least twenty-one times during their stay (see "Detailed Schedule of the Negro Delegation," in *PHWT*, 1:283–300).

23. *WHAH*, 134.

24. *WHAH*, 134–35.

25. Bayard Rustin, "Even in the Face of Death," in *Down the Line: The Collected Writings of Bayard Rustin* (Chicago: Quadrangle, 1971), 103. Originally published in *Liberation*, February 1957.

26. For Ralla Ram, see Myra Scovel, *I Must Speak: The Biography of Augustine Ralla Ram* (Allahabad, India: North India Christian Literature Society, 1961). He served as general secretary of the Student Christian Federation Association of India, Ceylon, and Burma from 1928 until 1947.

27. "A Great Christian from India," *Spelman Messenger* 48 (October 1931): 24–25. Thurman was then teaching at Spelman, and he might have met Ralla Ram at that time, though neither man mentions this. In 1945, during the founding conference of the United Nations, Ralla Ram was in San Francisco and spoke at Fellowship Church (HT, *Footprints of a Dream: The Story of the Church for the Fellowship of All Peoples* [New York: Harper and Brothers, 1959], 65).

28. Sue Bailey Thurman had been on a Pilgrimage of Friendship to Europe in the late 1920s, and Ralla Ram had been part of a four-person, three month "Mission of Friendship" from India to the British Isles in 1932 (Dixie and Eisenstadt, *Visions of a Better World,* 72).

29. "Committee on Negro Delegation to India," 13 March 1934, Howard Thurman Papers Project Files. Ralla Ram's words are quoted by committee member Luther Tucker.

30. "General Principles to Be Followed in Sending to the Student Christian Movement of India a Deputation of Negro Representatives by the Student Christian Movement of the United States," Committee on the Negro Delegation to India, 6 April 1934, Howard Thurman Papers Project Files.

31. Frank. T. Wilson, "Minutes Regarding the Decision of the Personnel of the Proposed Delegation to India," 19 April 1934, Howard Thurman Papers Project Files.

32. Frank. T. Wilson, "Minutes Regarding the Decision of the Personnel of the Proposed Delegation to India," 19 April 1934, in Howard Thurman Papers Project Files

33. "Committee on Negro Delegation to India," 13 March 1934, Howard Thurman Papers Project Files.

34. "Minutes of the Committee on the Negro Delegation to India," 10 April 1934, Howard Thurman Papers Project Files.

35. HT, "India Report," in *PHWT,* 2:122–23.

36. Thurman to Winnifred Wygal, 24 March 1934, in *PHWT,* 1:178–79.

37. HT, "India Report," in *PHWT,* 2:122–23; *WHAH,* 104. In the initial list of names considered by the India Committee, Sue is listed second, right after Howard, but her name has a strike-through ("Committee on Negro Delegation to India," 13 March 1934).

38. See the formal invitation, in Betty Harrington to Sue Bailey Thurman, 24 May 1934, Howard Thurman Papers Project Files.

39. Herbert King to HT, 11 October 1934, Folder 36, Box 23, HTC; Shelton Hale Bishop to HT, 1 May 1935, Folder 51, Box 23, HCT; HT to Grace Virginia Imes, 5 December 1934, in *PHWT,* 1:225–26. See also Paul Hutchinson to Winnifred Wygal, 14 March 1935, in *PHWT,* 1:245–46.

40. HT to Elizabeth Harrington, 6 September 1934, Folder 36, Box 23, HTC; *WHAH,* 116.

41. HT to Joseph Baker, 4 December 1934, in *PHWT,* 1:222–24.

42. Thurman felt that for many Indian Christians, conversion had left them with confused and uncertain identities. Thinking of them, he quoted Carl Sandberg's

poem about a flying fish: "Child of water, child of air / Wing thing, water thing / I have lived in many half worlds myself / So I know you" (HT, "India Report," in *PHWT*, 2:129).

43. *WHAH*, 116. For both its American and its Indian sponsors, the Negro Delegation represented part of a broader rethinking of traditional mission work, away from evangelizing and toward "de-Westernizing" Christianity (see William R. Hutchinson, *Errand to the World: American Protestant Thought and Foreign Missions* [Chicago: University of Chicago Press, 1987]). Ralla Ram wanted a Negro Delegation because "in the mind of our people belonging to other faiths, Christianity is identified with western imperialism, and they all think that Christianity is part and parcel of a western cult. The purpose of suggesting a mission of this kind . . . is that our students throughout the country should see for itself that Christianity is universal in its scope" (A. Ralla Ram to Frank T. Wilson, 28 June 1934, in *PHWT*, 1:193–95).

44. HT to the Members of the India Committee, 20 December 1935, in *PHWT*, 1:314.

45. African American tourists were sometimes required to post five hundred dollars before entering Mexico (see HT to Hubert Herring, 10 November 1934; HT to Hubert Herring, 22 March 1935; and Sue Bailey Thurman to Susan Ford Bailey, March 1935?, in *PHWT*, 2:217–18; 248–49, 244–45).

46. HT to Robert R. Moton, 30 August 1935, in *PHWT*, 1:279.

47. *WHAH*, 105–7.

48. HT to Grace Towns Hamilton, 12 October 1934, Folder 37, Box 23, HTC. See also HT to Elizabeth Harrington, 6 September 1934, Folder 36, Box 23, HTC.

49. For South Asian interest in the Scottsboro case, see *PHWT*, 1:302, 330.

50. A. Ralla Ram to Frank T. Wilson, 28 June 1934, in *PHWT*, 1:193–95.

51. *WHAH*, 121.

52. *WHAH*, 108; *PHWT*, 1:317.

53. Herbert King to Sue Bailey Thurman, 27 October 1936, Folder 10, Box 24, HTC.

54. The question of the selection of Phenola Carroll is discussed in more detail in *PHWT*, 1:184–86. HT to Betty Harrington, 11 July 1935, Folder 46, Box 23, HTC; HT to Frank T. Wilson, 20 July 1935, in *PHWT*, 1:273–75.

55. HT to the Members of the India Committee, 20 December 1935, in *PHWT*, 1:312–18.

56. See Betty Harrington to HT, 7 February 1936, Folder 41, Box 23, HTC; and Channing H. Tobias to Ruth Taylor, 9 March 1936, in *PHWT*, 1:332.

57. For Thurman's positive evaluations of the Carrolls in his autobiography, see *WHAH*, 105, 112.

58. HT to Elizabeth Harrington, 13 May 1935, in *PHWT*, 1:258–60.

59. *WHAH*, 109.

60. *WHAH*, 109.

61. HT to Frank T. Wilson, 28 May 1935, in *PHWT*, 1:261–62.

62. Olive Thurman Wong, interview by Peter Eisenstadt, January 2012.

63. HT, "'Our Delegation' in India" (March 1936), in *PHWT*, 1:328–32.

64. HT, "Journey in Understanding" (June 1964), Folder 37, Box 6, HTC.

65. HT, "Colombo Journal" (October 1935), in *PHWT*, 1:300.

66. *WHAH*, 113.

67. Dixie and Eisenstadt, *Visions of a Better World*, xiv–xv.

68. HT, "Colombo Journal," in *PHWT*, 1:304.

69. HT, "Crossing the Great Divide: India," 33, Folder 11, Box 4, HTC.

70. For a more detailed account of the meeting at the Colombo Law Club, see Dixie and Eisenstadt, *Visions of a Better World*, xvi–xxii.

71. Thurman was particularly impressed by Alwaye College, the one college managed by the Indian Orthodox Church, an ancient, non-Western Indian Christian denomination (HT, "India Report," in *PHWT*, 2:124).

72. *WHAH*, 127–28.

73. While in Bombay, the Negro Delegation was entertained by a Black jazz pianist, who wrote to Thurman as "Dr. Jazz" (Dr. Jazz to HT, 18 February 1936, in *PHWT*, 1:327–28). Dr. Jazz did not further identify himself, and in the first volume of the documentary edition, Dr. Jazz was misidentified as Teddy Weatherford, due to my overenthusiastic research (*PHWT*, 1:327–28). Although Weatherford was in Bombay at the time, Dr. Jazz was almost certainly a far more obscure musician, Frank George Shriver (see Mary Louise Jackson to HT, 16 June 1936; and HT to Mary Louise Jackson, 23 June 1936, both in Folder 6, Box 24, HTC). Shriver had been in Asia for a number of years, originally as a member of Wilbur's Blackbirds (see "'Buddy' Letter," *Chicago Defender*, 5 January 1929).

74. For details of the tour's schedule, see "Detailed Schedule," in *PHWT*, 1:283–99.

75. *PHWT*, 1:187.

76. *PHWT*, 1:186–87.

77. *WHAH*, 135.

78. *WHAH*, 128–29; Dixie and Eisenstadt, *Visions of a Better World*, 92–95.

79. T. J. George to HT, 14 January 1936, Folder 1, Box 24, HTC.

80. Ch. John to Members of the India Delegation, 21 November 1935, in *PHWT*, 1:310–11.

81. "One Who Met Them, the Negro Delegation in Madras," *Guardian* (Madras), 12 December 1935.

82. T. K. Jagannathacharya to HT, 7 December 1935, Folder 51, Box 23, HTC.

83. *WHAH*, 118.

84. Kapur, *Raising up a Prophet*, 81.

85. Dixie and Eisenstadt, *Visions of a Better World*, 96; Kapur, *Raising up a Prophet*, 39.

86. Muriel Lester to HT, 21 January 1935; HT to Allan A. Hunter, 30 January 1935; HT to Muriel Lester, 30 January 1935, in *PHWT*, 1:231–33, 235–36, 236–37.

87. HT to Mahatma Gandhi, 9 September 1935; Mahatma Gandhi to HT, 6 October 1935, in *PHWT*, 1:279–80; 282–83.

88. HT, "Men Who Have Walked with God: Mahatma Gandhi" (6 July 1953), Folder 91, Box 11, HTC.

89. *WHAH*, 131.

90. HT, *Footprints of a Dream*, 24.

91. *PHWT*, 2:126.

1. Deep River

1. U.S. Bureau of the Census, *Twelfth Census of the United States, Population Schedule, Dade County, Florida* (Washington, DC: GPO), Roll T623–167. See *PHWT,* 1:xxxi.

2. Edward N. Akin, *Flagler: Rockefeller Partner and Florida Baron* (Kent, OH: Kent State University Press, 1998). For a brief overview of the African American history of West Palm Beach, see Kevin M. McCarthy, *The Hippocrene U.S.A. Guide to Black Florida* (New York: Hippocrene, 1995), 322–27.

3. Clarence Walker, principal of the Industrial High School for Negroes in West Palm Beach, wrote Thurman, "My attention has been called to the fact that this town has the honor of being the place of your birth." Thurman's response to Walker did not address Walker's claim (Clarence Walker to HT, 2 January 1937; HT to Clarence Walker, 14 January 1937, both in Folder 14, Box 24, HTC). When, in passing, he did state, as he did in 1964, "I was born and raised in Daytona Beach," as in *PHWT,* 5:25, in discussing Howard Thurman Day in that city, it was, I suspect, as much out of a disinclination to tell a more complicated story as any other motive. Usually, as in his autobiography, he did not mention his place of birth but spoke rather only of growing up in Daytona.

4. Leonard H. Lempel, "African American Settlement in the Daytona Beach Area, 1876–1910," in *Proceedings from the Florida Conference of Historians* (Orange Park: Florida Conference of Historians, 1993), 109. See also Harold D. Cardwell and Priscilla D. Cardwell, *Historic Daytona Beach* (Charleston, SC: Arcadia, 2004).

5. *WHAH,* 9–10; Landrum Bolling, "Conversations with Howard Thurman: Transcript of Howard Thurman Documentary," 8–9 January 1976, p. 3, Folder 33, Box 16, HTC.

6. *WHAH,* 9–10.

7. Gordon Parks, Deborah Willis, and Leonard Lempel, *Midway: Portrait of a Daytona Beach Neighborhood* (Daytona Beach, FL: Southeast Museum of Photography at Daytona Beach Community College, 1999), esp. Leonard Lempel, "Black Daytona Beach in the 1940s: A Community at the Crossroads," 59–67.

8. *WHAH,* 9.

9. HT, "Man and the Moral Struggle: Paul" (9 January 1955), Folder 3, Box 17, HTC. See also HT, "The Message of Amos" (25 May 1952), in HT, *Moral Struggle and the Prophets,* ed. Peter Eisenstadt and Walter Earl Fluker, (Maryknoll, NY: Orbis, 2020), 131–39.

10. *Polk's Daytona Beach City Directory* (Jacksonville, FL: Polk, 1900), 2–3.

11. William Adams, "Southern City Making Wonderful Progress," *Chicago Defender,* 10 July 1915.

12. Washington praised Daytona during a 1912 visit: "Florida Willing to Give Negroes a Chance," *Chicago Defender,* 16 March 1912, see David H. Jackson, "Booker T. Washington's Tour of the Sunshine State, March, 1912," *Florida Historical Quarterly* 81, no. 3 (winter 2003): 254–78.

13. Paul Ortiz, *Emancipation Betrayed: The Hidden History of Black Organizing and White Violence in Florida to the Bloody Election of 1920* (Berkeley: University of

California Press, 2005), 99; William Adams, "Daytona Will Celebrate on New Year's Day," *Chicago Defender* 18 December 1915.

14. Leonard R. Lempel, "The Mayor's 'Henchmen and Henchwomen, Both White and Colored': Edward H. Armstrong and the Politics of Race in Daytona Beach, 1900–1940," *Florida Historical Quarterly* 70, no. 3 (Winter 2001): 273–74.
15. *WHAH*, 9.
16. *WHAH*, 13; William Adams, "Daytona Kindergarten to Be Improved," *Chicago Defender,* 23 October 1915.
17. Ralph Bunche, *The Political Status of the Negro in the Age of FDR* (Chicago: University of Chicago Press, 1973), 451–54, 480–82.
18. "Race Doings," *Baltimore Afro-American,* 26 March 1898.
19. Lempel, "The Mayor's 'Henchmen,'" 277.
20. "A Pleasant Visit to Oldest American City," *Baltimore Afro-American,* 22 February 1912.
21. William Adams, "Florida," *Chicago Defender,* 18 November 1916.
22. Lempel, "The Mayor's 'Henchmen,'" 282. The Brooklyn Dodgers held spring training in Daytona Beach in 1946, Jackie Robinson's first season in organized baseball, because Dodgers president Branch Rickey determined that because of its Black political presence, it would likely be the most welcoming city in Florida for an interracial team (see Chris Lamb, *Blackout: The Untold Story of Jackie Robinson's First Spring Training* [Lincoln: University of Nebraska Press, 2004], 46).
23. *WHAH*, 10.
24. On sundown towns, see James Loewen, *Sundown Towns: A Hidden Dimension of American Racism* (New York: New Press, 2005).
25. *WHAH*, 10.
26. *PHWT*, 1:xxxix.
27. *WHAH*, 8.
28. Lempel, "The Mayor's 'Henchmen,'" 274.
29. *WHAH*, 11–12.
30. Bolling, "Conversations with Howard Thurman: Transcript of Howard Thurman Documentary," Folder 33, Box 16, HTC.
31. Roberta Byrd Barr, "A Creative Encounter: Interview with Howard Thurman," 14–15 February 1969, Part 2, p. 7, Folder 30, Box 16, HTC.
32. HT, *Footprints of a Dream: The Story of the Church for the Fellowship of All Peoples* (New York: Harper and Brothers, 1959), 17.
33. Bolling, "Conversations with Howard Thurman: Transcript of Howard Thurman Documentary," p. 63, Folder 33, Box 16, HTC.
34. Bolling, "Conversations with Howard Thurman: Transcript of Howard Thurman Documentary," p. 14, Folder 33, Box 16, HTC.
35. Byrd Barr, "A Creative Encounter: Interview with Howard Thurman," Part 1, pp. 3–4, Folder 30, Box 16, HTC.
36. Larry Eugene Rivers, *Slavery in Florida: Territorial Days to Emancipation* (Gainesville: University of Florida Press, 2002), 212. See also Clifton Paisley, *The Red Hills of Florida, 1528–1865* (Tuscaloosa: University of Alabama Press, 1989); and Edward E. Baptist, *Creating an Old South: Middle Florida's Plantation Frontier before the Civil War* (Chapel Hill: University of North Carolina Press, 2002).

37. U.S. Bureau of the Census, *Tenth Census of the United States, Population Schedule, Moseley Hall, Madison County, Florida* (Washington, DC: GPO, 1880), T9, Roll 130; *PHWT,* 1:lxxxn4, 7.

38. Larry Eugene Rivers, "Madison County—1830 to 1860: A Case Study in Land, Labor, and Prosperity," *Journal of Negro History* 78, no. 4 (autumn 1993): 233–44; U.S Census Slave Schedules for Madison County, Florida, 1860, NARA Microfilm Series M653, Roll 110; HT, *Jesus and the Disinherited* (New York: Abingdon-Cokesbury, 1949), 30; *PHWT,* 1: xxxi–xxxii.

39. Paisley, *The Red Hills of Florida,* 147–55.

40. Paisley, *The Red Hills of Florida,* 152.

41. Rosa Galphin, "John C. McGehee," *Florida Historical Society Quarterly* 4, no. 4 (April 1926): 187; HT, *Jesus and the Disinherited,* 30–31.

42. Rivers, "Madison County—1830 to 1860," 241; *Journal of the Proceedings of the Convention of the People of Florida, Tallahassee, January 3, 1861* (Tallahassee: Dyke and Carlisle, 1861), 8.

43. HT, "The Moment of Crisis IV" (7 March 1958), Folder 33, Box 12, HTC.

44. *WHAH,* 232

45. *PHWT,* 1:xxxi–xxxii.

46. See HT, "The Three Faiths of the Negro: Belief in His Ability, in Life, and in God," *Times of India,* 21 February 1936, in *PHWT,* 1:307. For accounts of remarkable enslaved and free Black calculators, see Sidney Kaplan and Emma Nogrady Kaplan, *The Black Presence in the Era of the American Revolution* (Amherst: University of Massachusetts Press, 1989), 167–70.

47. *WHAH,* 12–13.

48. Ortiz, *Reconstruction Betrayed,* 23, 38, 64, 169.

49. See *PHWT,* 4:243–44n1.

50. See *PHWT,* 1:xxxi. The 1900 census gives his age as fifty. Thurman states that at the time of his death, in 1907 or 1908, he was fifty-five, putting his birth in the early 1850s (HT, *Footprints of a Dream,* 15).

51. See Les Staniford, *Last Train to Paradise: Henry Flagler and the Spectacular Rise and Fall of the Railroad That Crossed an Ocean* (New York: Crown, 2002); and Dan Gallagher, *Florida's Great Ocean Railway: Building the Key West Extension* (Sarasota, FL: Pineapple, 2003).

52. For national attention to enforced and captive labor on the Key West Extension, see Pete Daniel, *The Shadow of Slavery: Peonage in the South, 1901–1969* (Urbana: University of Illinois Press, 1972), 95–107.

53. Bolling, "Conversations with Howard Thurman: Transcript of Howard Thurman Documentary," p. 6, Folder 33, Box 16, HTC.

54. *WHAH,* 4–5; HT, *Footprints of a Dream,* 15–16.

55. Bolling, "Conversations with Howard Thurman: Transcript of Howard Thurman Documentary," p. 10, Folder 33, Box 16, HTC.

56. *WHAH,* 5.

57. Bolling, "Conversations with Howard Thurman: Transcript of Howard Thurman Documentary," p. 7, Folder 33, Box 16, HTC.

58. *WHAH,* 18.

59. *WHAH,* 6.

60. *WHAH*, 7.

61. HT, *Footprints of a Dream*, 15–16 (this is the opening of the first chapter); *WHAH*, 4–6; Bolling, "Conversations with Howard Thurman: Transcript of Howard Thurman Documentary," pp. 10–13, Folder 33, Box 16, HTC.

62. See, for example, Benjamin Mays, *Born to Rebel: An Autobiography* (New York, Scribner's, 1971), 1–8.

63. HT, "The Fascist Masquerade" (1946), in *PHWT*, 3:158.

64. I have not seen, and do not have access to, the letter, written in the early 1970s, from Thurman to his daughter Anne, but several leading Thurman scholars who were able to briefly see the letter but not copy it have vouched for its existence and described to me its contents in general terms.

65. HT, "Man and the Moral Struggle: *The Great Hunger* [by Johann Bojer]" (18 December 1949), in HT, *Moral Struggle and the Prophets,* ed. Peter Eisenstadt and Walter Earl Fluker (Maryknoll, NY: Orbis, 2020), 93–101.

66. *WHAH*, 253.

67. *WHAH*, 15–16.

68. *WHAH*, 13. For Thurman's animosity to James Sams, see James Sams to HT, 15 December 1946, in *PHWT*, 3:210–11.

69. HT, "Religious Commitment" (unpublished typescript, ca. 1978), 6, Folder 25, Box 4, HTC.

70. HT, "The Binding Commitment: Concluding Chapter, With Head and Heart" (ca. 1978), 2, Folder 24, Box 4, HTC.

71. HT, "The Binding Commitment," 5, Folder 25, Box 4, HTC.

72. HT, "Religious Commitment," 6, Folder 25, Box 4, HTC.

73. Bolling, "Conversations with Howard Thurman: Transcript of Howard Thurman Documentary," pp. 3–4, Folder 33, Box 16, HTC.

74. *WHAH*, 7.

75. *WHAH*, 7; HT, "Modern Challenges to Religion III" (4 May 1958), Folder 42, Box 12, HTC.

76. *PHWT*, 1:12–13.

77. HT, "Religious Commitment," 10, Folder 25, Box 4, HTC.

78. HT, "Sunrise" (1919), in *PHWT*, 1:11.

79. *WHAH*, 8–9.

80. HT, "Mysticism and Social Change" (February 1939), in *PHWT*, 2:206.

81. Bolling, "Conversations with Howard Thurman: Transcript of Howard Thurman Documentary," p. 2, Folder 33, Box 16, HTC.

82. Lerone Bennett Jr., "Howard Thurman: 20th Century Holy Man," *Ebony* 33, no. 4 (February 1978): 85.

83. For "seekin'," see Margaret Washington Creel, *"A Peculiar People": Slave Religion and Community-Culture among the Gullahs* (New York: New York University Press, 1988), 285–95.

84. W. E. B. Du Bois, "The Souls of Black Folk," in *Writings,* by Du Bois (New York: Library of America, 1986), 364.

85. *WHAH*, 263.

86. Bolling, "Conversations with Howard Thurman: Transcript of Howard Thurman Documentary," p. 13, Folder 33, Box 16, HTC. See HT, *Footprints of a Dream,* 18,

for an instance in which Nancy diagnosed a spectral influence making her grandson ill.

87. HT, "Mysticism and Social Change, #5" (12 July 1978), in *Walking with God: The Howard Thurman Sermon Series,* ed. Peter Eisenstadt and Walter E. Fluker, vol. 2: *Howard Thurman on Mysticism* (Maryknoll, NY: Orbis, 2021).

88. HT, "Religious Commitment," 3, Folder 25, Box 4, HTC; HT, "The Binding Commitment, 2–3, Folder 25, Box 4, HTC.

89. *WHAH,* 15.

90. Jean Burden, "Meditation on Howard Thurman on the Occasion of His Memorial Service April 10, 1981," Howard Thurman Papers Project Files.

91. *WHAH,* 13.

92. Elizabeth Yates, *Howard Thurman: Portrait of a Practical Dreamer* (New York: John Day, 1964), 161, 163.

93. Bolling, "Conversations with Howard Thurman: Transcript of Howard Thurman Documentary," p. 4, Folder 33, Box 16, HTC.

94. *WHAH,* 266.

95. Bolling, "Conversations with Howard Thurman: Transcript of Howard Thurman Documentary," p. 5, Folder 33, Box 16, HTC.

96. *WHAH,* 19–20.

97. *WHAH,* 18; HT, *Footprints of a Dream,* 15; Bolling, "Conversations with Howard Thurman: Transcript of Howard Thurman Documentary," pp. 7–8, Folder 33, Box 16, HTC.

98. William Adams, "B.Y.P.U. Sunday School Hold Big Convention," *Chicago Defender,* 7 August 1915.

99. William Adams, "Successful Revival Is Held," *Chicago Defender,* 4 September 1915.

100. *WHAH,* 17.

101. For Owen, see HT to S. A. Owen, 6 March 1963, in *PHWT,* 5:9–10.

102. *WHAH,* 48.

103. William Adams, "Florida," *Chicago Defender,* 7 October 1916.

104. William Adams, "Florida," *Chicago Defender,* 23 December 1916.

105. *WHAH,* 17.

106. Adams, "Florida," *Chicago Defender,* 23 December 1916.

107. *WHAH,* 22.

108. William Adams, "Florida People Read the *Defender,*" *Chicago Defender,* 19 June 1915.

109. *WHAH,* 21–22. Leonard Lempel, the leading historian of Black Daytona, concluded that while some of the details of Thurman's version of the story "are most likely apocryphal," the story does reveal "the burgeoning political involvement of Daytona's Blacks during the 1920s" and Thornton's role in this (Lempel, "The Mayor's 'Henchmen,'" 273–74).

110. HT, "Religious Commitment," 14–16, Folder 25, Box 4, HTC.

111. *WHAH,* 25.

112. *WHAH,* 11, 21, 25, 26.

113. HT to Mordecai Wyatt Johnson, 18 June 1918, in *PHWT,* 1:2.

114. Adams, "Florida People Read the *Defender.*"

115. Eulogy for Mary McLeod Bethune, 23 May 1955, in *PHWT,* 4:124.

116. For an overview of Bethune's career, see Audrey Thomas McCluskey and Elaine M. Smith, eds., *Mary McLeod Bethune, Building a Better World: Essays and Selected Documents* (Bloomington: Indiana University Press, 1999).

117. *WHAH*, 13–14.

118. Bolling, "Conversations with Howard Thurman: Transcript of Howard Thurman Documentary," p. 13, Folder 33, Box 16, HTC.

119. HT, "Negro Spirituals and the Black Madonna" (16 October 1975), Folder 16, Box 14, HTC.

120. Bolling, "Conversations with Howard Thurman: Transcript of Howard Thurman Documentary," p. 16, Folder 33, Box 16, HTC.

121. Thomas Jesse Jones, ed., *Negro Education: A Study of the Private and Higher Schools for Colored People in the United States* (Washington, DC: Bureau of Education, Department of the Interior, 1917), 2:178.

122. Jones, ed., *Negro Education,* 2:162.

123. *PHWT,* 1:342.

124. Jones, ed., *Negro Education,* 2:162–78.

125. Thurman writes that after his success, an eighth grade was soon added to the junior high school in Daytona for Blacks (*WHAH*, 24; Bolling, "Conversations with Howard Thurman: Transcript of Howard Thurman Documentary," pp. 17–18, Folder 33, Box 16, HTC). Thurman was not the first Black Daytonan to get around the eighth-grade gap and attend high school. In 1916, when Thurman was a sophomore, at least six Blacks from Daytona were attending high school in Jacksonville, including Thurman and his sister Henrietta (William Adams, "Florida," *Chicago Defender,* 7 October 1916). For young women, the Bethune Institute had a secondary education program from shortly after its 1904 founding.

126. HT to Mordecai Wyatt Johnson, 18 June 1918, in *PHWT,* 1:2.

127. *PHWT,* 1:1–4.

128. Bolling, "Conversations with Howard Thurman: Transcript of Howard Thurman Documentary," p. 18, Folder 33, Box 16, HTC.

129. *WHAH*, 24–25.

130. Yates, *Howard Thurman,* 23.

2. "My People Need Me"

1. Landrum Bolling, "Conversations with Howard Thurman: Transcript of Howard Thurman Documentary," 8–9 January 1976, pp. 20, 18, Folder 33, Box 16, HTC.

2. *WHAH*, 25.

3. Bolling, "Conversations with Howard Thurman: Transcript of Howard Thurman Documentary," p. 20, Folder 33, Box 16, HTC.

4. *WHAH*, 25–26, 238–39; Bolling, "Conversations with Howard Thurman: Transcript of Howard Thurman Documentary," pp. 21–22, Folder 33, Box 16, HTC.

5. HT to Ethel Simons, 4 June 1919, in *PHWT,* 1:6–7.

6. HT to Ethel Simons, 13 July 1920, in *PHWT,* 1:9–10.

7. For a similar episode in 1936, see Herbert King to Sue Bailey Thurman, 27 October 1936, Folder 10, Box 24, HTC; Phyllis Case to HT, 11 December 1936, Folder 13, Box 24, HTC.

8. The school's transformations were not yet complete. It became a four-year college in 1941 and moved to Miami in 1968, where it is now Florida Memorial University (Florida Memorial University, "Our History," https://www.fmuniv.edu/history/).

9. Thomas Jesse Jones, ed., *Negro Education: A Study of the Private and Higher Schools for Colored People in the United States* (Washington, DC: Bureau of Education, Department of the Interior, 1917), 2:169.

10. *Register of Florida Baptist Academy, with Catalogue of Students* (Jacksonville, 1916).

11. *Register of Florida Baptist Academy.*

12. Jones, ed., *Negro Education,* 2:169.

13. *Register of Florida Baptist Academy.*

14. For details of Thurman's coursework, see *PHWT,* 1:342–51.

15. HT, "Africa Journal" (Autumn, 1963), in *PHWT,* 5:44.

16. *Register of Florida Baptist Academy.*

17. Jones, ed., *Negro Education,* 2:169.

18. *Register of Florida Baptist Academy.*

19. HT to Josephine Junius, 9 December 1917, Folder 1, Box 23, HTC.

20. Answer Sheet: "*Howard Thurman,*" enclosure in HT to Louise Daniel Hutchinson, 26 April 1971, Folder 4, Box 45, HTC. See also Bolling, "Conversations with Howard Thurman: Transcript of Howard Thurman Documentary," pp. 19–20, Folder 33, Box 16, HTC; and Elizabeth Yates, *Howard Thurman: Portrait of a Practical Dreamer* (New York: John Day, 1964), 46.

21. HT to Josephine Junius, 21 October 1917, Folder 1, Box 23, HTC.

22. HT to Josephine Junius, 9 December 1917, Folder 1, Box 23, HTC.

23. HT, "Religious Commitment" (unpublished typescript, ca. 1978), 3, Folder 25, Box 4, HTC.

24. Answer Sheet: "*Howard Thurman,*" enclosure in HT to Louise Daniel Hutchinson, 26 April 1971, Folder 4, Box 45, HTC.

25. Yates, *Howard Thurman,* 46; HT to Ethel Simons, 4 June 1919, in *PHWT,* 1:6–7.

26. Yates, *Howard Thurman,* 46.

27. See HT to Ethel Simons Meeds, 19 February 1965, in *PHWT,* 5:127–30.

28. HT to Ethel Simons, 4 June 1919, in *PHWT,* 1:6–7.

29. Roberta Byrd Barr, "A Creative Encounter: Interview with Howard Thurman, 14–15 February 1969, Part 1, p. 7, Folder 30, Box 16, HTC.

30. Bolling, "Conversations with Howard Thurman: Transcript of Howard Thurman Documentary," p. 23, Folder 33, Box 16, HTC.

31. Bolling, "Conversations with Howard Thurman: Transcript of Howard Thurman Documentary," pp. 23–24, Folder 33, Box 16, HTC.

32. Byrd Barr, "A Creative Encounter: Interview with Howard Thurman," Part 1, p. 7, Folder 30, Box 16, HTC.

33. *WHAH,* 26–27.

34. For late-in-life letters from Thurman, see HT to "Miss Junius" [Mrs. Josephine Harris], 22 May 1978, Folder 2, Box 48, HTC; and HT to Miss Simons [Ethel Simons Meeds], February 1980, Folder 2, Box 50, HTC.

35. Byrd Barr, "A Creative Encounter," Part 1, p. 7, Folder 30, Box 16, HTC.

36. HT to Nathan Collier, 30 August 1935, in *PHWT*, 1:277–78. Thurman returned to his alma mater for a commencement address (see "Hold Founder's Day at Florida Normal," *Chicago Defender*, 25 April 1931).

37. In Thurman's later years, support for students at historically Black colleges was one of the main activities of the Howard Thurman Educational Trust.

38. *WHAH*, 4.

39. *WHAH*, 253–54.

40. *WHAH*, 241–42, 232–33.

41. *WHAH*, 253–54; William Adams, "Florida," *Chicago Defender*, 9 September 1916; "Florida," *Chicago Defender*, 1 October 1916.

42. *WHAH*, 253–54; William Adams, "Florida," *Chicago Defender*, 8 June 1918.

43. HT, "The Sphere of the Church's Responsibility in Social Reconstruction" (July 1925), in *PHWT*, 1:41–43.

44. HT, "A 'Native Son' Speaks" (1940), in *PHWT*, 2:250–51 For African Americans in World War I, see Nina Mjagkij, *Loyalty in Time of Trial: The African American Experience during World War I* (Lanham, MD: Rowman and Littlefield, 2011); and Adriane Lentz-Smith, *Freedom Struggles: African Americans and World War I* (Cambridge, MA: Harvard University Press, 2009).

45. "Emmett J. Scott Invited to Deliver Commencement Address," *Chicago Defender*, 8 June 1918.

46. "Third Liberty Loan Honor Flag to Jacksonville, Fla.," *Chicago Defender*, 15 June 1918.

47. James Weldon Johnson, *Fifty Years and Other Poems* (Boston: Cornhill, 1917), 22. Collier and Johnson had been classmates at Atlanta University and remained friends (see "Along This Way," in James Weldon Johnson, *Writings* [New York: Library of America, 2004], 283).

48. Johnson, *Fifty Years and Other Poems*, 486–93.

49. "Experienced Men Wanted," "Why Should a Negro Fight," in Johnson, *Writings*, 631, 633

50. "Commander of Student Army Training Corps," *Chicago Defender*, 10 August 1918.

51. "Sec. Baker's Wife Sings for Soldiers at Howard U.," *Chicago Defender*, 14 September 1918.

52. "Kelly Miller Says the Outlook Is Hopeful," *Chicago Defender*, 27 September 1918. In a 1926 address in Cedar Falls, Iowa, according to a newspaper account "concerning the essential kinship of all peoples, Mr. Thurman said that all life is one. He cited the example of the westward march of the influenza epidemic" (HT, "Characteristic Christian Life Attitudes" [6 October 1926], Engagements Scrapbook, 1920–1930, Folder 1, Box 100, HTC; Howard Thurman Papers Project Files). This is one of the earliest statements of Thurman's belief in the unity of life, speaking to our shared vunerablities. It is also Thurman's only reference I know to the 1918–19 Spanish flu pandemic. There is no evidence that he was stricken, but he had a close call. Military camps were notorious sites of infection during the pandemic, and Thurman remained in Washington, D.C., until mid-September.

The first cases of Spanish flu were recorded in the city in late August, and the disease was epidemic in the city by the end of September, by which time Thurman had returned to St. Augustine for his senior year of high school.

53. HT to Mordecai Wyatt Johnson, 18 June 1918, in *PHWT*, 1:1–4.
54. *WHAH*, 27–28.
55. HT, "The Flag" (January 1920), in *PHWT*, 1:11–12.
56. HT, "Our Challenge" (February-March 1922), in *PHWT*, 1:20–22.
57. See Lurana Sheldon's poem "At Carrizal," which praised "negro troops" who supposedly "faced their death singing," in *Rendezvous with Death: American Poems of the Great War,* ed. Mark W. Van Wienen (Urbana: University of Illinois Press, 2002), 136–37.
58. *WHAH*, 22–23.
59. *WHAH*, 45.
60. For Thurman's only extended discussion of color bias among Blacks, see "What We May Learn from India" (1936), reprinted in *A Strange Freedom: The Best of Howard Thurman on Religious Experience and Public Life,* ed. Walter Earl Fluker and Catherine Tumber (Boston: Beacon, 1998), 208.
61. For Johnson, see Richard I. McKinney, *Mordecai: The Man and His Message: The Story of Mordecai Wyatt Johnson* (Washington, DC: Howard University Press, 1998); and Gary Dorrien, *Breaking White Supremacy: Martin Luther King Jr. and the Social Gospel* (New Haven, CT: Yale University Press 2018), 24–95.
62. In 1912 the YMCA started two annual summer conferences in North Carolina, one, at Blue Ridge, for whites, and one, at Kings Mountain, for Blacks. They would remain segregated, separate (and in their facilities, unequal) for decades.
63. Bolling, "Conversations with Howard Thurman: Transcript of Howard Thurman Documentary," p. 27, Folder 33, Box 16, HTC.
64. HT to Mordecai Wyatt Johnson, 18 June 1918, in *PHWT*, 1:1–4.
65. HT to Mordecai Wyatt Johnson, 18 June 1918.
66. Mordecai Wyatt Johnson to HT, 8 July 1918, in *PHWT*, 1:4–5.
67. HT to Mordecai Wyatt Johnson, 17 July 1918, in *PHWT*, 1:5–6.
68. HT to Mordecai Wyatt Johnson, 17 July 1918, in *PHWT*, 1:5–6. See David Setran, *The College "Y": Student Religion in an Age of Secularization* (New York: Palgrave Macmillan, 2007).
69. Gamewell Valentine, "Themes and Variations," *Atlanta Daily World,* 31 May 1937.

3. "The Personification of the Morehouse Ideal"

1. Samuel G. Freedman, "Parents' Ceremony Serves up Elements of 'Morehouse Gospel,'" *New York Times,* 21 August 2015.
2. Morehouse College Yearbook, in *PHWT*, 1:25.
3. See Peter Godwin Heltzel, "The Morehouse Gospel: Howard Thurman, Martin Luther King, Jr., and Prophetic Black Christianity," in *In The Beginning; The Martin Luther King, Jr., International Chapel at Morehouse College: A Festschrift in Honor of Lawrence Carter, Sr.,* ed. Echol Nix Jr. (Macon, GA: Mercer University Press, 2015), 65–80; and Peter Godwin Heltzel, *Resurrection City: A Theology of Improvisation* (Grand Rapids, MI: Eerdmans, 2012), 90–112.

4. HT, "Religious Commitment" (unpublished typescript, ca. 1978), Folder 25, Box 4, HTC.

5. HT, "Religious Commitment," 3, Folder 25, Box 4, HTC. Thurman presumably saw attending Worcester Academy as a form of "validation," a post–high school year prior to his entering Brown. It seems likely that Thurman had learned that John Hope, Morehouse president, had followed this trajectory, Worcester Academy and then Brown.

6. "Morehouse College Seventy-Fifth Anniversary Sermon" (15 February 1942), in *PHWT*, 2:293–301; HT, "The Public and Private Results of College Education in the Life of Negro Americans" (15 February 1967), in *A Strange Freedom: The Best of Howard Thurman on Religious Experience and Public Life,* ed. Walter Earl Fluker and Catherine Tumber (Boston: Beacon, 1998), 233–40.

7. *WHAH,* 35.

8. For the history of Morehouse, see Edward A. Jones, *A Candle in the Dark: A History of Morehouse College* (Valley Forge, PA: Judson, 1967); and Leroy Davis, *A Clashing of the Soul: John Hope and the Dilemma of African American Leadership and Black Higher Education in the Early Twentieth Century* (Athens: University of Georgia Press, 1998).

9. HT, "Morehouse College Seventy-Fifth Anniversary Sermon," in *PHWT,* 2:293–302.

10. HT, "Our Challenge" (January 1922), in *PHWT,* 1:21.

11. HT, "The Contribution of Baptist Church Schools to Negro Youth" (6 August 1938), in *PHWT,* 2:182.

12. HT, "Morehouse College Seventy-Fifth Anniversary Sermon," in *PHWT,* 2:293–302.

13. For Hope's early biography, see Davis, *A Clashing of the Soul.*

14. W. E. B. Du Bois, *Darkwater: Voices from within the Veil* (New York: Harcourt, Brace, and Howe, 1920), 27.

15. Davis, *A Clashing of the Soul,* 166–297.

16. Davis, *A Clashing of the Soul,* 251.

17. Davis, *A Clashing of the Soul,* 252, 248.

18. Davis, *A Clashing of the Soul,* 257–58.

19. Davis, *A Clashing of the Soul,* 273.

20. Mays, *Born to Rebel: An Autobiography* (1971; repr., Athens: University of Georgia Press, 2003), 90.

21. *WHAH,* 37. Thurman offers two dates when this discussion with Hope took place, either when he was an undergraduate (*WHAH,* 37), or when he returned to Morehouse as a teacher in the late 1920s (HT, *The Luminous Darkness: A Personal Interpretation of the Anatomy of Segregation and the Ground of Hope* [New York: Harper and Row, 1964], 13–14). There are difficulties with both dates, but Hayes had his first recital in Atlanta only in 1925. There were plans, unfortunately aborted, for Hayes and Thurman to collaborate on a recording of a spiritual-cycle of the life of Christ, with Hayes as singer and Thurman as narrator (Roland Hayes to HT, 25 August 1954, in *PHWT,* 4:94–95).

22. John Hope to W. E. B. Du Bois, 15 November 1924, cited in Davis, *A Clashing of the Soul,* 255.

23. Thomas Jesse Jones, ed., *Negro Education: A Study of the Private and Higher Schools for Colored People in the United States* (Washington, DC: Bureau of Education, Department of the Interior, 1917), 2:219.

24. *WHAH,* 33.

25. Davis, *A Clashing of the Soul,* 259.

26. Davis, *A Clashing of the Soul,* 175–78, 258.

27. *WHAH,* 39.

28. See Cameron McWhirter, *Red Summer: The Summer of 1919 and the Awakening of Black America* (New York: Henry Holt, 2011).

29. *WHAH,* 36.

30. Davis, *A Clashing of the Soul,* 177, 259.

31. Davis, *A Clashing of the Soul,* 259.

32. HT to John Hope, 20 June 1921; John Hope to HT, 28 June 1921, in *PHWT,* 1:17–18; 18–19.

33. HT to John Hope, 13 July 1926, Folder 1, Box 23, HTC.

34. Thurman is mentioned in passing in Ridgely Torrence, *The Story of John Hope* (New York: Macmillan, 1948), 329; HT to Lorimer Milton, 11 January 1949, in *PHWT,* 3:301–2.

35. Advertisement for Morehouse College, *The Crisis* 16, no. 13 (July 1918): 109.

36. Landrum Bolling, "Conversations with Howard Thurman: Transcript of Howard Thurman Documentary," 8–9 January 1976, p. 25, Folder 33, Box 16, HTC.

37. It is perhaps worth noting that several literary vignettes Thurman published in the Morehouse-Spellman literary magazine had a similar moral: women are smarter, wiser, and braver than their male counterparts (HT, "The Letter" [November 1922], in *PHWT* 1: 13–15; "The Ingrate" [February/March 1922], in *PHWT,* 1:15–16). He idealized motherhood in conventional evangelical language in "Regret Song," a poem appearing in the literary magazine in 1920, expressing the desire to "cry again at Mother's breast" and "feel her soft, god-like caress" so "A sweeter song I'd have to sing / In honor of my Risen King" (Howard Thurman Papers Project Files).

38. *WHAH,* 36.

39. For an example, see HT to Martin Luther King, Jr., 14 March 1956, in *PHWT,* 4:151–53.

40. *WHAH,* 36.

41. HT, "Religious Commitment," 3, Folder 25, Box 4, HTC.

42. HT, "Our Challenge," in *PHWT,* 1:20–22.

43. HT, "Our Challenge," in *PHWT,* 1:20–22.

44. HT, "Our Challenge," in *PHWT,* 1:20–22.

45. HT, "Our Challenge," in *PHWT,* 1:20–22.

46. *The Torch* [Morehouse College yearbook], excerpts, in *PHWT,* 1:25–29.

47. Jones, *A Candle in the Dark,* 199.

48. Clarence J. Gresham to HT, 29 December 1921, in *PHWT,* 1:19–20.

49. *WHAH,* 35.

50. Roberta Byrd Barr, "A Creative Encounter: Interview with Howard Thurman," 14–15 February 1969, Part 2, p. 7, Folder 30, Box 16, HTC.

51. *PHWT,* 1:22–25. He proposed something similar to his high school and college benefactor James Gamble (*WHAH,* 238).

52. HT, "Morehouse" (ca. 1978), Folder 3, Box 4, HTC.

53. Garrie Moore, "A Study of a Group of West Indian Negroes in New York City" (master's thesis, Columbia University, 1913).

54. For Garrie Moore, see *PHWT,* 1:xlix–l, lxxxiiin54. A tribute to Moore, co-written by Thurman, called him "Son of Morehouse, thou great source of power and inspiration," one who "whether working or sleeping" had "always dreamed of someday seeing Morehouse become the college of the Southland and a model for America" (F. W. Crawford, J. M. Nabrit Jr., and H. W. Thurman, "Professor G.W. Moore: An Appreciation," *Athenaeum* [April 1923]: 159–60).

55. For accounts of efforts to address Black poverty in Atlanta around Thurman's years in Morehouse, see Louie Davis Shivery, "The Neighborhood Union: A Survey of the Beginnings of Social Welfare Movements among Negroes in Atlanta," *Phylon* 3, no. 2 (2nd quarter 1943): 149–62; and Jacqueline Rouse, *Lugenia Burns Hope: Black Southern Reformer* (Athens: University of Georgia Press, 1989.) For Thurman on Beaver's Slide, see "'Relaxation' and the Peace Process" (1929), in *PHWT,* 1:146.

56. *The Torch,* in *PHWT,* 1:22.

57. Anthony M. Platt, *E. Franklin Frazier Reconsidered* (New Brunswick, NJ: Rutgers University Press, 1991), 62. For Frazier, see also Jonathan Scott Holloway, *Confronting the Veil: Abram Harris, Jr., E. Franklin Frazier, and Ralph Bunche, 1919–1941* (Chapel Hill: University of North Carolina Press, 2002), 123–56.

58. E. Franklin Frazier, "A Note on Negro Education," *Opportunity* 2 (March 1924): 75–77.

59. Edward Franklin Frazier, "New Currents of Thought among the Colored People of North America" (master's thesis, Clark University, 1920), 32, 36.

60. Frazier, "New Currents of Thought among the Colored People of North America," 14, 32.

61. *WHAH,* 40–41.

62. For Frazier's first widely circulated attack on the mores of the Black middle class, see E. Franklin Frazier, "La Bourgeoise Noire," in *Anthology of American Negro Literature,* ed. V. F. Calverton (New York: Modern Library, 1929), 379–88.

63. Frazier, "A Note on Negro Education."

64. *WHAH,* 40.

65. Barbara Dianne Savage, *Your Spirits Walk beside Us: The Politics of Black Religion* (Cambridge, MA: Harvard University Press, 2008), 205–37.

66. For Mays's biography, see Orville Vernon Burton, ix–lix, in Mays, *Born to Rebel;* and Randall Maurice Jelks, *Benjamin Elijah Mays, Schoolmaster of the Movement: A Biography* (Chapel Hill: University of North Carolina Press, 2012).

67. *WHAH,* 34.

68. *WHAH,* 41; *PHWT,* 1:l

69. Benjamin Mays, Memorial Tribute, in "Simmering on the Calm Presence and Profound Wisdom of Howard Thurman," special issue, *Debate & Understanding,* ed. Ricardo A. Millet and Conley H. Hughes (spring 1982): 87.

70. Benjamin Mays, "Address Given at Older Boys Conference," in *Sketches of Negro Life in South Carolina,* ed. Asa H. Gordon (1929; repr., Columbia: University of South Carolina Press, 1971), 203–11.

71. Benjamin Elijah Mays, "Pagan Survivals in Christianity" (master's thesis, University of Chicago, 1925), 56.
72. *WHAH,* 42.
73. *WHAH,* 43–44.
74. *WHAH,* 43–44.
75. *WHAH,* 43–44.
76. *WHAH,* 43–44.
77. Elizabeth Yates, *Howard Thurman: Portrait of a Practical Dreamer* (New York: John Day, 1964), 61.
78. *WHAH,* 43–44.
79. *WHAH,* 43–44.
80. Laurence Buermeyer et al., *An Introduction to Reflective Thinking* (Boston: Houghton Mifflin, 1923), 2. Thurman and his classmates must have had access to an early version of the book to use as their text.
81. John Dewey, *How We Think* (Boston: D. C. Heath, 1910), 13.
82. For community and contagion, see the four sermons Thurman delivered on "Community and the Will of God (I–IV)" (1961), Folders 7–10, Box 8, HTC.
83. *WHAH,* 265; HT to Dahlberg Peace Prize Committee, 4 September 1969, Folder 9, Box 44, HTC.
84. *PHWT,* 1:27–29.
85. Yates, *Howard Thurman,* 59–60.
86. *WHAH,* 28.
87. Benjamin E. Mays to Mary Jenness, 12 February 1936, in *PHWT,* 1:323–25.

4. "The Sound of Rushing Water"

1. HT, "Mysticism and the Experience of Love" (unpublished typescript, 1961), 5–6, subsequently published as *Mysticism and the Experience of Love* (Wallingford, PA: Pendle Hill, 1961). For Thurman's teaching the Bible class, see Luther Smith, communication with the author, April 2012. In the mid-1920s the Genesee River (not the Erie Canal) flowed under some well-developed areas in downtown Rochester (see Quinton Dixie and Peter Eisenstadt, *Visions of a Better World: Howard Thurman's Pilgrimage to India and the Origins of African American Nonviolence* [Boston: Beacon, 2011], 26).
2. *WHAH,* 45.
3. George Peck to HT, 18 January 1979, Folder 1, Box 49, HTC; HT to George Peck, 6 February 1979, Folder 2, Box 49, HTC. Newton Theological Institution had previously admitted African Americans, among them the pioneering historian George Washington Williams, who graduated in 1874.
4. *WHAH,* 46; HT, *The Luminous Darkness: A Personal Interpretation of the Anatomy of Segregation and the Ground of Hope* (New York: Harper and Row, 1965), 3.
5. Grant Wacker described Strong's magnum opus as a "hodgepodge of unintegrated insights" ("Augustus H. Strong," American National Biography Online, accessed 22 December 2019). For the history of RTS, see Leroy Moore Jr., "The Rise of Religious Liberalism at the Rochester Theological Seminary, 1872–1928" (Ph.D diss., Claremont Graduate School, 1966).

6. Elizabeth Yates, *Howard Thurman: Portrait of a Practical Dreamer* (New York: John Day, 1964), 77. For Thurman's apology, see HT to Mrs. William McCreal (Elizabeth Yates), 24 July 1965, Folder 7, Box 42, HTC.

7. For Rauschenbusch, see Christopher Hodge Evans, *The Kingdom Is Always but Coming: A Life of Walter Rauschenbusch* (Grand Rapids, MI: Eerdmans, 2004). In 1938 Thurman delivered the Rauschenbusch Lecture at Colgate Rochester Divinity School (see HT to Mordecai Wyatt Johnson, 3 February 1938, in *PHWT*, 2:119–20).

8. For Thurman's friendship with Pauline Rauschenbusch (1864–1949), Walter Rauschenbusch's widow, see Pauline Rauschenbusch to HT, 20 December 1939, Folder 13, Box 26, HTC.

9. Robert L. Kelley, *Theological Education in America: A Study of One Hundred Sixty-One Theological Schools in the United States* (New York: George H. Doran, 1924), 81.

10. *PHWT*, 1:2.

11. Roberta Byrd Barr, "A Creative Encounter: Interview with Howard Thurman," 14–15 February 1969, Part 1, pp. 9–10, Folder 30, Box 16, HTC.

12. *PHWT*, 1:25.

13. Byrd Barr, "A Creative Encounter: Interview with Howard Thurman," Part 1, pp. 11–12, Folder 30, Box 16, HTC.

14. *WHAH*, 46.

15. *WHAH*, 51.

16. HT, *The Luminous Darkness*, 3.

17. *WHAH*, 48.

18. Yates, *Howard Thurman*, 69.

19. Dave Voss to HT, 6 January 1965, Folder 1, Box 42, HTC.

20. *WHAH*, 48; Yates, *Howard Thurman*, 67, 69.

21. HT, "College and Color" (April 1924), in *PHWT*, 1:36–41.

22. HT, "College and Color," in *PHWT*, 1:36–41; Yates, *Howard Thurman*, 66.

23. *WHAH*, 49–51.

24. Yates, *Howard Thurman*, 64.

25. HT, "College and Color," in *PHWT*, 1:36–37.

26. HT, "College and Color," in *PHWT*, 1:36–37.

27. *WHAH*, 49; HT, "College and Color," in *PHWT*, 1:37.

28. HT, "College and Color," in *PHWT*, 1:39–40.

29. Yates, *Howard Thurman*, 66.

30. *WHAH*, 48, 53.

31. *WHAH*, 53. For his friendship with Jack Schooler, who continued to provide Thurman with his suits, see Jack Schooler to HT, 7 March 1945, Folder 13, Box 29, HTC. Thurman and Schooler continued to correspond into the 1980s.

32. It would move in 1928, with substantial support from John D. Rockefeller Jr., to a new location on the city's outskirts, housed in a beautiful neo-Gothic building, high on a majestic hill, and with a new name, the Colgate Rochester Divinity School.

33. *WHAH*, 46.

34. *WHAH*, 47.

35. Henry Adams, *Mont-Saint-Michel and Chartres* (New York: Houghton Mifflin, 1913).
36. HT, "The Gothic Arch" (undated, ca. 1970), Folder 27, Box 19, HTC. See also "The Gothic Principle" (1957), in which Thurman defines the architecture of a Gothic cathedral as "reaching for a realization that cannot be contained within the walls or within the stretch and expanse of the arches themselves" (in *PHWT*, 4:179).
37. Dave Voss to HT, 6 January 1965, Folder 1, Box 42, HTC.
38. Rochester Theological Seminary Transcripts, in *PHWT*, 1:350–51.
39. *WHAH*, 54. For Thurman's professors at RTS, see Luther E. Smith Jr., *Howard Thurman: The Mystic as Prophet* (1981; repr., Richmond, IN: Friends United Press, 2007), 21–33.
40. Evans, *The Kingdom Is Always but Coming*, 255. See also Ralph E. Luker, *The Social Gospel in Black and White: American Racial Reform, 1885–1912* (Chapel Hill: University of North Carolina Press, 1991).
41. *WHAH*, 54. For Robins, see Moore, "The Rise of Religious Liberalism," 199–215.
42. Yates, *Howard Thurman*, 63.
43. HT to Henry Burke Robins, 11 October 1934; Henry Burke Robins to HT, 15 October 1935, in *PHWT*, 1:207–9; 209–11.
44. Conrad Henry Moehlman, "Is Christianity Vanishing?," *The Baptist*, 25 April 1931, 524.
45. *WHAH*, 55.
46. Conrad Henry Moehlman, *The Christian-Jewish Tragedy: A Study in Religious Prejudice* (Rochester, NY: Printing House of Leo Hart, 1933), 3.
47. Grant Wacker, *Augustus H. Strong and the Dilemma of Historical Consciousness* (Macon, GA: Mercer University Press, 1985), 106.
48. *WHAH*, 55; Moore, "The Rise of Religious Liberalism," 172, citing Stanley I. Stuber, "Letter to the Editor," *CRDS Bulletin* 1 (May 1929): 272–73.
49. *WHAH*, 55.
50. *WHAH*, 55.
51. George Cross, The *Theology of Schleiermacher: A Condensed Presentation of His Chief Work* (Chicago: University of Chicago Press, 1911), 309.
52. Cross, *The Theology of Schleiermacher*, 182; *RTS Bulletin*, May 1916, 43–44; *RTS Bulletin*, May 1915, 20, latter two cited in Moore, "The Rise of Religious Liberalism," 184.
53. George Cross, *What Is Christianity? A Study of Rival Interpretations* (Chicago: University of Chicago, 1918), 166.
54. Moore, "The Rise of Religious Liberalism," 167.
55. HT, "Virgin Birth," in *PHWT*, 1:31–36. One of Thurman's main arguments, borrowed from leading anthropologists of the time, was that the myth of virgin birth was a product of the inability of primitive peoples to comprehend that most basic of the basic facts of life, that copulation, after a nine-month lag, can lead to procreation (see Edmund Leach, "Virgin Birth," in *Genesis as Myth and Other Essays* [London: Cape, 1969], 85–110).
56. HT, "Can It Truly Be Said That the Existence of a Supreme Spirit Is a Scientific Hypothesis?" (fall 1925), in *PHWT*, 1:54–67.

57. HT, "Can It Truly Be Said," in *PHWT,* 1:54–67.

58. HT, "Can It Truly Be Said," in *PHWT,* 1:54–67. There is one more aspect of "Can It Truly Be Said" that requires mention. There are fifteen instances of unacknowledged borrowings and overly close paraphrases from his sources, or, in other words, instances of plagiarism. Most are fairly innocuous, many borrowings from Laurence Buermeyer et al., *An Introduction to Reflective Thinking* (Boston: Houghton Mifflin, 1923), a text he had used in his 1922 course on reflective thinking, in a discussion, in his 1924 paper, on the Ptolemaic and Copernican world-systems. Thurman no doubt did not expect future scholars, a century on, to pick over all of his references, but this is one of the burdens of being sufficiently important to attract pedantic researchers. This was a class paper not intended for publication, and it is clear that Thurman was not entirely comfortable writing academic philosophy of this sort. The essay was largely a skein of quotations to begin with, and Thurman no doubt wanted to claim a higher proportion of the essay as his own prose than was warranted. As far as I know, it was a one-time indiscretion, and one can make of it what one will. In this way, too, of course, Thurman, unfortunately, was a forerunner of Martin Luther King, Jr. (see *PHWT,* 1:55, 65–66nn13–25). For King, see the essays in "Becoming Martin Luther King, Jr.—Plagiarism and Originality: A Round Table," *Journal of American History* 78, no. 1 (June 1991): 11–105.

59. HT, "The Basis of Sex Morality: An Inquiry into the Attitude toward Premarital Sexual Morality among Various People and an Analysis of Its True Basis," in *PHWT,* 1:71–107.

60. For Schreiner, see Ruth First and Ann Scott, *Olive Schreiner: A Biography* (New Brunswick, NJ: Rutgers University Press, 1991); Joyce Avrech Berkman, *The Healing Imagination of Olive Schreiner: Beyond South African Colonialism* (Amherst: University of Massachusetts Press, 1989); and Cherry Clayton, *Olive Schreiner* (New York: Twayne, 1997).

61. HT, "The Basis of Sex Morality," in *PHWT,* 1:92. For an account of the new sexual attitudes in the 1920s, see Paula S. Fass, *The Damned and the Beautiful: American Youth in the 1920s* (New York: Oxford University Press, 1977).

62. For the Pawling conference, see *WHAH,* 58–60; and HT, *A Track to the Water's Edge: The Olive Schreiner Reader* (New York: Harper and Row, 1973), xi–xii.

63. *WHAH,* 59–60.

64. *WHAH,* 59; *PHWT,* 1:92.

65. *WHAH,* 59.

66. *PHWT,* 92. Others at the Pawling retreat were interested in the study of sexuality. Thurman singles out the YWCA official Grace Louks as someone with whom he had extensive talks at Pawling (*WHAH,* 50). She would shortly be the coauthor of *The Sex Life of Youth* (New York: Association Press, 1929).

67. HT, "The Hunter," in *A Track to the Water's Edge,* 84–95. To somewhat complicate Thurman's narrative (and my retelling of it), his RTS seminary roommate, Dave Voss, who had the good habit of writing down the date he purchased a book on its flyleaf, wrote him in 1965 that "My copy of Olive Schreiner's *Dreams,* I note, was purchased on Oct. 24, 1924. Undoubtedly I made her acquaintance through you" (Dave Voss to HT, 6 January 1965). If Voss is correct in his date of

acquisition in the book and in his typing of the date in his letter, it meant that Thurman was likely familiar with Schreiner before the 1925 retreat.

68. HT, *A Track to the Water's Edge*, xi.
69. The book's title is drawn from "Three Dreams in a Desert," in HT, *A Track to the Water's Edge*, 56. Thurman quoted this allegory in the last sermon he ever delivered, "The Growing Edge," in October 1980 (in *PHWT*, 5:312). For Thurman's early efforts to publish a Schreiner anthology, see HT to Bill Worthy, 30 December 1942, Folder 17, Box 28, HTC.
70. Olive Schreiner, *Woman and Labor* (New York: Frederick A. Stokes, 1911).
71. HT, *A Track to the Water's Edge*, xii.
72. Clayton, *Olive Schreiner*, 81.
73. HT, *A Track to the Water's Edge*, xxviii.
74. HT, *A Track to the Water's Edge*, xi–xii, xxix.
75. HT, *A Track to the Water's Edge*, xxv, xxvii.
76. HT, "The Basis of Sex Morality," in *PHWT*, 1:74; Margaret Mead, *Coming of Age in Samoa: A Psychological Study of Primitive Youth for Western Civilization* (New York: William Morrow, 1928).
77. HT, "The Basis of Sex Morality," in *PHWT*, 1:82, 88.
78. HT, "The Basis of Sex Morality," in *PHWT*, 1:81.
79. It is interesting to note, and probably reflective of Thurman's exposure to feminism through Schreiner, that he does not cite in the thesis or bibliography any African American feminist authors, such as Anna Julia Cooper, Mary Church Terrell, or Ida B. Wells.
80. HT, "The Basis of Sex Morality," in *PHWT*, 1:88.
81. HT, "The Basis of Sex Morality," in *PHWT*, 1:89.
82. HT, "The Basis of Sex Morality," in *PHWT*, 1:91.
83. HT, "The Basis of Sex Morality," in *PHWT*, 1:91–92.
84. HT, "The Basis of Sex Morality," in *PHWT*, 1:88.
85. Works in Thurman's bibliography that take a generally positive view of homosexuality include Edward Carpenter, *Love's Coming of Age* (London: Methuen, 1924); and Havelock Ellis, *Sexual Inversion: Studies in the Psychology of Sex* (Philadelphia: F. A. Davis, 1924), vol. 2.
86. HT, "The Basis of Sex Morality," 96, 103.
87. HT, "The Basis of Sex Morality," 98.
88. On Reich, see Christopher Turner, *Adventures in the Orgasmatron: How the Sexual Revolution Came to America* (New York: Farrar, Straus and Giroux, 2011).
89. HT, "The Basis of Sex Morality," 103.
90. HT, "The Basis of Sex Morality," 98.
91. HT, "The Basis of Sex Morality, 104.
92. HT, *Jesus and the Disinherited* (New York: Abingdon-Cokesbury, 1949), 59.
93. *PHWT*, 1:103.
94. "God said, 'In the least Heaven sex reigns supreme; in the higher it is not noticed; but in the highest it does not exist'" (HT, "The Sunlight Lay across My Bed—," in HT, *A Track to the Water's Edge*, 82).
95. In Schreiner's original version, writing of a woman, unreturned love is a "kind of crown set up above her which she is always trying to grow tall enough to wear"

("The Buddhist Priest's Wife," in HT, *A Track to the Water's Edge*, 135). Thurman could use the phrase in many contexts, such as telling an audience in 1955 that "the possibility of a life of freedom under God is the crown that He holds steadily over our heads with the hope that as a nation we may grow tall enough to wear it" (*PHWT*, 4:118). Morehouse College has an annual Crown Forum of speakers, its title derived from another use of the Schreiner quote by Thurman: "Over the heads of her students Morehouse holds a crown that she challenges them to grow tall enough to wear."

96. HT, "Interview on 'Religion and Aging'" (May 1980), in *PHWT*, 5:307.
97. In HT, "From Man to Man," in HT, *A Track to the Water's Edge*, 153.

5. A New Prophet in Oberlin

1. Susan Hinman, "Howard Thurman—Prophet," *American Missionary* 82, no. 2 (March 1928): 111–13.
2. Conrad Henry Moehlman to Clarence Barbour, 28 October 1925, Folder 1, Box 23, HTC.
3. *WHAH*, 65.
4. *WHAH*, 31.
5. For Katie Kelley, see *PHWT*, 1:lxii.
6. Katie Kelley to Lucy Tapley, 18 September 1918, Deceased Alumnae Files, Spelman College, cited in *PHWT*, 1:lxii.
7. Katie Kelley to Lucy Tapley, 16 May 1921, in *PHWT*, 1:16–17. For the Anti-Tuberculosis Association of Atlanta, see Jacqueline Rouse, *Lugenia Burns Hope: Black Southern Reformer* (Athens: University of Georgia Press, 1989), 80–82.
8. *PHWT*, 1:lxiii; Cheryl C. Turkington, *Setting up Our Own City: The Black Community in Morristown, An Oral History Project* (Morristown, NJ: Joint Free Public Library of Morristown and Morristown Township, 1992), 58–62, with a group photograph including Kelley on page 60. During her time in Morristown, Kelley helped organize a Girl Scout troop and a Coleridge-Taylor Choral Society (named after the Afro-English composer Samuel Coleridge-Taylor). For Klan activity in Morristown during the mid-1920s, see Turkington, *Setting up Our Own City*, 47–49. I would like to thank Marc Korpus for obtaining a copy of this book for me.
9. *PHWT*, 1:lxiii.
10. *WHAH*, 53–54.
11. Katie Kelley-Thurman to Lucy Tapley, 9 April 1927, in *PHWT*, 1:116–17.
12. *WHAH*, 28.
13. *WHAH*, 36–37.
14. *WHAH*, 42.
15. *WHAH*, 44–45. After some initial hesitance, the church ushers allowed Thurman to sit in the family pew of a family away for the summer. Thurman found the church, ornate beyond his experience, "awe-inspiring." Hugh Black (1868–1953) was a Scottish Presbyterian who taught for many years at Union Theological Seminary.
16. *WHAH*, 17.

17. HT to Ethel Simons, 13 July 1920, in *PHWT,* 1:9–10.
18. See A. L. James 11 March 1959, in *PHWT,* 4:242–44; *WHAH,* 56–57. For Thurman's publication in Roanoke, see *PHWT,* 1:41–43.
19. *WHAH,* 56–57.
20. *WHAH,* 56–57.
21. For the titles of Thurman's sermons while in Rochester, see the chronology in *PHWT,* 1:xciv–xcvii.
22. HT, "The Faith of the American Negro" (Rochester, NY, 1925), Speaking Engagements Scrapbook, 1920–1930, Folder 1, Box 100, HTC.
23. HT, "Negro Youth and the Washington Conference" (December 1925), in *PHWT* 1:68.
24. HT, "Characteristic Christian Life Attitudes" (Cedar Falls, IA, 6 October 1926), Speaking Engagements Scrapbook, 1920–1930, Folder 1, Box 100, HTC.
25. *PHWT,* 1:xciv–xcvii.
26. HT, "The Perils of Immature Picty (May 1925), in *PHWT,* 1:47–52.
27. HT, "What Shall I Do with My Life?" (Rochester[?], 4 October 1925), Speaking Engagements Scrapbook, 1920–1930, Folder 1, Box 100, HTC.
28. Howard C. Thurman [*sic*], "Finding God," in Francis P. Miller, *Religion on the Campus: The Report of the National Student Conference, Milwaukee, Dec. 28, 1926 to Jan. 1, 1927* (New York: Association Press, 1927), 48–52, in *PHWT,* 1:110–15; Mordecai Wyatt Johnson, "The Meaning of God's Universal Fatherhood in the Relations of the Races," in Miller, *Religion on the Campus,* 80–94.
29. Thurman, "Finding God."
30. Daisy Rinehart, "The Call of the Open Sea," in HT, "Finding God" (see *PHWT,* 1:114n2). Thurman does not cite the author and either never knew or forgot the poem's source, attributing it in his autobiography to an "unknown author" (*WHAH,* 54).
31. Hinman, "Howard Thurman–Prophet."
32. John Dillingham to Friends, 24 January 1929, Folder 1, Box 23, HTC. Women's College of Alabama is now Huntingdon College. It was relatively unusual for Thurman to speak at white colleges in the South, though he spoke at many educational institutions that had no Black students and, needless to say, no Black faculty.
33. Swan Ella Owens to John Dillingham, 25 January 1929, Folder 1, Box 23, HTC.
34. Owens to Dillingham, 25 January 1929, Folder 1, Box 23, HTC.
35. In his autobiography Thurman wrote that after this awkward discussion, Cross changed the topic and told him that on his upcoming sabbatical in Europe he would find Thurman an appropriate European mentor, someone who liked Negroes—Cross had evidently rejected several possible mentors for Thurman based on this criterion. Cross would later write Thurman telling him he had found the right mentor but did not divulge his name to Thurman or anyone else before his sudden death (*WHAH,* 60–61).
36. For two accounts of the meeting with Cross, see *WHAH,* 60–61; and Elizabeth Yates, *Howard Thurman: Portrait of a Practical Dreamer* (New York: John Day, 1964), 77–79.

37. *WHAH*, 66–67; W. E. Bigglestone, "Oberlin College and the Negro Student," *Journal of Negro History* 56, no. 3 (July 1971): 198–219; James Moffatt, *A New Translation of the Bible Containing the Old and New Testaments* (New York: Harper and Brothers, 1922).

38. *WHAH*, 67, 69–70.

39. Mordecai Wyatt Johnson to HT, 16 December 1926, Folder 1, Box 23, HTC.

40. Frederick Bohn to J. L. Lobinger, 25 January 1927, Folder 1, Box 23, HTC.

41. *WHAH*, 73.

42. *WHAH*, 73.

43. Bigglestone, "Oberlin College and the Negro Student."

44. HT to Thomas W. Graham, 9 January 1926, in *PHWT*, 1:70.

45. HT to Mordecai Wyatt Johnson, 24 September 1926, Folder 1, Box 23, HTC.

46. HT to Johnson, 24 September 1926, Folder 1, Box 23, HTC.

47. *WHAH*, 76, "Religious Commitment" (unpublished typescript, ca. 1978), Folder 25, Box 4, HTC.

48. HT, "Religious Commitment," 8, Folder 25, Box 4, HTC; HT, "Africa Journal" (autumn 1963), in *PHWT*, 5:44; HT, "Religious Commitment" 8, Folder 25, Box 4, HTC.

49. HT, "Religious Commitment," 8, Folder 25, Box 4, HTC.

50. *PHWT*, 1:146; HT, "The Binding Commitment: Concluding Chapter, With Head and Heart," Folder 24, Box 4, HTC; HT, "Religious Commitment," 8, Folder 25, Box 4, HTC.

51. HT, "Religious Commitment," 8, Folder 25, Box 4, HTC.

52. Bosworth (1861–1927) died relatively soon after Thurman's arrival in Oberlin, and it is not clear how much time the two spent in study.

53. Kemper Fullerton, *Essays and Sketches: Oberlin, 1904–1934* (1938; repr., Freeport, NY: Books for Libraries Press, 1971), 158, 164.

54. *WHAH*, 70–71.

55. HT to Mordecai Wyatt Johnson, 20 September 1927, in *PHWT*, 1:117–18.

56. HT, "Higher Education and the Negro" (1927), in *PHWT*, 1:121. See also HT, "Negro Youth and the Washington Conference," in *PHWT*, 1:68.

57. HT, "The Task of the Negro Ministry" (October 1928), in *PHWT*, 1:140.

58. HT, "The Task of the Negro Ministry," in *PHWT*, 1:141, 142 .

59. HT to Mordecai Wyatt Johnson, 20 September 1927, in *PHWT*, 1:117–18.

60. HT, "The Task of the Negro Ministry" in *PHWT*, 1:142, 143–44.

61. HT to Mordecai Wyatt Johnson, 8 April 1927, Folder 1, Box 23, HTC.

62. HT to Mordecai Wyatt Johnson, 8 April 1927, Folder 1, Box 23, HTC. See HT, "Limitation of Intake" (1955), in *PHWT*, 4:99–104.

63. *WHAH*, 74; Rufus M. Jones, *Finding the Trail of Life* (New York: Macmillan, 1926), 10, 17.

64. Jones, *Finding the Trail of Life*, 159.

65. *WHAH*, 74. For Jones, see Matthew S. Hedstrom, "Rufus Jones and Mysticism for the Masses," *Cross Currents* 52, no. 2 (Summer 2004): 31–44; and Elizabeth Gray Vining, *Friend of Life: The Biography of Rufus M. Jones* (Philadelphia: Lippincott, 1958).

66. For the history of the study of mysticism, see Steven V. Katz, introduction to *Comparative Mysticism: An Anthology of Original Sources,* ed. Katz (New York: Oxford University Press, 2013), 2–23.

67. Rufus Jones, *Spiritual Energies in Daily Life* (New York: Macmillan, 1922), xi.

68. Thurman went to Philadelphia to lead a retreat at the University of Pennsylvania in the fall of 1928 and made contact with a longtime friend of Jones who facilitated the contact between the two men (HT, "Men Who Have Walked with God: Rufus Jones" [24 September 1950]), Folder 64, Box 11, HTC).

69. See https://travelingwithtwain.org/2011/11/14/philadelphia-pa/diversity-a-blind -spot-in-college-history/, accessed 24 December 2019.

70. *WHAH,* 74–76.

71. Douglass V. Steere, "Don't Forget Those Leather Gloves," in *Essays in Honor of Howard Thurman on the Occasion of His Seventy-Fifth Birthday, November 18, 1975,* ed. Samuel Lucius Gandy (Washington, DC: Hoffman, 1976), iii.

72. For Thurman on Eckhart, see the sermons "Men Who Have Walked with God— Meister Eckhart" (5 July 1953), Folder 56, Box 11, HTC; and "Meister Eckhart: From Whom God Hid Nothing" (15 October 1961), Folder 4, Box 14, HTC.

73. *WHAH,* 74–76.

74. Sue Bailey Thurman to HT, "Comments on Unpublished Biographical Draft of James Earl Massey" (ca. 1974), Folder 6, Box 17, HTC. I would like to thank Paul Harvey for sharing this document with me.

75. HT to Elizabeth Vining, 18 April 1956, Folder 8, Box 35, HTC.

76. Rufus M. Jones, *Social Law in the Spiritual World Studies in Human and Divine Inter-Relationship* (Philadelphia: John C. Winston, 1904), 150, 152. For Jones and Thurman and twentieth-century spirituality, see Leigh E. Schmidt, *Restless Souls: The Making of American Spirituality* (San Francisco: HarperSanFrancisco, 2005), 266–68.

77. Jones, *Social Law in the Spiritual World,* 188.

78. HT, "Mysticism and Social Change, #12" (19 July 1978), in *Walking with God: The Howard Thurman Sermon Series,* ed. Peter Eisenstadt and Walter E. Fluker, vol. 2: *Howard Thurman on Mysticism* (Maryknoll, NY: Orbis, 2021).

79. Hedstrom, "Rufus Jones and Mysticism for the Masses."

80. HT, "Mysticism and Social Change" (February 1939), in *PHWT,* 2:211.

81. Vining, *Friend for Life,* 219–22.

82. HT, "Mysticism and Social Change, Lecture XII" (19 July 1978), Folder 38, Box 8, HTC.

83. *WHAH,* 77.

84. At Howard University, Thurman taught about mysticism, as well as leading special seminars on Meister Eckhart and Rufus Jones (see *PHWT,* 2:xxx). As early as 1934, Thurman was offering to lecture on Eckhart (HT to Dorothy Phillips, 21 November 1934, Folder 38, Box 23, HTC). In 1950 and again in 1953 Thurman gave extensive sermon series on leading figures in the mystic tradition, including Eckhart and Jones, many of them drawn from Rufus Jones's canon of leading mystics. For a reprint of many of Thurman's 1950s sermons on mysticism, see Peter Eisenstadt and Walter E. Fluker, eds., *Walking with God: The Howard*

Thurman Sermon Series, vol. 2: *Howard Thurman on Mysticism* (Maryknoll, NY: Orbis, 2021).

85. Benjamin E. Mays to Mary Jenness, 12 February 1936, in *PHWT,* 1:323–25.

86. Lester Granger to Virgil Louder, 23 December 1941, Folder 6, Box 28, HTC.

87. Richard H. Bowling, "A Valley of Decision," *Norfolk Journal and Guide,* 10 December 1932; Lucius L. Jones Jr., "A Version of the Thurman-Bailey Nuptials," *Atlanta Daily World,* 14 June 1932.

88. HT, "Mysticism and Social Change," in *PHWT,* 2:201–2. Luther Smith, one of the pioneers of Thurman scholarship, discovered a copy of the lecture series in the archives of Eden Seminary in the 1970s. Thurman had been unaware of its publication and had assumed the lectures had been lost (Luther Smith, personal communication with the author, 2013).

89. HT, review of "A Survey of Mystical Symbolism," by Mary Anita Ewer, in *PHWT,* 1:203–5.

90. HT, "Mysticism and Social Change," in *PHWT,* 2:190–222.

91. HT, "The Mystic Way" (ca. 1938), Folder 27, Box 9, HTC.

92. HT, "The Mystic Way," Folder 27, Box 9, HTC.

93. HT, "The Mystic Way." Folder 27, Box 9, HTC.

94. HT, review of "A Survey of Mystical Symbolism," by Mary Anita Ewer.

95. HT, "Mysticism and Social Change," in *PHWT,* 2:213.

96. HT, "Mysticism and Social Change," in *PHWT,* 2:208.

97. HT, "Mysticism and Social Change," in *PHWT,* 2:191.

98. HT, "Mysticism and Social Change," in *PHWT,* 2:214.

99. HT, "Mysticism and Social Change," in *PHWT,* 2:214

100. HT, "Mysticism and Social Change," in *PHWT,* 2:216.

101. Albert J. Raboteau, "In Search of Common Ground: Howard Thurman and Religious Community," in *Meaning and Modernity: Religion, Polity, and Self,* ed. Richard Masden et al. (Berkeley: University of California Press, 2001), 157. For another version of the anecdote, see HT, "Mysticism and Social Action," in *Lawrence Lectures on Religion and Society* (Berkeley, CA: First Unitarian Church of Berkeley, 1978), 26.

6. "A Technique of Survival for the Underprivileged"

1. *PHWT,* 1: lxvii; *WHAH,* 77–78.

2. *WHAH,* 79–80; Leroy Davis, *A Clashing of the Soul: John Hope and the Dilemma of African American Leadership and Black Higher Education in the Early Twentieth Century* (Athens: University of Georgia Press, 1998), 292, 297, 301–4.

3. *WHAH,* 79–80.

4. *WHAH,* 79–80.

5. *WHAH,* 78.

6. Davis, *A Clashing of the Soul,* 227.

7. Davis, *A Clashing of the Soul,* 313–14.

8. HT, "Mysticism and Social Action," in *Lawrence Lectures on Religion and Society* (Berkeley, CA: First Unitarian Church of Berkeley, 1978), 22–23.

9. Davis, *A Clashing of the Soul,* 313–14.

10. See *PHWT,* 1:302, 330.

11. For Derricotte, see Winnifred Wygal and W. E. B. Du Bois, "Juliette Derricotte: Her Character and Her Martyrdom," *The Crisis* 41, no. 3 (March 1932): 84–87; Marion Cuthbert, *Juliette Derricotte* (New York: Woman's Press, 1933); Sarah Azaransky, *This Worldwide Struggle: Religion and the International Roots of the Civil Rights Movement* (New York: Oxford University Press, 2017), 29–31; and Lauren Kientz Anderson, "A Nauseating Sentiment, a Magical Device, or a Real Insight? Interracialism at Fisk University in 1930," *Perspectives on the History of Higher Education* 29 (2012): 75–112. Anderson's research uncovered the previously unknown fact that Derricotte's mother was white.

12. See *PHWT,* 1:53; and "Student Y.M.C.A. in Conference," *Baltimore Afro-American,* 5 June 1926.

13. "Tribute Is Paid to Juliette Derricotte, Noble Woman," *Chicago Defender,* 14 November 1931.

14. Cuthbert, *Juliette Derricotte,* 55. Cuthbert (1896–1989), was a "cherished friend" of the Thurmans (*WHAH,* 95). She taught educational policy for many years at Brooklyn College.

15. Sue Bailey Thurman in Jean Beaven Abernethy, ed., *Meditations for Women* (New York: Abingdon-Cokesbury, 1949), 97.

16. Juliette A. Derricotte, "The Student Conference at Mysore, India," *The Crisis* 36, no. 3 (August 1929): 282.

17. "Tribute Is Paid to Juliette Derricotte."

18. *PHWT,* 1:245–46.

19. For the Juliette Derricotte Scholarship Fund, see *PHWT* 2: xxi–xxvii, xlvi–xlviinn28–31. The Derricotte Fund was one of the first overseas studies programs specifically for African Americans. Sue Bailey Thurman raised money in the late 1930s by presenting a series of lecture-exhibits where, dressed in a sari, she played a sitar and discussed examples of Indian arts and crafts (see, for example, "Sue Bailey Thurman's Lecture in Florida Stimulates Group," *Atlanta Daily World,* 19 June 1936).

20. Wygal and Du Bois, "Juliette Derricotte," 85. Thurman borrowed the phrase about the ghosts from a poem by Hermann Hagedorn (see *PHWT,* 2:163n3).

21. See *PHWT,* 2:157.

22. *PHWT,* 1:121.

23. *PHWT,* 1:146.

24. HT, "The Message of the Spirituals" (October 1928), in *PHWT,* 1:129.

25. HT, "The Message of the Spirituals," in *PHWT,* 1:126–38.

26. HT, *Deep River* (Mills College, CA: Eucalyptus, 1945); HT, *The Negro Spiritual Speaks of Life and Death* (New York: Harper and Brothers, 1947). These two volumes were combined and published by Harper in 1955 in a single volume, with an expanded version of *Deep River.*

27. For the history of the spirituals, see Andrew Ward, *Dark Midnight When I Rise: The Story of the Fisk Jubilee Singers* (New York: Amistad, 2000).

28. "Preface to the Second Book of Negro Spirituals," in James Weldon Johnson, *Writings* (New York: Library of America, 2004), 737.

29. Curtis J. Evans, *The Burden of Black Religion* (New York: Oxford University Press, 2008), 4.

30. HT, "General Introduction" (1975), in *Deep River and The Negro Speaks of Life and Death* (1955; repr., Richmond, IN: Friends United Press, 1975), 3–4.

31. Raymond Wolters, *The New Negro on Campus: Black College Rebellions of the 1920s* (Princeton, NJ: Princeton University Press, 1975), 75, 37–38, 249–53.

32. Johnson, *Writings*, 737.

33. Alain Locke, "The Negro Spirituals," in *The New Negro*, ed. Locke (New York: Albert and Charles Boni, 1925), 199.

34. HT, "General Introduction," in *Deep River and The Negro Speaks of Life and Death*.

35. HT, "Religious Ideas in Negro Spirituals," *Christendom* 4 (Autumn 1939): 515.

36. For the African influence on slave culture and the spirituals, see Melville J. Hershkovits, *The Myth of the African Past* (New York: Harper and Brothers, 1941).

37. This was the perspective of the Society for the Preservation of the Spiritual, a whites-only organization in Charleston in the interwar years that sought to rescue the spiritual from its mistreatment by African American performers (see Ethan J. Kytle and Blain Roberts, *Denmark Vesey's Garden: Slavery and Memory in the Cradle of the Old Confederacy* [New York: New Press, 2018], 204–22).

38. HT, "Religious Ideas in Negro Spirituals, 515.

39. HT, "On American Slaves and the Bible," Annual Meeting of Chicago Bible Society Acceptance Speech, 3 May 1968, Folder 46, Box 6, HTC. See also HT, "A Balm in Gilead," in *"Deep River" and "The Negro Spiritual Speaks of Life and Death"* (New York: Harper and Brothers), 52–62.

40. HT, "Declaration of Independence: I" (29 July 1951), Folder 2, Box 14, HTC.

41. HT, "The Message of the Spirituals," in *PHWT*, 1:126–38.

42. *PHWT*, 1:138.

43. From Jerome Kern and Oscar Hammerstein II's *Showboat* (1927), in *American Musicals, 1927–1949*, ed. Laurence Maslon (New York: Library of America, 2014), 1:19.

44. "Nashville, October 10," *Topeka (KS) Plaindealer*, 21 November 1930.

45. HT, "General Introduction," in *"Deep River" and "The Negro Speaks of Life and Death."*

46. HT, "The Sphere of the Church's Responsibility in Social Reconstruction" (1924), in *PHWT*, 1:41–43.

47. HT, "'Relaxation' and Race Conflict," in *PHWT*, 1:144–52.

48. See Patricia Appelbaum, *Kingdom to Commune: Protestant Pacifist Culture between World War I and the Vietnam Era* (Chapel Hill: University of North Carolina Press, 2009).

49. For example, at the 1926 conference at which Thurman delivered "Finding God," of 1,500 persons surveyed, 70 percent supported some form of pacifism, whereas only 6 percent of those polled agreed to support "any war declared by the authority of my country" (Francis P. Miller, *Religion on the Campus* [New York: Association Press, 1927], 194–95).

50. Devere Allen, "Introduction" and "The New White Man," A. J. Muste, "Pacifism and Class War," and George L. Collins, "Pacifism and Social Injustice, all

in *Pacifism in the Modern World,* ed. Allen (Garden City, NY: Doubleday, 1929), xviii, 49–64, 91–102, 103–14.

51. *PHWT,* 1:145.

52. *PHWT,* 1:145.

53. *PHWT,* 1:145–46.

54. E. N. Davis, "Atlanta Postal Men's Program Very Good," *Atlanta Daily World,* 12 May 1932.

55. E. Franklin Frazier, "La Bourgeoise Noir," in *Anthology of American Negro Literature,* ed. V. F. Calverton (New York: Modern Library, 1929), 383.

56. *PHWT,* 1:147.

57. *PHWT,* 1:148.

58. *PHWT,* 1:147.

59. *PHWT,* 1:150.

60. *PHWT,* 1:147.

61. *PHWT,* 1:151.

62. *Catalogue of Spelman College, 1928–29* (Atlanta, 1928).

63. *WHAH,* 78–79, 81.

64. *PHWT,* 1:263–70.

65. HT, *Jesus and the Disinherited* (New York: Abingdon-Cokesbury, 1949).

66. HT, *Jesus and the Disinherited,* 15.

67. Susan Hinman, "Howard Thurman—Prophet," *American Missionary* 82, no. 2 (March 1928): 111–13.

68. HT, "The Sources of Power for Christian Action" (1937), in *PHWT,* 2:100.

69. On anti-Judaism within the Higher Criticism, see the work of Susannah Heschel, *Abraham Geiger and the Jewish Jesus* (Chicago: University of Chicago Press, 1998). Thurman relied on the work of the University of Chicago New Testament scholar Shirley Jackson Case, a male Shirley (see HT, "The Significance of Jesus I [1937], in *PHWT,* 2:46–47), while rejecting Case's invidious contrast of Judaism and Christianity.

70. HT to Mira B. Wilson, 6 May 1943, in *PHWT,* 3:333–34.

71. HT, "Good News for the Underprivileged" (1935), in *PHWT,* 1:264–65.

72. Jesse O. Thomas, "Urban League Weekly Bulletin," *Atlanta Constitution,* 28 February 1932.

73. "Tired of Being Underdog, Says Forum Speaker," *Baltimore Afro-American,* 19 December 1932; "Sincerity Will Not Work, Thurman Tells N.A.A.C.P.," *Baltimore Afro-American,* 4 April 1932. These early newspaper accounts are reportage, not verbatim accounts of Thurman's words, but he would make the same points often in his own writings, most prominently in *Jesus and the Disinherited,* 43.

74. "Tired of Being Underdog, Says Forum Speaker."

75. Verna Dozier, *Confronted by God: The Essential Verna Dozier,* ed. Cynthia Shattuck and Frederica Harris Thompsett (New York: Seabury, 2006), 24. Verna Dozier was a student at Howard in the 1930s and often heard Thurman preach.

76. "Thurman Says Education Is to Maintain Status Quo," *New Journal and Guide,* 17 February 1932.

77. Paul Harvey, *Moses, Jesus, and the Trickster in the Evangelical South* (Athens: University of Georgia Press, 2012), 132.

78. When asked by an editor of an African American magazine to participate in a forum on the color of God, Thurman responded, "I have no comment to make about the question as to whether God is black or white, because I do not know that the question has any relevancy for religious experience or religious faith" (HT to Ben Burns, 13 November 1956, Folder 1, Box 35, HTC).

79. "Tired of Being Underdog, Says Forum Speaker."

80. As related in the Book of Acts 22:28, when a Roman centurion in Jerusalem attempted to flog and arrest Paul, he used his citizenship to avoid punishment.

81. For Paul's critics in the nineteenth and twentieth centuries, with a discussion of Thurman, see Patrick Gray, *Paul as a Problem in History and Culture: The Apostle and His Critics through the Centuries* (Grand Rapids, MI: Baker Academic, 2016), esp. 94–96.

82. For earlier references to Paul's toleration of slavery by Thurman, see "'Relaxation' and Race Conflict," in *PHWT*, 1:148–49.

83. HT, *Jesus and the Disinherited*, 30–31.

84. HT, *Jesus and the Disinherited*, 32. Thurman's attitude toward Paul was more nuanced than simple rejection. In "Good News for the Underprivileged" Thurman called Paul a "flaming, mystic tentmaker" and "the first great creative interpreter of the Christian religion" (*PHWT*, 1:264), but his status as member of "a despised group" who had overcome some of the disabilities other Jews faced unavoidably registered "in the very ground of his underlying interpretation of the meaning of existence" (*PWHT*, 1:264–65). For two positive appreciations of Paul by Thurman, see two different sermons on Paul with the same name, "Man and the Moral Struggle: Paul" (9 October 1949), in HT, *Moral Struggle and the Prophets*, ed. Peter Eisenstadt and Walter Earl Fluker (Maryknoll, NY: Orbis, 2020), 41–52; and 9 January 1955, Folder 111, Box 11, HTC.

85. HT, "A 'Native Son' Speaks," in *PHWT*, 2:250.

86. *PHWT*, 1:264.

87. *PHWT*, 1:266.

88. *PHWT*, 1:269.

89. Faisal Devji, *The Impossible Indian: Gandhi and the Temptation of Violence* (Cambridge, MA: Harvard University Press, 2012), 6.

90. *WHAH*, 82.

91. *PHWT*, 1:cii.

92. *WHAH*, 83.

93. Ridgely Torrance, *The Story of John Hope* (New York: Macmillan, 1948), 329.

94. J. J. Mallon to HT, 6 August 1931, Folder 3, Box 23, HTC. Mallon was the warden, the chief executive, of the Toynbee Hall settlement house.

95. "Social News," *New York Age*, 3 October 1931; *WHAH*, 82–83.

96. *WHAH*, 82–83.

97. HT to John Hope, 29 June 1933, in *PHWT*, 1:173–74. This would become another favored catchphrase of Thurman. After the beginning of the Montgomery Bus Boycott, Thurman sent Martin Luther King, Jr., a copy of the recently published

Deep River inscribed with the same phrase. It is reprinted in *The Papers of Martin Luther King, Jr.,* ed. Clayborne Carson (Berkeley: University of California Press, 2007), 6:225.

98. Related to me by Walter Fluker, as told to him by his father-in-law (and Thurman's protégé) Melvin Watson. For Watson (1908–2006), see *PHWT,* 1:272n1.

99. Trudi Smith, *Sue Bailey Thurman: Building Bridges to Common Ground* (Boston: Thurman Center, Boston University, 1995), 7.

100. Jean Burden, "Meditation on Howard Thurman on the Occasion of His Memorial Services April 10, 1981" (1982?), Folder 18, Box 91, HTC .

101. *WHAH,* 84.

102. Sue Bailey Thurman, "Epilogue," in "Simmering on the Calm Presence and Profound Wisdom of Howard Thurman," special issue, *Debate & Understanding,* ed. Ricardo A. Millet and Conley H. Hughes (spring 1982): 91.

103. For Sue Bailey Thurman, see Smith, *Sue Bailey Thurman;* and Azaransky, *This Worldwide Struggle,* 26–28.

104. For Burroughs, see Evelyn Brooks Higginbotham, *Righteous Discontent: The Woman's Movement in the Black Church, 1880–1920* (Cambridge, MA: Harvard University Press, 1994).

105. Smith, *Sue Bailey Thurman,* 3–5.

106. Smith, *Sue Bailey Thurman,* 5–6. See Wolters, *The New Negro on Campus,* 230–75.

107. For Thompson, see Keith Gilyard, *Louise Thompson Patterson: A Life of Struggle for Justice* (Durham, NC: Duke University Press, 2017).

108. For African Americans in the YWCA, see Nancy Marie Robertson, *Christian Sisterhood, Race Relations, and the YWCA, 1906–1946* (Urbana: University of Illinois Press, 2007).

109. "Y.W.C.A Holds Conference in Atlanta," *Pittsburgh Courier,* 29 June 1929.

110. For occasions when Howard and Sue were at the same conference before their marriage, see "Joint Conference of 'Y's' in Florida," *Pittsburgh Courier,* 5 January 1929; "Student Confab Opens," *Pittsburgh Courier,* 15 June 1929; "Georgia Y Conference Closes Two-Day Meet at Atlanta U," *Chicago Defender,* 29 March 1930; [Untitled], *Topeka (KS) Plaindealer,* 21 November 1930.

111. Smith, *Sue Bailey Thurman,* 5–6.

112. Smith, *Sue Bailey Thurman,* 7–8.

113. "Thurman-Bailey Engagement Is Announced," *Atlanta Daily World,* 5 May 1932.

114. "Thurman-Bailey Engagement Is Announced," *Atlanta Daily World,* 5 May 1932; Lucius L. Jones, "Society Slants," *Atlanta Daily World,* 14 June 1932; "Thurman in Charge of Own Wedding Ceremony," *Atlanta Daily World,* 15 June 1932.

115. "Thurman in Charge of Own Wedding Ceremony."

116. Their daughter was named after Anne Spencer (1882–1975), who was a poet, active in the Harlem Renaissance, and who spent much of her life in Lynchburg, Virginia. Howard and Sue spent part of their honeymoon at Spencer's house and garden in Lynchburg (*WHAH,* 95).

117. Sue Bailey Thurman to Susan Ford Bailey, 12 February 1934, in *PHWT,* 1:175–76.

118. Burden, "Meditation on Howard Thurman on the Occasion of His Memorial Services April 10, 1981" (1982?).

119. HT, "Barren or Fruitful," in *PHWT,* 1:161–66.

7. In Black Athens

1. See Mordecai Wyatt Johnson to HT, 22 September 1926, in *PHWT,* 1:108–10; and *WHAH,* 77–78.

2. HT to Mordecai Wyatt Johnson, 8 April 1927, Folder 1, Box 23, HTC.

3. For Thurman's early appearances at Howard, see "Howard U Forms Rifle Club for R.O.T.C," *Washington Post,* 6 February 1927; "Pastor Will Speak on Gambling Rage," *Washington Post,* 27 April 1929 (Thurman was not the pastor in the headline); "H.U. Week," *Baltimore Afro-American,* 1 February 1930 (Thurman led the week of prayer at Howard from January 19–24); "Howard Is Visited by Carnegie Agents," *Washington Post,* 25 January 1931.

4. On the history of Howard University, see Walter Dyson, *Howard University, The Capstone of Negro Education: A History, 1867–1940* (Washington, DC: Howard University Press, 1941); Rayford W. Logan, *Howard University: The First Hundred Years, 1867–1967* (New York: New York University Press, 1969); and Zachery R. Williams, *In Search of the Talented Tenth: Howard University, Public Intellectuals and the Dilemmas of Race, 1926–1960* (Columbia: University of Missouri Press, 2009).

5. Although to be technical about it, he also spent twelve years as dean of chapel at Boston University, from 1953 to 1965. However, his duties at Boston University ended in the spring of 1962, so he spent only nine active years in Boston.

6. "Hoover May Be Booked as Howard University Commencement Speaker," *Baltimore Afro-American,* 4 June 1932.

7. Kenneth Janken, *Rayford W. Logan and the Dilemma of the African American Intellectual* (Amherst: University of Massachusetts Press, 1993), 204.

8. Logan, *Howard University: The First Hundred Years,* 379.

9. HT, Eulogy for Mordecai Wyatt Johnson, 12 September 1976, in *PHWT,* 5:278–81.

10. HT, Eulogy for Mordecai Wyatt Johnson, 12 September 1976, in *PHWT,* 5:278–81.

11. Benjamin E. Mays, *Born to Rebel: An Autobiography* (1971; repr., Athens: University of Georgia Press, 2003), 144; James Farmer, *Lay Bare the Heart: An Autobiography of the Civil Rights Movement* (New York: Plume, 1985), 185; Logan, *Howard University,* 51.

12. Logan, *Howard University: The First Hundred Years,* 83.

13. HT, "The Contribution of Baptist Church Schools to Negro Youth" (1938), in *PHWT,* 2:185.

14. Logan, *Howard University: The First Hundred Years,* 275. Between 1931 and 1941, the School of Religion faculty increased from two to four full-time professors, along with seven or eight part-time faculty members (see Anthony C. Siracusa, *The World as It Should Be: Religion and Nonviolence before King* [Chapel Hill: University of North Carolina Press, forthcoming]). I would like to thank Dr. Siracusa for sharing his manuscript with me prior to its publication.

15. "Johnson, "Inaugural Commencement Address at Howard University" (1927), in *Mordecai: The Man and His Message: The Story of Mordecai Wyatt Johnson,* ed. Richard I. McKinney (Washington, DC: Howard University Press, 1997), 257.

16. Lucius L. Jones, "Society Slants," *Atlanta Daily World,* 7 October 1932.
17. Emmett J. Scott to HT, 9 March 1932, Folder 6, Box 23, HTC. He certainly earned his salary. That first year at Howard, in the academic year of 1932–33, he had a five-five load, with fifteen hours of classroom time per week (see D. Butler Pratt to HT, 30 August 1932, in *PHWT,* 1:166–69). By 1941 his salary was $3,800 (HT to Jeannette G. Daboll, 10 July 1941), and $4,100 by 1944. By the time Thurman left Howard, in 1944, his salary had increased to $4,100 (Quinton Dixie and Peter Eisenstadt, *Visions of a Better World: Howard Thurman's Pilgrimage to India and the Origins of African American Nonviolence* [Boston: Beacon, 2011], 223n61).
18. Mays, *Born to Rebel,* 144.
19. Mays, *Born to Rebel,* 145–47; Siracusa, *The World as It Should Be: Religion and Nonviolence before King.*
20. Between 1927 and 1930 the *Chicago Defender* listed four conferences at which Thurman and Mays appeared together. In addition, Mays was a guest at Thurman's wedding, held at Kings Mountain ("Thurman in Charge of Own Wedding Ceremony," *Atlanta Daily World,* 15 June 1932).
21. Benjamin E. Mays to HT, 3 April 1940, Folder 2, Box 27, HTC; Benjamin E. Mays to HT, 31 July 1940, Folder 5, Box 27, HTC.
22. Farmer, *Lay Bare the Heart,* 136.
23. HT to Mordecai Wyatt Johnson, 20 January 1939, Folder 4, Box 26, HTC.
24. For Thurman's classes at Howard, see *PHWT,* 2:xxx.
25. Farmer, *Lay Bare the Heart,* 143, 145–46.
26. Farmer, *Lay Bare the Heart,* 143, 145–46.
27. James Russell Brown, "An Examination of the Thesis That Christianity in Its Genesis Was a Technique of Survival for an Underprivileged Minority" (masters' thesis, Howard University School of Religion, 1935). For Thurman's friendship with Brown (1909–1987), an AME minister who was the first African American chaplain in the U.S. Navy, see HT to James Russell Brown, 22 March 1945 in *PHWT,* 3:122–23. Other master's theses directed by Thurman included Lee C. Phillip, "A Critical Study of Two Minority Techniques in the Light of Christian Principles" (master's thesis, Howard University School of Religion, 1939); and Charles M Campbell, "Educating Young People on the Philosophy and Technique of Nonviolence" (master's thesis, 1941, Howard University School of Religion, 1941). These theses are cited and discussed in Siracusa, *The World as It Should Be: Religion and Nonviolence before King.* See also Paul Harvey, *Howard Thurman and the Disinherited* (Grand Rapids, MI: Eerdmans, 2020), 92.
28. Farmer, *Lay Bare the Heart,* 135–36.
29. Farmer, *Lay Bare the Heart,* 136.
30. HT to Ruth Cunningham, 18 January 1937, Folder 14, Box 24, HTC.
31. See HT, "The Sound of the Genuine" (1 May 1977), in *PHWT,* 5:281–86.
32. See Clarence J. Gresham to HT, 29 December 1921, in *PHWT,* 1:19–20.
33. Samuel L. Gandy to HT, 21 November 1938, Folder 2, Box 26, HTC.
34. Roberta Byrd Barr, "A Creative Encounter: Interview with Howard Thurman," 14–15 February 1969, Part 1, p. 3, Folder 30, Box 16, HTC.
35. HT to Melvin Watson, 26 July 1938, in *PHWT,* 2:178–79.

36. HT to Charles Barton, in *PHWT*, 2:321–23.
37. Harold B. Ingalls, "Howard Thurman: Being a Few Highlights on an Interesting Life," *Intercollegian*, April 1941, 137–38.
38. *WHAH*, 92; HT to Martha A. Biehle, 9 December 1937, Folder 5, Box 25, HTC; HT to E. A Yarrow, 8 July 1938, Folder 12, Box 25, HTC.
39. *WHAH*, 88–90.
40. For one such "adoption," see the account of the Howard years of the Cuban-America Evilio Grillo in *Black Cuban, Black American: A Memoir* (Houston, TX, Arte Público, 2000).
41. HT, Dean of Chapel Annual Report, 30 June 1944, in *PHWT*, 3:78.
42. *WHAH*, 90. Howard professor Alain Locke asked Thurman to invite a Bahá'í speaker to lead services, though Thurman's response is not extant (Alain Locke to HT, 24 June 1936, Folder 6, Box 24, HTC).
43. *WHAH*, 90. He made an exception for his friend Patrick Malin, who was fighting to change the discriminatory policies at Swarthmore College.
44. On the end of mandatory chapel services at Howard, see Raymond Wolters, *The New Negro on Campus: Black College Rebellions of the 1920s* (Princeton, NJ: Princeton University Press, 1975), 73–75; see also George M. Marsden, *The Soul of the American University: From Protestant Establishment to Established Unbelief* (New York: Oxford University Press, 1994), 334–45.
45. "Stimulating Questions Are Interesting Pastors of the City and of the Nation," *Norfolk Journal and Guide* 8 February 1930.
46. Benjamin E. Mays, "The Religious Life and Needs of Negro Students," *Journal of Negro Education* 9, no. 3 (July 1940): 332. Mays estimated that over three-quarters of the students at Howard were church members, an impressive figure but still considerably below the 95 percent–plus rates of church membership prevailing at most Negro colleges.
47. Bolling, "Conversations with Howard Thurman: Transcript of Howard Thurman Documentary," p. 58, Folder 33, Box 16, HTC.
48. Mays, "The Religious Life and Needs of Negro Students."
49. See George K. Makechnie, *Howard Thurman: His Enduring Dream* (Boston: Howard Thurman Center, Boston University, 1988), 59–60. Goodlett (1914–1997) was a 1935 graduate of Howard University, and he later became the Thurmans' personal physician in San Francisco (*WHAH*, 156). A man of many interests, Goodlett was chairman of the San Francisco branch of the NAACP from 1947–49, proprietor of the city's leading Black newspaper, the *Sun-Reporter*, and a powerful progressive voice in local Democratic Party politics. One of Goodlett's political protégés was Willie Brown (b. 1934), the longtime speaker of the California state assembly and two-term mayor of San Francisco. One of Brown's protégés was Kamala Devi Harris (b. 1964), an Afro-Indian woman, who in the fall of 2020 was elected vice president of the United States. Verna Dozier, *Confronted by God: The Essential Verna Dozier*, ed. Cynthia Shattuck and Frederica Harris Thompsett (New York: Seabury, 2006), 25. Dozier (1918–2006) graduated from Howard in 1937.
50. Farmer, *Lay Bare the Heart*, 135.

51. HT to Lewis Douglass, 10 April 1940, Folder 2, Box 27, HTC.

52. Grillo, *Black Cuban, Black American,* 75.

53. See James Hicks, "Big Town," *Baltimore Afro-American,* 8 January 1955.

54. HT to Lewis Douglass, 10 April 1940, Folder 2, Box 27, HTC.

55. Mary Emma Graham and Amritjit Singh, eds., *Conversations with Ralph Ellison* (Jackson: University of Mississippi Press, 1995), 329.

56. Although Thurman generally spoke extemporaneously, there were exceptions, and he often brought notes with him to the pulpit. In 1937 Melvin Watson congratulated him for leaving "your little papers and cards at home!" (Melvin Watson to HT, 14 April 1937, in *PHWT,* 2:29–30).

57. HT, "The Message of Ezekiel" (11 August 1952), in HT, *Moral Struggle and the Prophets,*ed. Peter Eisenstadt and Walter Earl Fluker (Maryknoll, NY: Orbis, 2020), 175–87.

58. Grillo, *Black Cuban, Black American,* 75.

59. *PHWT,* 1:25.

60. *Oberlin College News,* 19 March 1927.

61. *PHWT,* 1:cii.

62. See *PHWT,* 3:272–73n11. For Thurman and Fellowship Church's connection to Paton's novel, see *PHWT,* 3:271n1.

63. In 1937 he wrote his friend, the Smith College chaplain Ralph Harlow about a recent appearance at Smith: "In my ten years as a preacher the sermon that I gave in the Chapel yesterday was the worst exhibition of which I have been conscious. For some strange reason my mind didn't click" (HT to Ralph Harlow, 19 April 1937, in *PHWT,* 2:30–31). Harlow disputed Thurman's assessment (Ralph Harlow to HT, 9 May 1937, Folder 18, Box 24, HTC). In 1943 Thurman wrote of a sermon in which "there were not enough windows in my ideas and I was too overwhelmed by the weight of their meaning to do the greatest service for my hearers" (HT to A. Graham Baldwin, 3 February 1943, Folder 19, Box 28, HTC).

64. *WHAH,* 174–75.

65. HT, Dean of Chapel Annual Report, 1940–1941, Folder 69, Box 53, HTC; HT, Dean of Chapel Annual Report, 1943–1944, in *PHWT,* 3:75.

66. *WHAH,* 92–93.

67. HT, *Footprints of a Dream: The Story of the Church for the Fellowship of All Peoples* (New York: Harper and Brothers, 1959), 26.

68. HT, *Footprints of a Dream,* 26.

69. HT, [Madonna and Child] (1938), Folder 61, Box 6, HTC.

70. See HT, "The Strength of Corporate Worship" (8 April 1951), Folder 2, Box 12, HTC.

71. HT, "Mysticism and Social Change," in *PHWT,* 2:206.

72. G. James Fleming, "Preacher at Large to Universities," *The Crisis,* August 1939, 233, 251, 289.

73. Farmer, *Lay Bare the Heart,* 35.

74. *WHAH,* 87.

75. Bolling, "Conversations with Howard Thurman: Transcript of Howard Thurman Documentary," p. 58, Folder 33, Box 16, HTC.

76. HT to Roy Norris, 23 July 1938, in *PHWT,* 2:174–76.

77. In the 1941–42 academic year, there were 208 Black students attending accredited graduate schools of religion in the United States, 106 in predominantly white institutions, 102 in African American ones. Of the latter, 54 were attending Howard University (William Stuart Nelson, *Howard University School of Religion Annual Report, 1941–1942*, cited in Siracusa, *The World as It Should Be: Religion and Nonviolence before King*).

78. See *PHWT,* 1:333.

79. Qtd. in Kipton E. Jensen, *Howard Thurman: Philosophy, Civil Rights, and the Search for Common Ground* (Columbia: University of South Carolina Press, 2019), 53–54.

80. "Johnson Views Race Problem at NAACP Meet," *New York Amsterdam News,* 16 July 1938.

81. Carter G. Woodson, *The Mis-Education of the Negro* (1931; repr. Washington DC: ASALH, 2005), 54.

82. HT, "'Relaxation' and Race Conflict," in *PHWT,* 1:150.

83. "Thurman Says Education Is to Maintain Status Quo in US," *Norfolk Journal and Guide,* 17 February 1935. See also HT, "The Integration of the Ethical, Social, and Educational Program" (April 1938), in *PHWT,* 2:153.

84. HT, "The Integration of the Ethical, Social, and Educational Program," in *PHWT,* 2:153.

85. HT, "The Integration of the Ethical, Social, and Educational Program," in *PHWT,* 2:153.

86. When writing for himself, Thurman could be quite harsh about Black colleges, especially public Black colleges in the South that depended on funding from segregationist state legislatures. Writing that they were for the most part "a study in treachery," he went so far as to say that while he understood the need of Black educators for steady employment, those who worked in public segregated institutions had to remember their institutions were allowed to exist "to help the white man keep Negroes out of established universities" (HT, "The Higher Education of Negroes" [ca. 1950]), in Howard Thurman Papers Project Files).

87. HT, "'Relaxation' and Race Conflict," in *PHWT,* 1:146.

88. Thurman's views on education had affinities to the progressive educational theory associated with John Dewey and his acolytes such as George Coe, a professor of religious education at Columbia University who was an influence on Thurman's early thinking. George Coe (1862–1951) taught at Union Theological Seminary from 1909 to 1927. For his citation by Thurman in the 1920s, see *PHWT,* 1:39, 92–93, 149.

89. HT, "The Integration of the Ethical, Social, and Educational Program," in *PHWT,* 2:150.

90. HT, "The Integration of the Ethical, Social, and Educational Program, in *PHWT,* 2:152.

91. HT, "Commencement Address Delivered at the Tennessee A&I State College," in *PHWT,* 2:160.

92. HT, "The Integration of the Ethical, Social, and Educational Program," in *PHWT* 2:152, 161.

93. HT, "Commencement Address Delivered at the Tennessee A&I State College," in *PHWT,* 2:160.

94. HT, "The Integration of the Ethical, Social, and Educational Program," in *PHWT*, 2:153.

95. *WHAH*, 92.

96. HT and Frank T. Wilson to Fellowship of Religious Workers in Negro Colleges and Universities, September 1940, in *PHWT*, 2:261–64.

97. "Education and Social Stability: Examples of Negro Emancipation," *Madras Mail*, 4 December 1935.

98. See Jonathan Scott Holloway, *Confronting the Veil: Abram Harris, Jr., E. Franklin Frazier, and Ralph Bunche, 1919–1941* (Chapel Hill: University of North Carolina Press, 2002).

99. Ralph J. Bunche, "A Critical Analysis of the Tactics and Programs of Minority Groups, *Journal of Negro Education* 4, no. 3 (July 1935): 308–20.

100. HT to Mordecai Wyatt Johnson, 20 September 1927, in *PHWT*, 1:117–18.

101. Benjamin Elijah Mays and Joseph William Nicholson, *The Negro's Church* (New York: Institute of Social and Religious Research, 1933).

102. Mays and Nicholson, *The Negro's Church*, 278.

103. Mays and Nicholson, *The Negro's Church*, vi.

104. HT, "Review of Benjamin E. Mays and Joseph W. Nicholson, *The Negro's Church* (June 1933), in *PHWT*, 1:173.

105. Mays and Nicholson, *The Negro's Church*, 289–91.

106. *WHAH*, 90.

8. Delivering the Message of Nonviolence

1. Vincent Harding and Daisaku Ikeda, *America Will Be! Conversations on Hope, Freedom, and Democracy* (Cambridge, MA: Dialogue Path, 2013), 83. The story, as far as I know, does not appear elsewhere. Thurman might well have gone to Atlanta soon after his return to the United States in April 1936, though he did not speak publicly in Atlanta about his time in India until October 1936.

2. Peter Dana, "Dr. Thurman Speaks on Indian Question," *Pittsburgh Courier*, 29 August 1942.

3. HT, "What We May Learn from India" (1936), reprinted in *A Strange Freedom: The Best of Howard Thurman on Religious Experience and Public Life*, ed. Walter Earl Fluker and Catherine Tumber (Boston: Beacon, 1998), 200–210.

4. See *PHWT*, 2:xxxi.

5. Alice Sams to HT, June 1936, Folder 6, Box 24, HTC.

6. However, there might have been less financial reward from his rounds of speaking engagements than their sheer numbers might indicate. In 1941 he wrote a correspondent that his Howard University salary was "augmented by occasional engagements, but the net income above expenses from this source does not exceed $300" (HT to Jeannette Daboll, 10 July 1941, Folder 1, Box 28, HTC).

7. HT to A. Ralla Ram, 9 November 1936, Folder 11, Box 24, HTC. For the unpaid sabbatical, see Emmett J. Scott to HT, 8 October 1934, Folder 37, Box 23, HTC.

8. Herbert King, who knew Thurman as well as anyone, telegraphed asking about "three recent reports Howard suffering nervous collapse" (Herbert King to Sue Bailey Thurman, 27 October 1936, Folder 10, Box 24, HTC). Another friend

wrote Thurman that "we heard in this part of the country that you were not feeling at all well" (Phyllis Case to HT, 11 December 1936, Folder 12, Box 24, HTC).

9. Alice Sams to HT, June 1936, Folder 12, Box 24, HTC. He was not "feeling up to par," and even a restful retreat to New Hampshire "simply stirred up my weariness" (HT to John P. Whitaker, 25 August 1936, Folder 8, Box 24, HTC).

10. "He has never been known to travel without two things—a volume of detective stories and a book of poems. He is an authority on both types of literature, although he keeps the former as completely absent from his conversations as he most richly interjects the latter into sermons and discussions" (Harold B. Ingalls, "Howard Thurman: Being a Few Highlights of an Interesting Life," *Intercollegian* 58, no. 6 [April 1941]: 137–38). For Thurman's love of mystery novels, see also Samuel H. Archer to HT, 19 July 1938, in *PHWT*, 2:173–74.

11. Elizabeth Yates, *Howard Thurman: Portrait of a Practical Dreamer* (New York: John Day, 1964), 144.

12. *PHWT*, 4:227.

13. HT, *Jesus and the Disinherited* (New York: Abingdon-Cokesbury, 1949), 77–78. Thurman also mentions an incident in Texas in 1927 when he had to change trains late at night in a town in which there had been a serious racial disturbance. A Black man advised him to sit in a well-lit place in the colored waiting room, suitcase in view, so that any white man coming through would see that he was a stranger, and to not ask too many questions: "If you ask the ticket agent a question and he acts as if he didn't hear you, don't ask him a second time. You might get in trouble" (HT, *The Luminous Darkness: A Personal Interpretation of the Anatomy of Segregation and the Ground of Hope* [New York: Harper and Row, 1964], 31).

14. Samuel L. Gandy to HT, 21 November 1938, Folder 2, Box 26, HTC.

15. See Patricia Appelbaum, *Kingdom to Commune: Protestant Pacifist Culture between World War I and the Vietnam Era* (Chapel Hill: University of North Carolina Press, 2009), 25–44.

16. Earl Alcorn to HT, 23 February 1932, Folder 5, Box 23, HTC.

17. G. James Fleming, "Preacher at Large to Universities," *The Crisis,* August 1939, 233, 251, 289 A leader of the National Baptist Convention wrote Thurman that at a recent appearance, "numbers of white people were almost thrown into hysterics as they commented with me upon your marvelous delivery and the profound philosophy of your utterances" (Marshall Talley to HT, 3 March 1941, Folder 13, Box 27, HTC).

18. Fleming, "Preacher at Large to Universities."

19. Lester Granger to Virgil Louder, 23 December 1941, Folder 6, Box 28, HTC.

20. For the Howard Thurman Club in Detroit, see HT to Wilbur C. Woodson, 15 January 1935, in *PHWT*, 1:230–31; Edward C. Simmons to HT, 10 May 1937, Folder 18, Box 24, HTC; and Wilbur C. Woodson to Members and Friends of the Howard Thurman Club, 10 May 1937, Folder 18, Box 24, HTC.

21. Frank Wilson to Mordecai Wyatt Johnson, 22 September 1933, Folder 24, Box 24, HTC.

22. "NAACP Speaker Says Sincerity Won't Work: Dr. Thurman States That If Negroes Were Honest They Couldn't Survive," *Washington Tribune,* 30 March 1935.

23. Fleming, "Preacher at Large to Universities."

24. Susan F. Hinman, "Howard Thurman—Prophet," *American Missionary* 20, no. 3 (March 1928): 111–13. He went on to tell the interviewer that "seventy-five years from now, I believe, that phrase ["race relations"] will be obsolete; the problem will have been solved; but people will still be discussing human relations and the relation of God to man. There is a place for the discussion of race relations, but it is not what I do best. I avoid that subject, not because I am afraid of it, but because the fundamental problem is one of religion."

25. HT to J. Bernard Walton, 28 December 1934, Folder 39, Box 24, HTC.

26. HT to Mrs. E. R. Parks, 30 November 1936, Folder 11, Box 24, HTC. On this occasion Thurman nonetheless agreed to speak on "The Faith of the American Negro," perhaps because of Berea College's unique history as an integrated college in the Reconstruction and post-Reconstruction South.

27. William M. Ashby to HT, 2 February 1938; HT to William M. Ashby, 7 February 1938, in *PHWT,* 2:118–19, 120–21.

28. HT to Allan A. Hunter, 30 January 1935, in *PHWT,* 1:235–36.

29. HT, "To the Hecht Company," 23 May 1936, in *PHWT,* 2:8–9; HT to B. B. Huiell, 6 May 1937, Folder 18, Box 23, HTC.

30. HT to W. W. Mendenhall, 23 June 1936, in *PHWT,* 2: 11–13; HT to Celestine Smith, 27 May 1936, Folder 5, Box 24, HTC.

31. HT to Herbert King, 3 April 1937, Folder 17, Box 24, HTC. For someone who attended the alternative segregated Y conference at Kings Mountain, the Blue Ridge conference was especially egregious, but Thurman did preach at many churches, colleges, and schools that had no Black members or students, with the goal of "looking forward toward better days" (HT to Herbert King, 3 April 1937). At times this was an effort to help open the doors to Black students, as at Vassar (see HT to Henry Noble McCracken, 22 January 1940, in *PHWT,* 2:243–45).

32. HT to Henry H. Leber, 25 September 1936, Folder 9, Box 24, HTC.

33. HT to [Miss] Joe E. Brown, 15 January 1937, Folder 14, Box 24, HTC.

34. HT to B. F. Lamb, 18 August 1940, Folder 6, Box 27, HTC.

35. HT to Ruth Cunningham, 18 January 1937, Folder 14, Box 24, HTC.

36. HT, "Boston Chapel" (draft chapter of autobiography, ca. 1978), 23–24, Folder 14, Box 4, HTC.

37. HT, "Bold Adventure" (draft chapter of autobiography, ca. 1978), 13, Folder 13, Box 4, HTC.

38. HT, "Kingdom of God" (June 1938), in *PHWT,* 2:169.

39. Joseph Kip Kosek, *Acts of Conscience: Christian Nonviolence and Modern American Democracy* (New York: Columbia University Press, 2009), 126.

40. HT to Ralph Harlow, 6 November 1936, Folder 11, Box 24, HTC. In 1938, after Harlow had invited Thurman to speak at Smith College, and Harlow had pressing matters to attend elsewhere, Thurman understood: "I think it is far more important that you go to the National Convention of the Socialist party" (HT to Ralph Harlow, 15 March 1938, Folder 8, Box 25, HTC). Thurman was active in the Socialist Party–affiliated League for Industrial Democracy, an organization committed to "education for a new social order based on production for use and not for profit" (Mary Fox to HT, 2 May 1939, Folder 8, Box 26, HTC).

41. HT to Francis A. Henson, 18 October 1934, in *PHWT,* 1:211–12.

42. See John Nevin Sayre to HT, 26 December 1936, in *PHWT,* 1:227–28; and Allan A. Hunter to HT, 28 January 1935, in *PHWT,* 1:233–35. He was also a member of the national council of the short-lived Emergency Peace Campaign in 1936 and 1937 (Ray Newton to HT, 25 August 1936, Folder 8, Box 24, HTC).

43. HT to John Nevin Sayre, 26 May 1936, in *PHWT,* 2:9–11.

44. J. G. St. Clair Drake Jr. to HT, 4 August 1935, in *PHWT* 1:275–76. Drake would later become one of the most distinguished sociologists and anthropologists of his generation.

45. For the Delta Cooperative Farm, see HT to Sherwood Eddy, 9 November 1936, in *PHWT,* 2:18–19; and Sherwood Eddy to HT, 14 April 1937, in *PHWT,* 2:28–29. One of Thurman's protégés, Prentice Thomas, spent time on the farm. He later worked as a lawyer for the NAACP, where he tried, unsuccessfully, to get the organization more involved with the plight of Black sharecroppers (see HT to Prentice Thomas, 23 May 1938, in *PHWT* 2:154–56). For Kester, see Howard Kester to HT, 16 November 1934, in *PHWT,* 1:220–21; and Howard Kester to HT, 11 January 1940, in *PHWT,* 2:242–43.

46. Walter White to HT, 15 December 1934, Folder 39, Box 23, HTC. For Wilkins, see *PHWT,* 1:224. For Johnson, see *WHAH,* 95.

47. A. Philip Randolph to HT, 2 November 1936, in *PHWT,* 2:16–18. For Thurman and the National Negro Congress, see John P. Davis to HT, 29 October 1938, Folder 1, Box 26, HTC.

48. David Levering Lewis, *W. E. B. Du Bois: The Fight for Equality and the American Century* (New York: Henry Holt, 2000), 319. According to Lewis, Thurman never responded to Du Bois's invitation to attend the conference. For the second Amenia conference, see Lewis, *W. E. B. Du Bois,* 315–25. For Thurman's interest in Du Bois and his plans for a conference on a Negro youth movement, see HT to W. E. B. Du Bois, 24 March 1934, in *PHWT,* 1:177–78.

49. W. E. B. Du Bois to HT, 10 September 1935, in *PHWT,* 1:281–82; HT to W. E. B. Du Bois, 18 November 1935, Folder 50, Box 23, HTC. For Du Bois's travail with the Encyclopedia project, see Lewis, *W. E. B. Du Bois,* 427–33, 442–49.

50. For Thurman on the importance of interracial unionism, see *PHWT,* 2:251.

51. HT to Ralph Bunche, 4 November 1934, in *PHWT,* 1:216–17.

52. Kosek, *Acts of Conscience,* 126.

53. Ralph J. Bunche, "A Critique of New Deal Social Planning as It Affects Negroes," *Journal of Negro Education* 5, no. 1 (January 1936): 65. For Bunche and the Howard Conference, see Jonathan Scott Holloway, *Confronting the Veil: Abram Harris, Jr., E. Franklin Frazier, and Ralph Bunche, 1919–1941* (Chapel Hill: University of North Carolina Press, 2002), 69–75.

54. See Mary McLeod Bethune to HT, 13 November 1939, in *PHWT,* 2:238–39.

55. *WHAH,* 91.

56. See HT to Eleanor Roosevelt, 25 April 1944, in *PHWT,* 3:57–59; and *WHAH,* 141.

57. The literature on African Americans and Communism is extensive (see Mark Solomon, *The Cry Was Unity: Communists and African Americans, 1917–36* [Jackson: University of Mississippi Press, 1998]; and Walter T. Howard, *Black Communists Speak on Scottsboro: A Documentary History* [Philadelphia: Temple University Press, 2008]).

58. Thurman and Wilkerson coauthored a petition on India in 1942 (see HT to Alain L. Locke, 16 September 1942, in *PHWT*, 2:315–17). Wilkerson (1905–1993) taught in the Howard University Department of Education from 1935 to 1942, when he left to become a full-time official with the Communist Party, USA, and was one of its most prominent Black members. For Wilkerson, see Peter Eisenstadt, *Rochdale Village: Robert Moses, 6,000 Families, and New York City's Great Experiment in Integrated Housing* (Ithaca, NY: Cornell University Press, 2010), 284n67.

59. For Louise Thompson's 1932 trip to the Soviet Union and her friendship with Sue Bailey, see Erick S. McDuffie, *Sojourning for Freedom: Black Women, American Communism, and the Making of Black Left Feminism* (Durham, NC: Duke University Press, 2011), 62–77. For Thurman's officiating at the funeral of Thompson's mother, see "Hold Funeral Services for Mrs. Thompson," *Chicago Defender*, 4 March 1933. Both Thompson Patterson and Bailey Thurman were active in the National Negro Congress (see "Housewives Meet National Negro Congress," *Chicago Defender*, 6 November 1939; and T. E. B., "Chatter and Chimes," *New York Amsterdam News*, 11 November 1939).

60. For Thurman's friendship with Langston Hughes, see HT to Langston Hughes, 4 January 1937, Folder 14, Box 24, HTC. Thurman wanted Hughes to visit Howard for "one or two informal meetings at homes with students and faculty" (HT to Langston Hughes, 1 August 1940, Folder 6, Box 27, HTC; and Langston Hughes to HT, 21 July 1940, in *PHWT*, 2:260–61).

61. "Convocation at Howard," *Washington Tribune*, 3 November 1934.

62. Julius F. Hecker, *Religion and Communism: A Study of Religion and Atheism in Soviet Russia* (London: Chapman and Hall, 1933), 273.

63. HT to T. J King, 12 March 1935, Folder 44, Box 23, HTC.

64. Several months after his arrest, in a secret trial, Hecker confessed to being a spy and was shot several hours later (Alan Cullison, "Stalin-Era Secret Police Documents Detail Arrest, Executions of Americans," *Los Angeles Times*, 9 November 1997; Tim Tzouladis, *The Forsaken: An American Tragedy in Stalin's Russia* [New York: Penguin, 2008], 99).

65. "Dr. Johnson Explains His Stand on Communism," *Chicago Defender*, 17 June 1933.

66. "Claims Communism Is Help to Church," *Richmond News-Leader*, 10 April 1937.

67. Thurman continued to be interested in the Soviet Union's supposed abolition of racism and anti-Semitism in the 1936 constitution into the postwar period (see HT, "The Protestant's Dilemma Concerning Race" [October 1947?], Folder 63, Box 6, HTC).

68. See his wry look at the Communist effort to recruit Blacks in the 1930s in HT, "Materialism" (17 October 1948), Folder 17, Box 11, HTC.

69. *WHAH*, 119; E. Stanley Jones, *Christ's Alternative to Communism* (New York: Abingdon, 1935).

70. HT to Max Yergan, 15 January 1937, in *PHWT*, 2:26. For Yergan's (1892–1975) erratic career, from the YMCA, to an affiliation with Communism to a strident anti-Communism, see David Anthony, *Max Yergan: Race Man, Internationalist, Cold Warrior* (New York: New York University Press, 2006)

71. *WHAH*, 115.

72. HT to Juanita Harris, 10 August 1937, in *PHWT*, 2:41.

73. For the Howard school of international relations, see Robert Vitalis, *White World Order, Black Power Politics* (Ithaca, NY: Cornell University Press, 2015), esp. 11–14, 85–120.

74. Ralph J. Bunche, A *World View of Race* (1936; repr., Port Washington, NY: Kennikat, 1968), 2.

75. HT, "The Missionary Spirit and World Peace" (April 1935), in *PHWT,* 1:250. For the debate over labor practices in Liberia in the 1930s, see *PHWT,* 1:252n3.

76. HT, "Colombo Journal," in *PHWT,* 1:301.

77. HT, Colombo Journal," in *PHWT,* 1:302.

78. Sue Bailey Thurman, "The Negro and the Indian Press," *Atlanta Daily World,* 21 June 1936.

79. Sue Bailey Thurman, "The Negro and the Indian Press." Thurman was a great admirer of Joe Louis, and after Louis's famous first-round knockout of Max Schmeling, he hailed Louis's fisticuffs as marking "the passing of one more upward thrust of White Nordic Aryan supremacy" (HT to Herbert King, 7 July 1938, in *PHWT,* 2:172–73). In the late 1930s and early 1940s, Thurman tried to arrange his schedule to be in New York or Chicago at the time of big fights of Louis and other Black prizefighters. This ended after the famous fight between Louis and Billy Conn at the Polo Grounds in New York City on 18 June 1941, when the underdog Conn came close to beating Louis. Thereafter, probably because much of the crowd was vociferous in its rooting for Louis's white challenger, attending boxing matches "ceased to be a recreation, and for me its significance disintegrated" (HT, "Religious Commitment" [ca. 1978], 16, Folder 25, Box 4, HTC).

80. HT to Harold B. Ingalls, 24 May 1937, in *PHWT,* 2:32–34.

81. For the scholarship fund, see *PHWT,* 2:xxvi, 141n23. Thurman also tried to arrange an Indian scholarship for his protégé Melvin Watson at Alwaye College (the one Indian Christian college controlled by a native and non-Western Indian Christian denomination), but this did not take place (see Melvin Watson to HT, 14 April 1937, in *PHWT,* 2: 29–30).

82. HT, "What We May Learn from India." Much of this material was reused in Thurman's official summary to the India Committee of the Christian Student Movement, "India Report" (in *PHWT,* 2:121–42), which includes additional material but is less pointed. In the months after his return from India, Thurman gave other versions of this talk, speaking in Chicago ("The Experience of a Christian Ambassador in India," *Chicago Defender,* 11 April 1936); at Howard University ("Dr. and Mrs. Howard Thurman Back in States," *Atlanta Daily World,* 6 May 1936); and Atlanta ("India's Challenge to the Young Negro," *Atlanta Daily World,* 31 October 1936; and "Class Distinction among Negroes," 14 November 1936 [unidentified clipping in Howard Thurman Papers Project Files], and Philadelphia ("American Negroes and East Indians Suffer Alike," *Philadelphia Tribune,* 21 January 1937).

83. HT, "What We May Learn from India."

84. For the Anglo-Indians, see Evelyn Abel's *The Anglo-Indian Community* (Delhi, India: Chanakya, 1988).

85. HT, "What We May Learn from India," 209.

86. HT, "What We May Learn from India," 206–7; HT, "Class Distinctions among Negroes."

87. HT, "What We May Learn from India," 209–10.
88. "Lauds Gandhi in Stirring Chapel Talk," *Atlanta Daily World,* 4 November 1936.
89. HT, "The New Heaven and the New Earth" (spring 1958), in *PHWT,* 4:204–5.
90. HT, "What We May Learn from India," 208.
91. HT, "What We May Learn from India," 208.
92. HT to Joseph Baker, 4 December 1934, in *PHWT,* 1:223.
93. Gunnar Myrdal, *An American Dilemma: The Negro Problem and American Democracy* (New York: Harper and Row, 1994), 4.
94. Myrdal, *An American Dilemma,* 23.
95. HT to E. A. Yarrow, 26 April 1937, Folder 17, Box 24, HTC.
96. HT to Robert Holmes, 26 May 1937, Folder 18, Box 24, HTC. For the background to "The Significance of Jesus," see *PHWT,* 2:44–46.
97. For his attempts to publish "The Significance of Jesus," see HT to Herbert King, 25 September 1937, in *PHWT,* 2:92; William L. Savage to HT, 21 February 1937, in *PHWT,* 2:142–43; and Rufus M. Jones to Harold B. Ingalls, 7 December 1937, Folder 5, Box 25, HTC.
98. HT, "The Hope of the Disinherited" (1938?), Folder 58, Box 6, HTC.
99. *PHWT,* 2:159.
100. HT, "The Significance of Jesus I: Jesus the Man of Insight" (12 September 1937), in *PHWT,* 2:49. For the entire series, see *PHWT,* 2:44–92.
101. HT, "The Significance of Jesus I," in *PHWT,* 2:50–51. Thurman's views of the Pharisees as hidebound reactionaries are outdated. In his criticism of the "legalistic demands" of Pharisaic Judaism, Thurman dubiously quotes an extended passage written with the explicit purpose of convincing Jews of the ridiculousness of their religious practices (see "The Significance of Jesus I," in *PHWT,* 2:54n20, 77, and 81n8).
102. HT, "The Significance of Jesus I," in *PHWT,* 2:49–50, 51.
103. HT, "The Significance of Jesus I," in *PHWT,* 2:52
104. HT, "The Hope of the Disinherited," Folder 58, Box 6, HTC.
105. HT, "The Significance of Jesus II: The Temptations of Jesus (13 September, 1937), in *PHWT,* 2:54–60.
106. *PHWT,* 2:58. For Steffens, see *The Autobiography of Lincoln Steffens* (New York: Harcourt, Brace, 1932). Thurman, at some time in the early 1930s, met Steffens in California, and he was a significant influence on his social thought. He discussed their meeting, briefly, in *Jesus and the Disinherited,* 52–53, and again in HT, "Mysticism and Social Action," in *Lawrence Lectures on Religion & Society, 1977–1978* (Berkeley, CA: First Unitarian Church of Berkeley, 1978), 27.
107. *PHWT,* 2:86.
108. *PHWT,* 2:58.
109. Reinhold Niebuhr, *Moral Man and Immoral Society* (New York: Charles Scribner's, 1932).
110. HT, "Can We Be Christians Today," in *PHWT,* 2:251.
111. Thurman and Niebuhr met no later than 1927 (see HT, "Finding God" in *PHWT,* 1:110–14). They met again at the Kings Mountain conference in 1929 ("Student Confab Opens," *Pittsburgh Courier,* 15 June 1929). Niebuhr spoke at Howard in 1934 and again in 1935 (see HT to Reinhold Niebuhr, 8 January 1934; HT to

Reinhold Niebuhr, 28 December 1934, both in *PHWT,* 1:174–75, 229–30), and again (probably with some intervening engagements) in 1941 (see HT to Reinhold Niebuhr, 28 January 1941, Folder 11, Box 27, HTC).

112. Reinhold Niebuhr to HT, 13 March 1937, Folder 16, Box 24, HTC.

113. For Niebuhr's moderate civil rights stance in the 1950s, see Carol Palgrave, *Divided Minds: Intellectuals and the Civil Rights Movement* (New York: Norton, 2001), 42–46.

114. Cliff Mackay, "Political Strategy Needed—Neibuhr" [*sic*], *Atlanta Daily World,* 30 May 1932.

115. Niebuhr, *Moral Man and Immoral Society,* xvii.

116. For a comparison of the two men, see Ivory L. Lyons Jr., "The Idea of Sin in the Work of Reinhold Niebuhr and Howard Thurman: A Confluence Towards Justice" (Ph.D. diss., Claremont Graduate University, 1998).

117. For Niebuhr and the question of his neo-orthodoxy, see Gary Dorrien, *The Making of American Liberal Theology: Idealism, Realism, and Modernity, 1900–1950* (Louisville, KY: Westminster John Knox, 2003), 448–64. For Niebuhr and Thurman's connection, see Dixie and Eisenstadt, *Visions of a Better World,* 120–21.

118. *PHWT,* 2:58.

119. HT, "The Significance of Jesus III: Jesus and Love" (14 September 1937), in *PHWT,* 2:60–67.

120. HT, "The Significance of Jesus III," in *PHWT,* 2:63.

121. HT, "The Significance of Jesus III," in *PHWT* 2:64. In a kindred sermon, "The Perils of Preaching the Love Ethic of Jesus," Folder 6, Box 6, HTC, that Thurman delivered at the Boston University School of Theology on 18 October 1938, he called self-love, citing Niebuhr, the "self-regarding impulse."

122. For a similar passage, see Niebuhr, *Moral Man and Immoral Society,* 261.

123. HT, "The Significance of Jesus III," in *PHWT,* 2:65.

124. HT, "The Significance of Jesus III," in *PHWT,* 2:65.

125. *PHWT,* 2:217, 65. Thurman associated this phrase with Madeline Slade (1892–1982) or Mirabehn, a member of Gandhi's inner circle, who at Thurman's behest visited Howard in the year prior to his trip to India. The phrase caught on, and according to him, "for days afterward, half in jest, but with an undertone of seriousness, one student would say to another, 'You are a thief, look at your clothes! Or 'Are you a thief? You must be, with all that food on your plate'" (*WHAH,* 106–7).

126. *PHWT,* 2:216–17, 65–66.

127. Thurman, in 1952, spoke of Isaiah's visions of God's triumph as "a kind of utopian thing." When mankind loses "its self-regarding impulse; it will reorientate all of its egocentric compulsions" (HT, "The Message of Isaiah I" [15 June 1952], in HT, *Moral Struggle and the Prophets,* ed. Peter Eisenstadt and Walter Earl Fluker [Maryknoll, NY: Orbis, 2020], 154). See also Kipton E. Jensen, *Howard Thurman: Philosophy, Civil Rights, and the Search for Common Ground* (Columbia: University of South Carolina Press, 2019), 42–55.

128. HT, "The Significance of Jesus V: The Cross of Jesus"; "The Significance of Jesus VI: [Untitled]," (16, 17 September 1937), both in *PHWT,* 2:74–81, 81–91.

129. For other sermons and lectures of Thurman that made a similar argument about the strategies and tactics of radical nonviolence, see HT, "The Sources

of Power for Christian Action" (29 December 1937), in *PHWT*, 2:93–101; HT, "Christian, Who Calls Me Christian?" (30 December 1937–2 January 1938), in *PHWT*, 2:106–13; "The Perils of Preaching the Love Ethic of Jesus" (19 October 1938, Boston); HT, "Mysticism and Social Change" (February 1939), in *PHWT*, 2:190–221; "A Vision of God and Human Nature," 6–10 March 1939), in *PHWT*, 2:222–35; HT, "The Will to Segregation" (August 1943), in *PHWT*, 2:337–44.

130. HT, "The Significance of Jesus V," in *PHWT*, 2:78.

131. HT, "The Sources of Power for Christian Action," in *PHWT*, 2:100; "The Significance of Jesus VI: [Untitled]," in *PHWT*, 2:87.

132. HT, "The Significance of Jesus VI: [Untitled]," in *PHWT*, 2:87.

133. HT, "Mysticism and Social Change" (February 1939), in *PHWT*, 2:218.

134. "The Significance of Jesus VI: [Untitled]," in *PHWT*, 2:88.

135. HT, "The Sources of Power for Christian Action," in *PHWT*, 2: 96. The terms "shock method" or "shock treatment" used for a medical procedure were just beginning to enter the popular vocabulary in the late 1930s. The earliest use of the phrase "shock treatment" in the *New York Times* dates from 1936 ("'Sugar Shock' Is Used to Treat the Insane," *New York Times*, 24 September 1936). The earliest use of "shock method" is dated a few years later (Ritchie Calder, "Link to Heredity Is Seen in Anemia," *New York Times*, 24 August 1939).

136. "The Significance of Jesus VI: [Untitled]," in *PHWT*, 2:88–89.

137. HT, "Christian, Who Calls Me Christian?," in *PHWT*, 2:109.

138. Niebuhr and Thurman had enjoyed extensive conversations on the "ethical justification for coercion (see *PHWT*, 1:229–30). In *Moral Man and Immoral Society*, 241–56, Niebuhr criticized Gandhi for thinking that nonviolence did not involve coercion and argued that it was difficult to draw the line between violent and nonviolent coercion.

139. HT, "Mysticism and Social Change" (February 1939), in *PHWT*, 2:218.

140. HT, "The Significance of Jesus III," in *PHWT*, 2:62.

141. HT, "The Significance of Jesus V," in *PHWT*, 2:78.

142. HT, "Christian, Who Calls Me Christian?," in *PHWT*, 2:109.

143. The Significance of Jesus VI: [Untitled]," in *PHWT*, 2:87; HT, "The Significance of Jesus V," in *PHWT*, 2:89, 79.

144. HT, "The Perils of Preaching the Love Ethic of Jesus" (October 1938), Folder 6, Box 6, HTC.

145. HT, "The Mystic Way" (ca. 1938), Folder 27, Box 19, HTC.

146. *PHWT*, 2:77–78.

147. *PHWT*, 2:110–11.

148. HT, "Apostles of Sensitiveness" (February 1946), in *PHWT*, 3:170–74.

149. Rufus M. Jones, introduction to *The Power of Non-Violence*, by Richard B. Gregg (Philadelphia: Lippincott, 1934), 7–10.

150. Thurman wrote in 1934, "I am very sorry that to hear that the World Tomorrow has gone out of business as such. I feel there is no magazine that can quite take its place" (HT to Kirby Page, 5 September 1934, Folder 36, Box 23, HTC).

151. See Thurman's friend Douglas V. Steere, *The Peace Team* (New York: Fellowship of Reconciliation, ca. 1938); and Applebaum, *Kingdom to Commune*, 38–39.

152. HT, "Keep Awake!" (June 1937), in *PHWT*, 2:39.

153. A discussion of the recent refusal of an Edinburgh hotel to rent a room to an eighty-eight-year-old AME bishop was the only extended account of race in "The Significance of Jesus" series (*PHWT*, 2:86).

154. HT, "The Sources of Power of Christian Action," in *PHWT*, 2:93–101.

155. *WHAH*, 166.

156. HT to H. D. Bollinger, 19 January 1938, in *PHWT*, 2:116–18.

157. *WHAH*, 166. Thurman's introduction to the talk was not included in the published transcript of "The Sources of Power of Christian Action."

158. HT, "The Sources of Power of Christian Action," in *PHWT*, 2:100.

159. For another cite of Thurman dismissing moral reservations as a substitute for action, see Farmer, *Lay Bare the Heart*, 136.

160. HT to H. D. Bollinger, 19 January 1938.

161. *PHWT*, 2:110–11.

162. George "Shorty" Collins to HT, 18 January 1938, Folder 6, Box 25, HTC.

163. Hunter had wanted to write a book with profiles of the Christian pacifists Albert Schweitzer, Muriel Lester, Mahatma Gandhi, the Japanese pacifist Toyohiko Kagawa, and Thurman. It was never published in this form but appeared as *Three Trumpets Sound: Kagawa, Gandhi, Schweitzer* (New York: Association Press, 1939) (see Allan H. Hunter to HT, 28 January 1935), in *PHWT*, 2:233–35. Karl E. Downs, a prominent Methodist minister, called Thurman a "great prophet" (*Meet the Negro* [Los Angeles: Methodist Youth Fellowship, Southern California–Arizona Annual Conference, 1943], 168–69).

164. Ingalls, "Howard Thurman."

9. Footsteps of a War, Footprints of a Dream

1. Thurman to Christine Harrington, 24 November 1941, Folder 5, Box 28, HTC.

2. HT, "The Light That Is Darkness" (June 1940), in *PHWT*, 2:255.

3. Antonio Gramsci, *Selections from the Prison Notebooks,* ed. and trans. Quentin Hoare and Geoffrey Nowell-Smith (London: Lawrence and Wishhart, 1971), 556. Gramsci's remark dates from the 1920s, but since the *Prison Notebooks* had not been translated into English in 1941, the similarity was likely unintentional. There were other more plausible sources, such as the following lines from Matthew Arnold's "Stanzas from the Grande Chartreuse" (1855): "Wandering between two worlds, one dead / One powerless to be born."

4. Malachi 3:2.

5. Thurman to Muriel Lester, 9 September 1935, in *PHWT*, 1:280–81.

6. The Italian invasion of Ethiopia began on 3 October 1935. Thurman's party stopped in Djibouti on or about the same day. For the Negro Delegation on their port of call in Djibouti, see *PHWT*, 1:329.

7. Juanita Harris to HT, 25 July 1937; HT to Juanita Harris, 10 August 1937, in *PHWT*, 2:40–41; 41-42-42.

8. Joseph Kip Kosek, *Acts of Conscience: Christian Nonviolence and Modern American Democracy* (New York: Columbia University Press, 2009), 146.

9. A. J. Muste to HT, 9 September 1940; HT to A. J. Muste, 20 September 1940, in *PHWT* 2:264–65; 265–66. Thurman, an inveterate nonjoiner, added to Muste

that he was "willing to do what I can even though at the outset I must make clear that it will be very little." Nonetheless he remained an official of FOR until 1953 (see HT to A. J. Muste, 18 April 1953, in *PHWT*, 4:66–67).

10. Kirby Page, *How to Keep America out of War* (New York: American Friends Service Committee et al., 1939), 3–4.

11. Kosek, *Acts of Conscience*, 150, 155. For Holmes and Thurman, see *PHWT*, 3:180–82. Viewing the conflict as an imperialist war between moral equivalents was also the "line" of the Communist Party between the Hitler-Stalin Pact of 23 August 1939 and the Nazi invasion of the Soviet Union on 21 June 1941, after which the Party shifted to support an all-out military defense of the Soviet Union. The pacifists in FOR were rightly suspicious of Communist opposition to the war as purely opportunistic. Thurman continued to see the war as an imperialistic war, as in the letter to Christine Harrington, long after the Nazi invasion of the Soviet Union.

12. Allan A. Hunter to HT, 27 March 1939, in *PHWT*, 2:235–38. In the letter Hunter lambastes ex-pacifists who have fallen from the fold in the face of the threat of Hitler, especially Jews. The same year Hunter published profiles of leading European pacifists in *White Corpuscles in Europe* (Chicago: Willet and Clark, 1939).

13. Mahatma Gandhi, *The Gandhi Reader*, ed. Homer Jack (Bloomington: Indiana University Press, 1955), 319.

14. Faisal Devji, *The Impossible Indian: Gandhi and the Temptation of Violence* (Cambridge, MA: Harvard University Press, 2012), 119–50.

15. HT, "The Quest for Peace" (14 February 1940), Folder 5, Box 11, HTC.

16. HT, "San Francisco Journal" (July/August 1944), in *PHWT*, 3:85.

17. Kosek, *Acts of Conscience*, 155–56.

18. Herbert King to A. J. Muste, 27 October 1943, Folder 27, Box 28, HTC.

19. HT to Reinhold Niebuhr, 28 January 1941, Folder 11, Box 27, HTC. Niebuhr had spoken at Howard on 5 January (see "Dr. Niebuhr to Speak," *Washington Post*, 4 January 1941).

20. HT to Russell C. Barbour, 18 March 1940; HT to Russell Barbour, 31 May 1940, in *PHWT*, 2:245–46, 252–53.

21. Thurman to William Stuart Nelson, 29 August 1942, in *PHWT*, 2:311–13. Under the terms of the Selective Service Act of 1940, all men aged twenty-one to thirty-six were obliged to register for the draft. This was extended to men aged eighteen to forty-five after Pearl Harbor. Thurman was eligible for a 4-D deferment, available to ministers or divinity students, but he chose not to take it. There were apparently no consequences for Thurman in registering as a conscientious objector, such as having to serve in a Civilian Public Service camp. Some other prominent pacifists, such as A. J. Muste, did not register for the draft and suffered no adverse consequences, perhaps because the government sought to avoid trying prominent pacifists and enhancing their visibility, no doubt especially those near the upper limit of draft eligibility, like Muste and Thurman (see Kosek, *Acts of Conscience*, 165).

22. For Thurman and Farmer's draft status, see James Farmer to HT, 15 December 1944; HT to J. D. Pair, 18 December 1944, in *PHWT*, 3:100–101; 101–2. For Thurman's involvement with William Worthy, see William Worthy to HT, 24

October 1942, in *PHWT*, 2:321–22. For Thurman and Sutherland, see William Sutherland to HT, 1 June 1941, Folder 16, Box 27, HTC; and William Worthy to HT, 24 October 1942, in *PHWT*, 2:321–22.

23. HT to A. J. Muste, 20 September 1940, Folder 7, Box 27, HTC.

24. Kosek, *Acts of Conscience,* 184.

25. HT, Dean of Chapel Annual Report, 1942–1943, Folder 69, Box 53, HTC.

26. HT to James Russell Brown, 22 March 1945, in *PHWT*, 3:122–23.

27. HT to M. C. Merriweather, 9 February 1943, Folder 19, Box 28, HTC.

28. M. C. Merriweather to HT, 5 January 1945, in *PHWT*, 3:113–15.

29. HT to Patricia Van Blarcom, 17 April 1942, in *PHWT*, 2:302.

30. HT to Florence Cate, 1 May 1943, Folder 22, Box 28, HTC.

31. HT, "A 'Native Son' Speaks" (1940), in *PHWT*, 2:246–52, printed in the *Advocate,* 17 May 1940. A typescript of the lecture "The Negro in the City" is in Thurman's papers (Folder 7, Box 7, HTC).

32. Richard Wright, *Native Son* (New York: Harper and Brothers, 1940).

33. HT, "A 'Native Son' Speaks," in *PHWT*, 2:246–52. The second sentence is found only in "The Negro in the City."

34. HT, "A 'Native Son' Speaks," in *PHWT*, 2:246–52.

35. HT, "A 'Native Son' Speaks," in *PHWT*, 2:246–52.

36. HT, "A 'Native Son' Speaks," in *PHWT*, 2:246–52.

37. HT, "The Quest for Peace" (14 February 1940), Folder 5 Box 11, HTC.

38. HT to Marshall A. Talley, 28 March 1941, Folder 13, Box 27, HTC.

39. HT, "The Cultural and Spiritual Prospect for a Nation Emerging from Total War" (1945), in *PHWT*, 3:106.

40. HT, Morehouse College Seventy-Fifth Anniversary Sermon (15 February 1942), in *PHWT*, 2:295.

41. HT, "The Cultural and Spiritual Prospect for a Nation Emerging from Total War," in *PHWT*, 3:105, 108n6. By an act of Congress, daylight savings time, year-round, was mandatory for all states and was in effect from 9 February 1942 to 30 September 1945.

42. HT, "The Cultural and Spiritual Prospect for a Nation Emerging from Total War," in *PHWT*, 3:105.

43. HT, "The Cultural and Spiritual Prospect for a Nation Emerging from Total War," in *PHWT*, 3:105.

44. HT, "The Cultural and Spiritual Prospect for a Nation Emerging from Total War," in *PHWT*, 3:105, 108n8.

45. Or, as in the original, "War is essentially the health of the state" (Randolph S. Bourne, *Untimely Papers* [New York, B. W. Huebsch, 1919], 141).

46. HT, "Religion in a Time of Crisis" (August 1943), in *PHWT*, 2:345.

47. HT, "Religion in a Time of Crisis," in *PHWT*, 2:345.

48. HT, "Religion in a Time of Crisis," in *PHWT*, 2:345.

49. HT, "Religious Values in the Inter-War Period" (6 June 1942), Folder 27, Box 19, HTC.

50. HT, "Religious Values in the Inter-War Period," Folder 27, Box 19, HTC.

51. "The Moral Equivalent of War" (1910), in William James, *Writings* (New York: Library of America, 1987), 1281–93, is perhaps the most famous example of an

antimilitarist's admiration for the fervor of wartime commitment. Richard Gregg, in *The Power of Non-Violence* (Philadelphia: Lippincott, 1934), argued that "non-violent resistance is perhaps more like war than we imagined" (102), and the book is filled with discussions of military strategy. Another influential American introduction to Gandhian pacifism, Krishnahal Shridharani, *War without Violence: A Study of Gandhi's Method and Its Accomplishments* (New York: Harcourt, Brace, 1939), makes this pacifist invocation of war clear in its title.

52. HT, "Religion in a Time of Crisis," in *PHWT,* 2:345.

53. HT, "The Will to Segregation" (August 1942), in *PHWT,* 2:338.

54. HT, Dean of Chapel Annual Report, 1943–1944, in *PHWT,* 3:78.

55. For the text of the Atlantic Charter, see https://www.nato.int/cps/en/natohq /official_texts_16912.htm.

56. Peter Dana, "Dr. Thurman Speaks on Indian Question," *Pittsburgh Courier,* 29 August 1942.

57. Dana, "Dr. Thurman Speaks on Indian Question"; HT, "Religion in a Time of Crisis," in *PHWT,* 2:348.

58. HT, "The Will to Segregation," in *PHWT,* 2:338.

59. Erik Loomis, *A History of America in Ten Strikes* (New York: New Press, 2018), 140.

60. Danielle L. McGuire, *At the Dark End of the Street: Black Women, Rape, and Resistance—A New History of the Civil Rights Movement from Rosa Parks to the Rise of Black Power* (New York: Knopf, 2010), 22. See also Robin D. G. Kelley, "Congested Terrain: Resistance on Public Transportation," in *Race Rebels: Culture, Politics, and the Black Working Class* (New York: Free Press, 1994), 55–75.

61. HT, "The Fascist Masquerade" (1946), in *PHWT,* 3:152, 60n19.

62. HT, "The Will to Segregation," in *PHWT,* 2:339

63. HT to Kay H. Beach, 4 September 1942, in *PHWT,* 2:313–15.

64. HT, "The Religion of Jesus XII: The Great Moment" (3 March 1957), Folder 7, Box 12, HTC.

65. For the "Bold Adventure," see *WHAH,* 137–62.

66. For accounts of Thurman at the Khyber Pass, see HT, "The Historical Perspective," in *The Church for the Fellowship of All Peoples* (1947), in *PHWT,* 3:213–14; and HT, *Footprints of a Dream: The Story of the Church for the Fellowship of All Peoples* (New York: Harper and Brothers, 1959), 24. See also A. D. Dayala to HT, 9 February 1936, Folder 4, Box 24, HTC. Dayala was the vice principal of Edwardes College in Peshawar, who accompanied the Negro Delegation on their Khyber Pass excursion, and who had been deeply moved by meeting the Negro Delegation.

67. This was the wildest area of British India, the Northwest Frontier, the home of Pashtun tribes still largely unreconciled to British rule. Around the time of the visit of the Negro Delegation, the Royal Air Force was conducting bombing raids against unpacified tribes. Peshawar, as Thurman noted in a 1938 sermon, was one of the places on the planet were where "pellets of destruction that drop from engines of warfare flying through the breezes" were murdering "defenseless men, women, and women" (HT, "Kingdom of God" [26 June 1938], in *PHWT,* 2:169, 171–72n6).

68. Thurman was probably thinking of Alexander the Great, who invaded the Indian subcontinent in 326 BCE.
69. HT, *Footprints of a Dream,* 24.
70. *WHAH,* 136.
71. *WHAH,* 136.
72. HT, *Footprints of a Dream,* 24; *WHAH,* 136; HT, "The Historical Perspective," in *The Church for the Fellowship of All Peoples,* in *PHWT,* 3:213–14.
73. HT, "The Historical Perspective," in *The Church for the Fellowship of All Peoples,* in *PHWT,* 3:213–14.
74. The interracial service was noted with a "man bites dog" headline—"Both Races Worship in Same Church," *Chicago Defender,* 28 December 1935.
75. HT, *Footprints of a Dream,* 24.
76. HT, *Footprints of a Dream,* 24–25.
77. *The Church for the Fellowship of All Peoples,* in *PHWT,* 3:213.
78. For Marjorie Penney (1908–1983), the Fellowship Church of Philadelphia, and Fellowship House, see Stanley Keith Arnold, *Building the Beloved Community: Philadelphia's Interracial Civil Rights Organizations and Race Relations, 1930–1970* (Jackson: University Press of Mississippi, 2014).
79. Marjorie Penney to HT, 17 April 1936, Folder 4, Box 24, HTC.
80. HT to Marjorie Penney, 21 April 1936, Folder 4, Box 24, HTC.
81. For Thurman's appearances at the Fellowship Church in Philadelphia, see Marjorie Penney to HT, 25 April 1940, Folder 2, Box 27, HTC; and Quinton Dixie and Peter Eisenstadt, *Visions of a Better World: Howard Thurman's Pilgrimage to India and the Origins of African American Nonviolence* (Boston: Beacon, 2011), 222–23n49.
82. Marjorie Penney to HT, 22 October 1942, in *PHWT,* 3:318–20.
83. "Sinatra Starts Anti-Bias Tour," *Atlanta Daily World,* 26 April 1945. For the opening of Fellowship House in 1941, see G. James Fleming, "Racial Groups Work Together in Project," *Atlanta Daily World,* 30 April 1941.
84. Martin Luther King, Jr., *Stride toward Freedom: The Montgomery Story* (New York: Harper and Row, 1958), 96.
85. John Boles has written that before the Civil War, "the normative worship experience of blacks was in a biracial church" (John B. Boles, introduction to *Masters and Slaves in the House of the Lord, 1740–1870,* ed. Boles [Lexington: University of Kentucky Press, 1988], 10).
86. See Paul Harvey, *Freedom's Coming: Religious Culture and the Shaping of the South from the Civil War to the Civil Rights Era* (Chapel Hill: University of North Carolina Press, 2005), 107–68.
87. HT, "Men Who Have Walked with God XI: Meister Eckhart" (5 July 1953), Folder 4, Box 14, HTC.
88. In 1934 Thurman wrote to Pope Pius XI, "I appeal to you to consider the sad reflection on which the Catholic University of America [which did not admit Black students] casts upon the attitude and spirit of the Church Universal" (Folder 36, Box 23, HTC).
89. HT, *Footprints of a Dream,* 143–44; HT, "The Christian Minister and the Desegregation Decision" (May 1957), in *PHWT,* 4:173.

90. Race Relations Sunday was first held in 1923 on the Sunday nearest to Lincoln's birthday, celebrated at the same busy time of year as Negro History Week (see "Boost Plans to Worship with Whites," *Chicago Defender,* 28 October 1922; "Race Relations Sunday Program," *Norfolk Journal and Guide,* 27 January 1922; and George E. Haynes, *The Trend of the Races* [New York: Council of Women for the Home Missions in the United States and Canada, 1922]).

91. Lauren Kientz Anderson, "A Nauseating Sentiment, a Magical Device, or a Real Insight? Interracialism at Fisk University in 1930," *Perspectives on the History of Higher Education* 29 (2012): 105n8.

92. HT to John Nevin Sayre, 26 May 1936, in *PHWT,* 2:9–11.

93. The Church of the Crossroads, organized in 1923, described itself as an interracial place of worship, primarily for whites, Asians, and native Hawaiians, organized in 1923 (see Betty Hemphill and Robert F. Hemphill, *The Crossroads Witness* [Honolulu, HI: Church of the Crossroads, 1988]). Thurman spoke at the Church of the Crossroads in 1964 (see Howard Thurman Chronology, in *PHWT,* 5:lvvii).

94. For the Fellowship Church (Interracial) in Pasadena, see E. Stanley Jones, *The Christ of the American Road* (New York: Abingdon, 1944), 97; and "Here's Today's Events in Mission's Program," *Los Angeles Times,* 18 March 1941.

95. Cedric Belfrage, *A Faith to Free the People* (New York: Dryden, 1944), 262; Angela Dillard, *Faith in the City: Preaching Radical Social Change in Detroit* (Ann Arbor: University of Michigan Press, 2007), 140.

96. The latter's pastor, having heard of Thurman's efforts, enthusiastically wrote him that creating an interracial church was "the most critical and vital thing in the world (Dan B. Genung to HT, 29 February 1944, in *PHWT,* 3:36–37).

97. *PHWT,* 1:336.

98. For the Harlem Ashram, see Kosek, *Acts of Conscience,* 186; and Sarah Azaransky, *This Worldwide Struggle: Religion and the International Roots of the Civil Rights Movement* (New York: Oxford University Press, 2017), 89–91.

99. James Farmer, *Lay Bare the Heart: An Autobiography of the Civil Rights Movement* (New York: Plume, 1985), 149–50. Pauli Murray was also briefly a resident.

100. For the Newark Ashram, see Andrew E. Hunt, *David Dellinger: The Life and Times of a Nonviolent Revolutionary* (New York: New York University Press, 2006), 41–42, 68–69, 72, 79. For Sutherland, see *PHWT,* 2:320, 321n3.

101. A. J. Muste to HT, 14 March 1941; HT to A. J. Muste, 19 March 1941, in *PHWT,* 2:274–78; 278–79.

102. A. J. Muste to HT, 13 February 1943, Folder 19, Box 28, HTC. Muste at the meeting called for "a democratic people's peace." It is not clear if Thurman attended or spoke at the event (see "100 Pacifists Meet to Urge Peace Now," *New York Times,* 21 February 1943).

103. James Farmer, "The Race Logic of Pacifism," *Fellowship* 8, no. 2 (February 1942): 24–25.

104. HT to John M. Swomley Jr., 9 October 1941, Folder 4, Box 28, HTC.

105. For the origins of CORE, see Farmer, *Lay Bare the Heart,* 83–110; August Meier and Elliot Rudwick, *CORE: A Study in the Civil Rights Movement, 1942–1968* (New York: Oxford University Press, 1973), 4–14.

106. Farmer, *Lay Bare the Heart,* 110–12.

107. Bernice Fisher to HT, 20 January 1945, in *PHWT,* 2:323–24.

108. Pauli Murray, *Pauli Murray: The Autobiography of a Black Activist, Feminist, Priest, and Poet* (Knoxville: University of Tennessee Press, 1989), 238. For Murray, see Sarah Azaransky, *The Dream Is Freedom: Pauli Murray and American Democratic Faith* (New York: Oxford University Press, 2011); and *PHWT,* 3:99–100n5, 320–22.

109. HT to James Farmer, 11 March 1943, in *PHWT,* 2:328–30.

110. HT to Kay H. Beach, 4 September 1942, in *PHWT,* 2:313–15.

111. HT to Kay H. Beach, 4 September 1942, in PHWT 2: 313–15.

112. HT, *Deep Is the Hunger,* 37.

113. John Nevin Sayre, 15 December 1941, Folder 6, Box 28, HTC.

114. HT, "The Will to Segregation," in *PHWT,* 2:337–43.

115. HT, "God and the Race Question" (May 1946), in *PHWT,* 3:189.

116. HT, "The Cosmic Guarantee in the Judeo-Christian Message" (June 1944), Folder 11, Box 7, HTC.

117. HT, "The Will to Segregation," in *PHWT,* 2:337–43.

118. HT, "The Will to Segregation," in *PHWT,* 2:337–43.

119. HT to William Banks, 22 September 1942, Folder 14, Box 28, HTC.

120. HT, "The Will to Segregation," in *PHWT,* 2:337–43.

121. HT, "The Will to Segregation," in *PHWT,* 2:337–43.

122. HT, "The Will to Segregation," in *PHWT,* 2:337–43.

123. Samuel Williams to HT, 7 August 1943, Folder 25, Box 28, HTC.

124. HT, "The Will to Segregation," in *PHWT,* 2:337–43.

125. HT, "The Will to Segregation," in *PHWT,* 2:337–43.

126. HT, "The White Problem" (1944), in *PHWT,* 3:27–29.

127. HT, "The Will to Segregation," in *PHWT,* 2:337–43.

128. HT, "The Will to Segregation," in *PHWT,* 2:337–43.

129. A. J. Muste to HT, 8 October 1943 in *PHWT,* 3:1–2.

130. HT, *Footprints of a Dream,* 29.

131. HT, *Footprints of a Dream,* 29–30.

132. For Hope Foote, see *PHWT,* 3:xxvi, xlviin65; and Alfred G. Fisk to HT, 27 May 1944, in *PHWT,* 3:67n1.

133. HT, *Footprints of a Dream,* 30.

134. Alfred G. Fisk to HT, 15 October 1943, in *PHWT,* 3:2–4.

135. Alfred G. Fisk to HT, 15 October 1943, in *PHWT,* 3:2–4.

136. See HT to L. Maynard Catchings, 29 April 1943, in *PHWT,* 2:332–33.

137. See HT to W. L Wright (president of Lincoln University in Pennsylvania), 12 August 1943, Folder 25, Box 28, HTC.

138. HT to Benjamin E. Mays, 8 May 1943, in *PHWT,* 2:334–35. See also HT to Herbert King, 1 June 1943, in *PHWT,* 2:335–36; and HT to Henry P. Van Dusen, 21 June 1943, in *PHWT,* 2:335–37; HT to Members of the National Student Committee and Staff from Henry P. Duson et al., 14 June 1943, Folder 23, Box 28, HTC.

139. HT to Melvin H. Watson, 22 September 1943, Folder 26, Box 28, HTC.

140. HT to Melvin H. Watson, 22 September 1943, Folder 26, Box 28, HTC.

141. HT to L. Maynard Catchings, 29 April 1943, Folder 25, Box 28, HTC.

142. Herbert King to Alfred Fisk, 27 October 1943, Folder 27, Box 28, HTC.

143. HT to Alfred Fisk, 25 October 1943, in *PHWT,* 3:5–7.

144. Alfred Fisk to HT, 30 October 1943; Alfred Fisk to HT, 12 November 1943, in *PHWT*, 3:10–11; 11–12. For their meeting the previous July at the Mills College Institute of Interracial Relations (see Alfred Fisk to HT, 15 October 1943, in *PHWT*, 3:4n1).

145. HT, *Footprints of a Dream*, 31.

146. HT to Alfred Fisk, 1 December 1943, in *PHWT*, 3:16–17.

147. Albert J. Broussard, *Black San Francisco: The Struggle for Racial Equality in the West, 1900–1955* (Lawrence: University of Kansas Press, 1993), 185.

148. HT, *Footprints of a Dream*, 32.

149. HT, *Footprints of a Dream*, 31–32; HT, *WHAH*, 141.

150. HT to Alfred G. Fisk, 3 January 1944, in *PHWT*, 3:29–31.

151. HT to Alfred G. Fisk, 6 November, 1944, in *PHWT*, 3:30–31

152. Alfred G. Fisk to HT, 4 December 1943, in *PHWT*, 3:18–21.

153. HT to Alfred G. Fisk, 2 March 1944, in *PHWT*, 3:37–39.

154. *WHAH*, 141.

155. HT to William Gardner, 30 December 1943, in *PHWT*, 3:24–25.

156. HT to Mordecai Wyatt Johnson, 4 March 1946, in *PHWT*, 3:177–79.

157. HT to Jay Holmes Smith, 4 September 1942, Folder 14, Box 28, HTC.

158. Samuel Archer to HT, 2 May 1936, Folder 5, Box 24, HTC.

159. Samuel H. Archer to HT, 1 July 1938; HT to Samuel H. Archer, 26 July, 1938, in *PHWT*, 2:173–74; 176–78. Thurman had written to a member of Morehouse's board of trustees outlining the qualities they should look for in the next Morehouse president (see HT to Kendall Weisiger, 21 June 1938, in *PHWT*, 2:166–67).

160. HT to Russell C. Barbour, 31 May 1940, in *PHWT*, 2:252–53.

161. Nathan W. Collier to HT, 9 December 1940, in *PHWT*, 2:268–70.

162. Nathan W. Collier to HT, 9 December 1940; HT to Nathan W. Collier, 6 January 1941, in *PHWT*, 2:268–70; 271–72. Collier died shortly after this exchange, and the board of trustees of Florida Normal and Collegiate Institute unanimously asked Thurman to be Collier's successor (J. T. Brown to HT, 27 February 1941, in *PHWT*, 2:272–74). Thurman once again politely declined.

163. HT to S. W. Smith, 25 February 1941, Folder 12, Box 27, HTC.

164. HT to S. W. Smith, 26 March 1941, in *PHWT*, 2:281–82.

165. See J. A. Moore to HT, 28 April 1941, Folder 14, Box 27, HTC.

166. HT to S. W. Smith, 25 February 1941, Folder 12, Box 27, HTC.

167. HT, "San Francisco Journal" (July-August 1944), in *PHWT*, 3:84.

168. HT, *Footprints of a Dream*, 29.

169. Arthur Bierman and Jordan Churchill, "Alfred G. Fisk," *Proceedings and Addresses of the American Philosophical Society* 33 (1959–60): 117–18.

170. Alfred Grunsky Fisk (1905–1959) was raised in California, where his father was moderator of the Los Angeles Presbytery. He received his doctorate in philosophy from the University of Edinburgh, was a professor of philosophy at San Francisco State College, and had positions in various San Francisco Presbyterian congregations. He was an active member of the Fellowship of Reconciliation and, in Thurman's words, was a "voting socialist" (HT, "The Growing Edge" [6 October 1980], in *PHWT*, 5:314). For more on Fisk's biography, see *PHWT*, 3:xlvi–xlviin60.

171. Horace R. Cayton, "Tension Areas: Sanity and Progressive Forces Have Prevented Outbreak in San Francisco," *Pittsburgh Courier*, 18 September 1943.

172. Broussard, *Black San Francisco*, 189.

173. HT, *The Luminous Darkness: A Personal Interpretation of the Anatomy of Segregation and the Ground of Hope* (New York: Harper and Row, 1965), 2.

174. For Thurman's visits to Japanese internment camps in the summers of 1942 and 1943, see *PHWT*, 3:xlvin42.

175. Albert B. Cleage Jr., "Fellowship Church: Adventure in Interracial Understanding," NOW (October 1944), in *PHWT* 3:92.

176. Joseph James, "Race Relations on the Pacific Coast: San Francisco," *Journal of Educational Sociology* 19, no. 3 (November 1945): 166–78.

177. Langston Hughes, "Dixie in the Golden Gate," *Chicago Defender*, 6 May 1944.

178. Nathan Irvin Huggins, foreword to *Pioneer Urbanites: A Social and Cultural History of Black San Francisco*, by Douglas Henry Daniels (Philadelphia: Temple University Press, 1980), xiv–xv.

179. Charles S. Johnson, *The Negro War Worker in San Francisco: A Local Self-Survey* (San Francisco: American Missionary Association, 1944). For background on Johnson's survey, see Broussard, *Black San Francisco*, 136–42; and "San Francisco May Become Race Relations Test Tube," *Pittsburgh Courier*, 25 December 1943.

180. "Attorney General Fears Riot Spread," *Pittsburgh Courier*, 10 July 1943.

181. Cleage, "Fellowship Church," in *PHWT*, 3:92.

182. Alfred G. Fisk to HT, 30 October 1943, in *PHWT*, 3:7.

183. Virginia Scardigli to HT, 28 October 1943, Folder 27, Box 28, HTC. The group of protestors included Hope Foote, a member of the Sakai group. For Rustin's work with the San Francisco CORE group to attack restrictive covenants and segregated restaurants and places of recreation, see John D' Emilio, *Lost Prophet: The Life and Times of Bayard Rustin* (New York: Free Press, 2003), 55.

184. For example, "Dean Thurman on Leave to Establish Church," *Chicago Defender*, 19 February 1944; Dean Thurman Given Leave to Establish Interracial Church," *Pittsburgh Courier*, 19 February 1944; and "Howard Thurman Given Leave to Start New Church," *Atlanta Daily World*, 20 February 1944.

185. Thurman cherished these letters and subsequently printed most of them in a privately published volume: Alfred Fisk and Howard Thurman, *The First Footprints: The Dawn of the Idea of the Church for the Fellowship of All Peoples* (San Francisco: Lawton Kennedy, 1975). Much of this correspondence has been reprinted in volume 3 of *The Papers of Howard Washington Thurman*, ed. Walter Earl Fluker (Columbia: University of South Carolina Press, 2015).

186. The Sakai Group and some other early members had been partial to the name "the Neighborhood Church" (HT, *Footprints of a Dream*, 30), but Fisk and the board decided in February that the term "usually connotes a geographically restricted area" and gave the wrong impression of their intentions, and they settled instead on Fellowship Church (Alfred Fisk to HT, 17 February 1944, in *PHWT*, 3:33–36). Thurman's suggestion was the Church of All Peoples (HT to Alfred G. Fisk, 2 March 1944, in *PHWT*, 3:37–39), and the two names were combined. Pedants will note that it was first called the Church of the Fellowship of All Peoples.

Sometime in 1945, those involved opted for a more active preposition, calling it the Church for the Fellowship of All Peoples.

187. Alfred Fisk to A. L. Roberts, 24 December 1943, cited in *PHWT,* 3:xl, viin62.

188. Alfred Fisk to HT, 26 January 1944, reprinted in Fisk and Thurman, *The First Footprints,* 21–22.

189. Alfred Fisk, 17 February 1944, in *PHWT,* 3:34–36.

190. HT to Alfred Fisk, 12 November 1943, in *PHWT,* 3:11–12. In the same letter Thurman suggested that the main service be held in a local theater, with the church used only for vesper services.

191. Alfred G. Fisk to HT, 28 December 1943, in *PHWT,* 3:21–24.

192. For other correspondence from Fisk on the effort to obtain new quarters, see Alfred G. Fisk to HT, 17 April 1944, in *PHWT,* 3:49–54; Alfred G. Fisk to HT, 16 May 1944, in *PHWT,* 3:59–62; HT to Paul Robeson, 21 April 1944, in *PHWT* 3: 55–57; and HT, *Footprints of a Dream,* 45–46.

193. Alfred G. Fisk to HT, 13 March 1944, in *PHWT,* 3:39–41.

194. Alfred G. Fisk to HT, 16 May 1944, in *PHWT,* 3:59–62.

195. Alfred G. Fisk to HT, 8 June 1944, in *PHWT,* 3:69–71.

196. For Albert Buford Cleage Jr. (1911–2000), see Hiley H. Ward, *Prophet of the Black Nation* (Philadelphia: Pilgrim, 1969); and *PHWT,* 3:34n2.

197. Albert Cleage to Fred L. Brownlee, 18 January 1944, American Missionary Association Papers, Amistad Research Center, Tulane University.

198. HT to Alfred G. Fisk, 3 January 1944, in *PHWT,* 3:29–31.

199. Alfred G. Fisk to HT, 16 May 1944, in *PHWT,* 3:59–62; Alfred G. Fisk to American Missionary Association, 18 October 1944, American Missionary Association Papers, Amistad Research Center, Tulane University. Fisk wrote this latter letter in an effort to prevent Cleage from obtaining another ministerial position.

200. Ward, *Prophet of the Black Nation,* 54–55.

201. For the struggle to end segregation in the San Francisco shipyards, see Albert S. Broussard, *Black San Francisco,* 159–65. Joseph James, an influential founding member of Fellowship Church, was the lead plaintiff in a successful and landmark 1944 case brought against the perpetrators of the shipyard discrimination (see Charles Wollenberg, "James v. Marinship: Trouble on the New Black Frontier," in *Working People of California,* ed. Daniel Cornford, 159–79 [Berkeley: University of California Press, 1995]).

202. Alfred G. Fisk to American Missionary Association, 18 October 1944, American Missionary Association Papers, Amistad Research Center, Tulane University. For Fisk's opposition to discriminatory American Federation of Labor auxiliary locals, see Alfred Fisk to HT, 4 December 1943, in *PHWT,* 3:18–21.

203. Alfred G. Fisk to American Missionary Association, 18 October 1944, American Missionary Association Papers, Amistad Research Center, Tulane University.

204. Angelo Herndon to HT, 12 May 1944. Herndon (1913–1997), as a young black Communist in Atlanta, received unwanted celebrity as the central figure in a notable civil liberties case (see *PHWT,* 3:35–36n6; 62nn4, 5).

205. Alfred G. Fisk to HT, 16 May 1944, in *PHWT,* 3:59–62.

206. In early 1944 Cleage wrote about reading the *Daily Worker,* the Communist Party newspaper, and approved of the rioters in his native Detroit the previous summer

as protorevolutionaries, and their actions as an exemplification of the "Marxian interpretation of social change" of how people from the bottom orders of society "become the militant unafraid men and women willing to die for what believe" (Albert Cleage to Fred L. Brownlee, 18 January 1944, American Missionary Association Papers, Amistad Research Center, Tulane University).

207. Cleage, "Fellowship Church," 93. As Angela Dillard has noted through the 1950s, none of Cleage's "activities at the time placed him outside the mainstream of post–World War II civil rights activism" (Dillard, *Faith in the City*, 249).

208. Ward, *Prophet of the Black Nation*, 54–55.

209. HT to A. L. Roberts, 19 September 1945, Board of National Missions, Collections of the Department of History, Presbyterian Church (U.S.A.), Philadelphia.

210. See HT, Dean of Chapel Annual Report, 1943–44, in *PHWT*, 3:83; and Howard Thurman Chronology, in *PHWT*, 3:lix–lxii.

211. HT to Alice Sams, 2 April 1944, in *PHWT*, 3:44–45.

212. HT to Emerson O. Bradshaw, 16 March 1944, in *PHWT*, 3:41–42.

213. HT to Emerson O. Bradshaw, 16 March 1944, in *PHWT*, 3:41–42.

214. HT, Dean of Chapel Annual Report, 30 June 1944, in *PHWT*, 3:81.

215. Gunnar Myrdal, *An American Dilemma: The Negro Problem and American Democracy* (New York: Harper and Brothers, 1944).

216. HT, "The White Problem," in *PHWT*, 3:27–29.

217. HT, *The Greatest of These* (Mills College, CA: Eucalyptus, 1944).

218. HT, *The Greatest of These*, 2. "The Great Incarnate Words" had been earlier published in the Methodist magazine *motive* 4, no. 4 (January 1944): 24–26.

219. For the testimonial dinner, see HT to Eleanor Roosevelt, 25 April 1944, in *PHWT*, 3:57–59; "Dr. Thurman Gets Farewell Dinner," *Baltimore Afro-American*, 10 June 1944; HT, *Footprints*, 32; and Eleanor Roosevelt, "My Day, June 1, 1944," The Eleanor Roosevelt Papers Digital Edition (2008), accessed 19 January 2017, https://www2.gwu.edu/~erpapers/myday/displaydoc.cfm?_y=1944&_f=md056811.

10. In the Queen of Cities

1. *WHAH*, 141; HT, "San Francisco Journal," in *PHWT*, 3:84–88.

2. HT to Friends at Howard University, 21 October 1944, in *PHWT*, 3:96–100.

3. Jean Burden, "Howard Thurman, Modern Prophet," 13, Folder 2, Box 17, HTC. (This is a longer version of the article, titled "Howard Thurman," published in the *Atlantic Monthly*, October 1953, 39–44.)

4. HT to Friends at Howard University, 21 October 1944, in *PHWT*, 3:96–100. The International Institute, founded in 1919, was an offshoot of the YWCA's Department of Immigration and Foreign Communities. Annie Clo Watson, a prominent member of Fellowship Church, was the director of the San Francisco office, which during the war years was closely involved in questions concerning Japanese internment.

5. See HT to Thomas B. Foster, 25 May 1945, in *PHWT*, 3:128–29. See the daily meditations by Sue Bailey Thurman in Jean Beaven Abernethy, *Meditations for Women* (New York: Abingdon-Cokesbury, 1949), 97–127; and Sue Bailey Thurman, *Pioneers of Negro Origin in California* (San Francisco: Acme, 1952).

6. HT to Friends at Howard University, 21 October 1944, in *PHWT,* 3:96–100.
7. HT to Friends at Howard University, 21 October 1944, in *PHWT,* 3:96–100.
8. HT to Friends at Howard University, 21 October 1944, in *PHWT,* 3:96–100.
9. HT, "San Francisco Journal," in *PHWT,* 3:85–86.
10. HT, San Francisco Journal, in *PHWT,* 3:85–86.
11. *WHAH,* 145; HT, "San Francisco Journal," in *PHWT,* 3:85–86.
12. HT, "San Francisco Journal," in *PHWT,* 3:87.
13. Lewis Mumford, *Herman Melville* (New York: Literary Guild, 1929), 361.
14. HT, *Footprints of a Dream: The Story of the Church for the Fellowship of Peoples* (New York: Harper and Brothers, 1959), 38.
15. HT, *Footprints of a Dream,* 37.
16. In the "San Francisco Journal," he describes a relatively straightforward process of drafting the Commitment: "Sue and I had prepared the statement with Alfred's ok" (in *PHWT,* 3:87). In *Footprints of a Dream,* the Commitment was completed only after "day and night I wrestled with the problem" and "many rewritings" (37). In a 1949 sermon, Thurman said the Commitment was written by a nine-person committee working for several weeks (*PHWT,* 3:307). Since there were three major iterations of the Commitment, perhaps Thurman's comments refer to the drafting of different versions.
17. HT, *Footprints of a Dream,* 39.
18. HT, "The Commitment" (1944–49), in *PHWT,* 3:25–26, includes the texts of the three versions of the Commitment. George E. Haynes, of the Federal Council of Churches, thought the change from "Jesus Christ" to "Jesus of Nazareth" was not an improvement (George E. Haynes to HT, 19 September 1945, in *PHWT,* 3:142–43). On the other hand, the well-known liberal minister John Haynes Holmes felt that to single out "Jesus of Nazareth" while ignoring "Buddha, Zoroaster, and modern saints and prophets" was "disastrously limiting" (John Haynes Holmes to HT, 19 March 1946, in *PHWT,* 3:180–82).
19. HT, *Footprints of a Dream,* 38.
20. Like Fellowship Church, the South Berkeley Congregational Church had black and white copastors (see *PHWT,* 3:87).
21. HT, Footprints of a Dream, 40–43; HT to Friends at Howard University, 21 October 1944, in *PHWT,* 3:96–100.
22. HT to the Ministers and Board of Fellowship Church, 14 July 1978, Folder 2, Box 49, HTC.
23. HT, *Footprints of a Dream,* 38.
24. Albert Cleage wrote that when he arrived in San Francisco in February 1944, in the so-called "Negro District" (scare quotes in original), "Negroes made up about 50 percent" of the area's population (Albert Cleage, "Fellowship Church: Adventure in Interracial Understanding," in *PHWT,* 3:92). At the same time, the San Francisco Housing Authority—operating under the principle that "if a neighborhood had even a few African American residents, it should become an African American neighborhood"—was building public housing intended for Blacks and doing its best to turn a racially mixed area into one without racial mixture (Richard Rothstein, *The Color of Law: A Forgotten History of How Our Government Segregated America* [New York: Liveright, 2017], 27–29).

25. HT, *Footprints of a Dream,* 44.
26. *WHAH,* 93.
27. HT, *Footprints of a Dream,* 44.
28. HT, *Footprints of a Dream,* 44.
29. HT, *Footprints of a Dream,* 44.
30. HT, "The Will to Segregation" (August 1943), in *PHWT,* 2:339–40.
31. *WHAH,* 97; HT, "San Francisco Journal," in *PHWT,* 3:85.
32. HT, *Footprints of a Dream,* 46.
33. HT, *Footprints of a Dream,* 48, Alfred G. Fisk to HT, 13 March 1944 in *PHWT,* 3:9–41.
34. HT, *Footprints of a Dream,* 47.
35. "The Story of the Fellowship Church as Told by Dr. Thurman to Phillips Academy Students" (February 1947), Folder 14, Box 6, HTC.
36. See Earl Frederick Adams to HT, 7 August 1944, in *PHWT,* 3:88–90.
37. HT, "San Francisco Journal," in *PHWT,* 3:85.
38. HT, "San Francisco Journal," in *PHWT,* 3:85.
39. See Fisk's letter to HT of 30 October 1943 on the need for a church to address the rising racial tension among San Francisco's Blacks (*PHWT,* 3:7), and Fisk's original intention that Cleage would be involved in social service work, in two other Bay Area African American enclaves (see Alfred G. Fisk to HT, 10 January 1944, in *PHWT,* 3:32).
40. HT to Alfred G. Fisk, 3 January 1944, in *PHWT,* 3:29–31.
41. HT, *Footprints of a Dream,* 47; HT, "Fellowship Church," *Time* magazine, 26 July 1948, in *PHWT,* 3:275–78.
42. HT, "The Historical Perspective," in *The Church for the Fellowship of All Peoples,* in *PHWT,* 3:215.
43. HT, *Footprints of a Dream,* 47–48.
44. Landrum Bolling, "Conversations with Howard Thurman: Transcript of Howard Thurman Documentary," 8–9 January 1976, p. 95, Folder 33, Box 16, HTC.
45. Jacob A. Long to HT, 10 August 1945, in *PHWT,* 3:136–39.
46. HT to Thomas B. Foster, 28 February 1945, Board of National Missions, Collections of the Department of History, Presbyterian Church (U.S.A.), Philadelphia.
47. HT, *Footprints of a Dream,* 51. Thurman stated in an interview that at the time there were thirty-five church members (all but three of whom voted for an independent status), and it seems churlish to challenge him, but compared to most accounts of the number of church members, this seems quite low (Bolling, "Conversations with Howard Thurman: Transcript of Howard Thurman Documentary," p. 76, Folder 33, Box 16, HTC).
48. HT, *Footprints of a Dream,* 46–51.
49. Bolling, "Conversations with Howard Thurman: Transcript of Howard Thurman Documentary," p. 76, Folder 33, Box 16, HTC. For three years the church held services at one location, the Theater Art Colony, while the administrative offices were about ten blocks away.
50. HT, *Footprints of a Dream,* 54.
51. HT, *Footprints of a Dream,* 109. Jean Burden wrote in 1953 that Fellowship Church "is higher in white collar proportion than in manual laborer, but the latter is not

left out" (Jean Burden, "Howard Thurman, Modern Prophet," 18, Folder 2, Box 17, HTC).

52. HT to Friends at Howard [University], January 1946, in *PHWT,* 3:162.

53. For Thurman's plans, see HT to Charles Gilkey 19 February 1946; HT to Melvin Watson, 2 March 1946; HT to Mordecai Wyatt Johnson, 4 March 1946, in *PHWT,* 3:174–76; 176–77; 177–79.

54. Mordecai Wyatt Johnson to HT, 26 April 1946, in *PHWT,* 3:183–84.

55. HT to Mordecai Wyatt Johnson, 13 April 1946, in *PHWT,* 3:193–94.

56. Benjamin E. Mays to HT, 22 October 1946, in *PHWT,* 3:205–6; HT to Allan Hunter, 9 February 1946, Folder 26, Box 29, HTC.

57. HT to Emily Crosby, 20 May 1946, in *PHWT,* 3:195–96.

58. HT to William Stuart Nelson, 16 May 1946, in *PHWT* 3:194–95.

59. Alfred G. Fisk to Friends [War Service Unit], 15 September 1945; in Board of National Missions, Collections of the Department of History, Presbyterian Church (U.S.A.), Philadelphia.

60. Alfred G. Fisk to HT, 27 August 1946, in *PHWT,* 3:198–201.

61. HT to Adelbert Lindley, 14 March 1945, Folder 14, Box 29, HTC.

62. Thurman dedicated his 1959 history of Fellowship Church to the memory of the recently deceased Fisk (HT, *Footprints of a Dream,* dedication page).

63. Jane Sudekum, "S.F.—The City of Churches: Fellowship Group Has 285 Members," *San Francisco News,* 14 March 1949.

64. HT, "Trumpet Rises in the West," in *PHWT,* 3:329.

65. HT to Benjamin Mays, 21 September 1953, in *PHWT,* 4:73–74. Thurman's replacement was white, however, and there were reports that Black participation increased after he left (see Ruth Coffin? to HT, 11 December 1954, Folder 12, Box 33, HTC).

66. Virginia Scardigli to Elizabeth Jenks, 10 February 1947, Folder 7, Box 30, HTC.

67. HT to Peggy Bremer, 14 December 1954, Folder 12, Box 33, HTC.

68. HT to Peggy Bremer, 14 December 1954, Folder 12, Box 33, HTC.

69. HT, *Footprints of a Dream,* 121.

70. Virginia Corwin to HT, 25 September 1941; HT to Virginia Corwin, 1 October 1941, in *PHWT,* 2:288–89; 290–91.

71. HT, *Footprints of a Dream,* 121.

72. HT, *Footprints of a Dream,* 123.

73. "Intercultural Program and Workshop," in *The Church for the Fellowship of All Peoples* (1947), 9.

74. HT, "The Fellowship Church of All Peoples," *Common Ground* 5 (spring 1945), in *PHWT,* 3:124–28; HT, "Intercultural Program and Workshop," in *The Church for the Fellowship of All Peoples* (1947), 9.

75. HT, *Footprints of a Dream,* 124.

76. HT to Thomas B. Foster, 25 May 1945, in *PHWT,* 3:128–30.

77. The Intercultural Workshop, which was conducted from at least 1944 through at least 1947, was directed by Heather Whitton, a recent graduate of the Presbyterian Seminary at San Anselmo (north of San Francisco). In 1945 the program had twenty participants, aged ten to thirteen, with another, less elaborate program for younger children. For Sue Bailey Thurman, closely involved in its

planning, the workshop was "teaching tolerance through songs, dance, and art" (Dorothy Margaret Bailey, "'One World in Embryo' Aptly Describes This Intercultural Workshop," *Christian Science Monitor*, 14 September 1946). A photograph in a San Francisco newspaper that summer shows the smiling faces and entwined arms of a black, Japanese, Chinese, and white participant in the workshop (Emilia Hodel, "World Workshop for Youth," *San Francisco News*, 24 August 1945).

78. "Young Adult Group," in *The Church for the Fellowship of All Peoples* (1947), 8, ellipses as in original.

79. For an excellent history of the intercultural movement, what the author calls the "cultural gifts" movement, and its leading advocate, Rachel Davis Du Bois, see Diana Selig, *Americans All: The Cultural Gifts Movement* (Cambridge, MA: Harvard University Press, 2008).

80. Alfred Fisk wrote that the goal of intercultural programs was "accepting minority group cultural contributions without limiting members of those groups to the areas of cultural contributions with which they have been historically associated" (Fisk, "Stereotypes in Intercultural Education," *Common Ground* 7, no. 2 [December 1947]: 28–33). Fisk does not explicitly mention Fellowship Church by name in the article but seems to be clearly drawing on his experience in the church.

81. *The Church for the Fellowship of All Peoples* (1947), 10.

82. Selig, *Americans All*, 89.

83. "Fellowship Church," in *PHWT*, 3:275–78, ellipsis in original.

84. Burden, "Howard Thurman, Modern Prophet," 23–24.

85. HT to Ann Perry, 6 May 1948, Folder 22, Box 30, HTC.

86. HT, "Men Who Walked with God III: Brahman Mystics" (26 April 1953), Folder 4, Box 14, HTC; HT, *Footprints of a Dream*, 107.

87. HT, *Footprints of a Dream*, 90.

88. HT, *Footprints of a Dream*, 90–93; HT, "The Unfolding Idea: The Arts and Worship," *Growing Edge* (spring 1951), 5.

89. HT, *Footprints of a Dream*, 87.

90. *WHAH*, 152.

91. HT, *Footprints of a Dream*, 89–90; *WHAH*, 239–41.

92. *WHAH*, 141.

93. HT, *Footprints of a Dream*, 94.

94. *WHAH*, 247–48. For Thurman on music, see Harold B. Ingalls, "Howard Thurman: Being a Few Highlights on an Interesting Life," *Intercollegian*, April 1941, 137–38.

95. James Earl Massey, "Thurman's Preaching: Style and Substance," in *God and Human Freedom: A Festschrift in Honor of Howard Thurman*, ed. Henry J. Young (Richmond, IN: Friends United Press, 1983), 118–19.

96. HT, *Footprints of a Dream*, 67–69. Todd Duncan, a well-known baritone and former colleague of Thurman at Howard University, provided extensive financial support for the music program of the church. He is best remembered for creating the role of Porgy in the original 1935 Broadway production of *Porgy and Bess* (see Todd Duncan to HT, 31 December 1946, in *PHWT*, 3:211–12).

97. HT, *Footprints of a Dream*, 66–67; HT to Friend, January 1950, in *PHWT*, 4:12–17.

98. HT, *Footprints of a Dream*, 69.

99. HT, *Footprints of a Dream*, 66–67; HT to Friend, January 1950, in *PHWT*, 4:12–17.

100. Jean Burden, "Howard Thurman, Modern Prophet," 18, Folder 2, Box 17, HTC.

101. HT, *Footprints of a Dream*, 90.

102. HT, "The Strength of Corporate Worship" (8 April 1951), Folder 2, Box 14, HTC, elisions as in original.

103. HT, "The Meaning of Purpose in Religious Experience" (1964), in *PHWT*, 5:115. See also Stephen W. Angell, "Howard Thurman and Quakers," in *Black Fire: African American Quakers on Spirituality and Human Rights*, ed. Harold D. Weaver Jr. et al. (Philadelphia: Quaker Press of Friends General Conference, 2011), 63–95. For Thurman on three different varieties of worshipful silence, see HT, "Mysticism and Social Change" (1939), in *PHWT*, 2:205–6.

104. HT, *Footprints of a Dream*, 70.

105. HT, *Footprints of a Dream*, 70–72; HT, "To the Church of the Fellowship of All Peoples" (3 May 1948), in *PHWT*, 3:273–75.

106. Jean Burden, "Meditation on Howard Thurman on the Occasion of His Memorial Service, April 10, 1981" (1982), Howard Thurman Papers Project Files.

107. The earliest dateable tape recording from Fellowship Church is "Standing on Tip Toe," recorded 4 January 1948, printed in *PHWT*, 3:248–52. For the tape recording of Thurman's sermons, see introduction to *Walking with God: The Sermon Series of Howard Thurman*, vol. 1: *Moral Struggle and the Prophets*, ed. Peter Eisenstadt and Walter E. Fluker (Maryknoll, NY: Orbis, 2020), xi–xiii.

108. HT, *Footprints of a Dream*, 73–74. When, in 1953, Thurman was contemplating the move to Boston University, a good tape-recording system was one of his requirements (HT to Harold C. Case, 7 March 1953, in *PHWT* 4:57–60).

109. Contemporary events warranting immediate mention in sermons included the death of President Roosevelt (Hjalmar Petersen, "A Brief Historical Sketch and Visit with President Roosevelt," copy in the Howard Thurman Papers Project Files); the assassination of Gandhi (HT, "Mahatma Gandhi," in *PHWT*, 3:248–53); and the execution of the Rosenbergs (HT, Untitled Meditation, 21 July [June] 1953, Howard Thurman Papers Project Files).

110. Burden, "Howard Thurman, Modern Prophet," 23, Folder 2, Box 17, HTC.

111. HT, *Footprints of a Dream*, 72. However, for an excellent collection of sermons on explicitly Christian themes, see HT, *Sermons on the Parables*, ed. David B. Gowler and Kipton E. Jensen (Maryknoll, NY: Orbis, 2018).

112. HT, *Footprints of a Dream*, 72. See Eisenstadt and Fluker, eds., *Walking with God*.

113. HT, "Men Who Have Walked with God: Thomas a Kempis" (17 July 1953), Folder 28, Box 10, HTC.

114. HT to Alfred G. Fisk, 11 April 1944; HT to Alfred Fisk, 19 May 1944, in *PHWT*, 3:45–48; 62–65.

115. HT to Alfred Fisk, 19 May 1944, in *PHWT*, 3:62–65.

116. HT to George Thomas, 4 May 1946; HT to Mordecai Wyatt Johnson, 4 March 1946, in *PHWT*, 3:192–93, 177–79.

117. HT, "Interracial Church in San Francisco," *Social Action* 11, no. 2 (February 1945): 27–28; HT, "The Fellowship Church of All Peoples," *Common Ground* 5 (Spring

1945): 29–33, in *PHWT,* 3:124–28. In the period from 1945 to 1948 alone, Thurman visited persons interested in creating interracial congregations in Washington, DC; Newark, New Jersey; Portland, Oregon; Detroit, Michigan; Durham, North Carolina; Seattle, Washington; and Cleveland, Ohio (see *PHWT,* 3:liin166).

118. For King's familiarity with the *Growing Edge,* see Dixie and Eisenstadt, *Visions of a Better World,* 190.

119. The *Growing Edge* began publication in January 1949. It became a quarterly in 1953, eventually ceasing publication after Thurman left for Boston.

120. For a discussion of membership classes in the church, see HT, *Footprints of a Dream,* 55–56.

121. Burden, "Howard Thurman, Modern Prophet," 15, Folder 2, Box 17, HTC. However, in 1947 Thurman estimated that there were about 175 national associates, see "The Story of the Fellowship Church as Told by Dr. Thurman to Philips Academy Students, 20 February 1947, Folder 14, Box 6, HTC. The church and Thurman made a big effort to increase the number of national members in the early 1950s. HT, *Footprints of a Dream,* 56.

122. HT to Friends at Howard University, 21 October, 1944, in *PHWT,* 3:96–100.

123. HT, *Footprints of a Dream,* 116–17.

124. For Paton and Fellowship Church, see *PHWT,* 3:271n1; and Alan Paton, "The World at Our Doorstep," *Growing Edge,* spring 1950, 7, 8–11.

125. HT to Mrs. Harper Sibley, 24 August 1950, Folder 20, Box 31, HTC. See also HT, *Footprints of a Dream,* 106.

126. For the purchase of the church at on Larkin Street, see HT, *Footprints of a Dream,* 104–8. Thurman states that the purchase price was $30,000 with an additional $6,000 for repairs and refurbishing (105). Burden gives the purchase price as $40,000, almost all raised from "friends and national members" (Burden, "Howard Thurman: Modern Prophet," 15). Arthur U. Crosby was a Philadelphia insurance executive. His wife, Emily, was a longtime friend of Thurman and supporter of his endeavors (see *PHWT,* 3:196n1; 254n1).

127. *WHAH,* 165.

128. HT to Arthur P. Packard, 24 August 1950, Folder 20, Box 31, HTC.

129. HT to Arthur P. Packard, 24 August 1950, Folder 20, Box 31, HTC.

130. HT, *Footprints of a Dream,* 108, Nora Holt, "Hundreds Extol Religious Work of Dr. Thurman," *New York Amsterdam News,* 21 April 1951.

131. The articles in *Time* and the *Christian Century* are reprinted in *PHWT,* 3:275–78; 325–40. Burden's article was Jean Burden, "Howard Thurman," *Atlantic Monthly,* October 1953, 39–44.

132. Burden, "Howard Thurman: Modern Prophet," 26.

133. *WHAH,* 165.

134. HT, *Footprints of a Dream,* 116.

135. HT to George Thomas, 4 May 1946, in *PHWT,* 3:192–93.

136. In 1947 veteran peace activist Homer Jack identified eight interracial congregations of varying sorts, some actual churches, like Fellowship Church, others more along the lines of Fellowship House in Philadelphia, largely consisting of a regular interracial church service (Homer Jack, "The Emergence of the Interracial Church," *Social Action* 13, no. 1 [January, 1947]: 31–38). Half of the congregations, for reasons that are

not entirely clear, were in the Bay Area, what Federal Council of Churches executive George E. Haynes called an "Interracial Experiment Station" ("Along the Interracial Front: An Interracial Experiment Station," Department of Race Relations, Federal Council of Churches, 5 October 1945, Howard Thurman Papers Project Files).

137. Mark Wild, *Renewal: Liberal Protestantism and the American City after World War II* (Chicago: University of Chicago Press, 2019), 43.

138. Jack," The Emergence of the Interracial Church."

139. HT, "Special Meeting of Fellowship Church," 21 August 1950, Folder 20, Box 32, HTC.

140. HT to Adelbert Lindley, 14 March 1945. Folder 14, Box 29, HTC. Thurman was also worried that Fellowship Church, by attracting integration advocates from other local congregations, might hinder its progress elsewhere. He created a class of dual memberships for this purpose, but this was regarded by some other local churches as a sneaky way of stealing their members, HT, *Footprints of a Dream*, 54.

141. See the discussion of the state of the interracialism in the Protestant Church in 1959 in HT, *Footprints of a Dream*, 138–57.

142. HT to Arthur P. Packard, 24 August 1950, Folder 20, Box 31, HTC.

143. Benjamin Mays, "Dr. Benjamin Mays, Head of Morehouse College, Predicts: 'The Negro in the Next 50 Years,'" *Chicago Defender*, 19 August 1950. Thurman closed *Footprints of a Dream* by expressing hope that there will be a "common meeting place in which there will be no Negro church and no white church, but the church of God—that is the task we all must finish the work" (157). For King saying much the same thing, see *Strength to Love* (New York: Harper and Row, 1963), 57.

144. HT to John Overholt, 21 May 1951, Folder 30, Box 30, HTC.

145. Burden, "Howard Thurman, Modern Prophet," 19, Folder 2, Box 17, HTC.

146. Mary McLeod Bethune to HT, 30 April 1951. Folder 29, Box 31, HTC.

147. HT, *Footprints of a Dream*, 54.

148. HT to Wade Ellis, 20 January 1952, Folder 4, Box 32, HTC.

149. HT, *Footprints of a Dream*, 130.

150. HT, *Footprints of a Dream*, 130.

151. *PHWT*, 3:338.

152. HT, *Footprints of a Dream*, 129–30.

153. HT, *Footprints of a Dream*, 130.

154. HT to Friends of the Fellowship Church, August 1946, Folder 1, Box 30, HTC; HT to Willard Lampe, 30 October 1946, Folder 3, Box 30, HTC. In this latter letter Thurman proposed spending a half year in Iowa and a half year in San Francisco, but this proved unworkable. Thurman taught again at Iowa in the spring of 1948. The School of Religion, founded in 1927, was the first such school established at a public university, with a Protestant, Catholic, and Jewish professorship. Thurman was offered the Protestant professorship.

155. He had written a few months earlier of an opening at Stanford: "I wish we were far enough along in American education and democracy to consider a Negro for such a position. I know one very able man who could do the job most acceptably, but this is merely a pipe dream" (HT to Lynn White Jr., 10 December 1945, Folder 24, Box 29, HTC).

156. HT to Lorimer Milton, 20 October 1946, Folder 3, Box 30, HTC.

157. HT to Friend, December 1952, Folder 12, Box 32, HTC.

158. HT to Neil House, 21 October 1952, Folder 10, Box 32, HTC.

159. *WHAH*, 166–67. See also Dixie and Eisenstadt, *Visions of a Better World*, 138–44.

160. Walter Muelder to HT, 25 July 1952, Folder 7, Box 32, HTC.

161. HT to Walter Muelder, 1 August 1953 in *PHWT*, 4:45–46.

162. HT to Harold Case, 20 December 1952, in *PTWT*, 4:46–47.

163. Harold Case to HT, 26 January 1953, in *PHWT*, 4:52–53.

164. HT to Board of Trustees and Members of the Fellowship Church, 9 March 1953, in *PHWT*, 4:60–61.

165. Coleman Jennings to HT, 16 March 1953, Folder 15, Box 32, HTC.

166. Joseph Van Pelt to HT, 12 March 1953, in *PHWT*, 4:63. They later reconciled (see *PHWT*, 4:64n2).

167. Cardella Clifton to HT, 23 April 1953, in *PHWT*, 4:67.

168. Frank Boden Udale to HT, 2 April 1953, Folder 16, Box 32, HTC.

169. HT to Mrs. Ralph Smith, 10 March 1953, Folder 15, Box 32, HTC.

170. HT to Arthur Crosby, 21 March 1953, in *PHWT*, 4:64–65.

171. HT to Case, 7 March 1953, in *PHWT*, 4:57–60.

172. HT, *Footprints of a Dream*, 60.

173. *WHAH*, 162.

174. Thurman was fond of quoting these abysmal statistics from Frank Loescher, *The Protestant Church and the Negro* (New York: Association Press, 1948), 76–78 (see HT, *Footprints of a Dream*, 12). For more recent numbers, see Korie L. Edwards, Brad Christerson, and Michael O. Emerson, "Race, Religious Organization, and Integration," *Annual Review of Sociology* 39 (2013): 211–28; and Kathleen Garces-Foley, "New Opportunities and New Values: The Emergence of the Multicultural Church," *Annals of the American Academy of Political and Social Science* 612 (July 2007): 209–23. Garces-Foley found that 92.5 percent of Christian congregations remained dominated by a single ethnic or racial group, with 80 percent or more explicit in their ethnic identification, either on a congregational or denominational level.

175. HT, *The Creative Encounter: An Interpretation of Religion and the Social Witness* (New York: Harper and Brothers, 1954), 148.

11. Against the Hounds of Hell

1. HT to P. R. Hayward, 19 March, 1941, Folder 13, Box 27, HTC.

2. HT, *Jesus and the Disinherited* (New York: Abingdon-Cokesbury, 1949).

3. HT, *Footprints of a Dream: The Story of the Church for the Fellowship of Peoples* (New York: Harper and Brothers, 1959), 97.

4. Most of Thurman's early publications are available in the first two volumes of the *Papers of Howard Washington Thurman*, ed. Walter Earl Fluker (Columbia: University of South Carolina Press, 2009–19).

5. Rufus M. Jones to Harold B. Ingalls, 7 December, 1937, Folder 5, Box 25, HTC.

6. William L. Savage to HT, 21 February 1938, in *PHWT*, 2:142–43.

7. There were others who felt Thurman fell flat on the page. The distinguished man of letters J. Saunders Redding allowed that while Thurman might be "the greatest preacher in America . . . to read him is something else again, and so much of what seems to live in truth when it falls from the preacher's lips withers and dies when it is brought to the analysis and thought on the printed page" (Redding, "Book Review," *Baltimore Afro-American,* 15 December 1956).

8. HT, *The Greatest of These* (Mills College, CA: Eucalyptus, 1944).

9. Amos N. Wilder, "Review, Howard Thurman: *The Greatest of These,*" *Journal of Bible and Religion* 13, no. 4 (November 1945): 212.

10. HT, *Deep River* (Mills College, CA: Eucalyptus, 1945); HT, *Meditations for Apostles of Sensitiveness* (Mills College, CA; Eucalyptus, 1947).

11. *WHAH,* 216–17.

12. *WHAH,* 216.

13. George Thomas to HT, 18 April 1947, in *PHWT,* 3:222–25.

14. HT, *The Negro Spiritual Speaks of Life and Death* (New York: Harper and Brothers, 1947). In 1955 Harper and Brothers combined his Ingersoll Lecture with an expanded version of *Deep River,* in HT, *"Deep River" and "The Negro Spiritual Speaks of Life and Death"* (New York: Harper and Brothers, 1955).

15. Thurman was closest to John B. Chambers, and he delivered the eulogy at his funeral after Chambers's sudden death (see HT, *John B. Chambers, 1910–1955* [New York, 1955]). For Harper's role in promoting liberal Protestantism in the postwar years, see Matthew S. Hedstrom, *The Rise of Liberal Religion: Book Culture and American Spirituality in the Twentieth Century* (New York: Oxford University Press, 2013).

16. HT to Friends at Howard University, 21 October 1944, in *PHWT,* 3:96–100.

17. HT to Thomas B. Foster, 13 February 1945, HT to Thomas B. Foster, 28 February 1945, both in Board of National Missions, Collections of the Department of History, Presbyterian Church (U.S.A.), Philadelphia.

18. HT, "Modern Challenges to Religion III" (4 May 1958), Folder 42, Box 11, HTC. See also *WHAH,* 162. For Ayoka Murota, see HT to James C. Baker, 12 May 1947, in *PHWT,* 3:231–32n4. Even before Murota was hired, the church had a temporary Japanese American secretary, a Miss Ishida (see HT to Thomas B. Foster, 21 December 1944, in *PHWT,* 3:102–4).

19. For Dave Tatsuno, born Masaharu Tatsuno (1913–2006) in San Francisco, see HT to Friends at Howard, January 1946, in *PHWT,* 3:162–64.

20. Program, "The Fellowship Church," 3 June 1945, Howard Thurman Papers Project Files.

21. For John Yamashita, see HT to James C. Baker, 12 May 1947; and HT to Board of Fellowship Church, 12 July 1947, in *PHWT,* 3:230–32; 239–40.

22. For an early discussion of the changing status of Filipino Americans, see Sue Bailey Thurman, "'Dress Circle' Affords Best View of Conference," *Chicago Defender,* 19 May 1945.

23. Hjalmar Petersen, "A Brief Historical Sketch and Visit with President Roosevelt," copy in the Howard Thurman Papers Project Files.

24. The literature on the UNICO conference is immense. For an overview, see Elizabeth Borgwardt, *A New Deal for the World: America's Vision on Human Rights* (Cambridge, MA: Harvard University Press, 2005), 142–95.

25. HT to Thomas B. Foster, 25 May 1945, Board of National Missions, Collections of the Department of History, Presbyterian Church (U.S.A.), Philadelphia.

26. HT to Thomas B. Foster, 25 May 1945, Board of National Missions, Collections of the Department of History, Presbyterian Church (U.S.A.), Philadelphia.

27. *PHWT,* 3:130n2.

28. W. E. B. Du Bois, "The Winds of Time," *Chicago Defender,* 8 June 1945.

29. Ralph Matthews, "Watching the Big Parade," *Baltimore Afro-American,* 2 June 1945.

30. Sue Bailey Thurman, "'Dress Circle' Affords Best View of Conference"; "View of Confab's 'Dress Circle' Big Peace Factor"; "Feminine Personalities Brighten Frisco Parley," "Dress Circle Affairs Highlighted Parley," all in *Chicago Defender* 19 May, 26 May, 2 June, and 16 June 1945.

31. Sue Bailey Thurman, "'Dress Circle' Affords Best View of Conference." The NCNW had called several months before for the world powers to prepare "the blueprint of the post-war world" and "recognize that no lasting peace can be possible until the world is purged of its traditional concepts, and the practice of racial superiority, imperialist domination, and economic exploitation" (qtd. in Elizabeth Borgwardt, "Race, Rights, and Nongovernmental Organizations at the United Nations San Francisco Conference," in *Fog of War: The Second World War and the Civil Rights Movement,* ed. Kevin Kruse and Stephen Tuck [New York: Oxford University Press, 2012], 196). These positions were reiterated by the NCNW after the San Francisco Conference (see "Top Negro Leaders Map Strategy for All-Out Battle for Full Freedom," *Chicago Defender,* 29 June 1945).

32. Sue Bailey Thurman, "Dress Circle Affairs Highlighted Parley."

33. W. E. B. Du Bois, "Color Line Absent at Frisco, DuBois Finds," *Chicago Defender,* 5 May 1945.

34. "Hits Conference Charter," *New York Times,* 6 June 1945.

35. Sue Bailey Thurman, "Dress Circle Affairs Highlighted Parley."

36. Borgwardt, *A New Deal for the World,* 198. For White's surprisingly militant views on decolonization, see Carol Anderson, *Bourgeois Radicals: The NAACP and the Struggle for Colonial Liberation, 1940–1960* (Cambridge: Cambridge University Press, 2015).

37. "Co-Pastor of Interracial Church Views Racial Tension as Evidence of Progress," *Cleveland Call and Post,* 23 June 1945.

38. HT, "Letter in Support of 'United World Federalists'" (1960), in *PHWT,* 4:259–60.

39. HT, "The Inner Life and World-Mindedness" (1945), in *PHWT,* 3:108–13.

40. HT, "The Inner Life and World-Mindedness," in *PHWT,* 3:108–13.

41. HT, "The Inner Life and World-Mindedness," in *PHWT,* 3:108–13.

42. Henry Alonzo Myers, *Are Men Equal? An Inquiry into the Meaning of American Democracy* (Ithaca, NY: Cornell University Press, 1945).

43. HT to Henry A. Myers, 28 May 1945, in *PHWT,* 3:130–32. Myers had spoken at Rankin Chapel in 1941 and befriended Thurman and sent him a copy of his new book "in remembrance of that meeting" (Henry A. Myers to HT, 19 April 1945, Folder 16, Box 29, HTC).

44. Myers, *Are Men Equal?,* 7.

45. Myers, *Are Men Equal?,* 160, 161.

46. Thurman might have voted in his first presidential election in 1924, in New York State (if so, he probably voted for the Progressive candidate, Robert La Follette). Given that he probably did not vote in Atlanta in 1928 and was unable, like all Washington, D.C., residents, to vote in 1932, 1936, or 1940, it is likely that 1944 would have been the year of either his first or second vote for president.

47. *PHWT,* 3:87.

48. HT, "Apostles of Sensitiveness" (1946), in *PHWT,* 3:170–74.

49. HT, *Meditations for Apostles of Sensitiveness* (Mills College, CA; Eucalyptus, 1947). See also HT, *Apostles of Sensitiveness* (Boston: American Unitarian Association, 1956).

50. *WHAH,* 60–61.

51. HT, "The Will to Segregation," in *PHWT,* 2:340.

52. HT, "The Cultural and Spiritual Prospect for a Nation Emerging from Total War" (1945), in *PHWT,* 3:107.

53. For Thurman's support of FOR's Journey of Reconciliation, a forerunner of the Freedom Riders of the 1960s, see HT to George Houser, 14 October 1946, in *PHWT,* 3:204–5.

54. Program, "The Fellowship Church—San Francisco," 8 April 1945.

55. HT, "The Cultural and Spiritual Prospect for a Nation Emerging from Total War," in *PHWT,* 3:108.

56. HT, "Apostles of Sensitiveness," in *PHWT,* 3:173.

57. HT, "The Cultural and Spiritual Prospect for a Nation Emerging from Total War," in *PHWT,* 3:107.

58. HT, "The Fascist Masquerade" (1946), in *PHWT,* 3:145–62. The essay was originally published in *The Church and Organized Movements: The Interseminary Series, Volume Two,* ed. Randolph Crump Miller (New York: Harper and Brothers, 1946), 82–100.

59. Henry A. Wallace, "Wallace Defines 'American Fascism,'" *New York Times,* 9 April 1944.

60. For "The Fascist Masquerade" (1946) and its background, see *PHWT,* 3:145–46.

61. HT to Ruth Smith, 17 April 1946, Folder 28, Box 28, HTC.

62. HT, "The Fascist Masquerade," in *PHWT,* 3:148–49.

63. HT, "The Fascist Masquerade," in *PHWT,* 3:150.

64. Probably the best-known avowed American fascist was Lawrence Dennis, whose book, *The Coming American Fascism* (New York: Harper and Brothers, 1936), was included in Thurman's bibliography for "The Fascist Masquerade." Dennis was, almost certainly unbeknownst to Thurman, an African American passing as white (see Gerald Horne, *The Color of Fascism: Lawrence Dennis, Racial Passing, and the Rise of Right-Wing Extremism in the United States* [New York: New York University Press, 2006]).

65. See Frank A. Warren, *Liberals and Communism: The "Red Decade" Revisited* (1966; repr., New York: Columbia University Press, 1933), 39.

66. W. E. B. Du Bois, "As the Crow Flies," *New York Amsterdam News,* 27 January 1940.

67. For American fascism, see Alan Brinkley, *Voices of Protest: Huey Long, Father Coughlin and the Great Depression* (New York: Knopf, 1982), esp. 269–83; and

Robert Brinkmeyer Jr., *The Fourth Ghost: White Southern Writers and European Fascism, 1920–1950* (Baton Rouge: Louisiana State University Press, 2009).

68. *Chicago Defender,* 21 January 1939.

69. "Gone with the Wind," *Chicago Defender,* 13 January 1940.

70. Adam Clayton Powell Jr., "Soap Box," *New York Amsterdam News,* 3 December 1938.

71. "Text of Roosevelts Address at Gainesville," *Atlanta Constitution,* 24 March 1938.

72. For the Christian American Association, see George Norris Green, *The Establishment in Texas Politics: The Primitive Years, 1938–1957* (Westport, CT: Greenwood, 1977), 58–68: and Gilbert J. Gall, *The Politics of Right to Work: The Labor Federation as Special Interest, 1943–1979* (New York: Greenwood, 1988).

73. HT, "The Fascist Masquerade," in *PHWT,* 3:152.

74. HT, "The Fascist Masquerade," in *PHWT,* 3:152–53; "A 'Nationalist Party' Launched by Reynolds," *New York Times,* 8 January 1945. For Reynolds, see Julian M. Pleasants, *Buncombe Bob: The Life and Times of Robert Rice Reynolds* (Chapel Hill: University of North Carolina Press, 2000).

75. "Rout Klans or Face Civil War Governor Says," *Chicago Defender,* 30 December 1922; "Italian Fascisti Is Not Like U.S. Ku Klux Klan," *Chicago Defender,* 7 October 1922. The latter article argued that the comparison between the Klan and fascism was flawed because the Klan was far worse.

76. Thurman's analysis of American fascism as a middle-class tantrum follows influential works such as Alfred Bingham, *Insurgent America: Revolt of the Middle Class* (New York: Harper and Brothers, 1935).

77. HT, "The Fascist Masquerade," in *PHWT,* 3:156.

78. HT, "The Fascist Masquerade," in *PHWT,* 3:157.

79. For Thurman's concern about fifth columnists, see "HT, "The Fascist Masquerade," in *PHWT,* 3:150, and his source for much of his information in the essay, E.A. Piller, *Time Bomb* (New York: Arco, 1945).

80. "The Brown Scare," in Leo P. Ribuffo, *The Old Christian Right: The Protestant Far Right from the Great Depression to the Cold War* (Philadelphia: Temple University Press, 1983), 178–224.

81. HT, "The Fascist Masquerade," in *PHWT,* 3:155; J. Edgar Hoover, *Masters of Deceit: The Story of Communism in America and How to Fight It* (New York: Holt, 1958).

82. For the ways opposition to unionization among white southern politicians shaped the growing rejection of the New Deal after 1938, see Ira Katznelson, *Fear Itself: The New Deal and the Origins of Our Time* (New York: Norton, 2013).

83. See Neil McMillen, *The Citizens' Councils: Organized Resistance to the Second Reconstruction, 1954–64* (Urbana: University of Illinois Press, 1971).

84. HT, "The Fascist Masquerade," in *PHWT,* 3:148, quoting "Fascism!," *Army Talk: Orientation Fact Sheet 64,* 24 March 1945.

85. HT, "The Cultural and Spiritual Prospect for a Nation Emerging from Total War," in *PHWT,* 3:107.

86. HT, "The Quest for Stability" (April 1949), in *PHWT,* 3:312–13.

87. HT, "Modern Challenges to Religion: Secular Radicalism" (6 November 1948), Folder 16, Box 16, HTC.

88. *WHAH*, 145.

89. For the Civil Rights Congress, see Gerald Horne, *Communist Front? The Civil Rights Congress, 1946–1956* (Rutherford, NJ: Fairleigh Dickinson University Press, 1988). For more on Thurman and the Cold War, see Peter Eisenstadt, "Howard Thurman, Martin Luther King, Jr., the Cold War, and the Civil Rights Movement," in *North American Churches and the Cold War,* ed. Paul Mojzes, 194–205 (Grand Rapids, MI: Eerdmans, 2018).

90. HT, "*Time:* Fellowship Church," in *PHWT,* 3:275–78; HT to Marion and Gilbert Banfield, 3 August 1948, Folder 25, Box 30, HTC. If I were to hazard a guess, Thurman probably voted for Wallace in 1948.

91. Robert A. Meyners to HT, 9 April 1948, Folder 21, Box 20, HTC.

92. Jean Burden, "Howard Thurman, Modern Prophet," 20, Folder 2, Box 17, HTC.

93. "Community Relations Committee," in *The Church for the Fellowship of All Peoples* (1947), 10.

94. HT, *Footprints of a Dream,* 115.

95. HT, "The Meaning of Loyalty #1" (6 May 1951); HT, "The Meaning of Loyalty #3: The State" (20 May 1951), both in Folder 2, Box 14, HTC.

96. HT, Meditation [June] 21, 1953, Howard Thurman Papers Project Files.

97. The scholarly consensus, certainly since the release of the Venona transcriptions in the 1990s, is that Julius Rosenberg and probably Ethel, too, were guilty of espionage. But this does not excuse the prosecutorial misconduct and the political savagery that led to their execution.

98. HT, Meditation [June] 21, 1953, Howard Thurman Papers Project Files.

99. HT, "Freedom under God" (February 1955), in *PHWT,* 4:117.

100. SAC [Special Agent in Charge] Cincinnati to Director, FBI re Reverend Howard Thurman, Security Matter, in Howard W. Thurman, Main Investigation File, FBI File 100-417823, Federal Bureau of Investigation, US Department of Justice, in Howard Thurman Paper Project Files. The files also mention Thurman's alleged support for the Joint Anti-Fascist Refugee Committee and the Spanish Refugee Appeal, both created in 1940 to assist Loyalist refugees from Spain; the Institute of Pacific Relations, an organization that was accused of support for Chinese Communists and of harboring Communist supporters; as well two organizations of which he was indeed a long-term supporter and member, the Congress of Racial Equality and the American Civil Liberties Union (ACLU). Whatever his involvement in the other organizations, Thurman was broadly supportive of left-progressive causes. He did have contact and friendships with some members of the Communist Party, perhaps especially during the San Francisco years, such as Louise Rosenberg Bransten; see PHWT, 3:14n1, 39n4, HT to Paul Robeson, 21 April 1944, in PHWT, 3:55–57.

   In an effort to increase the number of African American Foreign Service officers, Thurman served as a public member of the selection board for Foreign Service officers in the fall of 1966; see HT to Joseph Palmer 2nd, 4 January 1967, in PHWT, 5:162–64. The FBI initiated an investigation into whether Thurman should receive a security clearance, and was evidently opposed to his receiving one, but this did not prevent him from serving on the selection board. In a memo dated 6 February 1967, FBI director J. Edgar Hoover wrote that given that Thurman had already completed his assignment, further investigations were moot, John Edgar Hoover to Director of Personnel Investigations, Civil Service Commission, 6 February 1967, in Howard W. Thurman, Main Investigation File, FBI file 100-417823. Other than this episode, there is no evidence that the material in Thurman's FBI file was used against him.

101. HT, "Speech at Lambda Kappa Mu Human Relations Award Dinner" (19 November 1955), in *PHWT* 4:132.

102. HT, "The American Dream" (1958), in *PHWT,* 4:216–17.

103. HT, "Freedom under God," in *PHWT,* 4:117–18.

104. HT, "The American Dream," in *PHWT,* 4:220.

105. For Thurman's statements against the development of nuclear weapons, see "Dr. Thurman, Six Others Urge End of H-Bomb Tests," *Baltimore Afro-American,* 8 May 1954; and "Use of A-Bomb Condemned," *New York Times,* 3 August 1955. For Thurman's support for the emergence of a nonaligned bloc of newly independent nations at the 1955 Bandung Conference, see Louis Lautier, "Explosion Certain in South Africa," *Baltimore Afro-American,* 30 April 1955. See also *PHWT,* 4:132.

106. According to Jonathan Rieder, in comparison to Thurman's other books, *Jesus and the Disinherited* has an "earthier quality in keeping with its concern with social oppression" (Rieder, *The Word of the Lord Is upon Me: The Righteous Performance of Martin Luther King, Jr.* [Cambridge, MA: Harvard University Press, 2008], 277).

107. Alice Sams to HT, 15 November 1938, Folder 2, Box 26, HTC.

108. Karl E. Downs to HT, 5 January 1948, Folder 18, Box 30, HTC. For Downs, see the entry in the online *Handbook of Texas,* https://tshaonline.org/handbook /online/articles/fdo43.

109. *WHAH,* 219.

110. Karl E. Downs, *Meet the Negro* (Los Angeles: Methodist Youth Fellowship Southern California–Arizona Annual Conference, 1943), 21.

111. Downs, *Meet the Negro,* 168–70.

112. Jackie Robinson, *I Never Had It Made,* with Al Duckett (New York: Putnam, 1972), 82–83.

113. Robinson, *I Never Had It Made,* with Duckett, 18–19.

114. Karl E. Downs to HT, 5 January 1948, Folder 18, Box 30, HTC. Downs in this letter recaps a phone conversation he recently had with Thurman about the topic of the lectures.

115. Harold Pflug to HT, 28 October 1938, Folder 1, Box 26, HTC.

116. HT to Aubrey and Marigold Burns, 23 April 1948, in *PHWT,* 3:270–73.

117. HT to Gretchen Conduitte, 23 April 1948, Folder 21, Box 30, HTC.

118. HT to Aubrey and Marigold Burns, 23 April 1948, Folder 21, Box 30, HTC.

119. See *WHAH,* 221; and HT to Aubrey and Marigold Burns, 23 April 1948, Folder 21, Box 30, HTC. But see Harmon's understanding of Thurman's contractual obligation in Nolan B. Harmon to HT, 23 April 1948, Folder 21, Box 30, HTC.

120. HT to Eugene Exman, 23 April 1948, Folder 21, Box 30, HTC.

121. *WHAH,* 219–20.

122. Nolan Harmon, the editor in chief of Abingdon-Cokesbury, was polite, enthusiastic, though firm in his suggestions in his surviving correspondence with

Thurman (Nolan B. Harmon to HT, 28 May 1949, Folder 5, Box 31, HTC; Nolan B. Harmon to HT, 7 October 1948, Folder 27, Box 30, HTC).

123. S. Jonathan Bass, *Blessed Are the Peacemakers: Martin Luther King Jr., Eight White Religious Leaders, and the "Letter from Birmingham Jail"* (Baton Rouge: Louisiana State University Press, 2001), 38–44, 233–36.

124. HT to Nolan B. Harmon, 24 August 1948, in *PHWT,* 3:286–89.

125. Thurman published an essay using that title in another publication in 1949, "The Religion of Jesus and the Disinherited," in *In Defense of Democracy,* ed. Thomas H. Johnson (New York: G. P. Putnam, 1949), 125–38. Thurman had suggested to the publishers another possible title, "Religion and the Disinherited" (HT to Donald Glover, 23 April 1948, Folder 21, Box 30, HTC).

126. *Jesus and the Disinherited,* 15.

127. From Pat Beaird, 1 November 1948, in *PHWT* 3:291–93.

128. HT, *Jesus and the Disinherited,* 29.

129. HT, *Jesus and the Disinherited,* 5.

130. HT, *Jesus and the Disinherited,* 11.

131. HT, *Jesus and the Disinherited,* 56.

132. HT, *Jesus and the Disinherited,* 33.

133. HT, *Jesus and the Disinherited,* 33–34.

134. HT, *Jesus and the Disinherited,* 35, 69.

135. HT, *Jesus and the Disinherited,* 46.

136. HT, *Jesus and the Disinherited,* 51, 56.

137. HT, *Jesus and the Disinherited,* 51.

138. HT, *Jesus and the Disinherited,* 58.

139. HT, *Jesus and the Disinherited,* 59. In this context, Thurman defends the Equal Rights Amendment as needed to end "the morally degrading aspects of deception and dishonesty that enter into the relationship between men and women."

140. HT, *Jesus and the Disinherited,* 65.

141. HT, *Jesus and the Disinherited,* 101–2.

142. HT, *Jesus and the Disinherited,* 70.

143. HT, *Jesus and the Disinherited,* 73.

144. HT, *Jesus and the Disinherited,* 70.

145. HT, *Jesus and the Disinherited,* 83, 82.

146. HT, *Jesus and the Disinherited,* 88.

147. Nolan B. Harmon to HT, 24 May 1948, Folder 27, Box 22, HTC.

148. HT, *Jesus and the Disinherited,* 29–30.

149. HT, *Jesus and the Disinherited,* 93–95.

150. HT, *Jesus and the Disinherited,* 95.

151. HT, *Jesus and the Disinherited,* 106.

152. HT, *Jesus and the Disinherited,* 98–100.

153. Jean Burden, "Meditation on Howard Thurman on the Occasion of His Memorial Service April 10, 1981," (1982), Howard Thurman Papers Project Files.

154. Janella Smith to HT, 24 April 1956, Folder 4, Box 35, HTC.

155. Janella Smith to HT, 24 April 1956, Folder 4, Box 35, HTC; HT to Janella Smith, 13 June 1956, Folder 6, Box 35, HTC.

156. HT, *Jesus and the Disinherited,* 100, 103.

157. HT, *Jesus and the Disinherited*, 101.
158. Howard Thurman, *Moral Struggle and the Prophets*, ed. Peter Eisenstadt and Walter Earl Fluker (Maryknoll, NY: Orbis, 2020), 147.
159. HT, *Jesus and the Disinherited*, 107.
160. HT, "Religious Commitment," 12, Folder 25, Box 4, HTC.
161. HT, *Disciplines of the Spirit* (New York: Harper and Row, 1962), 127.
162. Vincent Harding, foreword to *Jesus and the Disinherited* (1949; repr., Boston: Beacon, 1996), xii.
163. HT, *Jesus and the Disinherited*, 106.
164. "Hellhound on My Trail," Vocalion 93623, recorded 20 June 1937. For the history of interpretation of "Hellhound on My Trail," see Barry Lee Pearson and Bill McCulloch, *Robert Johnson: Lost and Found* (Chicago: University of Illinois Press, 2003), 22–25.
165. For the two images of the blues as representing accommodation or resistance, see R. A. Lawson, *Jim Crow's Counterculture: The Blues and Black Southerners, 1890–1945* (Baton Rouge: Louisiana State University Press, 2010), 1–22.
166. HT, *Jesus and the Disinherited*, 25–26.
167. HT, "The Message of the Spirituals" (October 1928), in *PHWT*, 1:129.
168. See Daryl Michael Scott, *Contempt and Pity: Social Policy and the Image of the Damaged Black Psyche, 1880–1996* (Chapel Hill: University of North Carolina Press, 1997), xiii. Scott's book does not mention Thurman.
169. Howard Thurman, *Moral Struggle and the Prophets*, 61.
170. *PHWT*, 1:146.
171. HT, *Jesus and the Disinherited*, 49–50
172. HT, *Jesus and the Disinherited*, 50–51, 55.
173. HT, "Freedom under God," in *PHWT*, 4:117.
174. HT, *Apostles of Sensitiveness*, 12.
175. HT, *Jesus and the Disinherited*, 109.
176. Harold L. Bowman, "Review: *Jesus and the Disinherited*," *Journal of Religion* 29, no. 4 (October 1949): 330; Irwin R. Bailer, "Review of *Jesus and the Disinherited* [and two other books]," *Journal of Bible and Religion* 18, no. 2 (April 1950): 132–34. See also Paul Davies, "Review: *Jesus and the Disinherited*," *Journal of Biblical Literature* 66, no. 3 (September 1949): 280.
177. Aubrey Burns, "Christianity and Minorities," *Southwestern Review* 34, no. 4 (autumn 1949): 395.
178. Charley Cherokee, "National Grapevine," *Chicago Defender*, 21 May 1949.
179. Gertrude Martin, "Thurman's Book Treats Problems of Oppressed," *Chicago Defender*, 11 June 1949. Other notices in the Black press include "Howard Thurman to Publish New Book in April," *Atlanta Daily World*, 29 March 1949; Albert Anderson, "Review: *Jesus and the Disinherited*," *Philadelphia Tribune*, 7 May 1949; and Marshall L. Shephard, "The Christian Church," *Baltimore Afro-American*, 25 June 1949.
180. J. Edward Miller to HT, 10 May 1949; HT to J. Edward Miller, 25 May 1949, in *PWHT*, 3:323–24; 324.
181. Alice Sams to HT, 4 May 1949, in *PHWT*, 3:319–20.
182. *WHAH*, 155–56.

183. Clayborn Carson, ed., *The Papers of Martin Luther King, Jr.*, 1:281, 245. For the influence of *Jesus and the Disinherited* on King, see Quinton Dixie and Peter Eisenstadt, *Visions of a Better World: Howard Thurman's Pilgrimage to India and the Origins of African American Nonviolence* (Boston: Beacon, 2011), 190–95.

184. Martin Luther King, Jr., to HT, 6 September 1966, in *PHWT*, 5:159–60.

185. Lerone Bennett Jr., *What Manner of Man: A Biography of Martin Luther King, Jr.* (New York: Pocket Books, 1968), 57–58. Another early reader of Thurman's book was the pacifist, Korean War conscientious objector, civil rights activist, and minister James Lawson (b. 1928), later recruited by King to work for the SCLC. He told an interviewer that "in '49 or '50" he read *Jesus and the Disinherited*. Its argument that "the Gospel of Jesus is the survival kit for people whose backs are against the wall" was "very powerful for me because it was my experience reaffirmed" (cited in Sarah Azaransky, *This Worldwide Struggle: Religion and the International Roots of the Civil Rights Movement* [New York: Oxford University Press, 2017], 211).

186. HT, "The Hope of the Disinherited," ca. 1938, Folder 58, Box 6. HTC.

12. Disciplines and Resources

1. HT to Board of Trustees Fellowship Church, 31 January 1953, in *PHWT*, 4:53–56.

2. HT to Board of Trustees Fellowship Church, 31 January 1953, in *PHWT*, 4:53–56.

3. HT to Board of Trustees Fellowship Church, 31 January 1953, in *PHWT*, 4:53–56.

4. Jack Kerouac, *Big Sur* (New York: Farrar, Straus and Cudahy, 1962). Olive and Victor had two children, Emily and Anton. The marriage ended in the 1960s, and Olive thereafter split her time between New York City and California, before her death in 2009.

5. Anne moved east with her parents, graduating from Boston University in 1954, and graduating from the BU law school in 1958. She had a number of jobs and positions over the years, including that of speechwriter to Massachusetts lieutenant governor Elliot Richardson from 1966 to 1968. She would, like her parents, relocate to San Francisco, and she remained active in the work of her parents and the Howard Thurman Educational Trust. In 1961 she married the photographer Carl Chiarenza, and they had one child, Suzanne. They later divorced. Anne Spencer Thurman died in 2001.

6. In the late 1940 Madaline Thurman was living in New York City, studying music and dance, when Thurman chided her for not keeping in touch (Madaline Thurman to HT, 1 May 1947, in *PHWT*, 3:225–27). Madaline soon moved to California, but her emotional health was fragile, and she would have several bouts of institutionalization for severe depression, involving electroshock treatments (see HT to John Overholt, 21 May 1951, Folder 30, Box 31, HTC; HT to Melvin Watson, 18 January 1955, in *PHWT*, 4:35–37; 111–12; and David Geddes to HT, 1 June 1956, Folder 6, Box 35, HTC). Madaline's hospitalization was a "very difficult period" for Thurman (*PHWT*, 4:36), one that he rarely talked about.

7. HT, *Footprints of a Dream: The Story of the Church for the Fellowship of All Peoples* (New York: Harper and Brothers, 1959).

8. *WHAH*, 169.

9. *WHAH*, 169
10. *WHAH*, 171.
11. "Boston: One" (unpublished draft of autobiography, ca. 1978), 20–22, Folder 14, Box 4, HTC.
12. According to Allan Knight Chalmers, after he joined the faculty of the BU School of Theology in 1948, he pushed for Thurman to be hired, discussing it with Dean Walter Muelder, and renewed the call for hiring Thurman after Case became president of BU in 1951 (Allan Knight Chalmers to HT, 25 March 1953, Folder 15, Box 32, HTC). Chalmers had spoken at Rankin Chapel under Thurman's supervision as early as 1932 (Alan Knight Chalmers to HT, 18 November 1932, Folder 14, Box 23, HTC).
13. Edgar S. Brightman to HT, 9 October 1946, Folder 3, Box 30, HTC.
14. See Jannette E. Newhall to HT, 23 March 1953, in *PHWT*, 4:65–66. Brightman had heard Thurman's Ingersoll Lecture, published as *The Negro Spiritual Speaks of Life and Death*, and pronounced it "one of the most brilliant and satisfying, both intellectually and spiritually, in the entire Series" (Edgar DeWitt Jones, *The Royalty of the Pulpit: A Survey and Appreciation of the Lyman Beecher Lectures on Preaching* [New York: Harper and Brothers, 1951], 402–3). Brightman was also, until his death, the main dissertation advisor for Martin Luther King, Jr.
15. Allan Knight Chalmers to HT, 25 March 1953, Folder 15, Box 32, HTC.
16. *WHAH*, 173–74. This was by way of the senior BU executive telling Thurman that, once he started to attend services at Marsh Chapel, "few times in my life have I had this kind of profound religious experience."
17. *WHAH*, 174.
18. HT, "Boston: One," 26. Thurman had been a frequent visitor to Boston and Boston University, with at least ten visits in the two decades before his appointment. His most important publication of the 1930s, "Good News for the Underprivileged," had originally been delivered at a preaching convocation at the university.
19. See Kathleen Kilgore, *Transformations: A History of Boston University* (Boston: Boston University, 1991).
20. Kilgore, *Transformations*, 247.
21. HT, "Biographical Essay," in *PHWT*, 4:xix–xx.
22. Kilgore, *Transformations*, 251–52.
23. J[ohn] W[esley] E[dward] Bowen (1855–1933) was born into slavery in New Orleans and was the second African American to be awarded a Ph.D. degree in the United States. In 1893 he joined the previously all-white faculty at Gammon Theological Seminary in Atlanta, where he remained until his retirement in 1932. Other African American Ph.D. recipients from Boston University of Thurman's acquaintance include J. Leonard Farmer Sr. (1886–1961), in 1918, the father of the civil rights leader and Thurman's colleague at Howard University; Willis J. King (1886–1976), in 1921 (who was Bowen's successor at Gammon Theological Seminary, serving from 1932 to 1944); and Samuel DeWitt Proctor (1919–1997), in 1950.
24. Gary Dorrien, *Breaking White Supremacy: Martin Luther King Jr. and the Black Social Gospel* (New Haven, CT: Yale University Press, 2018), 271.
25. Gary J. Dorrien, *The Making of American Liberal Theology: Idealism, Realism, and Modernity, 1900–1950* (Louisville, KY.: Westminster John Knox, 2003), 286; Paul

Deats and Carol Robb, eds., *The Boston Personalist Tradition in Philosophy, Social Ethics, and Theology* (Macon, GA: Mercer University Press, 1986).

26. Dorrien, *The Making of American Liberal Theology*, 300, citing Brightman, "The Unpopularity of Personalism," *Methodist Review* 104 (January 1921): 13.

27. Stanley High, "Methodism's Pink Fringe," *Reader's Digest*, February 1950, 134–38. See also Kilgore, *Transformations*, 229–30.

28. See Willis J. King, "Personalism and Race," in *Personalism in Theology: A Symposium in Honor of Albert Cornelius Knudson*, ed. Edgar Sheffield Brightman (Boston: Boston University Press, 1943), 204–24.

29. Leroy Moore Jr., "The Rise of Religious Liberalism at the Rochester Theological Seminary, 1872–1928" (Ph.D. diss., Claremont Graduate School, 1966), 124, 154.

30. *PHWT*, 1:39.

31. *PHWT*, 1:44.

32. An example from the BU years: in 1955 he stated that "the essence of good human relations is a fundamental respect for human personality" (*PHWT*, 4:132).

33. For a searching of the impact of personalism on Thurman and King, see Kipton E. Jensen, *Howard Thurman: Philosophy, Civil Rights, and the Search for Common Ground* (Columbia: University of South Carolina Press, 2019). See also Rufus Burrow Jr., *God and Human Dignity: The Personalism, Theology, and Ethics of Martin Luther King, Jr.* (South Bend, IN: University of Notre Dame Press, 2006).

34. G. James Fleming, "Noted Preacher to Head Boston U's Chapel Staff," *New York Amsterdam News*, 28 March 1953. For other typical comments, see "Boston University Employs First Fulltime Negro Professor," *Norfolk Journal and Guide*, 28 March 1953; "Former Ohio Pastor Named Boston Professor," *Cleveland Call and Post*, 28 March 1953.

35. "Baptist Pastor Is Named Preacher by Boston U," *New York Times*, 22 March 1953.

36. "Great Preachers: These 12—and Others—Bring America Back to the Churches," *Life*, 6 April 1953, 126.

37. Jean Burden, "Howard Thurman," *Atlantic Monthly*, October 1953, 39–44.

38. Jean Burden, "Meditation on Howard Thurman on the Occasion of His Memorial Service April 10, 1981" (1982), Howard Thurman Papers Project Files. The article was also used to demonstrate African American accomplishment as part of the Cold War propaganda struggle, broadcast on Voice of America and distributed by the US Information Agency.

39. Kilgore, *Transformations*, 251. Marsh Chapel was new, having opened only in 1950, next to the School of Theology, designed in a neomedieval style by the prominent architect Ralph Adams Cram. It was named, after his retirement in 1951, for the university's longtime president Daniel Marsh, who had written a book about it (Marsh, *The Charm of the Chapel* [Boston: Boston University Press, 1950]).

40. HT to Board of Trustees of Fellowship Church, 31 January 1953, in *PHWT*, 4:53–56.

41. HT to Board of Trustees of Fellowship Church, 31 January 1953, in *PHWT*, 4:53–56.

42. HT, *Footprints of a Dream*, 17.

43. "All University Religious Services, Daniel L. Marsh Chapel, Boston University," 20 September 1953, in Howard Thurman Papers Project Files. The same statement would remain in the weekly program throughout Thurman's years in Boston.

44. George K. Makechnie, *Howard Thurman: His Enduring Dream* (Boston: Howard Thurman Center, Boston University, 1988), 69.

45. Attendance figures are available in Thurman's annual reports as dean of chapel, which estimate average attendance of 226 (HT, Annual Report, Dean of Chapel, 1953–54), 286; HT, Dean of Chapel Annual Report, 1955–56, 225; HT, Dean of Chapel Annual Report, 1960–61, 300), the annual reports in Folder 27, Box 21, HTC. See also Makechnie, *Howard Thurman*, 41.

46. Makechnie, *Howard Thurman*, 41.

47. Beth E. Ruhde-Colgate, "A Thank You Letter to Howard Thurman," in *Common Ground: Essays in Honor of Howard Thurman on the Occasion of His Seventy-Fifth Birthday, November 18, 1975*, ed. Samuel Lucius Gandy (Washington, DC: Hoffman, 1976), 1–6.

48. Makechnie, *Howard Thurman*, 55.

49. Makechnie, *Howard Thurman*, 82.

50. Makechnie, *Howard Thurman*, 38–39, brackets in original.

51. Henry Bollman to HT, 7 January 1956, in *PHWT*, 4:150–51.

52. See HT, *We Believe*, 20 November 1959, in *PHWT*, 4:254–57.

53. HT, *We Believe*, 29 May 1965. See also *WHAH*, 174–75.

54. *WHAH*, 185–87.

55. *WHAH*, 185–87.

56. Makechnie, *Howard Thurman*, 25. In 1958, for a cookbook Sue edited for the National Council of Negro Women, Howard offered a recipe for one of his throw-everything-into-the-pot concoctions, a "June Commencement Soup" with ingredients including beef, peppers, onions, and various herbs with special meanings he assigned them: Marjoram (joy), basil (wisdom), thyme (courage), chives (usefulness), parsley (festivity), all dedicated "to his mother and grandmother, and all Negro women of the long past who have striven by dint of sacrifice and hard labor to educate the race" (National Council of Negro Women, *The Historical Cookbook of the American Negro*, ed. Sue Bailey Thurman [1958, repr., Boston, Beacon, 2000], 54).

57. Harold C. Case, *"Harvest from the Seed": Boston University in Mid-Century* (New York: Newcomen Society in North America, 1957), 15–16.

58. HT, Dean of Chapel Annual Report, 1953–54, in *PHWT*, 4:85–94.

59. HT, Dean of Chapel Annual Report, 1953–54, in *PHWT*, 4:85–94.

60. HT, Dean of Chapel Annual Report, 1954–55, Folder 27, Box 61, HTC.

61. HT, Martin Luther King Lecture, #2, 10 April 1975, Graduate Student Union, Berkeley, California, Folder 4, Box 16, HTC.

62. Trudi Smith, *Sue Bailey Thurman: Building Bridges to Common Ground* (Boston: Thurman Center, Boston University, 1995), 17.

63. HT, "Morehouse College Seventy-Fifth Anniversary Sermon" (15 February 1942), in *PHWT*, 2:293–302.

64. Lewis V. Baldwin, *There Is a Balm in Gilead: The Cultural Roots of Martin Luther King, Jr.* (Minneapolis, MN: Fortress, 1991), 300–301.

65. See in *PHWT,* 4:xlvn51.
66. For details on King's allusions to Thurman, see Dixie and Eisenstadt, *Visions of a Better World,* 192–93, 226n31. See also Walter E. Fluker, *They Looked for a City: A Comparative Analysis of the Ideal of Community in the Thought of Howard Thurman and Martin Luther King, Jr.* (Lanham, MD.: University Press of America, 1989), 112.
67. HT, Martin Luther King Lecture, #2, Folder 4, Box 16, HTC.
68. HT, Martin Luther King Lecture, #2, Folder 4, Box 16, HTC.
69. HT, Martin Luther King Lecture, #2, Folder 4, Box 16, HTC.
70. "Martin Luther King, Jr. Ceremony," 8 April 1968 (University of California at Santa Cruz).
71. *WHAH,* 254.
72. Major Jones (1919–1993), an early exponent of black theology, had a distinguished career as a teacher and as president of Gammon Theological Seminary from 1967 to 1985. Both King and Jones eventually interviewed for the position, but it went to another Thurman protégé, Samuel L. Gandy (see *PHWT,* 4:99n2, 97n4).
73. See A. W. Dent to HT, 1 December 1954; HT to A. W. Dent 14 December 1954, in *PHWT,* 4:96–98; 98–99. See also Peter Eisenstadt, "Did a Mediocre Letter of Recommendation for Martin Luther King, Jr. Change the Course of History?," History News Network and Time.com, December 2014.
74. Clayborne Carson, ed., *The Papers of Martin Luther King, Jr.* (Berkeley: University of California Press, 1992–), 3:73.
75. HT, *The Creative Encounter: An Interpretation of Religion and the Social Witness* (New York: Harper and Brothers, 1954).
76. HT, *The Creative Encounter,* 9.
77. HT, *The Creative Encounter,* 22.
78. HT, *The Creative Encounter,* 9.
79. HT, *The Creative Encounter,* 133. Thurman made one of his few explicit references to Joseph McCarthy in a 1956 lecture: "During the many weeks of the hearing involving the Secretary of the Army and the junior Senator from Wisconsin, a comment that I heard with great persistency was this: 'Unfortunately, there isn't anything that anybody can do about this situation.' Such is the despair growing out of a steady disintegration of the responsibility for the common life which each citizen is under obligation to preserve" (HT, *Apostles of Sensitiveness* [Boston: American Unitarian Association, 1956], 14).
80. HT, *The Creative Encounter,* 151–52.
81. HT, "Be Not Overcome by Evil" (16 May 1954), Folder 4, Box 16, HTC.
82. "Educators Comment on the School Decision," *Chicago Defender,* 22 May 1954.
83. "Mrs. Bethune Sees the School Ruling as a Milestone in U.S. History," *Chicago Defender,* 29 May 1954.
84. "Dr. Thurman Speaks to Bennett College Grads," *Norfolk Journal and Guide,* 19 June 1954.
85. "Students Told They Can Make America Over," *Baltimore Afro-American,* 6 March 1943.
86. HT, "Speech at Lambda Kappa Mu Human Relations Dinner," in *PHWT,* 4:135.

87. HT, "The Christian Minister and the Desegregation Decision" (May 1957), in *PHWT*, 4:170–78.

88. HT, "The Christian Minister and the Desegregation Decision," in *PHWT*, 4:170–78. See also HT, *Footprints of a Dream*, 138–57.

89. Paul Harvey has written: "For most of the 1950s, King still professed hope that white southern ministers could provide moral leadership. Speaking at Vanderbilt in 1957 King said, 'there are in the white South more open-minded moderates than appears on the surface. These are people silent today because of the fear of social, political, and economic reprisals'" (Harvey, *Christianity and Race in the South* [Chicago: University of Chicago Press, 2016], 167–68).

90. HT, "Love Your Enemies III" (9 October 1955), Folder 120, Box 11, HTC. The quote about Emmett Till was from a *Life* magazine editorial.

91. HT, "Love Your Enemies III," Folder 120, Box 11, HTC.

92. HT, "Speech at Lambda Kappa Mu Human Relations Dinner" (November 1955), in *PHWT*, 4:131–36. Georgia tried to ban teachers from membership in the NAACP; the murderers of Emmett Till were acquitted after a sham trial; the Rev. DeLaine fled his home in Lake City, South Carolina, after his house was firebombed and sprayed with gunfire; in Florida, citrus workers attending a union organizing meeting were wounded by shotgun blasts. For more details on the incidents mentioned by Thurman, see the annotation in *PHWT*, 4:135–36nn4–7.

93. HT, "The Light That Is Darkness" (25 May 1958), Folder 28, Box 6, HTC.

94. "7,000 S.C Teachers Told 'Seek Freedom,'" *Baltimore Afro-American*, 13 April 1957.

95. HT to John Overholt, 28 March 1957, in *PHWT*, 4:167–70.

96. HT to John Overholt, 28 March 1957, in *PHWT*, 4:167–70.

97. Carson, ed., *The Papers of Martin Luther King, Jr.*, 3:168–70.

98. Carson, ed., *The Papers of Martin Luther King, Jr.*, 3:178–79.

99. See HT to Martin Luther King, Jr., 14 March 1956; and Martin Luther King, Jr., to HT, 16 March 1956, in *PHWT*, 4:151–53; 153–54. Thurman's and King's paths did cross at several conferences over the next few years, but it seems unlikely that they had time for more than a passing conversation. They both spoke at the August 1956 convention of the National Baptist Convention in Denver ("15,000 Baptists to Attend Denver Session," *Chicago Defender*, 25 August 1956). Over the next several years they were both present at several other meetings; at the 1959 Religious Leaders Conference of the President's Committee on Government Contracts, with Vice-President Richard Nixon presiding ("Leaders See U.S. Job Parley as a 'Significant Meeting,'" *Baltimore Afro-American*, 23 May 1959), and at the Hampton Minister's Institute in 1962 ("Dr. King and Dr. Thurman Will Be Hampton Speakers," *Norfolk Journal and Guide*, 23 June 1962).

100. The inscribed cover of *Deep River* is reproduced in Carson, ed., *The Papers of Martin Luther King, Jr.*, 6:225.

101. *WHAH*, 254–55.

102. *WHAH*, 254–55.

103. "Statement Issued from Harlem Hospital," 30 September 1958, in Carson, ed., *The Papers of Martin Luther King, Jr.*, 4:502. Gandhi's famous statement to Thurman

was familiar to King (see Bayard Rustin, *Down the Line: The Collected Works of Bayard Rustin* [Chicago: Quadrangle, 1971], 103).

104. Martin Luther King, Jr., to HT, 8 November 1958, in *PHWT,* 4:231–33. This was a response (HT to Martin Luther King, Jr., 20 October 1958, in *PHWT,* 4:222–24).

105. Taylor Branch, *Parting the Waters: America in the King Years, 1954–63* (New York: Simon and Schuster, 1988), 245.

106. "My Trip to the Land of Gandhi," *Ebony* (July 1959), reprinted in Martin Luther King, Jr., *A Testament of Hope: The Essential Writings and Speeches of Martin Luther King, Jr.,* ed. James M. Washington (New York: HarperCollins, 1986), 23.

107. Karl E. Downs, *Meet the Negro* (Los Angeles: Methodist Youth Fellowship Southern California–Arizona Annual Conference, 1943), 168–69.

108. James Earl Massey to HT, 17 April 1956, in *PHWT,* 4:154–58.

109. James Earl Massey, *Aspects of My Pilgrimage: An Autobiography* (Anderson, IN: Anderson University Press, 2002), 65–66. For another account by Massey of his first hearing Thurman preach, see James Earl Massey to HT, 5 November 1971, in *PHWT,* 5:224–25.

110. James Earl Massey to HT, 17 April 1956, in *PHWT,* 154–58.

111. For Massey's efforts to write a scholarly study of Thurman (including an abortive attempt at a Thurman biography), see James Earl Massey to HT, 16 April 1974, Folder 16, Box 46, HTC; HT to James Earl Massey, 24 August 1974; Folder 20, Box 46, HTC; James Earl Massey, "Howard Thurman: Preacher" (unpublished biographical draft), Folder 7, Box 17, HTC; and Sue Bailey Thurman, "Comments on Unpublished Biographical Draft of James Earl Massey" (ca. 1974), Folder 7, Box 17, HTC. For Massey's published works on Thurman, see James E. Massey, "Bibliographical Essay: Howard Thurman and Rufus M. Jones, Two Mystics," *Journal of Negro History* (April 1972): 190–95; Massey, "Thurman's Preaching: Style and Substance," in *God and Human Freedom: A Festschrift in Honor of Howard Thurman,* ed. Henry J. Young (Richmond, ID: Friends United Press, 1983), 110–21.

112. Downs, *Meet the Negro,* 168–69.

113. *WHAH,* 177–78.

114. HT to Lloyd Smith, 6 October 1953, Folder 22, Box 32, HTC.

115. HT, *Disciplines of the Spirit* (New York: Harper and Row, 1963), 9.

116. *WHAH,* 177–78.

117. HT, "March 1, 1955," in "Course Material, 1955–71," Folder 1, Box 66, HTC; Rabbi Zalman M. Schachter-Shalomi, *My Life in Jewish Renewal: A Memoir,* with Edward Hoffman (Lanham, MD: Rowman and Littlefield, 2012), 91.

118. HT, "March 1, 1955," in "Course Material, 1955–71."

119. HT, *Disciplines of the Spirit,* 9–10.

120. HT, *Disciplines of the Spirit,* 96.

121. For accounts of Zalman Schachter-Shalomi's life, see Schachter-Shalomi, *My Life in Jewish Renewal,* with Hoffman; and Sara Davidson, *The December Project: An Extraordinary Rabbi and a Skeptical Seeker Confront Life's Greatest Mystery* (New York: HarperOne, 2014). For an evaluation of his religious thought, see Shaul Magid, *American Post-Judaism: Identity and Renewal in a Postethnic Society* (Bloomington: Indiana University Press, 2013). Rabbi Or N. Rose's "'My Black

Rebbe': Howard Thurman's Mentorship of Zalman Schachter-Shalomi," a paper in the author's possession, is the best overview of the friendship of Thurman and Schachter-Shalomi.

122. Zalman Schachter-Shalomi, "What I Found in the Chapel," in *My Neighbor's Faith: Stories of Interreligious Encounter, Growth, and Transformation,* ed. Jennifer Howe Peace, Or N. Rose, and Gregory Mobley (Maryknoll, NY: Orbis, 2012), 207–10. For other accounts of the initial meetings of Schachter-Shalomi and Thurman, see Davidson, *The December Project,* 75–77; and Or N. Rose, "On the Growing Edge of Judaism: Reb Zalman at Eighty," in *Tikkun Reader: Twentieth Anniversary,* ed. Michael Lerner (New York: Rowan and Littlefield, 2007), 145–49.

123. Schachter-Shalomi, "What I Found in the Chapel; Schachter-Shalomi, *My Life in Jewish Renewal,* 91.

124. Schachter-Shalomi, *My Life in Jewish Renewal,* 91.

125. Zalman Schachter-Shalomi, *The First Step: A Guide for the New Jewish Spirit,* with Donald Gropman (New York: Bantam, 1983), 6.

126. Zalman Schachter-Shalomi, interview by Peter Eisenstadt, 28 June 2012.

127. Rose, "On the Growing Edge of Judaism," 149.

128. Zalman M. Schachter, *The First Step: A Primer of a Jew's Spiritual Life* (Winnipeg, Manitoba: n.p., 1958), 1. I would like to thank Rabbi Or Rose for making a copy available to me.

129. HT to Zalman M. Schachter, 3 March 1959, in *PHWT,* 4:240–42; HT, "Annual Report: The Wider Ministry, 1962–1963" (September 1963), in *PHWT,* 5:14–35.

130. HT, "The Wider Ministry and the Concept of Community" (28 July 1963), Folder 45, Box, 13, HTC; HT, "Annual Report: The Wider Ministry, 1962–1963," in *PHWT,* 5:24.

131. If Thurman was confused as to the branch of Judaism to which Schachter-Shalomi belonged, it is understandable. Raised and trained in Orthodox (what is often called "Ultra-Orthodox" Judaism), he moved freely between the branches of Judaism. He was rabbi to a Conservative congregation in Winnipeg and received his doctorate in 1966 from the Reform Hebrew Union College. He later, as a founder of the Havurah movement, created his own unaffiliated branch of Judaism.

132. HT, "Annual Report: The Wider Ministry, 1962–1963," in *PHWT,* 5:24.

133. For an overview of the Jewish renewal and Havurah movements and Schachter-Shalomi's role within it, see Dana Evan Kaplan, *Contemporary American Judaism: Transformation and Renewal* (New York: Columbia University Press, 2009), 258–98, 387–93.

134. Zalman Schachter-Shalomi, interview by Peter Eisenstadt, 28 June 2012. Schachter-Shalomi died in 2014. If Thurman's friendship with Schachter-Shalomi was the highpoint of Thurman's philo-Semitism, it was part of a deep affinity with Judaism, with a religion where there was "no veil between the worshipper and God." He was friends with a number of rabbis who formed "my private reserve, my treasures of the spirit" (*WHAH,* 267–68). Rabbi Joseph Glaser (1924–1994), who served as executive vice president of the Central Conference of American Rabbis, the main Reform rabbinic organization, called Thurman his "teacher and

spiritual counselor," adding, "But for him, I would likely not have become a rabbi, nor seen the glories of the Jewish tradition as fully and vividly as this man" (Glaser, "Of Time and Timelessness," in *Common Ground,* ed. Samuel Lucius Gandy, 91–96). Other Jewish thinkers influenced by Thurman included his friend Rabbi Dudley Weinberg (see Dudley Weinberg, *The Efficacy of Prayer* [New York: Jewish Chautauqua Society, 1965]). Edward Kaplan, the future biographer of Abraham Joshua Heschel, was still a teenager when Thurman became his spiritual model and mentor. Kaplan has written extensively on Thurman; see "Howard Thurman: Meditation, Mysticism, and Life's Contradictions," in *Debate and Understanding,* ed. Ricardo A. Millet and Conley H. Hughes (spring 1982): 19–26; and "A Jewish Dialogue with Howard Thurman: Mysticism, Compassion, and Community," *Cross-Currents* (December 2010): 515–25.

135. See Walter N. Pahnke to HT, 6 September 1957, in *PHWT,* 4:193–98.

136. Ruhde-Colgate, "A Thank You Letter to Howard Thurman."

137. Walter N. Pahnke to HT, 13 November 1956, Folder 11, Box 35, HTC.

138. Walter N. Pahnke to HT, 6 September 1957, in *PHWT,* 4:193–98.

139. For Thurman's most extended exposition of this theme in print, see HT, *The Search for Common Ground* (New York: Harper and Row, 1971), 28–41.

140. HT to Rev. J. E. Dunn, 11 March 1937, Folder 16, Box 24, HTC. Rosicrucianism was an occult philosophy popular in early seventeenth-century Europe that had a revival in the United States in the early years of the twentieth century.

141. See his discussion of his meeting with Harrie Vernette Rhodes, a famous Minneapolis faith healer in HT, "Mysticism: Lecture 6" (April 1973), University of Redlands, Folder 27, Box 8, HTC.

142. Edgar Cayce (1877–1945) was a famous American psychic who went into regular trances during his readings with clients. Thurman received a letter on 27 October 1960 inquiring of Peggy Strong, a Fellowship Church member who had received a reading from Cayce: "Walter Pahnke, who visited us here at Virginia Beach last summer, also told us that you had spoken to him about Peggy's reading" (Gladys Davis Turner to HT, 27 October 1960, Folder 10, Box 38, HTC). For Thurman's friendship with the artist Peggy Strong, see *WHAH,* 239–41.

143. HT to J. Goodell Schultz, 4 November 1960, Folder 11, Box 38, HTC.

144. Aldous Huxley, *The Doors of Perception* (New York: Harper and Brothers, 1954), 73.

145. Coleman Jennings to HT, 14 November 1959, Folder 15, Box 38, HTC. Zalman Schachter-Shalomi was also interested in the spiritual dimensions of psychedelic substances and, under the direction of Timothy Leary, took his first LSD trip in the summer of 1962 (Rose, "My Black Rebbe").

146. HT, "Mysticism: Lecture 4" (April 1973, University of Redlands), Folder 27, Box 8, HTC.

147. Timothy Leary, *Your Brain Is God* (Berkeley, CA: Ronin, 1988), 8.

148. Walter Pahnke, "Drugs and Mysticism: An Analysis of the Relationship between Psychedelic Drugs and the Mystical Consciousness" (Ph.D. diss., Harvard University, 1963).

149. Timothy Leary, *Flashbacks: An Autobiography* (Los Angeles: J. P. Tarcher, 1983), 102. Leary misspelled Thurman's name as "Thurmond," and this misspelling has

unfortunately been repeated in much of the subsequent literature on the Good Friday Experiment.

150. Huston Smith, "The Good Friday Experiment," in *Cleansing the Doors of Perception: The Religious Significance of Entheogenic Plants and Chemicals* (Boulder, CO: Sentient, 2000), 99–103. Smith dedicated the book "to the memory of Walter Pahnke."

151. A tape recording of Thurman's 1962 Good Friday service is available at https://maps .org/news/multimedia-library/138%E2%80%931962-good-Friday-experiment, accessed 11 June 2020.

152. Robert Greenfield, *Timothy Leary: A Biography* (Orlando, FL: Harcourt, 1995), 182.

153. Don Lattin, *The Harvard Psychedelic Club* (New York: HarperCollins, 2010), 81.

154. Jeanne Malgren, "Tune In, Turn on, Drop Out: The Good Friday Experiment," *St. Petersburg Times,* 27 November 1994.

155. Lattin, *The Harvard Psychedelic Club,* 80.

156. Smith, *Cleansing the Doors of Perception,* 99–103.

157. Pahnke, "Drugs and Mysticism," 234.

158. Rick Doblin, "Pahnke's 'Good Friday Experiment': A Long-Term Follow-Up and Methodological Critique," *Journal of Transpersonal Psychology* 23, no. 1 (1991): 1–28; R. R. Griffiths et al., "Psilocybin Can Occasion Mystical-Type Experiences Having Substantial and Sustained Personal Meaning and Spiritual Significance," *Psychopharmacology* (August 2006): 1–16.

159. Noah Gordon, "The Hallucinogenic Drug Cult," *Reporter,* 15 August 1963, 35–43; HT to Shirley Katzander, 8 August 1963, in *PHWT,* 4:335–37. There is a tantalizing beginning of a discussion of how "a young friend of mine" became involved with Leary, cut short after only a few sentences (the tape ends) in a course Thurman delivered on mysticism at the University of Redlands in 1973 (see HT, "Mysticism: Lecture 4" [April 1973, University of Redlands], Folder 27, Box 8, HTC).

160. Timothy Leary to HT, 29 October 1962, *PHWT,* 4:333–35.

161. Like Thurman, Pahnke delivered the Ingersoll Lecture at Harvard, published as Walter N. Pahnke, "The Psychedelic Mystical Experience in the Human Encounter with Death," *Harvard Theological Review* 62, no. 1 (January 1969): 1–21. Thurman wrote a prayer that was read at Pahnke's funeral ("Howard Thurman Prayer, 1971," Folder 5, Walter Richards Collection of Walter Pahnke Papers, 1952–1971, Archives and Special Collections, Purdue University Library).

162. Luther Smith, communication with the author, July 2007.

163. The misconception persists that Leary was Pahnke's dissertation advisor (see Michael Pollan, *How to Change Your Mind: What the New Science of Psychedelics Teaches Us about Consciousness, Dying, Addiction, Depression, and Transcendence* (New York: Penguin, 2018), 45.

164. HT, Dean of Chapel Annual Report, 1954–55, Folder 27, Box 61, HTC.

165. HT, Chapel Committee Meeting, 29 April 1956, Folder 27, Box 61, HTC.

166. HT, Chapel Committee Meeting, 29 April 1956, Folder 27, Box 61, HTC.

167. HT, Dean of Chapel Annual Report, 1956–57, Folder 27, Box 61, HTC.

168. HT, Dean of Chapel Annual Report, 1960–61, Folder 27, Box 61, HTC.

169. Statement of Affirmation (undated, ca. October 1960), Folder 13, Box 64, HTC.

170. Statement of Affirmation (undated, ca. October 1960), Folder 13, Box 64, HTC.

171. Statement of Affirmation (undated, ca. October 1960), Folder 13, Box 64, HTC.

172. Statement of Affirmation (undated, ca. October 1960), Folder 13, Box 64, HTC.

173. Statement of Affirmation (undated, ca. October 1960), Folder 13, Box 64, HTC.

174. George Warmer to HT, 10 June 1960, Folder 6, Box 38, HTC; George Warmer to Jean Hodge, 28 October 1960, Folder 10, Box 38, HTC; HT, Dean of Chapel Annual Report, 1960–61, Folder 27, Box 61, HTC.

175. HT, Dean of Chapel Annual Report, 1960–61, Folder 27, Box 61, HTC.

176. *WHAH*, 181.

177. *WHAH*, 187.

178. *WHAH*, 180–81.

179. Will Herberg, *Protestant/Catholic/Jew: An Essay in American Religious Sociology* (Garden City, NY: Doubleday, 1955).

180. HT, Dean of Chapel Annual Report, 1953–54, Folder 27, Box 61, HTC.

181. HT, Dean of Chapel Annual Report, 1955–56, Folder 27, Box 61, HTC.

182. J. Wendell Yeo to HT, 11 July 1961, Folder 19, Box 38, HTC.

183. Chapel Committee Meeting, 29 April 1956.

184. *WHAH*, 169.

185. Harold C. Case to Margaret Harding, 9 July 1956, in *PHWT*, 4:164–65.

186. HT to Harold C. Case, July 1956, in *PHWT*, 4:165–67. This is a handwritten, unfinished letter that might have never been sent.

187. Harold C. Case to HT, 4 October 1957; HT to Harold C. Case, 15 October 1957; in *PHWT*, 4:198; 198–201.

188. HT, "Annual Report: The Wider Ministry, 1962–1963," in *PHWT*, 5:16–17.

189. HT to Harold Case, 29 April 1963, in *PHWT*, 5:10–12.

190. HT to Harold Case, 29 April 1963, in *PHWT*, 5:10–12; Robert Hamill to HT, 15 February 1963, Folder 2, Box 40, HTC.

191. George Makechnie to Harold Case, 6 February 1962, Folder 7, Box 39, HTC.

192. HT to Harold Case, 29 April 1963, in *PHWT*, 5:10–12.

193. Walter G. Muelder, "Apostles of Growth: Howard Thurman" (November 1965), Folder 10, Box 17, HTC.

194. Walter Fluker told me that Thurman confided this to him in one of their conversations.

195. HT to Harold C. Case, July 1956, in *PHWT*, 4:165–67.

196. HT to Harold C. Case, 23 July 1958, in *PHWT*, 4:234–37.

197. Richard Morgan Cameron, *Boston University School of Theology, 1839–1968* (Boston: Boston University School of Theology, 1968), 137.

198. HT to William Jovanovich, 4 April 1978, Folder 22, Box 48, HTC.

199. Roberta Byrd Barr, "A Creative Encounter: Interview with Howard Thurman, 14–15 February 1969, Part 1, p. 14, Folder 30, Box 16, HTC.

13. "The Stillness of Absolute Motion"

1. HT, Speech at Lambda Kappa Mu Human Relations Award Dinner (November 1955), in *PHWT*, 4:132.

2. See HT to John Overholt (March 1957), in *PHWT,* 4:167–69. This was in connection to a month the Thurmans spent in Edinburgh in the summer of 1957 as the guest of their friend Coleman Jennings. This was the first overseas trip Howard had taken since the trip to India. Thurman once described his ideal vacation to "just sit under a tree with somebody to scratch my back and pour lemonade down my throat" (HT to Melvin Watson, 16 May 1940, Folder 3, Box 27, HTC).

3. HT to William J. Trent Jr., 23 January 1960, in *PHWT,* 4:260–62.

4. HT, "The New Heaven and the New Earth" (1958), in *PHWT,* 4:204.

5. Stokely Carmichael and Charles V. Hamilton, *Black Power: The Politics of Liberation in America* (New York: Vintage, 1967).

6. Charles V. Hamilton to HT, 18 February 1960, in *PHWT,* 4:264–65. Hamilton drafted the voting rights bill that the Tuskegee Civic Association submitted to Congress in 1959 (see Robert J. Norell, *Reaping the Whirlwind: The Civil Rights Movement in Tuskegee* [New York: Knopf, 1985], 170).

7. HT, "Nonviolence and the Art of Reconciliation" (1963), in *PHWT,* 5:6

8. HT to E. H. Hall, 19 September 1960, Folder 9, Box 39, HTC. For Thurman's reflections on the trip and its reconstructed itinerary, see HT, "To Friends of the International Fellowship Community" (August 1960), in *PHWT,* 4:268–75. Although it is possible that the Thurmans made a brief return to India on this trip, it is my view, after examining the somewhat contradictory available evidence, that they did not.

9. HT, "To Friends of the International Fellowship Community" (August 1960), in *PHWT,* 4:270.

10. HT to Boice Gross, 19 September 1960, Folder 9, Box 39, HTC.

11. HT, "To Friends of the International Fellowship Community," in *PHWT,* 4:271–72.

12. HT, "To Friends of the International Fellowship Community," in *PHWT,* 4:271.

13. HT, "Windbreak . . . Against Existence" (Fall 1960), 7–9, in *PHWT,* 4:282–83; HT, "To Friends of the International Fellowship Community," in *PHWT,* 4:271

14. HT, "Windbreak . . . Against Existence," 7–9, in *PHWT,* 4:283.

15. Thurman cited this proverb as early as 1928 (see *PHWT,* 1:143).

16. HT, "Windbreak. . . Against Existence," in *PHWT,* 4:283

17. HT, "Windbreak. . . Against Existence," in *PHWT,* 4:284–85.

18. HT to J. Wendell Yeo, 16 March 1961, in *PHWT,* 4:300–304.

19. See HT, Dean of Chapel Annual Report, June 1944, in *PHWT,* 3:80.

20. HT to Boice Gross, 24 April 1962, Folder 9, Box 39, HTC.

21. HT to Boice Gross, 19 March 1963, Folder 8, Box 39, HTC.

22. Zalman Schachter to HT, 9 November 1964, Folder 11, Box 41, HTC.

23. HT to J. Wendell Yeo, cc'd to Harold Case and William Overholt, 10 May 1962, Folder 10, Box 39, HTC.

24. HT to Harold Case, 4 October 1962, Folder 15, Box 39, HTC; HT to Harold Case, 17 November, 1962, Folder 16, Box 39, HTC.

25. HT to W. Stuart MacLeod, 21 December 1962, Folder 17, Box 39, HTC.

26. *WHAH,* 188.

27. Thurman was interested in restoring Harriet Tubman's derelict house in Auburn, New York, as early as 1940 (see HT to Donal Cloward, 16 March 1940, Folder 1,

Box 27, HTC), and he subsequently spoke in Auburn ("Dr. Howard Thurman Speaks at 3rd Tubman Pilgrimage," *Norfolk Journal and Guide,* 29 October 1955).

28. See Linda J. Henry, "Promoting Historical Consciousness: The Early Archives Committee of the National Council of Negro Women," *Signs* 7, no. 1 (Spring 1981): 251–59; and Sue Bailey Thurman, *Pioneers of Negro San Francisco* (San Francisco: Acme, 1952).

29. Anne Thurman Chiarenza and Sue Bailey Thurman, *Freedom Trails of Negro History in Boston* (Boston: n.p., 1964). For the American Negro History Museum, see HT to Nathan I. Huggins, 30 June 1967, in *PHWT,* 5:169–73.

30. HT to James M. Nabritt Jr., 6 March 1962, in *PHWT,* 4:323–26.

31. HT, "Annual Report: The Wider Ministry, 1962–1963" (September 1963), in *PHWT,* 5:14–34.

32. But see his comment in 1936 in "What We May Learn from India," that both the Negro and "the white man, is a foreigner in a land stolen from the American Indian" (HT, *A Strange Freedom: The Best of Howard Thurman on Religious Experience and Public Life,* ed. Walter Earl Fluker and Catherine Tumber [Boston: Beacon, 1998], 209). Both of Nancy Ambrose's parents were born in South Carolina (see *PHWT,* 1:xxxii), which makes it unlikely that she had Seminole ancestry, since the Seminoles were originally part of the Lower Creek Nation in southern Georgia before migrating to Florida in the early nineteenth century. This of course does not preclude her ancestry from Native peoples living in South Carolina.

33. *WHAH,* 13. The Howard Thurman Educational Trust would take an interest in American Indian matters (see HTET Minutes of the Board of Trustees, 1 April 1970, HTET Papers, Morehouse College).

34. For details of the Saskatchewan trip, see *WHAH,* 242–47; HT, "The Wider Ministry and the Concept of Community" (July 1963), Folder 46, Box 13, HTC; and HT, "Annual Report: The Wider Ministry, 1962–1963," in *PHWT,* 5:19–23.

35. HT, "Annual Report: The Wider Ministry, 1962–1963," in *PHWT,* 5:22.

36. HT, "Annual Report: The Wider Ministry, 1962–1963," in *PHWT,* 5:23.

37. HT, "The Wider Ministry and the Concept of Community," 4–5, Folder 13, Box 46, HTC.

38. For background to Howard Thurman Day, see HT, "Annual Report: The Wider Ministry, 1962–1963," in *PHWT,* 5:25–27.

39. HT to Richard V. Moore, 5 March 1963, Folder 4, Box 40, HTC.

40. *PHWT,* 5:25–27; *WHAH,* 14.

41. HT to Richard V. Moore; HT to J. Owen Eubank, 31 May/29 July 1963 in Folders 5/7, Box 40, HTC.

42. HT, "Annual Report: The Wider Ministry, 1962–1963," in *PHWT,* 5:25.

43. See Leonard R. Lempel, "Toms and Bombs: The Civil Rights Struggle in Daytona Beach," in *Old South, New South, or Down South? Florida and the Modern Civil Rights Movement,* ed. Irvin D. S. Winsboro (Morgantown: West Virginia University Press, 2009), 87–112.

44. James C. Tanner, "Desegregation Today Will Score Its Widest Dixie Classroom Gains," *Wall Street Journal,* 3 September 1963.

45. "Negroes Push Drive at Daytona Beach," *New York Times,* 7 June 1963.

46. HT, "Annual Report: The Wider Ministry, 1962–1963," in *PHWT,* 5:18.

47. HT, "Religious Faith and Revolution" (1 July 1950), Folder 57, Box 11, HTC.

48. HT to Coleman Jennings, 11 July 1963, Folder 7, Box 40, HTC.

49. HT to Leonard Malone, 6 September, 1963, Folder 9, Box 40, HTC.

50. Gregory P. Downs, *The Second American Revolution: The Civil-War Struggle over Cuba and the Rebirth of the American Republic* (Chapel Hill: University of North Carolina Press, 2019), 16.

51. HT, "Non-Violence and the Art of Reconciliation" (1963), in *PHWT*, 5:7.

52. HT, "Non-Violence and the Art of Reconciliation," in *PHWT*, 5:5.

53. HT, "Non-Violence and the Art of Reconciliation," in *PHWT*, 5:7

54. HT, "The Will to Segregation," (1943), reprinted in *Fellowship*, May 1960, 47–51.

55. P. L. Prattis, "Horizon: Another Way," *Pittsburgh Courier*, 9 January 1965.

56. See HT to Congress of Racial Equality, 6 July 1966, in *PHWT*, 5:140–142.

57. Benjamin Mays, Memorial Tribute, in "Simmering on the Calm Presence and Profound Wisdom of Howard Thurman," special issue, *Debate and Understanding*, ed. Ricardo A. Millet and Conley H. Hughes (spring 1982): 86–88.

58. Lerone Bennett Jr., "Howard Thurman: 20th Century Holy Man," *Ebony*, February 1978, 70.

59. Gerald Horne, *Black and Red: W. E. B. Du Bois and the Afro-American Response to the Cold War, 1944–1963* (Albany: State University of New York Press, 1986), 250.

60. HT, "Mysticism and Social Action," in Garrett Hardin and Howard Thurman, *Lawrence Lectures on Religion & Society, 1977–1978* (Berkeley, CA: First Unitarian Church of Berkeley, 1978), 33–34.

61. Bennett, "Howard Thurman," 68.

62. HT to Jesse Jackson, 17 January 1973, in *PHWT*, 5:234–36.

63. HT, "Religious Faith and Revolution" (1 July 1950), Folder 57, Box 11, HTC.

64. HT to Leonard Malone, 6 September 1963, Folder 9, Box 40, HTC.

65. HT, "Africa Journal" (September 1963–February 1964), in *PHWT*, 5:39. Thurman's handwriting often verges on the indecipherable, accounting for lacunae in the transcription. Transcription was further complicated by some deliberate erasures to the journal, probably not by Thurman's hand. The "Africa Journal" in *PHWT*, 5:35–102, and its accompanying annotations discuss Thurman's time in Africa in more detail than is possible here.

66. HT to Balumu J. Mukasa, August 1932, in *PHWT*, 1:159–61.

67. *WHAH*, 194–95.

68. HT, "Negro Youth and the Washington Conference" (December 1925), in *PHWT*, 1:67–69.

69. *WHAH*, 195–96. William Leo Hansberry (1894–1965) taught at Howard from 1922 to 1959. For Thurman's interest in 1938 in arranging an extended trip to Africa and South Africa (see the correspondence in *PHWT*, 2:144–49).

70. *WHAH*, 195–96.

71. HT, "Africa Journal," in *PHWT*, 5:41, 45.

72. Walter G. Muelder to HT, 16 January 1953, in *PHWT*, 4:49–52; Kathleen Kilgore, *Transformations: A History of Boston University* (Boston: Boston University, 1991), 247. Its first director, William O. Brown, who led the program from its founding in 1953 until 1966, headed the African division of the Office of Strategic Services during the war and subsequently was chief advisor on African affairs at the State Department (see *PHWT*, 4:50, 52n8).

73. "B.U. Exercises Spotlight University as Center of Cosmopolitan Activity," *Boston Globe*, 4 June 1962; "Seven Who Received B.U. Honor Degrees," *Boston Globe*, 4 June 1962.

74. For Dike (1918–83), one of the first professionally trained, native historians of Africa, see HT, "Africa Journal," in *PHWT*, 5:85n, 86n8.

75. To trace the history of Thurman's decision to teach at the University of Ibadan, see *PHWT*, 5:35–36.

76. HT, "Africa Journal," in *PHWT*, 5:41.

77. See Synda Altschuler to Lost and Found Department, New York City Police Department, 20 September 1963, Folder 9, Box 40, HTC.

78. Esther J. Byrne was the sister of Lloyd M. Smith and wife of Carleton E. Byrne, all of whom helped underwrite the Thurmans' travels.

79. HT, "Africa Journal," in *PHWT*, 5:41.

80. HT, "Africa Journal," in *PHWT*, 5:38. The opening paragraphs of the "Africa Journal" suggest that Howard might have had an argument with Sue before leaving for the trip. (She was not in the stateroom and joined him in Africa several weeks after his arrival, flying to Nigeria.) In any event, the fact that he was "undertaking a major voyage out of the country without Sue" left him with "hurt and disappointment." The incident seems to have been something Thurman said—"The injury was done; the words uttered in making a single but clear point had no malice aforethought" (HT, "Africa Journal," in *PHWT*, 5:38). As in any marriage, that of the Thurmans had its strains and rough patches. At times Sue felt that Howard undervalued her contribution to his work, and the adoration of his admirers sometimes left her feeling like an appendage, the wife of Howard Thurman rather than an accomplished person in her own right. Some of these frustrations were poured out in a remarkable letter to her husband (see Sue Bailey Thurman, "Comments on Unpublished Biographical Draft of James Earl Massey," ca. 1974, Folder 7, Box 17, HTC).

81. Olive told me that she could look at her father objectively because in some ways she never knew him that well when she was growing up because she spent many years in boarding school (Peter Eisenstadt, personal conversation with Olive Thurman Wong, January 2012).

82. HT, "Africa Journal," in *PHWT*, 5:40. Thurman suggests that there was one candidate for the role of honorary son, though his name is erased. One possibility was the historian Nathan Huggins, whose relationship with Thurman is discussed in the final chapter.

83. HT, "Africa Journal," in *PHWT*, 5:44.

84. HT, "Africa Journal," in *PHWT*, 5:43, 46.

85. HT, "Africa Journal," in *PHWT*, 5:49. In 1960 Billy Graham (1918–2018) had an extensive preaching mission in Africa, which included stops in Lagos, Ibadan, and other Nigerian cities.

86. HT, "Africa Journal," in *PHWT*, 5:45.

87. HT, "Africa Journal," in *PHWT*, 5:44.

88. HT, "Africa Journal," in *PHWT*, 5:44.

89. Geeche and Gullah are African-influenced Creole languages spoken on the South Carolina and Georgia sea islands.

90. HT, "Africa Journal," in *PHWT*, 5:43, 49.

91. *WHAH*, 193.
92. HT, "Africa Journal," in *PHWT*, 5:49–50.
93. HT, "Africa Journal," in *PHWT*, 5:49–50.
94. *On Viewing the Coast of Africa* (San Francisco: Alfred and Lawton Kennedy, 1964?); *WHAH*, 193–94.
95. Gambia was granted full internally self-governing status on 4 October 1963. It achieved full independence from Britain on 18 February 1965. Its capital, Bathurst, was renamed Banjul in 1972.
96. HT, "Africa Journal," in *PHWT*, 5:50–54.
97. Asa J. Davis (1922–1999) had a doctorate in African history from Harvard and taught at Ibadan from 1962 to 1969 (see HT, "Africa Journal," in *PHWT*, 5:92n63).
98. From 1935 to 1942 Nkrumah studied at Lincoln University (Pennsylvania), earning two degrees (including a bachelor's degree in theology). Thurman often visited and spoke there during these years, raising the possibility, perhaps even the likelihood, that he heard Thurman speak or preach.
99. For African Americans in Ghana in the 1950s and 1960s, see Kevin K. Gaines, *African Americans in Ghana: Black Expatriates and the Civil Rights Era* (Chapel Hill: University of North Carolina Press, 2006).
100. See Robert B. Shepard, "Kennedy and America's African Model," in *Nigeria, Africa, and the United States: From Kennedy to Reagan* (Bloomington: Indiana University Press, 1991), 9–34. Many of the African Americans Thurman met in Ibadan were working for the U.S. government: William A. Reed and Vernon Johnson for the U.S. Agency for International Development, and William Jones for the U.S. Information Agency (see HT, "Africa Journal," in *PHWT*, 5:97n116, 100n141, 100n143).
101. HT, "Africa Journal," in *PHWT*, 5:60. The "parasitic women" for Schreiner was a woman whose "social conditions tend to rob her of all forms of conscious social labor, and to reduce her, like the field-bug, to the passive exercise of the sex function alone" (*PHWT*, 1:89).
102. HT, "Africa Journal," in *PHWT*, 5:60.
103. HT, "Africa Journal," in *PHWT*, 5:55–56.
104. HT, "Africa Journal," in *PHWT*, 5:62.
105. HT, "Africa Journal," in *PHWT*, 5:66.
106. E[ssien]-U[dosen] Essien-Udom (1928–2002), was educated in Nigeria before coming to the United States. His University of Chicago dissertation formed the basis of *Black Nationalism: A Search for Identity in America* (Chicago: University of Chicago Press, 1962). He taught at the University of Ibadan from 1963 to 1972 (see HT, "Africa Journal," in *PHWT*, 5:92n65).
107. HT, "Africa Journal," in *PHWT*, 5:67.
108. HT, "Africa Journal," in *PHWT*, 5:57.
109. HT, "Africa Journal," in *PHWT*, 5:68–69.
110. HT, "Africa Journal," in *PHWT*, 5:9–80.
111. HT, "Africa Journal," in *PHWT*, 5:69–74. For the history of Owo, see Roland Abiodun, "The Kingdom of Owo," in *Yoruba: Nine Centuries of African Art and Thought,* ed. Henry John Drewal and John Pemberton III, 91–116 (New York: Abrams, 1989); and G. J. Afolabi Ojo, *Yoruba Palaces: A Study of Afins of Yorubaland* (London: University of London Press, 1966), 38–42.

112. HT, "Africa Journal," in *PHWT,* 5:70, 74.

113. HT, "Africa Journal," in *PHWT,* 5:63, 71.

114. HT, "Africa Journal," in *PHWT,* 5:70.

115. HT, "Africa Journal," in *PHWT,* 5:63, 65.

116. HT, "Africa Journal," in *PHWT,* 5:71.

117. HT, "Africa Journal," in *PHWT,* 5:81.

118. "Nigeria Rebukes U.S.," *Chicago Defender,* 4 December 1963.

119. HT, "Africa Journal," in *PHWT,* 5:76.

120. HT, "Africa Journal," in in *PHWT,* 5:72–73.

121. HT, "Eulogy for President Kennedy," in *PHWT,* 5:103–7.

122. HT, "Africa Journal," 81. For Thurman's effort to circulate his eulogy, see HT, "Eulogy for President Kennedy," in *PHWT,* 5:107n2. Thurman's eulogy was included in *That Day with God,* ed. William M. Fine (New York: McGraw-Hill, 1965), 143–47, a collection of sermons and eulogies delivered after President Kennedy's assassination. Thurman reprinted it in his autobiography (*WHAH,* 208–11).

123. See HT to Joseph Palmer II, 4 January 1967, in *PHWT,* 5:162–65.

124. HT to Herbert King, 9 June 1963, Folder 6, Box 40, HTC.

125. HT, "Africa Journal," in *PHWT,* 5:83–84; *WHAH,* 188–91.

126. See HT to Maurice Friedman, 6 September 1963, Folder 9, Box 40, HTC.

127. HT, "Africa Journal," in *PHWT,* 5:84.

128. *WHAH,* 190.

129. HT, "Africa Journal," in *PHWT,* 5:83–84; *WHAH,* 194–95.

130. Roland Gittelsohn to HT, 25 January 1980, Folder 1, Box 50, HTC.

131. *WHAH,* 191.

132. There are discussions of the Thurman's post Africa/Israel plans in HT to Herbert King, 9 June 1963, Folder 6, Box 40, HTC; HT to Boice Gross, 1 July 1963, Folder 7, Box 40, HTC; HT to Lloyd M. Smith, 23 September 1963, Folder 9, Box 40, HTC; and Gene [K. Walker?] to HT, 14 January 1964, Folder 1, Box 41, HTC.

133. HT, "Journey in Understanding" (8 June 1964), 17, Folder 37, Box 6, HTC. This talk, one of Thurman's first after returning to Boston, drew heavily on the "Africa Journal."

134. HT, "Journey in Understanding" 17.

135. HT, "Journey in Understanding," 17.

136. HT, "Journey in Understanding" 4.

137. HT, "Desegregation, Integration, and the Beloved Community" (September 1966), in *PHWT,* 5:157.

138. HT, "Journey in Understanding," Constantine P. Cavafy (1863–1933) was a Greek-language poet who lived most of his life in Alexandria, Egypt. Thurman's quotation is from Louis Golding, *Good-Bye to Ithaca* (New York: Thomas Yoseloff, 1958), 8, as translated by John Mavrogordato in *The Poems of C. P. Cavafy* (London: Hogarth, 1951).

14. Common Ground? Coming Aground?

1. HT, "Desegregation, Integration, and the Beloved Community" (September 1966), in *PHWT,* 5:156.

2. HT, *The Luminous Darkness: A Personal Interpretation of the Anatomy of Segregation and the Ground of Hope* (New York: Harper and Row, 1965).

3. HT, *The Luminous Darkness*, 5, 93–94.

4. HT, *The Luminous Darkness*, 6, 3.

5. HT, *The Luminous Darkness*, 30, 85, 5.

6. HT, *The Luminous Darkness*, 23.

7. HT, *The Luminous Darkness*, 11, 26.

8. HT, *The Luminous Darkness*, 16.

9. HT, *The Luminous Darkness*, 16.

10. HT, *The Luminous Darkness*, 84.

11. HT, *The Luminous Darkness*, 84.

12. *WHAH*, 233–34; HT, *The Luminous Darkness*, 84, 93–94.

13. HT, *The Luminous Darkness*, 29.

14. HT, *The Luminous Darkness*, 30, 21.

15. For Reeb, and Thurman's eulogies for him and Liuzzo, see HT, "We Believe: On Jim Reeb" (12 March 1965), in *PHWT*, 5:130–38.

16. HT, "We Believe: On Jim Reeb," in *PHWT*, 5:130–38.

17. See HT to Congress of Racial Equality, 6 July 1966; HT to Don Smith, 19 August 1966, in *PHWT*, 5:140–43; 143–44. For allegations of anti-Semitism in CORE, see Alfred W. Halper to HT, 19 November 1965, Folder 11, Box 42, HTC.

18. Cited in Sean Scalmer, *Gandhi in the West: The Mahatma and the Rise of Radical Protest* (New York: Cambridge University Press, 2011), 210.

19. For Thurman's argument in 1940 that while Blacks in the South were "lynched, tortured, and intimidated," northern Blacks faced subtler but in many ways just as devastating forms of discrimination, see *PHWT*, 2:248–50.

20. James Farmer, *Freedom, When?* (New York: Random House, 1965), 112, 176.

21. HT, "Desegregation, Integration, and the Beloved Community," in *Benjamin E. Mays: His Life, Contributions, and Legacy*, ed. Samuel DuBois Cook (Franklin, TN: Providence House, 2009), 197–207. The essay was commissioned by Samuel DuBois Cook (1928–2017), who at the time was a professor of political science at Duke University (where he was the first tenured African American professor at a predominantly white university in the South). From 1974 to 1997 he was president of Dillard University. Thurman's essay is reprinted, along with a longer discussion of its tangled history, in *PHWT*, 5:147–59.

22. HT, "Desegregation, Integration, and the Beloved Community," in *PHWT*, 5:148–49.

23. HT, "Desegregation, Integration, and the Beloved Community," in *PHWT*, 5:151.

24. HT, "Desegregation, Integration, and the Beloved Community," in *PHWT*, 5:151

25. HT, "Desegregation, Integration, and the Beloved Community," in *PHWT*, 5:151, 153.

26. HT, "Desegregation, Integration, and the Beloved Community," in *PHWT*, 5:151.

27. For the origins, in the 1950s, of the distinction between integration and desegregation, see Peter Eisenstadt, "'Neighborliness Is Nonspatial': Howard Thurman and the Search for Integration and Common Ground," *Journal of Urban History* 46, no. 6 (2020): 1206–1221.

28. HT, "Desegregation, Integration, and the Beloved Community," in *PHWT*, 5:154.

29. HT, "Desegregation, Integration, and the Beloved Community," in *PHWT*, 5:155.

30. HT, "Desegregation, Integration, and the Beloved Community," in *PHWT*, 5:154.

31. HT, "Desegregation, Integration, and the Beloved Community," in *PHWT*, 5:155.

32. The phrase "beloved community" was first used by the Harvard philosopher Josiah Royce and soon became a popular phrase among progressives and liberal Protestants. The phrase was used by Martin Luther King, Jr., as early as 1956, who further popularized it (see Ralph E. Luker, "Kingdom of God and Beloved Community in the Thought of Martin Luther King, Jr.," in *The Role of Ideas in the Civil Rights South,* ed. Ted Ownby [Jackson: University of Mississippi Press, 2002], 39–54). For Thurman on the "beloved community," see Kipton E. Jensen, *Howard Thurman: Philosophy, Civil Rights, and the Search for Common Ground* (Columbia: University of South Carolina Press, 2019), 129–36.

33. HT, "Desegregation, Integration, and the Beloved Community," in *PHWT*, 5:156–57.

34. Thurman probably wrote about the beloved community only because Cook had assigned him the topic and the name of the essay (see Samuel DuBois Cook to HT, 4 March 1966, Folder 18, Box 43, HTC).

35. HT, "Desegregation, Integration, and the Beloved Community," in *PHWT*, 5:157.

36. Thurman's description of the highest stage of integration has much in common with an earlier attempt to provide a blueprint for his utopia (HT, "The Significance of Jesus III: Love" [1937], in *PHWT*, 2:60–67).

37. HT, "Desegregation, Integration, and the Beloved Community," in *PHWT*, 5:156.

38. HT, "Desegregation, Integration, and the Beloved Community," in *PHWT*, 5:156.

39. Robert Hamill to HT, 3 May 1965, Folder 17, Box 42, HTC.

40. See HT to Don Carver; and HT to Evans Crawford, both dated 17 April 1965, both in Folder 16, Box 42, HTC.

41. Rachel H. Libby to HT, 28 May 1965, Folder 17, Box 42, HTC.

42. Rosalie A. Ellis to HT, May 1965, Folder 17, Box 42, HTC.

43. HT to Lloyd M. Smith, 23 September 1963, Folder 9, Box 40, HTC.

44. HT to Coretta Scott King, 14 May 1974, Folder 17, Box 40, HTC.

45. See HT to Lorimer Milton, 11 January 1949, in *PHWT*, 3:301–2. For many years Milton was the president of Citizens Trust Bank, the largest Black-owned bank in Atlanta. He was chairman of the Howard University Board of Trustees from 1949 to 1972.

46. For instance, Thurman received $2,500 for teaching a course at Earlham College in early 1966 (see HT to Francis J. McTerman, 26 May 1965, Folder 17, Box 42, HTC). In 1976, when Thurman wanted to take a so-called "sabbatical," friends established a fund to replace some of the lost income from speaking and preaching engagements (HT to Luther Smith, 24 February 1976, Folder 14, Box 47, HTC; HT to Jean Burden, February 1976, Folder 14, Box 47, HTC).

47. HT, "Proposal for Negro Scholarship Fund" (1922–23), in *PHWT*, 1:22–25.

48. HT to Lloyd M. Smith, 31 October 1960, in *PHWT*, 4:294–96.

49. HT to John Overholt, 7 July 1961, Folder 19, Box 38, HTC.

50. HT, "Declaration of the Howard Thurman Educational Trust" (1961), in HTET Papers, Morehouse College.
51. HT to Frank T. Wilson, 24 June 1965, Folder 6, Box 42, HTC.
52. HT to Frank T. Wilson, 24 June 1965, Folder 6, Box 42, HTC; *WHAH*, 261. As an example of the sort of contributions made at the time of his retirement, WHDT-TV in Boston (where Thurman had recorded the *We Believe* broadcasts since 1959) made a five-hundred-dollar contribution to the Trust Fund (John M. Day to George Makechnie, 12 May 1965, Folder 5, Box 42, HTC).
53. The lawyer Francis J. McTerman wrote Thurman that the HTET could use its funds for "office expenses" after his retirement, and the Claremore Foundation could provide "life tenancy" for the Thurmans (Francis J. McTerman to HT, 6 May 1965, Folder 17, Box 42, HTC). The Thurmans, over the course of their married life, would never own their own home.
54. HT to Frank T. Wilson, 24 June 1965, Folder 6, Box 42, HTC. For the Trust's support of African American students and historically Black colleges and ancillary institutions, see "Trustees' Report for 1967"; "Trustees' Report for 1970"; and "1980–1981 Academic year Scholarship Awards" (probably a loose page from an HTET annual trustees' report, and according to which the awards totaled a little over $27,000), HTET Papers, Morehouse College. See also "The Trust at Work: New Revolving Loan Funds," *Listening Ear* 2, no. 2 (May 1974); HT to Nathan Huggins, 3 May 1971, with enclosure entitled "Description of Memorial Fund for Kathryn Ann Huggins," Folder 5, Box 45, HTC; and "The Jefferson County Library," *Listening Ear* 5, no. 2 (Winter 1977).
55. See "Woodcarving of Negro History Dedicated in Boston," *Jet*, 17 June 1965, 6; and Hollie I. West, "Carving Black History," *Washington Post*, 14 December 1971. For the quilt, see Walker, "Trustees' Report for 1967."
56. For a review of the Trust's activities, see "Spreading Our Wings: The Howard Thurman Educational Trust" (May 1980), HTET Papers, Morehouse College.
57. HTET Minutes of the Board of Trustees, April 1, 1970, HTET Papers, Morehouse College.
58. HT, "HTET, HT Notes—1971," HTET Papers, Morehouse College.
59. The Trust was supported by a number of benefactors who had long admired and supported Thurman's work since the Fellowship Church years, almost all of whom were wealthy white businessmen and their wives, committed liberal Christians who supported a variety of progressive causes. Probably the most important benefactors were a constellation of wealthy investors whose fortune came from the Ventura oil field in southern California, and who subsequently branched into many other business ventures. The matriarch was Eleanor Lloyd Smith, to whom Thurman dedicated *Meditations of the Heart* (New York: Harper and Brothers, 1955): "To Eleanor Lloyd Smith, in whom the inner and the outer are one." In addition, there was her son, Lloyd M. Smith, her daughter, Esther Byrne, and son-in-law, Carleton Byrne, wealthy industrialists, lawyers, and investors who supported Thurman in various ways (see *PHWT*, 4:42n1).
60. HT to Francis Geddes, 16 August 1960, in *PHWT*, 5:278.
61. For the gossip, see, for example, Grace [Huntzinger?] to HT, 20 February 1955, Folder 2, Box 34, HTC. For Thurman making very specific personnel

recommendations—"I think it would be a fatal blunder to even consider hiring Bob Smith"—see HT to Dryden Phelps, 19 January 1954, in *PHWT*, 4:74–75.

62. Thurman spoke at least three times at Fellowship Church in the summer of 1954, and three times in July 1955, four times in July 1955, as well as leading a retreat in 1956, two sermons and a retreat in July 1957, one sermon in August 1958, and two retreats in July 1959.

63. Clarence R. Johnson to HT, 19 March 1958, in *PHWT*, 4:207–9.

64. HT to George Britton, 24 February 1959, in *PHWT*, 4:237–39.

65. HT to Benjamin Mays, 21 September 1953, in *PHWT*, 4:73–74.

66. HT to the Board of Trustees of Fellowship Church, 19 May 1953, in *PHWT*, 4:71.

67. HT to the Board of Trustees of Fellowship Church, 19 May 1953, in *PHWT*, 4:71.

68. HT to the Board of Trustees of Fellowship Church, 19 May 1953, in *PHWT*, 4:71.

69. For Phelps, see HT to the Board of Trustees of Fellowship Church, 19 May 1953, in *PHWT*, 4:73n1.

70. Grace [Huntzinger?] to HT, 20 February 1955, Folder 2, Box 34, HTC.

71. HT to Dryden Phelps, 23 April 1955, in *PHWT*, 4:121–23; Frances Geddes to HT, 20 September 1958, Folder 1, Box 37, HTC.

72. HT to the Board of Trustees of Fellowship Church, 19 May 1953, in *PHWT*, 4:73n3.

73. HT to Francis Geddes, 1 September 1955, Folder 9, Box 34, HTC.

74. HT to Clarence R. Johnson, 19 March 1958, in *PHWT*, 4:207–9.

75. Francis Geddes to HT, 26 December 1959, in *PHWT* 4: 257–59.

76. HT to Francis Geddes, 25 January 1960 in *PHWT*, 4:262–64; HT to Francis Geddes, May 1960, in *PHWT*, 4:65–66.

77. Francis Geddes to HT, 3 August 1960, in *PHWT*, 4:265–67.

78. HT to Francis Geddes, 16 August 1960, in *PHWT*, 4:276–80.

79. HT to Francis Geddes, 16 August 1960, in *PHWT*, 4:276–80.

80. HT to Herbert King, 3 April 1964, Folder 4, Box 41, HTC. However, once Thurman returned to San Francisco, he and Geddes (no longer with Fellowship Church) reestablished their friendship (see Francis Geddes to HT, 27 January 1966), Folder 13, Box 42, HTC).

81. HT to Fellowship Church Congregation, 24 September 1970, in *PHWT*, 5:214–19.

82. HT to Minister, Board of Trustees, and Membership of Fellowship Church, 4 November 1974, in *PHWT*, 5:266–68.

83. HT, "The Growing Edge," 26 October 1980, in *PHWT* 5:311–18.

84. HT to John A. Taylor, 16 April 1968, in *PHWT*, 5:188–89.

85. *WHAH*, 222. The KPFK statement can be found in "Martin Luther King, Jr: Litany and Words in Memoriam," 7 April 1968, in *PHWT*, 5:179–80. For Thurman's statement reaching Boston, see J. Anthony Lukas, *Common Ground: A Turbulent Decade in the Lives of Three American Families* (New York: Knopf, 1985), 9. For the distribution of the KPFK statement, see HT to "Dear Friends," April 1968, Folder 16, Box 43, HTC.

86. See HT, "Interview on the Significance of the Life and Death of Martin Luther King, Jr." (7 April 1968), in *PHWT*, 5:173–76.

87. HT, "Martin Luther King, Jr.: Litany and Words in Memoriam," in *PHWT,* 5:183.
88. HT, "Interview on the Significance of the Life and Death of Martin Luther King, Jr.," in *PHWT,* 5:173–74.
89. HT, "Martin Luther King, Jr.: Litany and Words in Memoriam," in *PHWT,* 5:181.
90. "Martin Luther King, Jr. Memorial Ceremony" (comments delivered at the University of California at Santa Cruz, on 8 April 1968), Folder 11, Box 9, HTC.
91. HT, "Martin Luther King, Jr.: Litany and Words in Memoriam," 183, and "Martin Luther King, Jr. Memorial Ceremony," Folder 11, Box 9, HTC.
92. HT, "Martin Luther King, Jr.: Litany and Words in Memoriam," in *PHWT,* 5:179.
93. HT, "Martin Luther King, Jr.: Litany and Words in Memoriam," in *PHWT,* 5:183.
94. HT, "Interview on the Significance of the Life and Death of Martin Luther King, Jr.," in *PHWT,* 5:174.
95. HT, "Interview on the Significance of the Life and Death of Martin Luther King, Jr.," in *PHWT,* 5:174–75. For similar comments about the rioting after World War I, see *PHWT,* 2:250–51.
96. Frank Wilson to HT, 8 April 1968, Folder 16, Box 43, HTC.
97. HT to Frank Wilson, 10 June 1968, in *PHWT,* 5:196–98.
98. Unpublished preface to *The Negro Spiritual Speaks of Life and Death* (December 1968), Howard Thurman Papers Project Files.
99. HT, "South Pacific Journal," in *PHWT,* 5:212.
100. HT, "Surrogate Gods" (October 1976), Howard Thurman Papers Project Files.
101. HT to Mary Powell, 24 January 1969, Folder 1, Box 44, HTC.
102. Roberta Byrd Barr, "A Creative Encounter: Interview with Howard Thurman," 14–15 February 1969, Part 1, p. 1, Folder 30, Box 16, HTC. The textual history of this extended interview is messy, existing in five overlapping partial transcripts. For background to the interview, see *PHWT,* 5:xxiv, xlviin65.
103. Byrd Barr, "A Creative Encounter: Interview with Howard Thurman," Part 5, Folder 30, Box 16, HTC.
104. Byrd Barr, "A Creative Encounter: Interview with Howard Thurman," Part 5, Folder 30, Box 16, HTC.
105. Byrd Barr, "A Creative Encounter: Interview with Howard Thurman," Part 5, Folder 30, Box 16, HTC.
106. Byrd Barr, "A Creative Encounter: Interview with Howard Thurman," Part 3, Folder 30, Box 16, HTC.
107. For the possible book on Martin Luther King, Jr., see HT to William Robert Miller, 4 June 1968, in *PHWT,* 5: 94–96.
108. For a possible updated edition of *Jesus and the Disinherited* (with a new chapter on violence and nonviolence) and a possible book on Martin Luther King, Jr., see HT to William Robert Miller, 4 June 1968, in *PHWT,* 5:194–96; HT to Tad Akashi, 21 May 1968; Tad Akashi to HT, 14 May 1968, and 21 May 1968; all three letters in Folder 17, Box 43, HTC; HT to Tad Akashi, September 1968, Folder 21, Box 43, HTC.
109. HT, *The Search for Common Ground: An Inquiry into the Basis of Man's Experience of Community* (New York: Harper and Row, 1971).

110. George K. Makechnie, "Remembering Dr. Howard Thurman," *New Crisis* 106 (November/December 1999): 26–28.

111. HT, *The Search for Common Ground,* 95.

112. HT, *The Search for Common Ground,* 95.

113. For Thurman on community, see, in particular, Walter E. Fluker, *They Looked for a City: A Comparative Analysis of the Ideal of Community in the Thought of Howard Thurman and Martin Luther King, Jr.* (Lanham, MD: University Press of America, 1989).

114. For an early discussion of "the sense of community," see his Tennessee A&I Commencement Address (1938) in *PHWT,* 2:159–60. See also HT, "The Religion of Jesus V: Freedom" (9 December 1956), Folder 152, Box 11, HTC: "Jesus was convinced that the purpose of God in creating man is to establish community, to establish wholeness."

115. See also HT, "The Quest for Community" (2 August 1964), Folder 38, Box 6, HTC.

116. HT, "Community and the Unity of Life" (probably delivered at Taos, New Mexico, in March 1964), Folder 43, Box 7, HTC.

117. Lucille Withers to HT, 10 December 1965, Folder 12, Box 42, HTC.

118. On Thurman as an epitome of the "essential loneliness" of the person of faith, see Edward K. Kaplan, "Howard Thurman: Meditation, Mysticism, and Life's Contradictions," in *Simmering on the Calm Presence and Profound Wisdom of Howard Thurman,* special issue, *Debate & Understanding,* ed. Ricardo A. Millet and Conley H. Hughes (spring 1982): 19–26.

119. HT, *Mysticism and the Experience of Love* (Wallingford, PA: Pendle Hill, 1961), 19.

120. HT, *The Search for Common Ground,* 76.

121. For Thurman's likely source of the phrase, see A. Ann Silver to HT, 23 May 1936, in *PHWT,* 2:7–8; and HT, "The Growing Edge" in *The Growing Edge* (New York: Harper and Brothers, 1956), 177, 180.

122. "The Cosmic Guarantee in the Judeo-Christian Message" (June 1944), Folder 11, Box 7, HTC, was reworked as "Judgment and Hope in the Christian Message," published in 1948, and reprinted in *PHWT,* 2:242–47.

123. HT, "Community and the Will of God I" (1961), Folder 7, Box 8, HTC; "Community and the Will of God IV: Community and Christian Commitment" (1961), Folder 10, Box 8, HTC. At the same time, he stated that "I am not thinking in terms of a philosophical teleology" (HT, "Community and the Will of God II," [1961], Folder 8, Box 8, HTC). If Thurman was protesting too much here, and there is an undeniable "telic" dimension to his biological thought, he was probably contrasting his view of all life as goal-seeking to full-blown spiritual-biological teleologies, such as those of Pierre Lecomte du Noüy (1883–1947) or Pierre Teilhard de Chardin (1881–1955). For Thurman's interest in Lecomte du Noüy, see HT, *Footprints of a Dream: The Story of the Church for the Fellowship of All Peoples* (New York: Harper and Brothers, 1959), 75.

124. HT, "Community and the Will of God II," Folder 8, Box 8, HTC.

125. HT, "The Quest for Community" (2 August 1964), Folder 38, Box 6, HTC.

126. HT, *The Search for Common Ground,* 56–75. Thurman was particularly fond of J. Boone Allen's *Kinship with All Life* (New York: Harper and Brothers, 1954), by

an animal trainer who maintained one could develop a shared consciousness with animals of all sorts, as he did, from dogs to insects.

127. HT, *The Search for Common Ground*, 67.

128. HT, *The Search for Common Ground*, 1–2. In Thurman's introduction to his Olive Schreiner anthology, he approvingly quotes her as saying "all matter is alive, even so-called inanimate matter; a stone has no apparent energy and so *seems* dead, but life runs through everything (HT, *A Track to the Water's Edge: The Olive Schreiner Reader* [New York: Harper and Row, 1973], xxviii).

129. HT, *The Search for Common Ground*, 33.

130. HT, "Community and the Will of God IV: Community and Christian Commitment," Folder 10, Box 8, HTC.

131. Jessica Riskin, *The Restless Clock: A History of the Centuries-Long Argument over What Makes Living Things Tick* (Chicago: University of Chicago Press, 2016), 3.

132. Riskin, *The Restless Clock*, 308.

133. For Thurman on John Duns Scotus, who believed "that life is one," see HT, "The Quest for Stability" (1949), in *PHWT*, 3:316. Thurman had an epistolary acquaintance with Albert Schweitzer (see Albert Schweitzer to HT, 1944, Folder 12, Box 29, HTC; and Albert Schweitzer to HT, 23 September 1956, Folder 9, Box 35, HTC [both short letters in French]). See also HT, "Albert Schweitzer—Spiritual Genius," 7 July 1949, for Thurman's admiration for Schweitzer's belief in "reverence for life," in HT, *Walking with God: The Sermon Series of Howard Thurman*, vol. 1: *Moral Struggle and the Prophets*, ed. Peter Eisenstadt and Walter E. Fluker (Maryknoll, NY: Orbis, 2020), 11–19.

134. For Schreiner's Lamarckian views of evolution, see Carolyn Burdett, *Olive Schreiner and the Progress of Feminism* (Houndmills, UK: Palgrave, 2001). Thurman thought well enough of the Russian-English anarchist theorist Peter Kropotkin, the author of the anti-Spencerian, anti-Darwinian and communitarian evolutionary tract *Mutual Aid: A Factor in Evolution* (1902), to name one of his favorite dogs in his honor (*WHAH*, 234–37).

135. HT, "Community and the Will of God," Folder 7, Box 8, HTC.

136. HT, *The Search for Common Ground*, 8–28; HT, "Community and the Will of God IV: Community and Christian Commitment," Folder 7, Box 10, HTC.

137. HT, "Community and the Will of God I," Folder 7, Box 8, HTC.

138. HT, *The Search for Common Ground*, 42–55. See also "Community and the Will of God III: Community and the Prophet's Dream," Folder 9, Box 10, HTC.

139. HT, *The Search for Common Ground*, 46.

140. HT, "Community and the Will of God III," Folder 9, Box 10, HTC.

141. Victor Anderson, *Beyond Ontological Blackness: An Essay on African American Religious and Cultural Criticism* (New York: Continuum, 1995), 42–43.

142. HT, *The Search for Common Ground*, 77, 78; HT, "Community and the Will of God III," Folder 9, Box 10, HTC.

143. HT, *"Deep River" and "The Negro Spiritual Speaks of Life and Death"* (New York: Harper and Brothers, 1955), 59.

144. HT, *The Search for Common Ground*, 77.

145. HT, *The Search for Common Ground*, 91.

146. HT, *The Search for Common Ground,* 91.

147. HT, *The Search for Common Ground,* 83–87.

148. HT, *The Search for Common Ground,* 88–89.

149. HT, *The Search for Common Ground,* 97.

150. HT, *The Search for Common Ground,* 100.

151. HT, *The Search for Common Ground,* 92, emphasis in original.

152. "Co-Pastor of Interracial Church Views Racial Tension as Evidence of Progress," *Cleveland Call and Post,* 23 June 1945.

153. HT, *The Search for Common Ground,* 93.

154. HT, *The Search for Common Ground,* 93.

155. HT, *The Search for Common Ground,* 97.

156. HT, *The Search for Common Ground,* 96.

157. HT, *The Search for Common Ground,* 97–98.

158. HT, *The Search for Common Ground,* 102.

159. HT, *The Search for Common Ground,* 96.

160. HT, *The Search for Common Ground,* 103.

161. HT, *The Search for Common Ground,* 103.

162. HT, *The Search for Common Ground,* 103–4.

163. HT, *The Luminous Darkness,* 94.

164. George K. Makechnie, "Remembering Dr. Howard Thurman."

165. Stephen Jay Gould, *Bully for Brontosaurus: Reflections in Natural History* (New York: Norton, 1991), 338–39.

166. "It is always dangerous to read into the behavior of nature some great design or plan to human life" (HT, *Deep Is the Hunger: Meditations for the Apostles of Sensitiveness* [1951; repr., Richmond, IN: Friends United Press, 1973], 27).

15. With Head and Heart

1. HT, "South Pacific Journal," in *PHWT,* 5:207–8.

2. Coleman Jennings noted that Thurman during the Pacific trip wrote him that "slowly the depths of fatigue are being loosened" and of a promise made to Jennings and others that "never again would this happen" (Coleman Jennings to HT, 12 February 1970, Folder 14, Box 44, HTC). By speaking of Thurman's "depressed moods," I am reflecting the concerns expressed by Jennings and others at the time and not offering any sort of psychological diagnosis.

3. HT to Jean Burden, 14 February 1970, Folder 14, Box 44, HTC.

4. HT to Dudley Weinberg, 20 March 1970, Folder 15, Box 44, HTC.

5. HT to Dudley Weinberg, 20 March 1970, Folder 15, Box 44, HTC.

6. Edward Kaplan, interview by Peter Eisenstadt, 6 July 2015.

7. HT, "South Pacific Journal," in *PHWT,* 5:208.

8. HT, "South Pacific Journal," in *PHWT,* 5:209–10.

9. HT, "South Pacific Journal," in *PHWT,* 5:210.

10. HT, "South Pacific Journal," in *PHWT,* 5:210.

11. HT, "South Pacific Journal," in *PHWT,* 5:212.

12. HT to Coleman Jennings, 24 August 1966, Folder 20, Box 42, HTC.

13. HT to Herbert King, 9 June 1963, in *PHWT,* 5:12–14.

14. Frank T. Wilson to HT and Herbert King, 31 January 1966, Folder 13, Box 42, HTC.

15. HT to G. Murray Branch, 25 August 1966, Folder 20, Box 42. HTC.

16. Jean Burden (1914–2008) was a poet, journalist, editor, nonfiction writer, and public relations expert. For Burden, see HT to Jean Burden, 23 September 1974, in *PHWT,* 5:264–65n1.

17. Jean Burden, "Meditation on Howard Thurman on the Occasion of His Memorial Service April 10, 1981" (1982), Howard Thurman Papers Project Files.

18. Jean Burden, "Howard Thurman," *Atlantic Monthly,* October 1953, 39–44.

19. Berkley Hudson, "She's Well Versed in the Art of Writing Well: Poetry: Author, Editor and Teacher Jean Burden Shares Her Lifelong Obsession through Invitation-Only Workshops in Her Home," *Los Angeles Times,* 16 August 1992.

20. Burden, "Meditation on Howard Thurman."

21. Jean Burden to Howard Thurman, 2 September 1974, Folder 21, Box 46, HTC. Thurman replied: "What a beautiful and moving letter that touched and plumbed my deepest depths. There is no comment I can make but there is much to say when I see you face to face" (HT to Jean Burden, 23 September 1974, in *PHWT,* 5:263).

22. Jean Burden, "Meditation on Howard Thurman."

23. Jesse Jackson, Memorial Tribute, in "Simmering on the Calm Presence and Profound Wisdom of Howard Thurman, special issue, *Debate and Understanding,* ed. Ricardo A. Millet and Conley H. Hughes (spring 1982): 82–84.

24. HT, *Jesus and the Disinherited* (New York: Abingdon-Cokesbury, 1949), 108. See also HT, *Disciplines of the Spirit* (New York: Harper and Row, 1963), 77.

25. HT to Whitney Young Jr., 16 June 1966, Folder 18, Box 42, HTC. When two men first met is not clear, but they become closer after Thurman spoke at a National Urban League convention on the topic of "The Quest for Community" (see Whitney Young to HT, 19 March 1964, Folder 3, Box 31, HTC; and Edith Macy to HT, 14 August 1964, Folder 8, Box 41, HTC).

26. HT, "Eulogy for Whitney Young," in *PHWT,* 5:220.

27. HT, "Eulogy for Whitney Young," in *PHWT,* 5:221.

28. Thomas A. Johnson, "6,000 Here Attend Funeral of Young," *New York Times,* 17 March 1971.

29. HT, "Whitney Young: What Can I Do?" (4 April 1971). This was delivered at the First Unitarian Church of San Francisco two weeks after the original funeral in New York City on 16 March 1971 (reprinted in HT, *A Strange Freedom: The Best of Howard Thurman on Religious Experience and Public Life,* ed. Walter Earl Fluker and Catherine Tumber [Boston: Beacon, 1998], 260).

30. HT to Kivie Kaplan, 14 April 1967, in *PHWT,* 5:165–67. Thurman provides a long list of African American magazines, from *The Crisis* to the *Journal of Negro Education,* for which he has the "deepest admiration and respect." But he suggests that Black journals have had overwhelmingly Black readership in the past, and fears the same would happen with any new serious Black-interest journal.

31. Donald Szantho Harrington to HT, 20 June 1968; "Unitarian Calls for Black Aid," *Pittsburgh Courier,* 25 May 1968.

32. James Forman, "Manifesto of the National Black Economic Development Conference, 1969," in *Black Protest Thought in the Twentieth Century,* ed. August Meier, Elliott Rudwick, and Francis L. Broderick (Indianapolis: Bobbs-Merrill, 1971), 535–49.

33. HT to Frank Wilson, 2 July 1969, in *PHWT,* 5:202–4.

34. See Beth E. Ruhde-Colgate, "A Thank You Letter to Howard Thurman," in *Common Ground: Essays in Honor of Howard Thurman on the Occasion of His Seventy-Fifth Birthday, November 18, 1975,* ed. Samuel Lucius Gandy (Washington, DC: Hoffman, 1976), 1–6.

35. Irvin S. Moxley, "An Examination of the Mysticism of Howard Thurman and Its Relevance to Black Liberation" (D.Min. diss., Louisville Presbyterian Theological Seminary, 1974); Irvin S. Moxley to HT, 7 January 1974, Folder 13, Box 46, HTC. See also Hubert Lee Ivery, "The Spiritual Psychology of Howard Thurman: An Afrocentric Perspective" (Ph.D. diss., California Institute of Integral Studies, 1997). Anthony Sean Neal, *Common Ground: A Comparison of the Ideas of Consciousness in the Writings of Howard W. Thurman and Huey P. Newton* (Trenton, NJ: Africa World Press, 2015), argues the "confluence" in the thinking of Thurman and Newton is a result of their sharing "in the culture derived from the African Freedom Aesthetic" (133).

36. "Howard Told Main Problem Is Lack of Self-Appreciation," *Washington Post,* 6 June 1970.

37. "Jackson Sees Plot in Integration Guise," *Baltimore Afro-American,* 19 September 1970.

38. Walter Earl Fluker, *Ethical Leadership: The Quest for Character, Civility, and Community* (Minneapolis, MN: Fortress, 2009), 17.

39. George K. Makechnie, *Howard Thurman: His Enduring Dream* (Boston: Howard Thurman Center, Boston University, 1988), 81.

40. Madison Davis Lacey Jr. and Henry Hampton, "Interview with Jesse Jackson: Question 10," 11 April 1989, Eyes on the Prize II Interviews, Washington University Digital Gateway Texts, http://digital.wustl.edu/e/eii/eiiweb/jac5427.0519 .072marc_record_interviewer_process.html. Thurman used the phrase as early as 1932: "To what do I appeal when I want to convince myself that I am somebody?" (HT, "Barren or Fruitful" [1932], in *PHWT,* 1:161).

41. Jackson, Memorial Tribute, in "Simmering on the Calm Presence and Profound Wisdom of Howard Thurman," special issue, *Debate and Understanding,* ed. Ricardo A. Millet and Conley H. Hughes (spring 1982): 82–84.

42. See Derrick A Bell Jr. (1930–2011) to HT, 27 February 1978, in *PHWT,* 5:286–90; and Paul Smith, interview by Peter Eisenstadt, 29 February 2016.

43. For Vincent Harding (1931–2014), see Vincent Harding to HT, 14 July 1973, in *PHWT,* 5:249–54; and for more detail on Thurman's relationship with the historians discussed in this chapter, see Peter Eisenstadt, "Three Historians and a Theologian: Howard Thurman's Impact on the Writing of African American History," in *Reconstruction at 150: Reassessing the Revolutionary "New Birth of Freedom,"* ed. Orville Vernon Burton and Brent Morris (Charlottesville: University of Virginia Press, forthcoming).

44. Harding, "Black Power and the American Christ" (January 1967), reprinted in Gayraud S. Wilmore and James H. Cone, *Black Theology: A Documentary History, 1966–1979* (Maryknoll, NY: Orbis, 1979), 35–42.

45. Vincent Harding, *Beyond Chaos: Black History and the Search for the New Land* (Atlanta: Institute of the Black World, 1970), 21.

46. Vincent Harding, introduction to *For the Inward Journey: The Writings of Howard Thurman,* selected by Anne Thurman (Richmond, ID: Friends United Press, 1991), xiv. See also the testimonial, Rosemary Freeney and Vincent Harding, "For Howard Thurman: Brother, Father, and Comrade," 5 November 1974, Folder 21, Box 46, HTC.

47. Vincent Harding, "Introduction," in *For the Inward Journey: The Writings of Howard Thurman,* xiii.

48. Vincent Harding, *There Is a River: The Black Struggle for Freedom in America* (New York: Harcourt Brace Jovanovich, 1981).

49. Harding, *There Is a River,* xviii–xix. For Thurman's assistance in finding Harding a publisher, see Vincent Harding to HT, 14 July 1973, in *PHWT,* 5:253n11.

50. Harding, *There Is a River,* dedication page.

51. Henry Abelove et al., *Visions of History* (New York: Pantheon 1983), 234.

52. Rachel E. Harding and Vincent Harding, "Biography, Democracy and Spirit: An Interview with Vincent Harding," *Callaloo* 20, no. 3 (Summer 1997): 693–95.

53. Lerone Bennett, *Before the Mayflower: A History of the Negro in America, 1619–1962* (Chicago: Johnson, 1962). For Bennett, see Lerone Bennett to HT, September 1968, in *PHWT,* 5:199–201; and James West, "*Ebony* Magazine, Lerone Bennett, Jr., and the Making of Modern Black History, 1943–1957" (Ph.D. diss., University of Manchester, 2015).

54. Lerone Bennett Jr., "The Challenge of Blackness," in *The Challenge of Blackness* (Chicago: Johnson, 1972), 33–44.

55. Bennett met Thurman as early as 1956 at a Morehouse alumni gathering (see Lerone Bennett and W. E. Cross to HT, 6 June 1956, Folder 6, Box 35, HTC).

56. Lerone Bennett to HT, September 1968, in *PHWT,* 5:199–201.

57. Lerone Bennett, "Howard Thurman: 20th Century Holy Man," *Ebony* 33, no. 4 (February 1978): 68–70, 72, 76, 84–85.

58. Lerone Bennett, Memorial Tribute, in "Simmering on the Calm Presence and Profound Wisdom of Howard Thurman," special issue, *Debate and Understanding,* ed. Ricardo A. Millet and Conley H. Hughes (spring 1982): 71–72.

59. Alfonzo A. Narvaez, "Nathan I. Huggins, Educator, 62; Leader in Afro-American Studies, *New York Times,* 7 December 1989.

60. HT to Nathan Huggins, 24 November 1964, Folder 11, Box 41, HTC.

61. For Huggins, see HT to Nathan I. Huggins, 30 June 1967, in *PHWT,* 5:169–73.

62. Nathan Irvin Huggins, *Black Odyssey: The Afro-American Ordeal in Slavery* (New York: Vintage, 1977), 250.

63. Nathan I. Huggins, "Afro-American History: Myths, Heroes, Reality," in *Key Issues in the Afro-American Experience,* ed. Huggins, Martin Kilson, and Daniel M. Fox (New York: Harcourt Brace Jovanovich, 1971), 14.

64. Huggins, "Afro-American History: Myths, Heroes, Reality," 14.
65. Huggins, "Afro-American History: Myths, Heroes, Reality," 17.
66. Jackson, Memorial Tribute, in "Simmering on the Calm Presence and Profound Wisdom of Howard Thurman," special issue, *Debate and Understanding,* ed. Ricardo A. Millet and Conley H. Hughes (spring 1982): 82–84.
67. HT to Samuel D. Cook, 1 April 1971, Folder 4, Box 45, HTC. Thurman was writing to Cook, describing a recent conversation with Lerone Bennett.
68. Lerone Bennett Jr., "Listen to the Blood," *Ebony,* November 1985, 185–94.
69. HT, "Black Pentecost: Footprints of the Disinherited" (May 1972), in *PHWT* 5:225–34.
70. Acts 2:5, 2:8.
71. *PHWT,* 5:227–28, 30; Burden, "Meditation on Howard Thurman."
72. HT, "America in Search of a Soul" (1976), in HT, *A Strange Freedom,* ed. Fluker and Tumber, 265–72.
73. HT, "America in Search of a Soul," in HT, *A Strange Freedom,* ed. Fluker and Tumber, 268.
74. HT, "America in Search of a Soul," in HT, *A Strange Freedom,* ed. Fluker and Tumber, 272.
75. HT, "America in Search of a Soul," in HT, *A Strange Freedom,* ed. Fluker and Tumber, 271.
76. "Spreading Our Wings: The Howard Thurman Educational Trust" (May 1980), HTET Papers, Morehouse College.
77. The transfer of Thurman's sermons from reel-to-reel recordings to cassettes was facilitated by a grant from the Lilly Foundation and the hard work of HTET's Joyce Sloan, who supervised the technical work in San Francisco (see HT, "Dear Friends of the Trust," *Listening Ear* 4, no. 1 [June 1976]; and HT, "For Your Information," *Listening Ear* 5, no. 1 [spring 1977]). By 1975, the Trust was distributing $50,924 in grants while spending $22,449 in tape editing and related services ("Financial Highlights, 1975").
78. Burden, "Meditation on Howard Thurman."
79. The first off-site listening room was established in 1973 at the farmhouse of Ellen Bartell Klemperer (1912–1995), a wealthy trustee of the HTET who lived in Richmond, Indiana. She would be the main force behind the listening-room program throughout its existence. Klemperer was an active Quaker and helped arrange for the Friends United Press (also in Richmond) to republish in the 1970s Thurman's out-of-print books. For Klemperer on her experiences in South Africa, see Ellen Klemperer to HT, 13 July 1979, Folder 14, Box 49, HTC; see also Anna Pearce, *Simply Living: The Story of Compassion and the Wonderbox* (Saffron Walden, UK: Box, 1989), 109; and *WHAH,* 261–62.
80. For the recordings released by the Trust and the history of the listening rooms, see *PHWT,* 5:xx–xxi.
81. Luther Smith to Paul Smith and Lorenzo Traylor, 6 September 1974, Folder 21, Box 46, HTC.
82. HT to Walter E. Fluker, 11 September 1979, Folder 16, Box 50, HTC. All participants in this seminar received essentially identical letters from Thurman.
83. For the HTET seminars, see *PHWT,* 5:xxii–xxiv.

84. Tyrone L. Burkette, "Conversation with Dr. Howard Thurman," enclosed with Tyrone L. Burkette to HT, 17 April 1980, Folder 4, Box 50, HTC. Walter Fluker reports a similar male-female ratio in his seminar.

85. Walter Fluker, interview by Peter Eisenstadt, 14 April 2016.

86. HT to Samuel Gandy, 29 January 1975, Folder 1, Box 47, HTC.

87. HT to Samuel Gandy, 29 January 1975, Folder, Box 47, HTC.

88. HT, "Memorandum to the [HTET] Board," 26 October 1979, Folder 17, Box 49, HTC.

89. HT, "Memorandum to the [HTET] Board," 26 October 1979, Folder 17, Box 49, HTC; Paul Smith to HT, 12 February 1975, emphasis in original; see Thurman's response (HT to Paul Smith, 17 February 1975), both in Folder 2, Box 47, HTC.

90. Morrison F. Smith to HT, 25 March 1980, HTET Papers, Morehouse College.

91. Walter Fluker, interview by Peter Eisenstadt, 14 April 2016.

92. *A Conversation with Howard Thurman* was directed and produced by Mischa Scorer (b. 1939), a prolific British director of documentaries. For its San Francisco premiere, see "'The Life and Thought of Howard Thurman': A Documentary," *The Listening Ear* 5, no. 1 (Spring 1977). The transcript of the entire conversation is available as Landrum Bolling, "Conversations with Howard Thurman: Transcript of Howard Thurman Documentary," 8–9 January, 1976, Folder 33, Box 16, HTC. Bolling (1913–2018) was director of the Lilly Endowment from 1973 to 1978. For Bolling, see *PHWT,* 5:xlvi–xlviin47. For the television production, see *PHWT,* 5:xxi–xxii, and 5:xlvin46.

93. Elizabeth Yates (1905–2001) was a prolific author of novels and nonfiction books on many topics, and for many audiences, often Christian-themed. *Amos Fortune: Free Man* (1950), her biography of an eighteenth-century African who was enslaved in New England and who subsequently purchased his freedom, won the Newbery Prize for children's literature, the first on an African American subject (Yates, *Amos Fortune: Free Man* [New York: Dutton, 1950]). See Margaret Trudell, *Elizabeth Yates: A Biography and Bibliography* (AuthorHouse, 2003). Her married name was Elizabeth Yates McGreal.

94. HT to Herbert King, 9 June 1963, Folder 6, Box 40, HTC. Yates came down to Boston that summer two days a week to interview Thurman (Yates, *Howard Thurman,* 10).

95. Roberta Byrd Barr, "A Creative Encounter: An Interview with Howard Thurman," Part 1, 14–15 February 1969, Folder 30, Box 16, HTC.

96. Elizabeth Yates McGreal to HT, 16 December 1963, Folder 12, Box 40, HTC.

97. HT to Richard J. Walsh Jr., 4 August, 1964, Folder 8, Box 41, HTC.

98. HT to Luther Smith, 12 September 1974, Folder 21, Box 46, HTC.

99. For Thurman's first attempt at an extended autobiographical sketch, see *Footprints of a Dream,* 15–28.

100. See HT to Jean Burden, February 1976.

101. He wrote that his daughter Anne Spencer was a "collaborator and sounding board [who] gave three years of her life to this project, bringing to it her training and experience as a critic and editor. Without her work this book would not have been published" (*WHAH,* xii).

102. HT to Jean Burden, June 1976, Folder 18, Box 47, HTC.

103. Bianchi, "Religion and Aging," interview with Howard Thurman, 6 May 1980, in *PHWT,* 5:302–7.
104. HT to Luther Smith, 24 February 1976, Folder 14, Box 47, HTC.
105. William Jovanovich (1920–2001) became the head of the publishing firm Harcourt, Brace in 1954. In 1970 it was renamed Harcourt Brace Jovanovich. He was a generous benefactor for the Trust and gave ten thousand dollars to Fellowship Church (HT to Leroy Jackson, 9 February 1980). For Jovanovich, see *PHWT,* 5:lin157.
106. HT to William Jovanovich, 27 April 1976, Folder 16, Box 47, HTC; Author's Guild Survey: Trade Book Contract Financial Terms, 1976?, Howard Thurman Papers Project Files
107. For Daniel Collins, see *PHWT,* 5:253n11.
108. HT to Winthrop Knowlton, 25 June 1976, Folder 18, Box 47, HTC.
109. William Jovanovich to HT, 7 October 1978, Folder 5, Box 49, HTC.
110. Jack Schooler to HT, 20 September 1980, Folder 8, Box 50, HTC.
111. Advertisement for *With Head and Heart, New York Times,* 25 November 1979.
112. Vernon E. Jordan Jr., "Group W Commentary #145: Howard Thurman," 3 December 1979, Folder 19, Box 49, HTC.
113. Otis Moss Sr. to HT, 6 November 1979, Folder 18, Box 49, HTC. See also Genna Rae McNeil to HT, 21 November 1979, Folder 18, Box 49, HTC.
114. Ron Smith to HT, 26 November 1979, Folder 18, Box 49, HTC.
115. Ethel Simons Meads to HT, 27 January, 1980, Folder 1, Box 50, HTC.
116. "*With Head and Heart: The Autobiography of Howard Thurman,* by Howard Thurman," *Kirkus Reviews,* 15 September 1979.
117. Doris Grumbach, "Nonfiction in Brief," *New York Times,* 6 January 1980. For Grumbach, see *PHWT,* 5:299n2.
118. Benita Eisler, "Keeping the Faith," *Nation* 230 (5–12 January 1980): 22–25. For Eisler, see *PHWT,* 5:299n3.
119. HT to Richard A. Chartier, 17 April 1980, Folder 4, Box 50, HTC.
120. Benjamin E. Mays to HT, 7 April 1980, in *PHWT,* 5:297–300.
121. Mays's unfortunate comment about "groups of Jews in the East" is out of keeping with a lifelong support of Jews and opposition to anti-Semitism (see Benjamin E. Mays to HT, 7 April 1980, in *PHWT,* 5:299n4). In 1961 President Kennedy considered appointing Mays ambassador to Israel (Benjamin E. Mays, *Born to Rebel: An Autobiography* [1971; repr., Athens: University of Georgia Press, 2003], 231–32).
122. Ed Kaplan to HT, 27 January 1980, Folder 1, Box 50, HTC; Benjamin E. Mays to HT, 7 April 1980, in *PHWT,* 5:297–300.
123. HT to Richard Newman, 29 February 1980, Folder 2, Box 50, HTC. Richard Newman (1930–2003), an ordained Presbyterian minister, spent most of his career as a distinguished editor, bibliographer, and historian of African American life and religion. If I may be allowed a personal note, Dick Newman was a friend and mentor. When I first was considering taking a position with the Howard Thurman Papers Project, at a time when I knew nothing about Howard Thurman, he encouraged me to do so.
124. Richard Newman, draft of review of *With Head and Heart,* enclosed with Richard Newman to HT, 19 February 1980, Folder 2, Box 50, HTC. The review appeared

in the *Newsletter of the Afro-American Religious History Group of the American Academy of Religion* 7, no. 1 (spring 1980), 9; it was reprinted in Richard Newman, *Black Power and Black Religion: Essays and Reviews* (West Cornwall, CT: Locust Hill, 1987), 221–22.

125. For Thurman's place within the history of American spirituality, see Leigh Eric Schmidt, *Restless Souls: The Making of American Spirituality* (Berkeley: University of California Press, 2012), 266–68.

126. To Frank E. Drumwright Jr., 8 December 1977, Folder 17, Box 48, HTC.

127. Gil Bailie, *Violence Unveiled: Humanity at the Crossroads* (New York: Crossroad, 1995), xv.

128. "Keep Awake!," in *PHWT*, 2:39.

129. HT, *Deep Is the Hunger*, 98.

130. HT, "South Pacific Journal," in *PHWT*, 5:212.

131. Thurman resigned from the National Council of FOR in April 1953, unable to give the organization sufficient time, but this did not mean any "relaxation of my concern with concern for peace in all the dimensions to which FOR is dedicated" (HT to A. J. Muste, 18 April 1953, in *PHWT*, 4:66). In 1957 he wrote a testimonial for a FOR promotional folder (HT, "[Fellowship of Reconciliation Testimonial]," 8 October 1957, Folder 8, Box 36, HTC), and he continued to support FOR-related efforts, such as signing newspaper statements (see HT to A. J. Muste, 2 March 1962, in *PHWT*, 4:317).

132. HT, "Letter in Support of United World Federalists" (1960), in *PHWT*, 4:259–60.

133. HT, "Two Options" (1961), in *PHWT*, 4:297–300.

134. *PHWT*, 5:135

135. "Vietnam: America Must Decide between a Full-Scale War and a Negotiated Truce," *New York Times*, 19 February 1965; "Who Is Blocking Negotiation on Vietnam—Now?," *New York Times*, 18 June 1967.

136. HT, *The Search for Common Ground*, 91.

137. HT to Edward Kaplan, 14 April 1967, in *PHWT*, 5:167–68.

138. HT, *Jesus and the Disinherited*, 59.

139. Sue Bailey Thurman was a delegate to the first Inter-American Congress of Women in 1947 ("Mrs. Thurman Will Represent Women at Guatemala Meeting," *Norfolk Journal and Guide*, 23 August 1947).

140. HT, *A Track to the Water's Edge*, 97–116

141. Walter Fluker, communication with the author, 19 September 2016.

142. Marshall C. Grigsby to HT, 7 April 1980, Folder 4, Box 50, HTC. Adena Joy was an assistant minister at Fellowship Church from 1949 to 1951, and Thurman wrote of her that "for two years, the church had the rare experience of having a woman, Miss Adena Joy, serve as the assistant minister. What was so rare not that the fact that she shared in the religious leadership of the church, but that she carried some of the responsibility in the pulpit in the absence of the minister" (HT, *Footprints of a Dream*, 102–3). For Joy, see HT to Friend (January 1950), in *PHWT*, 4:15n2.

143. HT to Dr. and Mrs. Marshall Grigsby, 17 April 1980, Folder 4, Box 50, HTC.

144. *PHWT*, 1:99–100.

145. Havelock Ellis, *Studies in the Psychology of Sex: Sexual Inversion* (Philadelphia: F. A. Davis, 1901); Edward Carpenter, *Love's Coming-of-Age: A Series of Papers on the Relations of the Sexes* (London: Methuen, 1924).

146. HT, "Mysticism and Social Action," in *Lawrence Lectures on Religion and Society* (Berkeley, CA: First Unitarian Church of Berkeley, 1978), 18.

147. See Douglas Morgan Strong to HT, 26 October 1978; and HT to Douglas Morgan Strong, 31 October 1978, in *PHWT,* 5:290–94; 294–95. Douglas Morgan Strong (b. 1943) was one of the first openly gay Unitarian Universalist ministers.

148. The Thurmans were close to Pauli Murray and helped her through a difficult period in her life when she was deeply conflicted over her gender and sexual identity (see *PHWT,* 3:320–23). For the lesbianism of Winnifred Wygal, a YWCA official close to Thurman in the 1930s, and who played a crucial role in arranging the India trip, see Linda W. Rosenzweig, *Another Self: Middle-Class American Women and Their Friends in the Twentieth Century* (New York: New York University Press, 1999), 138–40.

149. After working as a United Methodist minister in his native state of Montana, Pfleiderer came to San Francisco in the early 1970s to work with the city's gay and lesbian community. In 1979 he was called to the Pilgrim United Church of Christ congregation in San Francisco, serving until 1982. He was ordained into the ministry of the gay- and lesbian-oriented Metropolitan Community Church (MCC) shortly before his death, from AIDS, in December 1982 (for Pfleiderer, see *PHWT,* 5:ln123).

150. John W. Pfleiderer to HT, 24 January 1979, Folder 8, Box 49, HTC.

151. John W. Pfleiderer to HT, 24 January 1979, Folder 8, Box 49, HTC.

152. HT, "Man and the World of Nature," in *PHWT,* 2:101–6.

153. HT, "Extract of Sermon at St. Thomas Church" (16 July 1965), Folder 6, Box 42, HTC; "Sense of Kinship Is Termed Vital," *New York Times,* 28 June 1965. Thurman prepared this extract from this sermon from memory, after receiving a request for its text from an official of the National Audubon Society (Charles H. Callison to HT, 29 June 1965; HT to Charles H. Callison, 16 July 1965, Folder 6, Box 42, HTC).

154. HT to Jean Burden, 14 February 1970, Folder 14, Box 44, HTC.

155. HT, "Extract of Sermon at St. Thomas Church" (16 July 1965), Folder 6, Box 42, HTC.

156. HT to William Irwin Thompson 15 January 1976, Folder 13, Box 47, HTC.

157. HT to Guy Murchie, 19 January 1979, Folder 8, Box 49, HTC. See Guy Murchie, *The Seven Mysteries of Life: An Exploration in Science & Philosophy* (Boston: Houghton Mifflin, 1978).

158. For an overview of New Age thinking, see Catherine L. Albanese, *A Republic of Mind and Spirit: A Cultural History of American Metaphysical Religion* (New Haven, CT: Yale University Press, 2007), 496–516.

159. For a discussion of Thurman and New Age thought, see HT, *A Strange Freedom,* ed. Fluker and Tumber, 8.

160. Henry Miller to HT, 12 April 1966, Folder 20, Box 42, HTC. Edward Kaplan met Henry Miller in Paris in 1959 (when Kaplan was a teenager) and subsequently urged the two men to meet (Edward Kaplan, interview by Peter Eisenstadt, 6 July 2015).

161. For Schachter-Shalomi's New Age sympathies, see *Paradigm Shift: From the Jewish Renewal Teachings of Reb Zalman Schachter-Shalomi* (Northvale, NJ: Jason Aronson, 1993).

162. See Sam Keen, *Fire in the Belly: On Being a Man* (New York: Bantam, 1991), 159–60; Mozella G. Mitchell, "'The Shaman's Doorway': Techniques of Myth and Ritual in Thurman," in "Simmering on the Calm Presence and Profound Wisdom of Howard Thurman," special issue, *Debate and Understanding,* ed. Ricardo A. Millet and Conley H. Hughes (spring 1982): 27–36. Keen dedicated a book to Thurman, *Beginnings without End* (New York: Harper and Row, 1975).

163. HT, "Africa Journal," in *PHWT,* 5:58–59.

164. Burden, "Meditation on Howard Thurman."

165. HT, "Mysticism and Social Action," 18.

166. HT, "Mysticism and Social Action," 18.

167. Sam Keen, Memorial Tribute, in "Simmering on the Calm Presence and Profound Wisdom of Howard Thurman," special issue, *Debate and Understanding,* ed. Ricardo A. Millet and Conley H. Hughes (spring 1982): 90.

168. J. Anthony Lukas, *Common Ground: A Turbulent Decade in the Lives of Three American Families* (New York: Knopf, 1985).

169. J. Anthony Lukas, foreword to HT, *The Search for Common Ground* (1971; repr., Richmond, ID: Friends United Press, 1986), xi.

170. *A Conversation with Howard Thurman,* 22 January 1976.

171. For Thurman's health in the 1950s, see Donyelle C. McCray, "Howard Thurman," in *Can I Get a Witness? Thirteen Peacemakers, Community Builders, and Agitators for Peace and Justice,* ed. Charles Marsh, Shea Tuttle, and Daniel P. Rhodes (Grand Rapids, MI: Eerdmans, 2019), 52–53.

172. HT to Jean Burden, 25 February 1974.

173. Burden, "Meditation on Howard Thurman."

174. HT to William Jovanovich, 23 April 1980; see also HT to Frank P. Wilson, 9 April 1980, both letters in Folder 4, Box 50, HTC.

175. HT, *For the Inward Journey.*

176. HT to John A. Taylor, 17 April 1980, Folder 4, Box 50, HTC.

177. HT to Richard B. Deats, 17 April 1980, Folder 4, Box 50, HTC.

178. HT, "The Sound of the Genuine," *Spelman Messenger* 96, no. 4 (Summer 1980): 14–15.

179. "The Growing Edge" (26 October 1980), in *PHWT,* 5:311–18.

180. See Tina Wall to Lee, 24 February 1981, Folder 14, Box 50, HTC.

181. Burden, "Meditation on Howard Thurman."

182. Keen, *Fire in the Belly,* 159; Sue Bailey Thurman, "Epilogue," in "Simmering on the Calm Presence and Profound Wisdom of Howard Thurman," special issue, *Debate and Understanding,* ed. Ricardo A. Millet and Conley H. Hughes (spring 1982): 91.

183. HT, *Walking with God: The Sermon Series of Howard Thurman,* vol. 1: *Moral Struggle and the Prophets,* ed. Peter Eisenstadt and Walter E. Fluker (Maryknoll, NY: Orbis, 2020), 159.

184. HT, "'Concluding Chapter' Head and Heart" (unpublished draft), Folder 24, Box 4, HTC.

185. Bianchi, "Religion and Aging," interview with Howard Thurman, in *PHWT*, 5:302–11.
186. Keen, *Fire in the Belly*, 159–60, emphasis in original.
187. Walter Fluker, conversation with the author, no date.
188. Sue Bailey Thurman, "Epilogue," in "Simmering on the Calm Presence and Profound Wisdom of Howard Thurman," special issue, *Debate and Understanding*, ed. Ricardo A. Millet and Conley H. Hughes (spring 1982): 91.
189. "Memorial Services Celebrating the Life of Howard Thurman" 16 April 1981, HTET Papers, Morehouse College.
190. Benjamin E. Mays to Gerald Freund, 5 December 1980, Folder 12, Box 50, HTC.
191. "Calendar of Events," *Atlanta Daily World*, 12 May 1981.
192. Benjamin E. Mays, Memorial Tribute, in "Simmering on the Calm Presence and Profound Wisdom of Howard Thurman," special issue, *Debate and Understanding*, ed. Ricardo A. Millet and Conley H. Hughes (spring 1982): 86–88. (This is a reprint of Mays's baccalaureate sermon.)
193. Vernon E. Jordan Jr., "Our Fallen Heroes: Thurman & Louis," *Los Angeles Sentinel*, 30 April 1981. See also Vernon Jarrett, "One More Unsung Black Hero Gone," *Chicago Tribune*, 17 April 1981.
194. For Thurman on Louis, see HT to Herbert King, 7 July 1938, in *PHWT*, 2:172–73.
195. HT, "Mysticism and Social Action," n *Lawrence Lectures on Religion and Society* (Berkeley, CA: First Unitarian Church of Berkeley, 1978), 35.
196. For a short overview of Thurman scholarship, see *PHWT*, 5:xxxvii–xxxix.
197. The children's book is Kai Jackson Issa and Arthur L. Dawson, *Howard Thurman's Great Hope* (New York: Lee and Low, 2008). An excellent film (in which, in the interests of full disclosure, I was a talking head) is Martin Doblmeier, prod. and dir., *Backs Against the Wall: The Howard Thurman Story* (Journey Films, 2019).
198. "Biographical Essay," in *PHWT*, 5:xlii
199. Nathan Huggins, Memorial Tribute, in "Simmering on the Calm Presence and Profound Wisdom of Howard Thurman," special issue, *Debate and Understanding*, ed. Ricardo A. Millet and Conley H. Hughes (spring 1982): 82.
200. Vincent Harding, foreword to HT, *Jesus and the Disinherited* (1996 repr.), xii.
201. Lerone Bennett, Memorial Tribute, in "Simmering on the Calm Presence and Profound Wisdom of Howard Thurman," special issue, *Debate and Understanding*, ed. Ricardo A. Millet and Conley H. Hughes (spring 1982): 71.
202. Gil Bailie to HT, 20 April 1978?, Folder 21, Box 48, HTC.
203. Alvin I. Fine, Memorial Tribute, in "Simmering on the Calm Presence and Profound Wisdom of Howard Thurman," special issue, *Debate and Understanding*, ed. Ricardo A. Millet and Conley H. Hughes (spring 1982): 76.
204. *WHAH*, 162.
205. Lerone Bennett Jr., "Search for Common Ground," *New York Amsterdam News*, 18 April 1987.

Selected Bibliography

Printed Primary Sources (Collections)

Thurman, Howard Washington. *For the Inward Journey: The Writings of Howard Thurman*. Edited by Anne Spencer Thurman and Vincent Harding. New York: Harcourt Brace Jovanovich, 1984.

——. *Howard Thurman: Essential Writings*. Edited by Luther E. Smith. Maryknoll, NY: Orbis, 2006.

——. *The Papers of Howard Washington Thurman*. Edited by Walter Earl Fluker. Vols. 1–5. Columbia: University of South Carolina Press, 2009–19.

——. *Sermons on the Parables*. Edited by David B. Gowler and Kipton Jensen. Maryknoll, NY: Orbis, 2018.

——. *A Strange Freedom: The Best of Howard Thurman on Religious Experience and Public Life*. Edited by Walter Earl Fluker and Catherine Tumber. Boston: Beacon, 1998.

Books by Howard Thurman

The Greatest of These. Mills College, CA: Eucalyptus, 1944.

Jesus and the Disinherited. New York: Abingdon-Cokesbury, 1949.

Deep Is the Hunger: Meditations for the Apostles of Sensitiveness. New York: Harper and Brothers, 1951.

Meditations of the Heart. New York: Harper and Brothers, 1953.

The Creative Encounter: An Interpretation of Religion and the Social Witness. New York: Harper and Brothers, 1954.

Deep River: The Negro Spiritual Speaks of Life and Death. New York: Harper and Brothers, 1955.

The Growing Edge. New York: Harper and Brothers, 1956.

Footprints of a Dream: The Story of the Church for the Fellowship of All Peoples. New York: Harper and Brothers, 1959.

Mysticism and the Experience of Love. Wallingford, PA: Pendle Hill, 1961.

Disciplines of the Spirit. New York: Harper and Row, 1962.

The Luminous Darkness: A Personal Interpretation of the Anatomy of Segregation and the Ground of Hope. New York: Harper and Row, 1964.

The Centering Moment. New York: Harper and Row, 1969.

The Search for Common Ground: An Inquiry into the Basis of Man's Experience of Community. New York: Harper and Row, 1971.

A Track to the Water's Edge: The Olive Schreiner Reader. New York: Harper and Row, 1973.

The Mood of Christmas and Other Celebrations. New York: Harper and Row, 1973.

The First Footprint: The Dawn of the Idea of the Church for the Fellowship of All Peoples. San Francisco: Lawton and Alfred Kennedy, 1975.

With Head and Heart: The Autobiography of Howard Thurman. New York: Harcourt Brace Jovanovich, 1979.

Secondary Sources on Howard Thurman

Bennett, Lerone, Jr. "Howard Thurman: 20th Century Holy Man." *Ebony* 33, no. 4 (February 1978): 68–70, 72, 76, 84–85.

Burden, Jean. "Howard Thurman." *Atlantic Monthly,* October 1953, 39–44.

Dixie, Quinton, and Peter Eisenstadt. *Visions of a Better World: Howard Thurman's Pilgrimage to India and the Origins of African American Nonviolence.* Boston: Beacon, 2011.

Fluker, Walter E. *They Looked for a City: A Comparative Analysis of the Ideal of Community in the Thought of Howard Thurman and Martin Luther King, Jr.* Lanham, MD: University Press of America, 1989.

Gandy, Samuel Lucius, ed. *Common Ground: Essays in Honor of Howard Thurman on the Occasion of his Seventy-Fifth Birthday, November 18, 1975.* Washington, D.C.: Hoffman, 1976.

Harding, Vincent. Foreword to *Jesus and the Disinherited,* by Howard Thurman. Boston: Beacon, 1996.

Harvey, Paul. *Howard Thurman and the Disinherited.* Grand Rapids, MI: Eerdmans, 2020.

Jackson, Kai Issa, and Arthur L. Dawson. *Howard Thurman's Great Hope.* New York: Lee and Low, 2008.

Jensen, Kipton E. *Howard Thurman: Philosophy, Civil Rights, and the Search for Common Ground.* Columbia: University of South Carolina Press, 2019.

Makechnie, George K. *Howard Thurman: His Enduring Dream.* Boston: Howard Thurman Center, Boston University, 1988.

Mitchell, Mozella G., ed. *The Human Search: Howard Thurman and the Quest for Freedom—Proceedings of the Second Annual Thurman Convocation.* New York: Peter Lang, 1992.

———. *Spiritual Dynamics of Howard Thurman's Theology.* Bristol, IN: Wyndham Hall, 1985.

Neal, Anthony Sean. *Howard Thurman's Philosophical Mysticism: Love against Fragmentation.* Lanham, MD: Lexington, 2019.

Pollard, Alton, *Mysticism and Social Change: The Social Witness of Howard Thurman.* New York: Peter Lang, 1992.

"Simmering on the Calm Presence and Profound Wisdom of Howard Thurman." Special issue, *Debate & Understanding,* edited by Ricardo A. Millet and Conley H. Hughes (spring 1982).

Siracusa, Anthony C. *The World as It Should Be: Religion and Nonviolence before King.* Chapel Hill: University of North Carolina, forthcoming.

Smith, Luther E. *Howard Thurman: The Mystic as Prophet.* Lanham, MD: University Press of America, 1981.

Yates, Elizabeth. *Howard Thurman: Portrait of a Practical Dreamer.* New York: John Day, 1964.

Young, Henry James. *God and Human Freedom: A Festschrift in Honor of Howard Thurman.* Richmond, ID: Friends United Press, 1983.

Illustration Credits

Images here are reproduced by kind permission of the Thurman estate and the following image and rights holders:

Emory University Stuart A. Rose Manuscript, Archives, and Rare Book Library: Pages 28, 34, 391

Howard Thurman Papers in Boston University: Pages 20, 233, 276, 280, 293, 378

Journey Films: Page 30

Marc Korpus: Pages 17, 224

Moorland-Spingarn Research Center, Howard University: Pages 141, 147, 153

Robert W. Woodruff Library, Atlanta University Center: Page 67

State Archives of Florida: Pages 42, 48

Index

Entries for works by Howard Thurman appear under Thurman, Howard: works of.

Mays, Benjamin: on Black church, 156–57; on *Brown v. Board of Education,* 287; on Christianity, 74–75; and criticism of Morehouse as Black institution accepting segregation, 73–75; as Fellowship Church associate, 236; Festschrift for, 341; on John Hope, 65; on Howard University chapel services, 147–51; Howard University hiring of, 142–43; Morehouse presidency, 208–9; and Morehouse theology, creation of, 61; *The Negro's Church* (with Joseph Nicholson), 156–57; on segregation of American Christianity, 238–39; on student radicalism, 64–65; and HT, relationship with, 143, 156, 318, 390; on HT as mystic, 115; on HT autobiography, 381–82; and HT death, 391–92; on HT resignation from Howard University, 227

McCarthyism, 286

McGehee, John C., 28–29

McTerman, Francis J., 487n53

Meads, Ethel Simons, 53, 380–81

Meet the Negro (Karl E. Downs), 261

Melville, Herman: *Moby-Dick,* 220

Merriweather, M. C., 190

Middle Passage, 324

Miller, Henry, 387

Miller, Kelly, 56

Milton, Lorimer, 57–58, 71, 100, 344

Mirabehn (Madeline Slade), 439n125

miscegenation, 94

Mis-Education of the Negro, The (Carter G. Woodson), 153

Mitchell, John, 368

Mitchell, Mozella, 377, 387

Moby-Dick (Herman Melville), 220

Moehlman, Conrad Henry, 87, 97, 279

Montgomery Bus Boycott, 285–86

Montgomery Improvement Association, 285–86

Mont Saint Michel and Chartres (Henry Adams), 87

Moore, Garrie Ward, 71–72, 75

Moore, Richard V., 315–16

Moral Man and Immoral Society (Reinhold Niebuhr), 176–77

Morehouse, Henry Lyman, 62

Morehouse College: and Association with Spelman and Atlanta University, 119; and criticism of, as Black institution accepting segregation, 73–75; and General Education Board, 124; history of, 64, 65; and manhood, 67–68; and oration, practice of, 100; racial violence on campus, 120; student conduct, 65–66; Thurman interment at, 49, 61. *See also under* Thurman, Howard: education

Morgan College, 240

Morristown Neighborhood House Association, 98

Moss, Otis, Sr., 318–19, 380

Mount Bethel Baptist Church (Daytona), 31–33, 38–40, 100–101

Mount Zion Baptist Church (Oberlin), 97, 106

Moxley, Irvin Stuart, 369

Muelder, Walter, 241, 278, 302, 306, 343

Mumford, Lewis, 220

Murchie, Guy, 387

Murder in the Cathedral (T. S. Eliot), 150

Murota, Ayoka, 247

Murray, James, 40–41

Murray, Pauli, 200–201, 385, 446n99, 500n148

Muste, A. J., 187, 199–200, 204, 384, 442n21

Myers, Henry A.: *Are Men Equal?,* 250–51

Myrdal, Gunnar: *An American Dilemma,* 173, 216–17

mysticism, 111–12, 113, 293. *See also under* Thurman, Howard

NAACP, 64, 167, 289

Nabritt, James, Jr., 70

National Baptist Convention, 188

National Conference of Christians and Jews, 190

National Council of Negro Women (NCNW), 43, 140, 249. *See also* Bethune, Mary McLeod

Thurman, Howard (*continued*)
and nonviolence, 310, 351; economic and societal revolution, necessity of, 342; as inspiration and mentor to leaders of CRM, 318–19; and Kennedy assassination, 330–32; March on Washington (1963), 319–20, 337; and massive resistance, 288–90; personal spiritual exploration and social change, 286–88, 291, 317; and revolution/fear, release of, 317–18; as on sidelines of movement, 318–20, 382; skepticism of social change, 341–42; and white liberals, 337–38, 351; and white ministers, hope for change, 287–88
— education: and college, choosing of, 61–62; Columbia University summer courses, 75–77, 89; and Florida Baptist Academy for high school, 50–54; high school at Florida Baptist Academy, 47–54; importance of, 52; and Morehouse, 49, 61–63, 66–67, 70–73, 78; and Oberlin seminary, 108–9; and Ph.D., decision not to pursue, 108–9; and Rochester Theological Seminary (RTS) (*see* Thurman, Howard: Rochester Theological Seminary); seminary application rejection because of race, 80
— family life: and Anne, 137, 322; finances of, 12, 206–7, 312, 343–44, 363; and Katie Kelley, 9, 67, 97, 109, 112, 117–18, 133–34; and Olive, 99, 112, 117, 133–34, 322; and Sue Bailey, 136–38, 482n80. *See also individual family members*
— at Howard University: arrival at, 140; and counselor, in demand as, 145–46; Fellowship Council, creation of, 146; and Johnson, 139–43, 208; limitations on HT, 208; mysticism, teachings on, 115; as professor, 143–46; and Rankin Chapel, 146–51, 159; resignation from, 227–28, 235; salary of, 142; and San Francisco, leave of absence for, 207–8;

tenure at, 140; and World War II, enlisted students and alumni, 190, 194
— intellectual influences. *See* Bethune, Mary McLeod; Cross, George; Johnson, Mordecai Wyatt; Jones, Rufus M.; Moehlman, Conrad Henry; Robins, Henry Burke; Schreiner, Olive
— leisure and pleasures of: baseball, 262, 275, 284; boxing, 437n79; cooking, 283; ice cream making, 40–41; painting, 232; poetry, 52–53; reading, 160; traveling by ship, 308, 363–64
— life and views, general: on American materialism, 109–10; audiences, racial makeup of, 161–63, 190–91; and Communism and Soviet Union, 167–69; on community, 330, 355–62, 384, 386, 388–89; compensation of, 159; and decolonization movement, 311–12; demand for HT as speaker, 313, 343; and Juliette Derricotte, 121–22; on education, role of, 154–55; as empath, 66–67; on enslavement and emancipation, 63; FBI interest in, 259; and Fellowship Church (Philadelphia), 197; and feminism, 90–96, 384–85; and gambling, 40–41; on gay rights, 385–86; health in decline, 389–90; hellhound, use of as image, 217; increasing volume of writing, 244–46; interviews with, 378–79; on Japanese internment, 210–11; and Herbert King's death, 366; on MLK assassination, 350–53, 355; lecture circuit schedule, 160–63, 182–83, 239; legacy and continued relevance of, 392–94; and liturgical dance, incorporation of, 150; and music, 232; overseas travel, 134, 308–9, 310–12, 334–35; overseas travel, South Pacific cruise, 363–65, 366; overseas travel, to Israel, 332–33; and overwork, exhaustion from, 12, 111, 363–64; on pain and joy, 134; and performance and theater, 149–50; philanthropy, desire for, 71, 344; and politics, 251–57, 259–60;

preaching style of, 147–51, 281–82, 291; as prophet, 97, 183, 387; recordings of sermons, 234–35, 375–76; and reflective thinking, 75–77; on FDR and New Deal, 167; scholarship on, 161, 392; and slavery, 128–29; and socialism, 77; and spirituals, 245–46, 269–70; televised, 150; topics of, 235; and train travel, segregation, 160; unworthiness, sense of, 48, 52

— and mysticism: definition of, 116; on advising what people should do, 383; and affirmation mysticism, 113–14, 116–17; and Christianity, separation from, 114, 116; and environmentalism, 386–87; and Hindu mysticism, 18; on his death, 390–91; identification as mystic, 115; and Rufus Jones, study with, 112, 151; Khyber Pass epiphany, 196; and "life," 357–58; mystic experiences of, 20–21, 40–41, 79; and New Age thinking, 387–88; and the occult, 298; and origins of, 82, 111–12; and psychedelic drugs, 298–301; and race and segregation, 114–15; and relaxation, 129–30; religions coming together, experience of, 296–97; and sermons, style of, 151; and social issues, 116; teaching of, 115, 143, 292–94

— and organizations: and ACLU, 464n100; and CORE, 200–201, 340–43, 464n100; and FOR, 186–87, 189, 199–200, 384; and NAACP, 289; and Socialist Party, 165–67; and Student Christian Movement, 90–92, 146, 156–57, 173–83; on UNICO/UN, 250; and YMCA, 51, 58–59, 74, 90–92, 136, 206

— pacifism and nonviolence: and British imperialism in India, 158–59; and citizenship, 337; and civil disobedience, 201; and Fellowship of Reconciliation, 166; and Gandhi, meeting with, 1–8; and Jainist concept of ahimsa, 5–6, 199; models and theories for, 166, 181; on nuclear weapons, 384; and

oppression, method to challenge, 126–28; organizations, affiliations with, 383–84; religious implications of, 181–82; and self-immolation, 6, 180; and Vietnam War, 384; and WWI, 56–57, 407n52; and WWII, 185–90, 192–94, 250, 334

— pilgrimage to India: conclusion of, 16; and Gandhi, visit with, 20–21; Howard University leave, unpaid, 141, 159; India Committee, 9–13; and India press, 170–71; and Khyber Pass, 196; and MLK, similar trip, 158; Negro Delegation, 1–8, 9–12, 13; planning and preparations for, 9–12; and race and imperialism, 169–73, 196; and racism in India compared to in U.S., 171–73; return home from, 159; speaking engagements and topics, 12, 16–19; and World War II, early conflicts of, 185–86

— and race: on affirmation of race versus limitations of race, 246; and American Indians, 173, 314–15, 334, 345, 359; and Black citizenship, 191–92; and Black history, 313, 345, 373–75; and Black leadership, relationship with, 166–67; and Black nationalism, 68–70; and Black patriotism, 56–59; on Black personhood, 104–6; and Black separatism, 359–61, 368–72; and Daytona, 77–78; on generation gap, 353–55; interracial institutions, need for, 192; and interracialism, perils of, 205–6, 214–15; on navigating white world, 364; and pacifism, 77, 127–30; psychological violence of racism, 68–69, 80–81; and racial pride, 369; and RTS, experiences at, 82–83; segregated accommodations when lecturing, 182–83, 215, 216, 408n62; on segregation, 153–57, 201–3, 223–24; and "sensitiveness," 251–52; and Social Gospel, limitations of, 177–78; as transcending race, 367–69; and unity, 172–73, 175; and uplift versus integration, 225;

Thurman, Howard (*continued*)
on white liberals, working with, 65;
and World War I, no change in race
relationship, 66–67. *See also* Thurman,
Howard: pilgrimage to India
— relationships with prominent indi-
viduals: and Lerone Bennett, 372; and
Jean Burden, 366–67; and Alfred Fisk,
228; and Vincent Harding, 371; and
John Hope, 66–67, 134; and Nathan
Huggins, 372–73; and Mordecai
Wyatt Johnson, 57–60, 140–42,
208; and Kelley family, 134; and
MLK, 283–85, 289–91, 425n97; and
Benjamin Mays, 143; and Reinhold
Niebuhr, 176–77; and Florence Read,
119–20
— at Rochester Theological Seminary
(RTS), 82–83, 85–89; and faculty,
relationship with (*see* Cross, George;
Moehlman, Conrad Henry; Robins,
Henry Burke) ; student paper, "The
Basis of Sex Morality," 90–96; student
paper, "Can It Truly Be Said," 81–82,
89–90; student paper, and plagiarism,
instance of, 415n58; student paper,
"Virgin Birth," 89
— in San Francisco: decision to go,
195–96, 206–10, 218; and Fellowship
Church, opening of, logistics, 212–13;
fundraising and administration,
responsibilities of, 207; as home, 275;
networking, 219; return to, 344–45,
349–50; as writer, comfort with,
245–46. *See also* Fellowship Church
(San Francisco)
— theology and religion: on action
versus intention, 182–83; and the arts,
231–33; on Black church, 156–57;
childhood development of nature
mysticism, 36–37; and Christianity, divisions in, 81, 238, 255; and
Christianity, symbols of, 281; and
Christianity and colonialism, 7; and
Christianity as tool of the powerful,
10–11, 16, 21; and Christianity as
transformation of society, 177–82;
on church as institution, criticism of,
110–11; and citizenship, 59, 130–33,
173–75, 337; and evangelicalism, 39,
58–60; inclusive Christianity, desire to
create, 21; interracial churches, desire
for, 196–97, 203–4; and Jesus, religion
of (as separate from Christianity), 16,
38, 106, 130–33, 264–65; and Jews,
relationship with, 294–97, 475n134;
and life, unity of, 250, 302–5, 315,
345, 356–58, 379–80, 407n52; and
Paul, letters of, 132–33; and personal
property, 178; and philosophy, study
of, 75–77; and politics and social
agitation, separation of, 230–31; and
Quakers, 233–34; HT's father's experiences with church as formative, 32
— works of: "America in Search of a
Soul" (1976), 374–75; on the American Dream (1950s), 260; "Apostles
of Sensitiveness" (1946), 251; "Barren
or Fruitful" (1932), 137–38; "Be Not
Overcome by Evil" (1954), 287; "Black
Pentecost" (1972), 374; "Christian,
Who Calls Me Christian?" (1937),
183; "The Christian Minister and
the Desegregation Decision" (1957),
288; "College and Color" (1924),
83–85; "Community and the Will of
God" (1961), 357, 358; "The Cosmic
Guarantee in the Judeo-Christian
Message" (1944), 356–57; *The Creative
Encounter* (1954), 286–87; "Deep
River" (1928, 1930)/*Deep River* (1945,
1947, 1955), 123–24, 126, 245; "Deseg-
regation, Integration, and the Beloved
Community" (1966, 2009), 341; *Dis-
ciplines of the Spirit* (1963), 268, 294;
"The Fascist Masquerade" (1946), 252–
57; for Federation of Saskatchewan
Indians (1962), 314–15; "Finding God"
(1926), 103–4; "The Flag" (1920), 57;
Footprints of a Dream (1959), 275;

Women's College of Alabama, 104

Wong, Olive Thurman. *See* Thurman, Olive Kathleen

Wong, Victor, 275

Woodson, Carter G.: *The Mis-Education of the Negro,* 153

Woodward, C. Vann: *The Strange Career of Jim Crow,* 288

Woolworth sit-in, 309

World Fellowship Committee, 218

World Student Christian Federation, 9, 121

World Tomorrow, 181

World View of Race, A (Ralph Bunche), 170

World War I, 54–59, 66

World War II: destruction of, 252; and draft, 188–90; and federal government, role of, 193; Hiroshima, bombing of, 247; and imperialism as cause of, 185–88; and Japanese internment, 210–11, 218, 247; Jews, genocide of, 184–85; Pearl Harbor, 185, 442n21; and race relations, 193, 194–95, 200–201, 202–3

Worthy, William, 188–89

Wright Richard: *Native Son,* 191

Wygal, Winnifred, 11, 500n148

Yamashita, John, 247

Yates, Elizabeth: *Howard Thurman,* 378–79

Yergan, Max, 169

YMCA, 58–59, 60, 79, 103–4, 205–6

Young, Whitney, Jr., 367–68

YWCA, 121

Recent books in

The American South Series

*Facing Freedom: An African American Community in Virginia
from Reconstruction to Jim Crow*
Daniel B. Thorp

*Capital and Convict: Race, Region, and Punishment
in Post–Civil War America*
Henry Kamerling

*The Uplift Generation: Cooperation across the Color Line
in Early Twentieth-Century Virginia*
Clayton McClure Brooks

The Risen Phoenix: Black Politics in the Post–Civil War South
Luis-Alejandro Dinnella-Borrego

Designing Dixie: Tourism, Memory, and Urban Space in the New South
Reiko Hillyer

*A Deed So Accursed: Lynching in Mississippi
and South Carolina, 1881–1940*
Terence Finnegan

*Radical Reform: Interracial Politics in Post-Emancipation
North Carolina*
Deborah Beckel

*Religion and the Making of Nat Turner's Virginia:
Baptist Community and Conflict, 1740–1840*
Randolph Ferguson Scully

From Yeoman to Redneck in the South Carolina Upcountry, 1850–1915
Stephen A. West

What Reconstruction Meant: Historical Memory in the American South
Bruce E. Baker

*Black, White, and Olive Drab: Racial Integration at Fort Jackson,
South Carolina, and the Civil Rights Movement*
Andrew H. Myers

*Murder, Honor, and Law: Four Virginia Homicides
from Reconstruction to the Great Depression*
Richard F. Hamm